THE SEARCH FOR
THE ANCIENT ORDER

A History of The Restoration Movement
1849-1906

BY

EARL IRVIN WEST

Vol. 2
1866-1906

Remember the days of old,
Consider the years of many generations:
Ask thy father and he will show thee;
Thine elders and they will tell thee.
—Deut. 32: 7.

DEDICATION

*To the Irvington Church of Christ, Indianapolis,
Indiana and to its elders—Charles Dean, John Smith,
Lewis Hurley, Gillespie Embry, and Loyd Gaines—without
whose patience and understanding this history could never
have been written, this volume is affectionately dedicated.*

DAVID LIPSCOMB

CONTENTS

viii

ACKNOWLEDGMENTS

The author acknowledges the assistance of a host of friends in making this volume possible. He expresses his gratitude to Olan Hicks, editor of the *Christian Chronicle* and to Homer Hailey, teacher of Bible at Abilene Christian College for valuable suggestions on the manuscript; to E. C. Coffman of Houston, Texas and John T. Lewis of Birmingham, Ala. for help on the chapter of Austin McGary; to C. E. W. Dorris of Nashville, Tenn. for the use of his library and suggestions on the manuscript; to Ben F. Taylor of Newcastle, Indiana for his assistance on the study of James A. Harding; to Monroe Hawley of East St. Louis, Illinois for assistance on the chapter on Liberalism; to Enos Dowling of Indianapolis for the use of the Butler University collection of restoration material; to B. C. Goodpasture, editor of the *Gospel Advocate* for valuable information on David Lipscomb; and to the countless other friends whose words of encouragement have helped vitally in producing this work.

PREFACE

All around the room my silent servants wait—
My friends in every season, bright and dim,
angels and seraphim,
Come down and murmur to me, sweet and low;
And spirits of the skies all come and go
Early and late.

Thus sang Proctor the praises of his books. "A taste for books is the pleasure and glory of my life," wrote Gibbon. "I would not exchange it for the riches of the Indies." Cicero thought that a room without books was like a body without a soul. Jeremy Collier said, "Books are a guide in youth and an entertainment in age. They support us under solitude, and keep us from being a burden to ourselves. They help us to forget the crossness of men and things, compose our cares and passions, and lay our disappointments asleep." "He that loveth a book," someone said, "will never want a faithful friend, a wholesome counselor, a cheerful companion, an effectual comforter."

A wise man wrote, "Of making many books there is no end; and much study is a weariness of the flesh." He who would undertake to add another publication to the endless parade of books marching before the attention of men should have something more than personal interest in doing so. The only excuse the author offers for the writing of this volume is that he feels there is a definite need for it. His method of writing has been colored by the consciousness of this need. Every attempt has been made to make the book easily readable and understandable. No one is more conscious than he of the lack of literary finesse the volumes could claim. The author is also conscious of departing from routine standards of historians in inserting many quotations that others might regard useless. Most historians it is true would have passed these controversies with much less attention. The author realized that many who read these volumes will not have this material accessible to them, that unless it was inserted here, many would remain ignorant of it. The volumes, therefore, have been written, not with the intention of meeting the high standards of literary criticisms, but to supply the need in the church of the present day.

It can hardly be denied that young preachers are filling the church today who have but scant knowledge of the historical background of the issues the church now faces and did face less than a century ago. But there is nothing new in this. When John F. Rowe visited one of "our colleges" in 1883, he asked a professor if the students were taught the rise and progress of the "current reformation," and whether they were acquainted with the literature of "our distinctive plea." The professor replied: "they have not; and as for myself, I have not read up." Rowe then remarked:

And yet we establish colleges and ask the brethren to support them, with the avowed object of training young men to know the Bible, to know the plan of salvation, to know the difference between our distinctive plea, and the shibboleths of sectarian parties and to understand the ground reasons of our separation from all entangling alliances with the sect world. If the country is to be flooded with a hungry horde of pastors who are unacquainted with the aims and objects of the fathers of the Reformation, we see no practical benefit in "Bible Colleges." The title is a misnomer and the pretension is a sham.[1]

There is a timeliness in these words which has not diminished with the passing years.

If any reader regards any of the pioneers of the restoration or any of the quotations given here from them as an authority today, he misses the point of the history. This attitude is disastrous to the search for the ancient order. In the final analysis it is the New Testament that is the authority. The pioneers would be the last to insist that their words be the present standard for the church.

Too, there is something merciless in our ability to forget the heroes of the past, and their battles for the truth. This is what Sir Thomas Browne calls, "the iniquity of oblivion." The author feels some satisfaction in lifting some of the outstanding pioneers from an engulfing darkness. Most historians have brushed aside men like David Lipscomb, Moses E. Lard, Ben Franklin and Jacob Creath, as inconsiderate legalists who lacked true spiritual attainments. On the contrary they were men who deeply loved the truth, and accepted the chastisement of others rather than

---

[1]John F. Rowe, "Lift Up A Standard For The People," *American Christian Review,* (Oct. 18, 1883) p. 332.

renounce their convictions. They are men who need to be remembered, and it is hoped these volumes will help do this.

Therefore, in presenting this work to the public the author feels that if it fulfills the need, and inspires the church to greater work in channels of loyal adherence to great and true principles, all his time and effort will have been repaid. It is with that desire that these volumes are sent forth.

INTRODUCTION

There is no chapter in church history this side af apostolic days more thrilling to the lover of truth than that of "the restoration movement." At the beginning of the nineteenth century there burst forth throughout the country a general wave of spiritual and religious unrest. It began in England with such men as Glass and the Haldanes, and in this country with Mr. O'Kelly, Abner Jones, Barton W. Stone and others. Men were fighting their way out of the maze of sectarian and denominational errors and prejudices. The cry of their hearts was, "Back to the Bible and to the Christ of the Bible."

The list of these early pioneers of the spirit of religious liberty was swelled by names such as that of Thomas Campbell and his son Alexander, Walter Scott, John Smith, John Rogers, the Creaths and scores of others who came later. The heart thrills today as one reads of their struggles for truth, the joy of their souls in finding it, and the urgency with which they proclaimed it everywhere. From rented halls and borrowed meeting-houses in the cities and towns to the school-houses and brush arbors of the back-woods, they heralded the newly discovered message of the ancient gospel of Christ and the apostles. Honest men and women of all sections gave a listening ear. The waters of rivers, creeks and man-made reservoirs were kept agitated by those sturdy pioneers as day by day they brought to be immersed the converts to the ancient faith. Like a great rolling tide, sweeping everything before it, the movement swept onward into the west, into the south, and across the ocean into England. Men began to wonder if the complete overthrow of sectarianism and the restoration of the true faith were not to be the "millennium" of the apocalypse.

But alas! the day came when men within the ranks of the church began to betray the faith by tendencies to compromise with those without, allowing the world and human errors of judgment to weaken and destroy the force of their plea. Their attitude toward the Scriptures changed. The temptation to be like the nations about them was more than some dared resist. Innovations entered and departures resulted—but not complete and entire! Noble men arose here and there with unsheathed sword to declare, "Hitherto thalt thou come, but no further; and here shall thy proud waves be stayed." A remnant was rescued from the tide of digression and the plea for the ancient order of things was saved. The cause of Christ began again to invade the ranks of sectarianism and worldliness till once more the number of God's people in the States and abroad can be numbered in the hundreds of thousands. God still had his "seven thousand" who refused to bow the knee to Baal.

In this second volume of his history, Mr. West has done a monumental work in gathering together facts and statements of the period long hid from the public's view. He has spent months delving into the literature of the movement from its beginning to the turn of the present century. With painstaking care he has sifted and sorted these materials, till he has given to the general public a clearer picture of the spirit and struggles of the men of that day than has any other historian.

In the past we have been treated to historical sketches and books written from the viewpoint of the liberal wing—men bereft of sympathy for the conservatives and their position, and oftentime by those lacking in sympathy for the Bible itself. In this particular volume, the author deals with the underlying causes of the division that came within the ranks of Christians—a division which resulted in the two groups known as Christian Churches and Churches of Christ. From contemporary writings and authenticated traditions Mr. West brings to light many facts hitherto lying silent and undiscovered in the periodicals of the times. He seeks to let such men as David Lipscomb, Ben Franklin, Tolbert Fanning and those laboring with him on the one hand, and Isaac Errett, W. K. Pendleton and their co-laborers on the other, present their own arguments and sentiments for the positions assumed. For the first time the Gospel Advocate, the American Christian Review and other contemporary periodicals among the conservative wing are allowed to express fully the sentiments of those opposing the innovations.

In reading this book one is able to see more clearly than before what were the issues in the controversy, and to appreciate more deeply the convictions of men who stood against what they considered to be innovations leading to digression and apostasy. But besides this rich outlay of historical data, the reader will find such chapters as the one on the colorful life of Austin McGary and his contributions to the cause in Texas most entertaining and stimulating.

Second to the Bible, a study of this period with its great aims and oppositions, its faithful and its deserters, its trials and its victories, will do more to enlighten and strengthen, to warn and direct the Christian than any other literature known to the present writer. Enlightenment is one of the greatest bulwarks against error. As it continues to fire the hearts of men and women with enthusiasm and greater determination, and to arouse a deeper consciousness of the rich heritage of present-day Christians, this book will live long, ever contributing to a better understanding of the restoration of primitive Christianity in this present generation.

Mr. West is comparatively a young man, but an untiring and thorough student. It is a pleasure and an honor to be asked to write this introduction. Brother West was a student in classes conducted by me in Abilene Christian College in the thirties. I have followed with interest his persistent study of history and his diligence in seeking the truth on the issues discussed in both volumes of THE SEARCH FOR THE ANCIENT ORDER. And, although he writes from the viewpoint of the conservative body, he has sought to keep bias and prejudice completely out of the story. His aim has been to present truth as the historian should present truth. For him I predict a continued useful life in the service of God, and for his book that it shall be reckoned among the most valuable brought forth by members of the church of Christ in this generation.

HOMER HAILEY

Abilene, Texas
June, 1950

CHAPTER I

REBIRTH OF THE GOSPEL ADVOCATE

It was late in the year 1865. A horse and buggy moved slowly up a lonely pike south of Nashville, Tennessee. The lone occupant of the vehicle was a squat middle-aged man. There was nothing in his appearance to suggest that he was a preacher, nor was there anything in his disposition to admit the fact. He was a farmer, and his home was twelve miles south of Nashville on a small country road. "This thoroughfare," as J. M. Barnes later described it, "is what the Hillsboro Pike becomes after it ceases to be a Pike."

The horse and buggy crept into the city limits, and then moved toward the center of town. The streets were crowded with blue clad soldiers under orders to keep peace. Here and there loitering aimlessly, were young men still wearing the gray. Silent and sulking, they had returned from the war to houses that were burned to the ground, and farms that were gutted by war's havoc. They shrank reluctantly from plunging into the task of rebuilding the glory that had belonged to the South.

The horse and buggy pulled up before a dingy printing office and the occupant stepped down, tied the horse, and pushed through the doorway. An armload of papers was laid on a table—all written in longhand. The printer picked them up and scanned the copy of the first issue of the *Gospel Advocate* that would be published after the war between the states. The date on the top would read, January 1, 1866. Above the date would be the names of the editors, T. Fanning and D. Lipscomb. The front page would also say that this would be Vol. VIII and No. 1.

In a moment David Lipscomb returned through the door, untied his horse, stepped back into the buggy and directed his horse toward his farm.

The cessation of a war usually brings as many problems as it settles, and this was certainly the case of the war between the states. Probably the nation had not seen a period when she was more demoralized than in those first few years after this conflict. The South was beaten and suffering badly. Her fields were without crops, her cities for the most part lay in shambles; her youth lay dead on the battlefields; her uncultured slaves were now free, some arrogantly defying their former masters, and creating strong resentment against the black race. All in all it was a picture of desolation and ruin the like of which no section of the nation had ever previously known.

E. G. Sewell lived south of Nashville and the impression of the war was vivid in his mind. Speaking of his experiences, he wrote:

He has again and again stood in his yard or sat in his house and heard cannons booming like distant thunder, when he knew great battles were raging and human lives were every moment being rushed into eternity, while others were lying wounded and helpless, bleeding and agonizing, upon the cold ground. He has listened to skirmishing with small arms, when cavalrymen could be seen dashing and retreating, while the fire of small arms was too rapid to count. It takes a man of quiet nerve to remain unmoved while such things are going on so close by.

We were living about halfway between the two great battles, one close to Franklin, Tenn., the other near Nashville, Tenn., during General Hood's noted raid against the forces then encamped at these two places. We could hear the cannonading almost equally well at both places. After the battle at Franklin, when the Union forces fell back to Nashville, and the other side soon followed, the people living along the way had the stragglers from both armies to feed. By the time the two armies had passed toward Nashville, homes were emptied of all they had on hand to eat, and our prospects looked gloomy as to feeding our own families; but while the armies were getting ready for the great battle near Nashville, we had time to hustle out, go to mill, get up some meal and flour, hunt up a little meat and such like, to live on again. By the time we did this the Nashville battle was fought. Hood and his forces fell back south, followed by the Union forces; then the stragglers from both armies had to be fed again. So we were again cleaned up of what we had to eat and were again ready to begin to stare hunger in the face; but before we got very hungry the armies passed on again, and again the people were fortunate enough to find supplies to keep hunger down a while longer. . . .[1]

The industrial North fared much better, but with the assassination of President Lincoln found it hard to control animosity against the South, even though few southerners welcomed the news of Lincoln's death. Inflation, hunger, hatred, rapacity—these swept over the country. The whole nation was enveloped in a

---

[1]E. G. Sewell, "Reminiscences of Civil War Times," *Gospel Advocate*, Vol. XLIX, No. 27 (July 4, 1907), p. 424.

cloud of gloom.   Just what the result would be nobody really knew.

Wise observers have pointed out that the condition of a nation politically reflects itself in the condition of the church.   Certainly the condition of the country in those first years following the close of the Civil War was reflected in the Church.   Probably the restoration movement knew no days of greater conflict than it was now to see.   The controversies over instrumental music and the missionary society now began to rage, picking up momentum with the passing of years.   Many brethren attempted to walk cautiously, fanning the flames as little as possible.   W. K. Pendleton wrote in the *Millennial Harbinger:*

Upon the threshold of this new year of 1866, we desire to renew our vows, and to devote with increasing zeal our energies to the sacred cause of humanity, religion, and truth. . . .

The world is suffering for the restoration of apostolic Christianity; the great heart of the times pants for something which it does not see in our present divided Christendom.[2]

Ben Franklin, contemplating the general religious condition of the times, wrote:

The religious condition of the country is alarming; terribly alarming.   The sectarian establishments in this country are tottering, crumbling and tumbling into one general chaos in all quarters.[3]

Franklin went on to point out that Episcopalian clergymen were fleeing into Roman Catholicism; the Methodist and Presbyterian churches were divided, and the courts were filled with disputes over their church property.   Infidelity seemed to be having a grand jubilee.   Meanwhile, Franklin held out that the only hope for the world was in the cause for which he and his brethren were pleading.   They alone had the answer, and yet, their internal condition made them incapable of carrying on successfully.   To accomplish the great work set before them, Franklin urged that they must (1) "set themselves in order in the house of the Lord," (2) "gather together in one harmonious and glorious union," and (3) go to work in earnest to convert the world.

---

[2]W. K. Pendleton, "Introduction," *Millennial Harbinger,* Vol. XXXVII, No. 1 (January, 1866), pp. 3, 4.

[3]Ben Franklin, "Introductory Address," *American Christian Review,* Vol. X, No. 1 (January 1, 1867), p. 4.

There were those like David Lipscomb who looked upon the war as divine punishment for evil in the nation. He wrote:

In days that are past, God blessed us with all the bounties of life. We grew rich, and in this world "had our good things." We hoarded our riches, and spent them upon our passions and vain desires. How little we consecrated to God and the good of our fellow man! God in his providence sent a fatal besom of destruction over our land, and how fearful the desolation! Where once abounded wealth, and comfort and happiness, what deep poverty now much more abounds; what pressing want; what sorrow of heart that refuses comfort for those who are not. Shall we, in beginning life anew, again pursue the same course that brought us to so disastrous an end? Shall we not, with the first dawn of returning peace, from our pinching necessities, consecrate the first fruit of our toil to the Lord, as the earnest of a more fruitful discharge of our duties for the future, as almoners of his manifold grace and stewards of his bounty?[4]

The moral in the words is as interesting as the general picture of the desolated condition of the land.

Yet, despite the demoralized condition of the brethren and the internal strife that prevailed, the church had enjoyed a substantial growth. In 1867 Ben Franklin wrote, comparing the condition of the church that year with that of twenty years previous. In 1847 the church had between one hundred and fifty thousand and two hundred thousand members, but twenty years later the number was conservatively estimated at a half-million. Moreover, in 1847 the work was just beginning in Iowa and Michigan, but by the postwar period, it had penetrated into Kansas, Nebraska, California, Wisconsin, Minnesota, Jamaica, Australia, Wales and New Zealand. Twenty years before, gospel preachers were numbered in the hundreds, but in 1867, they could be numbered in the thousands. Twenty years before there were eight or nine monthly papers and one weekly, but in 1867 there were twenty-five regular publications in the brotherhood. The brethren in 1847 were distributing no tracts at all, but twenty years later were spreading over one hundred thousand a year. Finally, in 1847, Franklin pointed out that there were only two colleges among the brethren,

---

[4]David Lipscomb, "The Advocate," *Gospel Advocate*, Vol. VIII, No. 1 (January 1, 1866), p. 3.

but twenty years later, there were ten colleges and not less than forty or fifty high schools.[5]

The records of the American Christian Missionary Society for those early post-war years show the strength of the church in various localities. B. U. Watkins reports in 1866 that there were sixteen churches in the state of Minnesota with a total of one thousand members. Kansas boasted of sixty-nine churches with three thousand, one hundred members. California had opened up now and mission work was being done there. Robert Graham, upon moving from Fayette, Arkansas, went to San Francisco, arriving there on July 18, 1865, becoming the harbinger of gospel truth to this section of the Pacific coast. On foreign fields the Jerusalem mission was closed, but the Jamaica mission was still open, although in 1866, it was being maintained only by native preachers. The next year, J. O. Beardslee was back on the island, but again stayed only one year, abandoning the work once again to the natives. The corresponding secretary of the Society reported in 1868 that the missionary organization was doing work in Jamaica, Nebraska, East Virginia and in the city of Troy, New York. Barrow was in Nebraska where in the previous year, he had baptized one hundred and forty-six persons. The state now had twenty-two congregations with two thousand members.

In the South the church, although in destitute circumstances, was recovering. P. S. Fall was still in Nashville. Justus M. Barnes preached in Alabama. J. S. Lamar was in Georgia. W. H. Hopson was in Virginia. The war had made contact between the churches virtually impossible. Brethren in the South began planning meetings where they could revive interest among themselves. The church in Murfreesboro, Tennessee, in their Lord's Day meeting on April 8, 1866, decided to send an invitation to the churches of the South, including Kentucky, Missouri, and Maryland to come together in a general consultation meeting, to discuss the needs of the church. W. H. Goodloe, evangelist at Murfreesboro, sent out the invitation, and accordingly the meeting was conducted early that summer.

But of all the attempts to get back to normality in the South, there is none more significant than the republication of the *Gospel Advocate*. When the war began, it became impossible to con-

[5]Ben Franklin, "Now and Twenty Years Ago," *American Christian Review*, Vol. X, No. 13 (March 26, 1867), p. 100.

tinue publication of the *Advocate*. All mail service was immediately stopped. The *Advocate* could neither be distributed nor could material reach it. Added to this the high state of excitement in the South produced a corresponding slackening of interest in a religious publication like the *Advocate*.

When the *Gospel Advocate* made its reappearance on January 1, 1866, the most noticeable change was the replacement of William Lipscomb as a co-editor by his younger brother, David. For the next forty years the name of David Lipscomb was to be the most prominent one in the churches of the Southland. No man did more to stabilize the church during the critical years ahead. Certainly no study of the restoration movement from 1866 to 1906 could be complete without a knowledge of this great man.

Franklin County, Tennessee, in the year 1831—the year David Lipscomb was born—was hardly more than a wilderness. Mail service was unknown. Newspapers never reached back into the farm homes. A stagecoach line from New York to New Orleans ran through the county near the farm of Granville Lipscomb. A tavern was located not far away where the stages changed horses on the journey. News came in from the outside world in this manner. Roads were but winding snake-paths of mud. Life was rugged, simple, primitive and difficult. Clothes were of the home-spun variety, and meals consisted, not of the dainties of modern-day living, but primarily of that which was grown on the farm. Schooling was hard to secure, and the man who could read and write was looked upon as an educated individual.

Here into Franklin County moved Granville Lipscomb from Virginia in 1826. He was the oldest of ten children born to William and Ann Day Lipscomb. There is much about the early life of Granville Lipscomb, David's father, that we would like to know, but apparently will never know. It seems probable that he was born in Louisa County, Virginia about the year, 1800. Granville Lipscomb might have married before leaving Virginia for Tennessee. Information on this is scant. In 1896 David Lipscomb met an elderly woman by the name of Betsy Broadaway who went to school with Granville Lipscomb's first wife in Spottsylvania County, Virginia. Granville was the oldest of ten children; Dabney was the fifth child, and John was the youngest.

These three boys were very devoted to each other. Soon after arriving in Franklin County, their father was killed by a falling tree, the first major tragedy they experienced in their new home.

Following the Revolutionary War, North Carolina paid her soldiers by giving them land grants in the valley of the Cumberland. The Tennessee Historical Society has the journal of John Lipscomb who served as an Ensign in the company of Capt. William's Sixth North Carolina Regiment. He is described as a "happy-go-lucky, waggish fellow" who left his home state on April 25, 1784 to journey to Nashville. John Lipscomb's journal begins when Lipscomb left the Holston on June 11, 1784.[6]

It is not likely, however, that this John Lipscomb was the same individual who was an uncle to David Lipscomb but who had the same name. The latter John Lipscomb would have been too young to have been the same person.

All three of these boys—Granville, Dabney, and John—were members of the Primitive Baptist Church that met on Bean's Creek in Franklin County. Granville was a deacon, and a very devout man. The *Christian Baptist* was circulated in their neighborhood and all three read it. They determined that they would take the Bible as their only rule of faith and practice, and so stated their position to the Baptist Church. They were immediately tried for heresy and excluded from Baptist fellowship. At Winchester, not far from them, was a Newlight Church, a congregation established on the principles advocated by Barton W. Stone. The three brothers immediately became identified with this congregation. Later, however, Granville Lipscomb and his wife were united with the church near Owl Hollow in Franklin County.

After accepting the New Testament as their only rule of faith and practice, the boys thought it wise to give their time to a diligent study of the scriptures. Soon they concluded that slavery was against the will of God, and determined to do something about it. All three boys were now married, and had families. They owned farms and a few slaves, although the exact number is not known. Carrying out their convictions, they moved in 1835 to

---

[6]John P. Brown, *Old Frontiers* (Kingsport, Tenn., Southern Publishers, Inc., 1938), pp. 232-239.

Sangamon County, Illinois, near Springfield. Here the slaves were freed. Among the first recollections of his life, David Lipscomb later recalled, was the year spent in Illinois. Here, two sisters and a brother died. In a short while his mother also died. Disheartened by these tragedies, all of which took place in such a short time, Granville decided to take the remainder of his family back to Franklin County. When he returned to Tennessee, David was the youngest of his three children. All three were down with malaria fever and were "as much dead as alive." Mrs. F. C. Van Zandt, a neighbor lady, warmly mothered David Lipscomb in those critical years. Parenthetically it might be noted that in a few years Mrs. Van Zandt and her husband moved to Texas. Isaac Van Zandt, her husband, was elected to the Texas Congress. He was later sent from the Republic of Texas to the United States as a minister, and helped to negotiate the treaty of annexation for Texas.

David Lipscomb attended a Sunday School class taught by his father at the Salem Church in Franklin County. No child ever had a more consecrated father. Each night before retiring the children listened to their father read a portion of Scripture and comment upon it.

A Baptist preacher by the name of Elder "Billy Woods" was a near neighbor of the Lipscomb's, and although Granville Lipscomb highly regarded him, he had no patience with his doctrine. Young David, then a lad of less than six, often heard his father speak of Woods' "false doctrine," but in his youthful mind could not distinguish between a "false doctrine" and a "falsehood." David promptly informed Woods one day that according to his father, Woods was "such a liar."

At the age of thirteen David and his brother, William, went to Virginia to spend a year with Lipscomb's grandfather, who was a deacon in the Baptist Church at Lower Good Mine in Louisa County. There was an active Sunday School in which the pupils memorized scripture. Lipscomb during this time memorized the four gospel records in addition to the book of Acts. He argued with his grandfather that baptism was for the remission of sins and refused to join the parade of young people to the mourner's bench.

In those early days it was unusual for a farmer to accumulate much wealth. If he eked out a living, stayed out of debt, and reared a family with an average amount of food, he considered himself successful. But Granville Lipscomb, through industry and thrift, became a moderately wealthy man. He married again, bought a few slaves, and earned a livelihood above the average for that day. Still he was very religious. The slaves were assembled regularly for worship. The Bible was read to them. The slaves were given instructions in how to read and write by a member of the family. In later years Lipscomb was heard frequently to remark that some of his best religious impressions came from an old negro woman. Probably she was one of these slaves.

The year, 1845, was an important one for David Lipscomb. He was now fourteen years old. Tolbert Fanning, who only recently had opened Franklin College, near Nashville, made a journey through Franklin County, preaching on the way. Young David was just recovering from typhoid fever. He spoke to no one about it, but made up his own mind to send for Fanning. When Fanning tested David by asking him why he wanted to be baptized, David replied, "to obey God." With this statement, Fanning baptized him in a box.

In January, 1846 Lipscomb entered Franklin College, and three years later graduated from this institution, delivering the valedictory. Here, he was constantly under the influence of Tolbert Fanning, an influence from which Lipscomb never escaped. Lipscomb was truly Fanning's protegè. He adopted that fearless independence of mind so characteristic of Fanning, and consequently in later years showed no reluctance at standing alone upon his convictions. Lipscomb adopted Fanning's attitude toward many of the issues of the day. Holding the same position as Fanning on such issues as missionary societies, christian participation in war, and in a measure, on church organization, it is not likely an exaggeration to say that Lipscomb portrayed the attitude of Fanning in his own life more than of any other living man.

As a student, Lipscomb decidedly was above the average although not probably at the top of the class. Tolbert Fanning's class record has come down to us. A survey of Lipscomb's record will prove of interest. The record is monthly and runs from January to July, 1846.

January		February		March	
English	8	English	8	English	8
Mathematics	8	Mathematics	8	Mathematics	9
Nat. Hist.	6	Nat. Hist.	7	Nat. Hist.	8
Music	5	Music	6	Music	6
Physics	8	Physics	9	Physics	10
Punctuality	9	Punctuality	9	Punctuality	10
Deportment	8	Deportment	9	Deportment	9
				Sacred Hist.	5

April		May		June	
English	8	English	8	English	9
Mathematics	9	Mathematics	9	Mathematics	8
Nat. Hist.	7	Nat. Hist.	8	Nat. Hist.	7
Music	6	Music	6	Music	6
Physics	10	Physics	9	Physics	7
Punctuality	10	Sacred Hist.	7	Punctuality	10
Deportment	10	Deportment	10	Deportment	10
Sacred Hist.	8	Sacred Hist.	8	Manners	5

July	
Latin	5
Greek	6
Mathematics	8
Music	6
Physics	7
Punctuality	10
Deportment	10
Manners	5

It would seem as though Lipscomb's poorest grades came in "manners," a fact which is especially interesting. Years later Lipscomb recalled that the last "whipping" he ever remembered getting was for stealing a kiss from a "cherry-lipped Baptist lass" while a student at Franklin College.

Upon graduation from College, Lipscomb moved to Georgia and became the manager of a large farm. It is unlikely that his stay in Georgia was over two years. Shortly we find him back in Franklin County, working on a farm. About this time the Nashville, Chattanooga, and St. Louis railway, which was to pass through his father's farm, was being laid so Lipscomb worked on the project, cutting away some of the high ground.

In a short while he owned a farm of his own, and even had a few slaves. He was well on his way to becoming a highly successful farmer.

David Lipscomb, like his father, had a tremendous interest in the Christian life, and, like his father, devoted a considerable portion of his time in studying the Scriptures. He had given very little *to* of his time to thinking about being a preacher. To him, every man who was a Christian, should dedicate his life to the service of God in whatever way and manner he could. He did not regard preaching as a profession. At no time in his life did he like to be thought of as a preacher. He had a natural timidity. In later years he could rarely stand before an audience without a feeling of embarrassment. He was merely a Christian doing what he could to serve the Lord, who earned his living by farming. He once wrote:

I started out to preach believing preachers were appointed by laying on of hands. I failed to submit to it, because I did not care to be considered a preacher. I began preaching because I thought I could do some work in that line that would be helpful, and all the help that could be given was needed then. I have had no ambition for official places or honors in the church or out of it. I desired to do what I did as a layman. I did not know how long I would continue in the work or when I would quit it. I did not wish to continue a day longer than I could do good. I soon saw that Barnabas and Saul had preached ten or twelve years before they had hands laid on them, and those scattered abroad from Jerusalem, both men and women, "went everywhere preaching the word." I felt sure with these examples that I was on safe ground in preaching what I could. Then I did not care for anyone to feel any responsibility for supporting me. So I preferred that kind of work.[7]

In 1875 Ben Franklin went to Franklin, Tennessee, to conduct a protracted meeting. Prior to this he had only a slight acquaintance with Lipscomb. On this trip he became better acquainted with him. Franklin later wrote his impression of David Lipscomb in the following words:

Brother Lipscomb is a plain and unassuming man, with the simplicity of a child. He has good native sense, much power and influence, and is greatly devoted to the cause. There is not the least danger of his ever turning *clergyman*. He has not an inkling

---

[7]Quoted by E. A. Elam, "An Endorsement," *Gospel Advocate,* Vol. XLVII, No. 24 (June 15, 1905), p. 369.

in that way. He lives in utter disregard of the notions of the world, puts on no airs, wears just such coat, hat and pants as suit him. We were much pleased with him as far as our short acquaintance went.[8]

Simplicity in life, and thorough devotion to the cause of Christ—these were David Lipscomb's two marked characteristics. By 1852 he had become a successful farmer. Having studied his Bible considerably, he was eager to use his influence to promote the cause of New Testament Christianity. As a young preacher, he looked with great admiration upon Jesse B. Ferguson, then a popular preacher for the church in Nashville. Very shortly there came the rumblings of discontent, bursting into war between the *Christian Magazine* and the *Millennial Harbinger*. The experience common to youth came now to him. Observing older brethren in whom he had confidence fall into violent conflict, brought disillusionment. But this dreadful experience was worth a thousand sermons. Lipscomb had learned not to put too much confidence in men. At first he seriously considered going back to the church of his fathers, the Primitive Baptist. But a closer study of the Bible revealed Ferguson's errors to him. He became stabilized, and weathered the storm. He was now a wiser man, having learned to trust man less and God's word more.

Lipscomb informs us that his first attempts at preaching the gospel took place only three or four years before the opening of the Civil War. Thus his first sermons were delivered about 1857 or 1858. However, before this time he had been actively serving in the church. In the summer of 1855 one finds Lipscomb at Salem, Tennessee, where he is serving as secretary of the executive committee of the "Christian Churches in the Mountain District" of Tennessee. He announces a cooperation meeting to be held in Woodbury, Cannon County, to start on the fourth Sunday in September, 1855.[9]

George Stroud of Warren County, Tennessee, was the first to suggest to Lipscomb that he should publicly proclaim the gospel. Lipscomb went with him to a Lord's Day appointment. Previously he had studied carefully about ten verses of Scripture and felt he was fully prepared to discuss them. When he stood up to

---

[8]Ben Franklin, "Visit in Tennessee," *American Christian Review,* Vol. XVIII, (1875), p. 220.

[9]David Lipscomb, "no title," *Gospel Advocate,* Vol. I, No. 3 (September, 1855), p. 88.

speak, however, he read the verses, but could not remember what he had planned to say. He finished reading the chapter, hoping the thoughts would come to him, but they did not. He was greatly embarrassed, and sat down in confusion. He asked Stroud to preach. Stroud was so taken back that he got confused, and could not preach, and the meeting closed, a great embarrassment to both.

After services both men took dinner at the home of a brother, neither mentioning the events of the occasion. After dinner, they mounted their horses, and rode off together. Finally Stroud spoke.

"Brother David," he said, "I hope you will not let this discourage you."

Lipscomb replied courageously: "Well, Brother Stroud, I will not be discouraged, if I can help it; but I confess that it is enough to discourage a young man to see a man who has been preaching fifty years make such a failure as you made today."

The war came in 1861. Lipscomb had fully made up his mind what he would do, having become thoroughly convicted that a Christian could have no part in it. He now lived on a farm at the edge of Nashville, and preached regularly. He publicly spoke out against the war, and took no part either in Southern or Northern politics. He was, however, denounced by men of both sides, but this did not deter him from preaching his convictions. He wrote letters to public politicians, stating his position. He lived apart from the war as much as possible, took care of his farming, and preached the gospel.

The disastrous effect of the war upon the South made Lipscomb decide, even before the war ended, to take more active steps to revive and reunite the scattered and discouraged brethren. He determined that when the war ended, the *Gospel Advocate* should be reborn to aid in this purpose. Then the question of editorship came before him. Fanning could not handle it alone, and Lipscomb himself did not feel competent. Furthermore, he was comparatively unknown as a preacher or writer. He had published only one article in any brotherhood paper, and it was not under his own name. We are never told just what this article was and when and where it appeared. In the hope of securing an editor for the *Advocate,* Lipscomb took a trip to Lexington, Kentucky, in the fall of 1864 to attend a meeting of the Kentucky Christian Missionary Society. Upon the recommendation of J. W. Mc-Garvey, a brother was urged by Lipscomb to move to Nashville and edit the *Advocate*. Who this brother was we are never told. McGarvey himself promised to write for the *Advocate*, but never did. The reason undoubtedly is found in the *Advocate's* opposition to Missionary Societies of which McGarvey was an ardent supporter.

The prospectus had been released sometime before January 1, 1866, when the *Gospel Advocate* appeared. It well declared the platform to be adopted by the *Advocate's* editors.

Our purpose is to maintain the right of Jesus Christ to rule the world, the supremacy of the Sacred Scriptures in all matters spiritual, and to encourage an investigation of every subject connected with the church of Christ, which we may consider of practical interest. "The Kingdom of God" was a real, permanent institution, "the pillar and support of the truth," upon a proper appreciation of which the welfare of the world and the happiness of man depend; her origin, organization, history, labor, and mission; her relation to worldly powers, civil, military and religious, and her final triumph, will occupy much of our attention. The education of the world for Christianity, and the training of Christians for immortality, will constitute an important part of our labor.[10]

It will be of great interest to study in more detail the editorial policy adopted by Lipscomb and Fanning, for in a large measure it shows the character of the two men. The war had left the brethren South and North filled with hatred. Neither Lipscomb nor Fanning could escape the conviction that brethren who had taken part in the conflict had abandoned God and the Bible. But the main suffering was now a thing of the past, and it was their desire to build upon something better and to put the church on a more substantial basis for the future. Consequently, in the "Salutatory," Fanning wrote:

After an anxious and painful silence of four dreary years, we thank God most devoutly for the favorable auspices under which we are permitted to address you. No one has "set on us" to injure us physically, or intellectually; and we trust to Heaven, that it is our privilege to send our kind greetings to thousands from whom we have long been separated. While it is not our

---

[10]T. Fanning and D. Lipscomb, "Prospectus of Volume VIII of The Gospel Advocate," *Gospel Advocate*, Vol. VIII, No. 2 (January 9, 1866), p. 32.

purpose to make many promises, we feel that it is due to our brethren and the cause of our Master to say that it is our earnest wish to cooperate with all good men in setting forth the claims of the Messiah to the lost of earth. We have no local or peculiar institutions to defend, and nothing new to set forth. We will cheerfully labor with our fellow servants in the Kingdom of Christ in promoting every interest suggested in the word of life; and it shall be our constant study to oppose every cause antipodal to the reign of the Messiah. We earnestly desire to cultivate the most kindly feelings towards all men, and should we consider it incumbent upon us, to oppose the views and practices of any of our race, we hope to be able to do so in the spirit of love and meekness. Yet we desire to act independently, and when called by duty to oppose error and forewarn the deluded, we trust that we may be able to do so in the fear of God.[11]

The rebirth of the *Gospel Advocate,* then, in 1866, had a direct relationship to the general feelings among brethren North and South. Lipscomb wrote later:

The fact that we had not a single paper known to us that Southern people could read without having their feelings wounded by political insinuations and slurs, had more to do with calling the *Advocate* into existence than all other circumstances combined.[12]

With these facts generally stated, it is little wonder that the *Advocate* in the years immediately ahead was often accused of harboring a sectional spirit. It was not the purpose of either Lipscomb or Fanning to make the *Advocate* a paper exclusively for the South. In short, it was not to be sectional. Yet, neither of the men would deny that he felt a deep sympathy for Southern people. The bulk of the brethren North felt that the *Advocate* was championing the rights of Southern people, so they looked upon Lipscomb's strictures on civil government as "sour grape" psychology, since the South had been beaten in the war. This background considerably aided the *Advocate's* growth in the South, but hindered it in the North, where it had little or no influence. In years to come, this fact was to have more significance. The *Advocate* opposed bitterly the use of instrumental music and the missionary society. Consequently, churches in the South for the

---

[11]Tolbert Fanning, "Salutatory," *Gospel Advocate,* Vol. VIII, No. 1 (January 1, 1866), p. 1.

[12]David Lipscomb, "The Advocate and Sectionalism," *Gospel Advocate,* Vol. VIII, No. 18 (May 1, 1866), p. 273.

most part stayed loyal to earlier restoration principles. In the North, where the *Advocate* was little read, and where the *Christian Standard* was more extensively read, the majority of the churches went with the general movement, accepting innovations. Thus the innocent and proper motives of Fanning and Lipscomb became the occasion for further alienations.

The editors of the *Advocate* assumed a thoroughly independent position, fully resolved that they would submit themselves only to Christ. Fanning remarked:

We have received several letters from brethren assuring us that if we will defend certain peculiar interests and submit a satisfactory platform, we shall have a very large patronage indeed. In reply, we respectfully suggest that in our early youth we repudiated all human creeds in religion, and we have never regretted it. We now see no adequate cause for changing our position.[13]

Upon the rebirth of the *Advocate,* the editors followed in a measure that attitude which they took in 1855 when the *Advocate* was first born. They wanted the columns of their paper to be used as a means of having open and free discussions of all questions of interest to the church. It was not the original purpose of the editors in reviving the *Advocate* to wage war on the missionary society, but of freely discussing the issue in the desire that unity might be achieved. Consequently, Lipscomb wrote:

Any Christian Brother shall have the same freedom to our pages, on any subject that we may deem of interest, that the Editors themselves have. In one word the *Gospel Advocate* shall not be partisan for or against Missionary Societies, nor for or against Christians engaging in war or politics, but shall be open to us free, full and candid investigation of the matters from those occupying positions on these and other practical questions as **our** space will admit.[14]

To open a paper to full and candid discussions of all questions that effect the interest of Zion always presents the problem of personalities. No matter what attitude the editors assumed, they opened themselves to criticism from the readers. While asking for full discussions of all issues, Lipscomb made no effort to steer away from personalities, realizing the futility of such an attempt.

[13]Tolbert Fanning, "Our Platform," *Gospel Advocate,* Vol. VIII, No. 1 (January 1, 1866), p. 13.

[14]David Lipscomb, "Errata—Our Future," *Gospel Advocate,* Vol. VIII, No. 45 (November 5, 1866), p. 717.

Some years later, when F. D. Syrgley was criticized for inserting personalities into his articles, he tersely replied that whenever he saw a good-sized chunk of error lying around separate and apart from a personality, he would attack the error and let the personality alone. Lipscomb determined that he would watch closely the general spirit conveyed through these discussions, and would insist upon Christian charity and kindness being shown on every hand. Lipscomb had much to say on this subject at various times.

In announcing certain changes in the *Advocate* for 1868, Lipscomb restates the old policy in the following words:

Our purpose in the future, as in the past, shall be to encourage the free and full investigation of every subject having a practical bearing upon the spiritual welfare of the human family and the Kingdom of our Redeemer. We shall always demand that all investigations be conducted in a kind, Christian spirit. All vain theorizing on impractical questions and endless learned and unlearned theories and logomachies, and all personal strifes and contentions, shall be rigidly kept out of the *Advocate*.[15]

Men become identified with issues and thus cannot avoid being noticed. Lipscomb felt that carrying unrestrained personal quarrels desecrated the paper. He writes:

We intend hereafter, more rigidly than in the past, to exclude all personal quarrels and bickerings. The *Advocate* was not established to attack, nor to defend, the characters of individuals, either its Editors or others. It hereafter shall be desecrated to no such ends. It matters but little to the great interest of the cause of God in the world whether I or any other man be a hypocrite or not. Principles and institutions that effect the interest of humanity, not men, shall demand our attention. It is only as men become identified with such principles and institutions that we shall ever notice them.[16]

Nathan W. Smith of Jonesboro, Georgia, had been a faithful preacher during the war, and had undergone great suffering during the conflict. On one occasion he felt that he had been personally abused in the *Advocate*. While attempting to smooth over ruffled feelings, and, at the same time, to set forth the *Advocate's* policy, Lipscomb wrote:

The *Advocate* was never established to emblazon before the world the personal shortcomings of the brethren. The most pre-

[15]David Lipscomb, "Our Next Volume," *Gospel Advocate*, Vol. IX, No. 43 (October 24, 1867), p. 842.
[16]David Lipscomb, "Errata—Our Future," *Gospel Advocate*, Vol. VIII, No. 45 (November 5, 1866), p. 717.

cious earthly treasure the earth possesses is the character of her true and worthy children, and faults personal in their nature, of which we are all, to a greater or less extent, guilty, will never be lightly paraded to the public, to the detriment of the cause or the annoyance of any brother.[17]

Like other editors, Lipscomb frequently received criticism from brethren who did not like to see discussions and personalities carried on in the press. Such criticisms, he thought, generally indicated a lack of understanding of the role of a periodical. Papers possessed no authority. They were but clearing-houses for ideas; avenues by which brethren came to a mutual understanding. That they were abused was readily admitted. On the whole point, Lipscomb once wrote:

Some of our brethren are very fearful of discussion of questions that continually arise among the brethren. They seem to think the time will come when there will be no difference of sentiment, no discord or jars, no need for the investigation of subjects connected with the interests of our Master's Kingdom. They seem to think if there are differences of sentiment, they had better not be discussed. It makes a bad impression upon the world. . . . Do you wish to make the impression that there are no differences, when differences do exist? That would be to perpetuate a deception upon the public, to act a falsehood. . . . And yet, there is a matter of conducting discussion, a proper spirit in which it must be done, in order that the greatest good may be, thereby, effected. Personalities, bitterness of feeling, and unkind inuendoes are unworthy of Christian men, and always harm the cause they are used to sustain. Bitterness is not force, nor is personal denunciation argument. We hope our scribes will remember these things, and like David of old, forget all personal insults and indignities in their holy indignation at insulted and injured truth, and in the name of Christ, with Christ's spirit, battle manfully for the truth as it is in Christ the Lord.[18]

After the first few issues of the *Advocate* appeared at the close of the war, Fanning gradually withdrew himself into the background. Almost the entire editorial work was done by David Lipscomb. When Fanning was asked why he did not write more, he replied:

The *Gospel Advocate* we consider ably edited without a line from us. We are not disposed to flatter, but we find Brother D.

---

[17]David Lipscomb, "Letters from Nathan W. Smith," *Gospel Advocate,* Vol. X, No. 4 (January 24, 1868), p. 85.
[18]David Lipscomb, "Discussion," *Gospel Advocate,* Vol. VIII, No. 6 (February 6, 1866), pp. 83, 84.

Lipscomb a strong and vigorous writer, an earnest man, and one who knows and loves the truth. Of course, he is mortal—has faults, is not an angel, but we know not where to find a writer amongst the brethren better qualified to instruct in apostolic Christianity.[19]

In those early years following the war, the *Gospel Advocate* had great difficulty in getting on a sound financial basis. There were times when it looked as though it might be forced to cease publication. Were it not for the sacrifices of David Lipscomb, it unquestionably would have ceased. During 1866 and most of 1867 he lived twelve miles from the office and had to ride this distance on horseback. This took a great amount of time, and often the *Advocate* was sent out without any proofreading. As an effort to avoid this, Lipscomb lived apart from his family for days, staying in unwarmed quarters, and munching cold lunches. Such personal sacrifices kept the *Advocate* going when otherwise it would have failed.

After the war, and for many years following, it was generally known that Lipscomb's health was very frail. He went to the consultation meeting at Murfreesboro in June, 1866, but had to return early because of illness. By the spring of 1867 he was in "constant pain." It was evident something had to be done. His condition he describes as "general biliary derangement, torpidity of liver, costiveness, alternated with a looseness of bowels." He complains that for several years he had known "severe paroxisms of pain." Upon hearing that a physician in Cleveland, Ohio, could cure such conditions by a "water cure," he determined to try it. He went to Cleveland via Cincinnati, visited congregations on the way, heard several preachers, met and talked with Isaac Errett. The water cure, he thought, helped him temporarily. For many years he suffered occasional hemorrhages that each time they occurred caused several days of suffering. The last of December, 1879, he took a severe cold and coughed so often and so violently that he had grave doubts that he would ever recover. Doctors declared his trouble to be "related to" asthma. In later years his health greatly improved, but until he was fifty years of age he constantly knew frail health.

Lipscomb's ill health received considerable attention from many

---

[19]Tolbert Fanning, "Why Do We Not Write More?" *Gospel Advocate,* Vol. VIII, No. 35 (August 28, 1866), p. 560.

brethren, especially from those who did not agree with his position. The *Advocate* has gained a reputation for speaking out against things that were wrong, but the feeling existed that it went to an extreme. L. B. Wilkes, one of the editors of the *Apostolic Times,* probably expressed the popular attitude of brethren toward the *Advocate* when he wrote:

The *Advocate* is sound in the faith; sometimes, I have thought, it is a little too sound—so straight that it leaned a little over. But its faults, and I think it not wholly free from them, generally lean toward the safe side.[20]

Now this being "too sound," as Wilkes put it, was at times laid to the ill health of David Lipscomb. Isaac Errett put it in the following words:

We like Brother Lipscomb for one thing—his entire frankness. There is nothing of the assassin in his warfare—no sulking about the pathway of his opponent with cowardly insinuations, ready to hurl them murderously at the reputation of an unsuspecting and unarmed antagonist. He comes into the field armed *cap-a-pie,* publishes his cause of quarrel, throws down the gauntlet, and waits, in true knightly posture, for an honorable tilt. He may, perhaps, be charged with an excess of frankness. We are inclined to think that ill health and a somewhat atrabilarious temperament lead him sometimes to indudge in gloomy apprehensions which give an undue soberness to many of his editorials. But we always know where to find him; and if we must have a controversy, we prefer to deal with an open and honorable disputant.

Lipscomb's reputation for having an "excess of frankness" was, at times, made the butt of a joke. Before his father. Ben Franklin, died, Joseph Franklin was a loyal devotee of the truth, and was one of the spiciest writers in the *Review.* He came to Nashville in December, 1877, and visited many brethren, David Lipscomb being among the number. In his characteristically pungent style, he later remarked: "Brother 'Dave' has a mighty fine way about him, but he don't mean it all." He was striking, of course, at Lipscomb's "excess of frankness."

In the years immediately after the war, the *Advocate* had great difficulty securing enough subscribers to continue. In 1866 the paper had no office, but was printed on contract by another

---

[20]L. B. Wilkes, "The Gospel Advocate," *Apostolic Times,* Vol. I, (1869), p. 12.

concern. Nashville was then occupied by a large Federal army. Living conditions were bad; labor was high. Postal facilities were very limited. Only the larger thoroughfares had postal facilities at all, and these were inadequate. Lipscomb had not the funds to put into the paper to make it go. In the spring of 1866 he announced that the *Advocate* did not have enough subscribers to carry it through the year without serious loss to the editor. By the fall of 1867 the condition was worse. The October 17th issue was delayed, and Lipscomb explained that this was due to lack of funds. Five hundred dollars had been given to him to buy a press. He loaned this money out with the understanding that he could get it back at any time. Unfortunately, this promise fell through. During the fall of 1867, Lipscomb begged brethren to send him one thousand subscribers. The *Advocate* reached a financial crisis that year, and closed out with the November 7th issue.

The paper appeared again in 1868, greatly enlarged, and changed in some details. Even though Lipscomb was not financially able to make this improvement, he went ahead upon the theory that brethren would support it if it were a better periodical. This year, Lipscomb assumed full responsibility for the editorship. The year before P. S. Fall had become a co editor. Fanning also was a co-editor. A new feature of the paper was an "Alien's Department" edited by Dr. T. W. Brents, consisting of essays on fundamental Bible teaching, intending to instruct the alien on how to become a Christian. These essays were later collected together into a tract called "The Gospel Plan of Salvation," which later became the book by the same title.

The year 1868 saw the *Gospel Advocate* emerging from the financial storm. By June, Lipscomb announced that the *Advocate* was now on a self-sustaining basis. By October, he suggested that it was past the crisis and in better condition than ever. Throughout the year 1869, Lipscomb carried the load alone. Both Fanning and Fall had become too preoccupied with other matters to take an interest in the *Advocate*. Elisha G. Sewell was now invited to move to Nashville. The invitation was readily accepted, and Sewell became co-editor of the *Gospel Advocate* January 1, 1870.

In later years David Lipscomb was to exert a tremendous

influence upon the course of the church in the South, an influence
which cannot be exaggerated and must not be underestimated.
The interest that lay closest to his heart was the welfare and
purity of the church. He was a giant in Israel in those days.
John F. Rowe spoke of him in the following words:

The *Gospel Advocate* is to hand, and, as usual, full of valuable
thought and interesting reading. Brother David Lipscomb, with
his efficient aids, is doing a large and good work, for which the
Master alone can bestow a corresponding reward. I know Brother
David well, and have always had the most undoubted assurance
that the welfare of society and the purity of the church were the
interests that fill his great heart.[21]

There were some, like V. M. Metcalfe, who believed that Lipscomb was providentially the man provided for those critical days
of the restoration movement when men were abandoning the
appointments of God for human opinions. It took a courageous,
intelligent man, and withal a charitable one to sweep back the tide
of innovations then engulfing the church. In view of this Metcalfe wrote:

He is getting old, and in the course of nature will not be here
many more years to earnestly contend for the purity of the church
and simplicity of the gospel. I don't know of a brother who is
more frequently misquoted and misunderstood than Brother Lipscomb. While everybody concedes that he is a man of ability, yet
few know his real worth. I have known him intimately for over
twenty-five years, and I have never known a more godly or self-
sacrificing man. Many suppose from his writings that he is a
cross, ill-natured, sour old man, yet just the reverse is true. He
is tenderhearted and loving as a child—can be led to do almost
anything unless he thinks it wrong; then all the earth can't move
him. He is loyal to the teachings of the Bible. I have never known
a man just like him in all of his makeup. I believed that God in
His providence has used him in the last twenty-five years as he
has no other man to elevate the standard of the church of Christ
and keep it pure from innovations. God has given him wisdom
and power for accomplishing good. He has not been unfaithful.[22]

The Lipscomb story—his controversies, his activities, and his
teachings—will largely fill the history into which we now launch.

---

[21]John F. Rowe, "Items," *Christian Leader,* Vol. 1, No. 2 (October 14,
1886), p. 4.

[22]V. M. Metcalfe, "Our Bible School," *Gospel Advocate,* Vol. XXXV,
No. 22 (June 1, 1893), p. 341.

CHAPTER II

ISAAC ERRETT

Any estimate which one places upon the work and ultimate influence of Isaac Errett will be colored largely by the individual's viewpoint. Historians among the Disciples of Christ invariably look upon Errett as the one who saved the restoration movement from becoming "a fissiparous sect of jangling legalists." This group hails Errett as the prophet of spirituality and liberalism. His life stands, therefore, as the epitome of that type of thinking, which, after the Civil War swept over the church. A closer investigation may raise some doubts about the validity of this claim. But, whether we regard Errett as the champion of liberalism and "saviour" of the church from "jangling legalism," or as the prophet of digression, still, his influence in the restoration movement is so important that a chapter must be devoted to him.

Errett was the fifth child of Henry and Sophia Kemmish Errett, and was born in New York City on January 2, 1820. His parents were very devout and belonged to a very strict religious sect. His membership in this sect went back to November, 1810 at which time this group consisted mainly of emmigrants from Scotland. The "holy kiss" seems to have been regularly practiced along with other peculiar religious observances.

Henry Errett, however, did not live long. He died in 1825, when young Isaac was only five years old. Isaac scarcely remembered his father. In this respect, as in many others, the experience of Isaac Errett was the antithesis of David Lipscomb. Lipscomb remembered his father, and hardly recalled his mother. Isaac Errett's mother, upon the death of her husband, was compelled to open a boarding house to earn a living for her family. Despite her difficulties her children were sent regularly to worship services where they listened to long speeches, endless prayers, and great theological discussions.

When Errett's mother married a Scotchman by the name of Sauter, the family moved to a farm in Somerset County, New Jersey. Here the boys in the Errett family learned to work long hours on the farm. Their stepfather was a hard-working man,

23

a strong disciplinarian, and with his enthusiasm for money, sometimes forgot to take into consideration the full welfare of his family. In 1832 he emigrated to Pittsburgh with his family where he set up a saw-mill, and put the boys to work. They worked from daylight until dark. They built up a resentment for their stepfather. Although he provided them with a home, he gave little love and tenderness. His life was occupied with making money. It was a mistake which he in later years realized.

The church in Pittsburgh borrowed freely from the Scottish background of its members. The "holy kiss" was practiced—at least for a while. Strict discipline was maintained. If a member of this church married an individual who was not, he could look for a public and personal chastisement from the leaders in the congregation. "Foot washing" was never practiced but was seriously considered.

The lives of the great pioneer preachers all display varied childhood backgrounds. Just how far the background of Isaac Errett influenced his thinking is difficult to say. Errett's youthful training made him thoroughly acquainted with the very strict interpretation of the letter of the law. This was his religious background and he rebelled stubbornly against it. His later outlook tended to react against what he considered a following of "the letter of the law." On the other hand, men like Jacob Creath, Jr., who knew in their youthful days the tyranny of human creeds and human opinions, became thoroughly obsessed with the conviction that any departure from the strict letter of the law would lead to apostasy. Consequently, Jacob Creath—and many like him—reacted violently against the projection of human opinions, and human innovations into the work and worship of the church. Certainly some significance is to be attached to these backgrounds.

Isaac Errett, and his older brother, Russell, were very close. Being religiously inclined, they acted together on nearly all important matters. So, in the spring of 1833, when both boys heard Elder Robert McLaren preach, each was baptized by him in the Allegheny River. They were now members of the church in Pittsburgh, and each was faithful in every way.

About this time Isaac Errett began thinking of his future. He secured a position in a bookstore where he worked (here) for nearly a year. In the meantime he decided that he would become a printer, and became an apprentice under a Mr. A. A. Anderson, editor of a paper called "The Intelligencer." Errett contributed several articles for this periodical, which friends observed, definitely indicated superior talent, a foreglance of his later greatness as a writer. In later years, after he began editing the *Christian Standard,* and his writings were before the brotherhood continually, Errett displayed an elegance of style, and a power of diction that few could equal. Perhaps this early experience contributed to this end. He stayed with the printing business under Mr. Anderson until 1839 when he resigned to accept a position as a teacher in a school in Roberson Township, Allegheny County, Pennsylvania.

It was during this time that he began to develop into a preacher. The church in Pittsburgh had various social meetings at which the young people were invited to speak. Errett spoke frequently. The older people noted at once his sincerity, his interest in spiritual affairs, and gave him more and more encouragement. His first "regular discourse" was delivered on April 21, 1839. His subject was the promise which God made to David that his kingdom would not fail. As the custom of the church was to set apart its evangelists with a solemn ceremony, Errett was thus "set apart" on June 18, 1840.

The Pittsburgh church was singularly fortunate in the fact that some of the outstanding preachers frequently visited and delivered discourses there. It was Errett's good fortune to hear Alexander Campbell, Thomas Campbell and Walter Scott on various occasions. It can be safely assumed that he heard many of the other prominent evangelists such as Samuel Church.

For the four years following his being set apart as an evangelist, Errett's fortunes were cast in Pittsburgh. Sometime in 1840 a new congregation was established in this city on Smithfield Street. In October Errett resigned his teaching position to devote his full time to preaching for this congregation. Here he baptized his first convert, Mrs. Sarah Ann King. Here, too, Errett became acquainted with Miss Harriet Reeder, and on October 18, 1841, they were married. But the church at Pittsburgh, like most congregations in those days was indifferent toward the preacher's salary. Errett cast his eyes in the direction of a more fertile field where he could more capably support his family.

In 1844 Errett moved to New Lisbon, Ohio on the Western Reserve. Here the eloquence of Walter Scott had blazed forth many years before, and through his proclamation of the plan of salvation the church had been planted. The congregation, at the time Errett went there, appears to have been in a bad condition but the nature of that condition is not explained. Errett, however, rode the storm and managed to see a measure of peace and growth come to the work.

It was five years later, on March 28, 1849, that he moved to the church at North Bloomfield, Ohio. But again, Errett ran into some of the old trouble—poor support. The next spring, by mutual agreement with the congregations, he began preaching part-time for the church at Warren, Ohio. For the next six years his labors were given mainly to the Warren congregation. He frequently went on evangelistic tours, and on one such tour, held a meeting at Bethany in 1854. While still at Warren, he debated Joel Tiffany, a Universalist. It was while Errett was preaching at Warren that his name came more frequently before the brotherhood until he assumed a more prominent role.

In political sentiment Errett was pronouncedly a man of the North. He looked upon slavery as a great evil. When the Fugitive Slave Law was passed requiring northern people to return run-away slaves, Errett remonstrated. He considered this to be against Christian principles. The sermon which he delivered at Warren in 1851 on the "Design of Civil Government And The Extent of Its Authority" clashed with the views of Alexander Campbell. Campbell printed it in the *Millennial Harbinger* as a very capable rebuttal, and replied. Errett's rejoinder was printed and Campbell answered it in footnotes.

In spring of 1856 Errett made plans for a move from Ohio. Michigan was attracting him. He purchased a farm near Lyons, and on May 9, 1856 made his transfer from Ohio. For the next few years his work was to be done in this state. In 1857 he became the corresponding secretary for the American Christian Missionary Society and held this position until 1860. Meanwhile, he traveled extensively in evangelistic efforts. In Michigan his labors extended to Ionia and Muir. In 1861 he was made a co-editor on the *Millennial Harbinger*. The same year he was an agent for securing funds for Bethany College.

The war came, and Errett threw his influence solidly behind the North. He made frequent political speeches, often going into camps to make rousing addresses to the boys in blue. He applied to the Governor for a commission as a colonel that he might raise corps to take to the field. The Governor refused, saying he had given out all the commissions that he could. Errett's brother, Russell, was a Major in the Union army. His son, James, enlisted, but severe illness prevented any active participation. J. W. McGarvey wrote Errett in an attempt to enlist his opposition to Christian participation in this carnal engagement. Errett however, refused. The cause of the Union was too close to his heart so he did all within his power to promote it.

Late in 1862 Errett considered casting his fortunes with the church in Detroit. For a number of years there had been a small congregation in the city, and it now met in the City Hall. Late that year a group left this congregation to start another church on Jefferson and Beaubian. The separation in the church appears to have been peaceable, although it seems evident that there were serious differences among the brethren. Alexander Linn, brother-in-law to Colin Campbell, was with the old congregation. Linn was as loyal to the truth as a man could be, and was one of the future leaders in the battle against digression in Detroit. Richard Hawley and Colin Campbell, on the other hand, were the chief men in the new congregation, and were liberal in spirit and outlook. They employed Isaac Errett as their new preacher. The building, which had been purchased from the Congregationalists, was dedicated by W. K. Pendleton on January 11, 1863.[1]

During these Civil War years, and particularly while Errett was in Detroit, his liberal attitude appeared. Errett had been laying the ground-work for the one-man pastor system in the *Millennial Harbinger*. He carefully, however, avoided dissension. The articles were conducted in the form of a dialogue, with "Eusebius" suggesting the ideas Errett wanted to put across.

But, soon after taking up the work with the church in Detroit, Errett published what he called "A Synopsis of The Faith And Practice of The Church of Christ." The "Synopsis" consisted of ten articles setting forth the faith and practice of the church, in

---

[1]W. K. Pendleton, "The Cause in Detroit," *Millennial Harbinger,* Fifth Series, Vol. VI, No. 1 (January, 1863), pp. 27-31.

addition to a series of by-laws, emphasizing the regulations of the order and business of the church. Most brethren felt that the "Synopsis" amounted to a creed. Those interested in reading it may find it in full in *Lard's Quarterly,* September, 1863, pp. 95-100. There was strong objection to this "creed." Ben Franklin published it in the *American Christian Review,* and voiced his opposition. But the strongest objections came from Moses E. Lard:

There is not a sound man in our ranks who has seen the preceding "Synopsis" that has not felt scandalized by it. I wish we possessed even one decent apology for its appearance. It is a deep offense against the brotherhood—an offense tossed into the teeth of a people, who, for forty years, have been working against the divisive and evil tendency of creeds.[2]

Also while in Detroit, Errett secured a name-plate to put over the office-door. On it was engraved the words: "Rev. I. Errett." At this early stage in the restoration movement it was enough to shock the brotherhood. This was looked upon by many as a definite departure from apostolic principles. Neither Jesus nor his apostles, nor an evangelist in primitive times set himself aside by this "popish" designation, the brethren reasoned. The very fact that Errett selected such a designation as "Reverend" indicated to many that he had a closer affinity to Rome than to ancient Jerusalem. The fuller discussion of this issue is reserved to a later chapter, but it is enough to note here Errett's general viewpoint.

On April 7, 1866, the first issue of the *Christian Standard* came from the press. Isaac Errett was the editor. To relate the full story of the establishment of this paper involves many little known details. The chief source of information has been J. S. Lamar's, "Memoirs of Isaac Errett," which is such a biased production that the full facts are not revealed. To Lamar Errett was an idol. His two volumes on the life of Isaac Errett, which were first published in the *Christian Standard* in 1892 in serial form, show him to be utterly incapable of grasping the point of Errett's opponents. The volumes are wordy and extravagant, and seldom is Errett spoken of except with an adjective such as "sweet," "pious," "godly," "spiritual." The opponents of Errett were

---

[2]Moses E. Lard, "Remarks on the Foregoing," *Lard's Quarterly,* Vol. 1, No. 1 (September, 1863), p. 100.

invariably "earth-born spirits," "legalists," etc. Those who agreed with Errett were the "leading minds in the brotherhood;" those who disagreed, were "disgruntled," "jealous," etc. When it came to writing that phase of Errett's life that dealt with his controversies with other men, Lamar was incapable of doing justice to Errett's opponents. That he relied much on his imagination is evident, and the result, so far as it respects these controversies, is as much fiction as history. When Lamar's articles appeared in the *Christian Standard,* there were those who answered them, presenting some of the fiction. David Lipscomb was one. L. F. Bittle was another. Bittle appraised Lamar's treatment of the establishment of the *Christian Standard* in the following words:

It is well that the people be informed of the facts in regard to the origin of the Christian Standard. Brother J. F. Rowe knows a great deal about the matter. Will he not give an impartial statement of the case? J. S. Lamar, like the majority of biographers, feels bound to eulogize his hero and to make the most of the latter's deeds and motives. But the result is fiction not history.[3]

But why was the *Christian Standard* established? Was there a particular need for the paper? That certain brethren felt there was need for such a paper is obvious else it never should have been started. But as to what that *need* was is a different question. Lamar pointed out the inadequacy of the currently published religious papers. He writes:

There were several weeklies, also, among them the "Review" and "Gospel Advocate," but these were not satisfactory. They were regarded as being narrow in their views in many respects, hurtful rather than helpful to the great cause which they assumed to represent. I would say nothing here derogatory of the editors of these papers. They represented and fostered that unfortunate type of discipleship to which allusion was made in a previous chapter—a type with which the leading minds among the brotherhood could have no sympathy. We may credit these writers with sincerity and honesty, but we can not read many of their productions without feeling that we are breathing an unwholesome religious atmosphere. They seem to infuse an unlovely and earth-born spirit, which they clothe, nevertheless, in the garb of the divine letter, and enforce with cold, legalistic and crushing power. The great truth for whose defense the Disciples are set, demanded a

---

[3]L. F. Bittle, "The Truth in History, " *Octographic Review,* Vol. XXXV, No. 32 (August 9, 1892), p. 6.

wiser, sweeter, better advocacy—an advocacy that should exhibit the apostolic *spirit* as well as the apostolic *letter*.[4]

Thus Lamar assures the reader that the *Christian Standard* was needed because the *Gospel Advocate* and the *American Christian Review* were edited by men of "unlovely and earth-born spirits" who were cold, and legalistic. Now the fiction in this is easily discernible. Plans for starting the *Standard* were under way by 1864. The *Gospel Advocate* had appeared as a small, monthly paper from 1855 to 1861, having ceased because of the war. The first issue of the *Advocate* as a weekly did not appear until January, 1866. In April that year Isaac Errett wrote to David Lipscomb requesting back copies of the *Advocate* saying he had not yet seen an issue of it. Yet this paper which Errett had not seen was the occasion for starting the *Standard*. To state that brethren were influenced to establish the *Standard* because of the "earth-born spirit" of the *Advocate* but betrays the prejudice Lamar felt and shows the undying contempt in which he held the *Advocate*. This is the element to which Bittle referred when he accused Lamar of resorting to his imagination—not to facts.

The *American Christian Review* was being printed as a weekly before this time by Ben Franklin. It was widely received; indeed, it was the most popular paper in the brotherhood, and it was this fact that worried an element of prominent men in the brotherhood. Franklin, on almost all issues before the church, stood opposed to Errett, Pendleton, and preachers of kindred thought. The editor of the *Review,* they considered "narrow" and "bigoted." Knowing Franklin's popularity with the majority of the brethren, it was their constant fear that Franklin's "narrowness" would fasten itself upon the brotherhood, and prevent the restoration movement from following along more "liberal," "progressive" lines. No person can go back to the study of this period and fail to see that the chief reason for the establishment of the *Christian Standard* was to kill the *Review,* and lead the brotherhood away from Franklin's influence into these more liberal channels.

The fact that the Civil War was in progress only aggravated the situation. Ben Franklin announced himself opposed to Christian participation in the war, insisting that he would not kill those

---

[4] J. S. Lamar, *Memoirs of Isaac Errett,* Vol. 1 (Cincinnati: The Christian Standard Publishing Co., 1893), pp. 300, 301.

people that he had for years been trying to convert to Christ.   He announced that the *Review* would not discuss war and politics. When the American Christian Missionary Society passed its resolutions backing the Union and denouncing the South, Franklin remonstrated.   Indeed, this did more than anything else to turn him against the Society.   He saw at once that it could be a powerful weapon for evil.   Isaac Errett was connected with the Society, and had endorsed the war resolutions.   His close friend, James A. Garfield, who was influential in starting the *Christian Standard,* stood by his side.   Garfield had forsaken the pulpit for a name in politics, had fought in the Union army, from Shiloh across to Chickamauga, and then resigned to be elected to Congress from his home district.   Garfield, too, severely denounced the South, even advocating the confiscation of all their lands and property.   Franklin strictly refused to allow the *American Christian Review* to become the mouthpiece for agitating hatred among brethren.   In 1867 while David Lipscomb was in Cleveland to get a water cure for his sickness, he met Isaac Errett for the first time.   Errett preached in Cleveland then and edited his paper from there.   At this time Errett heaped abuse upon Franklin.   He informed Lipscomb that the *Standard* was started because Franklin refused to allow them to publish their views on the duty of Christians to support the government in time of war.[5]

Thus, that the *Christian Standard* was started in part to kill the influence of Ben Franklin and the *American Christian Review* is plainly evident.

There is another factor regarding the establishment of this periodical which comes to us from John F. Rowe, and is completely ignored by Lamar.   In 1864 there lived at Corry, Virginia, a wealthy brother by the name of G. W. N. Yost.   Rowe was then an agent for the Missionary Society, and the Society, upon learning of Yost's wealth, sent Rowe over to get a part of it. Yost was in the oil business and at that time was making about one thousand dollars per day.   He had taken a particular liking to Rowe, and donated to him five hundred dollars, requesting that he secure a preacher and some singers, come to Corry and hold a meeting.   Anything left over should go to the Society.   Rowe

---

[5]David Lipscomb, "The Truth of History," *Gospel Advocate,* Vol. XXXIV, No. 28 (July 14, 1892), p. 436.

secured the services of A. W. Way, and the church was established at Corry. Yost paid for the erection of a meeting house.

Yost tried to prevail upon Rowe to settle in Corry. He volunteered to start and pay for a paper to be published from there. Rowe informed him that a first-class paper was needed, but should be published from a larger city, preferably New York. Yost requested Rowe to edit it, but Rowe refused, insisting however, that he would consent to be an associate-editor. When Yost asked him to recommend an editor, Rowe named Isaac Errett. Errett then lived in Muir, Michigan. Rowe wrote him, and his letter was signed jointly by J. H. Jones, who was then engaged in a gospel meeting with him, who was also a close personal friend of Errett. We are not told what Errett's answer was at this time, but that a correspondence ensued which kept the idea alive.

To get the full Rowe story it will be necessary to anticipate some events. The result of Yost's proposal to Rowe of a paper was a gathering at Newcastle, Pennsylvania in the home of the Phillips brothers. Here, the *Christian Standard* was organized. Errett insisted upon publishing it from Cleveland; Rowe, from New York. Errett suggested to Rowe that the paper would have no associate-editor, but left it open for Rowe to write any department he chose. Rowe selected the department of "Book Reviewer," but in a few months received word from Errett that this department would be edited by B. A. Hinsdale. Errett then proposed that Rowe write one article a month for which he was to be paid one hundred dollars. Rowe confesses that he wrote four articles and then broke all connection with the paper.[6] Thus, Rowe informs us that the *Christian Standard* was at first the result of Yost's suggestion to start a paper for Rowe, but that Errett saw fit slowly to push Rowe out of any place of responsibility.

Here, we have in its earliest stages two threads of action, each contributing to the establishment of the paper. The first was the desire to kill the influence of Ben Franklin and the *American Christian Review*. There melted into this stream of thought another which, happily for the Errett group, approached at the right time to furnish the occasion for carrying out the former

---

[6]John F. Rowe, "Reminiscences of The Restoration," *American Christian Review*, Vol. XXIX, No. 24 (June 10, 1886), p. 188.

purpose—Yost's desire to establish a paper just for John F. Rowe.

Referring again to Lamar's theory on the establishment of the *Christian Standard,* there is yet another angle to investigate. Lamar indicates that there was a popular clamor for the *Standard.* He says, first, that this clamor came from the "leading minds" whom he suggests were "wiser, sweeter, better" than the "unlovely and earth-born spirits" that dominated other periodicals. On this point David Lipscomb wrote:

In one word, Brother Lamar's theory as to the origin of the *Christian Standard* is, that the whole enterprise was projected by the "leading minds among the brotherhood" and that those "leading minds" were "wiser, sweeter, better" than the "unlovely and earth-born spirit" which dominated such papers as the *American Christian Review, Lard's Quarterly,* and the *Gospel Advocate,* and inspired such men as Benjamin Franklin, Tolbert Fanning, Moses E. Lard, David Lipscomb, E. G. Sewell, and Phillip S. Fall. Such is Brother Lamar's theory.[7]

But were these men "wiser, sweeter and better" than these other brethren? Certainly in no one's estimation but their own, and in this case they were not exactly altogether free of prejudice. It was not without point that Lipscomb called Lamar's attention to the contrast in character of these men. James A. Garfield was every inch a Union man. He led an army, made up greatly by members of the church, into the battles of Shiloh and later, Chickamauga. Returning from the war, he thundered wildly against the South. Errett himself preached war sermons, applied for a commission, and otherwise encouraged war. While this was going on, David Lipscomb preached openly in the South against Christians fighting either for South or North. Active opposition was raised against him. After preaching a sermon in middle Tennessee against Christians going to war, a man, standing in the doorway of a church building, said if he could get a dozen men to help him, they would hang David Lipscomb.[8] Lipscomb found it difficult to believe that Errett's group were "sweeter, and better" than Franklin, Sewell, Fall, Lard, and Fanning.

These facts abundantly show that Brother Lamar's talk about the brethren who started the *Christian Standard* being "wiser,

---

[7]David Lipscomb, "Concerning the Width and Sweetness of Things," *Gospel Advocate,* Vol. XXXIV, No. 24 (June 16, 1892), p. 370.
[8]David Lipscomb, "Correction," *Gospel Advocate,* Vol. XXXIV, No. 29 (July 21, 1892), p. 453.

sweeter, better" than the brethren who differed from them is the veriest twaddle. It is time to call a halt to such palaver. The plain truth is that "our brethren" differ among themselves on some points. The *Christian Standard* merely represents one party in those differences—simply that and nothing more. The brethren in one party are neither wiser nor sweeter than those in the other, save in their own estimation.

All this is perhaps none of my business, but in justice to such men as Harding, Lipscomb, Elam, Smith, Sewell, Larimore, Taylor, Butler, Kurfees, Wilmeth, Burnet, Brents, Gowen, Creel, Bryant, Grant, Northcross, and hundreds of others, I protest against the complacent self-righteousness and brazen egotism which sneers at those who differ from Brother Lamar and *Christian Standard* as "being narrow in their views of scripture truth" and "unlovely and earth-born spirits" with whom "the leading minds among the brotherhood" can have no sympathy.[9]

Lamar's explanation that the *Christian Standard* was the result of a demand from the brotherhood indicates that he again relies more upon his imagination than upon facts. For a year and a half after starting, the *Standard* came near being a financial disaster. The stockholders washed their hands of the paper and gave it to Errett. This fact alone does not necessarily reflect against the merit of the paper. The *Gospel Advocate* during this time came near going under. The truth is that those were hard times financially, and people with limited means did not subscribe freely to new papers. Lamar was not frank enough to face this fact. His hero-worship of the *Standard* would not permit it. He was dedicated to the task of showing that the whole brotherhood was up in arms against the *Review, Quarterly, Advocate*, etc., and were clamoring for the *Standard*. In trying to sustain this position, it is a curious fact that Lamar was never able to see his own contradictory statements. Writing of the association which was formed to establish the paper, he says,

The association was not only to issue the paper, but to publish books, tracts, etc., and the paper itself was *wanted;* "everybody" had been calling for it, and its circulation would certainly be very large. . .

But in the same paragraph Lamar adds:

. . . The "Standard" with all its backing, had to establish a

---

[9]David Lipscomb, "Concerning the Width and Sweetness of Things," *Gospel Advocate,* Vol. XXXIV, No. 24 (June 16, 1892), p. 370.

character for itself, and win its own way, little by little, to popular favor and support. . .

"Everybody," he insisted, wanted the *Standard,* and yet, by way of apologizing for the disappointingly small subscription list, he urged that the *Standard* had to win its way little by little. Again, Lamar explains the low subscription:

Still, the brotherhood as a whole had not, at this time, been educated up to this high standard. Their leading weekly, before the appearance of Mr. Errett's paper, was the "American Christian Review" edited by B. Franklin of Cincinnati—which, though in some respects strong and influencial, was run on a lower plane, and catered to a lower taste. *Its* readers, therefore, missed in the "Standard" the tone to which they had become accustomed, and that slugging sort of belligerency which had been weekly exhibited for their delectation and applause. Many, consequently, who most needed the blessed influence of Mr. Errett's gentler and sweeter spirit, had to be trained and schooled to appreciate it.[10]

There is no way to harmonize such statements; they are plainly contradictory. To say that the whole brotherhood wanted the *Standard* and then apologize for its small circulation which nearly caused it to fail on the ground that the brotherhood as a whole was not yet educated *up* to such a standard, is a plain contradiction of facts. The plain truth of the matter is that Ben Franklin was the man of the people. There were a few men with both money and position who disliked Ben Franklin's close adherence to the scriptures, and who were determined to sell the church over to their liberal ideas. The fact that a hundred thousand dollar concern went broke in the attempt attests the fact that Franklin's influence was far more powerful than they imagined.

This lengthy discussion has been necessary because of the prevalent misunderstanding regarding the establishment of the *Christian Standard.* We turn our attention now to the events which led to the birth of this periodical. How far-reaching Rowe's letter to Errett in 1864 regarding the establishment of a paper may be hard to say. Nevertheless, in May, 1865, the idea of starting a paper gained momentum. During the month, the Ohio Christian Missionary Society met at Ashland, Ohio at which time a conference was held privately among some individuals to discuss the project. A committee was appointed further to investigate the possibilities.

---

[10] J. S. Lamar, *Memoirs of Isaac Errett,* Vol. I, p. 334.

Of all procedures of preparation, the most significant was a meeting held at the home of the wealthy Phillips brothers—Thomas W., Charles M., I. N., and John T., who lived at Newcastle, Pennsylvania. The date was December 22, 1865. Those present included Isaac Errett, J. P. Robison, W. K. Pendleton, James A. Garfield, C. H. Gould, John F. Rowe, J. K. Pickett, J. B. Milner, O. Higgins, E. J. Agnew, John T. Phillips, C. M. Phillips, Thomas W. Phillips and W. J. Ford. J. P. Robison was selected as chairman and W. J. Ford was requested to serve as secretary. T. W. Phillips then proposed the following resolutions:

RESOLVED, First that the present aspect of affairs, in connection with the religious interest of the "current Reformation," requires the aid of a new religious weekly newspaper.

RESOLVED, Second, that in order the more surely and successfully to effect the establishment and support of such a weekly, a joint stock company should be formed to raise the means necessary, and to direct the conduct of the same.[11]

The resolutions, being considered separately, were passed upon and accepted.

The next order of business was the selection of a site for the location of the new periodical. C. H. Gould recommended Cincinnati; Robison, with the encouragement of Errett, recommended Cleveland; Rowe advocated New York. Cleveland was finally agreed upon as the site. The committee on legal affairs relative to the obtaining of a charter and getting the necessary papers for organizing was then appointed with James A. Garfield, J. P. Robison and W. S. Streator selected. This meeting was adjourned with the understanding they should meet again four days later in Cleveland.

Accordingly, the meeting in Cleveland was held on December 26, 1865. The capital stock of the corporation was set at one hundred thousand dollars to be sold in shares of ten dollars each. The name of the company was selected as "The Christian Publishing Association." The price of the paper was fixed at two dollars and fifty cents a year, with the first issue scheduled to appear in April, the following year. J. H. Jones moved that Errett be made the editor-in-chief, and the motion was carried unanimously.

---

[11] J. S. Lamar, *Memoirs of Isaac Errett*, Vol. I, p. 302.

From this time events moved more rapidly. The charter for the corporation was obtained January 2, 1866. A Board of Directors was appointed consisting of James A. Garfield, W. S. Streator, J. P. Robison, T. W. Phillips, C. M. Phillips, G. W. N. Yost, and W. J. Ford. The first meeting of the Directors was held February 14, that year. Streator was appointed president; W. J. Ford, secretary; and J. P. Robison, treasurer. These three men, according to the rules of the corporation, were to form the Executive Committee. It was agreed that Isaac Errett, as editor-in-chief should manage all business of the paper and select his own associates, subject to the approval of the Executive Committee. At this meeting the title, *Christian Standard* was selected for the periodical.

Regarding the name of the paper, Errett wrote later:

We propose, therefore, to lift up the *Christian Standard,* as a rally point for the scattered hosts of spiritual Israel; to know only "Jesus Christ and Him crucified: His cross, His word, His church, His ordinances, His laws, and the interests of His kingdom."[12]

Prospects for the success of the *Standard* looked very hopeful. It had immense wealth behind it, in addition to the cooperation of certain men of influence. The subscription list of the *Christian Record,* then being published in Indianapolis with Elijah Goodwin as editor, was turned over to the *Standard.* Thus the new paper had about eight thousand subscribers immediately given over to it.

The direction a new periodical proposes to travel at once indicates the viewpoint of its backers. In those days it was customary for such a new-born enterprise to start with a "Prospectus," so the *Christian Standard* followed the custom. Their prospectus read:

A joint stock company, under the name of The Christian Publishing Association, proposes to publish, in the city of Cleveland, Ohio, a weekly religious newspaper, to be called "The Christian Standard." Isaac Errett, editor.

The "Standard" proposes—

1. A bold and vigorous advocacy of Christianity, as revealed in the New Testament, without respect to party, creed or an established theological system.

2. A plea for the union of all who acknowledge the supreme

---

[12]Isaac Errett, "Our Name," *Christian Standard,* Vol. I, No. 1 (April 7, 1866), p. 4.

authority of the Lord Jesus, on the apostolic basis of "one Lord, one faith, one baptism."

3. Particular regard to practical religion in all the broad interests of piety and humanity. Missionary and educational enterprises, and every worthy form of active benevolence, will receive attention. While the "Standard" is designed to be preeminently a religious paper, it will freely discuss the moral and religious aspects of the leading questions of the day, in literature, education, moral and political science, commerce—in short, all that bears seriously on duty and destiny.

4. A Christian literature, involving a review of books and such discussions of literature, science and art as may serve to excite inquiry and promote the intelligence and taste of its readers.

5. A faithful record of important religious movements in the old world and the new. While it is intended to make the "Standard" an organ of the interests and movements of the brotherhood of Disciples, it will not fail to present such a view of the teachings and proceedings of all denominations and benevolent societies as will keep its readers posted in all the important affairs of the religious world.

6. Such a summary of political, commercial and general intelligence as is suitable for a family and paper.

Scriptural in aim, catholic in spirit, bold and uncompromising, but courteous in tone, the "Standard" will seek to rally the hosts of spiritual Israel around the Bible for the defense of truly Christian interests against the assumption of popery, the mischiefs of sectarianism, the sophistries of infidelity, and the pride and corruptions of the world.

The editor will be aided by an able corps of contributors.

The "Standard" will be published in quarto form, suitable for preservation, and will be about the size of the Cincinnati "Commercial." The first number will be issued in March or April next.

Terms, two dollars and fifty cents a year, invariably in advance. No club rates. Address

ISAAC ERRETT
Cleveland, Ohio.

Nearly all of the papers published this prospectus. There was one notable exception—the *Gospel Advocate*. Lipscomb had two reasons for refusing to encourage the *Standard's* circulation. The *Standard* was an advocate of the missionary society, to which Lipscomb objected. He wrote:

The Standard is edited with ability, and in a fair and liberal spirit. It is the only weekly now that is an advocate of the organizations of human societies in religion. Whether from a refusal upon the part of the conductors or not, articles upon but one side of this question ever appear in the Standard.[13]

Another objection Lipscomb had was that the *Standard* was too favorable to Christians participating in politics and taking active part in wars. To encourage the circulation of the *Standard* would have, from his point of view, been to encourage Christians to kill their fellowman. But in his objection, Lipscomb is charitable. He says,

It (the Christian Standard) is ably edited by Elder Isaac Errett, a man whose reputation for ability and polish as a writer and speaker, certainly is second to that of none among our brethren. The Standard, in its matter and execution, bears all the marks of both pecuniary and mental ability, skillfully used.[14]

When the first issue of the *Standard* appeared, Errett gave the promise that it would contain a variety of material to make it interesting. He proposed to give a record of activities of the various denominations; a practical application of Christian principles, and special attention to the Christian ministry. He made it clear that he intended to be independent.

In regard to the general style, tone, and spirit of the paper, we can only say that we have an ideal which we shall strive to realize. We shall seek to be gentle and courteous, but we are determined to be independent. Deference to the counsels of age and experience; respectful attention to the suggestions of friend and foe; suitable regard to honest convictions and prejudices—these we can promise: but, after all, our own convictions must control us. We forewarn our readers that we set out, not to please them, but to please God; to strike sturdily at error and wrong, and to utter freely our convictions, on grave and weighty themes, which can only be made profitable by free and manly discussion.[15]

In the spring of 1866 Isaac Errett moved from Michigan to Cleveland, Ohio where he set up his office in the rear of 99 Bank Street. The first issue was brought from the press of Fairbanks, Benedict & Co., on April 7, 1866. The motto was: "Set up a Standard; Publish and Conceal Not." The first number was destined to become a memorial edition, for just as it was in the process of being drawn up, the aged Alexander Campbell passed

---

[13]David Lipscomb, "Our Exchanges," *Gospel Advocate,* Vol. IX, No. 4 (January 24, 1867), pp. 72, 73.

[14]David Lipscomb, "An Explanation," *Gospel Advocate,* Vol. VIII, No. 26 (June 26, 1866), p. 425.

[15]Isaac Errett, "Salutatory," *Christian Standard,* Vol. I, No. 1 (April 7, 1866), p. 4.

away. Some of the front page of the first issue was devoted to a memorial of Campbell.

The first five years of publication were extremely difficult ones. The first year the paper did not pay expenses. Subscribers complained that the price was too high, so in October, 1867, Errett dropped the subscription rate to two dollars. At a meeting of the executive committee on April 15, 1867, a resolution was passed to discontinue the paper after January 1, 1868 unless more subscribers were forthcoming. By December that year, however, despite the fact that the subscription list was in little better condition, the committee decided to continue its publication throughout the next year. A month later the stockholders decided to abandon the whole enterprise, and gave it to Errett to salvage from it what he could.

Prospects for the paper proved no better in 1868. Errett was having hard financial difficulties. During the spring, he received an invitation to move to Alliance, Ohio, to become president of Alliance College. The invitation was accepted with the understanding that he could continue to edit the paper. Errett announced:

We have made arrangements with the Christian Publishing Association, by which the *Christian Standard* has become our own property. This involves no change whatever in the character and aims of the paper. . . We will not conceal from our readers that we accept considerable risk in this arrangement; but we are encouraged from the past to hope for entire success. . .

It has already become public, but not in our columns, that we have accepted the Presidency of Alliance College. This will not, for some time to come, necessitate any change of location, as we shall not enter on our duties in the College until next August or September. Nor will it make the slightest change in the character of the paper. A few friends of other educational institutions have expressed fears that the *Standard* will become a special organ of Alliance College. These fears are all unfounded. The college has nothing to do with the paper.[16]

Instead of increasing, the subscription list slowly dwindled. Errett himself began to entertain serious thoughts of abandoning it. Just at this point Mr. R. W. Carroll, president of the firm, R. W. Carroll & Co., which had printed so many books published by

---

[16]Isaac Errett, "A Change," *Christian Standard,* Vol. III, No. 8 (February 22, 1868), p. 60.

the brethren, heard of Errett's plight, and proposed to buy the *Christian Standard* and retain Errett as editor. Errett gladly accepted the offer and on July 31, 1869 the first issue of the *Christian Standard* from Cincinnati appeared.

Being released from the College, the necessity no longer exists for its continuance here, and we therefore transfer it to Cincinnati as the most desirable center of operation.[17]

J. S. Lamar was now called to be associate-editor.

The arrangement with the R. W. Carroll Co. was that Carroll was to own the paper and use it as a business project. The new owner was not a member of the church, but a Quaker. While there is little doubt that this move saved the *Standard* from complete collapse, there were those who criticized it. One of the editors of the *Apostolic Times* wrote:

Brother Errett, were the editors of the *Apostolic Times* to sell out their paper to a company of infidels, and then engage themselves to said company to edit the paper, as in the interest of primitive Christianity, what would you think of the act? Would you defend it? If not, why?[18]

At any rate, the move was made; the *Standard* was saved, and the years ahead were much less difficult ones.

It will be unnecessary at this point to follow in detail the life of Isaac Errett from this year, 1869 to his death in 1888, or to follow his thinking through the controversies ahead, as these matters shall come before us often in the next chapters. Needless to say the ensuing years were ones of labor mostly centered around the paper, the missionary society, and preaching efforts. Errett's health gave way. By the year 1887 it was much worse. His friends suggested a trip overseas, and raised $1,500 for this purpose. So there came a significant event in his life—his overseas trip to Europe.

Errett's traveling companion was Z. T. Sweeney of Columbus, Indiana, who is perhaps best remembered by the name, "Zach." On the night of January 13, 1887 a farewell party was given in the basement of the Richmond Street Church in Cincinnati. Four hundred were present, among the number being Archibald McLean,

---

[17]Isaac Errett, "Removal of the *Christian Standard* to Cincinnati," *Christian Standard*, Vol. IV, No. 30 (July 24, 1869), p. 236.

[18]Anonymous, "Card from R. W. Carroll & Co.," *Apostolic Times*, Vol. I, No. 22 (September 9, 1869), p. 171.

secretary of the Foreign Christian Missionary Society, and many
of the local preachers. Farewell addresses were given and then
a round of refreshments made by the ladies. Six days later Errett
and Sweeney left Cincinnati, and on January 22, in the middle
of the afternoon, the steamer, "Umbria" eased its way out of New
York harbor with Sweeney and Errett aboard bound for Liverpool.

It was Sunday afternoon when the ship docked at Liverpool.
The next morning they were off for London on a train. W. T.
Moore, then in London, met them. He was pacing up and down
the platform when the train pulled in. Two or three days of
sight-seeing followed.

On Thursday evening, Moore, Errett and Sweeney went to the
famous Baptist Tabernacle to listen to C. H. Spurgeon. Spurgeon
was just back from his vacation, and this was his first sermon
upon returning. Errett glanced over the tabernacle and sized it
up as capable of seating about six thousand people. There must
have been half that many present at this mid-week service, he
thought. He listened to the singing, and was struck with the fact
that no mechanical instrument was used. So he says,

It proves that there can be edifying congregational singing without the organ, and that the organ is not absolutely essential to the
edifying performance of this part of public worship, even in large
assemblies.[19]

Spurgeon's sermon, he noticed, was very ordinary. How, then,
account for his reputation? Errett felt that the secret of Spurgeon's
power lay in his ability to adapt himself and his material to his
audience. The crowds, he noticed, were made up entirely of
common working people. Spurgeon's language was simple, his
illustrations homely and to the point.

From London, Sweeney and Errett went to Paris, then to Italy,
then to Africa, and finally to the Holy Land. Late in June, they
arrived back home. Sweeney's arrival at Columbus, Indiana par-
took of the nature of a political convention. The big tabernacle
was ready for him. Beautiful flowers were across the pulpit.
The organ was also decorated and a large sign across it read, "Welcome Home." Chairs were draped in red, white and blue. Flags
from every nation hung from the gallery. When the train arrived,

---

[19]Isaac Errett, "Letters of Travel—No. II," *Christian Standard,* Vol.
XXII, No. 9 (February 26, 1887), p. 68.

bearing "Zach" Sweeney, four great white horses, drawing an elegant landau, came down the street to meet it. Behind it came the Sunday School with a brass band. Following this came throngs of people, cheering his arrival.[20]

Upon returning home Errett settled down to his work, but his health was no better. The announcement which appeared in the *Standard* on December 22, 1888 came very much as a surprise to most readers:

Unexpectedly we are called upon to make the mournful announcement that Isaac Errett, our beloved chief, passed to his reward on the morning of Wednesday, December 19, at his home at Terrace Park, twelve miles from Cincinnati. . .
The funeral service will be held in Cincinnati, Saturday next, December 22, 10:30 A.M.[21]

The funeral service was held in the Central Church in Cincinnati at the appointed time. Robert Graham told the story of Errett's life; C. L. Loos described the elements of his character, and J. H. Garrison preached the funeral.

At the time of death men have a way of being charitable. Errett had made many enemies, who looked upon him as the man most responsible for leading the church away from its apostolic moorings into digression. Yet, these men tried to be charitable. J. Perry Elliott wrote in the *Christian Leader:*

Although I had known for sometime that Brother Errett's health was very feeble, I was not prepared to hear of his death so soon. One by one our old brethren are passing away, and now only a few remain of those who, fifty years ago, were so earnestly pleading for a return to the divinely-ordained order of worship. Brother Errett was greatly admired by a host of brethren, and will be sadly missed; and I question if any brother can be found who can satisfactorily fill his place as editor of the *Standard.*[22]

R. B. Neal of Louisville, Kentucky, wrote the news of Errett's passing to the readers of the *Gospel Advocate:*

Few if any have attained to the high eminence as a leader upon which he stood. I was reared and nurtured in some prejudices

---

[20]S. F. Fowler, "Reception to Z. T. Sweeney," *Christian Standard,* Vol. XXII, No. 28 (July 9, 1887), p. 222.

[21]Anonymous, "Death of the Editor-in-Chief of the *Standard,*" *Christian Standard,* Vol. XXIII, No. 51 (December 22, 1888), p. 822.

[22]J. Perry Elliott, "Sundries," *Christian Leader,* Vol. III, No. 1 (January 1, 1889), p. 4.

against the *Standard* and stand today opposing some of the influences of that paper, but association in office and mission work
with Brother Errett won my highest regards for him as a manly
and Christian gentleman. He stood by me in the hour of greatest
need. He was gentle, courteous, liberal, manly and yet, there was
something of the slumbering lion in his nature—those who once
aroused it cared not to repeat the experiment.[23]

In the *Octographic Review,* Daniel Sommer wrote the news.
He perhaps was a little more frank than some of the others, but
was kindly even so.

Elder Isaac Errett, founder and editor of the journal called
"Christian Standard" is dead. He died of bronchial affection
December 19 at his home near Cincinnati. He will be greatly
missed. For years we hoped that he would live long enough to see
the full development of the policies that he advocated. But it was
the Lord's will that he should not, and so we bow in submission.[24]

---

[23]R. B. Neal, "Elder Isaac Errett," *Gospel Advocate,* Vol. XXXI, No. 1
(January 2, 1889), p. 1.

[24]Daniel Sommer, "Publisher's Paragraphs," *Octographic Review,* Vol.
XXXII, No. 1 (January 3, 1889), p. 1.

Chapter III

THE SOCIETY CONTROVERSY (1866-70)

The meeting of the American Christian Missionary Society in October, 1865 showed a discouraging outlook for the cause of organized missions. Funds were slow arriving. John F. Rowe who was traveling in Ohio and Pennsylvania was the only agent for the Society in the field. The Jerusalem Mission had been closed and a committee favored keeping it closed. J. O. Beardslee had returned from the Jamaica mission, leaving it to native workers. The Society voted to reopen this mission when a man could be found to go.

By 1867 Beardslee had returned to Jamaica, but funds for the support of missionaries were but little better. W. K. Pendleton, in an effort to bolster morale delivered a forceful address in favor of the Society in 1866. At the 1867 meeting both J. W. McGarvey and Moses E. Lard delivered addresses in its behalf. By the next year Beardslee had returned from Jamaica, and the only missionaries the Society was keeping in the field were here in America. In Nebraska, in Virginia, and at Troy, New York the Society had men located. This year, Thomas Munnell took over as corresponding secretary, replacing John Schackleford. R. M. Bishop, former mayor of Cincinnati, was president, having been placed in this office upon the death of D. S. Burnet.

To a few brethren there seemed to be abundant evidence that the Society movement in the church was now dead. In California early in the fall of 1866 an annual convention voted to adjourn *sine die* for a "want of scripture precedent" for such conventions. Joseph Franklin, son of Ben Franklin, wrote in the *Review* the next year:

That "Our Societies" are falling into disesteem is evident from the fact that Presidents, Boards and Secretaries everywhere, last fall, filled their annual addresses and Reports with defenses and excuses for failure. Let them go. The Gospel was preached before them, during their existence in spite of them, and will be preached after they are dead.[1]

[1] Joseph Franklin, " 'Our Societies' and the Preaching of the Gospel," *American Christian Review*, Vol. X, No. 2, (Jan. 8, 1867) p. 10.

Perhaps the chief reason for the Society's decline in popularity was its "war resolutions." Many thought the Society had over-stepped its right in declaring itself favorable to the North. At the close of hostilities, the Society passed the following resolution:

Resolved, That we have great reason for thanksgiving to the Ruler of Nations, not only in return of peace to our suffering country, but also in the emancipation of the slave, and the trium-phant vindication of our free and beneficial government.

The resolution doubtless looked innocent enough, yet in that day it could only mean one thing: The Society was passing measures of a political nature. Tolbert Fanning and David Lipscomb were quick to see this implication, and to observe how it had stepped out of bounds. After pondering the above resolution, they wrote:

Is this resolution one of the objects of said meeting? Is it one of the means of disseminating the Gospel? This resolution has done that Society more injury than it will ever do it good. Is this a political or religious resolution? or is it both religious and political? . . . Those brethren who can believe that this is the way to disseminate the Gospel can do so; and those brethren who believe that political resolutions are the Gospel can do so; and those who desire to contribute to such an object can do so: *we cannot do it!*[2]

Despite the fact, however, that these "war resolutions" seriously hindered the Society, that which hindered it even more was the change in Ben Franklin's attitude toward it. In 1857 Franklin had served as corresponding secretary, and had often defended the Society. Too, Franklin had put himself in an enviable position. As editor of the *American Christian Review,* then the most popular paper in the brotherhood, he wielded an extensive influence. Even W. K. Pendleton admits: "It is the most popular paper amongst us, and wields an influence that should fill its editor with a pro-found sense of responsibility for its proper conduct, as regards all the great interests of the church."[3] As long as Franklin backed the Society, Society advocates could rest easy, but when he turned against it, these same advocates found themselves facing the most difficult struggle in the history of the organization.

[2]Tolbert Fanning and David Lipscomb, "A Reply to the Call of W. C. Rogers, Corresponding Secretary of the A. C. M. Society for Aid to Disseminate the Gospel," *Gospel Advocate,* Vol. VIII, No. 13, (March 27, 1866) p. 206.
[3]W. K. Pendleton, "Items," *Millennial Harbinger,* Vol. XXXIX, No. 12, (Dec. 1868) p. 712.

Franklin had during the war looked with some misgivings upon the actions of the Society. He became profoundly impressed with the fact that such societies could be instruments of evil as well as good. Through the years that he had defended their right to exist, he had never done so with his conscience fully acquiescing in his utterances. With all of his large heart he wanted the brotherhood to be united; nothing pulled harder upon the threads of his soul than that the church might be divided. There were times when he stretched his conscience almost to the breaking point, trying to back the things the brotherhood apparently wanted, when he himself felt they could not be defended. Finally, he could do it no longer. By December, 1866, he announced his change in position, and came out fully ready to clash with society advocates.

Woe be to that man who changes his position on any issue in religion! He can be sure that the brethren will never allow him to forget it. J. S. Lamar went back to 1858, the year Ben Franklin carried on his controversy with Oliphant of Canada, mentioned in our previous volume, and dragged a few skeletons out of the closet. He printed Franklin's answers to Oliphant in defense of the Society to remind Franklin and the brotherhood of the change. C. L. Loos, in commenting upon Lamar's item, wrote:

Now it is true that a man may change, and has a right to change his views. But when and how this could have taken place with the editor of the *Review* is very inexplicable to us. It must date from the very shortest possible period,—less than a year; and what could possibly have occurred within six months to effect so sudden and radical a transformation, we are unable to see. . . .[4]

Loos then referred to a meeting held by the Ohio State Missionary Society at Akron in the spring of 1866 which Ben Franklin had attended, saying that Franklin at that time was very much in favor of the Societies. Thus he dated Franklin's change somewhere between the spring of 1866 and the beginning of January, 1867. He wonders what could have happened in that period of time to cause this change and how Franklin would now meet the arguments for the Society that he himself had formerly made. Loos showed that, in spite of Franklin's opposition, he had no intention of laying aside the Missionary Society. He adds:

---

[4]C. L. Loos, "Bro. Franklin's Argument for the Missionary Society," *Millennial Harbinger*, Vol. XXXVIII, No. 5, (May, 1867) p. 243.

If anyone asks why we thus call attention to the course of the editor of the *Review,*—our answer is that Brother F. is using his influence in his paper to the detriment of a work most near and dear to us, and thousands among us ; and we are resolved to stand by this work, in true devotion while life lasts. . . . Nothing that our opposing brethren have said has had the slightest influence in weakening our convictions in this respect ; but has only made our attachment to the cause stronger.

Franklin, in answer to Loos, admitted that he had changed his views on the scripturalness of the Missionary Society. He furthermore admitted *trying* to defend the Society, but added that he was no longer willing to do so. With regard to his action at the Ohio State Missionary Society meeting in the spring of 1866, Franklin admitted being there and making a reply, but declares that Loos twisted it out of its context, for he was not upholding a Society, *as such,* but missionary work. Franklin adds that he went to that Society meeting with some misgivings already in his mind about their scripturalness. He had hoped to find something there to settle his mind on the subject, but came away disappointed, realizing there was no other course open to him but to oppose them.

W. K. Pendleton was another who remonstrated against Franklin for his change. He wrote :

Brother Franklin, we know, with many others, thinks that the Missionary Society at Cincinnati did some unconstitutional things during the war,—and we think so too ;—but we think that far too much ado has been made about this already. Many *Churches* did impudent and unchristian things also—and are doing them every year ;—but does this prove that churches are dangerous things and ought to be abolished? These are incidents of our human frailty and must be met with the wisdom and charity which are higher than passion and sweeter and more blessed than revenge.[5]

About this time J. S. Sweeney wrote to Franklin about his change, as follows :

There seems to be at present considerable excitement among the brethren all over the country, growing out of the controversy about the Missionary Society, and it has been of late not a little intensified by the position you have—or are supposed to have—assumed in reference to the question.[6]

[5]W. K. Pendleton, "Missionary Movements," *Millennial Harbinger,* Vol. XXXVIII, No. 3, (March, 1867) p. 147.
[6]J. S. Sweeney, "Sweeney to Franklin," *American Christian Review,* Vol. X, No. 20, (May 14, 1867) p. 156.

To this Franklin replied:

We did, under certain *limitations and restrictions,* to which we found finally the Society could never be held, defend the Society scheme against brethren Oliphant, Fanning, and others, but never saw our way exactly clear.

George W. Elley was yet another to remind Franklin of his change. Elley lived near Lexington, Kentucky, and was a Society devotee. He wrote to Franklin, suggesting that some were saying he was with the *Gospel Advocate,* as though this would make his action criminal. He wanted to know exactly what the attitude of Franklin was toward Missionary Societies. Franklin replied:

It is not *missionary work* to which we are opposed, but empty plans, schemes and organizations, after sectarian models, which have proved failures; expensive, cumbrous and lamentable failures in *doing missionary work,* filling our publications with speeches, reports and resolutions, as also unpleasant controversies and discouraging the brethren.[7]

Despite the risk involved, Franklin made this change. Some did not hesitate to remind him that his paper would be forced out of existence. But Franklin was undaunted. He wrote:

At all events, we have come to the time to rest the question whether *love and devotion* to the creation of a few individuals, in the form of an outside society, with laws and names unknown to the law of God, is sufficient to sink a man of more than thirty years' labor and devotion to the spread of the gospel, *solely because he will not go for the Society.*[8]

Thus Ben Franklin took his stand against the Society. His influence, together with the unpopular war resolutions, found the American Christian Missionary Society in 1866 badly in need of repairs and rapidly losing in popularity.

At this crisis, the Society invited its great apologist, W. K. Pendleton, to defend it. Pendleton's address before the convention of 1866 was intended to do just this. The importance of this address in a study of the society controversy cannot be overemphasized. It was published in the *Millennial Harbinger* for

---

[7]Ben Franklin, "Our Position Defined," *American Christian Review,* Vol. X, No. 11, (March 12, 1867) p. 84.

[8]Ben Franklin, "Prof. C. L. Loos and the Harbinger," *American Christian Review,* Vol. X, No. 24 (June 11, 1867) p. 188.

1866, beginning on page 494. In our previous volume, some reference was made to it, but it is fitting that more attention should be given here. So far as the Society's defense went, it is the *summum bonum* in arguments for it. Almost all arguments draw their force from it. Pendleton's address, too, took on added significance by the interpretation which he set upon some of the basic principles of the restoration movement, and which set the pattern for future thinking by the more liberal element.

In an analysis of Pendleton's arguments, we note first his answer to the charge that the Society meant "we are departing from original ground." It was freely pointed out to the Society advocates that the organization was unknown to the early restoration movement. Some charged that Campbell in the *Christian Baptist* definitely opposed them. Pendleton's answer to these charges showed his skill and displayed his eagerness to pin a charge on the Society's opponents which they had previously pinned on its advocates. To say the Missionary Society is wrong because it was unknown to the earlier restoration is but to follow human opinions, and this is contrary to the very genius of the restoration movement. Obviously, this was a weak rebuttal, and Pendleton seemed to sense it, but where prejudice rules, weakness is strength. To the charge that Alexander Campbell had earlier opposed the Society, Pendleton simply asserted that this was a mistaken impression. The merit of this answer has already been discussed, but, at any rate, Campbell's words in the *Christian Baptist,* taken at their face value, are not as far-fetched as Pendleton suggested.

Pendleton's second argument was given in answer to the charge that the Missionary Society was not scriptural. He says:

You say, "Your Missionary Society is not scriptural"—and you mean by this, that there is no special express percept in the Scriptures commanding it. We concede this without a moment's hesitation. There is none; but what do you make of it? Is everything which is not scriptural therefore wrong?[9]

That the scripture is silent about a missionary society, Pendleton readily admitted. He contended, however, that this did not make it wrong. Speaking again of the Society's opponents, he said:

----

[9]W. K. Pendleton, "Address, by W. K. Pendleton," *Millennial Harbinger,* Vol. XXXVII, No. 11, (Nov., 1866) p. 501.

· Does he say that it is not *positively and expressly* commanded; then we demand by what canon of interpretation does he make mere *silence* prohibitory? You reply, the canon which forbids anything as a rule of Christian faith or duty, for which there cannot be expressly produced a "Thus saith the Lord," "either in express terms or by approved precedent." . . .

The annunciation of this principle needs much comment. Earlier in the restoration movement Thomas Campbell had spoken that great motto, "Where the Bible speaks, we speak; where the Bible is silent, we are silent." The bulk of the brotherhood had interpreted that motto to mean that whatever is unauthorized is forbidden. To most brethren the expression was simple, and meant that these people who advocated a return to the ancient order would practice in their religious beliefs only those things for which they found authority either by direct command, apostolic example or necessary inference. They had used the motto to sweep everything before them. They had challenged every sectarian body of religious people the country over to show divine authority for their existence as a body. This was enough. Men, finding they were members of bodies unknown to Holy Writ, were freely abandoning them, and beginning to plead for others to follow them to safe, authorized ground. When, therefore, a group of brethren projected a Missionary Society, they naturally inquired of themselves, "Where is the authority?" Finding none, they said the Society had no right to exist.

Now Pendleton asserted that this view of that old motto is altogether wrong; that it was not at all what Thomas Campbell had in mind. With this he returned to study the early restoration. Campbell, and a few others, had formed the "Christian Association of Washington." It was before this group that this motto was first announced. Pendleton asserted that this association was not a church; that it took money for membership; that it had an Executive Board and a Secretary and Treasurer. In these respects the "Christian Association of Washington" was in itself nothing more than a Missionary Society. Pendleton was striking a telling blow. He pressed the point home:

Now it was this organization, which in the very act of forming itself, announced this canon! Did they mean to condemn themselves? Were they simpletons or hypocrites?

Obviously then, Thomas Campbell himself, the man who penned

the great motto, did not mean by it to exclude such organizations
as the missionary society. This was Pendleton's point, and it had
its effect.

Unfortunately at the time of this address Robert Richardson had
not yet written his monumental work, *Memoirs of Alexander
Campbell.* The story of what had happened when the Declaration
and Address was written had been handed down mostly by word
of mouth. True enough, articles of historical nature appeared
once in a while in the *Millennial Harbinger,* but these were not
exhaustive or critical. It remains a fact that the knowledge the
average man possessed in 1866 of happenings sixty years before
was only hazy. Pendleton was closely associated with Alexander
Campbell, having married in succession two of his daughters, and
had been vice-president under him at Bethany College. His knowledge of the early restoration therefore went unchallenged. He
was able to plant an interpretation of this vital principle of the
restoration in the hearts of many leaders that opened the floodgates for all innovations the liberals may desire.

But what are the facts in the case? What did Thomas Campbell mean by the great motto, "Where the Bible speaks, we speak;
where the Bible is silent, we are silent"?

Regarding the "Christian Association of Washington," it can
be said that those who comprised it were neither simpletons nor
hypocrites! Pendleton in this case was but a prejudiced juror
and was, therefore, incapable of sensing every side of the issue.
The terms as "simpletons" and "hypocrites" were but appeals to
prejudice. The truth is that these people—Thomas Campbell
included—were just coming out of sectarian practices and had yet
a very imperfect grasp of what it meant to "speak where the Bible
speaks and be silent where it is silent." Of the minds of these
people at the time the "Christian Association of Washington" was
formed, Robert Richardson informs us:

It is true, indeed, that the individuals who had been for some
time attending Mr. Campbell's meeting were, by no means, all
settled in their religious convictions, and that they differed from
each other, especially in relation to a proper gospel ministry. . . .
For, while all were disposed to confide in the Bible as the only
true guide in religion, yet there were those who, conscious that
they were imperfectly acquainted with its teaching, naturally experienced some misgivings as they felt themselves slowly drifting

away from the well-known shores and landmarks of their respecti\
religious systems into the wide ocean of Divine truth, which
seemed to them so boundless and as yet but imperfectly ex-
plored. . . .[10]

Speaking of Thomas Campbell himself, Richardson says:

Neither Thomas Campbell himself, however, nor those associated
with him, had a full conception of all that was involved in these
principles. They only felt that the religious intolerance of the
time had itself become intolerable, and that a reformation was
imperiously demanded.[11]

The above points W. K. Pendleton found it convenient to overlook. When Campbell announced his great motto and formed
the "Christian Association of Washington," neither he nor his
associates had yet a full conception of all that was involved. That
it was right to take only those things that were authorized, they
could not doubt, but to see in advance where this would lead them,
they could not.

Campbell's attitude toward infant baptism may be taken as
typical of his attitude. Soon after announcing his famous motto,
James Foster approached Thomas Campbell with the question,
"How could you, in the absence of any authority in the word of
God, baptize a child in the name of the Father, and of the Son,
and of the Holy Spirit?" Robert Richardson informs us that
Campbell's face changed color. He became irritated and offended,
and tersely replied, "Sir, you are the most intractable person I
ever saw."[12] A short time later Thomas Campbell did reject
infant baptism. On what ground? On the ground that there
was no authority for it in the word of God, the very principle his
motto had laid down. Why did Campbell not see, at the time he
announced his motto, that infant baptism was unscriptural? The
idea had never dawned on him then. Was he a "simpleton" or a
"hypocrite"? Obviously not. As Richardson explains, "He had
not yet a full conception of all that was involved in this motto."

Contrary to Pendleton's assertion, Campbell did mean to say
that whatever in religion is not authorized in the divine word
cannot be used. His application of this principle to the subject

---

[10]Robert Richardson, *Memoirs of Alexander Campbell,* Vol. I, (Cincinnati: Standard Publishing Co., 1897) p. 234.

[11]Robert Richardson, *Memoirs of Alexander Campbell,* Vol. I, p. 245.

[12]Robert Richardson, *Memoirs of Alexander Campbell,* Vol. I, p. 240,

óf infant baptism shows him to be applying it in exactly this manner.

At any rate, Pendleton brushed aside this interpretation of the motto, and put a new one on it. He affirmed that it was meant to be applied to creeds and confessions of faith as terms of communion and fellowship. In short, all Campbell meant to say was that human creeds and human opinions cannot be forced upon us. If we want to practice a human opinion, this is our liberty; but if someone wants to force one upon us, we have the right to refuse, Pendleton argued.

The annunciation of this interpretation of Campbell's great motto is significant. It can be safely said that the bulk of the brotherhood had not so understood it. But now, Pendleton's interpretation began to be picked up by leading minds of the more liberal type and put into use to sanction every human opinion they wanted to urge upon the church. Upon this interpretation of the motto was based every innovation which was brought into the church. The door was now down, and human opinions, as they applied to the work and worship of the church, multiplied. To try to sweep back the avalanche by calling for divine authority was like trying to dry up the ocean with a sponge. Pendleton's interpretation was picked up by Isaac Errett and the *Christian Standard* and then by J. H. Garrison and B. W. Johnson in the *Christian-Evangelist* to resound down through the years to the present. Nevertheless, an element remained to whom the call for divine authority still meant something. They believed that whatever in the practice of religion was not authorized by the word of God was wrong. The *Gospel Advocate* and the *American Christian Review* maintained this conviction down through the years.

These two types of thinking are responsible for even modern-day differences in religious practice. The use of instrumental music, missionary societies, and the many other practices, based on no divine authority, are but symptoms of the real trouble, which lies basically at this point.

To insist that nothing could be practiced in religion for which there is no divine authority was, to Pendleton, a horrifying thought. It was such a binding thing! It would make us too narrow and too strict. He said:

Let it not be said, then, that the disciples of Christ are to take the silence of Scripture on a given subject as a positive rule of prohibition against all freedom of action or obligation of duty. No rule could be more productive of evil than this.

To ask for divine authority for everything in religion would mean that we couldn't have church buildings, blackboards, lights in the building, etc., they argued. Men became fearful of what it would mean to ask for divine authority. They soon shrugged off the idea as something utterly ridiculous.

Basically, this fear is to be accounted for by a failure to consider the fact that man is connected with two realms—the worldly and the religious. In what type of business shall a man earn his livelihood? Shall he be a doctor, lawyer, business man, farmer, etc.? Give book, chapter and verse. What kind of car shall a man drive—Chevrolet, Pontiac, Ford? Give the scripture. These things belong to the world, and no scripture is needed or expected. So with the meetinghouses, lights, blackboards, etc. These belong to the worldly realm, and have never presented much of a problem.

Ancient Israel erected idols with her own hands and bowed down to worship them. Men tend to become infatuated with creatures which they make with their own hands, and become blind to their faults. W. K. Pendleton was an intelligent man and certainly thoroughly honest; yet, he was so infatuated with the society, the creature which his hands had formed, that he saw in everything the means to justify it.

The basic apology for the Society Pendleton based upon his conception of the church universal, and in this he followed closely the reasoning of Alexander Campbell. No man is prepared to see the Society as Pendleton saw it without beginning where Pendleton began. First, he filled his mind with the thought of the church in its universal aspect, ignoring for the time being the local church. God gave to the church—in its universal sense— the responsibility to convert the world. But God did not give the *method* by which the church—in its universal sense—was to convert the world. Therefore, whatever method the church—in its universal sense—uses is acceptable. The method is a matter of expediency. The church universal is left free to decide for itself. This is briefly the defense he made for it.

Some day somebody will do the cause of Christ a real service by taking the concept of the church universal, and giving it a

thorough analysis based upon the scriptures and upon church
history for the past two thousand years. The church is spoken
of in the New Testament in a universal sense. There is a body
of people characterized by the fact that they follow Jesus that
comprise the New Testament Church in its universal aspect.

There are some things about this truly significant. It is significant, for example, that the church universal has never known but
one officer—Jesus Christ himself, who is Head over the body,
King over his Kingdom. The apostles were the ambassadors of
this King to the church universal. They were not officers of
the church, were never appointed by the church and existed before the church did. The study of church history reveals the fact
that every time men thought in terms of the church universal, they
ended up by forming organizations which in their work substituted
themselves in the place of Christ. Roman Catholicism is the
highest embodiment of the church universal concept, and claims
that its pope is the vicegerent of Christ on earth. So far as the
church universal on earth is concerned, as viewed by a Romanist,
the pope is virtually Christ.

Protestantism thought in terms of the church universal, and
set up synods and conferences. These synods and conferences
have written creeds, created confessions of faith—in short, have
made laws for the church universal, a prerogative that belongs
to Christ. In the final analysis these synods and conferences
assume the position of Christ over the church universal. Some,
like the Baptist denomination, have tried to throw off the concept
of the church universal for a time, and insist upon strict congregational polity. Yet they invariably thought in terms of the
church universal and established associations which soon began to dictate to the local churches, a prerogative that again
belonged to Christ. In the restoration movement, brethren thought
in terms of the church universal, and with that concept formed
a Missionary Society. Looking back on this history, as we can
now, who can fail to see that this Society became the master,
and soon dictated to the churches, a prerogative which belongs only
to Christ.

That Christ intended for the world to be converted through
individual congregations being established in every local community and thence, exercising a saving influence over that community seems too obvious for dispute. The plan the author of Acts

lays down is that the gospel is to spread from Jerusalem, thence to Judea, then to Samaria and to the uttermost parts of the earth. The gospel radiated out, local congregations were planted, and exercised a saving influence upon the community. In one generation the gospel was sounded out to the whole earth, and that without a missionary society. It is an indictment, not against our organization, but against our individual religious fervor that the same is not done today. The only church organization known to the New Testament is that of a local church, not the church universal. The only officers of the church are those of the local church, not the church universal. The individual congregation of Christ's disciples is the only missionary society then known to the Scriptures.

THE ISSUES

Up to this point a general view of the Society controversy has been given. No analysis of the controversy as it respects the basic issues has been given. Broad, basic principles have been given, but now, in order to make the study of the controversy more complete, the issues must be considered.

The first charge that was hurled against the Society which was that it was a *substitute for the church*. The Society had no divine authority for its existence; it owed its inception to human wisdom and human opinions. Whereas God left the evangelizing of the world to local churches scattered throughout the world, the Missionary Society was, in effect, a substitute for God's plan. It implied an imperfection in the divine plan and suggested that human wisdom could improve upon divine. Therefore, as some men, particularly David Lipscomb, looked at the Society, man could only defend the Society by first defending his right to substitute human plans for the divine. This, in summary, was the most serious charge hurled its way.

In 1866 Tolbert Fanning and George W. Elley carried on occasional discussions in the *Gospel Advocate* over the Society. Fanning, as his custom was, placed this charge in the lap of Elley, feeling confident of his position. Fanning wrote:

These missionary societies are not composed of churches, but of individuals, by paying a certain amount of money. In the work accomplished by them, the credit is mainly given to them and not to the church. Indeed, according to President Elley's statement, these associations plant churches, set them in order, and supervise them generally. . . .

Our view is that, such societies are employed as *substitutes* for the churches, that they stand on ground the churches are entitled to occupy, and that they do, to all intents and purposes, usurp the authority of the churches, and thwart the designs of Jehovah. They make void the churches of Jesus Christ and the law of God.[13]

After the war, Jacob Creath, Jr., was no less an opposer of missionary societies than before. On the whole study of the realm of the church, Creath had a clear insight. His language was generally supercharged with denunciations which only served to bring down upon his head the anathemas of those favoring the Societies. He gave an excellent view of the church and societies when he wrote:

If some of our own preachers will come among us and preach the gospel, and not politics, we will help to support such a man. But if any man comes among us sent out by one of these humbug societies, we shall let him pass. Ancient Christianity was spread by individuals, and not by societies or proxies, as is the modern gospels. And when a man becomes worthless, and his brethren have no confidence in him at once, he seeks an office in one of these falsely called missionary societies. The Jerusalem Church spread the gospel, or her members did *individually,* after the resurrection of Christ, before another church existed to assist her, through Judea, Samaria, Phoenicia, Cyprus, Antioch, and to the uttermost parts of the earth in the first century of the Christian era. (Acts, chapters 1, 2 and 11.) As this mother and model church spread the gospel, so did the other churches individually (not from societies), such as Antioch in Syria (Acts 13), and Thessalonia sounded out the gospel in Macedonia and Achaia (1 Thess. 1, 8). Let any church now do the same as these ancient churches did; let each member do all he can to spread the gospel. If a church or person is not able to do anything to spread the gospel, nothing is required of that person. Christ never gathered where he did not strew. It is required of us, according to what we have, and not according to what we have not. . . .[14]

Creath was striking at something fundamental just here which many congregations have found it convenient to overlook. God never requires of an individual Christian, or a congregation of Christians, any more than it is possible to do. The need for a

---

[13] Tolbert Fanning, "The Advocate and G. W. Elley," *Gospel Advocate,* Vol. VIII, No. 40, (Oct. 2, 1866) pp. 627-28.

[14] Jacob Creath, "Missionary, and Other Organizations Besides the Church, for Carrying Forward the Work of God," *Gospel Advocate,* Vol. VIII, No. 3, (Jan. 16, 1866) pp. 41-42.

Society arose from the fact that local churches felt themselves incapable of sending out the gospel, so they established societies to do the work which God ordained for the church.

David Lipscomb developed this point even further. After pointing out that the societies were founded on the assumption that the churches cannot or will not do the work of God as well as societies, he charged that the societies actually hinder and stifle church action. When the Society prospers, the congregations become inactive, allowing the work to be taken over by these human organizations. Instead of promoting church action, they check it.

The fact that many individuals and churches in sympathy with this Society encourage church action, does not at all militate against the fact that the society itself has a tendency to destroy church operation. For just to the extent that an individual gives of his means to the society, he withdraws it from the church.[15]

This business of the society's being a substitute for the church was to Lipscomb a serious matter.

To operate through an institution of man's devising in preference to the church of God is, in our esteem, to exalt man as of superior wisdom and power to God. To call in question the efficiency of God's appointments, as the best (we had like to say the *only*), that can be ordained for the accomplishment of God's designs, is to call in question the wisdom or power of God. As highly as we respect Brother McGarvey (and there is no man living, of his years, that we had formed a higher appreciation of for his work) and his associates, there are questions here involving too high, holy and sacred interests, both to God and man, for us to yield an iota.[16]

The Missionary Society had no more ardent supporter than Thomas Munnell, who, for a time served as corresponding secretary for the American Christian Missionary Society. During much of the year 1867, he and David Lipscomb carried on a discussion over the Society through the pages of the *Gospel Advocate*. While there shall be occasion to refer to this correspondence in the future, it is interesting at this point as it reveals Lipscomb's basic objection to the Society.

A chief objection we make to your societies is, that they ignore the overruling and guiding hand of God, and organize a human

[15]David Lipscomb, "Destroying Church Cooperation," *Gospel Advocate*, Vol. IX, No. 6, (Feb. 7, 1867) p. 114.
[16]David Lipscomb, "Destroying Church Cooperation," *Gospel Advocate*, Vol. IX, No. 6, (Feb. 7, 1867) p. 115.

association to do that which God has reserved for himself. God says to man: you operate according to my directions in the various spheres, and with the instrumentalities I ordain for you. I will overlook, I will guide, I will harmonize the various parts, and direct the vast complicated whole forward to the accomplishment of the designed mission without a jar or a discord. All I require of you is to faithfully operate the parts I assign to you. The action of the societies seem to say: No, Lord, we are not content to operate in the limited sphere assigned to us; we will take a general oversight, and take upon ourselves the responsibility of harmony, and controlling the vast whole. We will sit in the place of God, and do His work. The great misfortune to the churches, Brother Munnell, is not a lack of cooperation—but a lack of *operation*. If man will only faithfully operate, then God will superintend the cooperation.[17]

Lipscomb saw the Society standing opposed to the very genius of Christianity when he wrote:

Human societies spread by organic force—the religion of the Saviour spreads as a leaven. Human societies are based on the right of man to form organizations through which he will worship his Maker. This is the fundamental error of Romanism.[18]

A year later, Lipscomb argued in the same vein in these words:

We feel just as sure that the missionary societies are corrupt and corrupting—the last one of them—as we do that human political organizations are corrupt. We feel just as sure that they are subversive of the Lord's institutions as we do that the societies and organizations of the Romish hierarchy are subversive of his appointments. They stand precisely upon the same footing—have the same living principles as these do.[19]

John T. Walsh saw ample reason to object to the Society on the ground, viz., it was a substitute for the divine plan to do the work of the Lord. Walsh wrote:

I think it is an undeniable truth, that men never departed from *primitive Christianity* until they lost faith in it. And no Christian ever yet adopted human systems and appliances until his faith becomes weak in the divine. . . . I repeat, therefore, that what we need is not a new plan of missionary work, but more faith in the old Jerusalem plan.

. . . We want *more faith and less machinery, more work and less talk,* more faith and less planning. The Lord has given us

    [17]David Lipscomb, "Discussion—Missionary Societies," *Gospel Advocate,* Vol. IX, No. 11, (Mar. 14, 1867) p. 208.
    [18]David Lipscomb, "Discussion—Missionary Societies," *Gospel Advocate,* Vol. IX, No. 23, (June 6, 1867) p. 446.
    [19]David Lipscomb, "The Societies," *Gospel Advocate,* Vol. X, No. 33, (Aug. 13, 1868) p. 763.

the plan, and bids us go work in his vineyard; but instead of going
to work with the tools He has furnished, we spend all the day in
making *new ones* which in our wisdom, we think will work better.
Let us quit it, and go to work with a hearty good will.[20]

The only Missionary Society the Lord ever owned, Walsh contended, was the church.

The church of Christ is the Lord's missionary Society. He is
its Head, and every member of it, male and female, young and
old, rich and poor, learned and unlearned, black and white, *is* a
LIFE-MEMBER AND DIRECTOR! The terms of admission
are *faith* and *obedience.* The terms on which they continue members consist in the observance of "all things WHATSOEVER I
have commanded you," and among the "all things" the injunction
to "give as the Lord prospers" us stands out prominently and
imperatively. *All must obey it!* and thus "show their faith by
their works! In a word, let original Christianity be restored in
faith and practice, and nothing else will be needed.[21]

No sooner had Ben Franklin changed his position on the Society
than he announced his first conviction that Societies took the
place of the churches, and were man-made substitutes for the church
of Christ. He writes:

The circumstance that they had no missionary societies in the
first age of the church, *of itself,* does not prove that we may not
have them. But the fact that the Lord ordained the congregations,
with their officers, and made it their work to convert the world
with the additional fact that we have their example in sending our
preachers, with the circumstance, that they had no missionary
societies, but the churches, proves that it is wrong for individuals
to create missionary societies, separate from the churches, as *substitutes* to do the work which the Lord appointed for the churches.
The congregations of the Lord, divinely appointed and constituted
societies or bodies, for the worship of God, fitted for every good
work—specially for the propagation of the gospel. The simple
question is, whether we shall honor the churches in working in
them and making them effective as the Lord's appointed societies,
in converting the world, or declare them *insufficient* to do the
work which the Lord committed to them, and *substitute* a creation
of our own hands, to do the work of the *churches ordained by the
Lord.* Others may do this latter, but we *cannot.*[22]

---

[20]John T. Walsh, "Reply to G. W. Elley," *American Christian Review,*
Vol. X, No. 25, (June 18, 1867) p. 194.

[21]John T. Walsh, "Reply to G. W. Elley," *American Christian Review,*
Vol. X, No. 25, (June 18, 1867) p. 194.

[22]Ben Franklin, "Explanation for Bro. G. W. Elley," *American Christian
Review,* Vol. X, No. 19, (May 7, 1867) p. 148.

Quotations could be multiplied *ad infinitim,* but these are enough to indicate the viewpoint of the chief opposers of Missionary Societies. The organization of the Society merely indicated that man had lost faith in primitive Christianity; that he felt that he could by his own human wisdom devise a better plan to convert the world than the Lord furnished. The implication was that the church was insufficient to do the work God committed to it, and so human wisdom was at liberty to devise a better system of operation. We close this particular point with the words of Hiram Christopher, which probably go beneath the whole principle to the real one:

The Missionary Society had its origin in a false pride and shame, and a desire to be like the denominations around us. With all our condemnations of denominationalism, we have yet not the independence of mind to discard their machinery. We are afraid that they will get ahead of us, and this fear leads us to adopt some of their machinery. The first of these human instrumentalities was the Missionary Society.[23]

The second defense was that the Society was but an expedient. The church universal was charged with preaching to the world, but God did not provide its method; therefore, it was left to human expediency to devise the best plan. This, of course, completely overlooked the fact that the church universal *was* given a method, the method being the work of the local congregation. The gospel radiated from Jerusalem to the "uttermost parts of the earth," local congregations being planted, and influencing a saving power upon their community. The local congregation, then, was the only missionary society that God ordained.

But advocates of the Society never tired of putting the Society on the plane of expediency, and then insisting that the whole controversy over missionary societies, was one of which plan to adopt. As a means of justifying themselves, charges of inconsistency were laid at the door of the Society's enemies who, it was said, were guilty themselves of working through human organizations. More shall be said of these charges.

The use of expediency as a defense for the societies was suggested by W. K. Pendleton, as has been seen already. Pendleton, beginning with the concept of the church universal, emphasized that since God made no provision for the *method* the church

<hr />

[23]H. Christopher, "Dr. Christopher vs. Missionary Society," *American Christian Review,* Vol. X, No. 27, (July 2, 1867) p. 211.

universal was free to adopt any of its own by which to convert the world. But Pendleton backed off carrying this line of reasoning on out to its logical conclusion, for his reasoning would lead to the conclusion, that since the local churches are incapable of spreading the gospel throughout the world, there must be a universal organization of the church with some sort of earthly controlling center that would overlook and direct the work of the local congregations.

In so far as the principle involved here is concerned, it is basically Romanism. To assert that the church universal, to do the work God gave it, must, by human wisdom, devise an earthly, central controlling station to direct the operations of the churches is to work on the same principle that led Romanism to the papacy. It would have been argued, of course, that this universal organization would have no power except as a *servant* of the church and not its *master.* The future of the restoration movement was to show that this reasoning was but idle dreaming. A society without some power or control would have been a helpless thing. If it could not, for a time, control the churches which were the *source* of its income, there were yet other controls it could have essential to its existence. It had to have the control of the *use* of its funds. It also had to have control over its missionaries. It is idle to say that a Society could exist without controlling *where* its funds would be spent, and *who* would be its employees, it missionaries. The only one control the society lacked, and it did not lack this completely, was the power to control the source of its income. As time went on, these churches *where* the Society had spent its money, in turn, became the *source* for other revenue.

No one saw more clearly the logical end of Pendleton's reasoning than David Lipscomb who studied the address carefully. Lipscomb wrote:

The only defense that can be made of these institutions is, that there must be a universal organization of the church of God with an earthly, central head, that overlooks and directs the operations of all the numerous local organizations or congregations. The premises that lead to this conclusion were laid down not very definitely by Brother Pendleton, in his last address at the last meeting of the Cincinnati society. The logical result of these premises, we gladly note, he shrinks back from declaring. This, to our mind, is the most objectionable ground the societies could be placed upon. Brother Pendleton's use of the terms, universal church in connection with the society organization, we think can have no other meaning.[24]

With many, there was an inability to comprehend churches co-operating without forming some sort of a human organization. Consequently, some advocates of the society conceived that the whole controversy was very simple in that some advocated *organized* mission work and some *unorganized*. This retort was flung by Thomas Munnell to David Lipscomb in their discussions of 1867, but Lipscomb replied that if two distinct bodies (churches) blend themselves into one organization, their works become the operation of the third body, and not a cooperation of the other two. It is this newly organized body that is working, and the churches, so far as this work is concerned, have lost their identity.

But, as mentioned before, the Societies, in defending their right to exist on the ground of expediency, continually charged that their opponents were inconsistent. It was commonly asked, "If you insist upon a "thus saith the Lord" for everything, where is your scripture for a meeting-house?" The answer to this one came in an effective way from Jeremiah Smith, brother of B. K. Smith, who preached in Indianapolis. Jeremiah Smith replied:

The advocates of missionary societies uniformly and trium- phantly, as they seem to think, appeal to building meeting-houses in justification of having missionary societies to spread the gospel and build up Christian churches; and claim that Christians are left by the Lord free to plan and devise as to both; and that they are necessary expedients to forward the Lord's cause and kingdom.

Is building a meeting-house any part of the Lord's kingdom, or of its institutions? Certainly it is not; for there is not a word said about it in the New Testament. It is not any more so than in building a dwelling-house, a barn, or opening and cultivating a farm is. Is the "sounding out of the word of the Lord," the conversion of sinners, the planting and building of Christian con- gregations, any part of the Lord's kingdom, or of its institutions? Certainly they are; for they are frequently named and enjoined in the New Testament. Then the argument is wholly fallacious: it is proving spiritual things by arguments pertaining to earthly things. . .[25]

Again, advocates of the Society affirmed its opposers were in- consistent in that they printed papers while having no divine

---

[24]David Lipscomb, "Destroying Church Cooperation," *Gospel Advocate,* Vol. IX, No. 6, (Feb. 7, 1867) p. 115.

[25]Jeremiah Smith, "Missionary Societies Human Expedients," *Gospel Advocate,* Vol. VIII, No. 49, (Dec. 4, 1866) p. 780.

authority for such.   Moses E. Lard was never too hearty a devotee of the Societies, although he could never refrain from the belief they did have a right to exist.   To him, it was similar to a paper, so he wrote:

I am printing a *Quarterly,* the avowed object of which is the propagation and defense of the gospel.   But this *Quarterly* is unknown to the New Testament.   Should I therefore abandon it?   Not an honest man in our ranks will affirm it.   But this *Quarterly* has precisely the same origin which the Society has— human discretion, and not only proposes, but actually does, the same work.   If, now, my *Quarterly* is right in itself, that is, if it has a just and legitimate existence, and may lawfully do the work it proposes, then the man does not live who can show that a missionary society *per se* wrong, and may not cause the gospel to be preached.   With emphasis, I plant myself here, and main- tain that the same argument which would rebate a missionary society because it originates not in the New Testament, and would deny to it the right to cause the gospel to be preached, must of necessity rebate the *Quarterly.*   And in candor I must go further, and say I have no respect for the dullness which perceives not the analogy nor the casuistry which denies to the resulting con- clusion its just weight.[26]

The article is strongly worded, as all of Lard's were; yet, it is one of the ironies of the restoration movement that Lard could never see the force of this argument as applied to instrumental music in the worship.   He opposed the instrument on the ground the New Testament was silent on it, yet this argument meant nothing to him when applied to the Society.

The same argument was put to Lipscomb by Thomas Munnell in their discussions of 1867.   Where is the authority for publish- ing the *Gospel Advocate?*   To this Lipscomb answered:

So far as the publishing of a paper is concerned, it is nothing more than teaching, exhorting, reproving by the written word, instead of the spoken.   The apostles set us the example of doing this.   Printing is nothing more than the multiplication of the copies of the *written* word.   Who says we have not example for this?   It has no organization about it, but is the work of an in- dividual in the church, and responsible to the church.   There is no more organization than there is in one individual writing a letter to a brother.   Now the editors of the Advocate are each responsible

---

[26]Moses E. Lard, "A Few Words on Missionary Societies," *Lard's Quarterly,* Vol. IV, No. 2, (April, 1867) p. 151.

to the church of which he is a member for what he writes and does.[27]

But by far, that which the advocates of the Society viewed as a more serious inconsistency on the part of the Society's opposers, was that men who objected to the Society on the ground it lacked divine authority, would also establish schools, and in them teach the Bible. Soon after the close of the Civil War, Tolbert Fanning led a movement to establish a large university in Middle Tennessee where Christians would teach. An "Educational Association" was organized to help raise the money. Fanning was never allowed to forget that such schools were human organizations exactly the same as the missionary society and without scriptural authority. Isaac Errett responded to Fanning in these words:

But he must allow us to say, that to us the absurdity is so glaring of opposing Missionary Societies on the ground of their lack of scriptural authority, and at the same time getting up human schemes of "Christian education," that it is hard for us to keep back the conviction that there is some other cause for this opposition to the Missionary Society than the mere lack of Bible authority.[28]

It is not likely that either Fanning or Lipscomb recognized this problem as being so great in the eyes of their opponents as it was. They gave what appears to be far too little space discussing this phase of the issue. To neither of them was there any real problem here, and it was difficult to admit the honesty of those who presented this argument. Lipscomb could but reply, "general education is not a work God has committed to the church."[29] Fanning would but say, "these matters are under the supervision of the worldly-wisdom side of our nature."[30]

The whole subject of the colleges teaching Bible will be more fully dealt with in a later chapter, so a brief word is all that is needed here. It is vital to see Fanning and Lipscomb's point of view. Man was a creature of a "worldly" side to them, and they particularly preferred this term. By it they did not mean evil, as we have sometimes come to associate the word, worldly.

---

[27]David Lipscomb, "Discussion—Missionary Societies—No. 3," *Gospel Advocate,* Vol. IX, No. 13, (March 28, 1867) p. 249.

[28]Isaac Errett, "Missionary Societies," *Christian Standard,* Vol. I, No. 33, (Nov. 17, 1866) p. 260.

[29]David Lipscomb, "Discussion—Missionary Societies—No. 3," *Gospel Advocate,* Vol. IX, No. 13, (March 28, 1867) p. 248.

[30]Tolbert Fanning, "Letter—No. 2," *Gospel Advocate,* Vol. IX, No. 15, (April 11, 1867) p. 281.

Instead, man, living as he did in the world, had to use this wisdom of the world. The matter of earning a livelihood, securing an education, making business investments, and a thousand and one other such details which a man carries on in his life, have nothing to do with religion, and consequently, the Bible does not advise a man whether he must be a farmer, doctor, lawyer, teacher; or whether he must go to school or not go, or whether he must invest in business or not. Such things are completely outside the realm or scope of Bible teaching.

It dawned on neither Fanning nor Lipscomb that because a Christian school-teacher taught the Bible while giving a general education, that he was doing the work of the church. Neither man had anything good to say for "theological seminaries" or schools that existed to prepare preachers, for this was the work of the church.

The crucial discussion, then, of the missionary society's right to exist centered in the concept of expediency, its apologists all the while charging that the opposition was inconsistent in decrying the missionary society while maintaining their own right to have meeting-houses, publish papers, and teach in colleges. Lipscomb and Fanning maintained that these latter functions were beside the subject, and insisted that the missionary society was a substitute, devised by human wisdom, for the church which was established by divine wisdom. It was, therefore, to be thoroughly rejected as unscriptural and contrary to the will and desire of God.

While the crucial point upon which the whole issue turned has been seen, it would be wise to look at some of the lesser issues involved. It was charged that the missionary society was a cause of division in the brotherhood. The restoration movement had been conceived upon the ground of the need for unity. It maintained that its plea was the only catholic ground upon which the religious world could be united. Later an element of brethren brought in innovations which were unknown to the scriptures. Brethren could not agree upon these, and to promote them was to abandon the only catholic ground whereby the world could be united. Consequently, David Lipscomb wrote:

We have long been satisfied that the only safe, scriptural, catholic ground upon which all Christians could stand, and work together in harmony as the people of God, was "The Word of God, the only rule of faith; the church of God, the only institution for the people of God."[31]

Perhaps, however, the most serious side issue to the whole controversy was the charge that the Society was a virtual dictator of the local congregations; it was the *master* instead of the *servant*. Admittedly, this fact was not as true in 1866 as it later came to be, but traces of this tendency were already abundantly evident. Especially did it show up in the experience of the *Gospel Advocate* upon its rebirth in 1866.

Prior to 1866 Tolbert Fanning had become thoroughly convinced that the Society was contrary to the will of God. As for David Lipscomb, this was not true. He informs us later that he had never seriously studied the question; certainly had no intentions of making it a cause of dissension with the brotherhood. In 1864, while contemplating the rebirth of the *Advocate* as soon as the war should end, he paid a visit upon a meeting of the Kentucky State Missionary Society, and tried to persuade a man, much in sympathy with the societies, to move to Nashville to edit the paper.

No sooner had the "Prospectus" been issued than Lipscomb got his first personal taste of the spirit of these Societies. On November 27, 1865 Thomas Munnell, soon after seeing a copy of the "Prospectus" wrote a letter to Lipscomb and Fanning.

Dear Brethren: Your Prospectus was handed to me today, with a request to use my influence for its circulation. Before I do so, I want to ask if it is to oppose our Missionary Societies? I have been laboring two years to build up our Kentucky Society, and could not favor the introduction of a paper to war against it all. I am told that anti-mission is to be one feature of the "Advocate." If the "Advocate" will come out and help us in all our good work, I could wish for it a large circulation in our State, otherwise, my influence, much or little, will be against it. I would be glad to see the Brethren cooperate in every good work, and hope we will be able to do so.

Two weeks later the following letter came from George W. Elley of Lexington, Kentucky:

Brethren: Your Prospectus, or circular, for a renewal of the "Gospel Advocate" was received some days since. It would have been noticed earlier, but for other and various demands upon my time. I am more than glad that Tennessee, and the

---

[31]David Lipscomb, "Convention Abolished," *Gospel Advocate,* Vol. IX, No. 4, (Jan. 24, 1867) pp. 70-71.

South, is to have a paper in their midst. Here, the impression exists with some of our leading men, that its editors are unfriendly to Missionary Societies, and if so, I fear that but little can be done for its circulation in our midst. . .[32]

It was evident from these two letters that these men, both officers in the Kentucky Society, would refuse to support any paper that would not support the society. Fanning's reply to both of these letters but shows his independence of mind as well as his determination that no group of men could start a human organization and then dictate the policy of the *Gospel Advocate.*

You will, doubtless, believe us brethren, when we assure you that we had not conferred together in reference to Missionary or other Societies unknown to Holy Writ; but we felt in our heart, that we should enjoy almost inexpressible happiness in once more cordially cooperating with our beloved Brethren, from whom we have long been separated, in every good work, without reference to differences of opinion. But alas! we knew not what a day would bring forth, and when we hoped to find a hearty welcome, we met with a new creed to which we were to subscribe, or be thrust from your fellowship. One which, neither we, nor our fathers knew, nor were able to bear, and we were plainly told that unless we could and would subscribe to doctrines which we had not studied, we must be regarded as enemies. Brethren, pardon us for very respectfully begging you to stop and think before you go too far. What have you done already? You have positively hurled us from your territory and Christian cooperation, unless we subscribe to, and promise to advocate something that you certainly could not pretend was authorized by Jesus Christ, or any of his apostles.[33]

Some years before Fanning had learned the lesson for himself that the Society could be a friend of no man who was not first a friend of it. To feel the indignation of the Society one needed only to let it be known that he was not one of its advocates. Ways and means would be found to limit his influence. Fanning found this to be true, when, in 1859, he attended the annual convention of the Society in Cincinnati. Isaac Errett was corresponding secretary, and carefully cut Fanning off. Of this Fanning later wrote:

Years ago I attended the annual meeting of the American Christian Missionary Society in Cincinnati, with the disposition

---

[32]Thomas Munnell, George W. Elley, "Missionary Societies," *Gospel Advocate,* Vol. VIII, No. 2, (Jan. 8, 1866) pp. 20-21.

[33]Tolbert Fanning, "Missionary Societies," *Gospel Advocate,* Vol. VIII, No. 2, (Jan. 9, 1866) pp. 20, 21.

to respectfully protest against the whole proceeding, but the managers hedged up my way—kept my mouth closed, except a little I was enabled to wedge in by telling some of my experience; but I went far enough to say to hundreds of preachers present, that most of the brethren in my section performed their labors through the church. This was said with the hope of provoking a discussion, but at the close of my experience—for nothing else could I get to tell—Brother Isaac Errett, the Grand Secretary, rose with a paper prepared, Resolved That there was no difference in fact, in doing our work through the church, as presented by Brother Fanning, and through other agencies. This was called by an editor years afterwards, "The courtesy and urbanity," of the society, through the influence of which Brother Fanning, "could not have much influence." In the first place, the Secretary and Society, were not willing for it to be seen that there is the least difference between God's plan and man's plan in doing religious work; and, secondly, by a flattering trick, the Secretary shut my mouth. This was worldly wisdom—shrewdness.[34]

Still another side-issue in the whole Society controversy revolved around the charge that the Society was a poor business investment in getting the missionary work done. In the spring of 1866, J. W. McGarvey wrote a series of articles in the *American Christian Review* on how to settle the controversy. McGarvey proposed that every rich man who could, should support independently an evangelist in the field. Then, every congregation that could, should also support an evangelist. Then, those congregations which independently could not support a missionary, should collaborate. "This agency," says McGarvey, "would be what a missionary society ought to be, and what they all must be, if they continue to be at all."

Lipscomb's answer was intended to show the carelessness of McGarvey's words. If McGarvey wanted every rich man to support a missionary, would this not leave the church out of it altogether? Actually McGarvey did not mean to say this, nor did Lipscomb mean to try to interpret him so, but the language of McGarvey was extremely weak. Relative to the third point in McGarvey's proposal, Lipscomb wrote:

We suppose Brother McGarvey means that a sufficient number of weak churches should combine to sustain one evangelist, not that all the weak churches in the world, or the United States, or one State, should unite in one unwieldy and complicated associa-

---

[34]Tolbert Fanning, "Letter—No. 2," *Gospel Advocate*, Vol. IX, No. 15, (April 11, 1867) p. 282.

tion, that swallows up and destroys the integritism, identity and sense of responsibility of the individual congregations, and with a machinery so expensive in its operations as to absorb from one-fourth to one-half of the contributions before it can be got into operation.[35]

Lipscomb goes on to say that if this is what McGarvey means, and if the brethren will really do this, then those who are opposing them will not raise a voice or pen against them again. The discussion would cease at once, Lipscomb promised, if brethren will go to work through local churches, and not through extra, expensive machinery like the society. He charged that at times from twenty-five to forty per cent of the total money received went to pay the expenses of employees of the Society.

It was only to be expected that in the heat of such a controversy passions should be aroused, and personalities should creep into the arguments. Apologists for the Society denounced in bitter terms the opposers. It was claimed that these opposers did not believe in "cooperation" or in "mission work." They were looked upon as bitter men, with no spirituality and little love for lost souls. C. L. Loos wrote:

The evidence from all quarters of our land, and from other lands, demonstrate that this great matter of missions—organized associations for cooperative efforts to send the gospel abroad—is really no longer a doubtful question among us; that it is decided and accepted. The whole matter has been thoroughly sifted in the past quarter of a century, and may now be regarded as settled. . . . those few who have been of late days persistently and noisely denouncing missionary associations, have, by the unsanctified bitterness and rudeness of their attacks, given full evidence of the causes of their opposition—a lack of knowledge, of an enlightened piety and a true spiritual culture. To attempt to teach such men is well-nigh useless, as it is almost hopeless.[36]

To charge men with lacking piety, having no knowledge of a true spiritual culture because they opposed the society was a grave and uncalled for charge. The whole controversy, on the part of Ben Franklin, David Lipscomb and Tolbert Fanning, was not intended to be a personal attack despite the personal element which was often injected.

Even one so famous for spiritual culture as W. K. Pendleton

[35]David Lipscomb, "The Way to Settle the Society Question," *Gospel Advocate,* Vol. VIII, No. 19, (May 8, 1866) p. 292.
[36]C. L. Loos, "Ohio Missionary Meeting," *Millennial Harbinger,* Vol. XXXVII, No. 6, (June, 1866) pp. 274, 275.

found it easy to thrust these abuses upon the Society's enemies. In his reply to Carrol Kendrick, he praises Kendrick by observing that his article had none of the "trivial captiousness of ill-natured opposition; no frivilous dogmatism; no irreverent treatment of the great work of preaching the gospel, no scoffing at the pious efforts of God's noblest men to extend the borders of Zion." Speaking of Kendrick, he remarks that "he would not throw an envious, or captious criticism across the path of the just, nor hinder the preaching of the gospel, though done by a missionary." Pendleton advised:

Let men who have missionary work, . . . take counsel together . . . and let us not be disturbed, or distracted in our work, by outside railers, who seem to rejoice in nothing so much as their own success in preventing the preaching of the gospel.[37]

Personal thrusts develop attitudes, and attitudes govern conduct. Franklin, Lipscomb and Fanning were quick to feel a righteous indignation at these bitter remarks. To be represented as men who were trying to prevent the preaching of the gospel was something uncalled for considering the fact they had dedicated their lives to the cause, and had consistently encouraged it from the beginning. They were opposed to that presumption on man's part which allowed him to create an organization to do the work which God gave to the church. It implied that God's plan was imperfect, and that man could improve upon it. It implied that human wisdom could improve upon the revelation of God's will in the scriptures. This assumption, along with all of its implications, these men totally rejected.

---

[37]W. K. Pendleton, "Divine Missionary Society," *Millennial Harbinger,* Vol. XXXVIII, No. 5, (May, 1867) p. 255.

CHAPTER IV

THE INSTRUMENTAL MUSIC CONTROVERSY
(1866-70)

The issue which was to find little abatement, and which was more directly to effect a division among brethren was centered around the use of instrumental music in the worship. Actually, of course, the use or non-use of the instrument was symptomatic of an attitude toward the scriptures. Because many felt the use of the instrument was in direct violation of a basic principle which was necessary to maintain if the church was to return to the ancient order, they vigorously opposed it. Although it was frequently contended that the use of the instrument was a comparatively innocent practice, advocated even by some very spiritual-minded men; when viewed from the standpoint that it transgressed upon a very dear and essential principle, many were unwilling to compromise with it. It was this point that gave the controversy its vehemence. Certainly no study of the cross-currents of feelings giving rise to division in the ranks of the advocates of restoration principles could be complete without a detailed analysis of the instrumental music controversy.

It is right, however, to preface this material with a brief account of the beginning of another religious periodical among the brethren, viz., the *Apostolic Times*. The only apology needed for this apparent departure from the analysis of the controversy is the importance of this paper to the controversy. The editors of the *Times* were set for the defense of the church against the use of the instrument, making their paper fill a vital role in the controversy.

Lard's Quarterly had hardly died in the year, 1868, until plans were immediately begun to establish a new paper. The greatest names in the brotherhood were enlisted in a splendid array of talent for an editorial corps. These editors were Moses E. Lard, John W. McGarvey, L. B. Wilkes, W. H. Hopson, and Robert Graham, and were leading men in the church. Wherever the plea for restoration was known, these names were household

73

words.   The last three mentioned are less known to the church today and perhaps stand in need of a brief introduction.

Lanceford Bramblet Wilkes gained his greatest fame with his series of debates with Jacob Ditzler, an ardent polemic of the Methodist variety.   One of these debates was published, and shows Wilkes' scholarship, thoroughness, and greatness.   Fame also came to him as an educator.   In 1856 he was president of Christian College in Missouri.   Before that, he and W. H. Hopson had started and conducted Palmyra Female Academy in Palmyra, Missouri, the home of Jacob Creath, Jr.   Additional fame came to him because of his excellent ability as a proclaimer of the word of God.   In 1853 he was the preacher for the church at Hannibal, Missouri, and he stayed here on and off until the close of the war.   In the fall of 1865 he moved to Springfield, Illinois to preach.   Later in life he moved west, and died in Stockton, California the first of May, 1901.

Wilkes was of sallow complexion, with light hair and blue eyes, weighing one hundred sixty pounds.   He was born in Maury County, Tennessee on March 27, 1824.   When only five years old, his family moved to Miller County, Missouri and here Wilkes grew to manhood.   He heard the gospel preached by J. M. Wilkes and J. H. Haden, and was baptized in the James River near Springfield, Missouri on the second Lord's Day in August, 1848 by J. M. Wilkes.   He entered Bethany College in the spring of 1849, but at the constant urging of J. H. Haden, came back that summer to Missouri and graduated from the State University under the presidency of James Shannon.   He possessed a well-disciplined mind richly stored with great knowledge which probably made him a candidate for an editor's post on the *Apostolic Times* while the plans were yet in their formative stages.

Aside from Lard and McGarvey the most familiar name among the editors to present-day students of the restoration is undoubtedly that of Winthrop H. Hopson.   Hopson ranked foremost among the pulpiteers of his generation, seconded only by Moses E. Lard himself.   In personal appearance Hopson was meticulously neat, tall, erect and dignified. The poorer, undignified class of people shrank at first from his presence, but soon Hopson would win them over by his humility and spirituality which made him "all things to all men."   Sometimes this portly dignity was used as the means of a joke on Hopson.   In 1859 he conducted an evangelistic meeting for the Eighth and Walnut Streets Church in Cincinnati. A writer of the *Western Christian Advocate,* a denominational periodical, went to hear and criticize Hopson. He timed Hopson's sermon—it was one hour and thirty-seven minutes to the tick. He says of him,

He had on a good pair of whiskers as well as a fair representation of the article *mustache.* These he stroked with great complacency for a time, and then took out a penknife and began to whittle his nails.[1]

As a preacher, Hopson was a very gifted speaker. Many men of his generation bore testimony of this fact. In 1853 Alexander Campbell held a meeting in Hannibal, Missouri which Hopson attended. At this time, Hopson was conducting the school at Palmyra with L. B. Wilkes. Campbell writes of Hopson:

. Brother Hopson is one of our most gifted preachers, and when an evangelist, was so laborious as not .to lose a day in the year. We cannot but regret that such a man as he should be confined to the sphere of a preceptor in any academy, male or female.[2]

Hopson's great reputation as a speaker grew out of his ability to make the truth plain to the common man. Ben Franklin enjoyed listening to him. Franklin writes:

While Dr. Hopson is a fine scholar, and instructive to the highest order of society, he is also emphatically *the man for the people.* He possesses, pre-eminently, the happy art of presenting great truths in the plainest and easiest terms, and thus making them not only clear and appreciable to the whole people, but, at the same time, so interesting that all feel sorry to see him close.[3]

. W. H. Hopson was a protegè of Samuel Rogers. Early in the decade of the 1840's, Rogers was preaching in the Gasconade Valley in Missouri when Hopson first came to him. Hopson was now tall, neat, graceful and slender. Hopson possessed letters from Abram Miller of Calloway County saying that Hopson wanted to be under Rogers' care as a preacher. Rogers put Hopson to delivering the discourses, and he himself would conclude with the exhortation. Hopson was now about eighteen years of age; yet he was clear, logical, and forcible, and child-like in

---

[1]Ben Franklin, "Doctor Hopson," *American Christian Review,* Vol. II, No. 7 (February 15, 1859), p. 26.

[2]Alexander Campbell, "Notes of Incidents in a Tour Through Illinois and Missouri," *Millennial Harbinger,* Fourth Series, Vol. III, No. 2 (February 1853), p. 66.

[3]Ben Franklin, "No Title," *American Christian Review,* Vol. II, No. 3 (January 18, 1859), p. 10.

his simplicity, and always humble. Hopson's wife was Rebecca Parsons, daughter of Col. James Parsons. Samuel Rogers also baptized this young girl.

Hopson's son-in-law was R. Lin Cave, who for several years preached for the Vine Street church in Nashville. In his old age, Hopson lived with his son-in-law, and died in Nashville on Friday evening, April 20, 1888.

Robert Graham, the last of the five editors of the *Apostolic Times* to be noticed, was born in Liverpool, England on August 14, 1822. Because his parents were rigid Episcopalians, young Graham was reared as a member of the Established Church. Very early in life he moved from England to America, and settled in Allegheny City, Pennsylvania where Samuel Church was the distinguished preacher. Graham at first became a member of the Methodist Church, but later, when he discovered that there were many phases of Bible teaching which he could not harmonize with the practices of this denomination, he was baptized by Samuel Church.

Graham, by trade, was a carpenter, but gave a part of his time to devoted study. The first of January, 1843 he entered Bethany College, then only recently having been opened. He paid his way through by working as a carpenter on some of the buildings of the College which were under construction. After graduation, he traveled extensively in the interest of the college, settling finally in Fayetteville, Arkansas. Although he moved around considerably in later life, his most noticeable work was done in this city.

Thus briefly have we been introduced to the men who were behind the *Apostolic Times*. The first issue of the paper was scheduled to be published by the middle of April, 1869. During the fall and winter of 1868-69 preparations were rapidly made to launch the paper. The very fact that it had such an array of editorial talent, gave its friends high hopes of success. It was announced that subscriptions would cost $2.50, and anyone who secured ten subscriptions would receive one free. We have in our possession a letter, written by Moses E. Lard to W. C. Huffman, and preserved for us by Minnie Mae Corum on the subject and written at this time. The letter reads,

Lexington, Ky. Mar. 11, 1869

Dear Brother Huffman,

Yours of the 6th inst with names and P. O. order for $25 is

duly rec'd for which accept our cordial thanks. Our paper will be out early in next month. We shall feel deeply obliged for a continuation of your efforts in its behalf. When out, the paper will be the largest and finest sheet ever issued in our ranks.

Yours most fraternally,
M. E. Lard.

The "Prospectus" for the *Apostolic Times* appeared in the December, 1868 issue of the *Millennial Harbinger*. The "Prospectus" of the paper is important as it informs one of the direction the periodical proposed to go. The Prospectus for the *Times* said:

In compliance with the wishes of many brethren, expressed through a period of several years, the undersigned propose to issue from the city of Lexington, Kentucky, a weekly paper bearing the above title. It will be issued as soon as three thousand paid subscriptions have been received.

The absorbing object of the paper will be the propagation and defense of the Gospel as it came, pure from the lips of Christ and of the apostles. On this grand theme it will decline even the semblance of a compromise. Whatever aids this, it will aid; whatever opposes this, it will oppose. To the primitive faith and the primitive practice, without enlargement or diminution; without innovation or modification, the Editors here and now commit their paper and themselves with a will and purpose inflexible as the cause in whose interest they propose to write.

The paper will bear itself high over all political issues and geographical boundaries both in its matter and spirit. It will stand neither for the North nor the South as such, neither for the East nor the West as such, but in all places and at all times for the Truth alone and its friends.

The paper will aim to foster with tender solicitude and profound sympathy all our great educational enterprises. These, it is true, will be held as subordinate to the higher interests of Christianity, but as subordinate to these only, and hence, as entitled largely both to our space and aid.

Much room will be devoted to General Church News and Church Statistics. It is proposed to make this feature of the paper one of peculiar interest.

Important literary and scientific books, especially religious books, will be appropriately noticed. But endorsement where not merited may not be expected. We shall praise only where we think it is due.

The labor of the paper has been properly divided and distributed among its editors, but as editors, they are all equal, all alike pledged to its success, and are jointly responsible for its matter and manner.

Each paper will contain eight pages, and each page five columns.

The paper will be of the finest quality, the type new, and the work executed in the best style.

The price of the paper will be $2.50 per year. But to every person who will send us ten names with $25, we will send one copy gratis.

All preachers and other brethren who may feel willing to do so, are hereby requested and urged to act as Agents in procuring and forwarding both names and money. Let names and money be sent in as soon as practicable. Large lists of names are solicited.

All communications of every kind to be addressed to "The Apostolic Times," Lexington, Kentucky.

If the paper is not issued, the money will be returned.

> Moses E. Lard
> Robert Graham
> Winthrop H. Hopson
> Lanceford B. Wilkes
> John W. McGarvey.[4]

The first number of the *Times* came off the press dated April 15, 1869. The Motto written across the top was, "The Bible Alone—Its faith in its purity, its practice without a change." The leading editorial was written by Moses E. Lard as a commentary upon that motto.

The Bible—first purge it of the corruptions of men, and then not a line does it contain which we decline to believe with a whole sound heart. What it does not contain, as matter of faith or matter of duty, we value not at the price of a single mill. For us it contains only the thoughts of God, and of Christ, and of those who spoke for them. Our love of these thoughts falls only a little below our love of him who paid the ransom of his life to save us; nor could we more readily consent to see them corrupted than we could to see that bosom smuttered on which we yet hope to recline a weary head when the present troubled life is ended. . .

There is in the Bible, especially in the New Testament, something called *the faith*. It is not of this exactly that our motto speaks. It is of the matter of our faith or what we are to believe. This matter must be kept pure, pure as when it dropped from the lips of him who is its source. . . But according to our motto, the Bible practice must remain unchanged. In this we especially allude to the practice of the primitive Christians, as prescribed in the New Testament. No changes must be wrung on this, neither must innovations be incorporated with it. But here a few distinctions seem called for. By practice we do not mean *every thing*

---

[4]W. K. Pendleton, "Prospectus for the 'Apostolic Times,'" *Millennial Harbinger*, Vol. XXXIX, No. 12 (December, 1868), p. 713.

done by the first disciples. We mean strictly those acts which they performed *as* Christians in obedience to divine direction. What they thus did we must do; what they thus did not, we must not do. In this respect their lives must be our model, their practice the law of our conduct.[5]

After the first issue of the *Times* appeared, considerable reaction was seen along different lines. Commenting upon the first appearance of the paper, W. K. Pendleton writes in the *Harbinger:*

We cannot be suspected of partiality or flattery when we say that, no paper among us has a more imposing Corps of Editors. They are brethren of high talent, large experience, approved "soundness," and deep devotion to the cause. . .

The first numbers bristle a little at the apprehension of hostile spirits somewhere in the regions of the air; evince a slight magnetic tremor, under the disturbing influence of some as yet not well determined antipolar forces, that call for watchfulness; and that give due notice that an eye is upon them.[6]

Neither Isaac Errett nor David Lipscomb appreciated very much seeing the *Times* begin. Both the *Christian Standard* and the *Gospel Advocate* were having difficult times getting started. The *Standard* was in 1869 going through its most critical year when at any moment the paper could be a serious financial loss. The *Advocate* had weathered the worst of its troubles, but even so the paper needed to be on a better basis. Isaac Errett, upon seeing the first issues of the *Times,* then wrote the following:

We have received the first number of this journal, the prospectus of which we published sometime ago. It is about the size of the *Standard,* has the same form, and *of course* presents a commendable appearance. . . On its editorial staff are men of established reputation both as preachers and writers, and we expect from them a bold and vigorous advocacy of the truth as it is in Jesus. Among our best minds there is much doubt as to the expediency of starting a new weekly. On this there is much to be said on both sides. For ourselves, whatever our private judgment may be, we cheerfully recognize the right of these brethren to start a new paper, and bid them welcome to this field of toil.[7]

It was customary for David Lipscomb to be frank even if it came to his own discredit. At various times he had tried to get every single editor of the *Apostolic Times,* except one, to write

---

Moses E. Lard, "Our Motto," *Apostolic Times,* Vol. I, No. 1 (April 15, 1869), p. 1.

[6]W. K. Pendleton, "The Apostolic Times," *Millennial Harbinger,* Vol. XL, No. 5 (May, 1869), pp. 294, 295.

[7]Isaac Errett, "The Apostolic Times," *Christian Standard,* Vol. IV, No. 18 (May 1, 1869), p. 141.

for the *Advocate*. They had all refused. Now that they had started the *Times*, Lipscomb was frank enough to recognize that they would hurt the circulation of the *Advocate*. Consequently he was not glad to see the *Times* published, and he would not cover up this fact.

We will not say we are glad of the proposal of publication, for we are not. We regret that these brethren could not find some one of the papers, already in existence, worthy to publish their productions, inasmuch as quite a number of them are barely supported now. . .

We regret it, because we are conscious they will, to some extent, injure the circulation of the *Advocate,* when it is not in a condition to bear the loss of a few hundred subscribers.[8]

The *Apostolic Times* editorially occupied what was after the war the popular middle-of-the-road ground. It, on the one hand, favored the missionary society; yet, on the other hand, it bitterly opposed instrumental music. For a few years this was the popular position, but as time went by, many could not see the consistency of such a position and it gradually faded out of existence. To oppose instrumental music as being a human addition to a divine *worship* was the same *in principle* as opposing the missionary society as a human addition to a divine *work*. Moses E. Lard and J. W. McGarvey could never see it this way. The *Christian Standard* saw the position, and on the same ground that it accepted the society it was led to accept the instrument. The *American Christian Review* and the *Gospel Advocate* saw it this way, and on the same ground they were led *not* to accept the society, also rejected the instrument. Clearly, the *Times* was not occupying a consistent position, but while the issue was yet in its definitive period, the *Times* represented a large bulk of the brotherhood.

THE CONTROVERSY

After the war, the practice of using the instrument in worship was gradually increasing, and in almost every case where it was brought into the worship a serious eruption was occasioned. But as yet, the instrument was not being introduced at a very rapid pace. In the spring of 1868 Ben Franklin hazarded the guess that there were ten thousand congregations in the brotherhood,

---

[8]David Lipscomb, "No Title," *Gospel Advocate,* Vol. XI, No. 4, (January 28, 1869), p. 73.

and not over fifty of them had used the instrument in worship. Even so, the practice was coming unless something could be done to stop it, and most enlightened brethren could see this. John Rogers, one of the great pioneers of Kentucky, died in 1867, and on his death-bed worried considerably over the ever-increasing introduction of the instrument.

In the larger city congregations the introduction of the instrument generally was accompanied with considerable anxiety in the brotherhood. In 1867 the church in St. Louis purchased a new building from the Episcopalians. The building was located on the corner of Seventeenth and Olive Streets. In the deal was a three thousand dollar organ. The question of what to do with the organ immediately arose. A staunch group, led by Dr. Hiram Christopher, brother-in-law of J. W. McGarvey, opposed the instrument, and so, it was not immediately brought into the worship. For two years the agitation continued. At this time the church had one elder, A. Johnson, who favored the organ. A meeting was held the first of the year, 1869 to vote on the matter. Seventy-eight voted for it, and ten voted against it, but the elder recommended putting off using it until after the spring semi-annual meeting of the American Christian Missionary Society which was scheduled to be held in St. Louis in May, that year. A popular vote was later taken which showed that one hundred and four favored using the instrument and twenty-four opposed it. The opposition, although in the minority, was determined enough that for two years the instrument was rarely used. A gathering storm indicated division was on the way. Late in 1870, Robert Graham, Isaac Errett, Alexander Proctor, I. N. Rogers went to St. Louis to quiet the trouble. A compromise was reached whereby the instrument, for the sake of peace, was kept out. This lasted only a few years when the advocates of the organ took control, and those who opposed it were forced to leave and establish another congregation.

In Akron, Ohio about this time a similiar situation occurred. Ben Franklin was invited in April, 1868 to conduct an evangelistic meeting. The church had in the past on various occasions used the instrument, but in Franklin's presence had always refrained. But on this occasion, Franklin went into the building and took his seat, waiting for the singing to start, and then for his time to preach. But when the singing began, so did the instrument.

Franklin, opposed as he was to the instrument, was faced with a serious problem of what to do. He informs us of his thoughts during these few moments:

We have not been more tried in a long time. While this was going off, we reflected and turned the matter in every way possible. What was to be done? We never felt more unhappy. Are brethren determined, we involuntarily thought, to deteriorate the worship into music, and compel us to endorse it? If we refuse to preach, it may, we further thought, create a lasting trouble, and some may blame us for it. We decided to preach, and did so, but with a heavy heart, in view of the worship having been thus degenerated before our face.[9]

Nine-tenths of the congregation, Franklin was convinced, did not want the instrument, but the influential one-tenth promoted it. As to his own position, Franklin explained it as follows:

We have no prejudice against an organ, melodeon, piano, violin, or Jews' harp, but we do not intend to worship with any of these, or even tacitly to endorse the use of them, or any one of them in worship. . . We intend no man shall quote us, while we are living nor when we are gone, as endorsing or in any way giving countenance to the evil complained of. If brethren will introduce the instrument into worship, *they shall themselves be held responsible. We shall not be.* We therefore desire brethren not to invite us to hold a meeting for them, if they intend to play on an instrument in their worship. *We know positively that it is safe to keep it out.*[10]

In Chicago, Illinois still another similiar circumstance occurred. A new church building was purchased at the corner of Indiana Avenue and Twenty-fifth streets. This congregation was newly organized in June, 1868, and moved into its new building on January 17, 1869. D. P. Henderson was the preacher, and the organ was put in over his protest.

The organ is but a common melodeon, and even this is tolerated under protest by Brother D. P. Henderson, who is preaching for the congregation, and who is very much beloved for his work's sake by the whole membership.[11]

In the summer of 1870 the church in Memphis, Tennessee put in the instrument. David Walk, the preacher, chiefly instigated

[9]Ben Franklin, "Notes by the Way," *American Christian Review,* Vol. XI, No. 20 (May 19, 1868), p. 156.
[10]Ben Franklin, "Notes by the Way," *American Christian Review,* Vol. XI, No. 20 (May 19, 1868), p. 156.
[11]C. W. Sherwood, "The Cause in Chicago," *Christian Standard,* Vol. IV, No. 8 (February 20, 1869), p. 58.

it, and put on a concerted drive to raise the necessary funds. At the same time the famous Christian Chapel in Cincinnati, corner of Walnut and Eighth streets underwent a change. A new building was secured costing one hundred and forty thousand dollars. Eight thousand dollars was spent for an organ. W. T. Moore was the preacher for this congregation. Upon the completion of the building, he preached a sermon on the subject, "It is Finished." Ben Franklin was ashamed, and severely condemned Moore for applying Christ's words on the cross to such a lavish expenditure of money in Cincinnati. Robert Richardson wrote Franklin adding his remorse to Moore's conduct and stating that Alexander Campbell would never have agreed to such an act. Franklin, a few years later, confided to a friend that he could have wept with joy at receiving such a letter.

With the gradual increase in the number of instruments being added to congregations, it was clear that the restoration movement was taking on a new color, one of which for the most part the earlier pioneers had never dreamed. J. W. McGarvey very accurately summarized the condition when he wrote:

We are moving; we are progressing; at least some among us are advancing. Whether you think the movement forward or backward depends very much upon the way you are going yourself. Once we had no men among us who were known to tolerate instrumental music in worship. After that there arose some who contended that whether we use it or not is a mere matter of expediency. More recently, a few churches have actually used it, and their preachers have approved, but have not often ventured publicly to defend it.[12]

The apology chiefly used for introducing the instrument was the rapidly changing world. The frontier had pushed on westward; larger cities were growing up in the mid-west. Science was making new discoveries. The train was increasing its speed and efficiency, tying the country closer together. New standards were arising, and consequently, society was raising its requirements. Some felt that a worship without an instrument was all right in a society that was accustomed only to the backwoods, but new standards of respectability were now set up, and the church to be progressive must meet these standards. So McGarvey wrote:

---

[12]J. W. McGarvey, "A Little Farther Along," *Apostolic Times*, Vol. I, No. 2 (April 22, 1869), p. 13.

This question of instrumental music is becoming a serious one. There are many who favor it, and who will listen to no argument against it. By the cry of progress and conformity, it is making its way over the heads and hearts of many of our best brethren and sisters. . .[13]

One N. A. Walker found himself doing a profitable business. He was a preacher, but also sold mechanical instruments. He was busy most of the time holding evangelistic meetings, and usually managed to sell an organ to the church while he was there. For the year, 1869, he reported that he baptized three hundred people, and used an organ in every meeting he conducted except one. J. B. Briney, who in these earlier years was much opposed to the organ, but who later turned to favor them, thought he detected in Walker's attitude a feeling that the organ helped to convert people to Christ. Briney replies very firmly:

I suppose he has an improved edition of the commission to this effect: "Go preach the gospel and play an instrument to every creature!" What a mistake the Saviour made in leaving the instrument out of the commission. When N. A. Walker can convert (?) three hundred persons per annum by the use of the instrument, while he might fail altogether with the simple gospel!

. . . With N. A. Walker I am personally unacquainted, but how to reconcile a disposition to travel through the country sowing the seed of discord and strife among brethren with the spirit of the Master, I know not. . .

He knows that its introduction has caused strife and contention in various places, and, in some degree, injured the influence of some congregations. He knows that some of his preaching brethren can not conscientiously preach for a congregation where an instrument is used. He knows that leaving the instrument off can do no harm, while taking it on must work mischief. He knows all this and much more, and yet he is going through the country introducing the instrument wherever he can, and organizing churches with it in. . .

Concerning him, I can only say to the brethren, "Ephraim is joined to his idols, *let him alone*.[14]

Many were not persuaded that the adoption of the instrument would mean progress at all, but instead a definite departure from apostolic principles. The clash in views was evident. In the quest for progress the instrument was being used over the protest

---

[13]J. W. McGarvey, "Brother Hayden On Expediency and Progress," *Millennial Harbinger*, Vol. XXXIX, No. 4 (April, 1868), p. 216.
[14]J. B. Briney, "The Organ or the Gospel—Which?" *American Christian Review*, Vol. XIII, No. 7 (February 15, 1870), p. 50.

of men who were conscientiously opposed to it. McGarvey propounded the following question to A. S. Hayden:

There is a view of this question which I wish to present directly to Brother Hayden, and all conscientious men who stand with him for the use of organs. It is this: You know that such are the convictions of a very large number of the best and most intelligent class of your brethren, that they will resist to the very last extremity the introduction of instrumental music in worship, and that they will never, while they live, permit it to rest anywhere in peace. Such being the case, how can you, in the light of apostolic teaching, press the innovation in the manner that you do?[15]

The whole question of division growing out of instrumental music received only minor attention between the years, 1866-70. By its very nature it is such a thought that sincere men will put off considering as long as possible in the hope it will not be necessary to consider it. Nevertheless, John I. Rogers laid down a pattern which the minority by and large found it necessary to follow in the years ahead.

In cases of rebellion, defection or corruption, our duty is simple. If the whole congregation, after all laudable means have been used, persist in the use of organs, or any other objectionable thing, we must withdraw from such disorderly congregations, and go where we can worship with a good conscience.[16]

Tests of fellowship over the organ were not frequently discussed during these years, although J. B. Briney speaks out forthright on it.

All of our brethren who favor the use of the organ, and some of those opposed to it, say that this must not be made a test of fellowship. Did those brethren ever seriously ask themselves this question—who is it that makes the organ a test of fellowship? . . . The New Testament Scriptures know nothing of the organ.— They are silent here. Our consciences will not allow us to worship with the new element. The others say, we have the majority. This is a question of expediency, and in all such questions the majority *rule*. The minority reply, you can give neither precept nor example for the use of the instrument. We desire to live in fellowship with the congregation in which we have seen so many happy days, but we can not do it if you bring in the new item of worship. We regard it as unauthorized and corrupting; as calculated to carnalize the worship. But, say the

[15]J. W. McGarvey, "Brother Hayden On Expediency and Progress," *Millennial Harbinger*, Vol. XXXIX, No. 4 (April, 1868), p. 217.
[16]John I. Rogers, "Objectional Language," *Apostolic Times*, Vol. II, No. 26 (October 6, 1870), p. 206.

majority, we have determined to use the instrument, and you can either accept that or withdraw from the congregation.   Here, now, is a new test of fellowship.   Who has made it?[17]

The question of division will be handled in another chapter; nevertheless at this point, some attention needs to be directed toward the subject if anything like a complete picture of the controversy is to be given.

It was stated at the outset of this chapter that the use or nonuse of the instrument in worship was founded on basic concepts of the religion of the New Testament.   Opponents of the instrument considered the use of the instrument to be in violation of an important principle.   Moses E. Lard expressed this in the following words:

The question of instrumental music in the churches of Christ involves a great and sacred principle.   But for this the subject is not worthy of one thought at the hands of the child of God.   That principle is the right of men to introduce innovations into the prescribed worship of God.   This right we utterly deny.   The advocates of instrumental music affirm it.   This makes the issue.[18]

Ben Franklin strongly had the same feeling.

There is not an excuse in existence for forcing this new element into the worship and imposing it on those who cannot conscientiously worship with it.   There is not a man anywhere who claims any authority for the new element, nor one whose conscience demands it.   There is not a saint who cannot without any violation of conscience worship without it. . . . We can remain on safe ground, the common ground and the ground on which we have stood in peace and war—on what is *written*.   The worship in all its parts—all its elements—is a matter of *revelation—divinely prescribed*.   Nothing is acceptable worship, only that which the Lord ordained.[19]

On the other side, friends of the organ planted their whole apology for its use squarely upon the matter of expediency as they had formerly done in the case of the missionary society.   The champion of this view came to be Isaac Errett and the *Christian Standard*.

Until the spring of 1870 Errett had remained silent upon the subject of the instrument.   The columns of the *Standard* carried

[17]J. B. Briney, "Who Makes the Test?" *Apostolic Times*, Vol. II, No. 22 (September 8, 1870), p. 169.

[18]Moses E. Lard, *Lard's Quarterly*, Vol. IV, No. 4.

[19]Ben Franklin, "Explanatory to Brother Franklin," *American Christian Review*, Vol. XIII, No. 21 (May 24, 1870), p. 164.

articles pro and con, but little or nothing came from its editor. It was the spring of 1870 before Errett finally broke his editorial silence and stated his position. Afterwards, N. A. Walker humorously remarked that heretofore "we both claimed Brother Errett until I believe we are both willing that the other shall now have him." Actually, Errett was sincere enough. He was not straddling the fence, but held that the instrument was an expediency, although an *unnecessary* expedient and, therefore, should be counseled against. To Errett's credit it must be admitted that he was following a profound conviction which he had announced much earlier in the *Standard*.

. . . In a matter of expediency, where we have no conscientious leanings toward or against a proposed scheme, we desire to shape our counsels so as to promote harmony; and this we can better do after watching the current of public sentiment.[20]

Believing, as he did, that the use of the instrument involved only a matter of expediency, he waited to see what the current of public sentiment was toward it. After sensing this current, Errett speaks out:

Hitherto, while allowing a limited range to the discussion of the question in our columns, we have refrained from any expression of our own opinion. The discussion, generally speaking, has not been to our taste. We disliked the dogmatical spirit in which it commenced, and have not seen a time until now when we thought the public mind in readiness for a calm and dispassionate judgment; if, indeed, we have yet reached the most favorable mood for satisfactory investigation. Nearly all that we have published in the *Standard* has been in opposition to the use of instruments, and some of the articles—as those from the pen of Dr. Richardson—have been strong, clear, and dignified. We have held back some able essays on the other side, hoping that the differences would be adjusted without much discussion; but we are satisfied, from numerous indications, that some suggestions are needed just now from those who have not hitherto shared in the controversy, and who have reserved their counsel for a time when both parties might be induced to listen.[21]

In the next week's issue of the *Standard* Errett wrote:

We may as well state now, that we intend to counsel against the use of instrumental music in our churches. Our object is to persuade brethren who favor such use to hold their preferences in

[20]Isaac Errett, "Missionary Societies," *Christian Standard*, Vol. I, No. 33 (November 17, 1866), p. 260.
[21]Isaac Errett, "Instrumental Music in Our Churches," *Christian Standard*, Vol. V, No. 18 (April 30, 1870), p. 140.

abeyance for the sake of *harmony;* for as the love of harmony is
that which leads them to see that the deeper and more precious
harmony of *soul* must not be sacrificed by the lovers of harmony
to the inferior harmonies of sound. . . . It is a difference of opinion.
It is wrong to make this difference a test of fellowship or an
occasion of stumbling.[22]

Thus Errett put instrumental music on the foundation of mere
opinion, at the same time counseling against its use. In still the next
week's issue of the *Standard* Errett elaborated upon his feeling
that the use of the instrument was a matter of opinion by saying:

Before proceeding to give our reasons against instrumental
music in public worship, we desire to elaborate more fully the
thought presented in our last article on this subject, namely, that
the real difference among us is a difference of opinion as to the
expediency of instrumental music in public worship, and therefore,
it is wrong to make this difference a test of fellowship, on one
hand, or an occasion of *stumbling,* on the other.[23]

No sooner had Errett expressed himself on the subject until the
Apostolic Times replied. W. H. Hopson expresses his satisfaction
at seeing the *Standard* speak out against the instrument, but declared a disappointment at the ground on which Errett counseled
against the instrument. L. B. Wilkes was glad Errett spoke out,
but declared that Errett gave an uncertain sound. Wilkes declared
that ". . . it will require some sharper thinking than I am capable
of to discern 'whether the snake that made the track is going
South or coming back.' "[24]

Two distinct attitudes toward the instrument now became
apparent. Errett championed that one which placed instrumental
music forth as an opinion, being neither right nor wrong in itself.
Over against Errett was Ben Franklin, who wrote strongly on
the other side in these words:

We put it on no ground of *opinion* or *expediency*. The acts of
worship are all prescribed in the law of God. If it is an act of
worship, or an element in worship, it may not be added to it. If
it is not an act of worship, or an element in the worship, it is
most wicked and sinful to impose it on the worshippers. It is
useless to tell us, *It is not to be made a test*. If you impose it on
the conscience of brethren and, by a majority vote, force it into

[22]Isaac Errett, "Instrumental Music in Our Churches," *Christian Standard,*
Vol. V, No. 19 (May 7, 1870), p. 148.
[23]Isaac Errett, "Instrumental Music In Our Churches," *Christian Standard,*
Vol. V, No. 20 (May 14, 1870), p. 156.
[24]L. B. Wilkes, "Instrumental Music," *Apostolic Times,* Vol. II, No. 9
(June 9, 1870), p. 68.

the worship, are they bound to stifle their consciences? Have you a right to compel them to submit and worship with the instrument? They stand on the *old ground,* where the first Christians stood, as we all admit, and where we have all stood. If you press the instrument into the worship, we care not whether you call it an *element* in the worship or an *aid,* and drive them away, because they cannot conscientiously worship with the instrument, *you cause division—You* are the *aggressor*—the *innovator*—you do this, too, for the accompaniment of corruption and apostasy, admitting at the same time that you have no conscience in the matter.[25]

Clearly, then, to Franklin instrumental music was no matter of opinion. Man had no right to add an element of human origin to the divine worship, for such inescapably had to be an innovation. The two views, championed by Errett on one side and Franklin on the other, were poles apart. Down to the present day they have been the fundamental reason why fellowship between the churches of Christ, on one side, and the Disciples of Christ denomination, on the other, is inconceivable. If the use of the instrument is purely a matter of opinion, then, admittedly, any dispute about it borders on the ridiculous. If, however, the instrument is a human innovation, an addition to the divine worship, then it is sinful to use it. This latter view being accepted, there is no possible, consistent ground for compromise with the former.

The whole field of expediency received a thorough investigation during these years, 1866-70. What is meant by expediency? What is excluded and what included? Relative to the subject, Moses E. Lard sounded an ominous note when he wrote:

> The subject of expediency, as interpreted by some of us, may yet prove the rock on which the reformation for which we are pleading goes to pieces. This is not said in the spirit of alarm; it is the utterance of a calm conviction. I do not deny that expediency is sometimes right, nor that the New Testament, in very special cases, sanctions it. Certainly not. . . . When we plead expediency to justify practices unknown to the apostolic age, we are not within the limits of the expedient. We are then violating the word of God. Expediency is no law for innovations, either in faith or practice; and he who pleads it to this extent has abandoned the only rule which can save us from ruin.[26]

---

[25]Ben Franklin, "Two Standards," *American Christian Review,* Vol. XIII, No. 24 (June 14, 1870), p. 188.

[26]Moses E. Lard, "Innovations in Divine Worship," *Apostolic Times,* Vol. I, No. 3 (April 29, 1869), p. 20.

A writer, signing his name "Alexis," writing in the *Christian
Standard,* was equally pessimistic on the outcome of the plea of
expediency. He wrote:

It was expediency that caused the Pope and Church of Rome
to make the change from immersion to sprinkling and pouring in
Christian baptism; and that caused the same "Church" to introduce the *organ* into the worship of God, or what was styled that
worship. From the Roman Catholics the Episcopalians got it;
and thus it has come on down to us of the present day. The chart
of God's word is the only safe guide in religion. As long as we
adhere to that, properly or correctly interpreted, there is no danger; but when we *leave* it, there is no telling where we will float
to or land.[27]

Some of the clearest thinking done on the subject of instruments
appears to have come from Robert Richardson, Campbell's biographer. In 1868 and 1869, he conducted a lengthy discussion in
the columns of the *Christian Standard* with H. T. Anderson.
Anderson's views of expediency is best summarized in these words
which he wrote:

I am no advocate for instrumental music in churches. But the
Doctor with his legalism cannot legislate it out of the churches.
I might easily say to him, where there is no law, there is no trans-
gression. There is no law against instrumental music in churches;
therefore, those who use it are not transgressors.[28]

Briefly, there was no law *against* the use of instrumental music;
therefore, it is permitted by expediency. This was one view of
expediency. Robert Richardson, an opponent of the instrument,
set forth the other side. Expediency, Richardson pointed out, is
not *without* the law, but *within* it. Before there can be expediency,
there must be law. To illustrate his point, he uses the subject of
Prayer. The Bible prescribes prayer, but expediency determines
the place, the space of time, and the posture of prayer. Then he
writes:

As it regards the use of musical instruments in church worship,
the case is wholly different. This can never be a question of
expediency, for the simple reason that there is no law prescribing
or authorizing it. If it were anywhere said in the New Testament
that Christians should use instruments, then it would become a

---

[27]Alexis, "Alexis on Instrumental Music in the Worshipping of God in
Christian Congregations," *Christian Standard,* Vol. IV, No. 19 (May 8,
1869), p. 145.

[28]H. T. Anderson, "Law and Expediency," *Christian Standard,* Vol. IV,
No. 24 (June 12, 1869), p. 186.

question of expediency what kind of instruments was to be used, whether an organ or melodeon, the "loud-sounding cymbals," or the "light guitar"; whether it should cost $50 or $500 or $1,000, and what circumstances should regulate the performance.[29]

Richardson's words summarize his point. "The use of musical instruments in church worship can never be a question of expediency, for the simple reason that there is no law prescribing or authorizing it."

On still another occasion, Richardson writes plainly of the subject of expediency:

My position was simply that, as expediency has to do with the manner, time, means and circumstances connected with the doing of things, no question of expediency can rightfully arise until it is *first* proved that the things themselves are *lawful* and proper to be done. I feared, and my fears have been fully confirmed by some who have since written on the subject, that expediency was supposed to occupy a wide sphere *beyond* the boundaries of law, and, in its jurisdiction, to be quite independent of law. My view is, that with us, it can have no place at all until law has first authorized something to be done, and that, therefore, its exercise must be restricted within the limits of some law, or rule of life and action.[30]

The one view of expediency was that whatever the word of God did not specifically disallow was permissable. Since the word of God did not condemn instrumental music, it was allowable. But, Richardson pointed out that nothing is expedient which is not first of all lawful. It is a command of God to pray, but it is left to expediency to decide the place, time, and circumstances. J. B. Briney emphasizes this further by saying:

Expediency cannot be allowed to affect the character of a divine ordinance. Whatever adds to, subtracts from, or in any way modifies a divine ordinance, affects its character. Such are the principles that must regulate the work of expediency in the kingdom of God.[31]

It was evident during the years of 1866-70 that the restoration movement was undergoing a change. This is plainly so as to relates to the question of instrumental music. Earlier the pioneers had resisted the use of the instrument as an innovation, but advo-

---

[29] Robert Richardson, "Expediency," *Christian Standard,* Vol. III, (1868), p. 409.

[30] Robert Richardson, "Expediency Once More," *Christian Standard,* Vol. IV, No. 10 (March 6, 1869), p. 73.

[31] J. B. Briney, "The Doctrine of Expediency," *Apostolic Times,* Vol. I, No. 7 (May 27, 1869), p. 55.

cates favoring it were now creeping out here and there. Early in 1870 Enos Campbell wrote an article for the *Millennial Harbinger,* signing his name "E," in which he favored using the organ. Alexander Campbell had now been dead four years. But Campbell's widow wrote to Enos concerning his article, in a letter dated March 28, 1870. The letter but indicates the change that had come over the brethren. The part bearing on instrumental music is given here:

. . . You know full well, too, that as sure as the morning and evening sacrifice was attended to, that the songs of Zion resounded in this old mansion. But never was instrumental music tolerated or called in to aid the worship in the family. No, the revered patriarch [Alexander Campbell] advocated the "melody of the heart" in unison with the "human voice divine" in the worship of the family and in the church; and if he were upon earth now, he would do the same. He wrote about it and spoke about it. That you are well aware of, and he never yielded to the teachings of men in regard to the matter. He never approved nor recognized "expediency" as a doctrine to introduce it into the worship of the living God.[32]

But yet, instrumental music was bound to come. Many would at first reject it, but once they were lulled into complacency by its soothing tones, they would be in the future unwilling to listen to any argument against it. Richardson observed:

The introduction of a musical instrument into a church is a triumph of the sensual over the spiritual. The innovation once affected, the sensual mind seeks to justify the act by plausibilities, as any error may be sustained, and to trust to Christian forbearance of those who are unconvinced, until the habit of hearing the instrument shall at length silence their scruples. There will be no joy, however, I fancy, at the great day, in a triumph thus gained over conscientious conviction, where the soothing strains of music are employed, not to "admonish" or enlighten, but to put to sleep, the guardian of the soul.[33]

---

[32]S. H. Campbell, "Letter From Sis Campbell," *Apostolic Times,* Vol. II, No. 13 (July 7, 1870), p. 99.
[33]Robert Richardson, "Expediency," *Christian Standard,* Vol. III, (1868), p. 409.

CHAPTER V

THE LOUISVILLE PLAN

It has already been seen that the American Christian Missionary Society emerged from the Civil War with considerable doubt as to any successful operations for the future. The "war resolutions" caused many brethren to cock an eyebrow. It became evident that a perfectly innocent-appearing organization could soon become a legislative body for the whole church. Society leaders, however, met this opposition by admitting the mistake, but declaring that such mistakes did not militate against the right of a society to exist. Moreover, the cessation of hostilities immediately turned the attention of the people to thinking of rehabilitation, which drew some attention away from the Society. The Society now faced the worst crisis of its entire history. Whether it should live or die would depend upon the course of events in the next decade.

The original minutes of the Convention meetings from 1866 to 1869 indicate the impending crisis. W. K. Pendleton was called upon in 1866 to defend the Society. Being the successor of Alexander Campbell at Bethany, and the close ally of Campbell, his voice was tantamount to that of the sage of Bethany. It will not be necessary again to traverse the ground of Pendleton's defense. It is only necessary at this point to notice what he says of the state of the Society among the brethren:

It can not be denied, that we have not grown in power and means of good, as there was reason to expect. Instead of a steadily swelling treasury, our contributions have been less and less liberal. Instead of establishing new missions, we have allowed some that were started with enthusiastic zeal, to perish in our hands. . .

Pendleton's speech doubtlessly boosted many despairing spirits among Society advocates, but the crisis was by no means over. More defenses were needed, and the next year both Moses E. Lard and J. W. McGarvey were called upon to speak "in advocacy of the right of the brethren to have a society."

Considerable criticism had been incurred by the Society for its policy of making membership contingent upon the payment of money. To avoid this criticism the Society had abandoned this method of raising money. The result had been a severe loss in finances. By 1868 Thomas Munnell, Isaac Errett, W. K. Pendleton, G. W. Elley, and A. R. Benton were ready to ask that the following resolution be adopted:

Resolved, That in view of the abandonment of life-membership and life-directorships, which have been the main and permanent sources of income to the Society, we recommend to the Board that they devise and carry out a plan of annual and life subscriptions, whereby a constant income may be secured, and a reliable basis laid for permanent operations in the cause of missions.

As an attempt to improve the organization of the Society, the number of vice-presidents was lowered from twenty-five to three. But still enthusiasm was lacking.

Enemies of the Society during these years were all but holding a jubilee. Tolbert Fanning expressed himself frankly that the Society was dead; David Lipscomb appeared to think that all that remained was to gather up the broken fragments of a wasted effort. Their joy was considerably heightened when Ben Franklin, in 1866, threw the influence of the *American Christian Review* against the Society. Franklin, influenced largely by the war resolutions of the Society, began to see in it a potential danger to the future of the church. Both Fanning and Lipscomb felt that Franklin belonged on their side, and there is little doubt that Society advocates viewed Franklin's friendship with considerable uneasiness. No man could champion the principles that Franklin held without sooner or later finding the missionary organization in direct contradiction to them. When, therefore, Franklin turned against the Society, considering his place and position in the brotherhood, it threatened to be a blow from which the Society could not recover.

Quite naturally if the Society was to recover, it would be much to its advantage to win Ben Franklin back to its side. If Franklin could never be made to be an *advocate* of the Society, something should be done to draw a halt to his outspoken opposition. To this end a movement began to win Franklin back, and to unite the opposing forces of the brotherhood behind the Society.

Robert Milligan, president of the College of The Bible, in Kentucky University, led the way for this move. In the October 16, 1866 issue of the *American Christian Review,* Milligan presented an essay in which he attempted to "place our Missionary

Society on a true and scriptural basis." It was intended to be a "golden mean" between extremes. His plan was to leave off a constitution, by-laws, and other such objectionable features, and to organize the society into district, county, state, and national organizations.[1] Later, the idea was suggested through the *Millennial Harbinger*. This plan received some semblance of support from Ben Franklin even if his endorsement is somewhat weak. Franklin wrote:

We have all the time since our first efforts in the work of the Lord, felt some scruples about Missionary Societies, formed after sectarian models, but for years tried to be satisfied that if they were confined exclusively to missionary work, they might be employed without objection. But, after writing more to reconcile the brethren to them and give them efficiency than any other man among us we were forced to the conclusion that there was no possibility of confining them *exclusively* to missionary work; that they opened the way for dangerous and mischievous elements to be thrown in, spreading contention in every direction; that such confederations were wrong in themselves; that their constitutions were nothing but annoyances, opening the way for amendments, modifications, or changes of some sort, distracting our meetings, and were not only useless but injurious. Having been compelled to this conclusion some four years ago, we have been unable to make any defense of these Societies deserving the name, or to advocate them in any effective manner since.[2]

Nevertheless, Franklin did agree that Milligan's plan was far preferable to the Society as it had been known.

By the spring of 1869, criticism against the Society had abated very little. In May that year, a semi-annual meeting was held in St. Louis at which the discussion ran high as to what could be done about all of the opposition. At a recess following one of the dinners, W. T. Moore proposed to W. K. Pendleton that they take a walk. As they walked, they discussed the Society, the opposition, and possible remedies. At the next session of these St. Louis meetings, W. T. Moore arose and suggested that a Committee of twenty persons be appointed to consider the whole question and present a report at the regular meeting in October that year in Louisville. This proposal was accepted and twenty persons were selected to discuss this subject. Among the twenty

---

[1] Tolbert Fanning, "Religious Service Through Human Organizations," *Gospel Advocate*, Vol. VIII, No. 45 (November 6, 1866), pp. 709-711.

[2] Ben Franklin, "Brother Milligan On Missionary Societies," *Millennial Harbinger*, Vol. XXXVIII, No. 1 (January, 1867), p. 14.

were, W. T. Moore, Isaac Errett, Moses E. Lard, Ben Franklin, C. L. Loos and W. K. Pendleton.

The annual convention of the American Christian Missionary Society was held October 19, 20, 21, 1869 in Louisville, Kentucky. The Committee of Twenty met together in Louisville prior to the meeting of the regular convention. Three days and nights were spent in the home of W. H. Hopson, who then preached for the church at Fourth and Walnut Streets in Louisville. Finally, the committee was prepared to present its plan before the convention.

R. M. Bishop, president of the Missionary Society, prefaced the presentation of the famed "Louisville Plan" with these words:

But the present meeting, brethren, is likely to prove one of the most important we have ever had. It can not be denied that we have reached a crisis in our missionary operations. For the past fifteen or twenty years our missionary efforts can not be regarded more than experiments. I do not mean by this to undervalue what we have done; for when we take into account all the circumstances, we have certainly done well. I mean simply that we have now reached a period in our history when we must do better, and that the experiences of the past ought to enable us to adopt such a plan of operations for the future as will be commensurate with the good work to be accomplished.

On Wednesday of the meeting the Committee of Twenty gave printed copies of the Louisville Plan to each person present, so that it could be carefully studied.[3]

W. T. Moore, chairman of the Committee of Twenty, presented the proposed plan to the Convention. It was adopted with only two dissenting votes—both L. L. Pinkerton and John Schackleford considering it impractical. Later Isaac Errett wrote:

It was gratifying to notice that the same spirit which characterized the sessions of the committee, largely prevailed in the deliberations of the convention. And we think it would be difficult to find a body, made up of from five to six hundred delegates, coming together from all points of the country, representing so many varied interests and phases of a religious movement, who would discuss questions of vital interest with more deliberation than was done at the Louisville convention.[4]

The Louisville Plan, as it was adopted, proved to be everything

---

[3]J. W. McGarvey, "The Great Missionary Convention," *Apostolic Times,* Vol. I, No. 29 (October 28, 1869), p. 227.

[4]Isaac Errett, "The A. C. Missionary Society," *Christian Standard,* Vol. IV, No. 45 (November 6, 1869), p. 356.

but a simple one. Briefly, it consisted of national, state, and district organizations. The national organization consisted of a General Board and a Corresponding Secretary. The General Convention was to appoint nine men, who, with the corresponding secretaries of the states, and the presidents of the state boards constituted the General Board. Likewise, the smaller societies were modeled on the same order. Each state was to have a general board and a corresponding secretary. The numerous districts were to have boards together with a secretary. It was the responsibility of the district secretary to visit all the churches in his district. The district board was to retain one-half of the funds it received, and send the other half on to the state board. The state board was to retain one-half of its funds and send the other half to the national, General Board.

The reaction to this Plan was varied. Ben Franklin seemed to have satisfied his conscience that all was well. He wrote:

In our estimation, it is the most simple, natural, and wise arrangement ever made, and that it will commend itself to all who desire to do anything beyond their own immediate vicinities for the spread of the gospel. We have never seen anything proposed that came near meeting with the same approbation in a convention.[5]

Franklin, although a member of the Committee of Twenty, had said nothing in all the deliberations, nor did he speak a word in the convention that adopted the Plan. He makes it clear, however, that he regarded the Louisville Plan as entirely different from any other. It was not modeled after any sectarian scheme, he thought, and possessed no ecclesiastical authority—the two features of the former society that worried him most. As Franklin viewed the Louisville Plan, it was simply an agreement to work in certain ways; this was not, he insisted, a *society* but an *agreement*.[6] This point of view, it must be added, is one Franklin did not long retain. Only two years later, he was back, vigorously pressing a stern opposition to the Louisville Plan on the ground that it was a Society as the others had been.

For six years—from 1869 to 1875—the Louisville Plan occupied wide attention. The records of the annual conventions

[5]Ben Franklin, "The Annual Missionary Convention," *Millennial Harbinger*, Vol. XL, No. 11 (November, 1869), p. 606.
[6]Ben Franklin, "Great Convocation," *American Christian Review*, Vol. XII, No. 44 (November 2, 1869), p. 348.

during those years reveal that there was a lack of brotherhood support to the Plan. The Convention of 1870 met in Indianapolis in the new church building then located at the corner of Ohio and Delaware Streets. The Plan was now one year old. R. M. Bishop, president of the Convention, reported that the Louisville Plan had been agreed upon by all State and District conventions since the previous year's meeting. There were no alterations in the constitution to suggest. A note of disappointment was sounded in that less funds were received than were expected, but Bishop reminds the brethren to keep in mind that the first year was in reality one of getting the machinery in motion. Then, too, some had openly predicted the Plan would be a failure and were withholding funds while waiting to see. The Corresponding Secretary, Thomas Munnell, reported that eleven states and thirty-six districts had been organized, but not enough funds had been received to do any foreign work. So, all in all, the one hundred and two delegates and six hundred observers to the convention found little news to cheer them.

This first anniversary of the Louisville Plan found the convention searching earnestly for some remedy for the wide-spread indifference to the Society. John S. Sweeney, chairman of a Committee on Press, mildly criticized the various brotherhood papers for their half-hearted support, and pleaded for more enthusiastic publicity. As still another attempt to bolster sagging morale, Thomas Munnell made an appeal to the women to help. Munnell says,

Realizing that, as a people, we have never opened the way for the women of our churches to unite in any broad enterprise with us, we propose to invite their vast, though unemployed abilities to "labor with us in the gospel," both as solicitors among themselves and as missionaries in suitable fields.

Four years later Munnell's plea for the women to help was realized in the formation of the Christian Woman's Board of Missions.

The second anniversary of the Louisville Plan saw the annual convention back in Cincinnati. The date was October 19, 1871. The president, R. M. Bishop, again spoke. Men were needed, he stressed, who were more spiritual, more prayerful, and men who gave less time to discussion. The Corresponding Secretary's report showed that $48,123.33 had been given by the churches to the district organizations. However, only $2,600 had ever reached the General Convention. This was barely enough to pay the secretary's salary, and certainly allowed none for foreign missions.

Theoretically, one-fourth of the amount given by the churches to the district boards was to be sent to the General Board for foreign missions. J. W. McGarvey, however, had presented a suggestion that the churches who gave the money be allowed to say where they wanted it spent. It was a good diplomatic stroke, intended to avoid the criticism that the Society was dictating to the churches. However, it proved a blow to the Louisville Plan for the churches were asking their money be spent near home instead of being sent to the General Board. Ben Franklin saw some great significance to this.

Why did not about ten thousand dollars of the forty thousand raised come into the treasury in Cincinnati? Simply because, on some account, the churches that raised it, the districts, or the States, did not hold themselves bound to send their money, or one-fourth of it, there. The churches raised it, and claimed the right to expend it where they thought it would do the best service. This demonstrates that, in the judgment of the churches, the Board in Cincinnati is not needed, and they have not therefore, sent money enough to pay running expenses.[7]

Still, the Society searched anxiously for some way to get the churches more behind it. Perhaps if they showed the congregations they were doing something, that would help! Try to get their minds off of discussion and on the action! Get a man in the foreign fields! Attention now turned to this. The Franco-Prussian war had just ended in Europe and the two countries of France and Germany were before the people. War had plundered the countries, and people were destitute. German universities were filled with Rationalism, and the nation was largely godless. A mission to Germany, then, was recommended, and warmly received. Dr. W. A. Belding personally offered two hundred and fifty dollars to the right man who would go. C. L. Loos delivered a warm speech on the subject. The scene of so much bitter contesting, Alsace-Lorraine, was the place of Loos' birth. He could speak German as well as English. It was suggested that Loos be the man to go, but Loos asked for time to think it over.

Action from the Society was also sought from another place,

---

[7]Ben Franklin, "General Convention," *American Christian Review*, Vol. XIV, (1871), p. 356.

and one closer to home. The two hundred and fifty thousand inhabitants of Chicago had gone to bed on Sunday evening, October
8, 1871—less than two weeks before the convention met in Cincinnati—only to be awakened at one o'clock in the morning by
one of the "most extensive and appalling conflagrations ever
known in this country." At 9:45 that evening a small fire had been
discovered at Halsted Street and Canal Port Avenue. A high
wind blowing from the southwest blew the flames across the river
at Twelfth Street. A general alarm had been sounded after midnight. Eighty-five thousand homes had been destroyed, eighteen
thousand buildings burned down and eighteen hundred acres of
land in the heart of the city lay waste. The fire had been checked
when General Phil Sheridan ordered some buildings blown up at
the corner of Wabash Avenue and Congress Streets.

O. A. Burgess, who had been preaching in Chicago, now
brought the full story before the Convention. Two wealthy
brothers in the church had lost a million and a half dollars. Isaac
Errett had been visiting in the city that Sunday, and had stayed
up until midnight, talking to these men about putting their money
in spreading the gospel. Three hours later, these men were ruined
financially.[8] At any rate, the Society was now given the opportunity to assist the cause in Chicago.

Still other action was demanded of the convention. Thomas
Munnell continued to insist that the women ought to be given
more active responsibilities to help the work. Then, too, the
Society, undoubtedly feeling that they were not being given the
publicity from the brotherhood they deserved, decided to publish
a paper themselves. O. A. Burgess, still feeling the danger of
too great a centralization, asked that the publication be an individual enterprise. W. C. Dawson, who, in only a few years
after this, abandoned the church for the Episcopalians, asked that
the Society run the paper, insisting that he feared no centralization
of power. But, all of these steps pointing toward great activity,
were not enough to bolster the sagging spirits of the Society
advocates.

The convention of 1872 met again at the Fourth and Walnut
Streets church in Louisville. By now the general outlook for the
Society was even darker. Ben Franklin had again convinced him-

---

[8]Isaac Errett, "The Chicago Fire," *Christian Standard,* Vol. VI, (October
14, 1871), p. 324.

self that the Louisville Plan was not a plan, but another Society, and the *Review* once again was turned against it. The nation was now in a dark economic depression. Little money was reaching the General Board. The brotherhood was filled with bickering and debate over the Louisville Plan. In the midst of such a crisis, R. M. Bishop urged the brethren to be settled and not waste time arguing. He declared that some had as their mission only finding fault. He ironically asks, "Must we continue to fritter away our resources and cramp our energies by attempting to settle the difference between *tweedle dee* and *tweedle dum* while the great world is begging us for the Bread of life?"

By the next year, the nation was in the middle of its financial panic. The Convention met back in Indianapolis, but conditions were still unimproved. Bishop was now in a fighting mood. He reviewed the history of the American Christian Missionary Society and the Louisville Plan. Then he turned his attention toward Franklin, criticizing the editor of the *American Christian Review* for changing his position. He requests of the Society that it make up its mind that it cannot satisfy some critics. He cried out, "They mean to oppose us no matter what plan we adopt."

Still the Society was considering some changes that might help. $186,700.91 had been given to the boards in fourteen states of which $7,396.31 had come to the General Board. But the Convention feared going ahead with plans to open a foreign mission on such a small income. Some feared they would not get this if they did not go ahead. C. L. Loos had not yet agreed to go to Germany. How to get more money was the question. R. R. Sloan then suggested that the General Board be allowed to go directly to the churches with its appeal for funds. Heretofore, this was left up to the district boards. This resolution was passed, and the General Board made its plans to do this.

Once before when the Society was threatened with disaster, it had called upon its champion apologist, W. K. Pendleton. Up to the year, 1874, the outlook had steadily grown worse. W. K. Pendleton was again called. The Convention was held in October in Cincinnati, at the Richmond and Cutter Streets church. R. M. Bishop spoke cautiously and thoughtfully reminding the convention that "we as a religious people" have reached a crisis. Success is nowhere in sight, so something drastic had to be done.

Churches were still not giving to the General Board, but instead were requesting that their funds be spent near home. As an attempt to answer charges against the Society, W. K. Pendleton then spoke. He reviewed the quarter-of-a-century history of the Society, recalling the names of the preachers who had been behind the Society, and of the glorious memories of associations with these preachers. When Pendleton had spoken in 1866, his speech served to steady the Society and prevent collapse. Now in 1874 his speech was like a shot in the arm. They convinced themselves more than ever that they were on scriptural ground, although some drastic changes were now in order. Considerable discussion was given to the subject of foreign missions and of changing the constitution. These changes were not to be brought about for another year. Perhaps, however, the most important event of that meeting had to do with the establishment of the Woman's Board of Missions.

Mrs. C. N. Pearre of Iowa City, Iowa on the morning of April 10, 1874 conceived the idea of a missionary society among the women. She, knowing Thomas Munnell's interest in the project, wrote to him about it. To this Munnell replied, "This is a flame of the Lord's kindling; and no man can extinguish it." Mrs. Pearre then contacted J. H. Garrison of St. Louis, then the editor of the *Christian* and got a favorable response from him. Isaac Errett visited Iowa City about this time, and encouraged Mrs. Pearre. He followed this by writing several favorable articles in the *Standard*. He suggested also that the women plan a meeting in Cincinnati that October at the same time the General Convention would meet to talk over plans.

In accordance with this suggestion the women met in the basement of the Richmond Street church while the General Convention met upstairs. Mrs. R. R. Sloan presided while Mrs. Pearre outlined her ideas. These meetings resulted in the formation of the Christian Woman's Board of Missions on October 22, 1874.[9] A vote was taken and the women's decision was to reopen the Jamaica mission which had been grossly neglected.

The Foreign Christian Missionary Society, organized in Louisville, Kentucky, October 21, 1875, was the direct result of the

[9]Elmira J. Dickinson, Helen E. Moses, Anna R. Atwater, *Historical Sketch of The Christian Woman's Board of Missions,* (Indianapolis: Christian Woman's Board of Missions, 1911), p. 5-9.

discontent over the Louisville Plan. The new society really had its genesis the year before at the Convention in 1874. W. T. Moore, noting the discussions on foreign missions and seeing that nothing was to be done, called a group of men together in the basement of the building. A committee was then appointed to make definite plans to present at the next year's convention. On this committee were W. T. Moore, Joseph King, A. I. Hobbs, Thomas Munnell and B. B. Tyler. The next summer this committee met in Indianapolis and drew up a tentative constitution for the proposed new Society. They wanted an American Board to work in the home field, with a Foreign Christian Missionary Society established to work in foreign fields. In October, 1875, then, when the annual convention met in Louisville, this committee presented its plans to the assembly. Errett delivered a speech, speaking tenderly of the dying love of Christ, until all eyes were wet with tears. W. T. Moore presented the plans to the convention which plans were readily adopted. The Foreign Christian Missionary Society now was born. Isaac Errett was elected its first president. The constitution called for life directors by a payment of $500, life members by a payment of $100, and annual members by a payment of $10.

The next issue of the *Christian Standard* carried the reports of the Convention, and the plans for the new society. "The Foreign Christian Missionary Society proposes not to be a rival of the General Missionary Convention but a co-worker with it," wrote Errett. The General Convention remained so that it consisted of voluntary association of members and not delegates of the churches. Writing of the need of such a society, Errett said,

A great many brethren have been anxiously waiting for years to see foreign missions initiated by the General Convention and stood ready to work with it. Nothing has been done. Nothing is likely to be done. The foreign fields are entirely unoccupied by us.[10]

Henry S. Earl was present at the 1875 convention that organized the Foreign Society. He had formerly preached for three years in England, and for ten years in Australia. He announced to the Society that his intentions were to go back to England right away. He was going whether the Society was organized or not,

---

[10]Isaac Errett, "Foreign Missions," *Christian Standard,* Vol. X, (1875), p. 353.

but proposed to go now under this Society. The Society could make little promise of financial aid, but did manage to send him five hundred dollars the first year and nine hundred the second.

No sooner however, had the Foreign society been inaugurated than Isaac Errett struck out defiantly at all who opposed the Societies:

We offer our sympathy to all those brethren who regarded our missionary convention as dead, and were eagerly and rejoicingly anticipating its funeral services. We have determined not to go on with our dying. This may be a severe affliction to them, but we hope they will bear it with becoming resignation. It will slaughter the reputation of a few false prophets, but it will carry joy and gladness to thousands and tens of thousands when they learn that the convention not only is not dead, but is developing a more vigorous life, and promises to increase and abound in effective labors for the spread of the gospel.[11]

Opposition

Having now surveyed the history of the Louisville Plan from its origin in 1869 to its death in 1875 when the Foreign Christian Missionary Society was started, our attention now goes back to this history to be studied from the point of view of its enemies. The minutes of the various convention meetings, from which the previous material was gleaned, show that the Louisville Plan was not widely received. Nor did all of the opposition appear in outspoken criticism of the Plan, for the very fact that most churches failed to support it indicated their opposition to it.

When the Plan first was announced, ironically enough most of the prominent preachers gave it their support. J. W. McGarvey referred to the Plan as the "New Missionary Scheme," and declared that it virtually destroyed the American Christian Missionary Society. It has already been seen that Franklin hailed it as something new, not a society but a *plan* whereby the churches could cooperate for evangelizing the world. Isaac Errett did not agree with the judgment of those who proposed the Louisville Plan but promised his support. W. K. Pendleton did not feel that it would answer all the criticism of the objectors, but agreed to support it. Moses E. Lard urged the brethren to get fully behind it.

---

[11]Isaac Errett, "The General Missionary Convention," *Christian Standard*, Vol. X, (1875), p. 348.

Despite the backing of these prominent evangelists, the churches did not rally to the new Plan. In Missouri it was strictly opposed, especially in Bates and Cass counties. D. B. Swink, writing in the *Christian Pioneer* cautioned that if the State Evangelist came to churches around this section of the state, advocating the Plan, he would be opposed "as a Sectarian under any other name." Swink referred to such men as a Brother Davenport, who lost little love on the Louisville Plan.

Those thoughtless brethren in the State Meeting, calling such men as Brother Davenport, croakers, has made them more determined than ever.—I tell you, brethren, the Louisville Plan we do not want, and will not have. Those that attempt to introduce it here will be responsible for the dissensions it causes.[12]

In Georgia the Louisville Plan caused resentment among the churches. Nathan W. Smith wrote from Jonesboro, Georgia on December 27, 1870 that not over three churches in the state would support the Plan if they knew what it was. It was their impression that it was a cooperation meeting to send out T. M. Harris. Smith writes: "What will be the result of this movement time will show. It has brought division and sorrow with pain of heart to some of our best brethren already."[13] Likewise in Mississippi, the Louisville Plan received a severe knocking around before it was ever accepted. J. H. Curtis wrote in the *Apostolic Times:*

May the Lord bless us and his cause in Mississippi. There is a puny, but would be "big injun—me," opposition to our great "Louisville Plan," and some pop-guns have squirted water on it, but they are impotent efforts, claiming rather our pity than contempt, for these assaults do not rise to the dignity of demanding grave reply after all that has been said. In our own State there is no opposition.[14]

David Lipscomb, however, found himself assuming no different attitude toward the Louisville Plan than he did toward the Missionary Society. True indeed, such Societies were always a potential threat to the liberty of the individual congregations, and Lipscomb opposed them on this ground. Still, the Louisville Plan and the American Christian Missionary Society were alike unknown to

---

[12]D. B. Swink, "The Louisville Plan," *Gospel Advocate,* Vol. XII, No. 42 (October 27, 1870), p. 991.

[13]N. W. Smith, "Church News," *Gospel Advocate,* Vol. XIII, No. 2 (January 12, 1871), p. 30.

[14]J. H. Curtis, "Louisville Plan," *Gospel Advocate,* Vol. XII, No. 36 (September 15, 1870), pp. 843-844.

the scriptures, and an attempt to substitute human wisdom for divine revelation. So, the announcement that the Plan had been adopted found Lipscomb just as opposed to it as he had ever been to the Society. Consequently, he wrote:

I am just as sure that the scheme is weak and impracticable as I am of anything undemonstrated. I am sure every congregation in the land will do ten times as much acting for itself and controlling its own means as it will to have its means sent up to Cincinnati and other places to have a board at Cincinnati and other points tithe and control it. This, the Plan contemplates. We feel sure that thousands of good brethren all over the country feel just as I do, that it is anti-scriptural in organization, subversive of the work and organization of the churches, inefficient in operation and corrupting in influence. Believing this, our consciences demand we should protest earnestly against it.[15]

Of course, Jacob Creath, Jr., "the iron duke of the restoration," could be counted upon to oppose it. To oppose all human institutions to do the work of the church was with him the magna charta of all principles of living.

When I am dead I should like for it to be engraved upon my tomb-stone—

"Here lies Jacob Creath, who opposed all Societies to spread the gospel except the individual churches of Jesus Christ, because he believed such Societies to be destructive of the liberty of the churches and of mankind.[16]

On The Louisville Plan Creath wrote:

These meetings are a violation and a departure from the form of sound words, from speaking of spiritual things in spiritual words —of being silent where the Bible is silent—which is the fundamental principle of our cause. We had as well look for all the acts and deeds of Papists and sects, and all their councils, as to look for the names or doings of these two meetings. They are to be rejected by our people. This one reason is sufficient for their rejection, and until they can find the names of these meetings in the New Testament, they are bound to abandon them. They want apostolic precept and example. They have no "Thus saith the Lord."[17]

[15]David Lipscomb, "Mississippi and Louisville Plan," *Gospel Advocate*, Vol. XIII, No. 2 (January 12, 1871), p. 38.

[16]Jacob Creath, "Letter From Jacob Creath," *Gospel Advocate*, Vol. XIII, No. 2 (January 12, 1871), p. 30.

[17]Jacob Creath, "Some Thoughts On the Great Guns Placed on the Ramparts of the Missionary Fortifications in St. Louis, Mo. in May, 1869 and Louisville, Ky., October 20, 1869," *Gospel Advocate*, Vol. XI, No. 48 (December 16, 1869), p. 1139.

The *sunnum bonum* of all arguments in defense of the Society by its advocates was to be found in the word, expediency. All discussions of the question eventually backed up to this word and settled here. Moses E. Lard, always an advocate of Societies, wished this point to be kept clear, and tried to use it to soothe down ruffled feelings. His article in the *Apostolic Times* was copied by David Lipscomb in the *Gospel Advocate* and considerably discussed. Lard wrote:

It should be remembered that the "Louisville Plan" is wholly unknown to the New Testament. By that book, therefore, it is neither required nor sanctioned; consequently, if good brethren see fit to oppose it, they should neither be blamed, especially when their opposition is temperate and courteous, nor spoken of slightingly. . . On the other hand, if good brethren think the "Plan" right—that is, consistent with the Scriptures, and wish to see it, as a probable means of good, fully put to the test, their convictions should certainly be respected, and ungentle things should not be said against them. If, in the end, the plan does not promise well, it will be abandoned. This will be its death. But if great good shall result from it, it seems to me that it will be difficult to defend opposition to it.[18]

David Lipscomb replies:

It is seen there the ground upon which the Louisville Plan is placed by him. "It is wholly unknown to the New Testament." "It is neither required nor sanctioned." We confess our surprise to see Brother Lard accept an institution in the kingdom of God on such ground. He opposes instrumental music. It rests precisely on the same ground. It is neither required nor sanctioned by the New Testament.[19]

Lipscomb had for sometime been convinced that the Society was an organization gotten up by power-thirsty men wanting some means to control the churches. Such convictions as this were deeply settled in his mind. To express them would give an opponent the right to accuse him of uncharitableness in judging the motives of another. Lipscomb realized this, yet the conduct of the Society seemed to amply prove his contention. When the Society started, the advocates claimed it to be a mere expedient. They claimed that they were merely unselfishly interested in spreading the gospel. If brethren did not want to work through

---

[18]Moses E. Lard, "Louisville Plan," *Gospel Advocate*, Vol. XII, No. 36 (September 15, 1870), p. 848.

[19]David Lipscomb, "Louisville Plan," *Gospel Advocate*, Vol. XII, No. 36 (September 15, 1870), p. 848.

the Society, they could refuse. It was, according to the society enthusiasts, one among a possible number of ways to preach, and men could use their own judgment as to whether they chose to work this way. Lipscomb always believed that this was so much propaganda designed to win favor. Actually, the Society proved to have little sympathy with any man who would not work through it, nor with any church which would not support it. Friends of the society admitted that since it was but an expedient, if the churches did not want it, it would be dispensed with. Certainly in that decade between 1865 and 1875 the Society had plenty of evidence that it was not wanted. Churches refused to support, and not enough money was received to pay the salaries of the officers. The minute it was left to the churches, upon the suggestion of J. W. McGarvey, to decide where their money should be spent, funds to the General Board were less than ever. The Society over the country had alienated brethren, divided churches. Why did it not go out of existence?

With the passing of years this question more and more was raised in David Lipscomb's mind. In 1892 the Society's Convention was held in Nashville, Tennessee. Largely through the efforts of David Lipscomb and E. G. Sewell together with the *Gospel Advocate,* the churches in middle Tennessee opposed the Society. The cause had grown there rapidly without it, and churches were at peace among themselves, all working hard in spreading the truth. Not over three preachers in middle Tennessee favored the Society. Yet, it held its annual Convention there in the hope of swinging some of these churches in line with it. Was the Society *really* interested in peace among the churches? Was it *really* indifferent to the method of spreading the gospel? Lipscomb could never believe so.

The Society worked furiously to convince the bulk of the brethren to ignore the opposition. Thomas Munnell, its corresponding secretary, wrote:

It is a cheap, shoddy piety that spends itself in finding fault and breathing suspicions of the motives and conduct of others. But it wants brains and genuine piety to organize the forces of a people numbering half a million, and bring out their resources into healthful development. We beg our brethren in all the states to turn a deaf ear to controversy and fault finding, and make a bold strike at their conventions for higher achievements the coming year. Strike a higher key, and raise a louder note, and sing a grander strain. . .[20]

W. C. Dawson, writing in the *Apostolic Times* of July 6, 1871, criticized harshly the opponents of the Louisville Plan and recommended brethren to stop subscribing to papers that opposed the plan. John T. Poe of Huntsville, Texas replied to Dawson very vigorously:

We are not surprised at this. We *are a little* surprised, however, to find this advocated so early in the race for clerical power. We expected to see it but not yet. We expect to see the time, too, if the Plan succeeds well, when all preachers will be required to subscribe to the Louisville Plan, or support themselves entirely in the work. Why? Because the Plan is to be made *popular,* like circuit-riding in the M. E. Church. If you want a support in the ministry, you must join the circuit. Send your name up to Conference (Convention) and have the preachers elect you. The Pope, or Bishop there, will assign you your field of duty.

It will take but a few years of the present state of things to require another great Reformation, to relieve the church from its thraldom. . .[21]

Ben Franklin, finally convinced that the Society was unscriptural did not swerve from a steady opposition to it. The Conventions themselves were the source of brotherhood troubles. Therefore, Franklin wrote:

The conventions themselves are the wrongs, and we cannot cure the evil by attending and trying to mend them. There is but one cure for them and that is to abolish them. The way to do that is not to attend them.[22]

Franklin now insisted that the differences have not been about evangelizing nor cooperation, but about forming ecclesiasticisms which grasp power, usurp authority to tax the people, and which also usurps authority to negotiate union with "other denominations." This ecclesiasticism also wants to employ "pastors" for churches and have the right to try heretics.[23] Franklin sensed this trend, and set himself for the remainder of his life, against it.

It may be at once seen that the controversy over the Society

---

[20]Thomas Munnell, "Missionary Work," *Christian Standard,* Vol. VII, No. 1, (August 17, 1872), p. 260.

[21]John T. Poe, "The Plan Again," *Gospel Advocate,* Vol. XIII, No. 33 (August 24, 1871), p. 783.

[22]Ben Franklin, "Anti-Missionary," *American Christian Review,* Vol. XVIII, (1875), p. 52.

[23]Ben Franklin, "Evangelizing," *American Christian Review,* Vol. XVIII, (1875), p. 28.

was moving out to a different sphere of argument. In its earlier years the controversy settled on expediency, and while this remained the core of the argument; brethren now sensed a different type of danger: that of a power-grasping ecclesiasticism to control the churches. On the other hand, the opposition found itself gradually moving into a more closely definitive period in its argument. If the Society were wrong because it was a human institution doing the work of the church, then where was the line to be drawn between the society and printing establishments, church buildings, etc. This effort to sharply define the principle of differences was to occupy some attention in coming years.

The Society appeared to its advocates as a comparatively innocent looking organization. Perhaps Robert Richardson best summarized the feeling of the friends of the Society on the question when he wrote:

In the discussion about Missionary Societies, it is, I believe, agreed upon by all parties, that to the church is committed the duty of propagating the Gospel. Those who approve of missionary societies, do not, however, regard the Societies at all apart or distinct from the Church. On the contrary, they consider the Missionary Society as a proper organization, through which the church can accomplish the work. They do not conceive the Society at all to be independent of the Church, but to be merely a convenient arrangement, through which the church may best carry on the work committed to her.[24]

What could be wrong with it when viewed in this light? Thoughtful people often raised this question in their own minds.

One such individual was L. C. Wells of Burksville, Kentucky. In 1873 Wells wrote to the editor of the *Gospel Advocate* presenting a defense of the Society, but earnestly desiring more light. Wells suggested that the word, society, if particularly odious be dropped. Like Richardson, he presented the Society as not separate and apart from the church, but the church systematically at work. He then presented an illustration. Suppose a congregation wanted to erect a meeting house. It would select two or three men to buy a site, purchase the material, employ workmen, etc. The church is at work, but working systematically through the men especially appointed for certain responsibilities. No one in this case would complain that they were not authorized by the

---

[24]Robert Richardson, "Missionary Work," *Christian Standard*, Vol. II, (1867), p. 201.

New Testament. Then to draw the parallel, he said the church is really God's missionary society. Suppose the church were to select a few men to oversee the missionary work, it would not be unscriptural. Suppose a few congregations went together and appointed a committee to look after missionary work, nothing could be wrong with this, he contended. Certainly this is not a society, but the congregations at work.

David Lipscomb replied that the building committee in the illustration is the church at work if it furnishes the means, and builds according to the wishes of the church and then ceases its function when it is done. But the Society maintains an organic existence distinct and separate from the church. It elects its own officers, and acts independently of one and all churches. If this institution really is the church, then it must follow that its officers also must be officers of the church, but certainly they were not.[25] Wells had been bothered by the whole problem, but when he received Lipscomb's answer, saw the distinction and changed his mind.

W. D. Jourdan wrote to the *Apostolic Times* early in 1872 drawing a line of distinction on the whole question. Jourdan wrote:

It is true, God has left out of law many things that, in the course of time, fall within the direction of the church, such as building houses of worship, of what material they shall be, at what place, or how large they shall be. But not so in relation to matters upon which he has expressed his will, here we must not add one word, much less make, and enforce any plan whatever. The Louisville Plan, to my mind, assumes the ground that God has given no plan for raising money to maintain his cause on earth, or if he has, that his plan has failed. . . If he has given no law or plan for this purpose, what necessity caused us to originate one? . . .

But if the Louisville Plan claims for itself an existence on the ground that the plan of God has failed, it shows, at least some friendship in the attempt to resuscitate or aid the failure of its maker; but what confidence could we have in its success, more than we could have in the plan of God?[26]

The opposition to the Louisville Plan was effective. The

---

[25]David Lipscomb, "Thoughts on Missionary Cooperation," *Gospel Advocate*, Vol. XV, (1873), pp. 721-726.

[26]W. D. Jourdan, "The Louisville Plan," *Apostolic Times*, Vol. III, No. 51 (March 28, 1872), p. 401.

churches refusing to support it, left the Society destitute of funds. The decision to abandon the Louisville Plan in 1875 and establish the Foreign Christian Missionary Society was significant in that it was also a decision to abandon all attempts to please the element opposing societies in the brotherhood.   Henceforth all efforts to promote the society were to be exerted among its friends, and no attempt would be made to even notice the opposition.   It was virtually an admission that there was division in the brotherhood, and an abandonment of any attempt to reconcile the opposing forces.   Indeed, by the year 1875, the brotherhood was already divided so far as the fundamental issues were concerned.   The next quarter of a century was merely an era when congregations, members, preachers were lining themselves up on one side or the other.

CHAPTER VI

KENTUCKY UNIVERSITY

As events were now developing, the entire brotherhood was to find itself seriously effected by troubles at Kentucky University at Lexington in that decade between 1865 and 1875. These unfortunate happenings helped create a certain type of thinking respecting the whole issue of human institutions, their place and work, which has continued to be a major problem.

The history of Bacon College has already been briefly recounted. Starting in 1839 at Georgetown, Kentucky, Bacon College later moved to Harrodsburg, where it found the attempt to be a first-class school filled with so many problems that it finally closed. At the instigation of John B. Bowman, new hopes were suddenly revived for the school in 1857. Bowman had the vision of making it into Kentucky University. Very quickly he raised sufficient funds to make this seem possible. Then came the Civil War. Despite the handicap of the war, the College remained open, but in 1865 a serious fire blasted its hopes. At this moment an invitation was extended for it to join forces with Transylvania University in Lexington, and so from that date, Kentucky University became a name closely allied with Lexington.

In 1862 John W. McGarvey moved from Dover, Missouri to preach for the Main Street Church vacated by the resignation of Dr. Winthrop H. Hopson. Three years later, when Kentucky University moved to Lexington, McGarvey was invited to join the faculty of the College of the Bible which was then under the presidency of Robert Milligan. McGarvey's name had by now become a household word among members of the church. His commentary on Acts of The Apostles was already before the public and widely acclaimed. His enthusiastic defense of the pioneer's older practice of not using the instrument of music had often found his name in the *Millennial Harbinger* and the *American Christian Review*. McGarvey, sensing the opportunity to extend his influence, readily accepted the position as teacher of Bible in the College of The Bible when it was offered to him in 1865.

The center of activities in the brotherhood was already passing

113

from Bethany to Lexington, Kentucky. Alexander Campbell, old and feeble in 1865, had substantially yielded the sceptre to his younger contemporaries. It was Campbell who had made Bethany, and his passing meant in a measure the passing of Bethany as the Jerusalem of the restoration. But natural causes were also at work. The frontier had pushed westward. Lexington was no longer a city on the far reaches of the west, but a cultural center of the western United States. The moving of Kentucky University together with the College of The Bible to Lexington was of great interest to the brotherhood.

That trouble was eventually due to arise in this University was but natural, and probably few informed brethren saw any method of avoiding it. Basically, there was a clash in ideologies for the school. This clash sooner or later had to be forced into the open.

Kentucky University opened at Lexington for its first session on October 2, 1865. The College of The Bible opened with thirty-seven students. As it was now organized the University was divided into five separate colleges, the College of Arts, Agriculture and Mechanical College, College of Law, Commercial College and the College of The Bible. John B. Bowman, who had raised all of the money, was the supervisor of the university officially known as the regent. Each College had its president, Robert Milligan was the president of the College of The Bible.

The Agriculture and Mechanical College was a more recent addition to the University. Congress had previously granted thirty-thousand acres of land to each state for each representative and senator that it had in congress for an Agriculture and Mechanical College. Three years had been allowed for each state to accept the offer. Two years went by and nothing was done in Kentucky to accept it. Finally, Transylvania had applied to have the A. & M. College annexed to it. But, about this time, Kentucky University was joined to Transylvania. Bowman, in the meantime, had raised one hundred thousand dollars and had purchased Henry Clay's home of four hundred and thirty-three acres at Ashland. At any rate, Kentucky University by 1866 found itself in possession of an A. & M. College together with a four hundred thirty-three acre experimental farm in nearby Ashland.

By now, however, some had already begun to wonder just where Kentucky University stood in relation to the brotherhood.

It had been their understanding that the University belonged to them. The largest percentage of funds donated to the school had been given by members of the church in the belief that the school would be run on thoroughly Christian principles. The charter was intended to make this clear. Regent Bowman was to have gathered around him a Board of Curators, and he, together with the Curators, was to supervise the school. The charter stated that at least two-thirds of these Curators should be members of the church. Section No. 8 of the Charter read as follows:

For the ownership and control of said university, at least two-thirds of the Board of Curators shall always be members of the Christian Church in Kentucky. At no time shall any member of the faculty be a member of the Board.[1]

Members of the church in Kentucky, therefore, gave freely to the university. They expected the faculty to be members of the church, and thought they were to see a university where they could send their children to secure an education that would heighten their respect for the church. When the faculty more and more became made up of individuals not in sympathy with the church and when the University began to annex the A. & M. College, which meant it had formed an alliance with the state, a rumble of discontent began to sweep over the brotherhood. Particularly was this true in Kentucky.

Bowman had gathered around him a Board of Curators largely imbibed with his own educational ideas. Both for their day were filled with "liberal" ideas for the school, but their language, clothed as it was with the verbiage long familiar to the brotherhood, caused considerable misunderstanding. Both Bowman and the Curators claimed they were running a university on "non-sectarian" principles. The brotherhood breathed a sigh of relief. But they were soon to learn that the connotation of "non-sectarian" was not necessarily fixed. Bowman conceived of the churches of Christ as another sect. Instead of making Kentucky University be sympathetic toward their cause, he would conceive of a school that would serve equally as well the denominations. For the first time many brethren realized that they were looked upon as a sect.

There was a certain ambiguity in the terms that made the real truth difficult to see. To announce to the brotherhood that the

---

[1]Moses E. Lard, "Who Owns Kentucky University?" *Apostolic Times,* Vol. III, (1871), p. 244.

school was "non-sectarian" satisfied them for they believed the school was sympathetic to them. But the denominations understood by "non-sectarian," that it advocated the principles of no one religious group. Such ambiguity those close to the school could sense. McGarvey sensed that the brotherhood was being deceived by Bowman and the Curators. Moses E. Lard, who had moved back to Lexington at the close of the war where he edited both *Lard's Quarterly* and later, the *Apostolic Times,* agreed with McGarvey. The feeling became more widespread. The church in Lexington soon became convinced that all was not well, and gradually, this idea went out of the brotherhood.

By the time the fall term of 1871 was ready to open, the undercurrent of feeling had picked up sufficient momentum that it was at the bursting point. Only a matter of days before the term opened, Ben Franklin addressed an article through the *American Christian Review* to Regent Bowman and the University.

True, we grant, it is not to be *sectarian,* but it is to be *Christian.* It must be under the control of *Christians.* The church of God is no *sect,* and the gospel of Christ is not *sectarianism.* . .

True, the Institution has the funds and can **exist without** regard to the *will* of the donors, or the chief men among us. But it can not get the patronage of *Christians* unless it is true to the cause in the interest of which it has been raised up. . . We are perfectly aware how pleased it is to talk about *liberal principles* and an *unsectarian* Institution. But the religion of Christ is *liberal,* and those who submit to it are *free,* in the highest sense, and charitable too ; but not, however, liberal, charitable and free enough to be unequally yoked together with *unbeliever* and *sectarians.*

. . . We must have some assurance that the Institution will be run with a more strict regard to the wishes of the donors and the chief men in the State before our embarrassment will be removed. We desire to know that the University is not only *nominally* turned over to the brotherhood, but run in accordance with their desires.[2]

Kentucky University felt financially capable of running her own affairs without the brotherhood's sympathy and proposed to do so. It was the realization of this danger that had led Tolbert Fanning and David Lipscomb to advocate that schools have no endowment and that they might die upon the death of their founders. Men would give money to richly endow a school

---

[2]Ben Franklin, "Kentucky University," *American Christian Review,* Vol. XIV, No. 39 (September 26, 1871), p. 308.

and after they died, the money would be used to destroy the very thing they had tried to erect. Ben Franklin, hoping to get Bowman to put the school on a more acceptable foundation, thought it wise to call his attention to the need of getting back to the old foundation.

The leaven of discontent had now worked the situation up to the bursting point. Bowman and several of his faculty attended the Main Street Church in Lexington where McGarvey preached. Bowman felt the pressure gradually pushing in on him. He, with thirteen members of his faculty, suddenly decided to leave the Main Street Church and go "around the corner" to establish the Second Christian Church. Moses E. Lard now jumped into the trouble, declaring that Bowman was violating the teachings of Matthew, chapter XVIII, and therefore, was guilty of disorder and schism. A vote was taken whether or not the church should withdraw from Bowman, and was sustained fifty to ten.[3]

The story of the "church war at Lexington" now blazed forth before the whole country. A brother of one of the men who withdrew was connected with the secular press in Lexington. Soon, the *Lexington Press* and the *Louisville Ledger* were filled with news stories of the trouble. Quite naturally, their sympathy lay with Bowman and the Curators. They declared that Kentucky University belonged, not to any one "sect" or "denomination" but to the people of Kentucky. They praised Bowman for his liberal stand, and denounced McGarvey and Lard as narrow-minded bigots who were jealous of Bowman's popularity and who were without a sufficient breadth of understanding and charity.

The *Apostolic Times* charged head-long into the fracas. It met the attack of the secular press by frequent references to the charter and to the history of the school, declaring that the school was owned by the brotherhood of Kentucky who had been the largest contributors to it. It declared that Bowman and his curators were not thoroughly honest with the brethren, and that the secular press was a partisan witness in the whole affair.

The *Cincinnati Commercial* picked up the story and ran its side.

Three prominent members and leaders in the Christian denomination, Moses E. Lard, J. W. McGarvey, L. B. Wilkes, who form-

---

[3]Ben Franklin, "A Church War at Lexington," *American Christian Review*, Vol. XIV, No. 46 (November 14, 1871), p. 364.

erly were residents of Missouri and came to Lexington since the University expanded into its present broad proportions, with a few others of less note, have been manipulating to get Regent Bowman out of the university and have it conducted according to their ideas of the fitness of things, which ideas happen to be of a rather sectarian and illiberal character.

News of the trouble spread into the brotherhood papers. J. M. Long of Chillicothe, Missouri, Bowman's ardent supporter, picked out the above article from the *Commercial,* and printed it in the *Christian Standard,* over the name, "Alumnus," along with comments of his own. Long had a standing grievance against Lard and McGarvey of two years previously when both men had severely criticized an article he had written for the *Christian Pioneer.* Long had written some articles for the *Apostolic Times,* but Lard and McGarvey had regarded them as unsuitable for publication. Now, however, Long took advantage of an opportunity to criticize them. After quoting the article from the *Commercial,* he concluded by saying,

The whole difficulty lies in the fact that the large hearted founder of Kentucky University is too broad and catholic for them. They want a college that shall be run on a narrow and strictly sectarian gauge. In view of this we would say that Kentucky University is not the college for them; it is not suited to their dimensions.[4]

Both Lard and McGarvey expressed their disappointment that Isaac Errett had allowed such an article to be run, especially since it was unsigned. Errett, however, explained that his only purpose in printing it was to elicit some denials of it.

Regent Bowman was thoroughly convinced that Lard and McGarvey had been planning a campaign to oust him from his position. McGarvey and Lard felt greatly embarrassed when Bowman presented a statement from Thomas D. Butler of Louisville, Kentucky, affirming this point. Butler was a member of the Fourth and Walnut Streets congregation in Louisville where W. H. Hopson preached. According to Butler, shortly after the *Apostolic Times* was started in the spring of 1869, Hopson received a letter from Lard and McGarvey. The letter requested Hopson to get a brother to write a question and send it to the *Times,* which letter was to ask the *Times* questions about the handling of Kentucky University by Regent Bowman. One

[4]Alumnus, "Regent Bowman and Kentucky University," *Christian Standard,* Vol. VII, No. 2 (January 13, 1872), p. 11.

question that was to be asked was, "Why is it that the Regent has employed only nineteen professors from the Christian Church whilst eleven of the professors in the university are from elsewhere?" Another question to be asked was, "Is John B. Bowman, who is only a Kentucky farmer, the fittest man for the Regency of Kentucky University while we have so many college-bred preachers in the State?"

Furthermore, according to T. D. Butler, Lard and McGarvey suggested that they were ready to start a war against the Regent but they knew it would not do for them to start it themselves. T. D. Butler charged that soon after W. H. Hopson received this letter, he confided the matter to him asking him to write these questions for the *Times*. Butler had refused and had stopped his subscription as a result. Now, Butler wrote these facts out, signed them, had them notarized, and gave them to J. P. Torbitt of Louisville, Kentucky, one of the curators of the school. Torbitt, in turn, gave the statement to Regent Bowman, who now used it against Lard and McGarvey.[5]

No sooner, however, had Bowman published such a letter than a strict denial came from W. H. Hopson that he had ever had such a conversation with T. D. Butler. Lard and McGarvey, moreover, emphatically denied that they had ever written such a letter. The matter was presented vigorously to the Fourth and Walnut Streets church, but neither Butler nor Hopson backed down from their previous statement. The result was this argument entered a stalemate. A committee in the Louisville church was appointed to go into the matter, but nothing could be proved. The result was a re-affirmation of confidence in both men, but a severe upbraiding of Butler for ever publishing such a thing even if it were true.

Ben Franklin now began to view the Kentucky University troubles with great alarm. He lashed out against Bowman, claiming the church in Kentucky had lost complete confidence in him. Bowman is charged with trying to turn a Bible institution into a secular institution.[6] R. M. Bishop, president of the American Christian Missionary Society, was one of the leading members of

---

[5]Anonymous, "The Lexington Difficulties," *Christian Standard,* Vol. VII, (April 6, 1872), p. 106.

[6]Ben Franklin, "Kentucky University," *American Christian Review,* Vol. XV, (September 24, 1872), p. 316.

the Board of Curators of Kentucky University. Franklin turned against Bishop. The speeches which Bishop delivered before the Conventions of 1872 and 1873 were presented while Bishop was still nursing the wounds of this conflict with Franklin over Kentucky University.

David Lipscomb had been watching the trouble with keen interest. It was characteristic of Lipscomb to view so many troubles as largely political in origin, and that was the way he viewed this, although Franklin denied politics had anything to do with it. Lipscomb charged that Bowman was a radical in politics and in sympathy with the "progressive" party in the church. He claimed the Regent had filled the Board of Curators with his radical political friends, and of filling the faculty with the same.[7] That Lipscomb probably had some ground for making such charges seems evident, but if so, they nowhere appear in the controversy itself.

In spite of the controversy that was raging the matter rocked on in that vein until the summer of 1873. An Executive Committee was now appointed to go into the matter and bring forth a decision. Bowman was chairman of the committee, which gave assurance that an impartial decision was out of the question. McGarvey, at any rate, was asked to hand in his resignation. At the instigation of many of his close friends, McGarvey refused. The Executive Committee, however went before the Board of Curators with its decision, and the Board officially dismissed McGarvey as a teacher. Shortly afterward, McGarvey wrote:

The purpose long cherished in the heart of John B. Bowman has at last been accomplished. Mordecai no longer sits at the king's gate refusing to bow down when the great Haman goes in and out.[8]

McGarvey had for sometime been considering the matter of ceasing to teach and to preach and write. Now that he was out of Kentucky University he determined to give his time to preaching, and to writing a new commentary on Matthew and Mark.

The churches of Kentucky took the dismissal of McGarvey as in effect an attempt to pull the university away from the brotherhood altogether. They had confidence in McGarvey, and knew

---

[7]David Lipscomb, "Kentucky University," *Gospel Advocate,* Vol. XV, (1873), p. 882.
[8]J. W. McGarvey, "My Removal," *Apostolic Times,* Vol. V, No. (October 2, 1873), p. 4.

him to be loyal to their principles. Many decided not to surrender without a fight. A petition, signed by many members of the church in Kentucky was handed to R. M. Bishop, chairman of the Board of Curators, but to no avail. By the next spring the brethren were determined to try again.

Meeting in Louisville, Kentucky on May 28, 1874 a group of brethren agreed to appeal the matter to the State Legislature to change the management of the University. Their proposal was that a Board of managers would be selected by the church in Kentucky to manage the school. These would be elected for five years. Each manager was to be a member of the church. When fifty congregations should propose it, a change in the management of the institution could at any time be brought about. A committee of twenty-one brethren was appointed to try to secure this legislation. When the State Legislature met, the vote in the House of Representatives was forty-eight for the change, and forty-seven against. In the Senate, the vote was sixteen for, and twenty against. Since a majority vote in both chambers was necessary, the measure automatically ended.

During the summer of 1874, matters at the college looked dreary so far as the brethren were concerned. Many students were leaving the school, not to return. It was evident that something drastic had to be done. Brethren now began to reconsider the subject. Kentucky University, with its alliance with the State, its A. & M. College, was not the Bacon College of 1847. The pet cub had grown to be a roaring lion and who knew what to do with it? Theoretically, Kentucky University was owned by the churches of Kentucky, but the State also had some claim to the school now. For the churches to try to maintain an ownership of such a University seemed to many ridiculous. How could the church in Kentucky, by its very nature, own such a school? James Challen thought along this line very clearly. Speaking of the University said, "Now this is a pretty business for the churches in any State to be burdened with." He pointed out that the churches could not look after Kentucky University. "Brethren," he declared, "stop this thing. There is evil and mischief in it that will outlive the movers of it."[9]

---

[9]James Challen, "Old and New," *Christian Standard*, Vol. IX, (January 17, 1874), p. 17.

As many brethren now thought about it, they began to see that the college could be an instrument of evil as well as of good. Ben Franklin now started out to write a series of articles entitled, "Educational," but which he did not finish. At any rate, he states a new conception that he had concerning the schools. It had never before occurred to him that a school might be a source of evil as well as of good. He stated an opinion that colleges ought to stay with secular work and leave the teaching of the Bible to the churches. He resolved to give this whole subject some careful consideration. The question he asked was, "Ought the *church* to build a college of arts and sciences and make it denominational?" He was determined to think this through and come to some more definite conviction about it.

David Lipscomb himself now cocks an eyebrow toward such schools as Kentucky University. His idea of schools, patterned mostly after those of Tolbert Fanning before him, had never been too closely related to that of many in the brotherhood. Fanning had never favored building up Franklin College with a large endowment that it might last through the years. On this point Fanning and Alexander Campbell had formerly differed. Fanning saw that good men might give to a college for an endowment, but years after they were dead, their money might be used to tear down the thing they were trying to build. Lipscomb had the same conviction. He wrote:

We think the most fatal mistake of Alexander Campbell's life, and one that has done much and we fear will do much more to undo his life's work, was the establishment of a school to train and educate young preachers. . .

We think the idea of taking young men and withdrawing them in a preacher's school to make preachers of them, results in evil in many ways, without one particle of good attached. Christ did not take his teachers from that class. . .

All schools conducted by Christians ought to teach the Bible thoroughly to all who attend no matter what their anticipations for life may be.[10]

During the early part of the decade of the 1870's, Joseph Franklin wielded a powerful pen for the ancient landmarks. He followed his father with the greatest of enthusiasm. Unfortunately in years to come a sadder chapter appeared in his life. Less than

---

· [10]David Lipscomb, "Schools for Preachers," *Gospel Advocate,* Vol. XVII, No. 15 (April 8, 1875), p. 346.

five years after his father died, he began showing signs of yielding his position, and yet later, threw all of his influence behind the very cause he had once fought so vigorously. As Joseph Franklin viewed the situation at Kentucky University, he was led to some extreme points of view. "The arguments in favor of Bible Colleges," he wrote, "are fallacious and the results do not justify expectations. He lays a very serious abuse down at the door of these colleges.

We have been promised trained men who could fairly represent us in the world of letters and science. What have we got? Occasionally there is one such (who would have had an education had there never been a Bible college), but for one such *scores* of pedantic striplings who prate about the illiteracy of our ablest men snivel because people prefer common sense instead of their dry speeches, and make indecent haste to sell out the reformation for the fellowship of sectarians.

Young Franklin goes on to conclude:

I believe, therefore, that the "Bible College" is just the same old sectarian *pod auger* we used to know as the "theological seminary." The current scandal of Kentucky University illustrates and enforces my argument.

During these years also, when Kentucky University was having its troubles, a series of articles made its appearance in the form of letters written to Jacob Creath, Jr. by B. F. Leonard who lived in New England. Leonard wrote under the name of L. E. Bittle. He never became widely known as a preacher, being more or less secluded in New England. Yet for a score of years beginning at this time, Leonard's writings carried great weight. His letters to Jacob Creath pretended to be written by an outsider, criticizing the brotherhood. The articles are at times rather severe, and were a vital factor in helping to mold a certain attitude toward the Bible Colleges. To Creath, Bittle wrote:

You have abandoned the old and more appropriate name of "Theological Seminary" for that of "Bible College"; but because you have thus exchanged names it does not follow that you have in hand an institution differing in any wise from that possessed by the "sects."[11]

Bittle lays the accusation before Creath that the brethren will not listen or pause to consider that such colleges may be wrong. "They take for granted that "whatever is, is right" and are seldom willing

[11]B. F. Leonard, "Letters to Jacob Creath," *Gospel Advocate*, Vol. XVI, (July 2, 1874), pp. 631-635.

to listen candidly to a person who demands of them a valid reason, or rather, who shows them that they have no such reason, for things which they hold or practice. Men like horses, love to travel in a beaten path with the wheels in the ruts."

Bittle's articles frequently cause one to wince a little, but they are good in that there is more truth here than one sometimes likes to admit. Against Bible Colleges he lays some pretty severe charges. "One charge that I have to bring against them is that just intimated—they are worldly. Like all other colleges, they are founded on money, not on the Bible." He points out that they have to have an endowment, talent and patronage. Their success depends upon courting the favor of the world. He charges that whenever a crisis occurs, they can be counted on to take the most popular side in opposition to all principles of right, if need be. He has a word of warning:

I may be misinformed, but I believe your Bible Colleges are no exception to the general rule. Their abuses may not yet be plainly manifested, but they will surely show themselves in all their deformity.

To prove his charges he asks Creath what the colleges had done to check the avalanche of innovations. He charged that they were all either silent or advocating the wrong side.

The troubles at Kentucky University between the years, 1871-75, largely planted the seeds for the controversy to arise in later years against the right of Christians to operate schools in which they could teach the Bible. So far as its lasting effect in the brotherhood is concerned, the controversy at Kentucky University did both good and evil. For some men it served the purpose of helping them to clarify their thinking that schools might later be started which would avoid the errors of the College of The Bible. Evil was done in that men used the controversy at Kentucky University to set them off on the road of wholesale denunciation of schools, no matter how organized, and no matter the principles beneath them. The churches of Christ have not yet outgrown the full effect of the troubles at Kentucky University nor are they likely to do so in this generation.

Going back now to the historical sequence of the University conflict, the future, from the summer of 1874, indeed looked dark. Nothing of great consequence happened to clear the trouble through the following winter. But by the next summer the Board of

Curators had become convinced that something needed to be done to regain the favor of the brotherhood. It was decided to give the College of The Bible over to the control of the "brotherhood of Disciples," with an understanding that a vigorous campaign for endowing the college would be pressed. In effect, the College of The Bible was now being separated from Kentucky University, so that the churches of Kentucky would now only look after this college rather than the entire University. The peace was likely the only sensible one that could be brought about under the circumstances, but it was probably little comfort to members of the church to see thousands of dollars formerly given to endow a university slip from them.

The Board of Curators now began taking more steps to get the College of The Bible on a more thoroughly acceptable basis. In June, 1875 the Board appealed to the Kentucky Christian Educational Society to appoint two professors for the College. The Educational Society immediately laid this matter before the Committee of Twenty-One, who theoretically represented the will of the churches. Meeting on June 24, 1875 in Louisville, the committee suggested Robert Graham as president of the College of The Bible. (Robert Milligan, former president had died a few weeks before.) John W. McGarvey was suggested as professor of Sacred History. So, with Graham and McGarvey constituting the faculty, the College of The Bible reopened in the fall of 1875.

Two years later it was evident to all that the brotherhood of Kentucky had not rallied to support Graham and McGarvey. The College of the Bible while virtually separate from Kentucky University was not organically separate. The brethren, despite their confidence in both Graham and McGarvey, could not wholly bring themselves to support the College. On July 10, 1877 the Kentucky Christian Education Society met again to discuss what plan to pursue. Meanwhile, the Board of Curators, who still controlled the College of The Bible, decided to dismiss Graham completely and put McGarvey on a part-time basis. This step was necessary due to the lack of funds. The action of the Board had virtually disbanded the College of The Bible. The Education Society for the time being could do nothing.

The churches in Kentucky immediately became alarmed. At a mass meeting of the brethren on July 27, 1877, it was decided that an independent College of The Bible should be formed in Lexington. At this meeting, they elected Robert Graham, president, and J. W. McGarvey, a teacher. I. B. Grubbs was also added as a teacher. For the next quarter of a century the College of The Bible was associated with these names.

As the curtain was being drawn on the drama of the troubles of Kentucky University, an unfortunate act seemed necessary to be played. The chief role was to be played by Moses E. Lard. The decision on the part of the brethren to establish an independent College of The Bible struck forcibly at the pride of both John B. Bowman and the Board of Curators. The decision virtually was an admission that the brethren had no confidence in them. Consequently they met the decision for an independent college with a bitter, non-cooperative spirit. They were strictly forbidden to meet in the class rooms of Kentucky University, so for a year the new independent college was forced to meet in the church building.

Bowman was thoroughly determined to continue the College of The Bible in connection with the University as a rival institution of the new independent school. Bowman now looked over the field for a president. What Bowman now needed more than anything else to accomplish his purpose of defeating the other college was a president for the College of The Bible that would be thoroughly acceptable to the brotherhood. To get one that was not was to be defeated before he started. A few years before he cared little for this, but now it was absolutely imperative. He turned his attention, therefore, to Moses E. Lard, who accepted the offer and became president of the College of The Bible at Kentucky University.

This was a strange sight indeed. To the brotherhood generally Moses E. Lard now seemed to be backing Bowman against his old friend, McGarvey and against the brotherhood at large in whose interest he had formerly worked. Such conduct from Lard seemed unexplainable to them. When they turned to Lard for an explanation, none was forthcoming. Brethren shook their heads and wondered. The periodicals of the brethren ignored the strange contradiction of Moses E. Lard. Scarcely did it appear to be discussed except in private conversations of brethren. Lard himself felt keenly his ostracism. He moved around silently. He wrote little, preached little. Despondency clouded his life; his disposition became somewhat saturnine. His wife became ill, and financial troubles piled in upon him. Life was miserable, so he turned to studying the Scriptures about the life to come, and had some strange misgivings. Then he developed cancer of the stomach. Lard went down to his grave in June, 1880 a sad, broken-hearted man, a much misunderstood man. But the brotherhood threw a mantle of charity over the last three years of his life, and chose to remember him for what he had been.

Actually, however, Lard had not forsaken the brethren at all in becoming president of the rival College of The Bible. Bowman, while consulting Lard about taking the presidency, had privately and confidentially promised that he would step down from the Regency after one year if Lard would take the position. Lard now saw an opportunity of saving Kentucky University for the brethren. When therefore, he became president it was with the hope that Bowman would step down and Kentucky University would be given back to the brethren. But this fact Lard could not tell the brotherhood as yet. Not having any way of explaining his position, he had but to take the criticism as working against their interests.

Under these circumstances the College of The Bible under Lard naturally failed. It was only a year in doing so. On June 11, 1878 Kentucky University offered the independent College of The Bible the use of its classrooms. Here the college met until 1895 when it built its new building which still is in use at Lexington.

CHAPTER VII

POST-BELLUM DAYS (1865-75)

"These are times that try men's souls," wrote Thomas Paine of those pre-revolutionary war days in colonial America. No less was that decade after the close of the war between the states a time to try men's souls—for the world, for the nation, and most of all for that half-a-million people in America pleading for a return to the ancient order of things. Internal problems were mounting; division and discord were threatening. The restoration plea was being put to its most severe test. The entire future course of the restoration was to depend upon the events of this decade.

These indeed were trying times for the world. The Franco-Prussian War found Europe once more in a baptism of blood. Russia, nursing the wounds of her Crimean War, was watching defiantly for another chance for a struggle in the Balkans which later came by a series of revolts starting in 1875. In England Prime Minister Benjamin Disraeli was slowly pushing English imperialism to the far stretches of the world. America, meanwhile, was trying to recover from her Civil War. A grateful nation put General U. S. Grant in the presidency. Unfortunately, however, he met with a financial collapse scarcely equalled by any in the history of the nation. In one year, five thousand business concerns failed. Three million wage earners were out of work. Republican Senator George F. Hoar declared that never had corruption gotten so firm a hold on a government as it did during Grant's administration. Postmaster-General Creswell swindled the government out of over three hundred thousand dollars.

Yet these were memorable days. The eloquence of Henry Ward Beecher thundered from Brooklyn. These were the days of Dwight Moody, Ira D. Sankey and Charles H. Spurgeon, days when David Livingstone was doing his final work in Africa; when the doctrine of papal infallibility was being shaped into dogma by the Vatican. These were times when the word, crisis, is written high over the passing of all events.

The restoration movement now launched into an era of intense controversy, both internally and externally. Debating became the custom of the day. Almost every issue of the brotherhood periodicals carried a news item of at least one debate. The following list may be suggestive of the times: In 1871 David Lipscomb met Jacob Ditzler at Gallatin, Tennessee; the same year Clark Braden debated Sam Binnus, a Universalist, at Reynoldsburg, Ohio. J. Carroll Stark met W. M. Rush, a Methodist, in Gallatin, Missouri. F. G. Allen debated Robert Hiner at Mt. Byrd, Kentucky on infant baptism. Braden met A. J. Fishback, a Spiritualist at Sturgis, Michigan. D. R. Lucas met D. B. Ray ("Battle Flag" Ray), a Baptist, at Clayton, Illinois. Jesse L. Sewell met John R. Strange, a Methodist, in Hart County, Kentucky. It was common for T. W. Brents and Jacob Ditzler to be debating during these years. Ditzler also found a frequent opponent in L. B. Wilkes. A. J. Lemons met N. Ramsay, a Baptist, in Arkansas. H. T. Wilson debated R. T. Hanks, another Baptist, at Pickensville, Alabama. J. S. Sweeney traveled to Sherman, Texas to meet Jacob Ditzler in 1875, etc.

That the restoration movement was deepening itself, may be indicated in the publishing of so many books. The appearance of McGarvey's commentary on Acts in 1862 set off a wave of interest in commentaries. Lard encouraged McGarvey to put his work through a revision and make it the crowning work of his life. By 1865 Lard was prepared to announce his intention to write a commentary on Romans, which, however, he did not complete for ten years. After Lard's announcement of this intention, W. H. Hopson wrote to W. K. Pendleton suggesting that Pendleton write one on Hebrews and C. L. Loos, one on John. As matters proved it was left to Robert Milligan to write the commentary on Hebrews and B. W. Johnson to publish one on John.

Other great books were in the making. In 1868 the saintly Dr. Robert Richardson presented to the brotherhood his first volume of "Memoirs of A. Campbell," but it was another year before his second volume appeared. "From beginning to end," writes W. K. Pendleton, "it shows evidence of an earnest and conscientious worker."[1] After the appearance of the second volume, James T. Barclay wrote:

---

[1]W. K. Pendleton, "Memoirs of A. Campbell—by Dr. R. Richardson," *Millennial Harbinger,* Vol. XXXVII, No. 1 (January, 1866), p. 43.

The ardently cherished expectations of the brotherhood are at last gratified in the happy completion of this great work—and truly a complete work it is!

To mention that it is executed in the happiest style of the gifted biographer, printed on the finest toned paper, and bears the finished imprint of Lippincott's great establishment, is to declare it worthy of a most conspicuous place in any library. . . . Nothing is hazarded by the assertion that no Christian preacher can afford to dispense with this invaluable Thesaurus of our ecclesiastical history. And the library of any Christian family that is minus this lucid evolution of primeval Christianity from the chaos of sectarianism is minus a great blessing.[2]

Late in 1867 there came from the press of R. W. Carroll & Company of Cincinnati, the book *Reason and Revelation* by Robert Milligan, a book which never proved as popular as his later one, "Scheme of Redemption," published in 1869. In 1870 Clark Braden's debate with G. W. Hughey, president of the Cairo district of the Methodist Church, was published. J. C. Clymore, a wealthy member of the church, spent four thousand dollars producing it. It was widely acclaimed as one of the great debates of the restoration, John R. Howard declaring that it sustained the same relation "to the present state of the controversy" as the Campbell-Rice debate did in its day.

T. W. Brent's famous work, "The Gospel Plan of Salvation" made its appearance during these years. In 1867, Brents edited an "Alien's Department" in the *Advocate*. Late in 1868 he prepared a series of tracts on the gospel plan of salvation and printed them in the *Advocate*. Later these tracts became the basis for his book.

As the church expanded her borders, she came more and more in contact with the denominational world, setting off strenuous conflicts. The deepening of the church found her leaders undertaking more exhaustive research resulting in the production of literature calculated to strengthen the church. Yet, another movement, synchronous with these, not quite so favorable to the church was also developing in that decade between 1865-75. With the word, progress, as its key, the church internally was attempting to expand into many forbidden areas. The missionary society and the instrumental music, discussed in previous chapters, were

---

[2]J. T. B., "Dr. Richardson's Memoirs of Alexander Campbell," *Gospel Advocate*, Vol. XII, No. 1 (January 1, 1870), pp. 1-3.

but two expressions of the attempt at progress. Back of these and underlying them were dangerous trends of thought. The history of the restoration cannot be recounted without some attention to these trends.

TRENDS

Moses E. Lard, writing in the spring of 1865, sounded an ominous note for the future of the church. Lard then wrote:

The prudent man, who has the care of a family, watches well the first symptoms of disease. He does not wait till his wife is helpless, and his children prostrated. He has learned that early cures are easy cures, while late ones often fail. On this experience he resolutely acts, and the world applauds his wisdom. Why should not the same judicious policy be acted upon in the weighty matters of religion? . . .

Our churches and people now stretch over a tract reaching from Maine to the farthest coasts of the Pacific, and almost from the Lake of the woods to Panama. Within this wide area exists one of the noblest brotherhood, *and within their hands only,* is kept the cause which is the last hope of earth. . .

But Lard goes on to express more vividly his picture of the future.

He is a poor observer of men and things who does not see slowly growing up among us a class of men who can no longer be satisfied with the ancient gospel and the ancient order of things. These men must have changes; and silently they are preparing the mind of the brotherhood to receive changes.[3]

While Moses E. Lard, writing in 1865, declared he saw a group of men growing up in the brotherhood, not content with ancient gospel, but wanting something different; observers writing in later years looked back and declared a great change had come over the church. L. F. Bittle wrote to Ben Franklin at the close of the decade under discussion, saying,

For the last few years your people have had a great deal of unpleasant controversy, and some harsh wrangling, over matters entirely unknown to the past generation of Disciples. They, too, had their troubles, no doubt, and some of them may have said bitter words in consequence of personal disagreements. But they never had anything like the alienation that now exists in certain places in regard to matters which should not be so much as named among a people who claim to stand before the world as the repre-

---

[3]Moses E. Lard, "The Work of the Past—The Symptoms of the Future," *Lard's Quarterly,* Vol. II, No. 3 (April, 1865), pp. 251-262.

sentative champions of the Bible, and the Bible alone, as the rule of faith and practice.[4]

Henry Hathaway was an old elder in the church at Covington, Kentucky where Ben Franklin had preached for many years. Late in 1868 Hathaway wrote to Franklin:

When I embraced Christianity the church was a city sitting upon a hill, all beautiful and joyous, a green spot in this world of sin. Now the pride of life, the lust of the eye and the lust of the flesh are crowding into Zion, the beautiful city of God.[5]

Indicative of the line of thought was the feeling at a meeting of brethren held in Louisville, Kentucky during the summer of 1868. David Lipscomb attended, found many pleasant things, but heard some unfavorable comments:

Some were saying it was useless to try to get back to primitive Christianity; could not be done, and if done, wouldn't be desirable in this present age. We heard the assertion made that without more organization than God gave the churches in the beginning, the world could not be evangelized. . .[6]

Robert Graham who was ordinarily a man of milder moods, saw there was a radical change underway in the church during these years. Graham wrote:

. . . there is among ourselves a falling off from the simplicity of the gospel, a conforming to the mode of the *other* denominations, the loss of zeal for the spread of the gospel for fear people will think us solicitous only to build up a party, the decrease of Bible reading and study among us of late, the growing disposition to recognize the distinction of clergy and laity in our churches, and among much more that might be named, our conforming to the unscriptural phraseology of sects, to say nothing of our adopting many of their anti-scriptural customs. With the uniform experience of past ages before us, the tendency of men to make the gospel popular under the plea of extending its influence, and that, too, even at the cost of its purity and power to save, should make us keen to detect and fearless in our condemnation of all departures from the faith.[7]

A catacysmic event has upset all the routine of living for society after the war and it sensed that its foundation had been

[4]B. F. Leonard, "Who Are Responsible?" *American Christian Review,* Vol. XVIII, No. 4 (January 26, 1875), p. 29.

[5]Henry Hathaway, "Covington Church," *American Christian Review,* Vol. XII, No. 1 (January 5, 1869), p. 2.

[6]David Lipscomb, "The Louisville Meeting," *Gospel Advocate,* Vol. X, No. 31 (July 30, 1868), p. 723.

[7]Robert Graham, "The Signs of the Times," *Apostolic Times,* Vol. I, No. 1 (April 15, 1869), p. 4.

shaken and started a search for a new one. Some believed that this change in society demanded a change in the church to fit the times.

The frontier had pushed to the west, and the mid-west found itself no longer a sparsely-settled wilderness but a deepening, rapidly-increasing settlement. Crude log cabins, the huts of frontier life, were being replaced by larger, more permanent homes. Railroad lines tied the towns together, and gradually industries grew in larger cities. As the cities grew, men lived on fixed incomes. The backwoodsman became an oddity. Culture, education, money—these came more and more to mark society.

When, therefore, the Civil War closed, thoughtful brethren contemplating the future, recognized that in certain areas changes must come. Preachers would change their styles of delivery; churches would build better meeting houses. There was little conflict over these points. Brethren were ready to admit the influence of environment in these realms; they were hardly prepared, however, to see the church undergo a complete change in those realms of scripture teaching where the authority of God's word was at stake. Conflict, fierce and unrelenting, was at this point inevitable.

The demand for progress among some took on various characteristics. In some cases it threatened the basic conception of what constituted a New Testament Church. There was a definite trend to make the church another sect among sectarians; another denomination in denominationalism. There was also abundant evidence of a definite revolt against the past. Men who symbolized the previous generation were set for a stormy session. Progress also courted a more fashionable appeal to the rich by what many considered an extravagant expenditure for church buildings. The cry for progress also demanded a new position for the preacher and a different content to his message. Many were convicted that if they had to surrender the fundamental teachings of the Bible, teachings the earlier pioneers held, they would refuse "progress" at all costs. It was this method of looking at the question that gave the controversy additional fierceness.

Ben Franklin stood as a living symbol of the past. Against all departures from the word of God, he steeled himself for a vigorous fight. He became, therefore, a target for the friends of "progress" in the church. In the spring of 1872 Franklin wrote:

It is now an undisguised fact that there is a party in the ranks
that have been troubled for years about *our influence,* or *the influence of the* REVIEW. The party in question have and do
now consider our influence in the way of what they desire to accomplish. We have known this for years and understood it
through and through, and had not at any time, and have not now,
a doubt about the cause of it. We have watched this opposition
closely, and thought about it, and the grounds of it, as well as
how the difficulty could be relieved. . .

Franklin stated that for years he had tried to be kind, ignore the
bad feeling against him, but now it could no longer be done.

Who are they that are against us? They are the men who think
that much of the work by A. Campbell will have to be *undone;*
the friends of the organ in worship; of extravagant, fine and
houses of worship, festivals, fairs, organ concerts in churches,
etc.[8]

Because Franklin refused to go along with the popular trend
of progress, he was spoken of as being a "millstone around the
neck of the reformation." It is interesting to ask the reason for
this.

Wherein are we a "millstone around the neck of the reformation?" In our decided and determined opposition to the departures being made from the primitive gospel. In our opposition
to church fairs, festivals, church concerts, organ concerts, useless
outlay in gorgeous and fashionable temples of folly and pride,
called "churches," instruments of music in worship, etc. We
have sinned against *Dr. Progress, Mrs. Fashion, Sirs Custom,* and
offended the taste of their friends and the *spirit of the world in*
general, and have thus become a millstone around the neck of
pride, folly, arrogance and self-importance in general, the lusts of
the flesh, the lusts of the eye, and the pride of life in general. . .
We have failed to appreciate church fairs, festivals and enter-
tainments, as a means of raising money for the Lord. . .
We have no scheme to defend, no hobbies to ride, nor enemies
to pursue. We have our Lord and His cause squarely before us.
To please Him and maintain his cause is all we have to do. . .
We are opposed to *no man,* but opposed to all *departures from
the faith.* We stand not in opposition to men but error. . .[9]

Trouble between Ben Franklin and Isaac Errett had been

---

[8]Ben Franklin, "The Editor of the Review," *American Christian Review,*
Vol. XV, No. 19 (May 7, 1872), p. 148.

[9]Ben Franklin, "Prophecy Revived," *American Christian Review,* Vol.
XV, No. 27 (July 2, 1872), p. 212.

smouldering for some time. The two men were not standing on the same foundation. During the years, 1871 and 1872, the two clashed bitterly on several issues. Errett began to refer to Franklin as an "alarmist." G. W. Rice, in answer to Errett, wrote:

But, after all, he appears to us to be more alarmed than any of those he would hold up to ridicule and to be laughed at. He is no alarmist himself. He never warns the people against danger either from within or without. No, no; in his view of things there is no danger. Henry Ward Beecher is no alarmist, either. Anything that has the semblance of religion is acceptable with him. Baptism, or no baptism, immersion, sprinkling, pouring, or no water at all. All, or either, or none. Who ever heard from him a note of warning against departures from the simplicity of the Apostolic Practice and worship? Did he reach his present position at a single leap? Was it not by small beginnings under the specious plea of *expediency?* a word that, with some among the Disciples, has become a screen and a vail to pull over the eyes of the confiding and unsuspecting; and behind which some of our wise ones and learned scribes, not excepting our humorous brother of the *Standard,* fly, when hard pressed for something to justify their departure from Apostolic practice.[10]

It was obvious that the abuse heaped upon Ben Franklin by the *Christian Standard* came not because Franklin was departing from the faith and introducing innovations. Franklin had undergone no change. The *Standard,* however, conceived its role to be that of "moving forward," adapting the church to changing environmental factors. Franklin resisted these changes, clinging to the older practices. Very correctly, then, did Franklin write:

We learn that a few men among us are now expressing regret that we are taking *such a course in our old days*—that we are *spoiling all we did in former years,* etc. In this they are like the man standing on the landing boat, who thinks the shore is coming to him; they think that change is in us, but are unconscious of the *change in themselves.* They point to nothing in which we have changed, nothing new in us. Their trouble with us is about the new things they are introducing, the new departure they are making, their *progression,* which is really retrograding. We have put a vast amount of hard work into this cause—the great reformatory movement in which we are engaged; and men whose voices are now still in death, and whose faces are no more seen among us, have put forth their best energies and most faithful efforts, till

---

[10]G. W. Rice, "Alarmists," *American Christian Review,* Vol. XV, No. 43 (October 22, 1872), p. 340.

they breathed their last breath; and we do not intend now to give up the work, nor the glorious principles for which we have so long battled, but intend to stand by these principles firmly till the last, and to the men true to them, and that intend to stand by them. . . .

What *course* are we pursuing that they regret? What principle or truth are we departing from? Can they tell? Not a man of them. What good work have we not stood to firmly from first to last? We defy them to point to one. What has happened false in principle or practice that we have not opposed squarely all the time?[11]

Franklin and men of a similar school of thought were looked upon as being "perverse" and "stubborn." A correspondent, signing his name "Carl Crab," wrote an article, entitled "Franklinian Stupidity," as a satire against these men.

The term at the head of this article is not used in any offensive sense, but simply as a brief descriptive phrase by which we recognize a large class of the brotherhood, of whom the editor of the *Review* is almost a perfect specimen.

It is the common conclusion among the more liberal and progressive brethren that the above-minded class have, for years past, been exhibiting a stubborn and perverse stupidity in reference to the progress of the age.

Long since they became a real pest upon the body ecclesiastic, by standing directly in the way of those grand conceptions being realized which the more literary, refined, and charitable brethren have presented from time to time for the adoption of the Christian brotherhood.

It is really provoking to think that so many propositions for the adoption of means and practices intended to popularize our religious movement, and break down these distinctions between us and the other denominations which have to some degree united them in opposition to us, should be so stupidly and perversely opposed.[12]

Twenty years earlier Franklin was regarded as a champion for the truth. Although he had not changed his position, and was still fighting for the same principles, Franklin was regarded as a "pest upon the body ecclesiastic" and a "millstone around the neck of the reformation." What strange bewilderment must have clouded the mind of Ben Franklin!

The trend toward denominationalism. The demand for progress was also characterized by the fact there seemed to be clear indi-

---

[11]Ben Franklin, "A New Phase," *American Christian Review,* Vol. XV, No. 47 (November 19, 1872), p. 372.

[12]Carl Crab, "Franklinian Stupidity," *American Christian Review,* Vol. XV, No. 14 (April 2, 1872), p. 105.

cations that the church was drifting to the status of another sect among the sectarians. Reference to the above correspondence by Carl Crab will show that the "progressive party" considered it provoking that anyone would resist their attempt to break down the barriers with the denominations and resist the attempt to popularize the church with these denominations.

L. F. Bittle, in another of his famous letters to Jacob Creath, struck at this general disposition:

The greatest danger that threatens you, as a religious brothererhood, is the rapidly growing disposition, manifested by your so-called educated men, to elevate your people into the dignity of a sect, a denomination, with a name, policy and organization in harmony with those employed by the various parties into which Christendom is so unhappily divided.[13]

Moreover, the addition of a new periodical, the *Christian Quarterly,* in 1869 aroused considerable fears for a time that it might be influential in leading the church into this conception of things. The editor was W. T. Moore. In 1859, a decade earlier, Moses E. Lard had announced his intention of publishing a periodical to be called *The Christian Quarterly.* The intention of calling it this title appears to have stayed with Lard almost to the time of the first issue, when he switched to the name *Lard's Quarterly.* The history of *Lard's Quarterly* has already been told. That it failed in the middle of 1868 because of the lack of subscribers is known. Now, at the beginning of 1869, W. T. Moore started a *Quarterly,* using the title that Lard had previously intended to use. As men, W. T. Moore and Moses E. Lard were the antithesis; either would have been glad to have reflected upon the other. Did W. T. Moore establish the *Christian Quarterly* almost as soon as *Lard's Quarterly* failed as a taunt to Lard? One can but wonder.

Moore was popularly regarded as a man of extreme liberal ideas. Sometime previous, he had been responsible for publishing Campbell's famous *Lectures on The Pentateuch.* In the introduction, he had written of the church as a denomination which had been founded by Thomas and Alexander Campbell and that it was a branch of the Baptist denomination. Then, more recently Moore had preached that the church of the New Testament was in a

---

[13]B. F. Leonard, "Letters to Jacob Creath—No. II," *American Christian Review,* Vol. XVI, (July 22, 1873), p. 225,

state of infancy, but that it needed to grow into manhood.[14] Moore, himself, said of the *Quarterly,* that ". . . its main contention was for a liberal interpretation of the Disciple movement and a support of all worthy enterprises in the interests of the movement."[15]

The appearance of the *Christian Quarterly* was hailed as a great step forward by most brotherhood periodicals. David Lipscomb, however, saw it to be an omen of evil things to come, and so he wrote:

Almost every paper among the brotherhood, to some extent, save the *Advocate* and *Apostolic Times,* has given an unqualified commendation of the first number of the *Quarterly.* Yet if some things and matters that are there given prominence be true or right, the present effort at return to Apostolic Christianity is a senseless and criminal movement. I refer to the article on "Indifference to Things Indifferent." Saying nothing in reference to the bitter, unchristian spirit that pervades it, the tendency of its matter is to destroy entirely the plea for conformity to the word and institutions of God. . . . We must express, too, candidly our fears of the influence of the *Quarterly* under its present management. A *Quarterly* should be eminently sound and discriminating in its teachings—a display of superficial learning is nothing.

Lipscomb proceeded to speak of W. T. Moore as one who had courted the "association and fellowship of the sects in their clerical association," and then added:

Now, brethren, without prejudice or querulousness we protest that such things are unpardonable in a *Quarterly;* that the tendency of these things is to destroy the moral power and spirit of the children of God. The tendency is to lower their claims as the churches of Christ and degrade them to a position of a mere sect among sects.[16]

The trend toward fashionable church buildings. There was perhaps no event that stirred up more bitter feelings than the opening of the wealthy Central Christian Church of Cincinnati, where W. T. Moore was the preacher. R. M. Bishop, president of the American Christian Missionary Society, former mayor of Cincinnati, and later, governor of Ohio, was one of its elders. At the opening of its new church building early in 1872, Ben Franklin

---

[14]David Lipscomb, "Indications of Progress," *Gospel Advocate,* Vol. XV, No. 22 (May 29, 1873), pp. 515-521.
[15]W. T. Moore, *Comprehensive History of the Disciples of Christ* (New York: Fleming H. Revell Company, 1909), p. 558.
[16]David Lipscomb, "Christian Quarterly," *Gospel Advocate,* Vol. XI, No. 17 (April 29, 1869), p. 395.

apparently felt that the time of the Antichrist was here, and he was less sure than ever that W. T. Moore might not be he. Instrumental music, missionary societies, and other similar steps had caused heated controversy, but nothing excelled the intensity and bitterness that arose when the Central Christian Church moved into its new building.

The Central Christian Church spent one hundred and forty thousand dollars for a new meeting house and eight thousand dollars for a new organ, the organ not having previously been used in this congregation. Ben Franklin attacked this as an appeal to the worldly, the carnal, and pride in human hearts. It was a positive indication that the church had surrendered the spirit of Christ for the spirit of the world, thought Ben Franklin.

That Franklin was both right and wrong in various phases of this controversy seems to us evident. That Franklin was right in opposing the introduction of the organ is readily admitted, but the principle would have been the same had the organ been given to the church. The spending of eight thousand dollars for an organ merely made it worse. That this congregation had apparently forsaken the spirit of Christ for the spirit of the world will appear more evident in the further remarks. The only question is, did the expenditure of one hundred forty thousand dollars indicate this worldly spirit?

Ben Franklin would have been the first to agree that the building of a church building was a matter left purely to human discretion. While God commands meeting for worship, the place of meeting is left to human wisdom. The cost, size, looks, and structure of that place of meeting is left to the discretion of man, for God does not legislate upon these matters. All of this Franklin recognized. But, was there a place where a line could be drawn between extravagance and necessity? It was right that these brethren should have a building to meet their needs. Was it human pride that caused brethren to want to erect a structure extravagant enough to attract the worldly great, and compare with the finest cathedrals of sectarianism? Franklin thought so, and truly the lesson of history appears much in his favor. It is a historical fact that churches spending extravagantly on buildings seldom remain satisfied with the simple gospel more than one generation.

The Central Christian Church was, in the days when Alexander Campbell published the *Christian Baptist,* known as the Sycamore

Street Baptist Church. It was a branch of the Enon Baptist Church located on Walnut and Baker Streets just above Third Street. The Enon Church had become so large that a new congregation had been proposed. Letters of dismissal were granted to one hundred and fifty members who formed the nucleus of the Sycamore Street Baptist Church. Jeremiah Vardeman, who was converted through reading the *Christian Baptist,* was the preacher for the Enon Baptist Church.

At first, the Sycamore Street Congregation had met in the Council Chamber on Fourth Street, then in Talbott's schoolhouse on Fifth Street, then in an upper room in an old copper shop on the corner of Vine and Columbia. After this, it built its own meeting house on Sycamore Street above Fifth. This was in the fall of 1828. James Challen was the first preacher for this new congregation, although he at times alternated with D. S. Burnet. Walter Scott preached here for a short time in 1829. In 1837 Campbell debated Purcell in this building.

Through hearing Alexander Campbell and through reading the *Christian Baptist,* the Sycamore Street Baptist Church had dropped its practices and begun working for a restoration. Since most members lived in the west part of town, its building was sold to the Methodists, and the church started meeting at Walnut and Eighth Streets. It was in this building that the first convention of the American Christian Missionary Society was held. Here, the church continued to meet until 1872.

In 1870 the congregation started the construction of a new building on Ninth Street near Central Avenue. The estimated cost was one hundred thousand dollars which reached to one hundred and forty before it was finished. In January, 1871, a lecture room was completed, and dedicated. A year later, the whole building was finished. For style, architectural beauty, it surpassed anything known to the brotherhood.

The dedication of the new building was held on February 11, 1872. The house was packed and the aisles were filled with chairs to seat the overflow audience. For the first time in the history of the congregation the sound of the organ came from behind the pulpit. W. T. Moore spoke on the words of Christ on the cross, "It Is Finished." He remarked that when Christ spoke those words it was both an occasion of sorrow and gladness —sorrow because Christ was dying, but gladness because his death meant the work of Christ in human redemption was finished. He applied these words to the building in which they were meeting.

Franklin's ire knew no limitations. He charged that the organ had been introduced over the protest of the majority:

Many pretty things have been said by those determined to make the church a fashionable place of resort and entertainment. They would not introduce the organ if it would create the least disturbance! if it would wound the conscience of any member of the church! etc., etc. But the "Central Christian Church" have put it in, knowing that an overwhelming majority of their brethren cannot worship with it, and flourish it before our faces in the public prints in their description of their extravagant building, in which they have expended more money than has been given to the General Missionary Society during the past ten years from all sources.[17]

Franklin, to make it clear that he was not an extremist, wrote in the next week's issue of the *Review:*

We are not unreasonable, nor an extremist, nor would any allusion we made, nor logic used by us, lead to having no house in which to live or in which to meet and worship; but there is a vast difference between a comfortable and plain house in which to live, or in which to meet and worship, and extravagant temples rivaling the worldly temples around us. We may and ought to have the former, but ought not to have the latter.[18]

Forty years earlier Franklin had come to Cincinnati to preach for the congregation on Sixth Street. On the way to worship that morning an old man advised him to remember that he was preaching to *people,* so preach the same in the city that he did in the country. A few years after that, when the Episcopalians erected a building costing one hundred thousand dollars, "we talked of it as an example of extravagance beyond all endurance." Then he recalled that Alexander Campbell had told the Baptists that the only thing that kept them from being as vain and pompous as the Episcopalians was the lack of means. "But," Franklin went on,

little did he think then that those professing to be Christians, Disciples of Christ, and standing with him pleading for the "ancient order of things" and the "gospel restored" would ever have opened the way for such a document as the one we reproduce in another column to be flourished before the world. This is the "gospel restored"—the "ancient order of things"—with a ven-

---

[17] Ben Franklin, "Central Christian Church," *American Christian Review,* Vol. XV, No. 8 (February 20, 1872), p. 60.

[18] Ben Franklin, "Central Christian Church," *American Christian Review,* Vol. XV, No. 10 (March 5, 1872), p. 76.

geance! This worldly and carnal display will send grief home to many hearts of the old saints. Many thousands now living will grieve.[19]

Reaction among the brethren was divided. Isaac Errett came to the rescue of the Central Church, declaring that such a price naturally sounded high to a country man. E. P. Belshe, however, backed Franklin ardently.

If the Pope should happen to visit Cincinnati and lose his way to the Cathedral, he might sit pretty comfortably in *Central* and take notes of the advancement of his religious institutions.[20]

Robert Richardson, biographer of Alexander Campbell, wrote Franklin, saying that Campbell would never have agreed to such an expenditure of funds. Going further, he writes:

. . . While I have no disposition to denounce or harshly to criticize the erring, I cannot but express my sincere regret at the course which the Central Church in your city has thought proper to adopt in relation to the matters above mentioned.[21]

Indicative of the drift in this congregation was the following advertisement which appeared in one of the secular papers:

GRAND ORGAN CONCERT

At Central Christian Church, Thursday Evening,
February 29, 1872, for the Benefit of the Ladies'
Furnishing Committee

PROGRAMME

PART I

1. Overture to Masniello—Auber; M. Dell
2. Offertoire, op. 23 in Ab.—Batiste; C. M. Currier
3. Solo and Chorus (organ arrangement)—Handel; Wilbur F. Gole.
4. Offertoire—Wely; Henry G. Andre
5. Organ Solo—Batiste; Henry J. Smith

PART II

1. Offertoire in G—Wely; M. Dell
2. Serenade—Schubert; Wilbur F. Gole
3. Selections—Henry J. Smith
4. Improvisation on Home Melodies; C. M. Currier

---

[19]Ben Franklin, "Central Christian Church," *American Christian Review,* Vol. XV, No. 8 (February 20, 1872), p. 60.
[20]E. P. Belshe, "Dim Religious Tone," *American Christian Review,* Vol. XV, (May 7, 1872), p. 149.
[21]Robert Richardson, "Brother Moore Again," *American Christian Review,* Vol. XV, No. 16 (April 16, 1872), p. 124.

5. Fantasie—Andre; Henry G. Andre
Admission, one dollar.
The Church will be opened at seven o'clock. Concert will
begin at eight.

After the above advertisement appeared, Ben Franklin copied it
and then added:

Reader, what say you of this? Primitive Christianity! Ancient
order of things![22]

The objection to the course of the Central Christian Church
lasted only a few months and was intensely bitter. As a controversy it was contemporary with that at Kentucky University, instrumental music and the Louisville Plan. Moreover, the same
parties were arrayed against each other in each case. The conduct
of the Central Church probably did more than anything else to
convince Ben Franklin and his associates of like-mind that the
opposition had completely forsaken the spirit of Christ in favor
of the world. The breach in the brotherhood was to grow wider.

The trend in preaching. The cry for progress also expressed
itself in new trends for preaching. Indeed, this was the point
where the drift now centered. Some brethren were becoming
extremely intolerant toward the preaching of the "first principles."
Preachers stressing these were less popular than before. The cry
for higher spirituality was everywhere heard. J. B. Briney, realizing a change had come over the content of the sermons, wrote
the following:

There are some among us who seem to have imbibed quite an
antipathy to first principles. They love to talk about a "higher
spiritual," a "deeper piety," a "broader love," etc. Were it not
that these men make such lofty pretensions to a "higher spirituality," you would be led to think that this is the very article they
most need. . . .

The man that is tired of the first principles of the doctrine of
Christ is tired of the only thing that can convert men to God, and
lift their souls in holy aspirations toward heaven. But when a
man says he is tired of first principles, what does he mean? Does
he mean he is tired of faith? No. He has much to say about
faith. It is his theme on all occasions. Does he mean that he is
tired of repentance? Certainly not. He is for repentance, *theoretically*, at least. What, then, is the substance of all this opposition to first principles and to the men who are devoted to them?
Simply this: "I am tired of baptism for the remission of sins."

[22]Ben Franklin, "Central Christian Church," *American Christian Review*,
Vol. XV, No. 13 (March 26, 1872), p. 100.

This is what you get when you simmer all this talk about a "higher spirituality," etc., down.[23]

Men were heard to speak frequently of "legalism" and "the spirit of the New Testament." Preachers were now preaching, not the "letter" of the New Testament, but the "spirit" of it, an attitude that Errett championed. J. S. Lamar, his biographer, defined the point of view as follows:

The conditions by which we are confronted, being wholly unknown to the apostles, their practice *cannot be* applicable to these conditions in letter, and must be pleaded only in its spirit.[24]

A class of men yet remained, however, who preached the first principles, who insisted upon a "Thus saith the Lord" in their preaching. Against this class of men, the ugly title of "legalist" was continually hurled. Ben Franklin, Moses E. Lard, John W. McGarvey, David Lipscomb, and Tolbert Fanning were now classed as "legalists." Some who laid claim to have progressed a little more had reached the point of denying completely that there was a law under Christ. This spirit, David Lipscomb saw arising, and wrote:

We have been pained for some time to see reproach cast upon those who insist upon faithful obedience to the law of God, as the condition of his blessing, as *legalists,* and the principle that required the submission as *legalism* . . . Some of our progressive brethren have even gone so far as to deny there is any law in the New Testament as there was in the Old. . . .

The tendency of our brethren's speculative distinctions on these subjects is to weaken the scene of obligation to comply with the full requirements of God's will, and to give people license to follow some impulse, passion or prejudice which they may conceive to be the suggestion of faith within, that becomes law to itself.[25]

Moses E. Lard, however, looked with some pathetic humor upon these more progressive men. He wrote:

They are partial to the "pious" in other sects; yet they pounce unmercifully upon the faults of their own brethren. They appear doubtful that their brethren are right in anything. They claim to have made greater progress in spirituality; in the inner life, and in the secret walks with God.

Are they less tyrannical than others? or more lowly in their look, in their walk, or in their talk? Eat they less than their

[23]J. B. Briney, "What We Need," *Apostolic Times,* Vol. III, No. 21 (August 31, 1871), p. 161.

[24]J. S. Lamar, *Memoirs of Isaac Errett,* Vol. II, p. 253.

[25]David Lipscomb, "Legalism and Obedience," *Gospel Advocate,* Vol. XIII, No. 17 (April 27, 1871), pp. 389, 390.

brethren of the vulgar rout; pray they more, or just less coarsely? Give they more than others to the cause of God; work they more assiduously, or grumble less? In what do they excel? I clamor, in what? . . . No one emotion of piety ever trembled in their souls to which their brethren of the baser sort are strangers. Closely as they have gone to the presence of God, so closely have gone we; deeply as they have drunk at the fount of spiritual life, so deeply have drunk we. Not a flower blooms on the tallest peak their feet have ever pressed whose fragrance we have not inhaled. These men lack the gift to see themselves as others see them.[26]

These "progressive" men, Lard went on to say, were sweet and pious as long as a sectarian was their mark, but they were "ferocious as a hungry hippopotamus" when a brother was to be dispatched. In the pulpit their greatest delight appeared to be to preach so that no one knew what they believed. Their greatest desire was to let the world know they were out of sympathy with their brethren. These men, in their pursuit of a "higher spirituality," had abandoned preaching on the gospel plan of salvation. Ben Franklin admits that "progress" is a good word, but he expressed a fear that brethren misunderstood it. These who cried for "progress" showed an extreme dislike for a "Thus saith the Lord" and for a "It is written," said Franklin. He agreed that men needed progress in knowledge, but he called upon these men to distinguish between progress and apostasy. He also pointed out that those who advocated progress would do well to improve upon their tempers. "We never allude to any of their progressive ideas," writes Franklin, "when we do not expect most harsh treatment." "These men who know more," he adds, "ought to show a little more patience until we learn better or die off."[27]

The place of the preacher. Not only had the demand for progress caused the type of preaching to be changed, but it brought also a change in the place and position of the preacher. Moses E. Lard, writing in 1865, declared this to be one of the symptoms of future apostasy. Whereas God ordained a group of elders to rule the local congregations, Lard declared that a new class of officers, unknown to the Bible, had now arisen. These were the "pastors," men who took the oversight away from the elders. Lard writes:

[26]Moses E. Lard, "The Progressive vs. The Sound," *Apostolic Times,* Vol. I, No. 1 (April 15, 1869), p. 1.
[27]Ben Franklin, "Progress," *American Christian Review,* Vol. XIV, (August 22, 1871), p. 268.

There is no such function or position in the church as that of pastorate to be filled by a special class of men different from the elders. . . . Now, in view of the truth as here stated, we cannot but feel alarmed at the disposition on the part of many of our churches—a disposition which is clearly on the increase, to create a new office in the church, and to fill it with a class of men wholly unknown to the Bible.[28]

In another chapter considerable attention will be given to the study of the pastor as he arose in the restoration movement. Consequently, only a word need be mentioned here. Before human innovations could get far in the church, a human organization over the local church had to be devised. The "pastors" of the church possessed greater authority than they deserved. Most of them were young men, born and bred of a more modern spirit. Their consent was readily given to the modern innovations. Those who did little consenting often did less opposing. Joseph Franklin wrote:

I steadfastly believe that the current innovations might have been kept out, or might be put out, if preachers were not afraid to attack them. The Jews cried, "Give us a king." God gave them Saul. The people now cry: "Give us pastors! give us music; give us fairs, festivals and lotteries! give us conventions and societies! Allow us innocent amusements! And God is giving them over to ungodliness and worldly lusts. Presently the profoundly respectable denomination, "The Disciples' Church," will receive the right hand of fellowship as an "evangelical church." And then God will raise up another people who will defend the honor of His name.[29]

It is not without some justification that later in the restoration many looked at the "pastor" as a potent cause of the departures.

Already in the restoration movement discussion was arising over the adoption of titles by the preachers which were then peculiar to the Protestant or Roman Catholic clergymen. Alexander Campbell had been averse to adopting such titles for himself. He wrote:

My name is Alexander Campbell, and by this *alone* I choose to be known among men. Neither *Mr.* nor *Rev.* nor *Bishop* accord with my feelings, calling nor the cause which I plead. . . .
Some of our acquaintance would, methinks, look very much abashed to be saluted *in the great day* with the title *Reverend,*

---

[28]Moses E. Lard, "The Work of the Past—The Symptoms of the Future," *Lard's Quarterly,* Vol. II, No. 3 (April, 1865), pp. 251-262.
[29]Joseph Franklin, "Preachers," *Gospel Advocate,* Vol. XV, No. 10 (March 6, 1873), pp. 234, 235.

Elder, Bishop, or *Deacon,* by him who will render to every man according to his works! And how the *Doctors of Divinity* will hang their heads in the presence of that *Paul* whom they have so often misquoted, and of that Saviour whose command, *"Be not called Rabbi,"* they have so often condemned; imagination cannot point, nor ink and paper describe.[30]

During the summer of 1853, the following question was sent to the *Millennial Harbinger:* "Is it in accordance with the teaching of the Head of the church for her Elders and Evangelists to assume the honorary title of Reverend?" A. W. Campbell answered it by saying:

The Christian Church has no honorary titles to confer upon any of her members. Her titles are all official, and refer to a work, or class of duties to be performed.

The titles of Reverend, Right Reverend, Most Reverend, Reverend Father in God, Reverend and Holy Father, Most Reverend and Holy Father, Lord God the Pope, are all titles of the same category, and we have placed them in the ascending series, from the positive of spiritual pride to the superlative of blasphemy.

These are all contraband wares in the city of our God, but very saleable and desirable in Babylon the Great, where the articles are manufactured. . . .[31]

Tolbert Fanning in no uncertain terms blazed away in condemnation of preachers who assumed the title of "Reverend." He wrote:

When Cornelius met Peter, he fell at his feet to REVERENCE him, but Peter took him up and said, "I am a man—worship God." It is idolatry, rank and vulgar, to worship any being in Heaven or upon the earth, save the Father, whom we approach through the Son. Rome taught her slaves to reverence the priests, Protestants have adopted the custom, and, worse still, modern infidels, and profane Unitarians, Universalists, and flesh-serving Spiritualists, most wickedly apply the term "Reverend" to their scoffing priests. God will not suffer this insolence forever. Let no good man assume titles which are alone applicable to Deity. We assert not too much when we state that all such Popish designations are of the enemy, and become not an humble follower of Jesus of Nazareth.[32]

While, then, preachers of the gospel had a strong aversion to wearing the title, Reverend, earlier in the restoration, by the close

---

[30]Alexander Campbell, "Bishops," *Millennial Harbinger,* Vol. I, No. 9 (September, 1830), p. 428.

[31]A. W. Campbell, "Queries," *Millennial Harbinger,* Fourth Series, Vol. III, No. 8 (August, 1853), p. 473.

[32]Tolbert Fanning, "The Term Reverend Applied to Man," *Gospel Advocate,* Vol. II, No. 6 (June, 1856), p. 192.

of the Civil War the name was beginning to find more frequent use. The church obviously was drifting into the full status of another denomination. The first person of any great significance to apply the title to himself was Isaac Errett. When he moved into the new church building at Detroit, accepting the position as its minister, he nailed up a beautiful silver doorplate inscribed with "Rev. I. Errett" on it. At the time considerable objection was raised against it, but to Errett it was an innocent enough title to assume. J. S. Lamar explains it thus:

. . . It is coming to be more and more widely understood that the Saviour's words do not prohibit the use of any designation which simply makes known *the fact* that the man to whom it is applied is a *preacher*. It is distinctions *among* preachers—the acceptance of high-sounding titles which elevate the parties *above* their brother ministers—that the divine word seems to forbid. The word *Reverend* before a man's name is universally understood to indicate simply that he is a minister of the gospel. It bears no significance of personal superiority or official eminence.[33]

The term admittedly found some struggle before it became acceptable to most preachers. Thomas Munnell, one of the leading liberal-minded men of this decade, wrote an article with reference to William Pinkerton, son of L. L. Pinkerton. Through no fault of Munnell's, the printer allowed the title "Rev." to be placed before his name. Brethren arose up in arms. Munnell correctly explained the error, but then added:

If I had called a minister of the gospel "Rev," I have no idea that it would be a sin against the Holy Ghost. Brother Walk states about the truth when he says it simply means that a man is a preacher, and is certainly a very brief statement of that fact. The term to me is not a desirable one on account of the abuse of it by others, but in itself it is as harmless as any other.[34]

Thus it is seen that in the decade between 1865-1875 the restoration movement had entered a period of transition. Old principles were being restored; old mottoes were being given new applications. When the full effect of this transition was to be later felt, the church resulting was to be vastly different than that proposed by the earlier pioneers.

Against these departures, the preachers tabbed "legalists" rebelled, and the restoration movement headed toward an era of

---

[33]J. S. Lamar, *Memoirs of Isaac Errett*, Vol. II, p. 278.
[34]Thomas Munnell, "My 'Rev.,'" *American Christian Review*, Vol. X, No. 27 (July 2, 1867), p. 209.

division. But, who was to be responsible for this division? L. F. Bittle wrote:

Elijah was not to blame for the drought and famine that for three years or more cursed the land of Samaria. He was not the troubler of Israel as Ahab said. It was the wicked king himself that by departing from the way of the Lord, and bringing in the religious devices of his idolatrous neighbors, had incurred the displeasure of the Almighty, and the prophet was but the instrument of divine vengeance.

So it is now. The folks that built costly meeting-houses to please the eye, and introduced organs to gratify the ear, and have since apologized for these things, against the protestations of a great brotherhood, are responsible for all the alienation that has in consequence occurred. The men who left the New Testament plan of evangelizing, and organized sectarian societies to usurp the authority of Christ by creating offices and delegating powers unknown to the apostles, thus rightful independence, and who still in spite of brotherly admonition and scriptural argument, persist in their wild schemes, are responsible for all the strife that their plans have enkindled.[35]

---

[35]B. F. Leonard, "Who Are Responsible?" *American Christian Review,* Vol. XVIII, No. 4 (January 26, 1875), p. 20.

Chapter VIII

THE RISE OF NEW LEADERS

Elisha G. Sewell and John F. Rowe were not closely related in work nor did they agree on some major points of controversy. Each, however, had great influence during the last quarter of the nineteenth century. Although each man was born about the same time—only three years apart—death, however, came to Sewell in 1924 and to Rowe, in 1897. Thus, Sewell's work extended a quarter of a century longer. The former was a prominent leader of the church in the south; whereas, the latter was equally prominent in the North. Each made his contribution and is deserving of a place in the history of the church of the nineteenth century.

E. G. SEWELL

"Old-timers" of today who remember the church in the South have the names, "Lipscomb and Sewell" stamped upon their memory. Seldom was one man mentioned without the other. The two first met at a gospel meeting held near McMinnville, Tennessee around 1858. E. G. Sewell was a student at Franklin College under William Lipscomb, David Lipscomb's older brother. This connection afforded Lipscomb and Sewell opportunities to renew their friendships frequently. Later, in 1870, when David Lipscomb found himself in need of help in editing the *Gospel Advocate,* he was sagacious enough to see in Sewell an ideal co-worker. From January 1, 1870 until Lipscomb's death in the fall of 1917, "Lipscomb and Sewell" formed a team in shaping the cause in the Southland.

The *Gospel Advocate* was conceived to spread the word and encourage the church to better work. Neither of its editors, therefore, wrote much about himself. This admirable modesty is unfortunate for the historian whose information is necessarily limited.

E. G. Sewell was born in the mountainous plateau region of Overton County, Tennessee near Wolf River on October 25, 1830. His birthplace was within one mile of the Kentucky State Line and about twenty-one miles from Livingstone, the county

E. G. SEWELL

seat. Prior to his birth, twelve children had already been born into the log cabin home of Stephen and Annie Sewell. When the thirteenth child was born, he was a boy—the eighth—and, like the other children, had to have a Bible name. Accordingly, he was christened, Elisha. All but one of the eight boys bore Bible names. The pair of twin boys was called Caleb and Joshua. Joshua had died in infancy. Four of the seven boys became gospel preachers—Isaac, Caleb, Jesse and Elisha.

Stephen and Annie Sewell, parents of Elisha G., were of English descent. Stephen had formerly lived on Clear River in North Carolina but had moved into East Tennessee where he married. He and his wife lived in a cabin of hewed logs. It was a double house of the type that was very popular in those early days. There were two rooms down separated by an open hall, and a half-story upstairs. There was a chimney at each end of the house. The upstairs was used for bedrooms. Glass windows were unknown to them.

Living conditions, compared to modern standards, were very poor. It is not likely, however, that they considered them so. In their own way they had comforts. They worked hard and sacrificed much. Their clothing was home-spun. Each boy was given a plot of ground to plant for himself. The crop he raised was sold and the money often used to buy clothing. On Christmas morning each child was given a suit of jeans, and a pair of shoes of undressed red leather. This, together with what they bought for themselves, lasted until the next Christmas.

The Sewells were all Baptists. Methodists were scarce in Overton County, the Baptists being most prevalent religious sect. Meetings were great occasions back in these rural churches, and were largely social assemblies. Newspapers were almost non-existent, and the preacher, who went from one community to another, was the chief source of news. His importance was thus magnified, despite the fact his ability as a preacher might be negligible.

Country meetings were generally conducted upon Saturdays and Sundays, and people from ten to twenty miles away attended. Saturday's social gathering was largely an exchange of news. People came with no intention of listening to any preaching. Frequently there were several preachers present for the Sunday services, and Baptist custom authorized each to speak. Since each was thought to be guided by the Spirit, the messages were impromptu, and pronounced for their longevity. Often a service which began on Sunday morning lasted on until three or four o'clock in the afternoon. Customs regulating the conduct of listeners were loose, so no one apparently minded how long the service lasted. People were continually getting up and walking out. Sometimes they would go to the spring a half-a-mile away, chat for half-an-hour and then get up and go back for another "hearing." The young people, of course, utilized the time in getting their "courting" brought up to date.

The Sewell family became interested in the restoration plea

through the conversion of an elder son of Stephen Sewell, William B. Sewell to the Church of Christ. In 1840 W. B. Sewell, E. G. Sewell's older brother, married a woman who was a member of the Church of Christ. W. B. in deference to his wife's wishes, occasionally attended services with her, and learned to appreciate them. Very shortly, he was partaking of the Lord's Supper with these people. So far as the Baptists were concerned he had crossed the rubicon—straight into the darkest heresy.

The Wolf River Baptist Church was a member to the Stockton's Valley Association of United Baptists, a strict group in protecting its orthodoxy. The charge against William B. Sewell came immediately before the Wolf River Baptist Church. As the trial continued, it was evident that this was a matter of house being divided against house; it was Sewell against Sewell. William D. Sewell, an uncle of E. G. and William B., acted as the moderator. At the trial, William B. raised his New Testament in one hand and the article of faith of the Baptist Church in the other, and asked to know by which he would be tried. People were divided, and William B. Sewell was voted out of the Baptist Church without a trial.

The Sewell boys—Jesse L., Isaac, Caleb and Elisha particularly —regretted deeply the course their brother had taken. Jesse L., the oldest of the boys, decided to convert him. William B. expressed a willingness to be converted if it could be shown from the scriptures that he was wrong. To this end Jesse searched the scriptures, but in the process was himself converted. Soon, Isaac and Caleb and the whole Sewell family, except E. G., had abandoned the Baptist Church for the return to apostolic ground. E. G. was younger than the other boys, consequently less versed in the scriptures. He refused to be moved by his family's decision, insisting instead upon studying the Bible for himself. Sewell, in the spring of 1849, started reading his New Testament. On the fourth Lord's Day of October that same year, he was immersed by Jesse L. Sewell, an elder brother. Thus, William B. Sewell, although himself never a gospel preacher, influenced his family, and through them preached the "unsearchable riches."

Family worship was a regular activity with the Sewells. Until Isaac and Caleb left home to teach, it was customary for them to conduct the worship. After this, it was suggested that E. G. conduct it. This became his first attempt at anything related to a public service for the Lord. In the fall of 1851, at the private house of a neighbor, E. G. preached his first sermon.

Education for E. G. Sewell came with great difficulty. As a youth he picked up what learning he could around the rural community, but this was inadequate. The acquiring of a wife, and soon a family, only increased the difficulty. On November 22, 1853 he married Miss Lucy Kuykendall near Cookeville, Tennessee, and for convenience and economy moved in with his father-in-law. Matthew Kuykendall, his wife's father, encouraged him to continue his education in spite of being married. Two years passed, and late in 1855 Professor G. A. Kuykendall took Sewell to Spencer, Tennessee to investigate Burritt College where W. D. Carnes was president. Carnes was sympathetic and encouraging so Sewell rented a house and began preparations to enter school in February, 1856.

Burritt College held Sewell only two years. He studied Latin, Greek and mathematics. A congregation of New Testament Christians met in the town. However, a doom fell over the school when W. D. Carnes left as president. One night Carnes' residence was burned. He could not escape the conviction that he had many enemies who were seeking to ruin him. He could not, therefore, be persuaded to remain longer at Spencer, so moved to East Tennessee University. Carnes' successors at Burritt disappointed Sewell, and before long, he was back to the home of his wife's parents, five miles north of Cookeville.

The same year Sewell moved to Franklin College to study under Tolbert Fanning and William Lipscomb. His return to the Kuykendall home found him in despondency so far as his educational possibilities were concerned. His wife and children demanded his time and money, and this responsibility left scarcely any probability of further education. Nevertheless, when he heard that Fanning and Lipscomb proposed to educate twenty young men at Franklin College with board and tuition free, he decided to look into it. He found he could make arrangements to go, but what was he to do about his family? Providentially, the way was revealed. An unmarried brother of his wife's proposed to open up a boarding house and school at Bloomington Springs but had no one to superintend it. Room and board were offered to Sewell's wife and three children if his wife would take the position. She accepted and on September 1, 1858 E. G.

Sewell entered Franklin College. By studying arduously Sewell completed his course here in one year, graduating in June, 1859.

After leaving Franklin College, he gathered up his family and went to the home of James C. Owen in Williamson County. Through the Civil War and for the next five years after, he spent his time preaching in Middle Tennessee. With the exception of a part of 1866 when he was in Mississippi, most of Sewell's preaching was confined to Wilson, Williamson, and Rutherford Counties.

Nothing enlarged the border of Sewell's influence more than his work on the *Gospel Advocate*. Beginning on January 1, 1870 and extended forward over fifty years, the name of E. G. Sewell became familiar to *Advocate* readers. Upon receiving the invitation from David Lipscomb to assist in the publication of the *Advocate,* Sewell accepted the opportunity with little reluctance. His family had continued to grow, and, as Sewell was absent so much from home, the task of caring for the family was getting to be too great for his wife. Too, his observation was that the *Advocate* was growing, and that he was being extended an opportunity to do a larger and possibly more influential work. Besides, Nashville was growing. Although the church in 1870 was weak in the city, possibilities existed for a large extension of the work. It was not therefore a difficult decision to make.

Edgefield, Tennessee lay east of Nashville across the Cumberland River. Long since it has become a part of Nashville proper. 801 Boscobel Street in Edgefield became the address of E. G. Sewell on January 1, 1870 and remained his address as long as he lived. This street was then in the outskirts of town. A large pasture across the street offered a good opportunity for the Sewell's to keep a cow. With the passing of time, however, the city grew, and Sewell's living changed with differing environmental circumstances.

Were one writing a biography of a military general, there would be much of the wild, the turbulent, the picturesque to recount to make the pages gleam with activity. But to recall the history of one of God's servants, a man who lived a quiet, peaceful life, there is little of the colorful and the romantic. The remainder of Sewell's life was occupied in preaching and writing. The first fifteen years in Nashville found him working earnestly to build up a congregation in East Nashville. Probably the greatest disappointment of his life came when this church adopted the innovations flooding the church. To recall the meetings Sewell held would be to little advantage.

Moderation in everything was one of his prominent characteristics. The impression he left upon all was that he wanted to please God and go to heaven. He made no effort to please men nor did he make any pretense to be great despite the fact that his was true greatness. He loved to read the Bible, and even upon the most unusual occasions would be found with the Bible upon his lap, almost completely oblivious to his surroundings. He was gentle, earnest, and persuasive in his appeals to sinners. His heart was filled with loving-kindness toward all men. In personal appearance he was always neat. Some remarked that E. G. Sewell was the "cleanest-looking" man they ever saw. He never appeared to be anxious about anything.

The Sewell home became known for its hospitality. As the church grew in Nashville, and the *Gospel Advocate* became more widely read and known, the city became a radiating point for the gospel in the South. Traveling preachers found themselves welcome at Sewell's home. He not only *extended* invitations to Christians, but in sincerity and earnestness, *urged* them to be his guests.

E. G. Sewell was methodical. F. B. Srygley stayed in the Sewell home while he conducted a tent meeting at Tenth and Fatherland Streets in 1891. At precisely the same time every morning Sewell would rap on the door and call out, "Well, preacher, are you ready for breakfast?" Syrgley was then a young man, and had always heard that a preacher should eat little "supper" if he were going to preach that night. Syrgley enjoyed eating too well to want to follow that counsel, and therefore, was glad of the advice Sewell gave him, "I always eat about the same amount whether I preach or whether I listen to some one else preach."

Death came to E. G. Sewell on Sunday, March 2, 1924 at 1:45 A. M. He died at his old residence, 801 Boscobel Street where he had lived fifty-four years. His funeral was conducted the next day at the Russell Street Church in Nashville with S. H. Hall and J. C. McQuiddy preaching.

JOHN F. ROWE

The *American Christian Review* was unquestionably the most influential paper in the brotherhood for over a quarter of a century after 1856. The editor, Ben Franklin, was, doubtlessly, the most popular preacher in the church after Alexander Campbell. For eleven years John Franklin Rowe served as an associate-editor under Franklin later to become his successor as editor of the

Review. Rowe, too, founded the *Christian Leader* in 1886, and served as its editor until his death in 1897. Thus, through a period of intense crisis the name of John F. Rowe was often before the church. Whether his lasting influence be regarded as important or not, it is a historical fact that he played a major part in the later years of restoration movement.

Martin Rowe and his wife, Martha Magdalena Alshouse Rowe

were a young couple living on a farm near Greensburg, Pennsylvania in 1827. Both were of German descent; poor but industrious, and devoutly Lutheran. To them was born on March 23, that year an infant son whom they named John Franklin. In accordance to their religious beliefs the infant son was taken to the Lutheran Church nearby and "conscripted in infancy" by sprinkling.

Migration was characteristic of the times. It was a common sight to see wagon trains pushing westward, and to hear friends and neighbors discuss moving. When, therefore, John Franklin was only twelve years old, his family migrated into Ohio and settled near Wooster. Here, John F. Rowe spent his childhood.

Being a farmer did not militate against his following some other occupation as well. Martin Rowe followed the trade of a bricklayer, and quickly taught this trade to John F. However, Rowe informs us that when he was twenty years old, he took up the trade of a shoemaker. This gave him a work he could perform in the winter time when the weather made bricklaying impossible. He worked every day from seven o'clock in the morning until nine o'clock at night, and saved small amounts of money. During these early years, he attended "Parrott's Academy." Educational opportunities were limited, so Rowe read extensively and became well informed on many subjects, especially history.

The winter of 1827-28, when Rowe was twenty years old, he first came in contact with the restoration plea. His associates were heard to speak contemptuously of the "Campbellites," who were then conducting a meeting at Bentley's School House. Meetings were commonly conducted with two preachers on the ground —one to do the preaching and the other the "exhorting." Almon B. Green, a logical and argumentative man, was the preacher, and J. Harrison Jones was the exhorter. A man of strong emotions, also tender and somewhat eloquent, Jones had strong persuasive ability with the sinner. Known affectionately to his many friends as "Uncle Harry," Jones became a close friend and adviser to John F. Rowe in later years. It was out of curiosity that Rowe went to the meeting at first, but soon he became interested and obeyed the gospel.

The event changed the whole course of his life. Jones was his constant companion, and by traveling with him, Rowe soon heard the greatest preachers of the restoration. Rowe gradually built up an attitude of hero-worship toward Alexander Campbell, the "sage of Bethany." Meanwhile, his sincerity and earnestness caused him to make friends easily. Sensing an ability in Rowe for great service in the church, the money was raised to send him to Bethany College.

It was September, 1850 when Rowe arrived at Bethany, carrying a letter of introduction from J. H. Jones. Rowe somewhat presumptiously took the letter to Campbell's study where he obtained his first glimpse of the famous preacher. Because there were no other chairs in the study, Campbell piled up some books for a seat and said jokingly to Rowe, "Please, Sir, take a literary seat." Jones had said to Rowe, "Tell Brother Campbell that we want him to make a man of you," and Rowe now passed on the message. Campbell replied, "That, my dear Sir, depends on the kind of material they have sent me." Rowe wilted momentarily but Campbell's simple manners soon put him at ease.[1]

John F. Rowe came to Bethany College with the intention of remaining only one year, but when Campbell urged J. H. Jones to arrange for another year, it was done. During this second year at school, Rowe started preaching. On one of these attempts he rode an old gray horse twelve miles, taking four hours on the journey, to preach a sermon he had gathered from some of Alexander Campbell's notes. After he started preaching, he stopped only after an hour and twenty minutes and then from pure exhaustion. When he returned home, he weighed and found he had lost four pounds in the last twenty-four hours.

Rowe's stay at Bethany later furnished many happy memories. Here he had heard Thomas Campbell deliver his last address, and was later in the funeral procession that took the elder Campbell's body up to the cemetery on the hill. At Bethany Rowe enjoyed the companionship of great men. Among these were T. M. Henley, O. A. Burgess, J. S. Lamar, J. A. Meng, and J. M. Barnes. While a college student, Rowe served as one of the editors of the *Stylus,* the college paper. He was also still a student when he married Mary Editha Pardee, daughter of Judge Allen Pardee of Wadsworth, Ohio, the marriage occurring in September, 1852. It is not unlikely that J. H. Jones figured in this, for Mary Pardee was Jones' sister-in-law. Graduation from college came

---

[1] John F. Rowe, "Reminiscences of the Restoration, No. 2," *American Christian Review,* Vol. XXIX, No. 18 (April 29, 1886), p. 141.

in July, 1854. John Schackleford was called "the beloved disciple";
O. A. Burgess was the "son of thunder"; J. S. Lamar was the
"son of consolation and good hope," and J. F. Rowe held the
"pen of a ready writer."

Upon departing from Bethany, Rowe went to spend the summer
at his wife's home in Wadsworth, Ohio. That fall he became an
agent for the Ohio State Missionary Society. He spent about
five weeks, in the company of John Reed, traveling over the
western part of the state. In the spring of 1855 he moved to
Springfield, Illinois at the invitation of W. A. Mallory, editor of
the *Christian Sentinel,* to be co-editor. Most of his work was
traveling in Illinois, getting subscriptions to the periodical. A
part of the time he had as his traveling companion C. D. Roberts.
Roberts was the financial agent for Alexander Campbell, who
was in Illinois buying up land for Campbell. This land later
contributed considerably to Campbell's wealth. These trips through
Illinois provided Rowe with a romantic life. He and Roberts
rode horseback constantly, and while hurrying across the fields
often scared up prairie chickens which looked like a thick cloud
floating away on the horizon.

During the time Rowe lived at Springfield he became acquainted
with Abe Lincoln, who was then a young lawyer in the same
town. Rowe once engaged Lincoln to try a suit for him, which
for some reason was stopped. He stayed at Springfield for two
years, and during the time encouraged the church to have Isaac
Errett conduct a meeting. Here their first child, Eugene Pardee,
was born. The *Sentinel,* however, was so much in debt that
Rowe could not be paid his salary, so he sold his furniture to pay
his landlord, left town, owing a note for $15.00. It was ten
years before he could pay it, and was following from state to
state with a threatening suit.

Financial difficulties followed Rowe most of his life. In 1857
he moved to Oskaloosa, Iowa, upon the invitation of A. Chatter-
ton, assistant editor of the *Evangelist,* to help raise funds to establish Oskaloosa College. The agreement was that after the
school was financially secure, Rowe would be made a professor.
The financial depression that year crushed many men, Rowe
being among the number. He was forced to return to his work
of bricklaying for two dollars a day.

The times were hard. Northwest of Oskaloosa, lived an old

preacher named Anderson, who had lost everything the winter before except a cow and two pigs. Rowe lived here for three days on a diet of prairie chicken and corn bread. The tame prairie chickens lolled on a fence while Rowe picked them off with a shotgun. Often he walked ten miles without pay to preach the gospel. Once he was forty miles from home without a cent and walked the whole distance. Before leaving Oskaloosa in the spring of 1859 to return to Wadsworth, Ohio, Rowe was forced to sell everything except his bed-clothing to pay his debts. Only because his father sent him $50.00 could he make a return trip.

Rowe's activity during the Civil War centered in Ohio. The summer of 1859 he worked as a bricklayer for $5.00 a day, at the same time preaching at Manchester. At the opening of the war, he preached in Holmesville, Ohio. It was Rowe's practice to take no part in the war or in politics, however, he once delivered an address to the Soldier's Aid Society. For two years he worked as a member of the Board of the Ohio Christian Missionary Society, but considering himself a "nonentity," he resigned. Because he secured five thousand dollars for the Society from the Phillips Brothers of Newcastle, Pennsylvania, the Society raised his salary two hundred dollars a year.

G. W. N. Yost of Corry, Virginia, a wealthy man, cleared a thousand dollars a day in the oil business. He and Rowe became fast friends. Yost's interest in establishing a paper, and Rowe's part in this, has already been recounted. The result of this series of incidents was the creation of the *Christian Standard.* Rowe never felt that he could understand Isaac Errett, so consequently, he gave little enthusiasm to his support for the *Standard.* Yost agreed to pay Rowe one hundred dollars a month as salary for Rowe to write on any brotherhood publication. When Rowe stated the facts to Ben Franklin, Franklin placed him on the *Review,* giving him a one hundred dollar bonus to begin. After that, Ben Franklin became John F. Rowe's idol.

It was 1867 that Rowe became connected with the *American Christian Review,* a connection he retained until the close of 1886. It is as a writer that J. F. Rowe is best remembered today. The brotherhood had few men that could wield a pen with Rowe's pungency and clarity. Ben Franklin certainly held this opinion for in 1872 he wrote him:

Brother Rowe has stood side by side with us in the columns

of the *Review* for years, as our readers can testify. We have but few men who can write as he can; certainly not a half a dozen.[2]

When the *Review* of February 12, 1878 appeared, Rowe was listed as the assistant editor. Franklin then said of him:

Long has he worked at our side, and well do we know how to count on him. His pen scarcely ever slips, nor is it ever still. Nor does he stop with *writing*, but he is an *incessant* preacher. He is fully out now as the successful preacher and writer. We trust the way is now open for him to be more abundantly useful than ever before. He is ready for the work and in it. The Lord strengthen his hands and encourage his heart.[3]

After the death of Ben Franklin, Rowe took over the editorship of the *Review*, Daniel Sommer wrote of him,

Critics, sharpen your pens; he is a good subject to work on. He will neither coax nor drive into either good or bad; but convince him, and he will go himself into whatever is right.[4]

The reader may have guessed already that John F. Rowe was never a prominent preacher. The harsh truth is that Rowe bordered upon a failure as a preacher. He declared that when he came from Bethany College, he possessed a great knowledge of the Bible which he had learned from Campbell, but lacked the ability to organize and present it. This was true. He had deep convictions, and a great knowledge of the Scriptures. He was a good student, never reaching the point that he felt he had enough sermons to retire from further study. W. O. Tomson said of him, "As a preacher, Brother Rowe is not what many call a pulpit orator. . . He is clear and forcible and convincing and never fails to send conviction to every honest heart."[5]

Shortly after the Civil War, Rowe moved to Akron, Ohio where he lived the remainder of his life. In the fall of 1886 he became the editor of the *Christian Leader,* a paper which he founded. His break with the *American Christian Review* that year will be studied in another chapter.

The last decade or more Rowe lost much prominence. It is not too difficult to understand Rowe's thinking, and to some extent

---

[2]Ben Franklin, "John F. Rowe," *American Christian Review,* Vol. XV, No. 48 (November 26, 1872), p. 380.

[3]Ben Franklin, "John F. Rowe on the Warpath," *American Christian Review,* Vol. XXI, (February 12, 1878), p. 53.

[4]Daniel Sommer, "The Present Editor," *American Christian Review,* Vol. XXI, No. 48 (November 26, 1878), p. 377.

[5]W. O. Tomson, "John F. Rowe," *American Christian Review,* Vol. XXIII. (June 15, 1880), p. 186.

throw a mantle of charity over these years. The church passed a period of intense trial. By 1880 the issues in the brotherhood had, for the most part, been thoroughly discussed. Men arrayed themselves up on the various issues, but the question that now forced its way to the front demanding serious attention was that of fellowship. Many had taken the position that the use of the instrument and the missionary society were wrong, unscriptural and sinful. But, it became evident by 1880 that many churches were going to use the instrument and support the society anyway. The influence of the *Christian Standard,* particularly throughout the North, had been great enough to become a rallying point for those advocating the instrument, and using the society. Whereas one group insisted the instrument was wrong, the other insisted it could be used. Could fellowship remain?

This question forced its way upon the church. There were some who had formerly strictly opposed instrumental music whose opposition subsided. J. B. Briney had stood vigorously behind the opposition to the instrument, but now wavered. So did Joseph Franklin, son of Ben Franklin. What happened with these more prominent leaders happened to many less known. Others remained loyal to old convictions. If instrumental music were sinful, there could be no fellowship with it, and ten million churches using it would not make it any more right than it had ever been. A serious division was threatening and Rowe shrank from it. He firmly believed instrumental music was wrong, but how to continue to fellowship advocates of it was a problem the full force of which he never met. Uncertain sounds came from him. A small organ, he declared was permissible, just so it was not a large one. Brethren naturally rebelled against him on the one hand. On the other, while some congratulated him for his liberal spirit, he was never ardently received because of his pronounced belief against the use of the instrument. His influence, therefore, in his last years was localized.

Rowe's death came at four o'clock in the afternoon of Wednesday, December 29, 1897. Ill health prevented his being at the *Leader* office since May of that year. As far back as two years previous, he had a heavy mental strain that affected his health. In May, 1897, he suffered a nervous breakdown. His friends advised him to take a vacation. That August, he and his wife went to West Virginia for a vacation and in October returned to

Cincinnati. By this time he was partially paralyzed. It was evident that he could not recover. So he returned to Akron, to spend his last days.

Still later he partially lost his power of speech. His last articles which appeared in the *Leader* through November and December in 1897 were written under the most adverse circumstances. He was in bed when he dictated the articles to members of his family, who, at times, asked him several times to repeat his statements. His last words were directed to his son, Fred L., who still resided in Cincinnati, and who managed the *Leader* in the absence of his father. Rowe said to members of his family, "Tell Fred not to waver—keep the *Leader* pure and clean." These were his last words.

The funeral was conducted at the home of his second son at one o'clock on Friday afternoon, December 31, 1897. F. M. Green, then residing at Kent, Ohio, and a close friend of the family, preached the funeral. He read the words of one of Rowe's favorite songs, "On Jordan's Stormy Banks I Stand," before preaching the sermon.

CHAPTER IX

THE PASSING YEARS (1865-1885)

The passing of a score of years following the Civil War witnessed a rapid transition in every phase of American life. The nation in 1876 celebrated its centennial, and many awakened for the first time to the realization that this was a growing country. After the peace treaty of 1783 the colonies had a combined area of 820,680 square miles, but a century later, 3,603,884 square miles. The population increased from 2,803,000 in 1783 to 44,-000,000 by 1876. The centennial celebration on July 4th in which thirty-eight states participated, indicated the growth of a century.

The cessation of hostilities following the war however, little abated the nation's political problems. Days of reconstruction were ahead for the South, but the passing of twenty years saw most of these problems settled. Poverty had followed in the path of the war. The ripest manhood in the South were dead or badly crippled. In the transition the South paid a heavy price. Money was scarce, and the panic which hit the nation in 1873 and which lasted for several years, further burdened the nation. This environmental circumstance, of course, reflected itself upon a point of emphasis among preachers. The man who was paid a thousand dollars a year was mercenary. The emphasis in the South was on preaching to the poor, David Lipscomb in the *Gospel Advocate* ever being their champion. Preachers farmed for a living, and gave what time they could to preach. While they should receive much praise for this, the fact is that most could not have done otherwise had they desired.

"Man's extremity is God's opportunity" says a very truthful maxim. Since the rich and powerful seldom have time to think of God, years of hard struggle against depression prove splendid time for the growth of the cause of Christ. Environmental factors all favored the growth of the church. The war had taught the more thoughtful people the need of searching for God, and the years of poverty made it more compelling. Too, the predominately rural population contributed to the growth. The automobile had not yet been invented so few people traveled far from home. A gospel meeting was a big occasion in the average rural community, when nearly everybody generally attended. The occasion was quite frequently as big a social event as a religious. This, too, was a suitable environment for great debates. Behind the seriousness of a religious discussion there was for the average person in a rural community an occasion for sport. Aside from the seriousness of the event, people came to enjoy themselves with this unusual event. Preachers seemed to sense this and injected personal thrusts and humorous stories at the expense of their opponents. In later years, however, people were to find their enjoyment and sport in other events, and, on the whole have insisted that debating be what it should be—a serious search for truth.

Society as a whole, then, was prepared for the gospel. When a preacher showed the willingness to make the sacrifice to preach to a rural community, he could be sure of a good audience. The physical equipment was hardly essential since any school house, brush arbor, or large shade tree would suffice. Given an average preacher one could be assured of baptizing thirty to sixty people. A preacher, who in the course of five years baptized less than five thousand people, apologized often for it.

The national census for 1870 ranked the churches of Christ fifth in size in the nation, having 2,822 local congregations. It was widely rumored that the church numbered some half-a-million. The feeling generally was that this report was inadequate, and that a more accurate report was needed. When the General Convention of the Missionary Society met in Cincinnati in October, 1879 a committee was formed to gather the statistics. F. M. Green, J. B. Briney, R. Moffett, Elias Sias and L. D. Carpenter were on this committee.

Census reports among the churches of Christ through the years have every reason to be inaccurate. Because the churches are locally independent, with no central headquarters, no power of compulsion can be made to the local churches to make them report. Some reluctance had been felt to be placed in the same category with denominational churches as census reports imply. When, therefore, F. M. Green wrote to David Lipscomb, urging him to assist in getting up the census, Lipscomb declined.

God had not made any specific law to King David against

numbering the children of Israel, but God condemned him when he did it, reasoned Lipscomb. David, upon discovering the number of his people, would have been inclined to place his confidence, not upon God, but upon the strength of numbers, thought Lipscomb. So he reasoned that the same inclination would be felt in the church. Moreover, he regarded the Missionary Society as a representative of only a small minority of the churches. To come before the world with a claim to be the representative of the churches in America would be false.[1]

The Society, however, gathered its statistics. A large majority of the churches, not having any sympathy for the Society, failed to report to it, so it was far from being accurate. The report, however, presents some idea of the general growth of the church up to the year, 1880.

States	Congregations	Preachers	Members
Alabama	35	28	3,250
Arkansas	56	15	5,928
California	49	38	5,775
Colorado	16	12	1,750
Connecticut	6	4	775
Dakota	7	5	675
District of Columbia	1	2	425
Florida	14	11	900
Georgia	73	48	9,850
Illinois	795	650	85,250
Indiana	675	580	78,950
Iowa	200	98	15,500
Kansas	125	78	16,860
Kentucky	595	485	79,525
Louisiana	12	7	1,500
Maine	7	5	725
Maryland	5	4	1,695
Massachusetts	7	5	1,200
Michigan	75	49	6,000
Minnesota	7	5	725
Mississippi	15	12	2,370
Missouri	565	395	60,900
Montana	6	4	675
Nebraska	75	41	13,580
New York	49	39	5,950
North Carolina	95	79	14,700
Ohio	425	217	45,500
Oregon	45	24	4,750
Pennsylvania	95	88	13,400
South Carolina	25	18	2,825
Tennessee	275	195	38,890
Texas	165	138	16,500
Vermont	3	2	425

[1]David Lipscomb, "Statistics Wanted," *Gospel Advocate*, Vol. XXI, No. 32 (August 7, 1879), p. 503.

Virginia	150	115	16,500
Washington Territory	1	1	75
West Virginia	65	48	7,750
Wisconsin	21	12	2,575
Wyoming Territory	1	1	95
Totals	4,768	3,488	563,928[2]

The centers of numerical strength may be readily grasped from the report. Illinois, Kentucky, Indiana, Missouri and Ohio were the numerically strong states. In Illinois, where there were over 85,000 members, the church was largely in rural areas. In 1871 Chicago had but two congregations. Twenty years later there were seven.[3] John S. Sweeney preached at this time for the church at Sixteenth and Wabash Avenues.[4]

Kentucky had eighty thousand members in 1880, but her strong centers were at Lexington and Louisville. The church at Lexington had been established on Main Street in 1834 by James Challen. Here, the Campbell-Rice debate was held in 1843. The church had always known good preaching. W. H. Hopson labored here from 1859 to 1862. The war caused Hopson to leave, and J. W. McGarvey followed him. During the battle at Richmond, Kentucky the building was used for a hospital, but aside from this, the war did not greatly disturb the growth of the church. By 1871, it was evident that the church had outgrown its old building. It was found that the First Presbyterian Church, corner of Broadway and Second Streets, had its building for sale at $15,000. The money was quickly raised and the house purchased. The first meeting in the new building was held on May 1, 1870 at which J. W. McGarvey spoke, relating the history of the church in that city.

In Louisville, the history of the church dated back to 1825 when P. S. Fall established a Baptist Church in this city. Fall became converted through reading the *Christian Baptist,* and began preaching apostolic principles. The Baptist Church divided, and the first congregation worshiping purely upon primitive grounds, was organized. In the next few years the location of the building shifted.

---

[2]David Lipscomb, "Those Statistics," *Gospel Advocate,* Vol. XXIII, No. 8 (February 24, 1881), p. 114.

[3]A. J. White, "Two Years in Chicago," *Christian-Evangelist,* Vol. XXXI, No. 4 (January 25, 1894), p. 57.

[4]C. W. Sherwood, "The Cause in Chicago," *Christian Standard,* Vol. IV, No. 8 (February 20, 1869), p. 58.

The church met first at Green and Sixth Street. Then it bought another house on Second Street between Jefferson and Market. A few years later it built on Fifth Street between Chestnut and Walnut. By 1860, it was ready to build again. On May 18th, that year, the cornerstone was laid for a new building at Fourth and Walnut. A basement was finished here by March 17, 1861. Then came the war, and the building could not be completed. For nine years they continued to meet in the basement-building. W. H. Hopson moved to Louisville to preach for this church in 1868. At that time the church numbered nearly six hundred members. Work was being pushed on the upper part of the structure. The first meeting was held in it on April 23, 1870. The building had been completed at a cost of one hundred thousand dollars. At this first service in the new building the aging Samuel Rogers was present as a visitor and led the first prayer. Hopson used as his text Jeremiah 6: 16.

The Fourth and Walnut Streets Church was the original church in the city. After the war, other congregations arose. By 1870 there was a congregation of over four hundred members on Chestnut Street. The year before a smaller congregation had been established on Jefferson Street.[5] In the spring of 1876 forty members began meeting in Robinson Hall. R. B. Neal, an energetic and capable preacher, was the leading spirit in its establishment. In September that year this group purchased a lot on Campbell Street between Main and Market, and the following March completed their building. On the 18th of the month, J. W. McGarvey preached the dedicatory sermon for the Campbell Street Church, using Jeremiah 6: 16 as his text. Moses E. Lard, who was then engaged in a meeting at the Chestnut Street Church, was present and spoke a few words.[6] The Campbell Street congregation later became the Haldeman Avenue Church.

At this time the Fourth and Walnut Streets Church claimed to be the largest congregation worshiping after apostolic principles in the nation. When J. S. Lamar left here in 1876, it had eight hundred members. That spring B. B. Tylor came to preach to be followed in 1882 by A. I. Hobbs. With this array of more

---

[5]W. H. Hopson, "The Walnut Street Christian Church, Louisville, Ky.," *Apostolic Times,* Vol. II, No. 6 (May 19, 1870), p. 45.

[6]J. W. McGarvey, "My Visit to Louisville," *Apostolic Times,* Vol. IX (April 12, 1877), p. 225.

liberal spirited preachers, the church finally adopted instrumental music, and went with the general "progressive" movement. In the western part of the city about this time a few disciples left the Fourth and Walnut Streets Church when the instrument went in. By 1884 their number had increased to one hundred and twenty members. Their meeting house was first a livery stable which was bought by the Methodists. The brethren purchased the building from the Methodists, remodeled it to suit their purposes. This congregation was known as the Portland Avenue Church. It was here F. G. Allen preached in 1879-80 while editing the *Old Path Guide.* "Weeping Jo" Harding and R. B. Neal had been his predecessors.

The report of the Convention for 1880 showed Indiana to be third in point of membership with seventy-eight thousand. Prominent congregations were found at Indianapolis, Bloomington and Bedford. John O'Kane preached the first sermon in Indianapolis in 1833 at the log cabin house of Ben Roberts, who lived at the corner of Market and Illinois Streets. After the war, this congregation, with around five hundred members, met at Delaware and Ohio Streets. In 1869 the church dropped the name, church of Christ, and called itself the "Central Christian Church." Northwest Christian University was founded in 1855, and was located at Fourteenth and College. This was in those days out in the country. It was hard for students to go to Ohio and Delaware Streets to the Central Church, so classes were started at the University early on Sunday mornings, which led to the establishment of a church across from the campus in 1868. Eventually this became the Third Christian Church. The Second Christian Church was a colored congregation at Fourteenth and Illinois Streets, established in 1866.

These early churches, like many others in the brotherhood, put in the instrument and generally went with the "progressive" movement. The Third Christian Church in Indianapolis put in the instrument sometime late in the 1870's. The exact date is not known. Twelve brethren who could not conscientiously worship with the organ began in 1878 to worship on South New Jersey Street in a Danish Chapel. Dr. Joshua Webb, one of the members, went from house to house preaching. Alfred Ellmore began a meeting here on May 2, 1880, which lasted for twenty-nine days and ended with forty-one baptisms.[7] Four years later while the church was meeting on Mulberry Street, John F. Rowe conducted a meeting for the same congregation. Rowe enjoyed a renewal of friendship with the editor of the *Indianapolis Journal,* John C. New *(later, Indianapolis Star),* who had been Rowe's classmate at Bethany College in 1854, and previously the assistant United States Treasurer.[8]

At both Bloomington and Bedford strong congregations were established. The church at Bloomington started in 1828. In 1879 it had one hundred and seventy-five members. W. B. F. Treat and I. N. Porch made Bloomington their home and preached constantly in the surrounding territory. J. M. Mathes, one of Indiana's stalwart pioneers, editor of the *Christian Record,* lived at Bedford. By 1880 he was getting old, but he knew well the history of the work in Indiana. In the earlier days when Indians were plentiful in Indiana, Mathes was offered the position as chief in one of their tribes because of his tall, stalwart physical frame. Although he refused, they gave him the title of "Big Fire." Mathes lived in a little country home near Bedford, was an elder in the congregation which exercised great influence in the southern part of the state.

The state of Missouri boasted sixty thousand members in 1880. Some forty-five years before this time T. M. Allen, Thomas McBride and Samuel Rogers were among the earliest preachers of the ancient order in the state. They had traveled from one settlement to another, each with a sleeping bag and a few provisions. Thomas McBride died years before, but in 1877 the ninety-year-old Samuel Rogers was living with his son, John I. Rogers, in Danville, Kentucky. However, death cut off his earthly life two years later. T. M. Allen had died in 1871.

There were three schools run by the brethren in the state during these years. Christian University, at Canton, was in 1876 divided into four colleges—College of Arts, College of Literature and Science, College of the Bible, and Commercial College. The brethren also supported Christian College at Columbia and a female school, which at this time had J. K. Rogers as president. There

---

[7] A. Ellmore, "Indianapolis Meeting," *American Christian Review,* Vol. XXIII, (June 29, 1880), p. 205.

[8] John F. Rowe, "Mission Work in Indianapolis," *American Christian Review,* Vol. XXVII, No. 17 (April 24, 1884), p. 133.

was also a female orphan school at Camden Point in Platte County.[9]

Ohio, fifth largest in the nation as it respected the numerical strength of the brotherhood, had been a rallying ground for the plea of the ancient order since Walter Scott had preached on the Western Reserve fifty years before. Cincinnati, the "Queen City of the West," had six congregations in the year 1880. The largest was the Central Church, where at this time David Walk preached, but where sometime earlier W. T. Moore gained fame. In one sense, this was the Central Church of the brotherhood. In 1868, B. A. Hinsdale wrote of this congregation: "It contains many elements of power—wealth, character, social position, and if it does not exert a very considerable influence in the city, it it not because the Lord has withheld His blessings."[10] R. M. Bishop, one of its elders, was mayor of Cincinnati during the Civil War, and in 1874 he was elected governor of Ohio. The meeting house cost over one hundred thousand dollars—a large sum for those days. The Central Church, however, became the seat for innovations—instrumental music and missionary societies.

Richmond Street, Eastern Avenue, and Fergus Street were the other three white congregations in the city. Ben Franklin had preached for the Richmond Street Church shortly after the war, but A. I. Hobbs was the preacher in 1880. Two colored congregations—one on Harrison Street and at College Hill were also found here.

Aside from these "strong hold" states for the church, the cause was realizing rapid growth in all regions north of the Ohio River and east of the Mississippi. In Minnesota and Wisconsin the cause yet remained weak, as it did in most of the New England states. B. U. Watkins reports from St. Paul at the close of 1875 that a small congregation is found in this city. And in New England the plea was hardly as well planted as in the states to their west. By 1876 Baltimore, Maryland, had but two churches. The original congregation here was the North Street Church. In 1840 the Paca Street Church was formed from it through a division. Through the years the little fellowship existed. In 1876

---

[9]Messrs. Davis and Durrie, "Christian Church at Fulton, Missouri," *Apostolic Times,* Vol. IX (April 5, 1877), p. 213.

[10]B. A. Hinsdale, "A Week in Cincinnati and Covington," *Christian Standard,* Vol. III, No. 2 (January 11, 1868), pp. 12, 13.

the North Street Church reorganized under the name Dolphin Street Church and a more active fellowship was realized.

The larger cities in Michigan soon had congregations. Grand Rapids, the second city of Michigan, had about twenty members to begin meeting in 1874. S. E. Pearre moved here in February, 1875, to become the first preacher. But Detroit still remained the stronghold. On August 3, 1842, Alexander Linn came to Detroit from Glasgow, Scotland. He found Thomas Hawley and his family conducting worship in Hawley's house, so Linn joined in with them, and thus began the church in Detroit. Linn was then in the mercantile business, but after 1870 he devoted his full time to preaching the gospel.[11] About 1869 the Plum Street Church was organized at Fourth and Plum Streets with thirty members. The older congregation was meeting on Washington Street and using the instrument. By 1882 Plum Street had three hundred members and was renowned for carrying on its work with the leadership of its elders and not employing a preacher.[12] In 1883 the Plum Street Church established a congregation at Fourteenth and Ash, erecting a building that cost $2,600.

The church was spreading west of the Mississippi. A steady stream of migration poured across the Mississippi following the war, swelling the population on the vast prairies and to the Pacific. In the fall of 1877 Pardee Butler asserted before the state meeting of the Kansas Christian Missionary Society that fifty thousand members of the church had left their homes in the east and moved into those territories lying between the Missouri River and the Pacific Ocean.[13] The first congregation in Kansas, however, antedated the war. Butler went to this state in the spring of 1855, and in June gathered a large crowd on the banks of Stranger Creek, Atchison County, on a land claim belonging to Caleb May. A month later the first congregation was established at near-by Mount Pleasant, and became known as the Round Prairie Church. The Topeka Church was slow in beginning. D. H. Johnston went here in 1865. Five years later he published a call for all members of the church to meet in the courthouse. Thirty members organized

[11]J. M. L. Campbell, "Alexander Linn," *American Christian Review*, Vol. XXV, No. 18 (April 27, 1882), p. 141.
[12]James A. Harding, "The Plum Street Church of Detroit, Michigan," *Gospel Advocate*, Vol. XXIV, No. 19 (May 11, 1882), p. 298.
[13]Pardee Butler, "Address to the Brethren in Kansas," *The Christian*, Vol. XV, No. 38 (September 20, 1877), p. 5.

themselves, renting a hall for three hundred dollars a year. Three years later they had two hundred members, when the financial depression hit the nation. Money could not be raised to pay rent, so the church disbanded.[14] At Wichita the first congregation was established on July 4, 1880, by T. J. Shelton and J. H. Rosecrans, who held a thirty days' meeting and added forty-three persons to the church.[15] Considerable activity, then, took place in Kansas. Pardee Butler asserted that in that part of the state lying north of the Kansas River fifty congregations had been established since the war. All but twenty died out by 1877, and these were in poor condition. Beneath the pessimism is the symbol of struggling life.

In Arkansas and Louisiana the plea for the ancient order was felt. The church at Little Rock felt the impact of the war. Though not dividing openly, the war engendered an undercurrent of hard feelings. When J. H. Garrison conducted a meeting for the congregation in 1877, he found it greatly discouraged. David Lipscomb visited here eight years later, and remarked that the congregation was about holding its own—nothing more. Small, struggling churches were springing up over Arkansas. On June 25, 1875, Joe Waldrop came to Fort Smith and found a small congregation three or four years old. At Alma, Russellville and Dardanelle little churches were existing. Over the entire section the influence of Robert Graham, who had lived at Fayetteville before the war, was still felt. At Hope and Prescott, congregations were organized in 1882. At Texarkana, J. C. Mason preached almost steadily in 1884 and 1885.

In New Orleans, as late as 1883, the church had a poor foundation. When a correspondent named "Zenas" visited here that year, he wrote:

. . . The church in New Orleans was planted by Alexander Campbell many long years ago. Many malign influences have dwarfed its growth. The baleful glare of Jesse B. Ferguson's "post mortem" gospel; the soul-chilling doctrine of Dr. Thomas' Elpis Israel; the "word alone" theory, and perhaps worldly conformity, have all contributed to its present depressed, uninfluential and lifeless condition.

The writer of this notice had supposed that the labors of such men as James Shannon, J. A. Dearborn, R. B. Roberts, Drs. John

---

[14]D. H. Johnston, "Topeka Church," *The Christian,* Vol. XV, No. 29 (July 19, 1877), p. 2.

[15]A. A. Glenn, "Christian Church, Wichita, Kansas," *American Christian Review,* Vol. XXIII, (August 3, 1880), p. 242.

R. McCall and A. A. Jones, William Edwin Hall and his potential "Iron Preacher," etc., had built up a large and influential church in this Southern city. He therefore expected to see crowded aisles and pews, of brethren residing in the city, and throngs of members of the church from Texas then in New Orleans, who were supposed to be anxious to hear a preacher of so much renown as David Walker. Imagine the writer's astonishment when, entering the auditorium, he saw a small assemblage of not more than forty, embracing in the number Sunday school scholars, teachers and visitors. A very intelligent looking brother engaged in teaching a class, consisting of one old colored sister, pointed toward the rostrum, and then, for the first time, I saw Dr. Walk. (the word doctor is used in its proper sense, teacher.) When Geranius found his father, "Marius, a destitute wanderer, a hunted outcast weeping amid the ruins of Carthage," he saw not a sadder countenance than that of Dr. Walk, at that time. The diminutive Sunday school was a sufficient explanation of the gloomy face. A brother named Allen, in a very sprightly and fluent way, expounded II. Tim. 1 to the Bible class of five or six men. He seemed to be anxious to teach, and, in his explanations, went doubtless was in earnest, and, perhaps, realized that expansion was as good as thoroughness. . .[16]

As the tide of immigration swept westward, members established small churches in the communities where they settled. At Denver, Colorado a small congregation was organized in May, 1873. Six years later another was established in the city, and A. I. Hobbs visited here in 1880 to attempt a union between them.

The tide of immigration swept across the prairies, scaled the mountains and rolled on to the coast of California. Brethren were plentiful enough in the state that already they were thinking about establishing their own schools. Pierce Christian College was located at College City in Colusa County, six miles west of the Sacramento River. It had an endowment of forty-five thousand dollars given to it by a Brother Pierce. W. J. Carpenter was president here in 1876. Hesperian College was located in Woodland, Yolo County, having a thirty-five thousand dollar endowment. B. H. Smith, formerly of Christian College, Missouri, was at this time the president. At Santa Rosa there was a Christian College built in 1872 by J. M. Martin. Florence College was located at Hollister. Alexander Johnson was president.[17]

---

[16]Zenas, "The Church of Christ in New Orleans," *Gospel Advocate*, Vol. XVII, No. 23 (June 10, 1885), p. 358.

[17]G. O. Burnett, "Our Colleges in California," *Apostolic Times*, Vol. VIII, (August 24, 1876), pp. 530, 531.

David Lipscomb declared that the 1880 census report of some thirty-eight thousand members was grossly an understatement. In middle Tennessee, where the influence of the *Gospel Advocate* was strongly felt, the church had a rapid growth. In West Tennessee the large growth was due largely to preachers like John R. Howard who had preached there much earlier. East Tennessee remained almost destitute of churches. By 1878 no effort had been made to establish the church in Chattanooga on a sound footing. Twenty members lived in that city of twelve thousand people, but there was no meeting house. The brethren of middle Tennessee neglected Chattanooga, and the General Missionary Society grasped the opportunity to plant itself in Tennessee by sending a preacher to the city. It gave the Society an inroad into the state and paved the way in a few more years for the establishment of a state missionary society.

Joseph Franklin visited Tennessee in the fall of 1877. At Gallatin he found a congregation but writes of it: "The congregation in Gallatin has been built up by a series of very successful protracted meetings under Brethren Hopson, Gano, and others, but seems to have been deficient in systematic and regular instruction of the Disciples."[18]   At Hendersonville a congregation had been established that spring. W. B. Wilson, a member of the Fourth and Walnut Streets church in Louisville, had moved to Hendersonville in the fall of 1876, where he went to work to build up a congregation. By the spring of 1877 it had only eight or ten members.

In Alabama, by 1885, the cause was still in its infant stages. There were no congregations in Athens, and Decatur, although a group of brethren were meeting in Huntsville. James A. Harding had held one or two very successful meetings here. At Tuscaloosa, a small church was established in 1881 by a Brother Beasley. At Falkville, there was a small church. Hartselle, thirteen miles south of Decatur had a congregation which was established in 1884. When V. M. Metcalfe visited Birmingham in 1882, he referred to it as a "magic city of ten thousand inhabitants" which had grown up in only ten years. There were more saloons in the city he thought, than any city he had ever

---

[18]Joseph Franklin, "Incidents of Travel in Tennessee," *American Christian Review,* Vol. XXI, No. 2 (January 8, 1878), p. 9.

seen, but no church after the New Testament order. Twelve members lived here in 1876 when J. M. Barnes arrived, but because they refused to hold regular meetings, Barnes would not return.

The cause in Alabama was hindered by the death of J. M. Pickens on February 3, 1881. Pickens lived in the northern part of the State and operated a small school near Mountain Home. T. B. Larimore, after leaving Franklin College, went to Pickens' home and taught school with him several months. This gave Larimore the idea for Mars Hill College. Pickens, however, was an excellent preacher, and did much to establish the cause in northern Alabama. But, on February 3, 1881, Pickens, with a young man by the name of William Davidson, walked down a road toward a neighbor's farm. Another youth jumped out of the bushes, shot at the Davidson man and killed him. Pickens knocked the gun from the killer's hand and ran. The assassin picked up the gun and shot Pickens three times, killing him instantly. Pickens was only forty-five years old, and ready to do his greatest work.[19]

A volume would be required to write the history of the church in each of the various states. These sketches can only convey a general impression of the growth of the cause.

STATUS QUO

In imparting a general view of the passing years something must be said about the state of the church.

A marked difference in the state of the brotherhood may be seen twenty years after the war. In the North the *Christian Standard* and the *American Christian Review* were locked in combat. Each paper represented a different type of thinking. Society as a whole was changing. The increase in population, the advancement of science, greater educational opportunities— these were inherent causes. The *Christian Standard,* keenly aware of this fact, assumed its greatest task to be that of redefining the earlier restoration principles in terms of the growing demand for progress. The *American Christian Review,* while not opposed to progress, clearly assailed the redefining process. The Bible truths were static, the Bible teaching the same thing in 1885 that it had taught in 1845, and any attempt to change the church, to alter

---

[19]Sarah E. Williams, "Particulars of the Death of J. M. Pickens," *Gospel Advocate,* Vol. XXIII, (February 17, 1881), p. 102.

the laws of God to conform with the changing environmental factors in society, the *Review* considered objectionable.

A point of contention was the familiar motto coined by Thomas Campbell in 1809: "Where The Bible Speaks, We Speak; Where The Bible is silent, We Are Silent." Isaac Errett saw that a redefining of this motto had to be made if the church was to conform to an age of progress. Errett therefore, wrote that Campbell meant *"that nothing should be urged as a term of Christian fellowship* for which there could not be a *thus saith the Lord."*[20] Errett declared that Campbell was too intelligent to teach that everything should be avoided in our religious belief and practice except those things for which there could not be found a "thus saith the Lord." W. K. Pendleton's address before the Society convention in 1866 had declared substantially the same thing. It is evident Errett's thunder was only that of Pendleton pitched in a higher key.

In January, 1884 John F. Rowe began a series of editorials in the *Review* on the explanation of the motto and directly attacked Errett's viewpoint. If Campbell meant that "nothing should be made a test of fellowship except that for which there could be found a thus saith the Lord," what an unusual principle this was on which to start a movement of restoration, wrote Rowe. What denomination ever wanted to make its peculiar beliefs and practices a test of fellowship anyway? If this be what Campbell meant, why not join the ranks of the denominations and give up this plea for restoration? Rowe saw in Errett's interpretation a trend toward making the church another denomination for every denomination wanted to be allowed to hold its basic peculiarities while fraternizing with others with different peculiarities. So Rowe wrote:

The serious trouble now with some of our people is, not that they wish to make *their* "human opinions and human inventions a term of communion," which, as a question of divine law and authority, does not seem to enter into their calculations; but the trouble is that there is a large party opposed, upon the authority of God's word, to the introduction of "human opinions," and especially "human inventions," "into the constitution, faith or worship of the church." If there is "no harm" in these innovations upon the prescribed order of heaven, why talk about "reforma-

---

[20]Isaac Errett, "The Basis of Christian Fellowship," *Christian Standard*, Vol. XIX, (January 12, 1884), p. 12.

tion" at all? Why talk of the restoration of the apostolic church? Why should we prate of Christian union upon the basis of the Bible? If we may infringe upon the order of heaven in one place, we may in every other place. Grant this assumption of power and "our providential mission" is at an end: we have already degenerated into a sect.[21]

The *Review,* therefore was prone to look upon the cause of restoration with great alarm. It seemed to them as though the *Christian Standard* would guide the church in complete departures from apostolic grounds. Innovations came into the church, with the encouragement of the *Standard.* The *Review* cried aloud of dangers, but the *Standard* was perfectly complacent. William Baxter, author of the biographies of Knowles Shaw and Walter Scott, a year before his death wrote to the *Review* in defense of the *Standard.* His articles were signed "BW," his initials reversed. He declared he could detect no dangers. To this Alfred Ellmore responded with a strongly worded article.

. . . Please read in the same paper an article from Brother G. W. Rice, in which he is straightening the crookedness of the *Standard* on mission work. He certainly knows that the *Standard is* and *has been,* for years, apologizing and excusing, which amounts to defending, the following list of departures, viz: The *organ and choir in worship; the employing of a* pastor *to take charge,* of the church, missionary societies, with their *salaried secretaries, ministerial associations,* etc. all of which are unknown to the New Testament.[22]

E. C. Weekly summarized the "status quo" in 1881 in the following words:

"Behold how good and how pleasant it is for brethren to dwell together in unity." The church of Christ, when first organized, was a unit: continued a unit until a human creed was made. We were once, as a religious people, a unit in our faith and worship. But how things have changed in some churches called Christian churches, within the last few years! Some of our editors and preachers are now contending for human institutions—organs, festivals, societies, etc.; while other editors and preachers are reviewing and exposing all such institutions and things as unscriptural and hurtful. Yet both parties say, "Where the Bible speaks, we speak; and where the Bible is silent we are silent."

[21]John F. Rowe, "The Silence of the Scriptures," *American Christian Review,* Vol. XXVII, (January 17, 1884), p. 20.
[22]Alfred Ellmore, "A Very Dull Scholar," *American Christian Review,* Vol. XXII, No. 7 (February 11, 1879), p. 53.

Yet they continue to controvert questions not found in the Bible. . .

Dear Brethren, do come back, and be satisfied with the purity and all-sufficiency of the holy Scriptures. Let us all unite once more in contending for the unity of the faith. "Let all envy and strife be put away from you and be kind one to another, forgiving one another as God for Christ's sake hath forgiven you.[23]

In summarizing the work for the year, 1877, J. A. Headington found sufficient cause for optimism.

Our own people, the chosen of God, during the past year have not been idle. Vast numbers have been added to the fold of Christ during the past year. Matters of doubt and uncertainty have been put to the test, weighed in the balances and found wanting. Great conventions, salaried secretaries and mammoth missionary schemes are below par at the closing out of the year 1877.[24]

PUBLICATIONS

Periodicals and books, spreading the plea for a return to the ancient order, were rushing from press telling effectively the story of the restoration.

On January 1, 1879 there was published at Louisville, Kentucky the first issue of the *Old Path Guide* by its editor Frank G. Allen, minister of the Portland Avenue Church. Its prospectus announced that it would be called *Apostolic Age,* but Allen, considering that it might be confused with the *Apostolic Times,* changed the name to *Old Path Guide.* Financially, the paper was a success. The first year netted the editor six hundred dollars, a tidy profit for those days. The *Guide* proved also to be a popular paper. Dealing less with the prominent issues than other periodicals, its pages contained solid material on the fundamental principles of Christianity. In stating the purpose of the *Old Path Guide,* F. G. Allen wrote:

In the providence of God the Old Path Guide is now started on its mission of love and loyalty to Christ. Its object will ever be to guide the world into the old paths in which men walked with God in the golden days of uncorrupted Christianity. Than this, it has no higher aspiration. That it may ever be true to this end, the divine aid is especially invoked. . .

---

[23]E. C. Weekly, "Condition of Things," *American Christian Review,* Vol. XXIV, No. 38 (September 20, 1881), p. 297.
[24]J. A. Headington, "The Passing Years," *American Christian Review,* Vol. XXI, No. 1 (January 1, 1878), p. 5.

F. G. ALLEN

The Old Path Guide has no sympathy with that form of liberalism which regards divine appointments necessary only for the weak—that divine legislation is not for strong men, but only for babes in Christ.[25]

Through sheer determination F. G. Allen had become a preacher of considerable influence in the brotherhood. His early childhood

---

[25]F. G. Allen, "Introduction," *Old Path Guide,* Vol. I, No. 1 (January, 1879), p. 1.

was not different from that of other pioneer boys in Kentucky. There were the same hardships—endless hard labor on the farm plus little or no opportunity for education. It was on March 7, 1836 that Sarah A. Allen gave birth to Frank G., her fifth child. But she was to be the mother of eight more of Francis Allen's children, and the thirteen were to present no easy task at rearing.

Both parents were Methodists, but not "fussy about it." His mother was not a "shouting" Methodist. His father though religiously inclined could never "get religion" at the Methodist altar. Despite this fact he believed Methodist doctrines, and lived and died a member of that church. Allen at the age of ten, joined the Methodists during a revival near his home at LeGrange, Kentucky. Even as a boy, he enjoyed church services. Years later Allen could remember the texts and the sermons the Methodist preachers delivered in his early youth. He wrote: "I had high regard for preachers, and from early life was fond of their company; and since I have become one myself, the society of good, faithful men of God brings me as near heaven as I shall ever be in the flesh.[26]

Occasionally Allen showed indications of a great character. He was an average boy in that he liked to hunt, and enjoyed too, being slightly mischievous. Many honestly believed that he would some day be a criminal and be hanged. Even his own father held this conviction. There were, however, glimpses of greatness in him. From the coon skins he sold he would purchase books to study by the fireplace. By sheer determination he overcame physical handicaps and frail health. He had the markings of an outstanding person, once the spark could be ignited in him that would cause him to put his full powers to work toward one, worthwhile goal.

Allen met Jennie Maddox in the summer of 1855 while he was working as a harvest hand for her uncle, and it appeared to be a case of "love at first sight." September 11, 1856 they were married. His wife's father, G. W. Maddox was an elder at Pleasant Hill Church in Oldham County, Kentucky. He was one of the most enlightened men on the Scriptures in the brotherhood. Allen became attached to his father-in-law, and learned the gospel from him. He was slow to accept the truth, since he

---

[26]Robert Graham, *Autobiography of Frank G. Allen* (Cincinnati: Guide Printing and Publishing Company, 1887), p. 13.

had looked upon "Campbellism" as the worst of all heresies. He discussed religious subjects at great length with his father-in-law, and in May, 1861 was baptized by William Tharp during a meeting at Pleasant Hill.

In August, 1862 Allen entered Emminence College. It was not easy for a married man with a family and no money to attend school. But he rented a house and three acres of ground at the edge of town so he could raise hogs. His wife raised chickens. Knowing he was short of funds, Allen decided to work more strenuously and crowd four years of school work into two. He was the only married man in the classes—that is, until J. B. Briney came along a year later to join him. However, by working too hard, Allen ruined his health, and was never again well. At Emminence, Allen formed a close friendship with I. B. Grubbs that remained through life.

Leaving school in 1864, Allen went first to Campbell County, Kentucky where he opened a school of his own. He preached some in the neighborhood, too. For the next ten years Allen preached, taught school, and conducted religious debates. In 1876 he became an editor on the *Apostolic Times* with I. B. Grubbs and Samuel A. Kelley. In 1879, while living in Louisville and preaching for the Portland Avenue church he began publication of the *Old Path Guide.*

The major publications of the brotherhood from the close of the war to 1885 remained the *Christian Standard, American Christian Review, Gospel Advocate,* and the *Apostolic Times.* The *Old Path Guide,* new in the field of religious journalism in 1879, realized great prominence through its short life. In 1885 it united with the *Apostolic Times* to form the *Apostolic Guide.* The *Times* and *Guide* each represented that type of thinking characteristic of the brethren in middle Kentucky for thirty years after the war. McGarvey, Grubbs, Allen, Lard, and S. A. Kelley each believed in organized societies and defended them vigorously upon the ground of expediency. They were, on the other hand, bitter enemies of the instrument in worship. Men of their mind in middle Kentucky were slow to agree that both the society and the instrument stood on the same principle. As the fact slowly dawned on many, the "middle ground" faded away. It was evident, therefore, to many of those central Kentucky preachers that some adjustment had to be made in their positions. F. G.

Allen showed signs of seeing the error of societies when death came to him in 1885. J. B. Briney, a devotee of the "middle ground" made his adjustment by adhering to the instrument, although in his earlier years he was staunchly against it. McGarvey himself was the last of the die-hards of the position. In his later years he moved from one congregation to another as the instrument was introduced, refusing to worship with one.

Various smaller periodicals exercised an almost entirely local influence. They were effective, however, as far as their influence went. In Missouri, the *Christian Pioneer* began republication in 1872. D. T. Wright and John R. Howard had issued the first number in 1861. Wright continued the publication until November, 1870. The first of 1872 he began to republish the paper, now having W. C. Rogers as co-editor, and putting it forth weekly from Chillicothe, Missouri.[27] *The Christian,* another Missouri publication, which later joined with *The Evangelist* to form the *Christian-Evangelist,* will be noticed in another chapter.

Early in 1876 W. E. Hall of New Orleans sent forth the first issue of the *Iron Preacher.* This paper was a successor of the *Southern Christian Weekly.* The same year the *Texas Christian* took the place of the *Texas Christian Monthly.* The Wilmeth brothers, J. R. and C. M., published it from McKinney.

Aside from periodicals, brethren were now giving considerable attention to writing books. In the spring of 1863, during the darkest days of the Civil War, McGarvey had sent forth his commentary on Acts. McGarvey was a young man—a little beyond thirty years of age—and to the present day his commentary has proved to be among the most popular books in the brotherhood. In presenting his commentary McGarvey wrote:

I have now ready for the press a commentary on Acts of Apostles, to the preparation of which, I have devoted all the time which I could spare from my ministerial labors, for three and a half years. The peculiarities of the work are chiefly these.

1st. It presents the real meaning of the text, as developed in the writings and teaching of our brotherhood, the only people of modern times who have understood and appreciated this book.

2nd. On every passage which presents any of the great issues of the day, the question is argued in full. In this way nearly all

---

[27]D. T. Wright, "Prospectus of the Christian Pioneer for 1872—Vol. 11," *Apostolic Times,* Vol. III, No. 45 (February 15, 1872), p. 354.

the issues which we have formed with the sectarian world come up for discussion in the course of the work.

3rd. It is adapted to circulation among sectarians and the unconverted, and contains much matter designed for the edification of the brethren.

4th. It contains a complete biography of Paul, the blanks in his history left by Luke being filled up with facts derived from the epistles.

5th. It contains a revision of the text, in which the common version is modernized and corrected.

6th. The text and comments are so confined that the latter will not read like a dictionary, as in most commentaries, but the whole will be continuous and connected, like any other book. It is a book to be read, and not merely a book of reference.[28]

The appearance of McGarvey's commentary on Acts in 1863 set off a wave of interest in commentaries on the New Testament. Brethren dreamed of the day in the near future when an entire set, written by the more scholarly men connected with the restoration would be before the world. Bosworth, Chase and Hall, prominent publishers of brotherhood books, announced in 1871 that eleven volumes of New Testament commentaries to be called "The New Testament Commentary" were in preparation. The writers were J. W. McGarvey, W. K. Pendleton, J. S. Lamar, Isaac Errett, C. L. Loos, Robert Richardson, W. T. Moore and Robert Milligan. A meeting was held in Cincinnati that year with the publisher and the writers to make all arrangements.[29] As it worked out only McGarvey, Lamar, and Milligan completed their assignments.

McGarvey's commentary on Acts has never been surpassed by any writer connected with the restoration. It was eagerly awaited by the brotherhood at large. Ben Franklin wrote:

The work he now proposes to bring before the people is one of much importance and merit, and we are assured it will have a widely extended and profitable circulation. It is a commentary on the part of the New Testament most needed and one of the kind demanded. We are satisfied this work will meet the expectation of the brotherhood as fully as any book that has appeared for many years.[30]

---

[28]J. W. McGarvey, "A New Commentary on Acts," *Millennial Harbinger,* Fifth Series, Vol. VI, No. 5 (May, 1863), p. 211.

[29]Bosworth, Chase and Hall, "A New Commentary," *Gospel Advocate,* Vol. XIII, No. 12 (February 23, 1871), pp. 279, 280.

[30]Ben Franklin, "The New Commentary on Acts," *American Christian Review,* Vol. VI, No. 19 (May 12, 1863), p. 74.

W. K. Pendleton received his copy soon after its publication, and wrote of McGarvey's book:

The good sense and sound judgment of its laborious and ingenious author are more and more revealed at every reading. One feels safe in following Brother McGarvey, for it is evident that he is conscientiously particular as to where he leads us. He loves the truth, and would go very far out of his way to correct even his own errors. Such men are not apt to recklessly impose upon others as accurate and certain, that of which they are themselves in doubt.[31]

David Lipscomb, who had a reputation for considerable reservation in giving praise, was jubilant with McGarvey's work:

Whatever may be the minor faults of his production, we think it one of the best volumes that has been issued from the press for a number of years. As a commentary upon this most important portion of Sacred Scripture, and upon the plan of introduction into the Kingdom of Heaven, therein developed, for clearness and justness of conception, and as an aid in understanding the varied instructions and allusions of the divine teachers, by a thorough inquiry into the different circumstances and stand points from which they spoke, it is superior to any work known to us. We heartily commend it to all of our readers who feel an interest in the understanding of this most interesting and important part of Holy Writ.[32]

W. H. Hopson not only commended the book, but issued with a valuable suggestion. He wrote of the book, "I regard it as a felicitous performance, decidedly creditable to the author and to Bethany College, his Alma Mater, and eminently useful to the cause of truth." Hopson then suggested that Moses E. Lard undertake a writing of a commentary on Romans; that W. K. Pendleton undertake to write on Hebrews, and C. L. Loos on John. He then suggested that others undertake writing until the whole New Testament is completed.[33]

Not all, however, hailed McGarvey's work as being so praiseworthy. John Shackleford, writing in the *Independent Monthly* in 1869 complained that it was published too soon; that five or six more years should have been given to it. Those knowing the bitterness with which Schackleford and his co-editor, L. D.

---

[31]W. K. Pendleton, "Commentary on Acts of Apostles," *Millennial Harbinger,* Fifth Series, Vol. VII, No. 1 (January, 1864), p. 38.

[32]David Lipscomb, "New Publications," *Gospel Advocate,* Vol. VIII, No. 1 (January 1, 1866), p. 10.

[33]W. H. Hopson, "A Suggestion," *Millennial Harbinger,* Vol. XXXVII, No. 1 (January, 1866), p. 43.

Pinkerton, were assailing the brotherhood on many points, will be likely to take his criticism with the proverbial grain of salt. He complained that McGarvey goes at the law of pardon much as a lawyer goes at a contract. McGarvey was, however, coldly logical and almost destitute of sentimentality.

Completion of the writings on the New Testament were not made altogether according to plans. Moses E. Lard announced in 1865 his intention to write a commentary on Romans. Eight years passed and the work was still not finished, Lard scarcely finding the time to proceed. In 1873 he went into almost complete oblivion, brethren frequently inquiring what became of him. An occasional reply came back that he was busy, writing his commentary. Finally, at the close of 1875 Lard announced that his commentary had been turned over to the printer.

McGarvey on Matthew and Mark; Lamar on Luke and Milligan on Hebrews were all forthcoming about the same time.

Aside from writing commentaries, increased interest was shown in other fields of writing. Attention to biographical material was manifest. After the death of Alexander Campbell in 1866, Robert Richardson produced the classic history of the restoration, his biography of Campbell. Thirty years earlier when Richardson had approached Campbell, revealing his ambition, Campbell was receptive. Campbell was only dead a short time when his widow asked Richardson to start the biography. Richardson's eyes were bad, so his daughter, Emma, was conscripted for amanuensis. It was his intention to complete the work in one volume, but it became evident that two would be necessary—possibly three. After completing the first volume in the summer of 1868, Richardson sent a copy to his friend, John R. Howard, accompanied with the following letter:

When I last wrote to you, I hoped to be able to comprise the whole in one volume, but afterwards found it best to make two vols., and publish them consecutively. Indeed to carry out my plan fully would require at least *three* vols., such as I send you. I must however endeavor to embrace what remains in another of equal size.[34]

The book required three years to be written, and was a financial loss for Richardson. He paid all publication costs himself, but the sale of the book was so limited that he lost money.

---

[34] John R. Howard, "Memoirs of Alexander Campbell," *Christian Standard,* Vol. III, No. 33 (August 15, 1868), p. 258.

Since Richardson's death falls within the score of years now being surveyed, a brief sketch of his life will not be out of order. A. E. Meyers visited the Richardson home early in the spring of 1876 and found him recovering from a stroke of paralysis which had come to him on February 18. His general health appeared good. Meyers commented that he "can not articulate any words distinctly," and was only with great difficulty that he could write at all.

On the morning of October 22 Richardson arose before six o'clock, apparently quite well. It was the Lord's Day. The morning was spent in reading the Scriptures, and afterward, Richardson ate a hearty lunch. That afternoon he took a little walk, then he retired earlier than usual. Suddenly the family heard unusually heavy breathing from his room, and dashed to see about him. It was evident that Richardson had another stroke. Without uttering another word, he slipped quietly into death. Three days later his body was laid to rest in the cemetery at Bethany.

Born in Pittsburgh, Pennsylvania on September 27, 1806, Richardson was the son of a wealthy Irish merchant, Nathanael Richardson. Although Episcopalian in religious background, the Richardson home became the stopping-off-place for Thomas and Alexander Campbell and more frequently, of Walter Scott. Scott early became Richardson's idol, for Richardson attended his school at Pittsburgh and later rode horseback many miles to get Scott to immerse him. He attended a medical school at Philadelphia and became a doctor.

Richardson, however, did not limit his interests to the medical profession, for he was first a Christian. He was a preacher, teacher and writer as well. As a preacher, he was somewhat diffident. His thoughts were excellent, but his flow of words was very uneven, making his sermons boresome to an audience. In any of the great gatherings of the brotherhood Richardson was never a featured speaker. In 1830 he began writing for the *Millennial Harbinger* under the title, "Discipulus." He was an elder in the Bethany church and a teacher in the college for twenty years.

The popular reputation Richardson has gained depicts him as a mild-tempered, soft spoken individual. This was not always the case. I. B. Grubbs says of him, "When earnestly opposing what he deemed seriously erroneous, he was somewhat caustic, and was sarcastic to a degree that made him formidable to an opponent."[35] Isaac Errett wrote:

Pure in life, studious in habit, retiring in his disposition, unostentatious in his labors, supremely devoted to truth for truth's sake, his service to the cause of Christ were great and valuable, and his genuine merit was greater than his fame. His real worth was known only to the few that were intimately acquainted with him.[36]

The publication of the *Life of Elder John Smith* caused a minor upheaval of animosity between the *Christian Standard* and the *Apostolic Times*. Petty jealousies were frequent. The *Christian Standard* in 1869 was near bankruptcy. The *Times,* on the other hand, was just beginning, its outstanding corps of ambitious editors probably a little ashamed that the subscription was no higher than it was. When on August 21, 1869 it was announced that the *Standard* would begin carrying in serial form John A. William's biography of Smith, which later would be put in book form, The *Times* vigorously protested. Obviously they had been outmaneuvered. Nevertheless, William's biography did increase the *Standard's* circulation and helped to put it over the crisis.

Two years before Robert Milligan announced to the world his publication *Reason and Revelation* the object of which was to set forth the province of reason in "matters pertaining to divine revelation," and to "vindicate the paramount authority of the Sacred Scriptures." The book was widely acclaimed as a leader in its field, but *Time,* the true evaluator of all books, was not so generous. David Lipscomb wrote of "Reason and Revelation":

Our author has done this work well. His reasoning is sometimes faulty; his conclusions on minor and secondary matters is not always correct, and his exegesis of scripture, in one or two instances, is not the proper one from our stand point. Yet the work as a whole is good, and far surpasses any work on these subjects known to us.[37]

One other major publication work occuring during these years needs some attention. In 1880 McGarvey's *Lands of The Bible*

---

[35] I. B. Grubbs, "Dr. Robert Richardson," *Apostolic Times,* Vol. VIII (November 9, 1876), p. 712.
[36] Isaac Errett, "Death of Dr. R. Richardson," *Christian Standard,* Vol. XI, (November 4, 1876), p. 349.
[37] David Lipscomb, "A New Work," *Gospel Advocate,* Vol. IX, No. 45 (November 7, 1867), p. 895.

was published. This book related to McGarvey's studies a year earlier in Palestine.

On Saturday, March 1, 1879 McGarvey celebrated his fiftieth birthday. The next day he preached at a joint meeting of the congregations in Lexington, a farewell sermon. The following day at three o'clock he left for Palestine. Monday morning McGarvey walked upstairs to his library, and looking for a moment over his books, he spoke aloud: "Good by, my dear old friends; and if I never see you again, God bless you for the good you have done me, and the happy hours we have spent together." Downstairs, he went to the kitchen to tell the servants good by. The old colored servant, Jim, was morose. He wanted to go to Palestine, too. But McGarvey joked that a whale might swallow him up to which Jim replied, "If he do, I can't he'p it. I want to go anyhow. I ain't never seen nuthin' and I want to see somethin' before I die." The work at the Broadway Church was turned over to H. Turner. Robert Graham and I. B. Grubbs agreed to keep the College of the Bible going. So that afternoon, McGarvey took the train for Philadelphia.

On March 5, 1879 on board the steamer, "Pennsylvania" McGarvey sailed for England. With him were his cousins, Frank Thomson, a farmer who lived near Lexington and W. B. Taylor of Elizabethtown, Kentucky, a former student of the Bible College.[38] McGarvey sent regular dispatches to the *Christian Standard* while W. B. Taylor wrote regular articles for the *Gospel Advocate*. It was on this trip that McGarvey drowned. The claim was his heart had stopped, but he was brought back in a matter of moments to life. Upon his return to Lexington, McGarvey wrote his book based upon his travels in the holy land.

THE PASSING PREACHERS

The years which now occupy our attention witness the passing of H. T. Anderson, a preacher known chiefly for his translation of the New Testament from Greek into English. His death occurred September 19, 1872 in Washington D. C. His last years were decidedly unfortunate ones. In his old age he could preach little. His business management had been very poor, and for

---

[38]J. W. McGarvey, "Letters of Travel," *Christian Standard,* Vol. XIV, No. 11 (March 15, 1879), p. 81.

his financial maintainence he was at the mercy of the brotherhood. His association was mostly among the Baptists. He evidenced decided leanings in their direction. Baptists were quick to take advantage of it, and from that day to this Anderson has been quoted frequently, much to the embarrassment of many gospel preachers.

Around 1870 a movement was started, repeated every few years since, of a reunion with the Baptists. T. J. Melish, once a member of the church, went to the Baptists. Later he left them and went to the Episcopalians. At this time, he was editing a Baptist periodical, *Journal And Messenger*. Early in 1871 Anderson wrote for the *Journal And Messenger* articles favoring the Baptists. He wrote:

I must be permitted to say for myself that I have been with the Disciples for nearly forty years, and I know them. . . I now have to say, after studying the Scriptures for forty years, and after having made a second translation of the New Testament, that the dispensation of the Gospel is a dispensation of grace; as such it must be received into the heart by faith and love, not by work or works.[39]

The implication the Baptists saw was, of course, that baptism was not necessary to salvation.

It was one of Anderson's conviction that the "form" of expressions used by the brotherhood were standing in the way of a union with the Baptists. These "forms" he deprecated. So he says,

I am in favor of a union with the Baptists, and I believe in it. My purpose in writing was to state, sharply, what I understood to be obstacles in the way of union, and to remove those obstacles. I think I have already affected some good in that direction. I know my brethren. I know that they have certain *forms of words* current among them, that are hindrances to their own progress. "Baptism for the remission of sins," is one of those forms; "law of pardon" is another. I know that for more than forty years they have been explaining themselves, and are yet unexplained. The form of words, "baptism for the remission of sins," is unexplainable, and should be thrown out of use. No one believes it, and yet it is constantly used.

. . . . You teach, "Baptism for the remission of sins." I teach,

---

[39] Isaac Errett, "H. T. Anderson on the Disciples," *Christian Standard,* Vol. VI, No. 8 (February 25, 1871).

"Christ crucified for the remission of sins." Which of us is most likely to reach the Baptists?[40]

In Anderson's case it is little wonder the brotherhood did not understand him, and so refused to support him.

These passing years also bring to our attention the death of James T. Barclay, whose last years were spent in northern Alabama. From the day he became ill—October 20, 1874—until his death, his son, J. J. Barclay was constantly by his side. At noon on Wednesday, October 28, at the age of 68 years, he died. The next day J. M. Pickens preached the funeral.[41]

The passing of Dr. L. L. Pinkerton should be briefly noted. In the more recent years Pinkerton's prominence in the brotherhood declined so that he was seldom used as a preacher. An unknown writer pens in the *Apostolic Times* a pathetically candid article:

It is well known to our readers that for some years past he has been to a great extent alienated from the Christian Church, having adopted some views in religious matters which were in direct antagonism with cherished convictions of the Disciples, and having become involved in much personal animosity toward conspicuous brethren. During this period he has not held membership in any congregation, and his services as a preacher ceased to be in demand, so that he sought secular employment and was, at the time of his death, employed by the Federal Government as a detective in the mail service.[42]

President Robert Milligan of the College of The Bible in Lexington went to his death on March 22, 1875. His life has been sketched in our first volume. J. W. McGarvey preached his funeral, and in it related an incident instructive of the value of guarding one's Christian influence. During the days of Milligan's illness, the doctor recommended a drink of whiskey for its medicinal value, but Milligan refused. He pointed out to the doctor that he was the president of the College of The Bible and that he would rather die sooner than allow some action of his cause one of the young men in the school to stumble. Richardson, then, very appropriately wrote of Milligan:

---

[40]H. T. Anderson, "H. T. Anderson's Reply," *Christian Standard,* Vol. VI, No. 12 (March 25, 1871), p. 90.

[41]Robert Richardson, "Dr. J. T. Barclay," *Christian Standard,* Vol. IX, (1874), p. 364.

[42]Anonymous, "Dr. L. L. Pinkerton," *Apostolic Times,* Vol. VII (1875), p. 32.

To the church here, however, the loss of Brother Milligan is no common calamity. High in position, great in influence, eminent in example, abundant in labors, his relations to the brotherhood at large were coextensive with the reformatory movement in which we are engaged, and to which he has been in many respects a valuable auxiliary. So amiable was he in spirit, so gentle and unobtrusive, so free from self-assertion and pretension, that his departure and the cessation of his labors may alone enable the brotherhood to realize their value and to appreciate properly the power of that beneficent influence which he constantly exerted while quietly and faithfully fulfilling the various public duties in which he was engaged.[43]

On October 10, 1871 at Columbia, Missouri died one of the great in Missouri preachers. Thomas Miller Allen stood beside Samuel Rogers as foremost in establishing churches early in Missouri. T. M. Allen was born in the Shenandoah Valley in Virginia on October 21, 1797. Both of his parents died when he was but a child. At the age of seventeen he enlisted as a volunteer in Captain Peter Hay's Company and served six months in a regiment of the Virginia Militia in the war with Great Britain.

The familiar figure of T. M. Allen around Missouri always was of a stout man with a crippled arm at his side. On May 10, 1816 he was returning to Virginia from a visit to Kentucky when six miles west of Washington, Pennsylvania a violent storm struck. A tree suddenly fell across his path, killing his horse and a young lady companion riding beside him. Allen received the crippled arm.

On March 24, 1818 he was married to Rebecca W. Russell, Barton W. Stone performing the ceremony. He settled on a farm near Lexington and studied law at Transylvania University. Allen was a Mason, being master of the lodge of which Henry Clay was a member. In 1822 he moved to Bloomington, Indiana where he practiced law. His law partner was James Whitcomb, who was later elected Governor of Indiana and then still later a United States Senator from Indiana.

Allen moved back to Kentucky early in 1823. In May of that year he was immersed by Barton W. Stone. He had heard Stone and E. R. Palmer preach at the residence of General Robert S.

---

[43]Robert Richardson, "Robert Milligan," *Christian Standard,* Vol. X (April 10, 1875), p. 116.

Russell who resided on North Elkhorn in Fayette County, Kentucky. Thereafter, Allen went to work for the Lord. He was a member of the "Old Union" congregation in Fayette County which Stone established with six members. In the spring of 1825 Allen began preaching.[44]

In the fall of 1836 he purchased a farm on Two Mile prairie in Boone County, Missouri. After settling here, he was influential in establishing congregations throughout the state. He proved to be moderately wealthy due to exceptionally good business judgment and successful farming. Before the war, he had been able to purchase several slaves. Their attachment became so great that when they were freed following the war, they refused to leave the Allen home.

Early in February, 1880 William Baxter went from his home in New Lisbon, Ohio to Newcastle, Pennsylvania for a meeting. Suddenly he became ill with typhoid fever. On February 11th he, too, passed away. Three days later Alanson Wilcox preached the funeral at New Lisbon.

Baxter was born in Leeds, Yorkshire, England on July 16, 1820, and came to America when he was eight years old. Although his parents belonged to the Church of England, young Baxter was baptized by Samuel Church into the Methodist Church at Allegheny City. Church later became one of the foremost proclaimers of the return to the ancient order, although in these early days he was in the Methodist. In 1841, after becoming converted to the restoration, Baxter entered Bethany College. Upon graduation, he preached a year in Pittsburgh, and then three years at Port Gibson, Mississippi. Later he preached at Baton Rouge, Louisiana. The war years he spent at Fayetteville, Arkansas with Robert Graham. After the war, he preached for the Sixth Street church in Cincinnati for two years before finally moving to New Lisbon.

Baxter was outstanding for his writings. He contributed several poems to the *Millennial Harbinger*. His book, *"Pea Ridge and Prairie Grove"* is one of the best stories of the activities of the brethren during the Civil War to be found. Later, he wrote

---

[44]Anonymous, "Death of Elder T. M. Allen," *Apostolic Times,* Vol. III, No. 30 (November 2, 1871), p. 235.

biographies of Walter Scott and Knowles Shaw. In these writings he gained fame, but was never an outstanding preacher.

The death of James Challen should be noted. Challen, born at Hackensack, New Jersey on January 29, 1802, died in Cincinnati on December 9, 1878. Challen's early life was spent near Lexington, his parents moving here when he was only seven. In earlier life he was skeptical of all religion, but under James Fishback, one of Kentucky's foremost Baptist preachers, was led into the Baptist denomination. After graduating from old Transylvania University, Challen preached for the Enon Baptist Church in Cincinnati. Through reading the *Christian Baptist* he was converted to the restoration, and led most of the Baptist Church to apostolic principles.

In 1834, after the death of his father and younger brother, Challen went to Lexington again, and established the Main Street congregation. In 1850 he moved to Philadelphia where he preached eight years. He moved, then, to Davenport, Iowa for ten years, and finally back to Cincinnati where he preached until he died.[45]

John O'Kane, pioneer preacher of Indiana, died on January 5, 1881. He had established the first congregation in Indianapolis in 1833. Out of the fifty-six years he had preached the gospel, twenty-seven had been spent in Indiana.

O'Kane was born in Rockbridge County, Virginia on September 22, 1802. His father, Henry O'Kane, was a scholarly schoolteacher, and left an imprint on his son which never left him. John O'Kane became an unusually good Bible scholar, being very proficient in Greek, and having an excellent knowledge of Biblical criticism. Joseph Thomas, the "white pilgrim" baptized young O'Kane in 1825, and almost immediately O'Kane began to preach.

Around 1830 O'Kane read an article in the *Christian Messenger* on baptism written by James Matthews. It caused O'Kane to completely change his views on baptism. Two years after this, O'Kane moved to Milton, Indiana and thus began his long life of work in this state.

He had the personal appearance of a good preacher. His slender six feet, two inch body stood erect, making O'Kane the embodiment of dignity in the pulpit. His voice was deep and solemn. He

---

[45]Isaac Errett, "Death of Elder James Challen," *Christian Standard,* Vol. XIII (December 14, 1878), p. 400.

stood nearly perfectly still all the time he preached. He was not eloquent, but his earnestness was impressive to an audience.

He was laid to rest in Bellefontaine cemetery in St. Louis.[46]

These events, then, present the reader some idea of what was transpiring between the close of the war and the year, 1885.

---

[46]L. H. Jameson, "John O'Kane," *American Christian Review,* Vol. XXIV, (March 15, 1881), p. 81.

CHAPTER X

A CHRISTIAN PRESIDENT

The attention of the brethren turned in June, 1880 toward the nation's capitol. There was a very definite reason. One of its members, a prominent gospel preacher was nominated by the Republican convention that year as its presidential nominee. The following November the public elected him to the nation's highest office—the presidency of the United States. James Abram Garfield had traveled that difficult road from the log cabin in the wilderness of Cuyahoga County, Ohio to the White House. It was a long, rough and toilsome way, but Garfield by sheer determination accomplished the fete.

There was nothing new in a leading member of the church seeking a political office. R. M. Bishop, an elder in the church in Cincinnati, was mayor of the city during the Civil War, and was elected Governor of Ohio in 1874. The father of D. S. Burnet, Jacob Burnet, was mayor of Cincinnati in earlier days. In 1880 preachers of the church apparently became very much interested in politics. D. R. Dungan, that year, was a candidate for Governor of Iowa but was defeated. J. M. Pickens ran for Governor of Alabama the same year and also was defeated. The citizens of Indiana got out a petition urging O. A. Burgess to run for Governor on the Republican ticket, but the urge was not strong enough to get him the candidacy. R. M. Gano of Dallas, Texas, one of the brotherhood's prominent Texas preachers, was urged by the Greenbackers of Texas to run for Governor, but Gano refused. The *Christian Preacher* wrote, "Brother Gano could do more good preaching the gospel than ten Congressmen could making laws, even if they always made good ones. The Gospel of Christ is superior to the Greenback gospel." Still later, Ira J. Chase was governor of Indiana in 1892. Chase was one of Indiana's gospel preachers before running for Lieutenant-Governor. J. A. Brooks was vice-presidential nominee on the Prohibition ticket in 1888.

The Populist State Convention of Texas nominated Addison Clark for Superintendent of Public Instruction in 1894. David

197

JAMES A. GARFIELD

Lipscomb complained that gospel preachers were forsaking the pulpit and seeking honors in governmental positions. From the small village to the nation, church members were filling offices ranging from constables now to the presidency. This tendency touches a study of the restoration on its periphery, and a consideration of it is of value to this total study to see the different points of view aroused in James A. Garfield's election to the presidency.

In 1831 the Western Reserve, in northeastern Ohio, was a dense wilderness, the scattered population being predominately New Englanders. James A. Garfield's parents were typical of the inhabitants. Abram, Garfield's father, was born in December, 1799. His mother, Eliza Ballou, was born in Richmond, New Hampshire on September 21, 1801. Both had immigrated from New England to the promising lands to their west. Settling in Cuyahoga County, they built a log cabin thirty by twenty feet long consisting of one door and three windows, and a puncheon floor. The roof was made of oak clapboards held down by long weight poles. The family slept on straw in the attic.

James Abram Garfield was born in this log cabin on November 19, 1831. The hardy pioneer parents worked hard to have a home for the children. In May, 1833 the beginning of a tragedy occurred. A forest fire broke out. The neighbors pitted their efforts against this demon of nature, finally conquering it, but Abram exhausted himself, caught cold and died. James A. was now only eighteen months old. The rearing of the family was left up to Garfield's mother who patiently labored to provide for it, and guide the children. Consequently, Garfield had a respect for his mother in later years that caught the admiration of the nation.

Garfield's brother, Tom, was eight years older. At night they slept together in the attic. Garfield would often kick the covers off, and half awake, would cry, "Thomas, cover me up." After a battle during the Civil War, Garfield lay on the ground beside a distinguished Union officer. The covers came off, and Garfield murmured in his sleep, "Thomas, cover me up." The words awakened him. Memories of the childhood days drifted before his eyes. He covered his face and wept softly.

At the age of sixteen, Garfield agreed to cut wood at twenty-five cents a cord and his board for his uncle who lived near Newburgh. All the while he entertained the dream of being a sailor. The idea was a disappointment to his mother who desired for her son something greater. But she patiently acquiesced temporarily in his planning, thinking the dream might be exploded. In July, 1847 Garfield went to Cleveland to a cousin, Amos Letcher, and secured a position running a boat on the Ohio and Pennsylvania Canal. At the end of the summer, he returned to his home, still determined to become a sailor, and thoroughly satisfied with himself for the summer's work.

Wise guidance was now needed. The mother suggested that he go to school so that he could teach school in the winter and work at the canal in the summer. Her hope was that an education would make him forget the canal work. The plan worked perfectly. Through the influence of Samuel D. Bates, a gospel preacher who lived at Marion, Ohio, Garfield decided to enter Geauga Seminary at Chester. So, on March 6, 1849 he presented himself to this school. The next winter he taught school, and the following spring returned to Geauga. During the summer of 1850 he worked as a carpenter near Chester, and that winter, returned to the seminary once more.

That same fall, Western Reserve Eclectic Institute was born at Hiram, Portage County, Ohio with A. S. Hayden as president. Garfield continued to finish his term at Geauga, and the following year transferred to the Eclectic Institute. He remained here until the fall of 1854 when he transferred to Williams College to study under the famous educator, Mark Hopkins. He graduated from this school in 1856 taking the highest honors in the class, and then, returned to Hiram to become president of the Eclectic Institute, a position he held until he entered the Ohio State legislature.

GARFIELD'S RELIGION

Elder A. A. Lillie went to a school house at Organge in March, 1850 to conduct a meeting. The school was located about forty rods from where Garfield was reared. During the meeting, Garfield came to him privately, frankly admitting that he had some skepticism, and asking for reassurance that the Bible was the word of God. Lillie, instead of censuring the boy for his doubt, admired his frankness and absolute honesty in seeking after truth. The next night, he preached a sermon on "What Is Truth?" that thoroughly satisfied Garfield's inquiring mind. At the close of the sermon, Garfield and seven others stepped forward. The next day all were baptized. The date was March 4, 1849.[1]

From his mother Garfield had learned the practical walks of the Christian life. Upon his leaving home, she asked him to remember that every evening at sunset she would be reading the Bible. It became Garfield's practice through life to pause at sunset and read the Bible, for he had the consciousness that he was now reading with his mother. Likewise did she teach him to

---

[1] F. M. Green, *A Royal Life* (Chicago: Central Book Concern, 1882), p. 153.

pray. While in the army, Garfield never forgot this, and was often referred to as the "praying colonel." Moreover, he was always faithful to meet with the church for worship. He met with the church in Washington D. C. for the first time in the fall of 1861 while he was yet in the army. Later, when president, Garfield attended every service, even to the regular social gatherings. He mixed and mingled with the people, shook hands with them, and inquired of their personal health. It was his constant conviction that "there is nothing that can make youth so shapeful, manhood so strong, and old age so beautiful, as the religion of Jesus Christ."

The first sermon Garfield preached was at Hiram in the winter of 1853-54. After that, he was a popular speaker in the town. Garfield and Alexander Campbell met in August, 1860. Campbell was then seventy-two and Garfield was only twenty-nine. The meeting was at Alliance, Ohio. Campbell preached in the morning, and Garfield spoke in the afternoon. In a letter dated June 19, 1855 Garfield wrote to a friend:

Your favor of the 4th inst was received about ten days ago, but I have been entirely unable to answer until this time. A day or two after it came I left for Pittstown, New York, to attend a yearly meeting of Disciples, where I spent some four days, and last Saturday I left again for Poestenkill, and spoke to the people Saturday evening, and three discourses on Lord's Day. . . We had good meetings in each place, and much interest. I cannot resist the appeals of our brethren for aid while I have the strength to speak to them. . . I tell you, my dear brother, the cause in which we are engaged must take the world. It fills my soul when I reflect upon the light, joy and love of the ancient gospel, and its adaptation to the wants of the human race. . . I long to be in the thickest of the fight, and see the army of truth charge home upon the battalions of hoary-headed error. . .[2]

Garfield's regard for the religious conception he espoused may be easily seen. While in later years, his political career far overshadowed his religious, he remained faithful to Christ until his death. His preaching was often criticized, it is said, by the older pioneers in that it dealt more in the ethical realm than upon the "first principles." Still members of the church never doubted his allegiance to these principles.

In the halls of Congress he later gained much fame as a debater

---

[2]F. M. Green, *A Royal Life,* p. 121.

on political issues. Earlier he was winning considerable fame as a religious debater. At Chagrin Falls in Cuyahoga County, Ohio he debated an infidel by the name of William Denton. Brethren were highly pleased with his success.

The family of Garfield needs special mention. At the time of his death, Garfield's family consisted of eight persons—himself, his wife, Lucretia Rudolph Garfield, his aged mother, and five children. His children were Harry, James, Mollie, Irwin and Abram. Two of his children had died in infancy.

During the winter of 1850, 51, Garfield taught school at Warrensville, Ohio. One of his pupils was a girl by the name of Mary L. Hubbell. Later she went with him to school at the Eclectic Institute. It was generally assumed around the school that they were engaged, although many felt that she was not suited for Garfield. Garfield himself soon came to realize this, but the affair had gone so far that to break it off without offending the girl became with him a major problem. Often he talked to his close friend, C. E. Fuller, about the matter, and Fuller's advice was to go ahead and break it. But considerable criticism came to Garfield over it.

Garfield first met Lucretia Rudolph, the girl he married, at Geauga Seminary in Chester. Her father, Zeb Rudolph, shortly afterwards moved to Hiram to open up a boarding house for boys attending the Eclectic Institute. Rudolph had four children— Lucretia, John, Joseph, and Ellen. At this time, 1851, Lucretia was about nineteen, the oldest child of Zeb Rudolph. She taught a school two and a half miles north of Hiram, and was only home on the week ends. By disposition, she was a little reserved although attractive. She and Garfield were married on November 11, 1858 by the president of Western Reserve College at Hudson.

Through their thirty-two years of married life, Garfield displayed a devotion to his wife that was the contributing factor to their marriage success. In those months previous to his assassination his wife was severely sick. The newspapers carried daily stories of her condition, and the country watched anxiously for her recovery. Garfield was deeply concerned, and often said he would resign his position as president if it would help his wife to recover. But just as news came forth that she was better, he was himself shot down.

The first years of their married life were spent at Hiram. Garfield purchased a small farm, adjoining the college campus. When he went to Washington as a congressman, he at first rented the property. There is no indication that Garfield was ever materially wealthy. After his third election to Congress, he borrowed money from an old army friend, and bought him a lot and built a house on it.

Garfield's national fame came first as a soldier before he gained popularity in politics. Shortly after the outbreak of the war, he applied to Governor Dennison of Ohio for a commission with the right to raise a regiment. On August 14, 1861 he was commissioned a Lieutenant-Colonel of the Forty-Second Regiment of Ohio Volunteers. Two days later he was mustered into service at Camp Chase, Columbus, Ohio. Many of the soldiers in Garfield's regiment came from students in Hiram College. (Western Reserve Eclectic Institute) Three months were spent in drilling the soldiers, and by the first of December, they were ready to march Southward toward the conflict.

On December 15, 1861 Garfield reported to General D. C. Buell at Louisville, Kentucky. General Buell was a stern soldier, and was somewhat skeptical of Garfield's ability. Nevertheless, an assignment was forthcoming. General Zollicoffer was advancing from Cumberland Gap through Kentucky to Mill Spring. Confederate General Humphrey Marshall was threatening to over-run the whole of eastern Kentucky. General Buell's plans called for a main drive on Bowling Green southward, but the attack could not be risked until the pressure from the east could be relieved. General George H. Thomas, then a rising colonel, was assigned the task of stopping Zollicoffer, and Garfield was assigned the one of halting Marshall.

Marshall was known to be encamped at Paintsville up the Sandy Valley with five thousand men. Garfield gathered four regiments of infantry and eight companies of calvary and drove on Marshall. The confederate general was forced to retreat from Paintsville to Prestonburg, but Garfield pressed the battle winning decisive victory. For this triumph, President Lincoln made him a Brigadier-General. The commission came on January 10, 1862, giving Garfield the distinction of being the youngest general in the army.

He was now summoned to return to Louisville, but upon his arrival found that General Buell was at Nashville, and was ordered to follow him there. When he got to Nashville, the battle at Shiloh was shaping up, and Buell had already gone to join Grant. Garfield was ordered to Shiloh, and on April 5 was reassigned to the Twelfth Brigade of the Sixth Division of the Army of Ohio. The Sixth Division was one of Ohio's most active early in the war. It fought in upper Virginia until late in November, 1861 when it was ordered to Louisville to join General Buell. The Sixth was on the way to join Grant at Donelson when it heard of the fort's surrender. It turned up the Cumberland to Nashville. It was the first of the Union armies to march through the city, and was the first to hoist the national flag over the Tennessee state capitol building.[3] Garfield joined the division in time to take part in the last day's fighting at Shiloh.

After the Shiloh battle, he pursued the enemy southward to Corinth, then eastward through northern Mississippi and Alabama. Later he made headquarters at Huntsville. In August that year he became ill with ague and was sent home. Early in the fall he reported to Secretary of War Edwin M. Stanton in Washington where he was detailed as a member of a court of inquiry to investigate the case of General McDowell. On November 25, he was detailed to try the case of General Fitz-John Porter in a trial which lasted forty-five days. This trial demonstrated Garfield's ability as a lawyer.

In January, 1863 he was ordered to report to Major-General Rosecrans at Murfreesboro, Tennessee. He was made Rosecrans' chief of staff to reorganize the Army of Cumberland into a more efficient fighting unit. During this time, General Grant was sweeping down the Mississippi basin, threatening to cut the confederacy in two. But Rosecrans was immobile. People inquired why. The President and the war department were pushing Rosecrans to advance against the enemy, but Rosecrans refused. He addressed letters to each of the seventeen generals under him, asking their opinions and all agreed that an advance was impossible.

Garfield had by now come to an independent decision but the same one that the President, the war department and General Grant had already reached. Unlike European wars, this war was not to be won by occupying strategic cities, for the South

---

[3]T. J. Lindsey, *Ohio at Shiloh* (Cincinnati: C. J. Krehbiel & Company, 1903), pp. 58, 59.

had no strategic points. Victory lay only in meeting the enemy and destroying her army and the sooner this could be done, the sooner the war would be over. Garfield, therefore, studied the matter thoroughly, and recommended to Rosecrans a march eastward against General Bragg. He figured that discounting the number of soldiers needed to remain in Murfreesboro and hold the city, Rosecrans would still have over sixty-five thousand with which to face the enemy. Rosecrans and his army generals disagreed, and let it be known that Garfield alone would be personally responsible for what happened. Garfield assumed the responsibility, and the army moved eastward fighting a series of battles climaxing in the battle at Chickamauga.

Chickamauga was Garfield's last battle, and here he won national fame. The prize at Chickamauga was the Rossville Road, and General George H. Thomas was told to hold it at all costs. The enemy got reinforcements, and beseiged relentlessly Thomas' right flank. General Thomas was swept back in retreat. Longstreet paused to reorganize the attack, thinking victory now certain. Enemy forces three times as strong as Thomas were surrounding him, and the general could not know it. Garfield made a daring run on a horse fully exposed to enemy fire to convey the news to Thomas. Thomas immediately retreated further saving the Army of Cumberland from complete destruction. The War Department now made Garfield a Major-General.

But Garfield's army career was now at an end. With no effort at all on his part, his friends had placed his name before the public, and had elected him as a representative of the nineteenth district of Ohio in the national Congress. Reluctantly, Garfield gave up an army career, and on December 5, 1863 took his seat in the House of Representatives at Washington.

His interest in politics went back only to about 1856. In the fall of 1855, while he was yet a student in Williams College, John Z. Goodrich, a Congressman from Massachusetts, delivered an address on the Kansas-Nebraska bill that held Garfield speechless. Afterward he confided in a friend that he was ignorant of this subject and would familiarize himself completely with it. Much later Garfield became one of the best informed men in the nation on slavery question. Up to this time he had been a Whig. He was disinterested in the Know-Nothing Party, but afterward became an ardent Republican. His first political vote was cast for John C. Fremont.

His first political speeches were delivered at Hiram in 1856. Three years later he began to speak at County Mass Meetings. That year he was elected to the Ohio state legislature. During the winter of 1861 he was admitted to the bar. In January, 1860 he took his seat in the Ohio legislature, becoming its youngest member.

For seventeen years he was a member of the House of Representatives. He delivered forty speeches before Congress, addresses that were classics in rhetoric and logic.

On the night of the assassination of President Abraham Lincoln, Garfield was in New York City. In the early morning it was learned that Lincoln was shot. The streets were immediately filled with silent crowds. There was no business transacted. People milled around—no laughter, no mirth, but each anxiously awaiting news of the President's well being. The morning papers blazed the story more fully. The president had died; Secretary Seward's throat had been cut, and attempts were made upon the lives of other cabinet members. It looked as though the government itself was being overthrown, and people feared for what news might yet be forthcoming. Posters asking the crowd to meet around the Wall Street Exchange were placed up, and fifty thousand came. They were angry. The South, they felt had caused this. Two men were heard to say, "Lincoln ought to have been shot long ago!" In a matter of moments their bloody bodies lay still on the ground—one dead and the other dying. A frenzy swept the crowd; silence changed to hateful words, and the swearing of vengeance. Suddenly, Garfield stepped out on a balcony before them all and spoke:

Fellow-citizens!

Clouds and darkness are round about Him. His pavilion is dark waters and thick clouds of the skies! Justice and judgment are the establishment of His throne! Mercy and truth shall go before His face! Fellow-citizens! God reigns and the Government at Washington still lives.[4]

The effective of this speech was to cool the rising temperature of the crowd, and put some semblance of reason back on the throne.

Garfield's reputation in politics was on the whole excellent. His

---

[4]F. M. Green, *A Royal Life,* p. 299.

enemies in the presidential campaign laid three charges against him which the nation never seriously accepted. It was charged with corruptly purchasing ten shares of stock in the Credit Mobilier Corporation. He was accused, also of fathering a bill in Congress to raise the salaries of the congressmen, and of a corrupt practice in the DeGalyer contract for the pavement of the streets in Washington D. C. The South had a strong dislike for Garfield due to his part in the war, and his strong Northern political bias. Once Garfield favored the confiscation of all southern property, a thing for which David Lipscomb found it hard to grant forgiveness.

Early in life Garfield had formed a resolution against seeking for a position, but to allow the position seek him. He went to the Republican Convention in Chicago on June 2, 1880 with no thought at all of receiving the nomination for a candidacy. Grant, Sherman and Blaine were the three most likely prospects to get the honor to carry the Republican banner in the coming presidential campaign. Garfield ardently backed John Sherman of Ohio. Thirty-three ballots were taken, and on none of them was the name of either man enough in the majority to receive the nomination. Garfield's name appeared on the thirty-fourth ballot. On the thirty-sixth he was swept into the position as the Republican party's candidate for the presidency. Three weeks later the Democrats nominated General Winifield Scott Hancock as his opponent.

As a matter of repeating a historical fact, Garfield was elected in November, and the following March 4th, was duly inaugurated into office.

That which proved the cause of so much trouble at the outset of Garfield's term of office proved to be the cause of his death in only a few months. Civil service examinations to fill governmental positions were as yet unknown. Close to one hundred thousand positions were to be filled either directly or indirectly by the President. Members of the church were quick to take advantage of Garfield's presidency. They flocked into Washington from as far away as Texas with letters from churches, thinking they would now have an easy picking of political jobs. But Garfield refused. He would not be guilty of appointing his own brethren for positions for fear of the charge of biasness. He said to his Chaplain Mullins: "Keep my brethren away from me; it annoys and wounds me for them to come asking for office be-

cause of our religious relations." Brethren would meet him in
public places, rush up to him, shake hands with him, and say,
"How are you, Brother Garfield?" Mullins stated that John B.
Bowman would have been made Secretary of Interior and B. A.
Hinsdale, ambassador to England except for the fact they were
members of the church.[5]

Charles J. Guiteau, a French Canadian by birth, and a "vagabond
and dead-beat" by profession came to Washington D. C. on Sunday evening March 6, 1881—two days after the inauguration
ceremonies. He stopped at the Ebbitt House for one day, and
then moved around in Washington from place to place. On
Wednesday, May 18th, he determined to kill the President. The
last of May he went into O'Mara's store, corner of Fifteenth and
F Streets and looked at the pistols. He came back on Wednesday,
June 10th and purchased a gun for $10.00. The next day he
spent practicing.

On Sunday morning, June 12th, Guiteau sat in the park across
from the White House. He watched the President and his family
come out, get in their carriage, and drive off to church. He
hurried to his room, got his pistol, and started to church. Garfield
entered the building at five minutes past eleven, during the reading
of the Scriptures. Dr. Bayton and wife, friends of the Garfields,
from Cleveland were his companions. F. D. Power, regular
preacher for the congregation, was out of town, and S. D. Moore
of Hagerstown, Maryland, was the visiting speaker. Guiteau
took a seat several rows behind Garfield. His intention was to
shoot the President then, but he feared hitting someone else. He
noted, however, that the President sat near an open window, and
determined upon another plan. Guiteau was outside the window
the next Sunday morning, but Garfield was out of Washington
on official business, thus thwarting the vile purpose.

On Saturday, July 2nd, Garfield arose early at the White House,
and spent the early hours attending to considerable executive
business. He was preparing to leave for a two weeks trip into
New England. First on the itinerary was a scheduled stop at
Williams College to address a graduating class. Other members
of the party went ahead to the Baltimore and Potomac Railroad
Depot to take their seats in the President's car. Secretary of State,

---

[5]Chaplain Mullins, "Garfield's Religion," *Gospel Advocate,* Vol. XXV,
(March 8, 1883), p. 156.

Blaine and Garfield drove up in a carriage as the time was nearing 9:30 A. M. The carriage stopped at the B Street entrance, and both men stepped out to walk arm in arm into the station. They passed through the outer "Ladies' Room," on into the main corridor. Just as they did Guiteau darted from behind a door directly in back of Garfield, lifted his gun and shot twice. The last shot was fired only four feet from Garfield's back. The President staggered and fell. Mrs. S. V. White, the woman in charge of the Ladies' Room was standing only six feet from the President and watched the deed. She was the first to reach him. She lifted his head and found he was deathly pale but still conscious. One of Garfield's sons rushed up, bent over his father, and began sobbing frantically. A Dr. Sunderland, a former Chaplain in the Senate, was near. He rushed to Garfield and said: "Mr. President, you are in the hands of the God you have long trusted, and I say to you that the heart of this whole people will go out to God in prayer that you may be spared." The President calmly replied: "I know it, Doctor. I believe in God and trust myself in his hands."[6]

In ten minutes a thousand people were at the depot. The President was placed upon a mattress, and vomited violently. He was carried to an office. The ambulance drove up, and surrounded by twelve mounted police, it moved the President to the White House. Meanwhile, the ticket agent grabbed Guiteau, and he was quickly placed under arrest.

The nation watched anxiously through the months of July and August and up to the middle of September. At times, there seemed to be indications that the President would recover. Finally, on September 19, the eighteenth anniversary of his famous ride at Chickamauga, Garfield passed quietly away. Some years earlier an agreement had been made between Garfield, Isaac Errett, Dr. J. P. Robinson and J. Harrison Jones that the survivors would attend and take part in the funeral services of the other. Each of these men, therefore, spoke at Garfield's funeral.

The election of a member of the church, and a former gospel preacher at that, to the presidency of the United States reflected itself in different ways upon the church. It is for this reason that Garfield's life needs to be told, and that a chapter on him needs

---

[6]John F. Rowe, "Universal Sympathy for Our Beloved President," *American Christian Review*, Vol. XXIV, No. 29 (May 19, 1881), p. 228.

to find a place in restoration history. The first reaction was one largely localized in the South.

During the Civil War, David Lipscomb became seriously impressed with the idea that the whole study of the relation of the Christian to civil government needed to be gone over completely. It became his conviction that the general conception held by most church members was wrong. Consequently, in reviving the *Gospel Advocate* in 1866 Lipscomb announced at the beginning that the subject of the Christian's relation to civil government would be thoroughly examined in succeeding issues. Point by point he proceeded to investigate the subject.

Lipscomb declared that there were currently three ideas of the relation of the church to world powers. The first was that the church should form alliances with world powers and use these powers to advance her own cause. This was the Roman Catholic idea. The second idea current was that the political governments are of divine origin and should be thus sustained for this reason. This is the Protestant idea. The third idea is that the two institutions—the church and civil governments—are two separate and distinct systems. Each was necessary in its own sphere. The church was perfect and needed no human help; that God allowed those who refused to submit to the divine governments—the church —to form governments of their own and in them to accomplish their own desired ends. While the Christian is to have no part in this government, he will quietly and meekly submit to it where its laws do not conflict with that of the church.[7] Of course, further elaboration was demanded.

Tolbert Fanning left the imprint of his own character profoundly upon Lipscomb. There is, however, no indication that Lipscomb borrowed his conception of the Christian's relation to civil government from Fanning, but that he was influenced in the direction he went by Fanning hardly admits of any doubt. When, after the war, several brethren urged Fanning to run for a political office, he refused. Undoubtedly with his turn of mind he could have been an outstanding success in politics. But in refusing political offices, Fanning explained his reasons:

To be sure, we do not affirm that no Christian man or woman ever ascended a throne, but we are quite sure that no Christian

---

[7]David Lipscomb, "The Church of Christ and World Powers," *Gospel Advocate,* Vol. VIII, No. 2 (January 9, 1866), pp. 28-30.

ever ruled a nation by the principles of Christianity. The fact is, that the laws of Christ are not suited for the government of any of Satan's subjects. We, moreover, give it as our candid conviction, drawn from scores of examples, that no Christian man can engage in human legislation, or give, even a part of his time to the affairs of human government without being greatly injured spiritually. We do not pretend to give a reason for it; but we simply state the fact of corruption attached to all that busy themselves in politics, and the ordinary excitements incident to human governments. Ambition and false pride, have led many of our brethren into legislative halls, state and national, but in every instance, they are swallowed up and lost in vice, or greatly injured by their associations and labors.[8]

Beginning therefore in 1866 at a time when the South lay prostrate from the war, Lipscomb started setting forth the Christian's relation to civil government as he conceived it. The idea was somewhat novel to the brotherhood and that it took more hold in the South than in the North can be explained on two grounds. Lipscomb was a citizen of the South, and hence the prejudice then so current against Northerners was not an obstacle to the spread of the idea. Then, too, the South was pyschologically prepared for such teaching. A deep sense of the futility of earthly things and of the instability of human governments filled the South, making a fertile field in which to plant the seeds of Lipscomb's theory. An analysis of this theory will prepare the mind of the reader to understand how the impact of Garfield's election was received in the South.

Civil government denoted to David Lipscomb governments founded by men in contrast to that founded by God, the divine. He writes,

We shall use the adjectives, civil and political, when connected with the institutions of earth, as indicating those of human origin, in contradistinction to those of divine origin. Civil government then, is a government founded by man for the well-being of the human family, in contradistinction from a government founded by God for man's well-being.[9]

Definitions now out of the way, Lipscomb goes on to inquire (1) as to the origin of each government. (2) the relation of each to the other at the beginning. (3) and the changes in each with

[8]Tolbert Fanning, "Shall the *Gospel Advocate* Take Any Part in State Matters?" *Gospel Advocate,* Vol. VIII, No. 3 (January 16, 1866), pp. 33, 34.

[9]David Lipscomb, "The Church of Christ and World Powers," *Gospel Advocate,* Vol. VIII, No. 4 (January 23, 1866), p. 56.

reference to the other through the years and how these changes were regarded by God.

Starting then, with the creation of the world, Lipscomb pointed out that God possessed all authority and assigned to each created object its functions and positions and powers. God empowered man to "subdue the earth," etc. (Gen. 1: 28) No man, it is suggested, can occupy any position, or possess any authority, apart from the appointment of God. Man is empowered with the right to subdue and control lower creation. But who governs man? Shall he govern himself? No! God reserves the sole right to govern and control the man. Man's assumption to rule himself is an interference of the divine prerogative. God has always made provision for exercising His right by keeping a government of his own before man. In the garden of Eden, He controlled man by direct commands. When Adam refused this government by yielding to the Satanic suggestion to control himself, he was driven from the garden. During the patriarchal dispensation, God governed man—those who would submit—through the fathers. When the family grew, God changed the government from a family to a nation. When the Jewish nation refused the government of God, that form of government was abrogated and the church was inaugurated. All the people of God who submitted to the government of God belonged to the church.

Turning from this brief history, Lipscomb now raised the question of the origin of human governments. His answer was that human governments owe their origin to that portion of the human family that refused to submit to the government of God, and who, in rebellion, set up their own government. The first reference to a human government, says Lipscomb, is in Gen. 10: 10. Here it is seen that this government originated in man's rebellion against the government of God. He writes, "In its beginning it was the embodiment of man's effort to throw off the rule of His maker."

Down through the history of the Old Testament what was the relation of the human government to the divine? Genesis, chapter fourteen, says Lipscomb, shows five kings, rulers in the earthly governments, at war with Abraham, a servant of God, one who submitted to the government of God. The history of the Jews shows that God forbade His people from forming alliances with human governments. (ef. Ex. 23: 31, 2; 34: 12, 16; 1 Kgs. 11: 2)

Every time an alliance was formed between the divine government, the Jewish nation, and the human government, the kingdoms of the world, the Jews became weak and disobedient. This nation is a type of the church. For members of the church to form alliances with human governments weakens them and makes them disobedient to God.

It was, therefore, a profound conviction of David Lipscomb's that for Christians to enter into politics was not only wrong in principle but sinful against God. He refused to vote and urged others to refuse. Likewise, of course, did he refuse to participate in carnal wars which were but strifes between political governments brought on by jealousy and greed. Human governments, owing their origin to man's rebellion against God, would be overthrown when men the world over would all submit themselves to the government of God.

With David Lipscomb no man believed anything who was not willing to suffer for what he believed. Suffer, Lipscomb surely did. On November 13, 1862 he induced the elders and evangelists of ten or fifteen congregations in Middle Tennessee to send letters to both the President of the Confederacy and the President of the United States at Washington D. C. declaring their intentions to have nothing to do with war on either side. At the beginning of the war, then, Lipscomb was accused by the South of being disloyal to the Confederacy. He was often threatened and one or two vowed to hang him, but he persisted in his belief. When the Federal troops took over Nashville, Lipscomb showed the same indifference as he had toward the South, and was accused by them of being a Southern sympathizer. The truth is, he would have nothing to do with either government; he would be a Christian and meekly submit no matter the government under which he lived.

Jacob Creath, Jr., who at the beginning of the war showed some bias in favor of Christians' participation, found himself gradually changing as the war progressed. Before long, he quite independently, had reached conclusions similar to those of David Lipscomb. After commending Lipscomb for his articles, Creath wrote:

In August, 1863 or 4, I was in the state of Illinois, preaching the Gospel, and one Saturday evening I was sitting in the shade reading the Bible, near a railroad, and a man walking on the

road turned in at the gate and came to me and addressed me thus:
"What," said he, "are you reading the good book?" "Yes" said
I, "it is a good book, provided people will obey it." He immediately
introduced the subject of the war which was then raging, and
justified the war from God's commanding Moses to kill the
Canaanites and Saul the Amalekites. I asked him if God had
given a command to men, under the Gospel, to kill each other
as he did to Moses and Saul to kill? He said if I called killing
men in war, murder, I did not understand the language. I told
him when you took a man's life, you had killed him, whether
privately or in war, and that I knew the distinction, when done,
between homicide, manslaughter, and murder in self-defense, or
a self-murdering defense, and returned him his compliment of
ignorance, and closed by saying to him, "Now, Sir, you are a
stranger to me, and I to you. I never saw you before, but I
presume you are some sort of a religionist, or sectarian, full of
war up to your chin. I will state a few facts to you for your
future reflection. Our Saviour whom you profess to follow, never
killed a man while on earth—he never commanded a man to be
killed—he never shed a drop of human blood, and the only time
when violence was used by one of his followers, he ordered him
to put up his sword, and wrought a miracle to heal the maimed,
and more than that he was murdered outright and downright by
God's elect nation. Now, sir, compare your pleading for wholesale murder with the life of him whom you profess to follow,
and slander by calling yourself one of his people." He was off
quickly. I learned afterwards he was a Presbyterian priest.[10]

Lipscomb had to defend his doctrine. It was charged that his
theory violated 1 Pet. 2: 13-14, and Romans 13: 1-5. Inspiration charges every soul to "be in subjection to the higher
powers for there is no power but of God; and the powers that be
are ordained of God." To this Lipscomb pointed out that every
person possesses some power but yet there is always a higher
power. Every soul must be, according to Lipscomb, in subjection to that power which is over it. A servant must be in
subjection to the "higher power" of the master; a child to that
of its parent; a citizen to the "higher power" of the magistrate;
and a magistrate to the higher power of God. "The powers that
be"—all of them are subordinate in the present dispensation to
Christ, he wrote.[11]

---

[10]Jacob Creath, "War and Peace," *Gospel Advocate,* Vol. VIII, No. 41
(October 9, 1866), pp. 650, 651.

[11]David Lipscomb, "Romans 13: 1," *Gospel Advocate,* Vol. VIII, No. 4
(January 23, 1866), pp. 59, 60.

Lipscomb pointed out that during the Civil War, both sides used Romans 13: 1-5 to justify killing in the war. The citizens of the Confederacy used it to prove that they had a right to slay the citizens of the North, and the citizens of the Union used it to justify their killing the citizens of the Confederacy. The Christian under the Confederacy thought Romans 13: 1-5 taught him to submit to the Confederacy, but at the same time, that verse was teaching him to rebel against another government, the Union. Was not the Union a "power that be" the same as the Confederacy? By submitting to either government the Christian was rebelling against another "power that be."[12] This dilemma led Lipscomb to believe that something was wrong with men's interpretation of this scripture. What was it?

In March, 1867 Lipscomb raised the question without answering it. Is it absolutely sure that Paul is speaking of the "powers that be" refers to civil governments? Possibly there was some doubt at this writing in Lipscomb's mind. Fanning had believed that "higher powers" referred to church authorities, those whom the Holy Spirit had made overseers of the flock. The overseers are to see that the law is obeyed. "They bear now the sword in vain" refers figuratively to the fact that he bears not the authority in vain, said Fanning, and the paying of tribute referred to paying contributions.

Lipscomb toyed with this idea a month or two and then rejected it. The "higher powers" did mean civil governments, but to understand Paul, chapters twelve and thirteen of Romans must be studied together. Chapter twelve closed by declaring that vengeance belonged to God. The next chapter shows that God takes this vengeance through His agents. Christians are not God's agents for this vengeance, but the civil government is. The wickedness of the world compels a work to be done which a good man cannot do. Christians are ministers of mercy; civil government, a minister of wrath. The civil government is ordained of God as a minister of God's wrath.[13] Hell is ordained of God as a place of the punishment of the wicked, but this does not justify a Christian in helping Satan. Nor does it justify him in assisting

[12]David Lipscomb, "Defense of the Government," *Gospel Advocate,* Vol. IX, No. 11 (March 14, 1867), pp. 215, 216.

[13]David Lipscomb, "The Higher Powers," *Gospel Advocate,* Vol. IX, No. 27 (July 4, 1867), pp. 521-525.

civil governments in being ministers of God's wrath.   So reasoned Lipscomb.

The statement of Lipscomb's theory presented problems to be answered one of which was that of withdrawal of fellowship. Lipscomb, teaching as he did, that it was wrong for Christians to vote, hold political office, etc., had the question brought before him: Should congregations withdraw fellowship from those who voted, held office, and fought in carnal warfares.   R. C. Horn of McKinney, Texas wrote Lipscomb in 1875 inquiring what to do about such people—disfellowship them or not.   Lipscomb answers by saying,

While saying this much, we are yet unwilling to say that we think a church ought as yet, to withdraw themselves from one for voting.   (The brethren will excuse us for not using the word, exclude.   It is not a scriptural word, nor does it convey a scriptural idea.)   The reason for this is, the brethren have not been sufficiently taught upon the subject.   The Scriptural means for correcting an evil has not been sufficiently used to resort to this extreme measure. We have spoken upon the subject, written upon the subject, talked publicly and privately upon the subject, having come as near making a hobby of the subject as any one, (expect to do it more in the future and have no dread of being called a hobbyist), yet we have never to a single individual taken the pains to present the subject in such fullness and with such earnestness, as to be ready to give him over to Satan for rejecting it.[14]

Lipscomb goes further and wrote:

Now if others have made such efforts to patiently instruct and persuade their brethren the truth on this subject, have exhausted all patience, forbearance and long suffering in teaching them the way of the Lord, publicly and from house to house, and they wickedly refuse to hear that law, then it may be right to withdraw yourselves from such.   But no Christian, observant of the laws of the Lord, can properly withdraw from a brother, aiming to do right, but ignorant of the truth of God.

For fifteen years, then, Lipscomb's position on the Christian's relation to the civil government had been permeating the South, and had picked up many adherents.   When, therefore, in June, 1880 Garfield was nominated for the presidency, Lipscomb wrote:

After days of wrangling and strife the better elements of the party seemed to triumph and they nominated Gen. James A. Garfield as the candidate for President.   General Garfield is a

---

[14]David Lipscomb, "Queries on Civil Government," *Gospel Advocate,* Vol. XVII, No. 17 (April 22, 1875), p. 399.

member of the church of Christ, was once a preacher, or as he prefers to style it, a lecturer among the disciples of Christ, went into politics, was a member of the Ohio State Senate at the breaking out of the war, went into the army, was a general for a time, became General Rosecrans' chief of staff, and in this position at the time of Rosecrans' march through Middle Tennessee to Chattanooga. Since the war he has been a member of Congress. We presume he has maintained his personal and religious integrity as well as any man with his surroundings and his position could. There have been some ugly charges made against him, but we think, not sustained. . .

But now, dear brethren of the South who wish and argue for good, pious, religious rulers, what are you going to do about Brother Garfield? Are you going to vote for him, or will you take up an ungodly Democrat, if they should nominate such a one? . . .[15]

In the predominately Democratic South, this was a bitter pill for members of the church to swallow. Whether to vote for a member of the church when his politics was Republican or vote for a Democrat who was not a member. Lipscomb wrote:

Many Christians justify themselves in voting and taking part in politics on the ground that Christian men are needed in politics and in official positions. If Christians are needed in politics, the purer the form of Christianity, the better. We have been sure that they were mistaken in this reason. I do not mean that they were conscious of insincerity, but that they deceived themselves. We intend to make this deception evident to all who are willing to be undeceived. Gen. Garfield is a member of the church of Christ. He is a man in good standing in that church. He is intimate with a great number of well-known and leading disciples of Christ. They all regard him as a man of honor and integrity. . .

His neighbors esteem him. They have repeatedly elected him to represent them in the highest positions of trust and honor in Congress, with constantly increasing majorities. His party in the Legislature of his State unanimously elected him to the United States Senate. They knew him. In Congress he is personally esteemed by both political friends and opponents. No man in Congress, we have been assured by his most determined political opponents, is more highly esteemed personally than he. He is popular and respected personally by all in Congress. Under these circumstances, no Christian can believe or report or take up the public evil reports against Garfield, without violating all the obligations of Christian brotherhood.

[15]David Lipscomb, "Words of Caution," *Gospel Advocate*, Vol. XXII, No. 26 (June 24, 1880), p. 401.

We say this much about him while having no sympathy whatever with his course. We have watched his course for years; we knew his character and position before the war, as a man of culture and refinement, with strong religious sentiment. We watched him to see the effect of the soldier's profession and work on his character. We were to him an unknown but interested observer of his course while in military power here in our State. We have watched his course with interest from the day he took his seat in Congress till now, to see what effect politics and political associations would have upon his earnest religious nature and strong resolute will. We have been strengthened by this observation of his course, in our conviction that no Christian can go into politics and maintain a Christian character; at the same time that politics are not aided by the intrusion of religion into its domain. But we are satisfied that we know of no man who has gone into politics, who has become so thoroughly identified with the affairs of government, and yet so well retained his Christian character and religious interest as has General Garfield.

We hold that wherein Gen. Garfield has not failed in religious integrity in the political arena, ninety-nine out of every hundred Christians would fail. Moreover, I do not believe in a hundred years past, so much of earnest, intelligent religious character, in one person, has come so near the Presidency as does now in the person of General Garfield. The chances are, that so much will not again for a hundred years to come.[16]

Lipscomb declared that if he did not believe that Christians had no business in politics, he would vote for Garfield himself.

But Lipscomb was a Southerner, writing to Southern readers who bore no good will toward Republicans. To get his point across he was charitable in the extreme. His readers mistook this charitableness for weakness, thinking that now since a Christian was running for President, he was surrendering his former point of view. Lipscomb, however, was intending to show he bore no bias against Garfield while yet declaring that a Christian had no business in holding political offices. From Hallville, Texas an old brother, John H. Cain, wrote in anger: "Brother Lipscomb: I am very old and feeble and do not wish to be insulted with your black Republican politics. You will please discontinue my paper."

The *Gospel Advocate* felt the reaction of Lipscomb's theory. Joseph Franklin, early in 1880, was announced as a new associate-editor. Joseph Franklin, son of Ben Franklin, was then going

---

[16]David Lipscomb, "Christians and Politics," *Gospel Advocate,* Vol. XXII, No. 29 (July 15, 1880), p. 449.

through a period of confusion and readjustment. Ten years earlier he had stood squarely behind his father, and steadfastly fought all human innovations. Upon his father's death and the assumption of the editorial chair by John F. Rowe, young Franklin changed. Turning from the *Review,* he went to the *Gospel Advocate,* but the election of Garfield and its repercussions in the *Advocate* caused him to suddenly announce his resignation. Meanwhile, Lipscomb found himself on the opposite side of the issue from John F. Rowe, so both men discussed the issue, which was carried in both the *American Christian Review* and the *Gospel Advocate* in the summer of 1880 while the candidates were lectioneering.

Garfield's election to the presidency turned the attention of the brotherhood—and the world—to the church in Washington, D. C. Garfield began regularly attending the church upon his first election to Congress in 1863. In the spring of 1869 the congregation purchased a small, frame building from the Methodists. Reporters sneeringly referred to this as the "Campbellite shanty." After Garfield's nomination, the church felt its own inadequacy, and cries went up for funds to build a new house of worship. V. M. Metcalfe visited this congregation late in 1880, and reported that the church had begun to use a small organ in its worship. He noted that Garfield seldom missed a single service, even to attending the social meetings.

Garfield Memorial Church was badly needed, thought many brethren. The task of raising funds was turned over to the Missionary Society. David Lipscomb was critical of the move— not that a meeting house was not needed but to build one because of Garfield, to refer to it as the "Garfield Memorial Church," was totally contrary to the principle of returning to the ancient order. G. W. Rice, publisher of the Review, however, thought such a building was not needed. He wrote:

A week ago I expressed my opinion about the proposed meeting-house in Washington City. I now repeat, such a house is not needed. The one now there is sufficiently large for all the purposes of the church at that place. It has been said as a good and sufficient reason for building a fifty thousand dollar house in Washington—we want and need a court church in Washington City, it being the seat of government of the United States—That we need and must have a large and elegeant house where the President and his family can attend and be seen. . .[17]

Both Lipscomb and Rice were objecting fundamentally on the same ground, although Rice couched his objections in strongly-worded terms. That Washington needed a new meeting house was evident. To build one in honor of President Garfield, to build one as a means of show, to parade the church before the government in Washington was a fundamentally carnal and worldly spirit. This is the seat of the objections.

Plans for the erection of the building went on even after Garfield died. By the spring of 1882 the congregation was ready to let out the contract. The cornerstone was laid July 2, 1882, the first anniversary of the shooting of the President. Five thousand people attended that simple service, among them President Arthur himself. B. A. Hinsdale delivered the major address. The new building, to be known as the Garfield Memorial Church was to be completed at a cost of $33,700, a rather costly project considering the times.

This hero worship, and calling a church, the "Garfield Memorial Church" was too much for Lipscomb. He wrote of Garfield:

His course was one of dishonor to the church; with ability and assured success as a servant of that church, he surrendered it for service in the worldly kingdom. If Garfield's career was acceptable, why not all young men of popular talents turn from the ministry to law, war and politics? Did I believe his course was acceptable to God, I would yet turn from the service of the church to that of the world. Is it strange when the church counts him who turned from service in her offices and works, to the work of the world, worthy of so much more honor than those who serve faithfully in her sanctuaries. . .[18]

Garfield more than any other man had proved to be the exception to the rule. Politics corrupted him less than it did any other person. For strength of moral character and of devotion to God the presidency has never known Garfield's equal.

---

[17]G. W. Rice, "Washington City Mosque," *American Christian Review,* Vol. XXIV, No. 11 (March 15, 1881), p. 85.

[18]David Lipscomb, "Hero Worship," *Gospel Advocate,* Vol. XXIV, No. 30 (July 27, 1882), p. 467.

CHAPTER XI

DARKENING HORIZONS

In 1865 Moses E. Lard argued that division was virtually impossible, for in the first place, the teaching of the church virtually condemned it, and furthermore, the churches had no ecclesiastical tribunal to declare it. Added to this, thought Lard, was the fact that the local autonomy of the congregations was a decided barrier to division. Three years later, Ben Franklin voiced his approval of Lard's sentiments. Reviewing the history of the restoration, he found in such cases as the Jesse B. Ferguson trouble, the war, slavery and the society controversy that the church had weathered these threats of division with no serious breach in its ranks. These facts were encouraging to the belief that division was out of the question.

The passing of another decade, however, made many less confident of continual unity. Some were now speaking of "organic union and disunion" among the brethren, inquiring fearfully if "organic disunion" will ever come. But David Lipscomb alleged that he had not the least fear of "organic disunion" for the reason there was no "organic union" among the churches to be broken. In the next place, he contended, any union which existed among the churches was not dependent upon any action of will or resolution of the members themselves. Lipscomb's explanation was there was no such thing as "organic union" among the churches in New Testament times. The New Testament never speaks of union of churches, but only of unity among all the people of God. Christ prayed that individually, all of His disciples might be one— not one in organic union, but one like the Father and the Son are one—in purpose, in love, in desire. That which made all disciples one in New Testament times was a common belief in the same person, Jesus, and a "walking in the light as he is in the light."[1]

W. B. F. Treat concluded that division was no longer out of the question. He preached for the church at Bloomington, Indiana and saw the congregation divided over the introduction of the

---

[1]David Lipscomb, "Union, True or False," *Gospel Advocate,* Vol. XXII, (June 10, 1880), p. 374.

221

organ.   After reviewing Lard's reasons why the church could not divide, Treat added:

But the last few years have been eventful ones in our history and by experience. we have received lessons which some of us had hoped never to learn.   It is strictly true that we can never divide while, as individuals and as congregations, we have the grand watchword with which this movement began: "Where the Bible speaks, we speak; where the Bible is silent, we are silent."

But it begins to occur to the minds of many that there is a possibility of division over things not in the Bible!   That any great number of men among us would insist on organizations, customs and practices not mentioned in the Bible, and force these into the Church, does not appear to have been included among the possibilities by the scribes who decided that we could never divide.[2]

Treat added:

If the worldly, unauthorized customs and practices that are popular with innovationists and sectarians are forced into the Church, over the protests of godly men, division is not only imminent, but it may become a necessity and a virtue!   The law of Christian unity is based upon the recognition of the supreme authority of Christ; and nothing in the gospel of Christ requires a believer to submit to unauthorized practice in religion.

R. B. Trimble of Mayfield, Kentucky also contended that it *was* impossible for the people of God to divide.   The very fact that a few people were dissatisfied with apostolic principles and abandoned these for "human innovations" did not imply that God's people had divided.   "They went out from among us because they were not of us."   So Trimble wrote:

There is now, ever has been, and ever will be division of sects. But that there is now, or ever will be, a serious division of the true children of God, is that which I do not believe.   That good and bad are caught in the gospel net, no one who is a discerner of events, or at all acquainted with Bible history, will, for a moment deny.   There are great fears expressed by some of the brethren that the church will be divided.   I have no fears of division among the true friends of Jesus.[3]

Trimble pointed out that those who would make the church another denomination, who would put in the organ, and champion the missionary societies were never really converted to the truth anyway.

---

[2]W. B. F. Treat, "Can We Ever Divide?" *American Christian Review,* Vol. XXII, No. 19 (June 6, 1879), p. 145.

[3]R. B. Trimble, "Are the Children of God Divided?" *American Christian Review,* Vol. XXII, (1879), p. 43.

If division must come, Lipscomb refused to regard it as the worst calamity possible. He wrote:

We have not doubted, for years, that if the course of adding innovation to innovation, pursued by many, is persisted in, that division and separation will come. Nay, it ought to come. God will cause it to come. . . If a separation will, and ought to come, it may be asked, how will it be brought about? All the true disciple has to do, is to firmly stand for the truth, and to be true to it. God in His providence will then bring it.[4]

Likewise, J. W. McGarvey, sensing that division was threatening, did not fear it as the worst of calamities. His article, first printed in the *Old Path Guide* in 1885 was copied into the *Gospel Advocate*.

. . . I have but little sympathy with those brethren who seem to dread disunion among ourselves as the direst of all evils. If we would inspire sensible men around us with a desire for union with us, we must be careful to show them that we do not and will not maintain unity with anything unscriptural, whether it shows itself within our ranks or outside of them. Truth first, union afterwards, and union only in the truth. This is our motto.[5]

With the passing of time the war drums beat a steadily increasing tempo. The danger of division was increasing hourly. The horizon was dark. By 1883 some declared that division was present. The editorials of John F. Rowe in the *American Christian Review*, which began in the fall of that year are among the best Rowe ever penned. The fever was now at its height, and Rowe's strongly-worded articles were intended to check the trend. To dip back into the past and breathe the atmosphere of these editorials is to give one a sense of the anxiety of the hour, and an appreciation of this crisis in the restoration.

Rowe compared the plight of the church in 1883 with the condition of ancient Israel.

As a people, we have not yet passed into actual captivity; but we see premonitions of such a captivity all around us. Of these premonitions, or prognostication, we shall speak hereafter. That there have been gross departures from the principles of radical reform, with which we started; that the original simplicity of the gospel has been shamefully marred by perversions of the truth; that the hearts of the righteous have been made sad by a secularized worship; that false rules of Bible interpretation have

---

[4]David Lipscomb, "Union and Schism," *Gospel Advocate,* Vol. XXV, (December 26, 1883), p. 822.

[5]J. W. McGarvey, "no title," *Gospel Advocate,* Vol. XXVII, (January 7, 1885), p. 7.

made powerless our distinctive plea; that efforts have been made
to destroy the independence and individuality of the congregations
of Christ; that efforts have been made to subordinate the congregations to the will and dictation of organized conventions—a concern
distinct and separate from the church of Christ, and *under whose
protecting wing every folly and innovation hides itself;* that many
mock at the proposition, "Where the Bible speaks, we speak;
where the Bible is silent, we are silent"; that all who stand upon
the original platform of principles, as enunciated by the Campbells,
and resist all innovations upon the apostolic order, are proscribed,
persecuted, and socially ostracized—are questions of the most
serious nature, and patent to all observing eyes.[6]

Rowe reported that letters were pouring into the *Review* office,
asking if this "reformation" were to go forward, or "to degenerate
into a sect." While it appeared that a division was inevitable,
Rowe affirmed there was no present danger of it.

As long as the evil which God pronounces against does not
take an organic form, and as long as a yoke of bondage is not
actually fastened on the necks of the people, an actual separation
need not take place. Until such a condition of things actually
confronts us, and before we are bound hand and foot by a system
of ecclesiasticism, we are morally bound by our pledges to the
great Head of the church, in our places to beat back the tide of
innovations, and by invincible courage and resistless pluck, hold the
fort, secure every possible advantage and repel the enemy.

Here was a call to resist all innovations. But, suppose in spite
of all struggles, the innovations sweep over the church anyway,
what then? In the same editorial Rowe added:

If, however, in their struggles at the post of duty and as faithful members in the one body, the true Israel of God are over-
powered and the church of Christ loses its apostolic identity by
the presence of organized ecclesiasticism and priestly domination,
in that it will become necessary, according to the mandates of
God quoted above, to actually separate and make a new rally
upon the original ground.[7]

About the same time Rowe declared that two distinct parties
were growing up in the church. One, he calls the "ancient order
of things," and the other, "the new order of things." Each stands
antagonistic to the other.

That there is rapidly growing up among us a new order of

---

[6]John F. Rowe, "Lift Up a Standard for the People," *American Christian
Review,* Vol. XXVI, (September 13, 1883), p. 282.
[7]John F. Rowe, "Lift Up a Standard for the People," *American Christian
Review,* Vol. XXVI, (September 13, 1883), p. 292.

things in contrast with the old order of things, as advocated by Alexander Campbell and his associates, is a fact that is becoming more apparent and pronounced every day. Anyone who will take the pains to read the *Christian Baptist,* edited fifty years ago by Alexander Campbell, and continuing seven years, will discover in reading his series of articles on *"The Ancient Order of Things,"* that, when placed in contrast with much of our church literature of the present day, and in contrast with much of our pulpit teaching there is growing up and taking form "The Modern Order of Things." It pains us to make this statement, but the fact is so patent and palpable that it is in vain to try longer to conceal it. We might as well prepare to meet the issue first as last. We are grieved to say that the line of separation is becoming more distinct every day. There are two classes among us—those who represent "The Ancient Order of Things" and those who represent "The New Order of Things." It is manifest that these two parties are not only not acting in sympathy, but that the men of the New Order of Things are determined to crush down, if possible, the Ancient Order of Things.[8]

In the intensity of a controversy like this one now raging, one finds at least the partial answer for the future course of the restoration. Why did so many churches in the North adopt the innovations? The answer is partially explained in the fact that the *Christian Standard* "outmaneuvered" the *American Christian Review* at almost every turn. John F. Rowe was of a positive conviction that the rise of innovations would divide the church. But while opposing innovations, Rowe did not act consistently in what he believed. There is, on the one hand, a leader of the forces opposing innovations who was not consistent; on the other there was a leader shrewd enough to capitalize upon these inconsistencies, and the reason is found for many churches and brethren who were "on the fence" favoring innovations.

Rowe, in opposing Isaac Errett published ten items on which the scriptures were silent, and charged that the *Standard* was promoting these, and therefore, causing division. Included were such items as the instrument of music, missionary societies, etc. But as a last item, Rowe accused the *Standard* of promoting "lesson leaves," Bible School Quarterlies, of which the Bible was silent. Errett was shrewd enough to single out the "lesson leaves" and ride it mercilessly. He had, of course, very little difficulty in

---

[8]John F. Rowe, "The Old and the New Order," *American Christian Review,* Vol. XXIII, No. 13 (March 30, 1880), p. 100.

making Rowe's position appear ludicrous, and since Rowe had declared "lesson leaves" to be in the same category with instrumental music and missionary societies, the answer to "lesson leaves" was the answer to all—so concluded the readers of the *Christian Standard.* What drove Rowe to such an extreme?

Moreover, Rowe in opposing the missionary society, charged their conventions with causing division. Yet, late in 1883 he recommended a mass meeting of the brethren who opposed innovations to get together in a conference and republish the principles on which they stood. So he proposed fighting conventions by forming an opposing convention. James A. Harding was quick to point out Rowe's inconsistency:

It is clear that if division comes in the ranks of this reformation, it will come through the conventions. Were the anti-organ, anti-missionary society men to do what their opponents have already done, that is, were they to meet in such mass meetings, an organic division would inevitably result. Such a division could not take place without the conventions. There would be nothing larger than a church to divide; for there would be among Christians no other organization than the local congregations.[9]

Why could not Rowe see his inconsistency? The answer is difficult to find; we only state it as an inescapable fact.

THE CAUSES OF DIVISION

Underlying the fearful fact of division were certain causes. As an attempt to understand the threat of division, it will be necessary to understand some of these causes.

The growing use of instrumental music. Despite the fact that during the war, the instrument was fought severely as an innovation, its use grew at first slowly and then more rapidly. Ben Franklin declared in 1867 that not ten congregations in the brotherhood were using the instrument, but by 1885 that number had greatly multiplied.

The story of its introduction in most cases is a story of division, law suits, and bitterness. In the summer of 1872 the instrument came into the church at Frankfort, Kentucky. This congregation for years had been accustomed to strife, and the introduction of the organ only fanned the flames more. About 1870 the church house burned and the necessity for a new building was pressed.

---

[9] James A. Harding, "Will We Divide?" *Gospel Advocate,* Vol. XXVI, No. 1 (January 2, 1884), p. 10.

T. N. Arnold, the preacher, raised the money. Mrs. E. H. Tubman of Augusta, Georgia, a wealthy widow who had proved a benefactor for the erection of many church buildings, came to the rescue. The building was finished the summer of 1872 and by August, the church was ready for the dedication ceremony.

Isaac Errett and W. T. Moore, neither of whom opposed the organ, came to Frankfort. Errett was to preach the dedicatory sermon and Moore continue with a protracted meeting. A minority in the church planned the program, and all the details were unknown to Arnold and the elders. On Saturday before the scheduled service it was learned that an instrument was to be used. A petition was gotten up objecting to the move, but in spite of their objection the organ was used. Great division followed for years to come.[10]

Late in 1880 the church in Bedford, Indiana, put in the instrument. Uncle "Stever" Younger, who had given one thousand dollars on a new building, had worked hard in building up the congregation. When the organ was injected into the worship, he and fifty others were excluded.[11] A short time earlier the church at Bloomington, Indiana, had a similar experience. W. B. F. Treat came to Bloomington in 1870 and preached for the church four years. Afterwards, he turned his attention to evangelistic work, although still making Bloomington his home. Weak preaching produced weak members in the years that followed. The sermons were mere lectures or moralizing, "such as would be popular in any sectarian church." The organ was introduced. Treat and some others left and began meeting in the courthouse. The introduction of the organ took place in November, 1877. In the following spring Ben Franklin came to Bloomington and conducted a meeting in the courthouse. Treat began preaching monthly here.[12]

On Sunday, June 26, 1881, the church at East Cleveland, where Jabez Hall preached, dedicated a new organ costing two thousand dollars. The church had tried to secure the services of Isaac Errett for the dedication, but another appointment kept Errett

[10]W. H. Hopson, "The Frankfort, Kentucky, Christian Church," *American Christian Review,* Vol. XV, (September 24, 1872), p. 317.

[11]W. H. Krutsinger, "Bedford (Indiana) Church Split," *American Christian Review,* Vol. XXIV, No. 3 (January 18, 1881), p. 21.

[12]Ben Franklin, "Bloomington, Indiana," *American Christian Review,* Vol. XXI, No. 23 (June 4, 1878), p. 180.

from being present.   The pastors of several denominational churches were invited, and a professional organist, from the First Methodist Church, was hired.   A. S. Hayden, who worshipped there, wrote the following to John F. Rowe:

Can you imagine how all this idolatrous affair looks to me, for it is naught else, it being the instrument first, middle, and last. The prophet Amos, in speaking of the manner in which Israel worshiped, uttered this language: "Woe to them that chant to the sound of the viol, or invent to themselves instruments of music like unto David."   If it was woe unto them then, what will it be to those who live in this day of the printed word and gospel light?

To this John F. Rowe remarked:

So far as our distinctive plea is concerned, that "Disciple Church" is gone.   Indeed, it was carried away into Babylon years ago, and this is one of our "missionary churches" too!   *Two thousand dollars* for an organ is what they call "missionary work."   We have our doubts that this church has contributed one thousand dollars in the last ten years for missionary work. . . . As Jabez Hall "the pastor," and "three of the wealthy brethren," have thrown down the fences, of course the members can go in and out and find pasture—which ministers to the flesh—in any of the "sister churches." Of course the communion table is open to all streaked, ring-necked and speckled sectarians.   Jabez Hall was educated at Bethany College.   Shades of Alexander Campbell!   How have the mighty fallen!   Yes, it is *"money* that makes the mare go."[13]

The church in Anderson, Indiana, which had long been divided, introduced the organ during April, 1882.   On March 15 that year, George P. Slade came for a meeting.   Four years earlier Slade had astonished the brotherhood by carrying on a one-sided discussion with McGarvey in the *Review* alleging that the Greek word *Psallo* included an instrument.   Possessing a natural bias for the instrument, Slade came to Anderson and used his influence to promote the organ.[14]

At Augusta, Georgia, still earlier Mrs. Emily H. Tubman gave a hundred thousand dollars for a new building.   The lot cost $35,000; the parsonage cost $10,000, and the meetinghouse $55,000. The persons planning the building left place for an instrument, but Mrs. Tubman refused to allow it.   She tore down a picture of John baptizing the Saviour and put in its place the words, "Repent

---

[13]John F. Rowe, "Organ Dedication at East Cleveland," *American Christian Review,* Vol. XXIV, No. 31 (August 2, 1881), p. 242.
[14]Charles R. Cravens, *History of the Central Christian Church* (n.p., 1925), p. 52.

and be baptized every one of you in the name of Jesus Christ for the remission of your sins," etc. (Acts 2: 38.)[15]

The Central Church in Cincinnati, one of the most prominent in the brotherhood, put in the instrument in February, 1871. A short time before, while the church still met in its old house, a vote had been taken on the instrument. T. M. Allen of Missouri happened to be visiting that day, and threw his weight against the movement, cutting off the use of the instrument temporarily.

Still the use of the organ increased. At Wellington, Kansas, the organ was introduced in 1884. At Bowling Green, Kentucky, there was trouble in the church in 1879. M. J. Ferguson, a graduate of Bethany College and Harvard University, aided in putting in the mechanical instrument. John T. Poe wrote from Texas: "The old church at Huntsville has put the organ *in,* and some of its best members *out.*" Carroll Kendrick, who had only recently moved from Texas to California, wrote in March that year that the new church in Santa Ana had just included the organ in its worship.

By 1885 other congregations were taking steps preparatory to introducing the instrument. When Mrs. Alexander Campbell returned to Bethany in June, 1884, she found the organ in the vestibule, it already having been used in the Sunday School and on two different occasions at church services during her absence. She wrote:

I have attended the worship of the church the last two days since I came, and am happy to say the sound of instrumental music grated not upon *my ear,* but most excellent, solemn, congregational singing, in which I heartily enjoyed uniting. I have worshiped in the church, but with a protest elsewhere to the organ. I must say, however, I could not endure to worship in the church at Bethany if the instrument which had introduced so many discordant notes amongst dear brethren and sisters was made part of the worship instead the music rising from the heart of God's children. . . .[16]

Mrs. Campbell was an ardent opposer of the use of the instrument all her life, borrowing her conviction undoubtedly from her husband.

With the cases of the introduction of the organ growing, op-

[15]Anonymous, "Items, Personals, Etc.," *Gospel Advocate,* Vol. XVIII, No. 3 (January 20, 1876), p. 72.

[16]Mrs. Alexander Campbell, "Letter from Mrs. Alex. Campbell," *American Christian Review,* Vol. XXVII, No. 29 (July 17, 1884), p. 227.

posers found themselves wondering what they should do. Should they cease their opposition and acquiesce to the majority rule? On the other hand, could one who believed its use sinful adopt its use? The problem was serious, nor was it likely that their solution would at first be uniform.

J. M. Mathes, one of Indiana's pioneer preachers, had always opposed the use of the instrument just as he had the missionary society. When the society was accepted by a majority of brethren in 1849, he surrendered his opposition in deference to their wishes. His last years were spent near Bedford, Indiana. He watched Indiana churches adding the instrument. He never relinquished his opposition, and yet wrote:

I am opposed to the organ in the worship, but make no *factious* opposition to it. I suffer no organ to drive me from my place in the church of Christ, nor from my duty as a disciple of Christ.[17]

Isaac Errett put the use of the instrument entirely on the plain of expediency. Consequently, when a brother wrote him, asking for advice on what to do when the instrument was introduced, Errett responded:

Unquestionably, in such a case the wishes and convictions of aged and wise brethren should be respected. The law of love requires us to waive our own preferences, even when such preferences are right, rather than destroy the peace of the church or wound the feelings of our brethren. God cannot bless rude and unfeeling attempts to overrule the judgment and scruples of good brethren by the force of numbers, even when such judgment and scruples may be forced in error. . . . But where a majority thus acts, the minority should firmly protest against the action, and rid themselves of responsibility, and then patiently endure until a change comes. Sooner or later, unless the fear of God is entirely lost, time works out a remedy for such evils.

When the question of what the minority should do when the majority voted in the organ was sent to the *Apostolic Times,* one of the editors replied:

If they make the organ a matter of opinion or expedient, as the organ party professes to do, then according to their own professions, they ought not to bring the organ in. They cannot do this without giving offense. But we put it on no such grounds as this. The worship of God is divinely prescribed in the law of God. The acts of worship are clearly set forth. These acts we can perform. This is the true worship when performed in spirit and in truth.

[17] J. M. Mathes, "The Organ Once More," *The Evangelist,* Vol. XVI, No. 13 (March 31, 1881), p. 197.

Majorities have no right to vote a new element into worship. No majority can compel a man to submit to something for worship that is not found in the divinely prescribed acts in the Scriptures. We will worship according to the Scriptures in every item, small and great; but we will not have anything imposed on us not found in the prescribed worship. We can, we trust, find some who will worship according to the Scriptures, with whom we can worship, and with these by the blessing of the Lord, we will meet and worship the Lord—the Jehovah.[18]

Shortly afterwards, a man wrote, objecting to the *Times'* attitude toward the introduction of the instrument, declaring, "This makes every man's conscience, and every man's notion of divine teaching in regard to worship, the basis of union." To this the *Times* replied that this is wholly incorrect, but that it makes the word of God the basis of union, and requires each man to adhere to the word of God. The *Times* asked, "The only question is, how long shall the minority hold membership in a congregation that has abandoned the word of God?"[19]

Ben Franklin, seeing the magnitude of the problem, simply wrote:

A new question is being started; it is this: "Do you intend to make the organ a bar of fellowship?" We do not propose to *make it anything*. We want simply to have nothing to do with it. . . . The question is not about bars of fellowship, but about *worshiping with the organ*. Can you compel brethren to *worship with the organ?* You certainly cannot. If you introduce the organ and drive persons from the worship with it, and who cannot do it in good conscience, you are the cause of the disturbance and will find yourself held responsible. We are certain the Lord does not require us to worship with the organ, and *we will not do it*. If any man brings into the worship a new and foreign element, and thus places pious people in such a position as to compel them to worship with the organ or not worship with him, he introduces the disturbing element and is to be held responsible for the trouble. In reference to such the commandment is, "Mark them who cause divisions," etc."[20]

But as the years passed, there seemed to be no means in sight to settle the question. Franklin inquired: "But what is to be

---

[18]Anonymous, "Two Questions and Four Answers," *Apostolic Times,* Vol. V, (April 24, 1873), p. 4.

[19]Anonymous, "The Organ and Conscience," *Apostolic Times,* Vol. V, (May 15, 1873), p. 4.

[20]Ben Franklin, "The Frankfort, Kentucky, Christian Church," *American Christian Review,* Vol. XV, No. 39 (September 24, 1872), p. 316.

done? How can we avoid strife? Let the organ come in and say nothing against it?" He admitted that there was much bitterness over the organ, but insisted that this bitterness was all on the other side, a statement not altogether too accurate. But he was firm, "We are in the right, and intend by the grace of God to maintain it."[21]

Some questions of differences among brethren might be settled by putting the question on the plain of expediency, but it was becoming increasingly obvious that this subject of the use of the instrument could not be settled on any such grounds. If a man honestly believed the use of the instrument to be a sin, who could expect him to participate with it? E. M. Schrock wrote to Ben Franklin saying: "If you prefer to worship without an organ, it is none of my business; and if I wish to use an organ, it is none of your business." This rather rude and harsh way of putting it was precisely the position of those defending the instrument on the grounds of expediency. But Franklin replied:

But now, "If you prefer to worship without an organ, it is none of my business; and if I wish to use an organ it is none of your concern." But suppose we both meet in the same congregation, how can this rule be carried out? Can you worship *with it* and we *without it?* No, sir; if you worship *with it,* we must worship *with it.* If we worship *without it,* you must worship *without it.*

It is not my course that "creates strife." The course of the organ folks in bringing the organ, which "is outside of the Bible" into the worship prescribed in *the Bible,* creates the strife, and frequently divides the church. They are the responsible party, the cause of strife and division.[22]

It was not possible for brethren who thought the instrument sinful to worship along side of those who thought it expedient. Opposers of the instrument were failing to see why, if the use of the instrument was outside the Bible, it was expedient to put it into the worship and divide the church. Unfortunately, Franklin's death in 1878 came in the middle of the conflict. Had he lived longer, it is but a matter of conjecture what course the restoration would have taken. One cannot escape the conclusion that some breathed

---

[21]Ben Franklin, "Question of Fellowship," *American Christian Review,* Vol. XVIII, (1875), p. 316.

[22]Ben Franklin, "no title," *American Christian Review,* Vol. XXI, No. 1 (January 1, 1878), p. 4.

easier now that Franklin was gone. J. M. Barnes sensed this and wrote:

No doubt there are men who claim to be brethren, that rejoice that he [Ben Franklin] is dead. But they should remember that, like Abel, "though dead, he yet speaketh." His great works will live far into the periods of the future, and the unborn will call him blessed. He was truly a great commander, one that could see far into the future, and as such often has he lifted his warning voice to the host, among whom he so nobly battled, and sought to lead to higher scenes and purer joys. Often has he pointed out to the brotherhood a Judas, with his innovations, and time has proven him correct. Men hated him then, and now they hate his name and influence. But, Brother Rice, there will grow out of the church of Christ, in the United States, a sectarian party. They will be composed of the progressive and organ element. Let them go; the sooner, the better. They are a curse to the cause we plead. I like Brother Lard's position, as expressed in his *Quarterly,* in regard to the organ, not to preach for a congregation that uses an organ. . . . We will fight for the truth against innovations.[23]

J. W. McGarvey, in 1881, wrote a series of articles on instrumental music in the *Apostolic Times* strictly insisting that its use was a positive sin. A year later, however, the rumor was spread abroad that McGarvey had changed his position. To make his position perfectly clear, McGarvey wrote in a letter dated May 10, 1883, the following:

I have not withdrawn my opposition to the organ. I would not hold membership with, nor contract to preach for a church using one. Its introduction against the conscientious protest of a minority is high-handed wickedness, and can be prompted by no spirit but that of the world and the flesh.[24]

Along with McGarvey was J. A. Meng of Moberly, Missouri. Writing in 1879, Meng declared that in the state of Missouri only six congregations were using the instrument. He was opposed to it, but what should he do about worshiping with these that used the organ?

Were I to go there, I would have either to worship with the organ at the expense of my conscience; or, if I got them to let it remain silent while I was there, I would have the satisfaction of knowing and seeing that some of the members were staying away.

---

[23]J. M. Barnes, "Correspondence," *American Christian Review,* Vol. XXII, No. 7 (February 11, 1879), p. 51.

[24]J. W. McGarvey, "Beliefs Here and There," *American Christian Review,* Vol. XXVIII, (March 12, 1885), p. 82.

Why staying away? Anything wrong about the things command-ed? No, not that. They could not "hear the organ's peal" in the worship of their lowly Redeemer. Why this trouble, this unpleas-antness, this non-fellowship? Any precept, precedent or necessary inference, in the way of that union sweet and dear esteem that should be manifest in all our actions toward one another? No. Nothing of the sort. But, instead of that, human devices have crept in, the leaders have turned the people away from the sim-plicity of the worship to serving idols; those idols are dearer than their brethren for whom Christ died, and those strongly resemble those people of whom the Lord said, by the mouth of the prophet, Hosea: "Ephraim is joined to her idols, let him alone."[25]

Thus there were two attitudes toward the organ. One insisted that its use was a matter of expediency; the other insisted that it was a human innovation into a divine worship and, therefore, sinful. Between these two positions it was evident that there was no compromising or midway point, a fact that has always perma-nently stood in the way of a reunion between the churches of Christ and the Christian Church. Here, then, was the point of departure; the parting of the ways, the instrument giving the impetus to a division which neither the war, slavery, the Ferguson fiasco, or even the missionary society had done.

The issue and the corresponding decision were brought squarely before the minds of the brethren. Most who opposed the instru-ment stood their ground, refusing all fellowship with it. Some, like Joseph Franklin or J. B. Briney, however, were backing off from the logical consequence of their own reasoning. They con-cluded that if other brethren could not be convinced the instru-ment was sinful, they should surrender and go along with them. Franklin soon abandoned the major principles of his father. His old friends were disappointed. W. S. Harper of Greenville, Ohio, expressed a great disappointment, and wrote an article imagining the delight the denominations were feeling in Joe Franklin's change. He pictures the denominations saying:

What a different man Brother Joseph is from his father! Old Ben was as unyielding as a pharisee, had the New Testament at his tongue's end, and his manner of presenting arguments was so overpowering that it was not safe to be in hearing distance of his harangues. He has robbed us of many of our most valued mem-bers. We had to build our fences high and strong against him. But, thanks be to God, the scales are changed. Old Ben was called

[25]J. A. Meng, "New Tests of Fellowship," *Gospel Advocate*, Vol. XXI, No. 11 (March 13, 1879), pp. 169, 170.

a Commoner; we will dub his son a Leveler. We must welcome Brother Franklin into our pulpits and to our homes.[26]

J. W. McGarvey found himself shut out in coming years. He never ceased declaring the use of the instrument to be sinful. When the churches in Lexington, Kentucky, were introducing it, McGarvey moved from one congregation to the other, refusing to stay where the instrument was used. Nevertheless, his major influence went with the side of the advocates of the instrument, but it is doubtlessly true he never felt fully at ease with his company.

In the South, David Lipscomb used the columns of the *Gospel Advocate* very little in discussing this issue. The question was raging furiously in the *Review* and the *Apostolic Times,* but Lipscomb seemed to be unconscious of any need for the discussion in the *Advocate,* feeling that these two papers were sufficiently discussing it. Too, he was waging war against what he considered the greatest of the evils facing the church—the missionary society. With Lipscomb one missionary society was far more dangerous to apostolic Christianity than "a whole orchestra of instruments." This did not mean that he entertained the slightest inclination toward the instrument. In the Southland closely following the Civil War, churches were poverty stricken and could not buy instruments. By the time they could financially afford to own them, they had been indoctrinated sufficiently against them. Meanwhile, as the controversy raged in the North, Lipscomb for the most part watched as an interested observer.

At first, Lipscomb shrank from drawing lines of fellowship against the proponents of the instrument. In 1871 he wrote:

. . . The *Times* and *Review,* if we have not misunderstood their teaching, have advised brethren to withdraw from and refuse to worship with a church that adopts the organ. While we condemn the organ certainly as wrong, unauthorized and corrupting, we have never decided that it is a Christian's duty to go to this extremity. Churches became corrupt in primitive times, and yet no such advice is given in the Scriptures. So we hesitate, while we heartily and earnestly condemn the innovation as at once the outgrowth and promoter of evil. . . .[27]

At the time of writing the above, Lipscomb felt a keen sense of the inconsistency of both the *Times* and the *Review.* Both papers

---

[26]W. S. Harper, "Spirit of Sectism," *American Christian Review,* Vol. XXVII, (February 28, 1884), p. 69.

[27]David Lipscomb, "Piece of News," *Gospel Advocate,* Vol. XIII, No. 12 (March 23, 1871), p. 277.

recommended withdrawing from churches using the instrument; yet, both papers favored at this time the missionary society. The war was now raging against the Central Church in Cincinnati for its new extravagant building and the adoption of the instrument. Lipscomb failed to see just why the *Times* and *Review* could back the Louisville Plan and yet condemn this church as worldly when money for the plan went to the very men behind this congregation. So he asked:

For ourselves, could we open the door of expediency sufficiently wide to take in the plan, we could certainly take the organ, too, without an extra effort, and we think it is not principle but prejudice that causes a person who accepts the one to reject the other.

It is evident that Lipscomb saw earlier than most men that the instrument and the society stood or fell on the same ground.

Lipscomb's first thrust against the use of the instrument came in 1878. "Although," he wrote, "not speaking much concerning it, we have not regarded it with indifference." While admitting that the instrument was used in Old Testament times, he argued that it is incompatible with the worship of the church.

Instrumental music passed away with the other appeals to the merely sensuous and imaginative in men. Instrumental music as a part of divine worship was associated with bleeding beasts as sacrifices and the incense offering. There is just as much reason and authority for the revival of either of these as for the revival of instrumental music in worship. They are both more directly the commands of God, and neither of them have been more clearly or definitely excluded from his worship than instrumental music. Those who adopt one cannot reject the other.

Those who introduce instrumental music give up heart worship of Christ for the formalism of Judaism. It is another indication of that which was the trouble in apostolic times and has been since, the tendency to go back to the forms, the ritualism, sensuousness of Judaism. It shows how difficult, even now, it is to appreciate and cling to that which is purely spiritual in nature.

It was not accidental, or incidental, or unintention, or an oversight that Christ and the apostles ignored and left out of their worship instrumental music. They did it advisedly, because the nature of the religion was contrary to such worship. When Christ and the apostles left it out, who dare replace it in their worship? The incense, as a sweet smelling savor, affects the imagination of some persons just as powerfully as does instrumental music others.[28]

[28]David Lipscomb, "Instrumental Music in the Worship," *Gospel Advocate*, Vol. XX, No. 35 (September 5, 1878), p. 551.

The flame of division leaped high in Louisville, Kentucky, and helped undoubtedly in setting a precedent for opposers of the instrument. Around 1881 the Fourth and Walnut Streets Church put in the instrument, causing several conscientious people to depart. A. I. Hobbs shortly afterwards came to this congregation as its preacher. While he had no part in the division, his actions seemed to sustain the introduction of the instrument. F. G. Allen, then editing the *Old Path Guide* in Louisville, said to Hobbs, "I have as little fellowship for a church that forces an organ in, and thereby drives good brethren out, as I have for one that practices infant sprinkling." However, Allen had made Hobbs associate editor of his paper, an action which appeared to be inconsistent. Meanwhile, from Hobbs there came constant taunts thrown at the brethren asking what they were going to do about the instrument; it was in and they could do nothing about it. To this James A. Harding worded a strong reply, and wrote:

I think it is high time to give them an answer based upon the word of God. What does the Bible say we should do with regard to schismatics? Let the Sacred Writings answer. Rom. 16: 17, "——"; 2 Thess. 3: 6, "——"; 2 Thess. 3: 14, "——"; Titus 3: 10, "——."

Now it appears clear to me that brethren Yancey, Cline, Hume, and others, were as inconsistent in going to those union meetings at Fourth Street Church, as were brethren Marshall and Stanley in fraternizing with those sectarians at Cynthiana. And it appears, furthermore, that brethren McGarvey and Allen are equally inconsistent in hobnobbing with these same and other factious people in missionary conventions, etc. . . . Let us follow the Scriptures and avoid these people. The innovators are rapidly gaining ground in Kentucky in the face of an overwhelming majority who are opposed to them, and who favor standing by apostolic teaching and practice in the worship, simply because those who are for the old paths do not stand firmly and consistently by what they believe to be right.[29]

Two years later A. I. Hobbs wrote in the *Apostolic Guide* on division, charging that there were "those who seem to be doing what they can to bring on a conflict which may result in division." Deeply deploring this condition, he strongly condemned those opposed to the instrument as causes of this division. To this Harding replied:

---

[29]James A. Harding, "Another Inconsistency," *Gospel Advocate,* Vol. XXV, No 21 (May 23, 1883), p. 323.

The First Church at Louisville determined to use an organ in worship. A number of the members, some of them among their oldest and best, could not agree to this. The Holy Spirit had left the instruments of music out of the worship, upon the institution of the church of Christ, and they thought it would be sinful to put back into the worship of God that which his Holy Spirit had deliberately taken out. They could not use the organ in the worship without doing that which they believe to be presumptuously wicked. In this they agree with many of the most pious and learned among all religious people who claim to be guided by the New Testament. But the majority of this church deliberately kicked these excellent people out of their number by bringing in the organ anyhow. The majority does not claim that the organ is necessary to the worship; it does not claim that the organ was used in apostolic times; it merely claims that it will make the music sound better; for the sake of having their ears tickled with a pleasant sound, they drove out the most excellent members; for the sake of a "box of whistles" they cut themselves off from a number of God's faithful children. This wicked work was done with the full sympathy and concurrence of A. I. Hobbs; since it was done, he has defended the church in its action. As F. G. Allen once said, so say I now, I have no more fellowship for a church claiming to be a church of Christ that will introduce an organ and thereby drive out good brethren than I have for a Methodist society. And what more, I intend to do what F. G. Allen has not done, I intend to stand by the statement, to carry it into practice as a preacher and an editor. I would as soon edit a paper conjointly with an infidel as with a man who has thus stabbed a church of God. Such a man does more harm to the cause than any infidel. The majority in this First Church of Louisville caused division contrary to the doctrine of Christ, and we are to mark them and avoid them, if we are to obey the Saviour.[30]

A year earlier Harding drove forcefully at the seat of the trouble:

There are many whom we are told to "mark" and "avoid"; men from whom we are to "withdraw" ourselves; men who trouble the churches of God by forcing upon them untaught questions; who gratify their own tastes by forcing organs and other such things into the worship, thereby driving numbers of the oldest and best members out. From such let us turn away.

It is worthy to remark that the things that are troubling the churches are the inventions of men; the organ, the human missionary society, the suppers and festivals for raising money, etc.,

---

[30]James A. Harding, "Christ Came to Us to Divide Us," *Gospel Advocate,* Vol. XXVII, No. 32 (August 12, 1885), p. 498.

are the bones of contention. . . . Did not the apostles get along without the organ? Yes! Are not these things divisive? Yes! They have rent more churches, alienated more brethren, and caused more heartaches among the children of God than any other things that have troubled the Zion of our King in this century.[31]

Harding's articles were fast helping to mold an attitude among the readers of the *Gospel Advocate,* and undoubtedly set a precedent when circumstances similar to those in Louisville would occur other places. The use of the instrument, being sinful, would not be tolerated, and brethren who thus considered them sinful were now quickly ready to draw lines of fellowship against the innovators.

The trend toward denominationalism. Turning now from the study of instrumental music as a cause of division, our attention now centers upon a trend—a trend toward making the church another denomination. On this trend more attention shall be given in another chapter. At this point it is enough to see it as a cause of alienation among brethren.

Sensing a danger that the church was drifting unconsciously into becoming just another sect, John F. Rowe wrote:

That which gives us the greatest apprehension is the tendency to drift unconsciously and imperceptibly into a miserable sect, a condition of things which is overtaking us because of the supreme indifference of our people on the question of a restored Christianity.[32]

The plea for a return to the ancient order as advocated by earlier pioneers embodied among other things the restoration of the New Testament Church. No one denomination laid claim to being identical with the New Testament Church, but claimed to be a "section" of it. Thus denominations were constantly referred to as "sectarian bodies." The restoration movement proposed the destruction of all denominations by replacing the identical church of the New Testament—an event to be accomplished by close adherency to the word of God, without addition, subtraction or substitution. A conviction that this principle of action was at once practical and scriptural was the driving force for many of the church members. The denominations refused to see the charitableness in the plea, but pressed the charge that brethren had started

---

[31] James A. Harding, "Will We Divide?" *Gospel Advocate,* Vol. XXVI, No. 1 (January 2, 1884), p. 10.
[32] John F. Rowe, "The Old and the New Order," *American Christian Review,* Vol. XXIII, (March 30, 1880), p. 100.

a denomination of their own—the last thing brethren were interested in doing. But, because they insisted upon not being a denomination, but rather identical with the church of the New Testament, their enemies called them narrow and legalistic.

After the Civil War, a trend set in among many brethren to reduce the church to the status of another denomination. Some openly defended using the word denomination with reference to the churches of Christ. That there were Christians in all denominations now began to be openly advocated. The term, Disciples of Christ, was now elevated to the dignity of a denominational appellation, and the Disciples of Christ denomination, with its "reverends" and "pastors," a royal sect among sects, was now a reality. Some openly declared that a return to the New Testament Church was not desirable if it were practical, as did W. T. Moore, when he spoke before an Indiana Convention in Rushville. W. B. F. Treat openly laid the charge at the door of Isaac Errett of having as his supreme desire the making of the churches of Christ another denomination among denominations.[33]

Symptomatic of this trend was the attitude toward the "pious unimmersed," and the growing practice of union meetings with the denominations. But this analysis of the trend will be further treated in another chapter.

The silence of the Scriptures. A third factor underlying the division was the attitude of the brethren toward the silence of the Scriptures. Thomas Campbell's reason for rejecting infant baptism was that the Scriptures were silent on this point. Lacking apostolic authority, the brethren refused to practice it. After the Civil War, this way of measuring religious practices was entirely abandoned by many of the more progressive fringe. Some, however, looked upon this abandonment as dangerous in the extreme. If man were allowed of his own free will to add anything he desired to the work, worship, and organization of the church, there was no end to what could be introduced. Man's desire being the limitation, caused brethren to see no ending of the innovations that could now be introduced. Jacob Creath wrote:

When a man leaps the falls of Niagara, can he stop before he touches the bottom over the falls? When a man leaves the *Bible alone,* there is no rest for him this side of Rome. The most that

---

[33]W. B. F. Treat, "President, Scribe, Affairs, Etc.," *American Christian Review,* Vol. XXIII, (June 15, 1880), p. 185.

can be said for all those persons who have ceased to the *silence* of the Bible is that they are only partly in the reformation.[34]

Creath proceeded to charge that they are standing a straddle of the line, having one foot in the reformation and the other in sectarianism. "They are neither on one side or the other," he wrote.

But the principle of remaining "silent where the Bible is silent" was, with David Lipscomb, a vital one. When John H. West of Murray, Kentucky, wrote Lipscomb in 1873 inquiring for light on the subject of instrumental music, Lipscomb replied:

We do not think anyone has ever claimed authority from the Scriptures to use the organ in worship. They only claim it is not condemned. It is used as an assister of the worship. Its service is part of the worship and very frequently a substitute for a portion of the worship. Our worship to God is regulated by the laws of God. We have no knowledge of what is well-pleasing to God, in worship, save as God has revealed it to us. The New Testament is at once the rule and limit of our faith and worship to God.

This is the distinctive difference between us and other religious bodies. Others accept the New Testament as their rule of faith, but do not make it the limit of their faith. They add other things as articles of faith and acts of worship than those contained in the Bible. We seek for things authorized, they for things not prohibited. Our rule is safe—theirs is loose and latitudinarian. Ours confines us to God's appointments. Theirs opens the worship and service of God to whatever will please men. Our rule limits man's worship to the exercises approved of in the Bible.[35]

On the same point Lipscomb wrote later:

The arguments in favor of the use of instrumental music in the worship have been chiefly a ridicule of the idea that we are limited by the New Testament in our worship. That that principle has been sometimes abused, misapplied, and by ignorant persons perverted, we are well aware. But the principle properly applied, is a good one, is the only safe one to guide Christians. The true work to be done is not to ridicule the principle, but to show its proper application and wherein it is or may be abused.[36]

Those prone to look upon the silence of the Scriptures as a measure of acceptable religious practice insisted that Campbell meant no such thing by his motto, "Where the Bible speaks, we

[34]Jacob Creath, "Our Reformation," *Gospel Advocate*, Vol. XXII, (1875), p. 1123.

[35]David Lipscomb, "The Organ in Worship," *Gospel Advocate*, Vol. XV, No. 36 (September 11, 1873), pp. 854, 855.

[36]David Lipscomb, "Instrumental Music in the Worship," *Gospel Advocate*, Vol. XX, (1878), p. 566.

speak; where the Bible is silent, we are silent." Nathan J. Mitchell, author of "A Pioneer Preacher of the Ancient Gospel," and the founder of many congregations in the Bald Eagle Valley of Pennsylvania, recalled that he frequently traveled with Thomas Campbell and heard him preach many times. He insisted that he knew what Thomas Campbell meant by his motto, and quotes Campbell as frequently saying:

The order of the primitive churches, as to worship of God, under the immediate personal teaching and supervision of the inspired apostles, was equivalent to a command to us moderns; and that the silence of the inspired apostles, on any theme, was to be sacredly and unscrupulously regarded as much as the positive teaching.[37]

As a side line of this point, the word liberty now came into popular vogue. Some insisted that the cause of restoration was intended to unshackle men from the bondage of "legalism," and insisted that the additions to the church which had been introduced were allowable on the ground of the liberty. But yet, in this David Lipscomb thought he saw a definite swing away from the understanding of the earlier pioneers. Liberty of opinion they did not conceive to give them free license to push something into the worship for which there was no apostolic authority and compel men to either accept it or get out. Times had indeed changed! So Lipscomb wrote:

This principle of holding of opinions is one that has greatly changed in its use since it was first laid down by the Campbells. With them opinions might be held as private property, but must not be taught or imposed upon others. A noted example of this was the case of Aylett Raines, who was a Universalist or Restorationist. He could hold this as an opinion, but he could neither teach it or create strife, or force it on others as a condition of union or fellowship. He, without surrendering the opinion as untrue, agreed he would hold it as private property and preach the gospel. He did this, and, it is said, in holding the opinion as private property, not preaching it, he lost sight of the position altogether. According to the present interpretation of the principle, Aylett Raines would have been at liberty to preach Universalism on every occasion he saw fit, and none could have said nay.

For a man to make an opinion a principle of action, where others must act with him, is to force them to conform to his opinion, or to withdraw from his association. When a man has an opinion

---

[37]N. J. Mitchell, "no title," *American Christian Review*, Vol. XXII, (February 18, 1879), p. 57.

that an organ is admissible in the church service, and forces it in, he compels every man to accede to his opinion, or to withdraw from the church. When a man holds the opinion that sprinkling is baptism, and insists on acting on that opinion, he forces everyone in the church to accede to his opinion, or to withdraw from the church. This is making an opinion the test of fellowship; making others accept and act on our opinion, or withdraw from the fellowship of the church.[38]

But one other question now seemed pertinent, viz., who was to be charged with the responsibility for this division?

THE RESPONSIBILITY

Late in the summer and early in the fall of 1883 John F. Rowe undertook to write a series of editorials in the *American Christian Review* entitled, "Lift Up a Standard for the People," the very title suggesting that this threatened to be a blow to the *Christian Standard*. Rowe's editorials were charged with implications of the unsoundness of the *Standard,* and of the fact it was largely instrumental in leading the restoration away from its earlier points of emphasis. Finally, Rowe climaxed his editorials with one entitled, "The Duty of the Hour," which David Lipscomb pronounced the finest Rowe had ever written. Rowe called for "frequent consultation" among the men of faith to "republish to the world our platform of gospel principles." It was a strongly-worded fighting challenge to stand firm against the mighty inroads of innovations then engulfing the brotherhood.

Isaac Errett at once accepted the challenge for a struggle. In the *Christian Standard* of November 24, 1883, Errett replied to Rowe, doing so by charging that there was a coalition of brethren who were set to create disunion, and capture as many preachers and congregations as possible. Errett, while admitting that this charge was based only upon rumor, even named the persons involved. They were supposed to be John F. Rowe, J. C. Holloway, Alfred Ellmore and D. L. Kincaid. Errett responded to Rowe by insisting:

This looks very much like a feeler, and is in harmony with much more that has appeared in that paper, only a little bolder. It may help our querists and our readers generally to interpret the foregoing utterances in their real import, if we state that there are rumors in the air to the following effect: That there is already a

---

[38]David Lipscomb, "Strange Developments," *Gospel Advocate,* Vol. XXVI, No. 11 (March 12, 1884), p. 166.

combination of men engaged in an organized effort to capture as many of our preachers and churches as possible, with a view to such a separation as is implied in the foregoing extracts; that the movement—which has been carefully concealed from public notice, except as it gleams forth in obscure intimations in that paper, and is practically a secret combination—is under the leadership of John F. Rowe, assisted by such men as D. L. Kincaid, J. C. Holloway, and A. Ellmore; that those whom they wish to gain, but are not quite certain of, are pledged to profound secrecy before they are informed of their plans; that their purpose is to spot both churches and preachers who are not in favor of their movement, and by importing men of their own stripe, to hold every inch they can; that every man who favors the *Standard,* or missionary societies, or will tolerate an organ, is unsound and marked as one who causes division and they are pledged to each other to do all they can to lay every preacher of this kind on the shelf, and assist their own men of finding fields of labor where they can be sustained; that the question of division is a fixture, unless the Missionary Society as an organization is abandoned. At present it is reported to be to all intents and purposes a secret combination—a conspiracy against the unity and peace of our churches.[39]

This editorial was as if a bombshell had been dropped upon the church. John F. Rowe replied vigorously, denying totally the charges Errett specified:

So far as I am personally concerned, I deny emphatically that I know of "a combination of men engaged in an organized effort to capture as many of our preachers and churches as possible, with a view of such a separation." We demand the proof or a retraction. Errett's charges continued to burn deeper. Rowe charged that Errett was but creating a sensation with which to increase the subscription of the *Standard.* Moreover, the journalistic ethics involved were not too flattering to Errett, Rowe thought. Serious charges were made based only on rumor to the effect that a secret combination had contrived to cause a major division in the church. Rowe wrote:

Are not panics started on "rumors," especially if they originate with responsible parties? If rumors of the insolvency of a reliable banking house are floated among the people, do not such "rumors" shake the confidence of the people and create a panic among the depositors? And are they not greatly injured by the wanton circulation of such base "rumors"? And yet, the writer has the

---

[39]Isaac Errett, "Is There a Combination to Create Division Among Us?" *American Christian Review,* Vol. XXVI, No. 48 (November 29, 1883), p. 380.

effrontery to say: "We regret that our *benevolent motive* is not understood or appreciated." Yes, it is the benevolence that a wolf has for a lamb! And yet the writer has the temerity to say that "their present air of injured innocence is uncalled for." A wolf might, with propriety, smack his lips and impudently vocciferate the same language of insult.[40]

Errett was called upon to prove his statements or retract them, neither of which was forthcoming. Alfred Ellmore wrote to Errett:

But you have arrested four men, and virtually charged them with treason against this divine union; and though you had the nerve enough to make the arrest, yet when it came to the trial in court, your knees smote together, your courage failed you, and you withered like a fresh-mown flower.[41]

But Errett refused to believe that this "secret combination" did not exist, and refused to retract his statements, while at the same time he refused to prove them. Rowe was now furious. He closes off with Errett by writing the following terse statement:

I hold the editor personally responsible as my wilful defamer and detractor, in an implied charge of leading in a secret combination to produce divisions, until he either sustains his implied charge by documented testimony or makes an honorable detraction.[42]

But on what was this rumor based? The whole affair owed its origin to a private conversation between D. L. Kincaid of Perry, Illinois, and H. T. Buff. Kincaid confided in Buff that he thought there was a division coming in the ranks of the brotherhood, an observation requiring no profundity to be sure. Kincaid remarked that he was saddened over it but nevertheless feared it was coming. He remarked to Buff that he had talked over this matter with Brother Holloway and Brother Wolfe, and both felt the same way. He said he judged from the recent editorials of John F. Rowe that he, too, must feel the same way. Buff then remarked that he would like to write about this matter. Kincaid replied that he did not want to get into the controversy and requested his name be withheld, but authorized Buff to use anything he had spoken to him. From this basis, Buff told Isaac

[40]John F. Rowe, "Adding Insult to Injury," *American Christian Review* Vol. XXVII, No. 1 (January 3, 1884), p. 4.
[41]A. Ellmore, "A Call for Proof," *American Christian Review*, Vol. XXVII, No. 3 (January 17, 1884), p. 21.
[42]John F. Rowe, "The *Standard's* Desperation," *American Christian Review*, Vol. XXVII, (January 31, 1884), p. 36.

Errett, and from him through the *Christian Standard* that a "secret combination" was being formed to cause division. Naturally, the four brethren charged felt great indignation, for there was no real basis for the charge.

Yet, once more, Errett proved to be the better of the two strategists, and Rowe lost considerable prestige among the opposers of the innovations. Coming as it did in that critical time when many were on the fence respecting the innovations, Errett won a singular victory.

Once before, in 1880, John F. Rowe had used severe language in condemning instrumental music, and announced that division was coming. Once before, Errett accused Rowe of construing to cause division in the church. Rowe had to give a defense, for he would not be construed as the cause of division. So he wrote: "We have never said that we would declare 'nonfellowship' because of the presence of the organ." He further stipulated that every congregation must act independently. If a congregation puts in the organ, and does it in the fear of God, "have I a right to interfere with the independent act of said church, and does the constitution of the kingdom of Christ allow me to break the peace of that church and throw it into confusion?" Rowe proceeded to point out that while he is opposed to the instrument, he would not cause division.

Why does not our critic discriminate between the fact of *opposing* an injurious practice and *compulsory toleration and endurance* of such a practice? We have never said that we would declare "non-fellowship" with any church because of the presence of the organ. . . . The organ is not the only thing we oppose, while we are compelled to tolerate and endure it. We have always been opposed to select choirs, but have endured and tolerated them. . . . Paul was opposed to paganism, but he preached in pagan temples. . . . God himself is opposed to polygamy and slavery, yet he tolerates and endures these evils. That is exactly our position on the organ question. We have *never* said that we intend to make the use of the organ "a test of fellowship" in the churches.[43]

Rowe was placed in a dilemma. On the one hand, he held that the use of the instrument was sinful; yet, on the other hand, he would fellowship preachers and congregations introducing the organ. This is precisely the position that Errett wanted Rowe to

---

[43]John F. Rowe, "Self-Contradiction," *American Christian Review,* Vol. XXIII, No. 17 (April 27, 1880), p. 132.

take. Despite the fact that Rowe could never see he was inconsistent, he lost considerable prestige in the brotherhood generally.
Because he believed the instrument to be sinful, Errett's party
connected with the *Standard* could not welcome him with open
arms. But because he would not stand behind the logical consequence of his own declarations on the subject, brethren who agreed
with him in opposing the instrument gradually placed less confidence in him as a leader in the church. On the diplomatic checker
board Rowe had played his man once more against Errett and
lost.

Standing beside Rowe in opposing the instrument were his two
stalwart generals, J. A. Meng and W. B. F. Treat. Both men
were powerful writers, and influential men, but both looked with
alarm at Rowe's inconsistency. J. A. Meng wrote to Rowe that
his attitude "is the very thing to make the advocates of every
possible innovation laugh and almost dance for joy." Meng
declares that none of the apostles knew of any such church independent as Rowe imagines. Each congregation, says Meng, is
independent so far as its own worship and work is concerned.
But all congregations are under the same King, and under the same
laws. Meng affirmed that if a thing like the organ is not prescribed, it is not lawful, and then cannot be introduced except in
violation of the constitution of the kingdom.

. . . The organ is *not* commanded, is *not* prescribed, is not lawful, consequently can't be expedient, and no one has any right
to contend for it in the worship who is willing to "Speak where
the Bible speaks, and be silent where the Bible is silent."[44]

W. B. F. Treat also spoke out against Rowe, concluding his
attack by saying,

But we shall pursue this subject no further. Brother Rowe is
wrong and no amount of bluster can make him right. While we
feel no disposition to "crack the whip of censorship over him,"
yet we must remember that his mistakes are of more consequence
than formerly because of the highly responsible position he occupies.

All of this had occurred in 1880 to conclude one of Rowe's attacks against the *Christian Standard*. That battle had ended with
Rowe losing considerable prestige. When therefore, in 1883 Rowe
pressed home the declaration that division was coming. Errett
managed once more to boil the issue down to a charge that Rowe

---

[44] J. A. Meng, "When Shall the Controversy End?" *American Christian
Review*, Vol. XXI, (March 19, 1878), p. 89.

was the cause of division, and Rowe once more backed into his corner, still declaring he would fellowship a church using the instrument, although he believed its use to be a sin. In 1867 Rowe had declared that an organ was permissible provided it was under the elders. Now, in 1884 he admitted that an organ was permissible provided it was a "little organ." The effect, of course, was disastrous. Errett had succeeded in maneuvering so as to drive a wedge between Rowe and men of his mind. Alienation now set in between Rowe and his own brethren. A coolness developed between W. B. F. Treat and Rowe, and the *Review,* with its own editorial corps badly divided, was in no condition to press a successful attack against the innovations being promoted by the *Christian Standard.*

Meanwhile, neither Isaac Errett nor John F. Rowe was prepared to accept the responsibility for the imminent division. Errett wrote in the *Standard* for October 19, 1872:

The greatest danger that we see is that of making *tests of fellowship* of opinions or expedients concerning which we have no right to judge one another. Let us be careful at this point and we are safe.[45]

Once more Errett wrote:

It is becoming growingly evident that the way is being thus prepared for an attempted division in our ranks, to the extreme dishonor and injury of the effort so prosperously for the last half century for the union of all Christians on a scriptural basis. . .

Let our brethren be on their guard against every attempt, secret or open, to create division among us. There is nothing to justify it. It can only be done by the introduction of false tests of fellowship. Generally our people are too well schooled in the principles of New Testament Christianity to be captured by factionists, and are too thoroughly devoted to these principles to tolerate, even for an hour, any proposal to be false to them, come under what guise it may.[46]

This reasoning was logical, provided of course, one agreed that the use or non-use of the organ was an *expedient* and not an *innovation.* Errett's warning, therefore, could not have any effect on thwarting division.

Others believed that the instrument was unauthorized in the

---

[45]Isaac Errett, "Alarmists," *American Christian Review,* Vol. XV, No. 45 (November 5, 1872), p. 357.

[46]Isaac Errett, "The Responsibility of Division," *American Christian Review,* Vol. XXVI, No. 51 (December 20, 1883), p. 404.

scriptures. It was the act of bringing in unauthorized practices that was causing division, not the opposition to these things. Errett wrote in the *Standard,* "We trust our brethren everywhere will frown on every attempt to produce alienation and division." G. W. Rice, publisher of the *Review,* replied:

So do we. This is sound doctrine. We do most sincerely echo it. But, are there now no elements of discord, alienation and division existing among us? Is the organ such? I think the *Standard's* editor will not deny that it has created much alienation and discord. Who is responsible for its introduction? Not us. We trust, therefore, the editor of the *Standard* and all other good brethren will frown on every attempt to introduce this element of discord and alienation.[47]

By 1885 division was upon the church. The issue was now clear, and for the next twenty years churches were to be placing themselves behind one principle of action or the other. Congregations were yet to know division.

The *American Christian Review* entered the new era badly divided internally. John F. Rowe had not proved to be a man with the foresight of his predecessor, Ben Franklin. Underlying this divided state, too, was the fact that men felt themselves fully as qualified, if not more so, to wear Ben Franklin's shoes as John F. Rowe had been. A roaring current of suspicion and jealousy flowed freely through the columns of the *Review.* In these critical years the cause of the ancient order could ill afford this, and it cost heavily.

---

[47]G. W. Rice, "Alarmists," *American Christian Review,* Vol. XV, No. 43 (October 22, 1872), p. 340.

CHAPTER XII

"PROPHETS OF LIBERALISM"

Whether in the halcyon days of the restoration there could be found the seeds for the later liberalism that swept the brotherhood, may be doubted. Certainly, however, it can never be questioned that these seeds are discovered buried deep in human nature. There are always those who believe they sense something in the "spirit" of a thing contrary to what may be found in its "letter"; or, who, reacting against what they consider a radical extreme of isolationism devote their energies to popularizing a movement. The restoration period came to know these individuals following the war between the states. The church appeared to them to be too narrow and restricted, and their ambition therefore was to lift the brotherhood to a "dignified church" in a world of denominationalism, commanding at least some respect from these religious bodies. With the passing of years the number of men to take the lead in this type of thought became legion. To mention a few they were B. B. Tyler, A. B. Jones, Alexander Proctor, George W. Longan, J. H. Garrison and W. T. Moore. In lasting influence the latter two are far more significant than the others. Before considering the liberal movement that arose in the church it is well to consider its two greatest promotors—J. H. Garrison and W. T. Moore.

Garrison's influence came chiefly from the paper that he edited, *The Christian-Evangelist,* and not so much from his pulpit work. There is little indication that Garrison was a superior preacher, although he was far from an inferior orator. As an editor, however, he reached masses where as a preacher he reached the few. The modern *Christian-Evangelist* is largely a product of Garrison's viewpoint, and its following stems from Garrison's liberalism.

Born in what was then Green County in the state of Missouri, Garrison was the twelfth child in a family of thirteen. The exact place was near Ozark, fourteen miles southwest of Springfield, and the date was February 2, 1842. Ten years before, Garrison's parents, James and Diana Kyle Garrison, had moved here from Hawkins County, in East Tennessee. These were the years of

250

migration when wagon trains moved from North Carolina and
Virginia into Tennessee and Kentucky and thence, on to Missouri
where rich land and plentiful game attracted the pioneer. Isaac
Garrison, grandfather of J. H., had fought in the Revolutionary
War, and following the conflict, had moved from North Carolina
into East Tennessee. He came on westward with his youngest
son, James, who was the father of J. H., and died in Missouri in
1836 at the old age of one hundred and four. Ten years after
James and Diana Garrison settled near Ozark, Missouri, J. H.
Garrison was born.

Garrison's childhood was similar to any other frontier boy.
Educational opportunities were difficult to receive, most youths
managing to eke out a few months of each year under some local
pedagogue. The winter of 1860-61 Garrison acquired his most
impressive bit of education at the feet of a "yankee" school teacher,
Professor Charles P. Hall who had opened an academy at Ozark.
With the outbreak of the war, Hall closed the school, went back
to New England, and later joined the Union Army.

Religion played an important part in frontier life. Garrison's
father belonged to the Missionary Baptist Church. Garrison himself was immersed into this church at the age of fourteen by a
cousin, Ephraim Way, and became a member of the Prospect
Baptist Church. As yet, that body of people calling for a restoration of primitive Christianity was completely unknown to him.

Garrison's childhood was routine—endless work on the farm,
interrupted occasionally by a few months in a country school,
seasoned some by a sprinkling of religious emphasis. But the
spring of 1861 saw this routine changing for a more definite course
ahead. Rumblings filled Missouri of a Civil War that threatened
to burst over the nation.

Missouri was more largely populated by immigrants from Kentucky and Tennessee, who filled the state with pro-southern sentiment. Still, Missouri's close proximity to Union territory gave
it a substantial dotting of Union sympathizers. The direction
Missouri would tend in those critical days was hard to determine.

In the spring of 1861, while political excitement filled the
country over Lincoln's election, a business firm had recently completed construction of a court house in Springfield, and announced that on a given Saturday, a Confederate flag would be
unfurled on top of it. In this area the country people were pre-

dominantly loyal to the Union and the city people, to the Confederacy. A large gathering was on hand. A man appeared on top of the building to unfurl the Confederate flag. A Union man raised a rifle and took aim, but before he could fire, Garrison pulled his arm down. He gave an address, arguing with the people to put up a Union flag since war had not yet been declared, and then defend it if someone tried to take it down. Garrison's speech postponed any immediate bloodshed.

A short time later news that a Confederate Army was moving on Springfield reached the countryside. When Garrison learned of it, he packed his belongings and rushed to join the Home Guards. He came to realize that there was no immediate danger, so returned to help in the wheat harvest. It was July 4, 1861 and Garrison was in the wheat field when he heard the distant roar of the cannon. Dropping his work, he ran to defend Springfield, a defense that proved futile. General Lyon led the small band of Home Guards in a battle ten miles south of Springfield on Wilson's Creek. Lyon was killed and the band of men was driven back.

Garrison entered more determinedly into the Union cause by abandoning the Home Guards and joining Company F of the Twenty-Fourth Missouri Infantry under Colonel S. H. Boyd. Garrison, on March 6, 1862 was shot in the left leg while taking part in the battle at Pea Ridge near Fayetteville, Arkansas. He lay on the battlefield all night with no one to dress his wound. After attention finally was given to him, he was sent home. However, when he was well enough, he was made a Captain in his company and finally a major, a rating which he had when the war closed.

Near the close of the conflict, Garrison was acting as chief clerk in the Provost-Marshal's office where he became acquainted with A. N. Harris of the Tenth Illinois Calvary. It was this acquaintance that changed the whole future course of his life. Desiring to send his two sisters northward to safety and at the same time, to locate them in a place where they could go to school, Harris recommended Abingdon College, a school operated by the brethren. Garrison followed through with the suggestion, but sometime later was surprised when the sisters wrote to him that they had united with the "Christian Church." Later, at the insistence of his sisters, he enrolled in the same school.

This event proved the changing point in his career. Up to

now he had dreams of a future in politics. But when he heard J. W. Butler, president of the college, lecture on the Bible, it changed his interests greatly. The Bible now became a living book. It was only a matter of time until Garrison, too, was abandoning the Baptist Church.

A series of quick events set the pattern for Garrison's life in 1868 and the year following. One was his selection of a wife. While a student in school, Garrison met Judith Elizabeth Garrett of Camp Point, Illinois and became fond of her. Meanwhile, J. H. Smart had met an older sister of Miss Garrett. In a double ceremony held at Camp Point on July 2, 1868, Garrison and Smart were married to sisters. Another event happening about this time to set the pattern for his life was his connection with J. C. Reynolds which led to Garrison's future work. Through Reynolds' encouragement, he preached his first sermon at Macomb, Illinois in 1868. About this same time, Reynolds was editing a paper called the *Gospel Echo.* He insisted that Garrison become an associate-editor. On January 1, 1869 the first issue of this periodical under their partnership was sent forth. Thus, in a short period of time Garrison had become a member of the church, settled down in married life, begun to preach and started a career in religious journalism.

It was not long before he realized that the *Gospel Echo* needed to be a weekly and not a monthly publication, and that, furthermore, it needed to be in a larger center of operation. In casting around for a future likely home for the home, he settled upon the city of Chicago. To this end, the September, 1871 edition of the *Gospel Echo* announced the prospectus for a new publication to be issued from Chicago and known as the *Christian Missionary.* The new publication was to begin in October that same year. Then came the great Chicago fire that destroyed a large part of the city. Garrison went to Chicago to determine what this fire had done to his plans, and found that the men who were interested in the paper financially were now unable to help. So, the plans were abandoned. Garrison wanted to move to St. Louis as the most central location in the country for a large publishing interest, but abandoned this due to the lack of funds. He moved to Quincy, Illinois and immediately laid plans to start publishing a paper.

Meanwhile, an approach was made from several leading brethren, George W. Longan being the spokesman, to join the *Gospel Echo* with *The Christian,* then being published in western Missouri. The merger of these two papers marked an interesting development in both papers. The *Gospel Echo* was first published in Carrollton, Illinois in January, 1863 by E. L. Craig. J. C. Reynolds bought the paper in 1868 and moved it to Macomb, Illinois, J. H. Garrison joining him the first of the following year as an editor.

The *Christian* traced its history back much earlier. D. Pat Henderson was co-editor with Barton W. Stone of the *Christian Messenger,* Henderson going on with it after Stone's death. In January, 1847 the *Christian Messenger* emerged with the *Bible Advocate* and was published at St. Louis by John R. Howard. The first issue of this paper had been published in August, 1842 by John R. Howard and S. B. Aden from Paris, Tennessee. In June, 1861 John R. Howard and D. T. Wright started the *Christian Pioneer* at Lindley, Missouri. On January 11, 1864 the office burned and Wright moved the paper to Chillicothe, Missouri. On November 3, 1870 the *Christian Pioneer* merged with *The Christian* of Kansas City.[1]

T. P. Haley, George W. Longan, Alexander Proctor, A. B. Jones and George Plattenburg were editing *The Christian* in the fall of 1871. They proposed to publish it on what they styled more "progressive" style, but because the brotherhood was not yet educated up to this, it was a losing proposition financially. In the fall of 1871 *The Gospel Echo And Christian* began publication from Quincy, Illinois. The next January, a part of the name was dropped so that it became *The Christian.*

A year later, *The Christian* moved to St. Louis. Garrison now began the organization of a stock company called the Christian Publishing Company with fifty thousand capital stock. The paper began operations from its new headquarters January 1, 1874.

Garrison in the meantime settled in St. Louis and continued his publication of the paper. There were, to be sure, financial reverses which at times threatened the paper's existence. In January, 1881, at the insistence of the Foreign Christian Missionary Society Garrison took leave to go to England to join forces with W. T. Moore. After a stay of less than two years, he was back at St. Louis.

[1]J. Edward Moseley, "The Story of the *Christian-Evangelist," Christian-Evangelist,* Vol. LXXVI, No. 1 (January 6, 1938), pp. 24, 25. Cf. Jesse H. Berry, "Elder D. T. Wright," *American Christian Review,* Vol. XIV, No. 33 (August 15, 1871), p. 261.

In 1882 another merger was negotiated which led directly to the establishment of the *Christian-Evangelist*. B. W. Johnson was at this time editing *The Evangelist* at Oskaloosa, Iowa when negotiations began for the merger.

Barton W. Johnson, editor of *The Evangelist,* had by 1882 made a name for himself in the brotherhood. This he did in spite of his frail health and diffident disposition. Johnson never pushed himself and in brotherhood gatherings was never prominent. He was, therefore, an ideal co-partner for a man as ambitious as J. H. Garrison. But, from the log cabin in Tazewell County, Illinois where he was born in 1833, Johnson had taken advantage of every opportunity to distinguish himself as a brilliant student of the Bible. Upon his graduation from Bethany College in 1856 he ranked among the foremost in his class. Soon after leaving Bethany, he was called to teach at Eureka College and very shortly became president. Beginning in the fall of 1863 he acted as an agent for the American Christian Missionary Society in Illinois. The following spring he became corresponding secretary upon the resignation of D. S. Burnet.[2] In 1864 he took the chair of mathematics at Bethany College where he stayed until after the death of Alexander Campbell. Then he preached at Lincoln, Illinois before finally moving to Iowa to become president of Oskaloosa College. It was while he was in this position that he accepted the position as editor of *The Evangelist.*[3]

Meanwhile, *The Evangelist* had grown steadily. It had bought out the *Christian Record* that J. M. Mathes had edited so successfully from Bedford, Indiana. Still later, it purchased the publishing firm of Bosworth, Chase and Hall which had printed so many brotherhood publications from Cincinnati. *The Evangelist* changed its name to the "Central Book Concern" and took up headquarters in Chicago to have a larger area in which to work.

Late in the summer of 1882 both *The Christian* and *The Evangelist* announced their intention of consolidating. It was not by now a financial necessity on the part of either, but only that both had come to recognize that they covered the same general geographical area, and that the merger would result in a substantial

---

[2] W. K. Pendleton, "American Christian Missionary Society," *Millennial Harbinger,* Fifth Series, Vol. VII, No. 9 (September, 1864), pp. 418, 419.

[3] J. H. Garrison, "Departure of a Christian Hero," *Christian-Evangelist,* Vol. XXXI, No. 24 (June 14, 1894), pp. 369-371.

saving in effort, time and finances. "The Christian Publishing Company" would result from the merger. Accordingly, the first issue of the new *Christian-Evangelist* came from the press dated October 5, 1882.

In 1885 J. H. Garrison went to Boston at the insistence of the American Christian Missionary Society. He had been assured that he could continue his publication of the *Christian-Evangelist* although separated by many miles from St. Louis. By October 15, 1886 Garrison was back in St. Louis satisfied that the experiment could not be successful.

Until his death in 1926 Garrison gave his entire ability to promoting liberalism among the pioneer preachers. While at first he met with continued opposition, in the course of time he won many to his position. From 1894-99 the stockholders behind the *Christian-Evangelist* showed increasing dissatisfaction with his policy and threatened a revolt. The trouble was finally settled when Garrison managed to buy out their interests. The story of this liberalism and Garrison's particular connection with it shall be related in another chapter.

WILLIAM THOMAS MOORE

It is not likely that the lasting influence of W. T. Moore is as great as that of J. H. Garrison. With the exception of the *Christian Quarterly* and the *Christian Commonwealth,* Moore published no paper that molded the mind of the brotherhood as did Garrison in the *Christian-Evangelist.* The *Quarterly* ran roughly only a decade. The *Commonwealth* was published in England, and therefore, very little touched the American brotherhood. Nevertheless, Moore was a man of influence. He played a vital part in the various organizations, especially in the Missionary Society, and in no small measure controlled its policy which in turn controlled the thinking of a large mass of brethren.

W. T. Moore was the son of Richard and Nancy M. Moore, and was a Kentuckian by birth. Moore was born in Henry County, August 27, 1832. He was a mixture of Scotch-Irish, his father being Irish, and his mother, Scotch. His parents had moved into Henry County from Virginia. Moore was only nine years old when his father died, leaving behind him a widow with six children. The burden of rearing the family fell largely on him, so he had little time for an education. By the time he was eighteen, he could only read and write, but at that, had read the Bible through extensively. In 1850 he entered an academy at Newcastle, Kentucky. In the fall of 1855 he entered Bethany College and graduated in July, 1858 as valedictorian of his class.

In October after graduating from Bethany, Moore succeeded P. S. Fall as minister for the church in Frankfort, Kentucky. He preached here until 1864. In June of this year he married Mary A. Bishop, second daughter of R. M. Bishop. Thus, Moore by marriage made close social ties with the leading men of his generation.

On January 1, 1865 he accepted the position as the preacher for the Central Church in Detroit, Michigan. When Kentucky University sent him an invitation a year later to become a professor, he resigned his work in Detroit and moved to Lexington. Hardly had he settled here until the Central Church in Cincinnati invited him to preach there. He accepted hoping to preach at this congregation and deliver lectures during the week at Kentucky University since the distance between cities was not so great. He found this too difficult so resigned at Lexington to devote his full time preaching in Cincinnati.

For twelve years, from 1866-78, Moore stayed in Cincinnati, then the "Jerusalem of the brotherhood." Here was headquarters for the American Christian Missionary Society. Here the *Christian Standard* started and prospered, and Moore saw it through those crucial years when it battled financial depression. Here too, was a city in close proximity to Lexington, the locality of the College of The Bible. If one were to take a map and draw oblong around Cincinnati and Lexington with each city as a focal point, he would have marked out the heart of the brotherhood geographically in 1866-78. In this "heart," W. T. Moore carried no small influence.

During those twelve years, the Central Church underwent many changes. The erection of a building costing $140,000 was but one of them. But possessing the finest building in the brotherhood was a high point of pride with the congregation.

In membership, in influence and in building, Central, Cincinnati became the cathedral church of the brotherhood. One of the notable architectural features of the edifice is a great rose window high in its front. The most influencial church paper of that day denounced Mr. Moore for this "aping of Rome" and a number of prominent preachers took up the outcry against his supposed departure from the faith.[4]

In 1878 Timothy Coop, a prominent wealthy business man of Southport, England visited Cincinnati and convinced Moore that he should move to England to help advance the cause there. Under the sponsorship of the Foreign Christian Missionary Society Moore went to England. He spent eighteen years preaching in Southport, Liverpool, and London, most of the time preaching in the West London Tabernacle and editing the *Christian Commonwealth*. While he was here in England, Moore's liberalism caused considerable criticism in the brotherhood, but since that, too, will be given later, it will not be dwelt upon here.

It was 1896 when W. T. Moore returned to America. He immediately became the first dean of the Bible College of Missouri which was affiliated with the State University at Columbia. Moore and J. H. Garrison had a summer resort, with a cottage by the lake, at Pentwater, Michigan, and the two men spent much of their summers together. In 1909 Moore moved to Indianapolis but when his wife's health failed, moved to Eustis, Florida, purchasing the old home of W. K. Pendleton. Just before leaving England, Moore's first wife died, and he married Miss Emma S. Frederick of Carthage, New York. After spending ten years at Eustis, Florida, Moore moved to Clearwater, in the same state. His death occurred in the fall of 1926 and his burial was at the Spring Grove cemetery in Cincinnati.

Moore distinguished himself in the pulpit. L. L. Pinkerton said of him,

His manner in the pulpit, whether of action or utterance, indicates deep earnestness. His style sometimes borders on the vehement, but never on the declamatory. The points in his discourses are generally well chosen, forcibly argued, and clearly illustrated, and, when practical, powerfully enforced. But his success as a minister is owing much less to his logic than to the warm and wide sympathy which pervades and vivifies it.[5]

It is enough here to sketch this brief biography of Moore. His place in the controversy over liberalism shall be noticed again.

---

[4]Anonymous, "Distinguished in Three Generations," *World Call,* Vol. VIII, No. 11 (November, 1926), p. 37.

[5]W. T. Moore, *Living Pulpit of the Christian Church* (Cincinnati: R. W. Carroll & Company, 1868), pp. 537, 538.

Chapter XIII

THE RISE OF LIBERALISM

A cataclysmic occurrence stirred the brotherhood violently late in 1889 when R. C. Cave delivered a sermon filled with rationalism to the Central Church in St. Louis. The sermon with its repercussions was reported in the *St. Louis Republic* for December 9, 1889. Cave asserted that Abraham and Moses were grossly ignorant of the true character of God, and denied both the virgin birth of Jesus and the bodily resurrection of Christ. He described the Bible as an evolution, not a revelation, and declared that there was no such thing as a divinely-given "plan of salvation." Added to this was his affirmation that water baptism was not found in the great commission. Cave declared:

He who brings himself, according to his measure of knowledge and ability, into obedience to the will of Christ and into oneness of life and character with Christ, is a Christian and entitled to all Christian privileges, among which is membership in the church. To this basis I invite men.[1]

On the Wednesday night following this sermon on Sunday Cave embodied these beliefs in a series of resolutions which were presented to the church. The first resolution read, "The Christian Church makes nothing a test of fellowship but that which a man's own conscience tells him is right or true. . . Strict loyalty to self is the real loyalty to God."[2] The other resolutions were built around this one. The upsurge of the matter was that Cave insisted these resolutions must be accepted by the church or he would resign, adding a touch of dogmatism to the assertions. Liberalists are never dogmatic!!!

Both R. C. Cave and the Central Christian Church of St. Louis were long known for liberal tendencies. This congregation resulted from the minority who in 1869 had attempted to introduce the instrument into the worship. By 1871 the church had a separate existence, and for the next decade fraternized often

---

[1] A. T. Degroot, W. E. Garrison, *The Disciples of Christ: A History* (St. Louis: Christian Board of Publication, 1948), p. 388.

[2] C. L. Loos, "A Protest," *Christian-Evangelist,* Vol. XXVII, No. 1 (January 2, 1890), p. 9.

with the denominations. Later, Joseph H. Foy was its preacher. In 1884 Foy left the church to join the Episcopalians where he might receive "larger latitude of opinion." Later, however, Foy returned. J. H. Garrison preached for this congregation with some regularity for fifteen years. When R. C. Cave came from Richmond, Virginia on December 9, 1888 to serve as minister, he found fertile soil in which to plant his liberalism. Cave is described as "highly educated" and a "masterly orator." In character he was irreproachable. He possessed a magnetic personality.

On December 1, 1889 Cave preached a sermon dealing with God's revelation to the Old Testament characters in which he affirmed that an understanding of God was native to the soul, and questioned the understanding of God held by these Old Testament characters.

David, Elijah and Isaiah—all the worthies, whose names adorn the pages of the Old Testament story, while they were eagerly reaching out after God, were groping in darkness and grossly ignorant of his true character. These old Jews had a conception of Jehovah far higher than that of the heathen world round them, but still sadly imperfect and frightfully false.

She (the church) is not called upon to defend the Abrahamic and Mosaic conceptions of God; on the contrary, she cannot defend them without being disloyal to Him who came to displace them and give the world a different and higher and truer conception.

We ask men to come to him (God) by Christ. And when we invite them to come to Him by Christ, *we do not mean that they shall come by virtue of any sacrifice that Christ has made to appease his wrath and render him willing to receive them;* but we mean that they shall come to him by Christ as their guide, their teacher, their exemplar, leading them to him.[3]

The first reactions were violent. One denominational preacher accused Cave of leading the church to the devil; a prominent Baptist clergyman said Cave was "verging on Ingersollism." O. A. Bartholomew, minister of the First Church, reported:

Against Dr. Cave personally I have nothing to say—I must say that Dr. Cave is not in accord with the church on any one point, and his teachings are entirely at variance with the doctrine accepted by the Christian Church. . . Dr. Cave, in assailing the Old Testament, assails the inspired word of God, which is the foundation of the church. The church does not agree with Dr. Cave in any such belief, as he sets forth, which are his own views

---

[3]*St. Louis Republic,* December 8, 1889, p. 26.

and not those of the Disciples. Why he remains in the church while holding and preaching these views I do not know.[4]

The next Sunday, December 8, Cave preached another sermon along the same line of thought as the first. Most of the congregation, captivated no doubt by his unimpeachable character, glowing personality and scholarly appearance, congratulated him. That evening he spoke on "The Beginning of Christ's Society" and invited men to come to Christ as they understood him, despite the fact they might not believe in miracles, or even in the Bible.

On the third Sunday, December 15, Cave preached to an overflow audience, again presenting his liberal views. At the conclusion of this sermon, a committee of brethren headed by Dr. R. M. King presented a series of resolution. No doubt these resolutions were the result of a gathering storm of opposition swelling up from the entire brotherhood. The resolutions in the main objected to a creed in any form and opposed any attempt to "fetter thought." They read,

Whereas a fellow minister, O. A. Bartholomew had said R. C. Cave was not in accord with the Christian Church

Whereas the Christian Church makes nothing a test of fellowship but that which a man's own conscience tells him is right or true, and that the very biggest exemplification of one's faith is shown in strict loyalty to self as the true essence of loyalty to God

Whereas, the Christian Church has no established written creed—

Whereas, the church recognizes no canon by which to judge man's orthodoxy

Whereas, the Central Christian Church acknowledges no ecclesiastical court

Whereas our only rule of faith and practice is loyal and faithful obedience to self

Resolved that the church unanimously support Cave

Resolved that disciples at Central Christian Church in no way approve any attempt of man to fetter liberty of thought, conscience or speech

Resolved that a copy of the above be placed on records of the church and sent to the papers.[5]

J. H. Garrison at first allowed the Cave matter pass with but little controversy. He was out of town when the resolutions were adopted but upon reading them the next day in the newspaper, called upon Cave. The next Wednesday night at Prayer

---

[4]*St. Louis Republic,* December 8, 1889, p. 26.
[5]*St. Louis Republic,* December 16, 1889, p. 8.

Meeting the service was turned over to a business meeting to discuss the resolutions. Garrison asked that another date be set to consider these resolutions, but he was refused. Cave insisted that a vote against them was a vote against him. Garrison promptly asked for a letter of dismissal for himself and his wife, and was followed by the same request from J. H. Smart and his wife. Later Garrison wrote out his objections to the resolutions insisting that they nullified the Bible as a guide.

Very shortly Garrison drew up a letter of protest signed by sixty members of the church, and on Friday, December 27 presented this at a special meeting. F. E. Udell acted as chairman of the meeting calling upon Cave to repeat his views, which Cave did. This meeting adopted Garrison's protest and Cave promptly resigned. On Sunday January 5, J. H. Garrison spoke to the church on "Earnestly Contending For The Faith Once Delivered to The Saints." Twenty-nine of Cave's followers asked for letters of dismissal. Dr. R. M. King announced that a meeting would be held the next day to form a new congregation organized on "the oldline Campbellite basis." The congregation was organized under the name, "West End Christian Church" and Cave was invited to be the minister.

Garrison, editor of the *Christian-Evangelist,* admitted that he was pained deeply at Cave's bold declarations. When he and Cave met together privately to talk the matter over, Cave assured Garrison of his deep convictions on these matters totally at variance with the views of most of the brotherhood. He admitted also that these views might cause a division in the Central Church, and asked Garrison's advice. Garrison advised him to go to another locality as soon as it was deemed wise, and establish another church upon his own views. Cave appeared to accept the suggestion, but Wednesday night, in the meeting that lasted until eleven o'clock, Cave appeared to be pressing his views, which led Garrison to ask letters of dismissal from the congregation for himself and his wife.

Most of the brotherhood reacted violently against Cave. The *Church Register,* edited by J. C. Creel of Plattsburg, Missouri, published the following article which we copy from the *Christian Leader.*

The course of Dr. Cave was not a surprise to some among us. He has been known to hold views at variance with the disciples for several years; and yet he has filled some of the best pulpits of the Church. His foibles have been withheld from public gaze and criticism by means not necessary to mention until the crash came, which follows such a course as regularly as conclusion follows premises, and one of our churches has half its membership buried beneath the debris of his rationalistic air-castle. But was he alone to blame? I tell you No. The disaster was invited rather than avoided. There is a false idea of liberality among us that is ruinous in its tendency. Utterances that discredit all that is held as sacred among us, and even the express language of the inspired writers, are excused as mere differences of opinion. The more rash a man's statements in regard to the Bible the better his chances for a hearing at the annual meetings of our conventions, lectureships, etc. The remark is not without foundation that, "We used to preach the gospel at our conventions, but we've quit it."

Speculative subjects are discussed to the almost entire exclusion of the gospel of Christ. Men are known to hold views not only not believed among us, but views which, if practiced, would render nugatory the very commands of the gospel; still the most sacred interests of the Church are committed into their hands by men who know they hold such views. This is plain language, but "the time for great plainness of speech has come. We speak that we do know and testify that we have seen." Do we wonder that such a result as the "Cave matter" should follow such a course as we have persued? The only wonder is that it was delayed so long.

Whenever men abandon the Bible as a standard of truth, and exalt their conceptions of truth to the dignity of a tribunal at whose bar the Bible itself is to be tried, there is not much uncertainty in respect to results.[6]

David Lipscomb saw in Cave's remarks something striking at the very foundation of the inspiration of the Bible. So he wrote:

The defection of R. C. Cave, of St. Louis, pains us more, though does not surprise us as we heard intimations of it heretofore. He is a man of irreproachable moral character, fine powers of mind, and extraordinary force and attractiveness as a public speaker. We have heard for some time, that he doubted the inspiration of the scriptures and called in question the miraculous conception of Jesus, and other truths vital to the Christian faith.

Recently he preached a sermon in St. Louis an approved report of which has been published in the St. Louis *Republic*. In it, he clearly repudiates the inspiration of the Old Testament. He says "Those old Jews had a conception of Jehovah far higher than that of the heathen world around them, but sadly imperfect and frightfully false." "All the presentations of him were imperfect

[6]William Cobb, "Some Things Developing," *Christian Leader,* Vol. IV, No. 7 (February 18, 1890), p. 5.

and more or less false." "Abraham and Jeptha were no more commanded by God to sacrifice their children, than the Hindoo mother is commanded to cast her child into the Ganges."

He says to the infidel, "There is and can be no conflict between you and us, as long as your attacks are directed against the Judaistic conception of Jehovah, whether you find it in the Old Testament story book, or nineteenth century creeds. Wherever found, it is false and dishonoring to the true God, and we invoke the Divine blessing upon your efforts to drive it from the world," and much of the same kind. While making no direct attack upon the New Testament, it is clear he rejects its teachings which conflict with his ideal of what God should be. He repudiates the idea that Christ suffered to satisfy the demands of God or law— or to ransom man or as a propriation for man—he is his example.

To talk of denying the inspiration of the Old Testament yet maintain the inspiration of the New, is too absurd to talk of for a moment. Robert Cave has a logical, investigating mind. He attacks the inspiration and truthfulness of the statements of the Old—but he cannot believe the New inspired. If the Old Testament is not inspired, the New cannot be. Jesus Christ and the apostles have unequivocally affirmed the inspiration of the Old Testament. They have staked their claims to inspiration on the inspiration and truthfulness of the Old. If the Old is not inspired of God and true, they were deceived or deceivers. Either of which is fatal to their claims. Christ refers to Moses as the law-giver sent of God, to Abraham as the friend of God, as seeing the day of Christ and rejoicing in it. And makes Abraham's bosom the type of heaven. Declares all true children of Abraham the children of God. The apostles from the beginning of their career quote the law and the prophets as the word of God—given by inspiration. "All scripture is given by inspiration and is profitable for doctrine, for reproof, for correction, for instruction in righteousness that the man of God may be perfect, thoroughly furnished unto all good works." This refers to the Old Testament scriptures. Again to Timothy "thou hast known the holy scriptures, which are able to make thee wise unto salvation, through faith which is in Christ Jesus." These scriptures pronounced holy and able to make man wise unto salvation, are none other than the Old Testament scriptures. For none other were in existence in the childhood of Timothy. Why holy? Why able to make wise unto salvation, if not from God?

Then to object to the Old Testament, because of the cruelty manifest in the commands given to Abraham and Jeptha, as abhorrent, and to accept the New with the crucifixion and death of Christ in it, is to strain at gnats and swallow camels. If Jesus suffered and died as the scriptures declare, by the will of God, unless the Bible reason for that suffering be accepted, it surpassed in abhorrent cruelty a thousand fold all the cruelties recorded in the Old Testament combined. The scripture reason for the suffering of Christ, explains and justifies the lesser sufferings inflicted by the will of God on others. . .[7]

By 1890 the brethren were more conscious of the inroads of rationalism into the reformation than they had ever previously been. Garrison, in reacting against it, enlisted the assistance of some leading brethren to write on the fundamental principles. These articles, printed first in the *Christian-Evangelist* were later printed in the book, *Old Faith Restated,* a symbol of the doctrinal reaction. The *Gospel Advocate,* likewise sensing the danger in this type of modernism to the restoration, enlisted the support of a number of leading brethren to write articles against rationalism and in defense of the inspiration of the Bible. These articles were printed in the *Gospel Advocate* for 1890, and were never collected together in book form as were those in the *Christian-Evangelist.*

Garrison's opposition to R. C. Cave probably elevated him in the estimation of many brethren. Still, it is a matter of simple fact, that many failed to be impressed. Brethren frequently agreed that Garrison was as bad as R. C. Cave in his beliefs, but his dwindling prestige demanded some retraction to boost the brotherhood's confidence in him. H. R. Tanner of Missouri tersely put it this way,

There is not a sensible man in Missouri or out of it who thinks that either Garrison or the congregation to which he belongs objected to Cave's doctrine. It was only an indignant brotherhood which made them turn on their brother pastor and hound him out of their pulpit.[8]

Though the criticism appears harsh, there is undoubtedly much truth to it.

David Lipscomb shared Tanner's conviction about Garrison. Cave, he felt, had been made the scape-goat when in reality Garrison had much more harmed the brotherhood by his friendly overtures to liberal-minded preachers than had R. C. Cave. So Lipscomb wrote:

[7]David Lipscomb, "Sad Apostasies," *Gospel Advocate,* Vol. XXXII, No. 1 (January 1, 1890), p. 6.

[8]H. R. Tanner, "Western Splinters," *Octographic Review,* Vol. XXXIII, No. 24 (June 12, 1890), p. 2.

Whenever a man begins to draw the distinction between believing in Christ, and believing in the Bible, which reveals Christ,
he does not believe in the Christ of the Bible or of God. And
he who rejects the Bible, rejects the Christ of the Bible. And he
is the only Christ that can save. All other Christs are the
creations of their own minds, deifications of their own conceptions.
There is a school of rationalism in the church of Christ, especially
in Missouri. We have spoken of it heretofore. They use terms
out of their ordinary meaning. They mean by inspiration, as
Longan calls it, "inspired genius." The revelations of God are
merely "the creations of genius," as Shakespeare and Milton's
works are. They do not mean that the Spirit of God enters into,
reveals the mind of God to man, and speaks through him.

The Bible is the "creation of genius," not the revelation of God
to man, by the Holy Spirit. Hence it is not the complete and
perfect standard of religious truth. It is all to be subjected to
the judgment of man, or to the spirit of holiness in man, as what
of the Bible is true and what is not. "Inspired genius" may yet
develop new revelations, and higher manifestations of truth. All
this is sheer and unmasked infidelity to God, and to his Son
Jesus Christ, and is a rejection of the Bible. It makes every man
a law unto himself. Because of the disingenuous and equivocal
use of the terms, the evil has been insideous in its workings, and
difficult to define and expose. For one, we felt a sense of relief,
when Cave declared his convictions in unmistakable terms. This
was fair and honest in him, to let the world know in unambiguous
terms exactly where he stood. The disciples owe to him a vote of
thanks for his candor, and so far as we are concerned, he has it.

I object to those who have been teachers in this school of infidelity making Cave a scape-goat, while those denying the Bible
to be of God, equally hurtful in their teaching, but less courageous
and candid, are petted as "esteemed brothers."

Let us go to the bottom and make clean work in purifying the
church of this corrupting infidelity. Longan and Proctor have been
the leaders in this school. Others follow after them. They do
not believe the Scriptures are given by inspiration of God, hence
that they are not the final and perfect revelation of God to man,
and the standard of truth.

But anything now, short of thorough denunciation and exposure of the whole system of destructive of all true faith in God,
as destructive as the claims of the Bible to be worthy the attention
of humanity, as dishonoring to God and degrading to Christ, and
a rejection of the Holy Spirit; and as destructive of all good to
man in time and eternity, is treason to both God and man. Let
us be true to the occasion and faithful to God, and great good
will come to the church through this development. If we compromise in this matter, and fail to stand firmly for God's word and

God's honor, we betray the Son of God afresh and deserve shame and everlasting confusion.[9]

F. D. Srygley, who in 1890 began as front-page editor for the *Gospel Advocate,* watched the whole procedure with his characteristic note of humor. He thought of Mark 16: 16, "He that believeth and is baptized shall be saved." The *Christian-Evangelist* had been very lavish in declaring that the pious unbaptized should be saved. Srygley wondered what would become of the pious unbeliever, and so wrote:

The *Christian-Evangelist* and the *Apostolic Guide,* and the *Christian Leader* and the *Christian Standard* and, in fact, about every body else of much consequence have been pitching into R. C. Cave for the sermon he recently preached in St. Louis. So far as I have noticed, every body has been trying to prove that he is not in harmony with the current reformation. Well, suppose he isn't, what of it? I don't know any body that is in harmony with the current reformation, for that matter. I mean to say, the current reformation concedes to any man the right to differ from it, and about every body of any consequence exercises that right now and then. To differ from "us, as a people" is not a very great thing after all. If R. C. Cave has done nothing worse than this, we are doing entirely too much cackling for the size of the egg. The Bible says, "He that believeth not shall be damned." That is the point I am watching. So far, I have not yet seen that point made. And yet, that is the very pitch and substance of the case. What must a man believe, to keep from being damned, and will R. C. Cave be damned some too for what he does not believe? That is the question. It is needless to talk about what "we as a people" do or do not believe. For my own part, I stand by the Book—"He that believeth not shall be damned." And this I understand to be just such *believing not* as is set forth in those few whereases recently passed so flippantly by our erring brethren of the Central Church in St. Louis. This thing must be fought to the end on that issue, and the *Christian Evangelist* may as well come down to the work at once. We have been lavish of our sympathy for the pious unimmersed. What, now shall we do with the pious unbeliever? Is any body going to be damned? If not, I am disposed to say, in the language of the inimitable T. W. Caskey, "You may as well convert hell into a calf pasture and be done with it."[10]

Meanwhile, Garrison found it extremely difficult to countenance

---

[9]David Lipscomb, "Those Sad Apostasies," *Gospel Advocate,* Vol. XXXII, No. 6 (February 5, 1890), p. 87.

[10]F. D. Srygley, "From the Papers," *Gospel Advocate,* Vol. XXXII, No. 3 (January 15, 1890), p. 33.

Cave's "clear conscience" where the peace and welfare of the church was at stake. Garrison wrote to Cave, "If you, my brother, can look at the wreck of the Central Church, which a year of your ministry has wrought, with its divided homes and its saddened and alienated hearts, and with the fearful burden it imposes upon those who propose to stand by their colors, with a 'clear conscience,' as you say, that is the severest possible condemnation of the sufficiency of conscience as a guide in matters of religion."[11]

Srygley, on the other hand, failed to be touched by Garrison's display of conscientious opposition. After all, Garrison's editorial policy had not wrecked one congregation but scores the nation over, who objected to the policies advocated by the *Christian-Evangelist*. Srygley, after copying Garrison's note to Cave, replies:

That is a touching paragraph, and now I am expecting some one to "take up the thread" of the brother's exhortation and say to J. H. Garrison: "If you, my brother, can look at the wreck of the whole brotherhood all over this broad land and in Texas too, which your editorial policy has wrought by way of pushing things many good brethren conscientiously believe to be corruptions of the worship—a wrangling brotherhood with its divided homes and saddened and alienated hearts, and with the fearful burden it imposes upon such men as McGarvey and Lipscomb who propose to stand by their colors on this society and organ question— if you can look on all this with 'a clear conscience,' that is the best possible evidence that you are a pretty bad sort of fellow too!" Verily it does make a difference whose ox is gored. In the language of the lamented Allen, "The case being altered, alters the case." When J. H. Garrison wants to push something which the brethren conscientiously believe to be a corruption of the worship, their conscientious convictions are small considerations, and he can not understand at all why they have such consciences anyhow. When R. C. Cave wants to push something which J. H. Garrison conscientiously believes to be a corruption of the worship, this matter of divided homes and saddened and alienated hearts, at once looms up as one of the biggest things in the whole business. As between R. C. Cave and J. H. Garrison in this matter of divided homes and such like things, there is precious little difference. My own opinion is that one of them is about as bad as the other if not worse. . . .[12]

Within less than a decade following the Civil War it was

---

[11]J. H. Garrison, "The Difficulty in the Central Church," *Christian-Evangelist,* Vol. XXVII, No. 2 (January 9, 1890), p. 23.

[12]F. D. Srygley, "From the Papers," *Gospel Advocate,* Vol. XXXII, No. 5 (January 29, 1890), p. 63.

thought by some that there was a strong inclination toward what is abstractly called "modernism" in Missouri. Then it was referred to as "rationalism," a term borrowed from German theological circles. Alexander Proctor and George W. Longan were especially singled out as accepting the usual theory of Biblical interpretation used by German and French Rationalists. Proctor and Longan rolled out the anathema of "legalism," especially directing it toward the editorial policy held by the *Apostolic Times* with Moses E. Lard and J. W. McGarvey the specific targets. Some of the strongest articles against this drift are to be found in the *Apostolic Times* between the years 1869-72. The term, legalism, however, although popularized by the *Christian-Evangelist* and re-echoed on down to the present day by men imbibed with the Garrisonian type of thinking, is one that those who use it most are least willing to attempt to define. What is legalism? Moses E. Lard wrote in 1871 in answer to Proctor which we copy from a later issue of the *Gospel Advocate*. Lard says,

Not to insist on obedience to these commandments is legalism. Against it, of late, not a little has been said, and nothing wisely. The term legalism I do not like. It is an offensive term, with a bad sense, as popularly used, and should, therefore, not be employed. *Obedience to the commandments of Christ is its exact equivalent, and should always be used in its stead.* But few men, however, could be found bold enough to speak against obeying the commandments of Christ. The result here would be too glaring. None could fail to see it, and few would hesitate to pronounce it infidelity. A more insidious method is adopted. Legalism is the thing inveighed against. But the act amounts to the same. Legalism and obedience to Christ's commands are the same. Hence to speak against that is to speak against this. Nor have I any respect for the man who masks the law of Christ, and then speaks against it, than I have for him who insults it indirectly.[13]

Thus Lard accused Proctor of making the idea of obedience to Christ under the guise of legalism, and fighting it under this name.

By the year 1890, David Lipscomb thought back over the last twenty years of his life and recalled many statements coming from Missouri preachers, all of which were closely allied to rationalism. He recalled that E. B. Cake, president of the Missouri Sunday School Convention and a frequent contributor to the *Christian-Evangelist,* had time and again declared that God and man were

---

[13]David Lipscomb, "Is Rationalism Rife in Missouri?" *Gospel Advocate,* Vol. XXXII, No. 12 (March 19, 1890), pp. 182, 183.

one. God talks to himself when he talks to man. Man hears and
obeys the voice of God when he does what his intuition directs
him to do.

In the April 16, 1886, issue of the *Apostolic Guide,* J. W. Mc-
Garvey began openly criticizing the tendency of Missouri preachers
to accept liberalism in their thinking. For the next decade or
more, McGarvey became increasingly conscious of the evil of this
type of thinking to the restoration movement. His famous works
on "Biblical Criticism," reprints from articles he wrote for the
Christian Standard, are indicative of his strong reaction. At any
rate, by 1886 McGarvey opened a campaign of criticism against
the "advanced thinking" promoted by the Missouri Christian Lectures. He charged that Hedric's sermon in the 1885 lectureship
on "The Philosophy of Remission of Sins" philosophized the
atonement into nothing but a moral influence on the sinner and
made the remission of sins into a mere turning of the sinner away
from sin. It made pardon a figment of the imagination, according
to McGarvey, and went so far as to deny possibility of pardon in
the government of God. At the same lectureship McGarvey
charged that Proctor had said that the Jewish idea of angels and
demons were superstitions borrowed from Babylonia. McGarvey
immediately thought it to be a shame that Jesus and his apostles
did not have more scientific eyes and more rationalistic study so
that they might have detected this. The same year, Longan had
said it was a "piece of foolishness" for man to regard it as real
history that the sun and moon had stood still, as the Biblical account affirms. The book of Job, Longan regarded, as not inspired.

Simpson Ely, president of Christian College at Canton, Missouri, wrote in the *Christian Register:*

The New Theology has been spreading with alarming rapidity
during the last ten years. A mutual admiration society has been
formed in Missouri, and when one member of the society would
make a bold rationalistic statement, the other members would
applaud.

Their very pompous actions would seem to say, "We are the
only advanced thinkers." This society cannot brook opposition.
Woe to the man that has the hardihood to question their position.
Those who attended our lectureship will doubtless remember how
the writer was throttled when he entered his solemn protest against
charging the inspired apostle Paul with fallacious reasoning. Now

the same man who charged Paul with fallacies, does, in the last *Christian-Evangelist*, deny that Mary and Elizabeth sang the beautiful psalms attributed to them by the sacred writers.[14]

Ely's last charges were directed toward Longan. But, according to Lipscomb, Longan had gone further, insisting that Matthew and Mark were confused upon the second coming of Christ, and therefore he denied their credibility. He also questioned the reasoning of Paul. Lipscomb charged that when the Scriptures say Jesus cast out demons, Longan understood that Jesus was a victim of heathen superstition.

Lipscomb now charged that this type of thinking and preaching had been going on in Missouri for ten years. Yet, the favorite writers for the *Christian-Evangelist* had been these very men promoting such "advanced thinking." When, therefore, Garrison appeared to be taken by shock at R. C. Cave's bold rationalistic assertions, Lipscomb joined with many others in questioning Garrison's sincerity. This type of thing had been going on under his nose for years, and he had constantly winked at it. What made him suddenly change? Too, Cave's attitude was a little strange. He had formerly preached for the Vine Street Church in Nashville, but had never proclaimed his beliefs on rationalism there. Why had he done it immediately upon coming to St. Louis where Garrison attended church? Was it not likely that he felt that here he was among friends, and could afford to do it? At least no one had appeared more shocked at Garrison's rebuff than Cave himself. Actually, by 1890, there was a mounting antagonism to this new Missouri rationalism from all quarters. Although the charge is hard in its bluntness, many believed Garrison's action to be a political move to reinstate himself in the eyes of many who were losing confidence in him. Garrison admitted as much when he wrote:

. . . Some have, in their earnest zeal, even questioned my own soundness in the faith. I have no censure for them, but urge them to be patient and see whether or not the *Christian-Evangelist* shall prove worthy of confidence the brethren have reposed in it in this trying ordeal.[15]

The charge is not altogether groundless when all the facts are

[14]David Lipscomb, "Is Rationalism Rife in Missouri?" *Gospel Advocate*, Vol. XXXII, No. 12 (March 19, 1890), pp. 182, 183.

[15]J. H. Garrison, "The Difficulty in the Central Church," *Christian Evangelist*, Vol. XXVI, No. 52 (December 26, 1889), p. 820.

considered. At least Lipscomb had no less confidence in R. C. Cave than he did Garrison and let the fact be known:

This whole system is rationalism and skepticism of the most bare-faced type. It destroys the credibility of the Bible, all ground of respect for it as the word of God, and man's faith in Jesus as the Christ, the Son of God. The man who defends these men or their teachings, whether he intends it or not, aids and abets the spread of rationalism and infidelity in the land. The man who can see no apostasy in this widespread adoption and advocacy of these destructive theories proclaims himself more than half an apostate and infidel. For a man to denounce R. C. Cave, who has honestly declared his unbelief, and carried it and himself out of the churches of God, and to overlook or close his eyes to these ruinous teachings in the church, and to defend and cherish the men who advocate them, as brethren, shows sectarian spirit, or a moral cowardice that unfits for membership in a church of God, and proclaims him unworthy to be accounted a disciple of the Lord Jesus. I would prefer membership in any sect of Christendom that holds to the Bible as the inspired and infallible word of God, however it might pervert its ordinances, than to be in fellowship with those who tolerate, cover up and cherish teachings denying the inspiration of the Scriptures, rejecting the Bible as the infallible word of God, destroying man's faith in it and in Jesus the Christ as the Saviour of sinners, or who affiliate with and sustain the men in this work of ruin to the best hopes of humanity. If the Bible is the word of God, let us hold to it. If not, let it go to the dogs. If it is not the inspired word of God, it is a book of fables and falsehoods.

Others besides Lipscomb and McGarvey sensed the leanings in Missouri. In December, 1878, Proctor delivered an address on "Rights and Ceremonies in Religion" before a Preachers' Meeting in Kansas City. In this discourse he took the position "that in the usual and scriptural sense of the words, there were no rites and ceremonies in the New Testament." One senses that somehow the ambiguity in the statement worried F. G. Allen as much as the facts, for Allen replied:

Somehow in the last few years, a number of our preachers in Missouri and some other states, have fallen into the habit of delivering addresses at these "Preachers' Meetings" and conventions that require a great deal of explanation. Sometimes they are months trying to get the people to understand what they meant and what they didn't mean. There is no necessity for this. What the Bible clearly teaches on any subject may be so presented that the people will understand it—cannot help but understand it. We are constitutionally shy of a speech that requires so much explanation.

We know nothing of the nature of Brother Proctor's explanation of his position, "that in the usual and Scripture sense of the words, there were no rites and ceremonies in the New Testament," but we are profoundly certain that it would require *a good deal of it* to enable us to "endorse the position."[16]

Indicative of the trend in the brotherhood was the revival of the controversy over the "pious unimmersed." From the earliest days of the restoration movement the question has constantly been asked, what shall become of the pious members of the denominations who die without being immersed? Preachers had proclaimed that the Bible taught baptism (immersion) to be necessary to salvation, but does this imply the unimmersed will be lost. Those who frankly faced this implication were considered uncharitable and legalistic. Those who managed to squeeze in room in heaven for the unbaptized somehow considered they had caught more the true spirit of the restoration and breathed a more spiritual atmosphere.

In a large measure this controversy revived itself around W. T. Moore while he was preaching in England. Timothy Coop, a wealthy English member of the church, felt that a trip to America to discover the reasons for success in the United States would probably help the English cause. He visited America and Cincinnati in 1878 and managed to persuade W. T. Moore to move to England. The Foreign Christian Missionary Society promptly made arrangements, and sponsored Moore in that foreign country.

Moore left for England in the fall of 1878, locating first at Southport. There was a small congregation of disciples here, but Moore ignored this church and rented Cambridge Hall, a large auditorium. He selected fifty persons for a choir, none of whom were members of the church, and proposed to set forth "undenominational Christianity." David Lipscomb complained that Moore was deceiving the people, and so wrote:

The movement is announced in language which all persons, not acquainted with Mr. Moore's position and mission, must understand to mean that, like Mr. Moody, he labors for no denominational object and does not seek to promote the increase of any special church, or party, but will leave his converts, uninfluenced, as to the sects they may please to join; than which nothing can

---

[16]F. G. Allen, "Editorial Notes," *Old Path Guide*, Vol. I, No. 2 (February, 1879), pp. 77, 78.

be further from the truth. In the only sense in which the people understand the term, Mr. Moore is intensely denominational, his mission is denominational—so much so that no one of the churches connected with the Missionary Society, whose agent he declares himself, would receive into its membership anyone of the most pious of Southport's believing people, who had not been immersed, and he is sent here for the purpose of planting or enlarging such churches.[17]

In 1881 Moore began publication of his paper called *Christian Commonwealth*. During the spring of 1885 he made a recommendation through his paper calculated for union among all the denominations when he advocated that the church accept into her fellowship all members of denominations who were sprinkled for baptism, and who sincerely believed this was right, but that they should understand the church itself would only practice immersion.

While both the *Christian Standard* and the *Christian-Evangelist* defended Moore, his proposal excited the ire of a considerable number of brethren. F. G. Allen led the way in attacking Moore. He charged him with being the pastor of a church four hundred strong in membership, which was really a mixed Baptist Church. Allen charged that if Moore would preach the whole truth of God, that church would not keep him for twenty-four hours. Although Allen had a strong tendency to defend the society, and did ; he found ample reason to turn his anger toward it. He declared that up to this time he had "kept his finger in his mouth" and would do so no longer. John F. Rowe joined Allen's crusade against Moore, both charging that the *Christian Commonwealth* gave news reports of denominational activities in England while ignoring the brotherhood there. The *Commonwealth* had much to say about "Reverend Alexander McClaren, D.D.," but nothing about an advocacy of a return to the ancient order of things.

Alfred Ellmore reviews the work of Moore in the past and expresses no surprise at his conduct. He wrote:

And while we have nothing personal against Brother Moore and certainly wish him well, in well-doing, we say that when the brethren are through with his labors over there, we wish them to send him on to some other heathen (?) nation, for, while we would regard him as a citizen, we have no use for him as a preacher of

---

[17]David Lipscomb, " 'Rev.' W. T. Moore, M.A., at Southport," *Gospel Advocate,* Vol. XX, No. 45 (November 14, 1878), p. 715.

the *ancient order* over here. We are perfectly satisfied he is not reliable as a leader and, therefore, speak out plainly.[18]

But David Lipscomb laughed up his sleeve in the typical "I-told-you-so" attitude. He believed the Society was fundamentally wrong, and anything it would do would be wrong. Moreover, he never doubted that the basic philosophy underlying the establishment of the Society was the conviction on the part of its friends that human plans could improve upon the divine. The Society itself represented a basic implication that God's way, the church, was unsatisfactory, and that man could improve upon it. The Society, to Lipscomb, represented man's attempt to change the divine plan. He regarded F. G. Allen as being inconsistent in "keeping his finger in his mouth," but apologizes for Allen on the ground that Allen had been reared in central Kentucky among the friends of the Society. Lipscomb never doubted that if Allen lived long enough he would stand with him in opposing the Missionary Society. For W. T. Moore, however, to allow people into the church upon sprinkling was, to Lipscomb, equivalent to Moore's assuming the authority to change the law of God. But so what? Wasn't this the basic philosophy that underlay the whole program of the Society? Lipscomb wrote: ". . . The same authority that changed the order of God in reference to the work of the church can change the faith. You have sown to the wind; you must reap the whirlwind."[19]

On October 29, 1885, the fourth anniversary of the publication of the *Christian Commonwealth,* a dinner was held in honor of the paper. W. J. Hocking delivered the toast of the evening. Hocking was a high dignitary in the Church of England. He told the story of a man driving a wagon in Texas with four bullocks drawing it. One was named Baptist, another Methodist, another Presbyterian, and another Episcopalian. A man passing by inquired of the driver why these animals had been given such a peculiar name. The answer was that the bullock by the name of Baptist was so called because he always headed for the water, the one named Presbyterian would do nothing except by rule, the one named Methodist was always kicking over the traces, and the

---

[18] Alfred Ellmore, "Our Foreign Missionary," *American Christian Review,* Vol. XXVIII, (August 6, 1885), p. 253.

[19] David Lipscomb, "How It Was Treated," *Gospel Advocate,* Vol. XXVII, No. 30 (July 29, 1885), p. 470.

one named Episcopalian was so called for he always held his head high. Hocking applied the story. W. T. Moore was the driver, and the various men at the dinner—Methodist, Baptist, Presbyterians, and Episcopalians—were the animals. Hocking then pronounced the *Christian Commonwealth* a "scriptural," "unsectarian" paper. The paper was declared to be evangelical but not sectarian, scriptural but not uncharitable, progressive but loyal to Christian principles.

F. G. Allen printed this material in the *Guide,* but only brought down the wrath of the *Christian-Evangelist* and the *Christian Standard* against him. Both insisted that if he were a gentleman he would apologize.[20]

W. T. Moore's sincerity in his action is hardly to be questioned no matter how much one may disagree with his action of taking into the church those that were unimmersed. Actually, Moore, Errett, and Garrison looked upon the situation in England as being analogous with that of Thomas Campbell when the latter in 1809 inaugurated the "Christian Association of Washington" when baptism was hardly a controversial question. "The case being altered, should have altered the case"—to use a pet phrase of F. G. Allen—but Moore could hardly see it. Neither Moore, Errett or Garrison were in precisely the same point with regard to advancement in knowledge in 1885 that Thomas Campbell was in 1809. Campbell acted consistently with his beliefs. If sprinkling or immersion had not yet entered a discussion of the Association, it was only because Campbell had not yet surveyed the field of thought on the subject. He was acting in perfect accord with the convictions he had at that time. With the passing years, he added considerably to his knowledge, altering his ideas radically as to the purpose and method of baptism. In point of knowledge, the Thomas Campbell of 1845 was not the Thomas Campbell of 1809, and whether with his advanced learning of scriptural principles, he would have acted the same way in 1845 that he did in 1809 is highly questionable. W. T. Moore ostensibly believed that immersion was the only baptism, and that it was in order to salvation. To waive this in the interest of Christian union as Moore did is not wholly analogous to Thomas Campbell, who in 1809 had not yet reached these convictions. It is understandable

---

[20]A Recluse, "Jottings at Home," *American Christian Review,* Vol. XXIX, No. 1 (January 1, 1886), p. 2.

that Moore's act should be interpreted by David Lipscomb, F. G. Allen and John R. Rowe as a presumptious act on his part aimed at displacing the law of God with his own human wisdom.

The whole question of where the "pious unimmersed" stood with regard to their own salvation and the fellowship of members of the church displayed two attitudes. The *Christian-Evangelist,* on the one hand, advocated the liberal spirit, displaying no reticence to shut its eyes on immersion when it deemed it wise, declaring at the same time that "the church of Christ believes that it is wiser to keep the spirit of a commandment than the letter." Of course, just how an individual kept the "spirit of a commandment," without doing what the commandment enjoined, the *Christian-Evangelist* never proposed to explain. To this attitude, F. D. Srygley replied:

This talk about the spirit and letter of commandments usually comes from men who want to *feel* goodish, but do as they please, in religion. . . . To put the whole thing in its simplest form, the theory is that any man who is right in *spirit or motive* will be accepted of God no matter what the outward form of his conduct may be. It puts man's salvation wholly upon the ground of his own honesty, and taboos the idea that anyone will be damned who has the *spirit of obedience,* no matter how grave may be his mistakes as to the *letter* of God's commandments. Much has been said against rationalists, but in my judgment they have done no more than follow this spirit-and-letter buncombe to its legitimate, logical consequences. The point is, does God require man to conform his life to an external standard, or does he leave him to determine his own course by an internal light? Is man guided in religion by revelation from without, or by a spiritual light and nature *within* himself? Did religion originate in miracle, and is it perpetuated by teaching, or is it innate with man in principle, and developed by evolution? This is the only issue, and there are but two sides to the question. Those who talk flippantly about keeping the *spirit* of a command while sneering at the *letter* of the law, or the exact thing commanded, are but the logical premises of which rationalists are the necessary conclusion, whether they so understand and intend or not. . . .[21]

As to the other attitude, F. D. Srygley in his own inimitable style, expressed the feeling of most members of the churches of Christ when he wrote:

Brethren, it is a waste of time to try to drag me into a discus-

---

[21]F. D. Srygley, "From the Papers," *Gospel Advocate,* Vol. XXXII, No. 33 (August 13, 1890), p. 513.

sion of this "pious unimmersed" question. As I understand the
New Testament, the "pious unimmersed" ought to be immersed.
And in case they are not immersed, I know of no promise in the
New Testament that they will be saved. But, as to whether God
will make allowance for honest mistakes, and save those who think
they are obeying him when in reality they are doing something he
has not commanded in lieu of what he has commanded, is a question for God to settle, and I decline to take any part in it.[22]

To this same attitude, Isaac Errett came in the last years before
he died. In 1888 Errett was scheduled to speak on the Missouri
Christian Lectureship on the subject, "The Grounds of Christian
Fellowship." This was only a few months before he died. Because
of Errett's sickness, someone else read the paper on that subject
Errett had prepared. For several years Errett had given every
indication of backing the receiving of the "pious unimmersed" into
the fellowship of the brotherhood. His strong supporting of W. T.
Moore on that issue is but one indication of Errett's tendency.
Still, in the address, Errett says:

My own conviction, not hastily reached, is that we cannot consistently receive into fellowship, in our churches, the unimmersed.
I say this with a full recognition of the Christian character and
eminent spiritual worth of multitudes of Pedobaptists, and agreeing
with Mr. Campbell fully in acknowledging them as Christians in
the sense in which he employs that designation in the quotations
I have made.[23]

The very fact that J. H. Garrison at the close of the address gave
it his hearty endorsement presents the enigma that was Garrison.

The student of the restoration is not likely to be long in recognizing that such questions as that of the "pious unimmersed" are
but symptomatic: the basic question relates to the conception of
the church. On the one side men of a more conservative turn of
mind conceived of the church as *the* New Testament Church. By
following the scriptures—without addition, subtraction or substitution—they believed they would have *the* apostolic church; it
would not be a *sect* of the church as the Protestant denominations
claimed they were, but *the* church. But the liberal ranks in the
brotherhood frowned disgustedly upon this conception. Men who
had it were "narrow and legalistic and had not yet caught the

---

[22]F. D. Srygley, "From the Papers," *Gospel Advocate,* Vol. XXXII, No.
13 (March 26, 1890), p .193.
[23]Isaac Errett, *The Missouri Christian Lectures, 1886-88* (Cincinnati:
Standard Publishing Co., 1888), p. 53.

spirit of the restoration" was a typical Garrisonian statement, later to be applied with sophisticated airs against the *Christian Standard*. But the development of a score of years between 1870 and 1890 was to show how far apart brethren were drifting in their thinking at this point.

In some circles the practice was constantly growing of fraternizing with the Protestant denominations. W. T. Moore, as we have seen, practiced it regularly in England. At Madisonville, Kentucky, J. W. Higbee held a union meeting with the "other denominations." At Rushville, Indiana, D. R. Vanbuskirk waits on the communion table, assisted by a Presbyterian and Methodist clergyman.[24] This disposition many could hardly countenance. The aim of the restoration they conceived to be the exalting of the New Testament Church by the destruction of all sectarian bodies. Protestantism was the enemy to be destroyed that the apostolic church might alone remain. John F. Rowe, therefore, wrote:

> We ask with all the seriousness of the judgment day before our eyes, and in view of our final accountability, can the Disciples of Christ affiliate with men who have produced such a mongrel of the holy and blessed religion of Christ? Can we in any sense identify ourselves with such sectarian bodies? Can we, in the fear of God, and as the conservators of the ancient order of things, religiously mingle with them and sit down at their communion tables? To do so is to return willfully into Babylonian Captivity. Religiously, we must remain a distinct people, or else give the lie to all our pretensions of restoring the apostolic church, in doctrine, in faith and obedience, in worship and in discipline.[25]

To avoid sounding too narrow and exclusive, some were willing to relegate the church into another sect in Christendom. In 1889 an editorial appeared in the *Christian Standard* saying:

> We claim to be part of the church of Christ; we claim that the faithful in our fellowship are members of the church of Christ, and that our churches are churches of Christ, and that one of our churches is *a* church of Christ; but that churches as a whole constitute a church of Christ or *the* church of Christ we most positively reject.[26]

---

[24]J. A. Meng, "Let Us Have the Documents," *American Christian Review,* Vol. XXV, No. 8 (February 23, 1882), p. 65.

[25]John F. Rowe, "The Duty of the Hour," *American Christian Review,* Vol. XXVI (November 1, 1883), p. 348.

[26]John F. Rowe, "The *Standard's* Surrender," *Christian Leader,* Vol. III, No. 38 (September 17, 1889), p. 4.

Nine years earlier J. H. Garrison wrote in *The Christian:*

If it be inquired, "What, then, is the name of our church?" we reply, if by the term *our* is meant those of us engaged in this reformatory work, *we have no church,* separate and distinct from that to which all other Christians belong. The idea that we have is the *sect idea.* It is an idea that has given birth to such names as "the Methodist Church," "the Presbyterian Church," "the Baptist Church," etc. To speak of ourselves as "the Christian Church" is to adopt this sect-idea and to put ourselves on the same basis with all other sects. It is not necessary for us to say to our readers that the church of God or the church of Christ, in New Testament usage, includes all the saved—all obedient believers in Christ. This is a well-known fact. What right have we to use these names in any narrower or more restricted sense? To do so is to use them in a sectarian sense.

If it be replied to this that these sectarian bodies, by adopting party names, have virtually repudiated the scriptural names, and are, therefore, not entitled to them, we answer that, as separate parties or bodies, they are not entitled to them; but that, unless the act of consenting to be designated by a party name, on the part of the individual Christians in these various sects, has served their bond of allegiance to Christ, so that they have ceased to be members of his body, they are a part of the church of Christ, which he purchased with his own blood, and should, therefore, be included in our use of the word church. But if the fact of their being members of a sect *has* dismembered them from the body of Christ, then are they not Christians, and our plea for *Christian union is* without meaning. The plea for the union of Christians is based on the idea that there is one family of God, one church of Jesus Christ, and that the members of this one family are one church, by reason of human weakness, ignorance and folly, in the past, are now scattered, and divided into parties and sects, wearing party names, rallying around party leaders and dogmas, and building up partition walls between those who have a common Saviour and a common destiny, and who should, therefore, love each other as brethren, and help each other along the pilgrim way to the "better country." To plead for the union of this divided family and to point out the way to its realization is a work of such grandeur and dignity as to commend it to the approbation of all conscientious, thoughtful and unbiased minds, and to the gracious favor of Heaven.

Again, in the July 15, 1880, issue, Garrison wrote:

In our last we were speaking of the impropriety of alluding to our effort at reformation or restoration as "the Christian Church," or "the church of Christ"—thus employing Catholic terms in a denominational sense. It is easy to see how this has come about. All denominational movements in Christendom are styled *churches,* with a prefix setting forth some leading doctrine or principle of such denomination. Adopting this style of thought, and conceiving of our movement as a separate church, with a proper aversion to unauthorized and unscriptural names, it was natural that the name Christian should be selected in preference to any other adjective, as best descriptive of *our* church. But the error lies either in conceiving of our religious movement as an ecclesiastical organization, answering to the name of church of God, and including all that the name includes in its scriptural usage, or else in regarding it as a denominational church, like the other churches about us.

Sometime ago there was a controversy between some of our papers on the question, "Are we a denomination?" It occurs to us there is another question lying behind that that will help to answer it. It is this: are we a *church?* If so, we are certainly a denominational church like the rest.[27]

Thus, germane to the spirit of liberalism arising in the brotherhood was the basic conception of the church. To Garrison there were Christians in all churches, and the purpose of the restoration was to unite all of these Christians. Baptism, far from being essential to church membership, could be cast aside, thus opening the doors of heaven to the pious regardless of their immersion or lack of it. The church in the final analysis was another sect and thus as denominational as the rest.

Nor can anyone doubt that this viewpoint was growing rapidly in popularity. B. B. Tyler, another of its champions, preached in New York, and became involved in a controversy with John F. Rowe. The New York preacher made it clear that baptism could be placed aside with him easily enough.

Let me as far as possible narrow the point of difference. I did not hold that immersion was the "dead fly." In this my brethren have misunderstood me. The dead fly, in my estimation, *was the insisting on immersion as the sine qua non of church membership.* I hold that as a large portion of the church of Christ (those considered by disciples as true members of Christ) are opposed to immersion, disciples ought to recognize their convictions.[28]

Later, Tyler proceeded to teach that all men are the sons of God, and in this sense only is Jesus the Son of God.[29] At Canton, Ohio,

---

[27]Joseph Franklin, "Sectarianism in the Reformation," *Gospel Advocate,* Vol. XXII, No. 35 (August 26, 1880), p. 545.

[28]B. B. Tyler, "A Word to Rev. Dr. Tyler," *Christian Leader,* Vol. IV, No. 23 (June 10, 1890), p. 1.

[29]B. B. Tyler, "In What Sense Is Jesus the Son of God?" *Christian Leader,* Vol. IV, No. 43 (October 28, 1890), p. 4.

in August, 1889, Tyler, speaking before a large gathering of brethren, taught that all men would be saved who did the best they
knew how, and in private conversation declared that unimmersed
people would be saved.   When it came to the subject of a union
with the denominations, Rowe found reason to give Tyler's strictures a vigorous examination.   Tyler had written:

The union of Christians is a subject very near to the hearts of
a great multitude of the children of God.   The interest increases.
Prayers in behalf of unity multiply.   Conferences to aid the cause
are becoming common.   Union is in the air.   Everybody feels it.
It is the watchword of the day. . . . Little by little we are finding
a common platform in that word which lives and will abide forever.
Coming out of the confusion of the Babylon of the great apostasy,
modern denominationalism seems to have been unavoidable; but
it was not so in the beginning.   The believers then were one heart
and one soul.   This was and is the will of our common Lord.   But
our denominationalism must not be confounded with the sectarianism so severely condemned by the Holy Ghost in the New Testament.   The sects condemned in the world of the Lord were companies of professed believers in the Son of God, turning away from
Jesus, from his truth and from his Church.   The denominations
of our time represent the efforts of godly men to return in faith
and in life to the religion of Jesus as he gave it to the world in the
beginning.   The various Protestant denominations represent stages
in the journey from Babylon to Jerusalem.

Rowe responded by saying, "Let us analyze this piece of sectarian
soft solder."

a. B. B. Tyler says, "The union of Christians is a subject very
near to the hearts of a great multitude of the children of God."
Well, sir, if a "great multitude are already the "children of God,"
why discuss Christian union at all?   The idea is superfluous and
preposterous. . . .

l. "Little by little we are finding a common platform."   "Are
finding" is in the present tense.   Paul says the "word of faith
which we preach is nigh thee, even in thy mouth and in thy heart."
If it is that near, it shouldn't take the honest, sectarian, theological
doctors long to find the jewel.   Again, does Brother Tyler pretend
to affirm that the Disciples of Christ are "little by little *finding* a
common platform"?   He found it some years ago, but it now
seems he lost it in the wide West, and that he is again "finding" it
in New York City!   Like the man who "got religion"—now he
has it, and now he hasn't. . . .

m. "But the good Lord will show us in his own good time the
way out of the present difficulty."   Please tell us by what means,
outside of his revealed will, God will "show us the way out"?   Are
we to have new revelations?   You had better spend your precious

time, my brother, in showing the denominations the way *in,* provided you regard yourself as being *in,* and not simply occupying a "stage" in the "movement from Babylon to Jerusalem." If the Lord in his own good time intends to show us the way out in the remote future, then, in that case, the Bible has actually ceased to be an infallible guide!

So much sophistry in so small a space we have not, in a long time, seen in a sectarian sheet of the deepest dye. Alas, alas, the "Grand Restoration" is only a "movement," and another denomination has been added to a troop of phatasmagoria.[30]

It was inevitable that with the rise of this liberal spirit it should eventually affect the schools operated by the brethren. Butler University in Indianapolis was in for more than one session of constant anxiety over the encrouchment of this spirit. In 1879 the university found itself in the midst of a war with the brethren over the question of whether or not only members of the church should compose the faculty. Love H. Jameson, president of the Board of Trustees, upheld using sectarians on the faculty, insisting that "our plea" was indefinite, and our principles broad and catholic. Jameson asked:

One of the most distinctive tents of Disciples, if I do not misunderstand them, is that sectarianism is wrong, and all Christians should be united. Holding such opinions, ought we to exclude a Christian man or woman from our faculty because they differ with us? . . .

F. G. Allen looked aghast at such a statement and replied:

With what singular uniformity do those who lend themselves to sectarian interests speak disparagingly and even contemptuously of the Restoration. . . . When men begin to champion sectarianism they have at once a strange idea of undenominational institutions, with them that institution which is composed and conducted in the interests of a number of denominations is undenominational; while that conducted by and in the interests of *no* denomination is *sectarian.*

With such men our plea for the restoration of primitive Christianity and the union of God's people on the Bible becomes at once a myth as unsubstantial and shadowy as the shade of Plato's ghost; or else a human creed to be condemned by an institution founded on the Bible alone, to the rejection of human creeds.[31]

---

[30]John F. Rowe, "An Apology for Sectarianism," *Christian Leader,* Vol. II, No. 8 (February 21, 1888), p. 4.

[31]F. G. Allen, "Butler University," *Old Path Guide,* Vol. I, No. 7 (July, 1879), pp. 269, 279.

But there were those who yet stood in opposition to this general trend toward making a sect out of the church. In this respect there are oddities in the restoration. F. M. Green was connected in sympathy with the *Standard*. He was secretary for the Society, and in 1886 was a member of the Ohio State Legislature, and thinking seriously about running for a United States Congressman. F. M. Green's father was Philander Green of Kent, Ohio. No greater contrast in men could be found than in Philander Green and his son. The father was as unyielding and determined as Jacob Creath. He opposed everything that looked like progression, but his son was the opposite, working hard toward it. As the elderly Green thought back over the restoration movement, he wrote:

I remember well when we had no meetinghouses to dedicate by professional dedicators or successful beggars for money. We had no organs to entertain the congregations, but the natural one the Lord had given to his children. We had no hired boys just out of college to play the clergyman and usurp the authority given to the heaven-ordained elders of the church of God. I have lived to see nearly all things we once preached and practiced changed to the modern, fashionable, sectarian practices, where all expedients are used to entertain the people and gain thereby the recognition of the conflicting sects about us, to become popular, and be considered orthodox and really, one of the branches of the church. . . .

When I became a member of the church almost fifty years ago, I never expected or dreamed that I would live to see the change in doing the Lord's work, as it is called, that I have seen.[32]

But Green comes to the battle fully ready to do his part in his declining years. Manby J. Breaker writes: "Christians are asked to unite on the basis of the primitive church in Jerusalem, but in reality no one wants to return to the condition of that church." Breaker goes on to say that the Jerusalem church had no Sunday School, lacked discipline and was badly organized. But Green went to work on Breaker. "The farther some people get from Jerusalem and primitive Christianity," he writes, "the better they feel." Breaker had said there was in the Jerusalem church no definitely stated terms of membership. Green says that of course the Missionary Society has membership on a money basis, and in this case every man knows when he has complied, but the Lord

---

[32]P. Green, "The Testimony of One of the Pioneers," *Gospel Advocate,* Vol. XXX, No. 7 (February 15, 1888), p. 12.

didn't have as much sense as men have, and so didn't give any terms of membership.[33]

In addition to the liberalism expressed in the general conception of the church, there was yet another tendency which must be noticed. This relates to the drift toward a centralized ecclesiasticism which would serve as the "voice of the brotherhood" to exercise a control over the preachers and the churches. The Missionary Society in most cases became identified as this centralized ecclesiasticism, and so the debate over the Society now entered a second phase.

In 1882 the Missouri State Convention adopted a constitution which assumed the oversight of all the schools operated by the brethren in the state. The State Convention insisted that "all schools demanding recognition allow the nomination of their trustees by the State Convention." Three years later only two schools had complied with the request—Christian University at Canton and the orphan school at Camden Point. F. G. Allen again took his finger out of his mouth and wrote:

The fact is, our conventions are making rapid strides in the footsteps of the post-apostolic church, which eventually led the great apostasy. If they do not soon become *legislative* in their action, it will be because their progress in that direction is arrested.

David Lipscomb said:

It seems to me that all hope that a society whose existence is itself an unauthorized usurpation, should refrain from unauthorized usurpation of power, is wholly against scripture and common sense. Like begets like.[34]

Rowe charged that the Convention was trying to control the school, and through the schools, to control the church.

B. Bowen read a paper before the Kansas City Alliance of Christian Preachers on September 1, 1888, deploring the "present distracted condition of the churches" He said:

The Christian Church has no protection against an incompetent and vicious ministry. If a man can deceive one congregation, he may wear, without contradiction, the name of Christian preacher. Our preachers are located with no reference to their peculiar abilities. . . .

[33]P. Green, "The Conclusion of the Whole Matter," *American Christian Review,*" Vol. XXIX, No. 40 (September 30, 1886), p. 316.

[34]David Lipscomb, "Societies," *Gospel Advocate,* Vol. XXIV, No. (October 5, 1882), p. 625.

. . . The brotherhood, then, ought to have authority over individual congregations.[35]

The *Christian-Evangelist* now took the lead in advocating some centralized control over the brotherhood, fearing centralization less than excessive individual liberty. Depicting the general tendency on this point is the following from Samuel Magee:

The *Christian-Evangelist* now advocates a conference, or some such institution with authority, to pass upon the ministerial qualifications of all preachers; that is, as to their moral fitness and doctrinal soundness, etc. Verily, this is progression with a quick movement. But who gave the *Christian-Evangelist,* managed by poor, fallible, sinful, uninspired men, the prerogative to legislate and to dictate for the great Head of the Church? Just as Christ commanded in the words of his commission, all disciples have authority to go out into all the world and preach the gospel, and who has authority to command otherwise? The creed of the Christian is personal, not doctrinal nor dogmatical. Paul's statement is, "I know whom I have believed," not "what I have believed." Paul was never alarmed concerning "the danger among us has always been in the direction of an extreme individualism rather than a tyrannical ecclesiasticism." This is the danger our progressive movement fears! . . .

. . . The state societies are everywhere taking advantage of every opportunity to foist an ecclesiasticism upon the churches of Christ. In Mississippi the State Society is making a desperate effort to secure and hold the title of all the church property in that state; in Kansas the Society has recommended that no preacher be employed unless indorsed by the Corresponding Secretary; in North Carolina the State Convention has, by a committee, "passed, ordained and placed on the roll of ministers" certain evangelists, and by the same committee "one candidate was rejected." How does this strike you? In Missouri the Society has taken control of all the educational institutions. I want to know from whence this authority is derived! Is not this whole thing a bold assumption? How long will the disciples of Christ submit to this assumption? How can we stand fast in the liberty wherewith Christ has made us free so long as we wear the collar of this man-made institution? . . .[36]

In October, 1882, James A. Harding attended the convention of the Society in Lexington, Kentucky, as an observer. Isaac Errett was the spokesman to raise money by selling life membership.

---

[35]B. Bowen, "Centralized Organization of the Christian Church," *Christian-Evangelist,* Vol. XXV, No. 37 (September 20, 1888), p. 581.

[36]Samuel Magee, "Missouri Letter" *Christian Leader,* Vol. IV, No. 47 November 25, 1890), p. 1.

When a man asked Errett if he could purchase a life membership for his eight-year-old son, Errett replied: "Yes, or for one eight days old. We have infant membership here, though not in the church." Although Errett made his statement in jest, events proved that the Society had accepted money for infant membership. Harding took the Society severely to task only to be taken to task himself by F. M. Green.

A few months later The Northeastern Iowa Christian Convention modeled itself after the Methodist conference. The Convention proposed to put the churches and preachers under its oversight; to select preachers for the churches, to form circuits of the weak churches, and to send preachers to those circuits, and in addition, to establish new churches which would belong to and be under the care of the convention. Harding now wrote:

Well, things are progressing! The General Convention has begun to admit babies and outsiders to its membership and directorship; the Missouri Society proposes, I am informed, to take an oversight over the colleges and schools of the brethren of the state; the Northeastern Iowa Convention proposes to control and direct the churches and preachers in its district. . . . Truly, the world moves! Thank the Lord, we of the *Advocate* haven't any State Convention down here to run us and to manage things generally.[87]

Now that the State Conventions and the Missionary Society had grasped more and more power, brethren of the *Advocate* frame of mind saw that it was dangerous to oppose these organizations. The Conventions and the Society would work against any preacher or any congregation or paper that would not dance to their tune. In Missouri, Dr. E. W. Herndon edited from 1882-89 the *Christian Quarterly,* aimed at the presentation of conservative principles where liberalism was running wild. When, however, Herndon printed an article on Christian Unity, insisting that to maintain this unity it was necessary to observe all God's appointments and institutions, Garrison saw in this an objection to the Missionary Society and promptly asked the brotherhood to cease subscribing to the *Quarterly.*

When J. W. McGarvey wrote the *Gospel Advocate,* inquiring, "Please tell your readers how much error a man must preach in

---

[87]James A. Harding, "The World Moves," *Gospel Advocate,* Vol. XXV, No. 17 (April 25, 1883), p. 266.

order to deny the faith and forfeit fellowship," F. D. Srygley was ready to answer.

As to how much error a man must preach in order to deny the faith and forfeit fellowship, if I may venture an opinion upon a rather limited observation along this line, backed by more than thirty years' experience of the *Gospel Advocate,* I would be frank to say the surest way to "forfeit fellowship" would be to modestly criticize the action of a General Convention or lovingly question the scripturalness of instrumental music in the worship. I have never done anything as heterodox as this, and hence my orthodoxy has never been questioned, nor has my fellowship yet been jeopardized. But I have made some edifying observations on this subject. While enjoying the loving fellowship of warm and confiding hearts, I have seen and felt that such men as the lamented Allen, the beloved McGarvey, and the fearless Lipscomb had indiscreetly forfeited their fellowship with us by their narrow policies of criticizing conventions and opposing organs in worship. A man may repudiate all of the Old Testament and a good part of the New, deny the miraculous conception of Jesus, boldly assert that God inspires men today the same as in apostolic times, presumptuously point out the mistakes of Paul and knowingly pronounce the whole story of Eden a myth—all this and much more he may do, without forfeiting his fellowship. But if he should go so far as to intimate that a General Convention can make a mistake or that an organ cannot be scripturally used in the worship, his orthodox scalp would be dangling at the belt of some bold defender of the faith before he had time to offer an explanation or apology. We draw the line *here*.[38]

Despite all opposition the liberal tendencies multiplied greatly, and with the passing of a few years grew so rapidly that the *Christian Standard* sensed a stopping point must be found somewhere and began to draw back somewhat. The relation between the *Standard* and the *Evangelist* was for the most part cordial although a coolness developed.

At first it arose over the Hymn Book. In a letter written April 3, 1885, by Isaac Errett to J. H. Garrison, who was then in Boston, Errett gave some hint as to the development of this "misunderstanding." Garrison had invited Errett to visit him in Boston, and Errett sent the following reply:

---

[38]F. D. Srygley, "From the Papers," *Gospel Advocate,* Vol. XXXII, No. 1 (January 1, 1890), p. 1.

STANDARD PUBLISHING CO.
No. 180 Elm Street
Cincinnati

April 3, 1885

Dear Brother Garrison:

Your favor of 1st inst. received. I had made up my mind to spend June in the East, especially that by personal observation I might be able to speak with emphasis as to the openings and the prospects there. At the same time, I fully appreciated the kindness of Brother Tyler in proposing to make a visit as pleasurable as possible. But the removal of Brother Mathews from the city necessitated new arrangements about the Bible Lessons—and the only solution of the difficulty was my consent to take back the work into my own hands. The third quarter's lessons must be prepared for issue in quarterly form before July 1, and this, in addition to my other work and the promises already made abroad, put it out of my power to go anywhere in June. I may be able, after a time, to transfer part of my other work to other hands. I would like to make the eastern trip sometime, and thank you for your kind invitation. I fear the hot season would not be a time when I could be of much service to you, as it is the season for vacation in religious matters; but I will keep the matter in mind and see what can be done in the future. It would please me to be able to make a statement as the result of my own observation that might call attention more definitely to the Boston enterprise, which I am very anxious should succeed.

I had a letter recently from the Chn. Publishing Co. I presume that, before long, we shall be able to come to some understanding about a matter in regard to which there ought to have been no misunderstanding.

Wishing you all prosperity in the arduous work you have undertaken,

Ever truly yours,

ISAAC ERRETT

Alexander Campbell had in 1864 turned the *Christian Hymnal* over to the American Christian Missionary Society. The *Standard* published the Hymnal until 1882, when the *Christian-Evangelist* took over its publication. The *Standard* promptly put out a rival hymnal, and a controversy that grew extremely hot before abating developed between the *Standard* and the *Evangelist*.

David Lipscomb in 1868 had written to Ben Franklin informing him that the American Christian Missionary Society was being used to build up the *Standard*. Although at the time Franklin doubted it, later he agreed. Commenting later, Lipscomb said:

It has been managed to build up the *Standard* until it has become rich, and so independent, that the Standard Publishing Company served a very practical and significant notice on the Society and the public, that if the Society refused to be subservient to its interest, it would destroy the Society.

As an illustration, Lipscomb referred to the Hymn Book question. Errett had an active part in securing the Hymn Book from Campbell for the Society. When the Hymn Book was revised, the Christian Standard Publishing Company put in a bid for its publication but was underbid. The Standard then published a rival book, and by this means sought to destroy the sale of the other book. Lipscomb interpreted it to mean that if any person dared to act contrary to the financial interest of the Standard, he could count on opposition. Lipscomb wrote:

It is a great lack of common sense, and an indication of ignorance of human nature, to think such institutions will not be run in the interests of designing and ambitious men.
They not only afford facilities for ambitious and selfish men controlling the affairs of the church, but they present temptations to lead men into selfish and corrupting courses; just as the opportunity to steal is a temptation to steal. The opportunity to acquire power tempts to do it, and the possession of it is a constant temptation to it for selfish ends. No man can endure constant temptation. We are not intending to say that we, or others, tempted as the *Standard* has been by its opportunities, would have done better. We are saying the temptation ought not to be offered any one[39]

In the controversy with Errett over the Hymn Book in 1883, Lipscomb revealed his feelings toward the editor of the *Standard*. He charged that a host of brethren, including Ben Franklin and Tolbert Fanning, had regarded Errett as a "trickster," that Franklin had no confidence in him, nor did the elders of the church in Detroit where Errett's ambition or financial interests were at stake. James W. Goss had said of Errett, "He is full of treachery—he won't do." L. L. Pinkerton had charged Errett to be a person who would back down on principle for the sake of popularity and gain. Lipscomb directly charged that Errett's character was not good for firmness and principle where these contradicted his own interests.

It was not, however, until after the turn of the century that any remarkable difference appeared between the *Christian-Evangelist*

[39]David Lipscomb, "Its Practical Working," *Gospel Advocate,* Vol. XXV, No. 21 (May 23, 1883), p. 326.

and the *Standard,* and the difference then largely settled on the matter of centralization and too hearty cooperation with denominational bodies. An organization was formed in February, 1901, by the Protestant churches of America called the "Federation of Churches and Church Workers." The membership was made up of a few local churches, not whole denominations. The next year at their Convention in Omaha, the Disciples of Christ took up the issue of whether they should join a proposed federation of Protestant Churches in America. Upon the suggestion of J. H. Garrison, E. B. Sanford presented the plan. Garrison presented a resolution to this effect at the Convention. J. A. Lord, editor of the *Christian Standard,* cocked an eyebrow and raised the question whether this would be "recognizing the denominations." W. E. Garrison, son of J. H. Garrison, replied that it would only be recognizing that the denominations exist, not that they ought to exist. Another mass meeting was held at Norfolk in October, 1907, at which time it was agreed that the Disciples of Christ should join the proposed Federal Council soon to be organized. There was only one dissenting vote—that of J. B. Briney.

Garrison, of course, backed heartily the decision to join the Federal Council. Of those opposed, he wrote:

Those voting in the negative no doubt believed they were more loyal to the principles of our movement than those who favored it. But as a matter of fact they had never caught a true vision of its real spirit, intent and scope, as it is understood and presented by our representative men.[40]

Such a statement is typically Garrisonian.

---

[40] J. H. Garrison, *Memories and Experiences*, p. 116.

Chapter XIV

DANIEL SOMMER

"Of late years I have said the time will come that we will go so far from Bible Christianity we can well say, 'We had a prophet among us, but did not know it.'" So wrote J. D. Tant to Daniel Sommer twelve years ago.[1] The truculent Daniel Sommer was particularly adapt at making close friends and fierce enemies—only he preferred to call them "friendly friends" and "unfriendly friends," never enemies. He found a martyr's satisfaction in thinking of himself as the "most hated" and "most loved" man in the "disciple brotherhood." Despite, however, the obloquy of his "unfriendly friends," Daniel Sommer was unmoved in championing points of view which the brotherhood charitably at times called his "extremes." No matter how one may view the full effect of Sommer's work, it cannot be denied that before the year 1906, the enigmatic Daniel Sommer was a force with which to reckon. He has left his mark—whether for weal or woe will remain for the future to reveal.

The story of Sommer's life is an inspiring one. Although reared in almost absolute poverty, by sheer determination he became the protegè of Elder Ben Franklin and one of the most popular preachers in the brotherhood. He was "strong in the faith and robust mentally and physically" as W. B. F. Treat once described him. The appraisal is not overdrawn. Sommer had complete confidence in the word of God, and a child-like trust in God's leadings. It can hardly be denied that he was spiritually a giant. He loved the Bible and studied vigorously. He prayed constantly, and devoted himself earnestly to the work of God. Like Tolbert Fanning he was of an extreme independent term of mind, and took no man as an authority in religion. He freely challenged the great men. His series of twenty-five articles entitled "'Disciples of Christ' Challenged" which were run in the *Apostolic Review* in 1935 and 1936 show a refreshingly independent approach to the writings of Alexander Campbell.

---

[1] J. D. Tant, "An Open Letter," *Apostolic Review*, Vol. LXXXI, Nos. 49, 50 (December 7, 1937), p. 5.

Physically, Sommer was a giant. His excellent bodily condition enabled him to stretch his earthly life from the normal "three score and ten" to "four score and ten." His worn out frame yielded to death on February 14, 1940, and was laid to rest in Crown Hill Cemetery at Indianapolis.

A little over ninety years before, Daniel Sommer was born in St. Mary's County, in the state of Maryland. The exact date was January 11, 1850.

Sommer's parents were both German. His father, John Sommer, was a Hessian, and his mother, Magdalena Wyman was a Bavarian. Both had emmigrated to America in 1835. They were married "at or near" Washington D. C. in 1840. John Sommer died a comparatively young man, at the age of forty-one. Daniel Sommer was only a child at the time, and consequently remembered little of his father. By trade, his father was a blacksmith. He worked hard, but unlike most Germans, saved little. Although not a drunkard, he did drink considerably, and consequently, too much of his money was lost in this way. When he died, he left his widow with no money and a large family. The future for the family looked dark.

Sommer learned that tribulation is a difficult but necessary school in which to learn patience and perserverance. When John Sommer moved his family near the village of Queen Ann in Prince George's County, Maryland around 1855, he contacted a severe cold in the process. The cold developed into pneumonia, causing his death. His penniless widow, burdened with a large family, went unselfishly to work. To earn money she sewed suits for the negro slaves owned by the rich plantation owners in that vicinity. Usually a slave was allowed two suits a year by his master, so naturally, they sought for the best seamstress to make the clothing to last the longest.

Queen Ann was a small village on the west bank of the Patuxent River, about thirty miles east of Washington D. C. There were no churches of any kind here, and scarcely anything else to give it the reputation of being a village. Here, Daniel Sommer spent some of his early years. The family lived in a log cabin, and each did some kind of work. Young Daniel set his traps, and in the winter brought in the game from his traps. The family lived for many days at a time on wild rabbit and corn bread.

In the spring of 1859 Daniel was hired out to do his first work. He was only nine years old, and the law said a boy could not do public work under the age of ten. But his employer was a friend and conveniently lied about his age. Hoswell Marguder, his employer, was building roads through that section of Maryland, and hired Daniel for a very small salary to help in the construction. Young Daniel arose before daylight, put his breakfast and lunch in a sack, and walked several miles to be at the place of work on time. He would walk back again at night, and fall exhausted upon the floor of the log cabin, only to have the process repeated the next day. Off and on he worked at this job through the fall of 1861. When the war came, workers were scarce and work plentiful, so the boys below army age secured their full share. Although the war raged about him, Sommer lived in almost complete oblivion of it.

He entered school first at the age of seven. At first, he was slow to learn and received considerable "teasing" about it. Nevertheless, he managed to take full advantage of his opportunities and advanced very well. His school days lasted only a few months each year for five years. He dropped out in the spring of 1862 to return to work. Until he entered Bethany College seven years later, he was never again inside of a school. Through the winter of 1862-63 he worked as a farm hand for four dollars a month and his board.

Up to the spring of 1863 Sommer had given very little thought to religion. His parents were nominally Lutherans, and had their children sprinkled by Lutheran ministers. But they gave no devoted time to practicing their religion. Along through young life, Sommer had picked up a few bad habits, common to boys of the world. He could curse a little, and in case of necessity found it easy to lie occasionally. Old fashioned thievery was out, but woe be to the person who left a penknife lying around without a guard. These habits, then as now, were hardly considered too bad for an irreligious boy who had never given serious thought about his responsibility to God.

In the spring of 1863 Miss Louisa V. Harwood, an adopted daughter of the store keeper in the village, decided to open a Sunday School in a private house and invite the children of the neighborhood. Sommer at first was but little interested but later changed his mind. The young teacher presented her lessons in an appealing manner so Sommer became interested. She encouraged the children to think about their soul's welfare and asked them to "repent and pray" to God. Sommer for one, took her seriously, and began for the first time to pray. It was not long until he was living an entirely different life.

At the close of 1863 Sommer left the plantation of William Fielder Howell where he had been employed, to work for Oden Bowie. Here, Sommer had some unpleasant experiences, due in the main to the fact that Bowie expected too much out of the farm hands. He left this farm on January 1, 1865 and the next day hired out to a farmer by the name of Mullikin. Sommer's mother, meanwhile, lived in a tenant house on the farm.

Before the close of 1864 Sommer had grown careless about his religion, lapsing into indifference. About this time a revival meeting was conducted among the Methodists in McKendry Chapel. Sommer was solicited as a likely candidate to come forward, "get religion" and "join the church." He convinced them that he had religion already, and so was promptly admitted into the church. He began now to be regular in attending Bible classes at the Methodist Church.

During the winter of 1866, Sommer chopped wood for a living. It was during this time that he heard of a group of people called the disciples of Christ. He heard it rumored that these people had no knowledge of "heart-felt" religion, and had no experience in conversion. They simply took the attitude, he heard, that if they did certain things, God was obligated to save them. The whole affair was rumored to be a cold, legalistic type of religion, and of course, was arduously condemned. So, when Sommer had a day off from work, he went down to a creek to observe a baptism being conducted by D. S. Burnet, whom Sommer understood to be the preacher for the church in Baltimore, but who was now here in the country conducting an evangelistic meeting.

In the winter of 1866 Sommer moved into Hartford County, Maryland. Here he had his first real contact with the restoration. At the "Mountain Meeting House," also called the "Jerusalem Church," there was a preacher by the name of Calderwood, commonly described as a man "too lazy to work between meals." Talk of him—evidently not too praiseworthy—and of his teaching often became the topic of conversation in the community. When Sommer went to work for a man by the name of John Dallas

Everitt, a member of the church, young Daniel was now placed directly in the line for some wholesome teaching. When he reminded Everitt that he had been baptized—sprinkled when he was a baby—young Sommer was promptly told he had not been baptized at all. Step by step, through discussion and research of the Scripture, Sommer was led. For a year the discussions continued and Sommer found his convictions slowly changing. Finally, in August of 1869 he was baptized by Elder T. A. Crenshaw of Middletown, Pennsylvania.

The question of selecting a life's work now renewed itself in Sommer's mind. His father had selected him to be a blacksmith because of his hardy physical makeup. Later, one or another possible vocation suggested itself. Now that Sommer was converted, and was intensively interested in the Bible, he began to toss about in his mind the possibility of preaching the gospel. When he spoke to some of the elderly men in the congregation about it, they encouraged him, but suggested that he first needed more education. Bethany College was the closest of the schools connected with the brotherhood. Besides, it was the most illustrous. Alexander Campbell's memory hovered spirit-like around it. His son-in-law, W. K. Pendleton, was now its president. C. L. Loos, a highly-respected educator, was connected with the school. Robert Richardson, although growing old, was still there. Sommer, therefore, prepared to enter Bethany College.

He came to Bethany in the same state of poverty that had characterized his entire life. Consequently he worked hard to pay his way, and went greatly in debt besides. His educational background was very limited—not having put in over five years, and those were disconnected and under inadequate circumstances in country school houses. Sommer entered Bethany far below other students both in educational background and financial security, but no student ever entered with more determination. At first, he took Latin, Greek, and algebra, but dropped the algebra to take rhetoric.

The first disappointment that Sommer felt with the brotherhood came during his student days at Bethany. He noticed that there were two classes of disciples in the church. One class believed that the Bible was a revelation to the saint and sinner. The other believed it was only a revelation to the sinner. The rule with the latter class was that God gave a revelation to tell the sinner how to become a Christian, but beyond that, the rule was "love God and do as you please." There were no laws governing the church, and in the final analysis, sincerity alone was sufficient. President W. K. Pendleton was a champion of this point of view.

"The smooth and compromising manner of President Pendleton," wrote W. B. F. Treat, "had no charms for him" (Daniel Sommer). He reacted violently against this. Although C. L. Loos was less addicted to this type of thinking, he was still the friend of human societies outside the church to do the work of the church, and in this connection Sommer had his first serious trouble.

The lady members of the church in Bethany decided to raise some money to buy new curtains, a new carpet and to paint the building. C. L. Loos, an elder in the congregation, gave a talk before the congregation one evening favoring the plan. A Ladies' Mite Society was organized and the announcement made that the hat would be passed that each person might give his mite to this work. The Mite Society held frequent meetings, which in Sommer's opinion degenerated into something very worldly. It was the custom of the church to invite different preachers among the students to speak at the Sunday evening services at the church. When Sommer received his invitation, he chose the first Psalm as a text, and closed the discourse with a severe blast at the Mite Society. This blow staggered the Society and in a matter of few days it died peacefully, but the blast shook Sommer's popularity considerably around the school.

The Mite Society was the first deviation from apostolic principles that Sommer found in the church after becoming a Christian. He was proud of the fact that he had publicly attacked it, and that his flagellations against all unscriptural practices were never known to stop as long as he lived. Sommer wrote:

I denounced publicly the first deviation from apostolic simplicity that I found among "disciples," and I have been acting on the same principle ever since. For a brief period I thought that "mutual teaching and exhortation" should be the order at the time of worship without what is called a "sermon." But I soon learned that when any one imitating the apostle Paul as a preacher was present at such a meeting then that one should be used as Paul was at Troas. Then for a brief period I thought that we should not offend the objector to classifying children and others in order to teach them in the meeting house. But I soon learned the evil results of doing nothing special for children on Lord's Day, and thus I turned from my mistake on that question. . .[2]

Sommer's self-appointed role as a critic of brotherhood activities cost him dearly in friends, and gave him a reputation not altogether too envious. It is seldom that an individual can voluntarily select the role of a critic but what he can become overbalanced in this department of his work, and go to an extreme. One can repose, however, in some felicity with the thought that it is better to have a watch dog that barks too much than one that barks not at all.

In the spring of 1871 Ben Franklin, editor of the *American Christian Review,* came to Wellsburgh, West Virginia to conduct an evangelistic meeting. Quite naturally, Sommer had heard of Franklin, as had nearly every member of the church. From what he had heard about Franklin, he rather liked him, but he wanted to go see him and be sure. He asked and secured permission to miss classes one day at the College and went to Wellsburg to be with Ben Franklin. It was a case of love at first sight, and the love was fully returned. The aging Ben Franklin took a liking to young Sommer, and Sommer in turn idolized Ben Franklin. To the day of his death, Sommer never ceased regarding Franklin as the quintessence of gospel preachers. Sommer could well recall that at this meeting he found Franklin brokenhearted. Franklin now lived in Cincinnati where the Central Christian Church was erecting its $140,000 meeting house and putting in it an $8,000 organ. This case of extravagance was unparalleled in restoration history. So thought Franklin. His spirit was low when he met Sommer and he poured out his heart to his young protegè, and Sommer drank it in at the same time— consciously or unconsciously—firmly resolving to duplicate this man's life in his own.

Sommer's stay at Bethany College covered less than three years. During the Christmas holidays of 1872, he went to a place called Dutch Fork in Maryland and conducted a meeting. He did not return to take the final examinations that year, and dropped out of school. On his occasional excursions into Maryland, Sommer, too, had had other interests in mind the nature of which was

---

[2]Daniel Sommer, " 'Disciples of Christ' Challenged—No. 18," *Apostolic Review,* Vol. LXXXI, Nos. 5, 6 (February 2, 1937), p. 8.

clearly revealed when on this return trip he married Miss Kate Way.

For a short time immediately following his marriage, Sommer preached for one of the churches in Baltimore. There were two congregations here. The Paca Street Church where D. S. Burnet had preached until his death, and the congregation for which Sommer now preached had long been divided. The Paca Street congregation now had a preacher, who, in Sommer's opinion, was somewhat less than a Christian as it respected his morals. Sommer's stay was somewhat shortened and occasioned by considerable inter-congregational animosity.

During the time he lived in Baltimore, however, Sommer made a fast friend of George Austen, one of the elders. Austen had succeeded in establishing congregations in the bordering territory, and was one of the leading men in the church in that day. He was a harsh critic of Sommer's at a time perhaps when Sommer needed this. After hearing Sommer twice on one Lord's Day, he wrote his young friend the following letter:

Your forenoon's discourse was only tolerable. At night I knew you had made a failure as soon as I heard your text. Your gesticulations were stiff and awkward; your intonations of voice were forced and unnatural; your outlines were only ordinary, and the filing-up was miserable.[3]

Such harshness was far from pleasant, but Sommer profited by it.

After a brief stay in Baltimore, Sommer moved to Kelton, Pennsylvania where he preached for the next five or six years. This congregation was one that George Austen had established. In the absence of any documentary evidence, it is not unlikely that Austen played some part in the changing of the locations.

At Kelton, Sommer took the opportunity for constant growth. Little of any significance came from him before the brotherhood. In 1872 he wrote his first article for Ben Franklin which was published in the *American Christian Review*. Three years later a few short articles appeared. Then there is silence until the fall of 1878 when Sommer wrote for the *Review*. Aside from these occasional flings at writing, Sommer kept busy in evangelistic meetings, his unusual ability becoming more widely known. From November 8 to December 14, 1878, he was in a meeting at

---

[3] Daniel Sommer, " 'Disciples of Christ' Challenged—No. 22," Vol. LXXXI, Nos. 13, 14 (March 30, 1937), p. 8.

Reynoldsburg, Ohio. A. E. Sprague who heard him through the entire meeting wrote of him:

He is a young man not yet in the prime of life; his voice strong and clear; his enunciations exceedingly good; his knowledge of scripture rarely excelled; his energy untiring; his manner and address pleasing; all these, together with his exemplary walk, and great reverence for the word of God, makes him a man of no ordinary ability.[4]

In the spring of 1879 while still living at Kelton, Sommer was bitten by a mad dog, which gave him hydrophobia. Two physicians attended him, dosing him heavily with lobelia.

He felt heavily the blow of Ben Franklin's death in the fall of 1878, for he and Franklin had corresponded frequently, and already Sommer had sent in a series of articles entitled, "Educating Preachers" which were aimed at the culpableness of Bethany College. When John F. Rowe took over the editorship of the *Review,* Sommer continued his writing for several months, but eventually dropped from the contributors.

While preaching in Kelton, in Chester County, Pennsylvania, Sommer had occasion to receive a high compliment from Ben Franklin. In April, 1878 Franklin wrote Sommer of a congregation needing a preacher. The particular place offered twice the salary Sommer was then receiving, and from every point of view was attractive. But Sommer declined, writing to Ben Franklin that he was needed at Kelton more than at the other congregation. Although Franklin regretted that Sommer would not make the move, he admired the spirit, and so wrote:

We like this letter, though it does not agree to what we had in view. It is in the spirit of the pioneers in our great work, and of the primitive men in the church. The question with Brother Sommer is not *how much money* he can make out of his fine gifts and the gospel, but *how much he can do* in the great work of saving men.[5]

In 1880 Sommer moved from Kelton, Pennsylvania to Reynoldsburg, Ohio, stopping by Columbus for a short time on the move. In 1883 he began editorial work on his own. Together with L. F. Bittle he started a small monthly paper called the *Octograph.* The name was coined by Bittle to denote the "writings of eight,"

---

[4]A. E. Sprague, "Daniel Sommer at Reynoldsburg, Ohio," *American Christian Review,* Vol. XXII, No. 4 (January 27, 1880), p. 30.

[5]Ben Franklin, "The Right Idea," *American Christian Review,* Vol. XXI, No. 20 (May 14, 1878), p. 156.

referring to the eight writers of the New Testament. The paper was thus to be thoroughly apostolic. Bittle is one of those little-known heroes of the restoration. For a few years, while the *Review* was published by Franklin, he flamed into brilliance be-fore the brotherhood in his opposition to the "digressive" tendencies. Among *Review* readers, he was extremely popular.

In the fall of 1884 Sommer moved to Martel, Ohio, and the following spring, on to Richwood. At this latter place the church had only seventy-five members and was unable to support a preacher. Besides they were deeply in debt. Sommer agreed to preach for them temporarily for nothing. The congregation was, when Sommer came, using an organ, supporting the missionary societies, and selling pies at church festivals to raise money. Sommer, of course, pitched heavily into these. J. J. Moss, one of the liberal preachers, came by, conducted a meeting, and the result was an open division in the congregation.

As a preacher, however, Sommer was continuing to gain a great prominence. George W. Rice, after hearing him preach, said, "As an earnest and clear-headed gospel preacher he falls behind no one in the rank. For zeal, devotion and earnestness in preach-ing the gospel I place him next to Brother Franklin."[6] On an-other occasion Rice said of Sommer's preaching:

It forcibly reminded me of the preaching of the pioneer days, when men were ready to spend and be spent in the restoration of the apostolic gospel and order of things. . .

He is so full of the gospel that he has thrown everything else overboard—knowing nothing else but Jesus Christ and him cruci-fied. By doing this, he fills every person so full of the gospel that all innovations are given up and forgotten where he preaches.[7]

Ben Franklin, too, had always high regard for young Sommer as a promising gospel preacher. Shortly before he died, Franklin conducted a meeting in Detroit. Speaking confidentially to O. M. Benedict of Sommer, Franklin said:

I consider Brother Sommer as one of the most promising young men in my whole acquaintance. God has given him a grand physique, a strong, grasping mind, a sharp pen, a fairly-ready

[6]George W. Rice, "Why I Am Now on the Review," *Octographic Review,* Vol. XXX, No. 24 (June 30, 1887), p. 1.
[7]George W. Rice, "Daniel Sommer as a Preacher," *Octographic Review,* Vol. XXX, No. 43 (November 10, 1887), p. 8.

tongue, and his heart is attuned to the grand principles of this great *Restoration movement.*[8]

When Edwin Alden, owner of the *American Christian Review,* presented the paper for sale in the summer of 1886, Sommer was quick to take advantage of the opportunity to purchase it. The following spring the name was changed to *Octographic Review.* For the next seven years the paper was published first from Cincinnati, then from Richwood. All of the while, Sommer was casting about for a better location. Indianapolis immediately appealed to him due to its central location in the heart of the great brotherhood. But he was not adverse to moving it somewhere else. For a short time brethren in Missouri made a bid for it, but this did not materialize. Gradually Sommer became more and more in demand as a preacher in the state of Indiana, a fact which made Indianapolis seem more than ever like the best location from which to publish the *Review.* Early in 1894 then Sommer moved to this city. His office was at first at 66½ North Pennsylvania Street, but in two or three months was moved to West Udell Street in north Indianapolis. The first issue of the *Octographic Review* to come from Indianapolis was dated March 20, 1894.

The church in Indianapolis had grown considerably since John O'Kane had conducted the first evangelistic meeting there in 1833. Out of O'Kane's effort had gradually developed what became known as the Central Christian Church. With the establishment of Northwestern Christian College in 1855 in the city, members of the church were attracted to the city. When, following the Civil War, the instruments of music began filling all the churches, brethren who opposed these found themselves forced to start their work all over again.

Taking the lead in this new birth was Dr. Joshua Webb. Born on August 13, 1809 in Columbiana County, Ohio, Webb was baptized by Elder William Schooley when he was only fifteen. At the age of twenty-one he began to preach. He spent his entire time preaching for the next seven years, and usually with marked success. At Beaver Creek in Maryland the whole Lutheran Church dissolved its denominational status and adopted the name, Christian. At this time the Lutherans, becoming alarmed, sent their favorite, S. K. Hoshour of Hagerstown, Maryland to confound Webb, but

---

[8]O. M. Benedict, "To the Readers of the Review," *American Christian Review,* Vol. XXX, No. 1 (January 6, 1887), p. 5.

Webb succeeded in leading Hoshour to restoration principles. Webb's health broke and he ceased preaching. He studied medicine for three years, and practiced in Maryland and Ohio before coming to Indianapolis in 1865. He promptly became a member of the Central Church.

In 1878 after the Central Church had introduced the organ, Webb withdrew and began meeting with a few in what was called the Danish Church on South New Jersey Street. Shortly afterwards, Webb purchased a frame house from the Sixth Presbyterian Church, and had the building on the back of his lot behind his home on Mulberry Street. This congregation met three times every Sunday. The forenoon service consisted of short talks from the members—never any preaching. In the afternoon, they had Bible study, and of course, these were conducted without lesson leaves. At night, there was an evangelistic service.

When John F. Rowe visited Indianapolis in the fall of 1887 he found seven congregations, consisting of fifteen hundred members. The number included those using the organ. A new congregation had recently been established in West Indianapolis by Abram Plunkett. Wesley Davidson was one of the elders. The congregation had over a hundred members. It had not added any "innovation." On Home Avenue the "Third Church" had recently been established. D. R. Vanbuskirk was a leading member here. The congregation had three hundred and fifty members. The next year, 1888, Z. T. Sweeney, who was then riding a high crest of popularity, spoke at the dedication of a new church building.

Rowe had made frequent excursions into Indianapolis. When he visited the city again in 1890, he found a new congregation meeting on Madison Avenue. Two years later he came back to the city and went with J. W. Perkins, J. Perry Elliott, H. I. Shick and B. N. Davis to the newly founded North Indianapolis congregation. Rowe preached in the forenoon and Perkins in the evening. The congregation had only twenty members, nearly all of whom were young married people.

When, therefore, Daniel Sommer moved to Indianapolis in 1894, he identified himself with this church in North Indianapolis, and until his death preached off and on for this congregation. Sommer's first major activity in Indianapolis was to announce a ten week's Bible Reading to begin in May, 1894 and close the last of July. The cost was to be about fifty dollars. A dozen young men or so came to the Bible Reading. In later years, he lost some of his ardor for these readings insisting that it gave young men the idea they were preachers long before they were ready to preach.

Sommer never distinguished himself as a religious debater although he did engage in several during his life. His first debate was held with a German Baptist in Ray County, Missouri. Before the discussion, Sommer wrote, "Debating will be new business to me and I have no idea that it will be enjoyable." It did prove enjoyable, however, and Sommer found considerable satisfaction in this type of teaching.

It will not be needful to trace the life of Daniel Sommer through the years to his death in 1940. Much of this would be relatively modern history with which the average reader would already be acquainted. These facts of his life are given that cover the years of his life that relate especially to those covered in this volume. On some points of study with which this volume deals Daniel Sommer plays a prominent role.

Any estimate that one may place upon the life's work on Daniel Sommer will understandably be colored by the background of the biographer. We could wish in this matter as in all others to be true, honest, and charitably objective. That Daniel Sommer was a great preacher, possessing a great mind and heart, no person at all acquainted with his life can for a moment doubt. He was fearless, independent, and ambitious. Deploring as violently as he did the "digression" that swept the churches, it was hardly possible for him to look with any charity or much understanding upon anything, whatever it was, that played any part in causing this "departure."

Sommer's experiences at Bethany College found him departing from school with absolute disgust at the idea that a preacher needed a college education. The trouble at the College of The Bible in Kentucky University found the two men Sommer admired most— Ben Franklin and Jacob Creath, Jr.—turning against Bible Colleges. Sommer was a young preacher; they were older preachers. Their turning against these colleges at a time when Sommer's heart was already chafing at the bitter memory of Bethany, helped form a conviction in Sommer's heart. Too, Sommer could never think of himself in any role except the successor of Elder Ben Franklin, whom he regarded as the greatest gospel preacher since apostolic times. Franklin in his latter years opposed colleges, and the man who wore his mantle would be likely to do the same.

That Sommer went to extremes at times, even he himself admitted. In championing for a short time the view that preaching had no place at the morning worship, he saw soon was an extreme and abandoned this course. For our part we are not willing that his extremes should blind us in seeing the real greatness in the man, nor shall our willingness to see his greatness stand as an obstacle to our seeing his extremes.

Sommer's point of view on issues that developed before 1906 will be discussed in other chapters.

Chapter XV

THE REVIEW'S TROUBLES

In the August 26, 1886 issue of the *American Christian Review* there appeared a very startling report in the form of an editorial, making public the fact that the *Review* was having critical financial times. More than this, the editorial announced the resignation of John F. Rowe and George W. Rice—the former as editor and the latter as publisher. Brethren had little knowledge of any trouble, and so sat tensely waiting to see what would happen. Soon the facts came forth, but before they had finished doing so, the *Review* was injured seriously.

In 1873 the nation had experienced a severe financial panic. During this time, the *Review* was threatened. Edwin Alden, a business man who made his money acting as an advertising agent, came to the paper's financial aid by paying its debts as well as those of George Rice, the *Review* publisher. These totaled about fifteen thousand dollars. From that day, it was agreed that Alden should use the *Review* for his advertising, but the editorial policy would be directed by Ben Franklin. Alden was to have no say about how the *Review* should be run editorially, nor was he to do any advertising out of harmony with Christian principles. This arrangement had proved very satisfactory. In spite of the fact he was not a member of the church, his relations to Ben Franklin and Rice during those years was very cordial.

But, early in 1886, Alden faced the fact that his business was losing money. Before long he was fifteen thousand dollars in debt. Nothing remained for him but to sell the *Review* to save himself from complete bankruptcy. He immediately, therefore, began negotiations with two men—A. E. Childs and Geroge F. Hussey, neither of whom was a member of the church, and to them the *Review* was turned over.

Alden in conducting the whole transaction had failed to consult with either Rowe or Rice. Actually he was under no obligation to do so since he was the paper's owner. Rowe and Rice, true to human nature, felt left out. The new owners of the *Review* were strangers to them, and it is not unnatural that they should feel some misgivings as to the future. Moreover, the fact that Rowe would have liked to purchase the *Review* for something around nine thousand dollars doubtlessly influenced his revolt against Alden, so Rowe threw a gigantic bluff in the hope of getting the paper himself. It was a big chance, but if it succeeded, he would be able to purchase the *Review* at almost half its real value. Rowe took the chance and lost. Unfortunately he injured not only himself but the cause of which he was a symbol.

The editorial of August 26 was written by a Presbyterian preacher in Cincinnati and published over the names of Rowe and Rice. Why they induced this preacher to write the editorial for them is hard to explain. The editorial accused Alden of taking money that did not belong to him and of manipulating the business to his own selfish ends. Alden remained silent in the face of their accusations for some time. At first, brethren as a whole sympathized with Rowe. The idea of trying to edit a paper owned by a member who was not even a member of the church was enough to arouse their sympathy. In later years, however, Alden seems to have completely vindicated himself in their good graces by establishing a reputation for honesty despite the blow he received.

Three weeks after his first editorial appeared, the September 16, 1886 issue of the *Review* came out with the brief announcement from George W. Rice that John F. Rowe had been forced out as the editor of the paper. Rice proposed to carry on until further developments. The next issue of the paper appeared with W. B. F. Treat as the editor.

Fifty-one year old Treat was a short man with grey eyes, auburn hair and a heavy beard. He had been connected with the *Review* while Franklin edited it, but had found himself very often in disagreement with Rowe. He was a native of Morgan County, Indiana, and had been preaching for thirty years, although at one time he had served four years in the State Legislature of Indiana as a Senator. For a short time he had been associate-editor of the old *Christian Record* which had been edited by J. M. Mathes at Bedford, Indiana.[1]

The affair aroused Rowe's suspicion. Several months before the sale of the *Review,* Treat had resigned his work on the paper.

---

[1] J. W. Perkins, "Briefs Here and There," *American Christian Review,* Vol. XXX, No. 1 (January 6, 1887), p. 5.

After the trouble between Alden and Rowe, Alden had taken a trip and talked privately with Treat about becoming editor. Rowe, not knowing this, wrote to Treat, asking his advice about starting another paper. Treat advised both Rowe and Rice to do this, but afterwards explained that Rowe had asked him between two courses, one of which was starting another paper, which in his opinion would be more desirable. Treat said he did not think much of either action, but of the two, starting another paper seemed more desirable, and had so advised Rowe. At any date, when Treat, after advising Rowe to start another paper, was announced as editor of the *Review,* Rowe immediately concluded that a conspiracy to kill his work and influence had been under way.[2]

No sooner had Rowe left the *Review* until he made immediate plans to start another paper. His new paper he would call the *Christian Missionary* but later changed his mind and called it the *Christian Leader.* The first issue appeared dated, October 7, 1886, and its make-up and appearance was the *Review's* twin. Across the top was written: "One Faith, One Lord, and One Immersion." J. Logan Richardson, brother of Robert Richardson, Campbell's biographer, was the publisher of the *Leader.* John F. Rowe was editor and Alfred Ellmore, corresponding editor. In the first issue Rowe stated the purpose of his periodical:

It will be the constant aim of this journal to bring men and women in spiritual contact with Christ and His apostles. . . We shall aim to glorify the church of Jesus Christ, and not waste our time on the glorification of human missionary societies. . . We shall strive to build up in every congregation an intelligent and competent eldership, and, if possible, we shall by the grace of God, avoid all angry controversies with our brethren.[3]

In the next issue of the *Leader,* the editor laid down an eight-point program designed to be a guiding policy for the periodical. The *Leader* should be, (1) "thoroughly apostolic, yet abreast of the times." (2) It should not shun to declare the whole council of God. (3) While courteous to all men, the *Leader* should uncompromisingly present only God's standard of righteousness. (4) It must avoid all untaught questions that gender strife. (5) It must do nothing through strife or vainglory. (6) Bible thoughts

[2]John F. Rowe, "Overture for Reconciliation," *Christian Leader,* Vol. I, No. 8 (February 22, 1887), p. 4.

[3]John F. Rowe, "*The Christian Leader,*" *Christian Leader,* Vol. I, No. 1 (October 7, 1886), p. 4.

should be expressed in Bible language. (7) It should avoid all personal wranglings. (8) It should make an agressive battle for the truth.[4]

The immediate effect of establishing the new paper was a dividing of the forces of the old *Review*. Alfred Ellmore, who had been connected with the *Review* for many years, left it to join Rowe on the *Leader*. W. H. Krutsinger of Ellettsville, Indiana who had written Indiana items frequently for the *Review* transferred his editorial labor to the *Gospel Advocate*. Afterwards, Krutsinger writes:

There is no more *American Christian Review*. The paper that Franklin founded and ran until his death is a thing of the past. The best thing you can now do is to take and read the *Gospel Advocate*.[5]

The *Christian Messenger,* published at Bonham, Texas carried an article directing the old readers of the *American Christian Review* to subscribe to the *Leader,* a statement that solicited strong resentment from Treat. These petty differences, however, were indicative of things to come.

Meanwhile, the months of October and November, 1886 passed, and Edwin Alden felt that he must sell the paper, the deal with Childs and Hussey having failed. The issue of December 9, 1886 announced that business negotiations were under way for the paper to be purchased by a "prominent evangelist," who would act as owner, editor and publisher.[6] Two weeks later the *Review* announced that Daniel Sommer had purchased it. On the front page of this issue was a large picture of Elder Ben Franklin, indicating not only Sommer's admiration of the deceased gospel preacher, but the determination to return to the editorial policy of the great Hoosier preacher.

The fact of Daniel Sommer's purchasing the *Review* came as a blow to Rowe and his editorial corps on the *Leader*. There is every reason to believe that Rowe still had considerable hopes of securing its ownership. J. L. Richardson dangled the bait before Alden, offering through the *Leader* to buy the *Review* but

---

[4]John F. Rowe, "The Kind of Paper Wanted," *Christian Leader,* Vol. I, No. 2 (October 14, 1886), p. 4.

[5]Daniel Sommer "Peculiarly Unfortunate," *Octographic Review,* Vol. XXX, No. 19 (May 26, 1887), p. 1.

[6]W. B. F. Treat, "Important Notice," *American Christian Review,* Vol. XXIX, No. 50 (December 9, 1886), p. 398.

"not at a price double its value." It is not likely that anything would have pleased Rowe more than to purchase it at his own price, not at Alden's. When, therefore, Daniel Sommer entered the discussion, Alden went the second mile in making a financial arrangement whereby the "prominent evangelist" could make the purchase.

David Lipscomb had watched the negotiations with some interest. When Alden first attempted to sell the *Review* to Childs and Hussey, Lipscomb wrote, "We presume this will not in any way seriously modify the *Review*. The work of the *Review* is needed especially in Ohio, and we would dislike to see anything occur that would cripple its influence in the least." Shortly after Sommer bought the paper, Lipscomb wrote:

Brother Daniel Sommer, a man of most excellent repute, as a true and faithful Christian and a teacher of the Bible, has bought the *Review*. This removes the objectionable feature of the ownership, and we think the publishers of the *Review* and *Leader* ought to make an earnest effort to combine the two papers. Their circulation must be within the same section and among brethren who ought to work together in harmony. We know, under these circumstances, there must be clashing interest and partisan spirit excited. . . We know the subscriptions of the two combined will not be more than sufficient to sustain one paper so as to enable it to do effective service. We have only the kindliest feeling toward all persons concerned; and, while we think it not well for men not Christians to have the power to appoint and dismiss teachers for Christians, we wish to say that we have had dealings with Mr. Edwin Alden as advertising agent for fifteen years past, and although we lost by his failure, nothing ever occurred to induce the belief that he was not an honest, fair-dealing man.[7]

The December 23, 1886 issue of the *American Christian Review* was the first to carry the name of Daniel Sommer as "proprietor and publisher." W. B. F. Treat was listed as editor; Dr. J. C. Holloway, George T. Smith, and J. W. Perkins were corresponding editors. The paper was now published at the northwest corner of Fifth and Vine Streets in Cincinnati.

Daniel Sommer's assumption of control of the *Review* was the signal for the beginning hostilities. John F. Rowe opened the cannonading with vociferous barrage in the January 18, 1887 issue of the *Christian Leader*. Rowe charges that Sommer is

---

[7]David Lipscomb, "A Friendly Suggestion," *Gospel Advocate*, Vol. XXIX, No. 4 (January 26, 1887), p. 54.

deceived and that an "outsider" still owns the *Review*. Sommer rejoins with the accusation that Rowe had deliberately plotted the overthrow of the *Review* and had trumpted up some false charges against Alden. Moreover—and this hurt Sommer worse —Rowe, says Sommer, stole the subscription list of the *Review* in order to start the *Leader*. Readers of the two papers for some time were let in on the flagellations Rowe and Sommer each gave the other. Meanwhile, readers of the *Christian Standard* and *Christian-Evangelist* found additional reason to believe that the opposers of the society and instrumental music lacked Christianity, and the *Leader-Review* warfare increased the popularity of their point of view considerably.

The history of the *Review* for the past decade was now brought out for an inspection. Who was the person Ben Franklin had in mind to be his successor as editor of the *Review?* There could be little question that Franklin, well-meaning though he was, had unconsciously encouraged a jealous spirit among his admirers. As a means of encouraging young men, Franklin held out to them the possibility that they might succeed him as the editor of his paper. Several young men, each one thinking of himself as fit to wear Franklin's mantle, found themselves jealous of each other, and that jealousy split the forces of those who opposed innovations in the North.

W. B. F. Treat declared that a few months before Franklin's death he spent two weeks with him, and they had discussed his successor. According to Treat, Franklin had mentioned James A. Meng, L. F. Bittle, Daniel Sommer, Joel A. Headington, but John F. Rowe was definitely placed "at the foot of the list." Treat testifies that Franklin stated his confidence in Rowe was completely gone. Franklin had charged that Rowe was "the same color as the bush he was in." In Ohio, where the Society was strong, Rowe favored the Society, but in Pennsylvania where it was opposed, Rowe had opposed it.[8] There can be little doubt that L. F. Bittle was Franklin's first choice except for the fact that Bittle's health would probably have prevented his attending to the rigors of the editorship.

It will be recalled that Franklin's death occured unexpectedly. It was therefore left to George W. Rice, the publisher of the

[8]W. B. F. Treat, "The Conspiracy," *American Christian Review,* Vol. XXX, No. 8 (February 24, 1887), p. 60.

Review, to name the successor. The decision was by no means simple. Joel A. Headington was opposed to Rowe and threatened to quit the paper if Rowe were named as editor. Rowe, on the other hand, would do the same if Headington were chosen. Rice, after taking all things into consideration, decided in favor of Rowe. At the time of making his choice, he wrote:

I know that his [Ben Franklin] mind settled on Brother John F. Rowe as his successor. Believing that to be his wish and will, I have placed Brother Rowe in that position. This I have done without any hostility to anyone else. Brother Rowe has been connected with the *Review* as contributor and assistant editor longer than anyone else, and has had more of Brother Franklin's correspondence than any other brother that has ever contributed to the columns of the paper. . . .[9]

Daniel Sommer, on the other hand, seemed to question very little in his own mind that he himself was Ben Franklin's choice of a successor. In the spring of 1878, six months before Franklin's death, the editor received a letter from Sommer. The letter was never published, so one can only judge what was in it by the answer it received. In a letter to Sommer, dated May 30, 1878, Franklin replied that Sommer's letter to him had caused him to think much of the qualifications of a successor. The man, Franklin confessed, that he liked most was Bittle, but he feared Bittle's health would not permit him to edit a paper. Therefore, Franklin wrote that the only thing he could do was to open the way for some man in the brotherhood to make himself a record, "to write himself into the confidence of the brethren." Franklin stated to Sommer that he had recently thought of Sommer as a likely successor for the following reasons: (1) Sommer was a young man —then only twenty-eight. (2) He had good bodily health. (3) He had industry, endurance, perseverance and determination. (4) He had sufficient education. (5) He had had severe experiences for a young man. (6) "I believe you intend to keep the faith," wrote Franklin.

The *Review* editor then proposed that Sommer begin writing himself into the confidence of the brethren. Franklin advised Sommer to write under some name, like LUTHER, and advised Sommer to write about some "live issues."[10]   Acting upon this

---

[9]G. W. Rice, "Brother Franklin's Successor," *American Christian Review,* Vol. XXI, No. 46 (November 12, 1878), p. 364.

[10]Daniel Sommer, "History," *American Christian Review,* Vol. XXX, No. 9 (March 3, 1887), p. 65.

advice, Sommer prepared a series of articles on "Educating Preachers," signing them "Evangelist." The articles began to appear in
October, 1878, the same month Franklin died. Sommer, therefore, lacked the time to "write himself into the confidence of the
brethren" that he might be Franklin's successor. Nevertheless,
enough had been said to him by Franklin to lead him to believe
that he was the veteran editor's real choice of one to succeed him.

When, therefore, Rice announced John F. Rowe to be the new
editor of the paper in the fall of 1878, Sommer disagreed. He
immediately wrote to Rice announcing his intention to stay with
the *Review,* but no one can fail to see his disagreement of the
choice. Sommer's letter to Rice said in part:

I am not an aspirant, and I hold myself above narrow and
ungenerous thoughts. From the time of Brother Franklin's death
my constant prayer was *that* one might be chosen editor who
was best fitted for the position. *I acquiesce in what you have done
as the best for the present,* and in this time of its need I intend to
stand by the *Review* with whatsoever power I may have. No petty
considerations shall turn me from it. I am thinking about the
interests of our brotherhood, and not about individual and personal
aggrandizement. While your columns are open to me I intend to
write for the *Review,* pay or no pay.[11]

It would be a "dull scholar" indeed who could not see that Sommer's concern over an editor for the *Review* did not involve some
personal interest of his own in the position.

For two years events proceeded with Sommer continuing his
sporadic writing for the paper. Rowe, sensing in Daniel Sommer
a competitor to his editorial position, found it hard to keep his
ruffled emotions quiet. Rowe hardly greeted Sommer's attempt
to "write himself into the confidence of the brethren" cheerfully.
When, in the spring of 1880, Sommer negotiated arrangements to
move from Kelton, Pennsylvania, to Reynoldsburg, Ohio, he arrived at the latter city on May 1st, only to plunge into conflict
with Rowe. Two or three days later Mrs. M. R. Lemert approached him with a letter she had received from Rowe. Mrs.
Lemert was a very forward woman, having gained some degree
of prominence in her discussions in the *Review* with leading preachers. The letter from Rowe to Mrs. Lemert was not made public.
Nevertheless, Sommer assured his readers that it came as a terrible

[11]Daniel Sommer, "History," *American Christian Review,* Vol. XXX, No.
9 (March 3, 1887), p. 65.

shock to him.   One can but surmise that it must have been a
personal thrust.

Sommer immediately discontinued writing for the *Review.* Three
years later he and L. F. Bittle began publication of the *Octograph,*
perhaps in an attempt to "write himself into the confidence of the
brotherhood."   In purchasing the *Review,* Sommer states his
reasons as being:

One of our purposes was to save the enterprise of Benjamin
Franklin's grand life from ruin; another was to occupy a position
in which we could do the greatest possible good, and in order to
do this our purpose was to lift the *Review* out from its entangle-
ments.[12]

The vituperations between Rowe and Sommer continued for
several months, but eventually each grew weary of the struggle
and swore off putting such personal thrusts before the public.
The armistice undoubtedly helped both periodicals.   Actually the
whole warfare did little except to gratify the personal pride of
each.

With the passing of time the feelings mellowed, and notable
changes came in both papers.   In the spring of 1887 both George
W. Rice and J. L. Richardson abandoned the *Leader.*   "Time has
mellowed the whole matter," Rice wrote, "and then added that he
could now see that Alden's sale was not a "sham," and so offered
his apology to Mr. Alden.   Richardson confessed he was in error
in advising Rowe to publish another paper, and made public his
confession through the *Review.*   Alfred Ellmore, one of the popular writers and preachers of the time, went with the *Leader.*
There was nothing personal in his action.   He had made the
promise to Rowe and Rice when the trouble first occurred, and he
went with the *Leader* to keep his word.   Ellmore wrote:

The all-important question with me is, "what is my duty?"   I
am anxious that the right prevail.   I seek not caste, fame or wealth,
but duty.   An humble seat just inside the door is all I ask.   Life
is too brief and too precious to be thrown away.   But I would
rather fail sustaining the right than triumph in wrong.   I would
rather die with the few, being right, than to live and prosper with
the many in the wrong.[13]

However, Ellmore's stay with the *Leader* was not calculated to be

---

[12]Daniel Sommer, "The *Review's* Farewell," *American Christian Review,*
Vol. XXX, No. 11 (March 17, 1887), p. 81.
[13]Alfred Ellmore, "Wheat and Chaff," *Christian Leader,* Vol. I, No. 11
(March 15, 1887), p. 4.

of long duration. In the fall of 1893 the *Leader* changed its form, doubtlessly copying the *Christian-Evangelist*. About the same time Alfred Ellmore is noticeably dropped from among the contributors. The reason, he explains later, is that John F. Rowe had gone over to the "digressive element," alluding, of course, to Rowe's willingness to worship with a "small organ," but not, "O ye gods," said Rowe, a large one.

Meanwhile, Sommer's editorial work began in earnest. He made definite changes that he thought would contribute to the success of the paper, the first major change being the dropping of all secular advertising. It was the custom generally to advertise frequently in the papers everything from Royal Baking Powder to Hood's Sarsparilla. Most papers could not have eked out an existence through the lean years without this advertising. Sommer thought the practice so deplorable that he dropped it immediately, and began frequent criticisms of other papers who did advertise. The *Gospel Advocate* had by advertising sustained itself and was at the time in no financial position to drop them. Sommer made a lengthy attack on the *Advocate* for its practice, and David Lipscomb watched, but like F. G. Allen, had "kept his finger in his mouth." He considered Sommer "a good man and in many respects a most excellent teacher," yet Lipscomb felt Sommer "looks at things from a narrow and selfish standpoint."

On the whole the *Advocate's* relation to Daniel Sommer during the first part of Sommer's editorial labors was very cordial. James A. Harding, then riding the crest of popularity with his work in the *Advocate,* often found the enigmatic Sommer hard to understand. In an editorial printed in the *Review,* February 3, 1887, Sommer wrote on "Which Is the More Excellent Way?" Sommer attacked those preachers who preached where the organ was used, but in doing so insisted that it be silent. For this Harding found strenuous objections, although David Lipscomb advocated the same. If a congregation, reasoned Lipscomb, will not keep the organ silent out of respect for God, why should it do so out of respect for *me?* But on this point a considerable number of preachers who were all united in their disagreement of the use of the organ found room for contention. W. B. F. Treat, while preaching for the church at Martinsville, Indiana, which used the instrument, was content to work along with the church in he hope of leading them back. But Harding looked with dismay on the practice, and wrote:

. . . He [Daniel Sommer] is the present owner and publisher of the *American Christian Review,* and is also one of the chief writers for that paper. He has been regarded as one of the most earnest, faithful and powerful of the younger class of writers and speakers among the disciples (he is, I presume, yet under forty), and also as one of the most apostolic in his teachings. He was a great favorite with Brother Benjamin Franklin, the founder of the *Review.* For a number of years Brother Sommer has edited and published a small periodical called the *Octograph,* but of late he has obtained possession of the *Review,* a paper that has always taken a leading rank among us of those that oppose the missionary societies, fairs, festivals, organs, etc.

But within the last few months there has been a change all around in the management of the paper, and it appears that this is to be followed by a very decided change in its tone. . . . It has a new owner, a new editor-in-chief, and a new staff of editorial contributors, and (if I am not mistaken) it is beginning to show a very different spirit from that manifested by its bold, aggressive and devoted founder. A truer, nobler, grander man than Benjamin Franklin I think I never met. I read his writings for nearly a quarter of a century; that is, from the time I was about ten years of age till he died. He was often in my father's house (they were intimate friends), and I knew him well. He often spent months in our region conducting protracted meetings, and, when he did, it afforded me great pleasure to hear him preach, and to go with him from house to house, for I realized that there was in our midst indeed "a prince and a great man," a notable leader of the hosts of God. No other man was holding back so mightily the tide of innovation that was sweeping in upon us; no other was so vigorous in the endeavor to eradicate the seeds of division and the causes of stumbling.

Since his death I have watched the course of the *Review* with great interest, and I have seen much in it that was good, very good, and much that was evidently written in bad spirit and poor taste.

When Brother W. B. F. Treat became editor of it, I was glad, for I said, "Whatever may be the merits of the Rowe-Rice-Alden embroglio, a strong, true man is at the helm." But, much to my disappointment and sorrow, it was but a little while till I learned that Brother Treat was even then preaching regularly as the hired minister of a church that uses an organ with every song they sing, notwithstanding his supposed opposition to the pastor and the organ.

When Brother Sommer appeared as the owner and publisher of the paper, my hopes revived, for I had known of him, through some of the Detroit brethren, as a sturdy, faithful, resolute, apostolic man; but when this article which we are about to review appeared, my confidence in the *Review's* remaining true to the Divine teaching was sadly shaken. However, such has been my confidence in Brother Treat and my hope for Brother Sommer that, I think, there is not a man who would be happier than I were my fears to prove groundless. . . .[14]

Nothing very serious, however, developed from Harding's objections. For some reason the truculent Harding found Sommer slightly objectionable it seems, and the two men hurled their criticisms back and forth for years.

The last copy of the *American Christian Review* came before the public March 17, 1887. Sommer announces that the *Review* will henceforth be united with the semimonthly *Octograph,* and its new name would be *Octographic Review.* The name coined by L. F. Bittle was intended to be suggestive of the fact that the *Review* was to be thoroughly apostolic. The term "American" to Sommer was too local, and the term "Christian" was too sacred to be used in connection with a human enterprise. However, the term "Octograph" proved to be too burdensome, and in 1914 the name was changed to *Apostolic Review,* a name the paper held until Daniel Sommer's death.

The patrons of the *Review* found it difficult to familiarize themselves with the new name. It was odd, clumsy, and conveyed no real meaning to the average reader. The name *American Christian Review,* on the other hand, was alive wih tradition, and had come to symbolize everything bold, vigorous and truthful in the restoration. *The Christian Standard* tersely commented on the new title, "It is to be hoped that none will claim that this name is the outcome of seeking Bible names for Bible things."[15]

Meanwhile, Sommer had bright visions for the future welfare of his paper. Cincinnati was hardly the place to publish the *Review,* and in the spring of 1887, Sommer thought of Indianapolis as the logical place. He wrote:

At this juncture we venture to say that Cincinnati is not the most central place. For years we have thought of Indianapolis as the city above all others from which the publication that would

---

[14]James A. Harding, "The More Excellent Way—A Reply to Brother Sommer," *Gospel Advocate,* Vol. XXIX, No. 11 (March 16, 1887), p. 173.

[15]H. McDiarmid, "Editorial Items," *Christian Standard,* Vol. XXII, No. 17 (April 23, 1887), p. 133.

work a revolution should be issued. On this subject we have not changed our mind. Indiana was the home of the *Review's* founder, and doubtless is the state in which his influence was largely felt. Indianapolis is the city in which about fifteen lines of railroad center. Besides, it is perhaps more nearly than any other city in the center of our great brotherhood. In due time the *Review* expects to recover from her wounds and recuperate wasted forces and move westward. But for the present it is here in a beautiful town in a beautiful country which probably has as little iniquity to the square inch, as good health, as good and upright citizens as any other place that can be found eastward of westward, northward or southward.

Four months later Sommer wrote again after visiting in Indiana:

Something over four weeks ago we left home for this state (Indiana), and we must confess that the more we see of it the better we like it. The utter absence of aristocracy is delightful to a plain man. People seem to estimate each other at the point of character and regardless of wealth or grammar. They do not affect to despise either, but character seems to be the highest criterion. . . . Brethren of Indiana, we still think favorably of Indianapolis as the future home of the *Review*. It is a central place with excellent facilities. The Lord willing we shall get there, and we hope all the people will say, "amen."

According to a dream, therefore, that Sommer had entertained for some years, he moved the *Review* to Indianapolis in 1894.

Thus the *American Christian Review* had passed through an intensely interesting, if stormy, history. The *Review* of Ben Franklin's day died when Franklin died in 1878. The *Review* of John F. Rowe lived from 1878 to 1886. The newborn *Octographic Review* with its successor, *Apostolic Review,* ran from 1887.

CHAPTER XVI

SONS OF THUNDER

In the course of time, if one remains loyal to principles of truth, he is likely to see victory shine out from the darkness of despair. At the close of the Civil War, David Lipscomb and E. G. Sewell went patiently to work in a war-trodden South to build apostolic Christianity. Their paper, the *Gospel Advocate,* was an unostentatious periodical hardly promising of any great influence. The few disciples were scattered, the mails were just opening, and srong, influential preachers almost nonexistent in their latitude. They remained true to their convictions. Occasionally they were laughed at, but in the process of time, the preaching which they had done in schoolhouses and in brush arbors counted where they could see it. The teaching of the *Advocate* took root. Congregations grew stronger, and younger men began dedicating their lives to preaching the gospel. By 1890 Lipscomb and Sewell were beginning to catch a glimpse of the sunset, but around them had arisen a young corps of preachers whose adventures portray the romance of the era.

James A. Harding, F. D. Srygley, F. B. Srygley, E. A. Elam, J. D. Tant, M. C. Kurfees, T. B. Larimore and T. R. Burnett were now entering their prime. The stories of each of these men, in addition to others, would make, if completely told, thrilling reading. Their sacrifices would cheer the hearts of more modern gospel preachers, and furnish inspiration for the church at large. The stories of two—Fletcher Douglas Srygley and James A. Harding —are told here for the reason that they influenced in a major way the movement that is being studied. In some respects both were similar. Each was an intrepid soul. The logic of James A. Harding, and the fierceness with which he went at an opponent, added nothing to the felicity of his enemies. While Srygley used less of the real arts of a logician, he was, however, of a fiery temperament that shrank in fear of nothing. He had a masterful and humorous method of meeting every attack. To Harding and Srygley for at least a decade the restoration in the South can give credit for some of its coloring.

319

F. D. SRYGLEY

T. R. Burnett once declared that in Texas, F. D. Srygley was called "the Mark Twain of the Reformation." If so, it is little question but that he deserved the sobriquet. After becoming front-page editor of the *Gospel Advocate* in November, 1889, he gave to the paper a punch and wit that undoubtedly widely increased its influence. The *Advocate* during these years had a well-balanced editorial force. David Lipscomb's articles were deep and thought-provoking. E. G. Sewell's thoughts elegantly flowed through his words. J. C. McQuiddy kept abreast of the happenings of the brotherhood, and both T. R. Burnett and F. D. Srygley gave the paper humor enough to brighten up every crisis. Burnett was no doubt right in viewing the *Gospel Advocate* of those years in the following light:

Srygley's brilliant periods, Sewell's smoothly flowing leaders, McQuiddy's newsy items, old David's heavy artillery, this scribe's pointed paragraphs—here is a bill of fare that will edify a man who loves good eating, and will give a digressive saint the dyspepsia.[1]

For a time there was some talk going via grapevine that F. D. Srygley was being specially groomed to take Lipscomb's place as editor of the *Gospel Advocate*. The rumor seemed altogether ill-founded as Srygley well recognized, but even so, the application of a little humor to the case seemed appropriate:

A private letter from Texas, as well as hints from other quarters, would indicate that a few brethren are troubled to decide whether I am a proper person "to wear David Lipscomb's mantle after he dies." Seeing I have been in feeble health for several years, and that eminent physicians long ago decided I was beyond the aid of medical science and doomed to a premature grave, while D. L. is in vigorous health with every prospect of living to a green old age, I feel but little interest in the question. I think I can "rustle" around and keep a mantle of my own as long as I live, and the way D. L. is tearing around among rationalists just now, I am inclined to think his mantle will be pretty well ripped up by the time he is done with it.[2]

Rock Creek, Alabama, where Srygley was born, was a country post office "twelve miles from the nearest point on any railroad" in the rough, mountain country of Colbert County. It was six

---

[1]T. R. Burnett, "Burnett's Budget," *Gospel Advocate,* Vol. XXXVI, No. 23 (June 7, 1894), p. 9.
[2]F. D. Srygley, "From the Papers," *Gospel Advocate,* Vol. XXXII, No. 12 (March 19, 1890), p. 177.

F. D. SRYGLEY

miles to the nearest country village. It was here "in the hill country of north Alabama" that F. D. Srygley was born on December 22, 1856. His parents were James H. and Sarah Jane Srygley—poor, hard-working, devoted country people.

Sarah Jane Coats Srygley, his mother, was thoroughly devoted in her religious life and left the imprint of her convictions upon her sons. She was born into a Presbyterian family on November 7, 1831, and her father, Benjamin Coats, was a Cumberland Presbyterian preacher. She was baptized by J. M. Pickens, one of North Alabama's prominent preachers, soon after the close of the war. Immediately after she was immersed in August, 1866, she and her husband established a congregation at Rock Creek. Although for years the number of disciples was only about eight or ten, they were faithful in their religious duties.

Srygley's father, James H., a poor laborer, settled in the mountains of North Alabama, west of Huntsville soon after the Indians were removed. At the time he settled in North Alabama, the richer plantation owners were beginning to purchase the rich land along the Tennessee River, so from one of them Srygley's father secured a job splitting rails. His pay was fifty cents a hundred plus his board.

It was twelve miles from his home to the place where he worked. He would walk the distance through the trails in the woods about sunup on Monday mornings. From Monday morning until Saturday night he could split fifteen hundred rails, and on Saturday night he would walk the twelve miles back home again. He spent Sundays chopping wood for his wife and looking after her provisions so she could be taken care of until he arrived home again the next Saturday. It was a hard life, scarcely promising of a future.

The Srygleys had five boys—F. G., F. W., F. D., F. B., and F. L. F. D. and F. B. were the only two that were preachers. One may naturally wonder why all the boys were named with their names beginning with an "F." There is hardly a way to find out. To the inquisitive F. D. Srygley wrote in the summer of 1880, "Those who are curious to know why all of our names commence with an F may write to our dear mother who lives at Rock Creek, Alabama, inclosing stamp to pay return postage." If anyone wrote, the answer was never published.

The little Rock Creek congregation shared in common with the other churches the hardships of life in the South after the close of the war. People had no money and could only give to the Lord's work what little they could raise on their farms. As late as 1876 members of the church in Lauderdale, Alabama, lacking money, were contributing wheat, corn, flour, meal, cloth, etc., to the church. At a time when the church needed ready cash, it merely sold some of its stored-up produce. About this time when "Weeping Joe" Harding was trying to build a meetinghouse at South Tunnell in Sumner County, he took gifts of chickens, hauled them to Nashville and sold them to raise the money to build the house. People had no money, and the small band at Rock Creek shared alike in this.

T. B. Larimore was called from Tennessee to Rock Creek to preach for the small congregation. It was about 1868 or 1869. It was Larimore's first time to meet F. D. Srygley, then a poor country boy in his early "teens." Thirty years later, Larimore vividly recalled the scene:

More than thirty years ago, I went from Nashville, Tennessee— my native state—to Alabama, to Rock Creek, to the new historic Rock Creek meetinghouse. My mission was to preach the word. The church there then numbered seven souls. As, the first time, I approached the door of that old log cabin "meetinghouse"—a penniless stranger in a strange land—I saw, standing about thirty feet away, to the right and in front of me, twenty feet from the path that I was traveling and thirty feet from the door I was approaching, a bright, little, black-eyed bareheaded, barefooted boy; a picure of health, happiness, and peace, and contentment; perfectly beautiful—to me—then as, on memory's page, now. His cheeks were rosy; his eyes were black. Faultless in form and feature, he stood, silent, motionless and erect.

He was standing there to see the "preacher" as he passed, probably not caring to ever be nearer him than then. Instinctively I turned toward him, went to him, took his little right hand into mine, put my left arm around him, and led him into the house. From that day to the day when, in the delirium of death, he, suddenly recognizing me, enthusiastically grasped me by both hands and thrilled my soul with an expression I can never forget, he was my devoted friend.[3]

No man ever had a closer friend than Larimore did in F. D. Srygley. It was exactly so—from that moment that Srygley first saw Larimore until the day when Srygley died, he was a firm admirer of T. B. Larimore. Srygley would often say in later years, "I'll criticize him [Larimore] when he needs it, if I want to; but no other man shall do it." Throughout their lives, they corresponded frequently, and when Larimore would come in the vicinity where Srygley lived, they were constantly together.

The first book Srygley wrote was entitled, "Larimore and His Boys." It recounted, besides the life of Larimore, the lives of some of the boys who studied under Larimore at Mars Hill College near Florence, Alabama. But there was one book that Srygley wanted to write to make the crowning work of his life. It would

---

[3]T. B. Larimore, "F. D. Srygley," *Gospel Advocate,* Vol. XLII, No. 35 (August 30, 1900), p. 54.

be a complete compilation of the life and letters of Larimore. Srygley was younger by thirteen years than his friend, and he entertained some hope of living beyond the time of his former teacher. His ambition was to wait until after Larimore died, and then compile the story of his life, believing he could die in peace if he could but accomplish his.

But as the century was nearing its close, Srygley became painfully aware that his end was drawing nigh. Larimore had been invited to hold a lengthy meeting at Nashville, the meeting beginning in December, 1899, and lasting for over two months. Srygley felt that he had better strike then. Reluctantly did Larimore agree to the undertaking. Miss Emma Page, a teacher of the Fanning Orphan School, and later Larimore's second wife, was employed to take down Larimore's sermons. Srygley worked against time to gather letters and information, but early in the summer or late in the spring the material was turned over to the printer.

Srygley was already sick when the first copy of the book came from the press. He was in bed when he examined it. Naturally he found many mistakes; some errors to be corrected, but on the whole he was well pleased. At the time, Larimore was near Nashville in a meeting, and came to pay a visit on his dying friend. Srygley, from his bed, asked Larimore to get him the book. After pointing out an error or two in it that he wanted corrected, he said to Larimore: "I would love to live to read it and all that may be said about it in the press, revise it and perfect it; then I suppose my work would be about done. I now think of nothing else that I want to do." Later he added, "I may be mistaken, of course, but I honestly believe, the Bible excepted, it is the best book I have ever seen." He loved the book because he loved its subject.

In the month of August, before becoming eighteen years of age, F. D. Srygley was baptized by T. B. Larimore. For a long time Srygley had been wanting to be immersed, but had been taught that children need not hurry, so had waited until after he was seventeen. Larimore's school near Florence had been opened only three years before, so Srygley made plans to become one of its students. His plan was to go to school in the winter and preach in the summer.

The summer of 1876 Srygley left home "with a pair of saddle-bags on my shoulder" to join John Taylor in a preaching tour through northern Alabama. John Taylor was an old preacher, then over seventy, and Srygley was only nineteen. Srygley loved this old preacher for the sacrifices he had made. Nearly twenty-five years later Srygley took what profit he had made from "Larimore and His Boys" and remembered Taylor. A part of the profit from the sale of the book went in paying expenses for a little girl to attend the Fanning Orphan School. About two hundred and fifty dollars was spent in paying salaries for preachers who were in destitute fields. Eight dollars was spent to buy a gravestone for John Taylor. Srygley had known poverty. His heart was with the poor, and with any preacher, who would sacrifice to preach to the poor.

But, as he and Taylor went out in the summer of 1876 to preach, they planned for hardships. Taylor had a good horse; Srygley had none. It was decided that both of them should ride together when the roads were bad, and take turns riding when the road was good. However, a good brother offered Srygley a colt "whereon yet never man sat," but he had to walk five miles to get it. During this summer's preaching, they preached often in private houses, under brush arbors, and in school houses.

That winter, Srygley was back in school, but the next summer was out preaching again. This time he and Henry F. Williams of Maury County, Tennessee went forth together. Of the occasion, Larimore wrote:

Our two worthy young brethren, Henry F. Williams, of Maury County, Tennessee and Fletcher D. Srygley of Colbert County, Alabama left Mars Hill a few days ago, to begin their summer campaigns. They are noble young soldiers. They are entirely worthy of all the confidence that brethren and friends may repose in them. They love the ADVOCATE and will wield a strong influence in its favor.[4]

Young preachers are not likely to spend *all* their time in preaching. Most will find sometime for the more amorous affairs of life, and Srygley was no exception to the rule. He "wooed and won" Miss Ella Parkhill of Mars Hill, Alabama, and on December 15, 1878 found himself with a sixteen-year-old bride. Of course, Larimore performed the ceremony.

Two little girls—Mamie and Jeffie—were soon born, but Mamie, the first, died in infancy. The child's funeral was held and the baby was tearfully borne to the cemetery near Rock Creek. After

---

[4]T. B. Larimore, "Correspondence," *Gospel Advocate,* Vol. XIX, No. 27 (July 5, 1877), p. 423.

the funeral, Ella wept bitterly for a tiny curl she had forgotten to clip from the child's head. Friends tried to console her, but she refused their tenderness. Late one night, Srygley went out to the cemetery, reopened the grave, clipped a curl, and took it back to his sorrowing wife. But in a matter of a few months, she followed her little girl to the grave.

It was December, 1880, being only a few months out of school, that F. D. Srygley moved to Paris, Texas. His stay in Texas was short-lived. Having made the acquaintance of John T. Poe, then living at Longview, Srygley one day walked with Poe out into the woods. The two sat down and Srygley spoke thoughtfully saying, "Brother Poe, I am going into the larger cities; I feel I have a work to do I cannot accomplish in Texas." Something discouraged him, and he turned his footsteps back toward Tennessee.

There is little question but that Srygley felt he could do considerable good through his writing. He had natural writing ability, worked hard at it, and the ability to treat a subject with that kind of concern it demanded. However, before that time came when he and David Lipscomb found mutual acquiescence on major issues, Srygley's editorial career was somewhat stormy.

Very early in this career did Srygley and Lipscomb find themselves in disagreement. Srygley was a mere youth, only twenty-two years old, whereas Lipscomb was nearing fifty when they had their first disagreement. It is possible, if not probable, that Srygley shared a common sentiment, felt in those earlier days that David Lipscomb was a "sour old man," and this seemed to have lead to a natural aversion to agreeing with Lipscomb. At any rate, Lipscomb wrote in 1879, advising the participation in sports. He commented that man needed more rest and relaxation; that he himself had had poor health the past several years, a thing he attributed to his lack of sufficient diversion. Srygley took exception. It was better for a Christian to spend an afternoon in visiting the sick than in some sporting event. Srygley succeeded in calling on himself a mild castigation.

Two years later, however, Lipscomb and Srygley sparred off on more serious matters—this time the subject of the Missionary Society. It was customary for T. B. Larimore to stear clear of controversial subjects within the brotherhood which left room for some of his younger admirers to doubt the importance of opposition to them. Later, some of Larimore's "boys" caused considerable anxiety in the brotherhood in the South over these issues that Larimore refused to oppose. It might have been a different story had Larimore indoctrinated these youths earlier against them. This is one of the few just criticisms to be made of Larimore's work.

Apparently lacking in any trepidation whatever, young Srygley marched against the senior editor of the *Gospel Advocate* late in 1881 on the subject of the Society. Srygley made no contribution in the way of new arguments for the Missionary Society. The fact that a host of noble pioneers disagreed with Lipscomb weighed heavily with Srygley. While not a forceful advocate of the Society, it was difficult for Srygley to see that it could not be excused on the ground of expediency. Lipscomb was kind but positive in his disagreement. He confessed his belief that Srygley was unduly prejudiced and therefore, had not come fully to understand the real issue involved. Srygley took personal offense, thinking Lipscomb had been too hard on him, and withdrew his support from the *Advocate*.

F. G. Allen had within recent years begun publishing the *Old Path Guide* from Louisville, Kentucky and toward this paper Srygley now turned. Allen, an extremely forceful writer, commanded the respect of the more conservative bulk of the brotherhood, who occupied the "middle ground," viz, they favored the missionary society but opposed the use of instrumental music. The College of The Bible at Lexington was an educational center of this type of thinking, and a host of preachers flowed from its halls to melt here and there into the brotherhood activities. The passing of a decade made it increasingly certain that this middleground would pass out of existence. Some who saw it viewed the inevitable with bitterness. Such did Moses E. Lard. The majority, however, jumped from their sinking isle across the roaring currents of the controversies to the *Christian Standard*. They reluctantly accepted the use of the instrument, but their number gave a decidedly conservative coloring to the *Christian Standard* which it has in its own way retained through the years. J. W. McGarvey, who had furnished the music to inspire the vanguard of that hapless army of preachers, was oddly enough doomed to be its rearguard, being the last of that school of thought to pass. In the last five years of F. G. Allen's life he showed signs of leaning more and more to David Lipscomb's point of view. His life was cut down in 1886, but Lipscomb never doubted that had Allen lived longer, he would have stood solidly behind the *Advocate*.

When, therefore, Srygley left the *Advocate,* he became an ardent supporter of the *Old Path Guide,* and backed its editorial policy. Suffering severely from Bright's disease in 1884, he retired from the editorial staff of the *Old Path Guide*. For the next five years Srygley sat on the side-lines watching as best he could the current of events glide past. On December 26, 1888 he married again— this time Miss Jennie Scobey, daughter of James E. Scobey of Hopkinsville, Kentucky. His health was still poor, and Miss Jennie knew it. Later, F. B. Srygley declared that she had added ten years to his brother's life.

Upon the death of F. G. Allen, Russell Errett, owner of the *Christian Standard* took over the *Old Path Guide*. Srygley saw its editorial policy change, and watched the paper as it apologized for the use of the instrument of music in worship, and Srygley's ardor for the *Guide* cooled. The old wounded feeling against David Lipscomb healed some with the passing of time, and, although Srygley could not yet see entirely the way Lipscomb did, he decided that Lipscomb's "extremes" were on the side of safety. Having prepared his manuscript for "Larimore And His Boys," he and his wife made a trip to Nashville late in 1889 to see about getting it published. He met Lipscomb again. We are left to surmise the conversation they must have had. Judging from the fact that with the November issue that year, Srygley began his editorial work as "Front Page Editor" of the *Advocate,* old feelings were forgotten, and a basis of understanding reached.

No sooner had Srygley begun writing for the *Advocate,* than many waved the hand of despair. Was not Srygley known to favor the Society? Had he not been on the editorial staff of the *Guide,* a "progressive" paper? What then was wrong with David Lipscomb?

It is doubtful if many men have fully grasped the greatness of David Lipscomb, but in the attempt to do so one must not overlook the fact that it was his constant aim to be firm for the truth, oppose the wrong, and yet forbear with human weaknesses. Stating the principle on which he had worked all of his life, Lipscomb once wrote:

We have noticed those most extreme on one side are liable to run to the other extreme. Let your moderation be known to all men. Be firm for truth, steadfast in the maintainence of right, yet forbearing to the weaknesses of our fellowmen, knowing we also are liable to be drawn aside, and as we judge others, God will judge us. We have often borne with men that were wrong, tried to get them right, often failed, but have never regretted the forbearance. Be true to the truth, oppose the error, but forbear with humanity.[5]

On this principle David Lipscomb acted. But he learned that it is difficult for an individual to love truth, stand by principle, and yet not bear personal animosity. He who tries it may often find that his own brethren will most doubt his altruism.

Lipscomb felt that Srygley was still wrong, but that he was coming in the right direction; therefore, as a Christian he must forbear. Srygley had not reached that point of view that Lipscomb had, but he was going that direction. To forbear in such case might incur the wrath of some brethren, but it would win the individual. Srygley, aware of the criticism Lipscomb was getting, wrote on the serious subject in a vein of levity.

Speaking of boycotting, it might be well to say I am boycotted by extreme partisans on both sides of the progressive ditch and not on very good terms with myself just now. I have been giving attention for some weeks to certain extreme parties in Alabama, and Missouri, and now I find myself besieged and completely cut off from my base of supplies by extremists on the other side of the question in Arkansas and Texas. The *Firm Foundation* puts it this way: "If the *Advocate's* policy is to shelter, defend and praise every "progressive" that will work for it, we think it may safely calculate on getting "thirty thousand subscribers" soon. But if the paper is to be a faithful exponent of the views of Lipscomb, Srygley, Aten, *et al*, it will have to cut a broad swath— "weed a wide row"—so wide that we need not expect it to uproot every plant not planted by our heavenly Father. Those new men will slight their work when they come to some of the human plants, and D. L. may look out for criticism frequently." This is bad news from Texas, with several townships yet to hear from, and the latest news from Arkansas, as reported in the *Christian Preacher*, adds despair to defeat. The *Preacher* puts it thus: "The *Gospel Advocate* has recently added to its editorial

---

[5]David Lipscomb, "Thirty Years' Work," *Gospel Advocate*, Vol. XXXVIII, No. 2 (January 9, 1896), p. 20.

force, F. D. Srygley and A. P. Aten—the former a racy writer; and the latter a very elegant one. Both have been on the editorial staff of the *Guide,* and are known to be progressive. How they can consistently work with the *Advocate* we do not understand. We sometimes fear the "Old reliable" may be made to capitulate by a modern Trojan horse scheme."

Speaking of horses, I wish I had a Trojan horse, or any other kind of a horse, that I might ride him out of this mess. If I only had a "Texas plug," a "Mexican broncho," or even a hobbyhorse, I might yet be saved. As to how I work with the *Advocate,* I understood it on Paul's theory, "If meat make my brother to offend, I will eat no flesh while the world standeth," and considering that I have to tussel with all intolerant extremists on all sides of all questions, I find it pretty hard work on decidedly light diet.[6]

Srygley's interest in brotherhood periodicals was not limited to his writing, for he owned a half-interest in the *Old Path Guide.* When the Courier Publishing Company was organized in Dallas to publish the *Christian Courier,* Srygley purchased two hundred and fifty dollars worth of stock in that paper. In view of the fact that the *Christian Courier* was intended to be the *Christian Standard* of the west, Srygley was placed in an inconsistent light as owning stock in a company while editing for another paper directly opposed to it.

The Srygley family migrated from Alabama to Coal Hill, Arkansas about this time. F. D. Srygley moved here in October, 1885. Two years later, his mother followed. Soon a colony of three hundred or more had located here, most of them being Srygley's relatives from Alabama. A few disciples met and built a respectable meeting house. Srygley lived here about four years, until he moved to Nashville to work on the *Gospel Advocate.* While at Coal Hill, he worked as a real estate agent, preaching some on the side as he was able.

Early in the year, 1900, Srygley went back to Coal Hill for a visit. His mother had died the previous August. He tried to preach at Marianna, Arkansas but the doctor sent him home, knowing he was in a dying condition. From May until August, 1900, Srygley spent most of the time in bed, waiting for the end. He refused to allow any public announcement to be made of his

---

[6]F. D. Srygley, "From the Papers," *Gospel Advocate,* Vol. XXXII, No. 12 (March 19, 1890) p. 177.

condition. Consequently, the announcement of his death came as a surprise to many readers of the *Gospel Advocate*.

J. C. McQuiddy broke the news through the *Advocate* with the following announcement:

On the morning of August 2 our dear brother, associate, and friend, F. D. Srygley, breathed his last. He was sick for about two months; but as it was his request and desire, no mention was made of his sickness. His affliction was heart disease, which produced dropsy.

We feel very deeply the loss, and know that this announcement will bring sadness to many hearts. He has been one of the editors of the Gospel Advocate since November, 1889. During all these years he has been a vigorous, clear, and forceful writer. He loved his work, wrote with great ease and rapidity, and has often said to me that he expected to spend his life in writing books and in the defense of the gospel of Christ. He was true to this purpose, for he wrote to the very last, and before the paper containing his last editorial work had reached our readers he was dead. But his work is not dead, and will continue to live to bless thousands. While his life was a short one, being hardly forty-four years old, yet he lived much and did much that will live on to ennoble and purify. In the later years of his life he spent much of his time evangelizing in destitute fields. In these years he did far more of this work than any preacher known to me. Often have I heard him say that the wealthy churches could easily secure the best preachers to preach for them, while the poor could not, adding that the Saviour went among the poor while he was on earth. The many truths he has taught and impressed so forcibly cannot die. His work in showing that what constitutes one a Christian makes him a member of the one body cannot be in vain. God will raise up others to carry forward this teaching.[7]

JAMES A. HARDING

The outbreak of the Civil War in the spring of 1861 nearly paralyzed the work of the church for a time. Nevertheless, Moses E. Lard in the fall of that year ventured over to Winchester, Kentucky to assist J. W. Harding in a gospel meeting. In the course of the meeting J. W. Harding's thirteen-year-old son, James A., was baptized. He was the oldest child of J. W. and Mary E. McDonald Harding, and the parents took great delight in the fact that he became a Christian.

---

[7]J. C. McQuiddy, "F. D. Srygley," *Gospel Advocate,* Vol. XLII, No. 32 (August 9, 1900), p. 505.

J. A. HARDING

J. W. Harding was at home in Kentucky. For ninety-seven
years he lived around Winchester, traveling but little from there.
His father, Amos Harding, had moved into Kentucky from Boston

around 1820. Having become a tailor, he followed that trade for a number of years. In 1839 he obeyed the gospel, and after that he preached on Sundays, and worked either as a tailor or a merchant through the week. He married Mary E. McDonald in 1844, and to them fourteen children were born. J. W. Harding was throughly devoted to the work of God. He was an elder in the Court Street Church in Winchester, Kentucky until the instrument of music was forced in in 1887. Thereafter, he and fifteen others left and became the nucleus for the Fairfax congregation. Harding was active here until he died in 1919.

But the name of James A. Harding was destined to become much more familiar than that of his father. Although from very early in his life Harding intended to be a preacher, his first work was teaching school. Harding later recalled that the first pay he ever received was for teaching. When he was seven years old, his mother had employed a colored girl about fourteen who wanted to learn to read. Harding had just completed the "first reader," so he passed his knowledge on to her, forcing her all the while to get her lessons up well. If she were slothful, he flogged her, the same as his teacher did him. He took the colored girl through the second and third readers. One day her father gave him a sack of watermelons for teaching "his gal" to read.

Harding very largely paid his own way through school by teaching. At the age of sixteen he entered an academy taught by J. O. Fox, an eminent Kentucky educator, to prepare for entrance to College. He paid his board and tuition by teaching. It was the fall of 1866 that Harding entered the renowned school. Alexander Campbell had died the previous March, but the memory of Campbell permeated every phase of the school. Harding finished at Bethany in the spring of 1869, and then prepared to go back to Kentucky.

Harding intended to make the preaching of the gospel a lifetime career at this time. About the time James A. Harding was born, his father began preaching. It was nothing unusual for him to lead fifty to a hundred to Christ in the course of a gospel meeting. This impressed young Harding.

As far back as I can remember I had it in mind to preach when I became a man; so when I was about 19 I began to seek for opportunities to speak in the school houses away back 8 or 10 miles from town.[8]

Upon leaving Bethany College, Harding went to Hopkinsville, Kentucky and taught school. He stayed with the school five years, and attended faithfully the congregation in the town. Here, he met the daughter of Judge John B. Knight, a prominent member of the church, and married her. Three children were born to them, two of whom died almost immediately. In five years, his wife also died. Harding's second wife was Miss Pattie Cobb of Estill County, Kentucky.

While teaching school at Hopkinsville, Harding made the acquaintance of V. M. Metcalfe, a popular Kentucky preacher. They first met in 1870. Metcalfe was one who pushed Harding to preach. Often on the way to an appointment, he would stop by Hopkinsville, and take young Harding with him in his buggy. Before long, he had Harding preaching.

When Harding left Hopkinsville in 1874, he fainted because of malaria fever and was taken in a carriage to Winchester to recover. Just as he was recuperating, an old brother, John Adams came to get him to go back into the country and hold a protracted meeting. Harding protested vigorously that he had never held a meeting and had no meeting sermons. Adams talked roughly to him, and reminded Harding that he had been brought up in church and Sunday School and besides had been to Bethany College, and that he ought to be killed if he could not preach, and for him to "shut his mouth," get his horse and go hold that meeting. Harding went and held his first protracted meeting.

Usually every great man has one outstanding quality that he epitomizes. Harding's's most outstanding quality was his faith in God. It was with him a settled conviction that if he did the work God wanted him to do, God would look after him, even to the performing of a miracle if necessary. He could have no doubt that if he ceased his school work and devoted all his time to the work of the Lord, God would care for him. It was not unusual for Harding to be found hundreds of miles from home, getting ready to depart for the depot without a cent in his pocket. If someone inquired how he expected to ride a train with no money,

---

[8]James A. Harding, "Why I Became a Preacher," *Christian Leader and the Way*, Vol. XX, No. 11 (March 13, 1906), pp. 8, 9.

he could expect the answer that God would look after him. If Harding had an appointment to preach at a certain place on Sunday, and if a storm arose Saturday night, washing out a bridge so the train could not travel, it was a matter of certainty with Harding that God had caused that, and for some reason God did not want him to make that appointment.

Harding's absolute trust in God excites the admiration of all who study his life. However, in his own day, as now, the men were legion who believed Harding went to an extreme in his views on divine providence. In 1883 Harding and J. C. McQuiddy carried on a lengthy discussion in the *Gospel Advocate* on divine providence. Neither moved the other from his views.

James A. Harding very quickly became a prominent preacher. In 1882 Lipscomb made Harding a corresponding editor for the *Gospel Advocate*. For the next five years Harding's weighty thrusts in the *Advocate* helped establish the cause in Tennessee where the *Advocate* was especially circulated. He was fearless in his exposures of what he considered wrong. In 1882 he visited as an observer the annual convention of the Society which met at Lexington, Kentucky. Isaac Errett presided. Harding heard infant membership in the Society encouraged. He came home more thoroughly convinced than ever that the Society was an instrument of harm to the church, and set to work denouncing the organization. He was beset by anathemas and denials from F. M. Green and Isaac Errett, but undaunted, Harding stayed with it until he established his point. In 1899 Harding made a visit to Dallas, Texas. Here he met T. R. Burnett, who gives perhaps what is the best description of Harding in print:

Physically, he is a fine specimen of the genus homo, weighing perhaps over two hundred pounds, and has a large blue eye and a big red head. His fat, flush cheeks and thick, red neck indicate that he is of thoroughbred stock or has been fed well at the pie counter. He has doubtless made "full proof of his ministry" among the yellow legged chickens of the blue grass regions of Tennessee. I take it that he wears a No. 17 collar, sleeps well at night, has a conscience void of offense toward God and man, and is full of a laudable ambition to do a great work for the Master's cause. In personal appearance and manner of address, he is very much like Brother C. M. Wilmeth, only he is larger in size. Like Brother Wilmeth he fills his sermons with illustrations. It is no uncommon thing for his eyes to fill with tears while he is speaking, but this is rather a help, and not a hindrance to his speech. . .

He is in all respects the soundest gospel preacher that I have heard preach in Texas. He believes the Bible from "lid to lid."[9]

His quick mind made him particularly adept in controversy. G. G. Taylor was giving an accurate appraisal when he wrote,

His mind is quick and his speaking ability extraordinary. His memory is excellent and he possesses the rare gift of calling to his service momentarily whatever is available for, and advantageous to, his cause. He is always prepared for any emergency, and his zeal and honesty make for him friends on both sides of the controversy. Take him altogether he has few equals in the controversial field.[10]

But Harding's controversy was not limited to the columns of the Advocate. One of his first public discussions was with a Dr. Hayes, presiding elder in the Methodist Church, South. This occurred at Middletown, Kentucky, May 19-27, 1880. Perhaps his most famous discussion was held in Nashville with J. N. Moody, a Baptist preacher. Harding followed this debate with a lengthy meeting on Foster Street with over a hundred additions to the church.

It was true that Harding was no less adept in evangelistic work as in debating. V. M. Metcalfe watched his young protegè with considerable interest. Upon learning in the spring of 1882 that Harding was to preach for the small mission at Huntsville, Alabama, Metcalfe wrote:

Brother Harding is an old-style, solid gospel preacher, and the church that gets him to hold a meeting for them and expects him to go home as soon as he gets up an interest, will be disappointed. I learned he expects soon to commence a meeting at Huntsville, Ala. They could not have made a better selection in a preacher. I would urge the brethren in the surrounding country to attend the meeting and get acquainted with Brother H. He will do you good. Men of his strength, faith and earnest piety are seldom found. May the Lord bless him and all his faithful, struggling children.[11]

After closing a meeting with the famous Plum Street Church in Detroit in 1887, a correspondent wrote of him,

---

[9]T. R. Burnett, "Brother Harding in Texas," *Gospel Advocate,* Vol. XLI, No. 32 (August 10, 1899), p. 510.

[10]G. G. Taylor, "The Sulphur Debate," *Gospel Advocate,* Vol. XXVI, No. 25 (June 18, 1884), p. 394.

[11]V. M. Metcalfe, "Notes of Travel," *Gospel Advocate,* Vol. XXIV, No. 24 (June 14, 1882), p. 367.

A man of sterling character and wonderful memory. In my estimation as well as that of others he is a born orator, worthy of mention, with the same daring spirit which characterized the apostle Paul. . . From his well-stored mind a stream of seeming inexhaustible information flows forth, containing instruction for young and old, the rich and poor in every work of life.[12]

Fortunately Harding was strong physically, making it possible for him to do strenuous work. J. W. Higbee wrote of him,

Brother Harding is about thirty-four years of age, and very stoutly built. This enables him to endure a large amount of work without showing any signs of weariness. He is a faithful and earnest student of the Scriptures for he has reached the healthful conclusion that there is but one absolutely good book in the world and that book is the Bible. Not that he underestimates the value of other books or fails to study them, for he does not, but in his carefulness he has imbibed the spirit of the German proverb which truly affirms that the better is always a great enemy of the best; that is, the richest devotional books and newspapers are enemies if they keep one from reading the Bible.[13]

In 1891 James A. Harding and David Lipscomb established the Nashville Bible School. For nearly a decade Harding was one of the leading spirits in this school. In April, 1899 Harding edited a paper called *The Way*, which later united with the *Christian Leader* to become the *Christian Leader And The Way*.

After ten years with the Nashville Bible School, James A. Harding was providentially permitted to open the Potter Bible School at Bowling Green, Kentucky. The Nashville Bible School, at the close of its tenth session, could hardly see how it could lodge the number of pupils wanting admission the next session. C. C. Potter and his wife proposed to Harding to devote one of their farms to a Bible school and erect the proper buildings if he would secure the necessary faculty. The Potters had a one hundred and forty acre farm two miles from Bowling Green, the proceeds of which they wanted to use to support the school. Harding agreed to the proposal, and plans were immediately begun to erect the buildings for the new school. Potter's idea was that each college should be self-supporting. When in later years the Potter Bible School failed to support itself, he paid all outstanding bills and locked the doors.

---

[12]Vivian, "Plum Street Church of Christ," *Christian Leader,* Vol. I, No. 17 (April 26, 1887), p. 3.

[13]J. W. Higbee, "The Madisonville Meeting," *Gospel Advocate,* Vol. XXIV, No. 24 (June 15, 1882), p. 373.

Albert T. Potter and Mary J. Dunn were married February 15, 1866 and to this union was born two children: a daughter who died in infancy and a son, Eldon S. Potter. Albert Potter died September 28, 1873. Six years later, his younger brother, Clinton C. Potter, married his widow. No children were born to them. Both cared tenderly for Eldon S. Potter. Eldon never married. His death occurred October 9, 1899. This sadness over his death was a hard blow to C. C. Potter and his wife. When the opportunity of starting a Bible School came to them, they grasped it and named it in honor of Eldon S. Potter and as a memorial to him.

Upon the decision to start a Bible School at Bowling Green, C. C. Potter felt concerned over David Lipscomb's reaction, and so determined to take a trip to Nashville to find what Lipscomb's attitude would be. He was overjoyed to hear Lipscomb say, "I wish there was a college in every county." About this time Lipscomb, in announcing plans for the eleventh session of the Nashville Bible School, wrote:

. . . There will be some changes for the future. Brother Harding and Brother Armstrong go to Bowling Green, Ky., to begin a similiar school near that place. This comes of no disagreement or trouble in the faculty here; but means were offered to start a similiar school there, and Brother Harding thought it would be best to accept and use this means, and the rest of us acceded to his ideas. It has never been our idea to build up a school to monopolize the teaching of the Bible, but one of our aims has been to excite others to do likewise. We would be glad to see a school in which the Bible is taught to every pupil in every church in the land; indeed, we do not think children can be reared in the nurture and admonition of the Lord at home or at school without daily instruction in the word of God. . .[14]

His death occurred on May 28, 1922, and he was buried at Bowling Green.

---

[14]David Lipscomb, "Nashville Bible School," *Gospel Advocate,* Vol. XLII, No. 23 (June 6, 1901), p. 361.

Chapter XVII

REARGUARD ACTION

By 1890 the issues dividing the church were largely before the public. Little new in the way of arguments was being offered. Many had already weighed the thought and cast their lot with different sides. So serious a matter as an open breaking of fellowship comes with spiritual men only as a last resort. One of the most determining factors in this break is occasioned by the last-ditch fighting of the rearguard. Here, the battle is often the most intense. The straggling remnants of an undecided host found neutrality no longer possible, and now must plunge into the issues. As the break in fellowship now became more obvious, attempts to place the blame occupied men's attention. Fealty to principles of truth transcended personal interest. Fierce flagellation, dynamic onslaught of the enemies' ramparts, the last bitter cries of wounded pride—these naturally preceded zero hour. Finally came the silent, almost unnoticed, separation of ways, and in the distance was heard the mournful requiem of Israel, sobbing over a broken and battered Zion.

Rearguard action was not peculiar to any one front North, South, East or West—between the years, 1890 and 1906, but this chapter concerns itself with the last-ditch struggle in Tennessee. Through these years the life's work of David Lipscomb was put to the test. By the dawn of the twentieth century Lipscomb could see remarkable differences in the status of the church in Tennessee. Gold, silver, wood, hay or stubble? What had he built? The slow, burning fires of opposition were now to test it.

GOSPEL ADVOCATE

The *Gospel Advocate* had literally grown beside with the church in Tennessee. David Lipscomb liked to say this was the oldest publication in the brotherhood, beginning, as he avowed, with the *Christian Review* in 1844 and coming down through its successor, the *Christian Magazine*. So much had Ben Franklin liked the *Christian Review* as edited by Tolbert Fanning, that he called his paper the *American Christian Review* after Fanning's paper.

If David Lipscomb's point be granted, that the *Gospel Advocate* began with the *Christian Review,* certainly some justification could be found for the claim that this was the oldest periodical in the brotherhood. Reviewing a fifteen year history of his connection with the paper, Lipscomb, writing at the beginning of 1881, could well recall the trials he had met. Never, he declared, had it been his intention to make money from the *Advocate.* In fifteen years he had never made over five hundred dollars, and most of that had been made during the year, 1880. For the first four or five years of the paper's existence, he had given most of his time—and money—to keeping it going.

Lipscomb's bitter experiences had taught him to appreciate T. R. Burnett's "Texas proverb" which said,

There is more joy in a printing-office over one sinner who pays in advance, and abuses the editor on every occasion, than over ninety and nine church members who take the paper and sing its praises and puff the editor, but never contribute one cent to keep him out of the poor-house.[1]

The policies Lipscomb used were hardly the best guarantee of a growing subscription list. But still it grew. At the close of 1880, there were 3,200 subscribers; five years later the list had more than doubled. This happened despite the fact Lipscomb was especially proud that he had never asked anyone to subscribe to the *Advocate.* Frequently, he had given the paper to individuals, and asked them to examine it, and if they felt it worthy, to act accordingly; but he never pushed subscriptions.[2]

Moreover, Lipscomb used the *Advocate* to oppose whatever tendencies he thought wrong. It is safe to say that this is hardly an appeasement policy for the masses. When, therefore, a correspondent wrote to Lipscomb asserting that he was ashamed of the *Gospel Advocate* because of its "wrangling," Lipscomb replied:

I have no doubt Brother Harding, Brother Allen, and every honest lover of the truth, regrets the necessity of controversy with brethren, or anyone else. The necessity of the controversy arises from the disposition in man to sin and to go into error. So long as that disposition continues, so long the necessity of controversy will continue. That disposition is constant, is unceasing

---

[1]T. R. Burnett, "Burnett's Budget," *Gospel Advocate,* Vol. XXXVII, No. 9 (February 28, 1895), p. 131.

[2]David Lipscomb, "The *Gospel Advocate,*" *Gospel Advocate,* Vol XXIII, No. 2 (January 13, 1881), p. 15.

in seeking to work. It must be met with remonstrance, with arguments, with exposure. These must be constant as that. No movement for the better, even when originated by God himself has ever lasted one generation without the introduction of evil and wrong. That wrong must be met and exposed, or the error triumphs. Our movement is not different from others. The truth must be maintained by watchfulness, fidelity to the truth; by conflict from without and within. Whenever a church is not engaged in active conflict with error within itself, it is floating down a broad stream to an open hell. Those who introduce error are responsible for the controversies. A man who will not oppose error when it presents itself is a traitor to God, to Christ who died to root out error and establish truth. . .

Brethren complaining indiscriminately at all when engaged in controversies, those who oppose as well as those who introduce error throw their influence for the error. It says, let error be introduced without opposition—error with quiet is preferable to truth with controversy. . .[3]

But the *Gospel Advocate* gradually grew into a large concern. Early in 1871 its office was moved to 36 Cherry Street between Union and Church. J. T. S. Fall, the "best Job Printer in the City" published it, so in connection with the printing of the paper, a "first class Book and job printing office" went with it. Twenty years later, the *Advocate's* business increased thirty percent in one year. That was in 1889-90. The same year the office moved to 232 North Market Street. A "first-class" office had been equipped, and presses were now being run by electricity.

In a large measure the *Advocate's* growth may be contributed to the bettering of economic conditions throughout the South. The close of the Civil War left the South in desolation, but as this condition improved, the *Advocate's* financial condition did the same. But that is only a part of the story. The paper never lost touch with the common man, and managed to carry items somewhat "off the beaten track" that appealed to its readers. If Louisiana strawberries were selling for twelve cents a quart in Memphis the previous week, the *Advocate* announced it. Nor did the paper become so serious about weighty problems to forget the lighter side. When a boy wrote Lipscomb and Sewell in 1876 saying, "I have a pet Raccoon, if you want it you can have it," Lipscomb could reply, "We don't wish the animal for our

---

[3]David Lipscomb, "Queries," *Gospel Advocate,* Vol. XXVII, No. 45 (November 11, 1885), p. 711.

use and fear it would be a disastrous speculation to go into the 'coon business.' " When, in the summer of 1879, Russell Errett married Mary Glass, a Catholic, of Cincinnati, the *Advocate* jibbed: "May the snows of many winters whiten the head of this young editor Er-rett should come to pass that his fondness of his glass should cease." With the addition of a younger corps of writers later, levity became more the order of the day and Lipscomb's "heavy artillery" thundered less frequently. J. C. McQuiddy, the "office editor," compiled a column of "Miscellany" each week in which most anything might be found. But, once in a while, something like the following would fill it:

William Lipscomb, Jr. is sick this week. J. C. McQuiddy is at the World's Fair, E. G. Sewell is off holding protracted meetings, David Lipscomb is greatly crowded with outside duties connected with the closing of the Bible School, the Fanning Orphan School and other matters, and the first page man is writing an extemporaneous speech which he has been notified he will be unexpectedly called on to make at a commencement occasion in a few days. This explanation will account for nearly anything.[4]

Each year David Lipscomb's editorials not only set forth the perfect felicity he found in abiding solely by the word of God, but the growth of the paper so dear to his heart. At the beginning of 1886, he wrote:

This number begins the twenty-eighth volume of the *Advocate* and the twenty-first year of our connection with it. Over one thousand weekly visits have been made by the *Advocate* to its readers during the last twenty years, very few of which failed to have something from our pen. During this time we have doubtless said many things in a style that was not the best and some things that had better never been said. But we have a clear conscience that what we have said has been at all times with a view to honor God and promote His cause on earth. We begun our course with a firm conviction that the path of safety to man and honor to God can be found in a faithful adherence to His revealed will and to the examples approved by God in faith, in worship and in work. We believed then that efforts to substitute human inventions for the ways approved by inspired men, would be a cause of division and strife among the disciples, and would, also, by accustoming men to look to their own wisdom for help, lead to a reliance upon the wisdom of men rather than upon the wisdom of God, for guidance. It weans away from God, from His

---

[4] J. C. McQuiddy, "Miscellany," *Gospel Advocate,* XXXV, No. 2 (June 1, 1893), p. 344.

word, from His appointments. It leads to reliance upon human wisdom, human inventions, human strength. It breaks down faith and trust in God; it leads to rationalism, to the exaltation of human wisdom, and human expedients, and to infidelity.

A number of persons prominent among those pleading for the return to the primitive order, has gone out from among us. They all traveled the same road. Beginning with the adoption of human experiences, they all have followed the pathway until they set aside all divine appointments that fail to accord with their judgment.

As a man has faith in God, he will implicitly follow God in His approved worship and manner of work. As he lacks faith in God, and trusts human wisdom, he will forsake, set aside God's approved acts of worship and modes of work, and follow the suggestions of human wisdom instead. "Blessed are the poor in spirit,"—those without spiritual wisdom or resource, without confidence in their own spiritual strength or wisdom, is the first condition of possessing the Kingdom of God; because in the consciousness of their own lack of wisdom they are willing to rely upon God, trust His wisdom, and be led by Him in and through His own appointments, and leave the results in His hands. To return to the primitive heaven-approved ways of the Church of God requires a stronger faith in God,—less faith in man. Whomsoever we trust, we will follow. If we trust human wisdom, our own or another's, that we will follow. These things, then are tests of our faith in God.

Twenty years' experience and observation in the workings of the Church, have confirmed me more strongly in the conviction that the stronger our faith in God, the more closely we will seek to follow His approved order in faith, in work, in worship. And the more closely we follow God's approved examples, the stronger our faith in Him will grow. "A closer walk with God" we will seek. On the other hand, observation teaches clearly that the adoption of human inventions and devices in faith, in work, in worship, gradually lead further and further from God; and one innovation but prepares for a dozen others to follow. This has been the pathway in which every denomination in Christendom has traveled away from God. We are not better than others; if we travel the same pathway, we will like them wander from God. The besetting sin of the Jews, of all nations, of every tribe and kindred of earth, is to forget that God will be worshipped only in His own ways, and that the wisdom of man is foolishness with God.

We trust and pray as we grow older that we may more and more learn to trust God, and strive to walk continually more and more closely in His approved ways, that we may more and more distrust human wisdom and human inventions in religion. Our future course in the *Advocate* will be in accord with this prayer. Will all who believe that man's good will be promoted by an unshaken trust in God, and a faithful walk in His ways, work with us in promoting this end? As we have labored the past twenty years of our life to this end, with increased confidence in the wisdom of the course, we consecrate the remainder of it, be it long or short, with the help of our Father, to a more complete devotion of all our powers to this work.[5]

Four years later Lipscomb wrote again:

This is the fifty second and last number of the 32d volume of *Gospel Advocate.* This closes the 25th year of my editorial labor on the *Advocate.* Over twelve hundred and fifty numbers have been issued within this time. Very few of these numbers have gone out that did not carry some word of teaching and instruction, exhortation and warning from my pen. During this time, I have tried to be true to the word of God and faithful to his teachings. To maintain his teaching has been the leading and supreme aim of my labor. I have wished to succeed in the publication of the *Advocate,* and have not been indifferent to the esteem and approval of my fellowmen. But the controlling desire of my heart and the leading effort of my life have been to understand and teach the word of God, and to be faithful to him in all of his requirements, loyal to him in maintaining his church and all his services as he gave them. This has been the key note of my labor from the beginning. I now anticipate it will be to the end. . .[6]

The years stepped by quickly. Six more soon passed, and the senior editor wrote:

Thirty years is an average lifetime. A comparatively small proportion of the human family devote thirty years after they grow to the affairs of life. The last number of the Advocate closed thirty years of work for me in editing and publishing the Gospel Advocate. I began with the first week of January, 1886. The last number closed the year, 1895. I lacked a few days of being 35 years old when I published the first number. I now lack a few days of being 65 years old.[7]

When the last *Advocate* of the nineteenth century was being prepared, Lipscomb gave himself to some fond reminiscences. He was knocking at the door of three-score and ten, and was all but laying aside his life's labors. His faltering pen scratched out these words:

   [5]David Lipscomb, "Our Work," *Gospel Advocate,* Vol. XXVIII, No. 1 (January 6, 1886), p. 6.
   [6]David Lipscomb, "Twenty-Five Years' Labor," *Gospel Advocate,* Vol. XXII, No. 52 (December 24, 1890), p. 829.
   [7]David Lipscomb, "Thirty Years' Work," *Gospel Advocate,* Vol. XXXVIII, No. 1 (January 2, 1896), p. 4.

This number of the Gospel Advocate is the last one for the century, and closes thirty-five years of work I have given to the Advocate. This is considered an average lifetime, and usually spans the period of one man's active labors. I had earnestly desired by this time to have closed up my business relations with the *Advocate* and the publishing company, that the business might rest on younger shoulders and that I might write only as I had something to say. I have not been able to do so. The difficulty has been to find a suitable person willing to do the work and meet the responsibilities for the pay there is in it. This, too, in the face of the impression made by many that it has been a source of profit to those who manage it.

There are not many names on our list now that were there thirty-five years ago. The generation then living has passed away, and a new one has arisen. A few that then were with us still linger on the shores of mortality, while the great number are gone. The rest must soon follow.

While my general health is now much better than it was when I began this work, I feel very sensibly the infirmities of age creeping over me, and the incurable disease, old age, will soon finish its work. I do not now believe I will dread or shrink from the change when it comes. I have tried through three score years and ten to keep a conscience void of offense toward God and man. I remember when yet a youth my desire was to go through the world without any one's being able to say he was worse off by my having lived in it. I have tried to keep that before me through life. This falls far short of the ideal placed before man by God. This, if it were successfully lived up to, is only a negative life. The ideal God puts before man is, while injuring and harming none, to help all whom we can help. To do no evil is well; to do all the good in our power is the work to which God invites every human soul. I have tried to do that which would help my fellow-men. I have not always succeeded. I have not tried to do what would please them. I have tried to please them for their good to edification. I have tried to get them to be pleased with that which would build them up, do them good, and fit them for the service of God forever. Only in seeking the good of others can man find his own true good; only in seeking to live up and save others can he save himself. If all men could realize this, how it would change this world of woe into a heaven of bliss. . .[8]

The passing years made not only David Lipscomb conscious of his coming demise, but many others as well. Some were reflecting upon the loss to the cause in the Southland. When "Uncle

---

[8]David Lipscomb, "The Closing Year and Century," *Gospel Advocate,* Vol. XLII, No. 52 (December 27, 1900), p. 824.

Minor," V. M. Metcalfe, paid a visit to the Nashville Bible
School in 1893, he came away and penned his reflections about
Lipscomb, saying:

He is getting old, and in the course of nature will not be here
many more years to earnestly contend for the purity of the church
and simplicity of the gospel. I don't know of a brother who is
more frequently misquoted and misunderstood than Brother Lipscomb. While everybody concedes that he is a man of ability,
yet few know his real worth. I have known him intimately for
over twenty-five years, and I have never known a more godly
or self-sacrificing man. Many suppose from his writings that he
is a cross, ill-natured, sour old man, yet just the reverse is true.
He is tender-hearted and loving as a child—can be led to do
almost anything unless he thinks it wrong; then all the earth
can't move him. He is loyal to the teachings of the Bible. I
have never known a man just like him in all of his makeup. I
believe that God in His providence has used him in the last
twenty-five years as he has no other man to elevate the standard
of the church of Christ and keep it pure from innovations. God
has given him wisdom and power for accomplishing good. He
has not been unfaithful.[9]

On May 23, 1906 a reunion was held in Nashville of the former
students and teachers of the Nashville Bible School. Both E.
G. Sewell and David Lipscomb spoke. While David Lipscomb
did not possess the eloquence of E. A. Elam or T. B. Larimore,
nor the wit of F. D. Srygley, nor the logic of T. W. Brents,
there was something about him—his sincerity, his devotion to
God—that made him a remarkable speaker. At this particular
reunion James A. Harding came, and, having listened to the
two sermons by Lipscomb and Sewell reflected:

. . . They are seventy-five years of age, Brother Sewell being
a few weeks the older. They have done far more for the cause
of Christ in Tennessee than any other two men, I believe. I
have been more intimately associated with Brother Lipscomb. In
my judgment, since Campbell died, no man among us has been
so powerful with the pen. At seventy-five he is still an in-
tellectual giant. He is not an orator; but no orator has ever
moved me as he does. Had I not clinched my teeth and pressed
my lips together, I would have sobbed aloud; and in spite of me
the tear would flow. It is said that when Pitt spoke at his best, a
torrent of logic, red-hot with passion, flowed like a rushing river.
But when David Lipscomb speaks of truth that enlightens the

---

[9]V. M. Metcalfe, "Our Bible School," *Gospel Advocate,* Vol. XXXV, No.
22 (June 1, 1893), p. 341.

mind, warms the heart and mightily moves the will, fills me. He is the Nestor of the brotherhood, the sage of Nashville, one of the greatest of the great men of the ages. He is not as great as Brother Sewell in some things; each would have been incomplete without the other. A fortunate union has been their long association as editors of the *Gospel Advocate*. May God greatly bless them both.[10]

Nor was an appreciation for David Lipscomb's work lacking in more extended areas. J. T. Showalter, then field editor of the *Octographic Review,* wrote of the *Advocate's* influence in these words:

Through that paper Brother Lipscomb has done a grand work for the church of the living God. Those that follow innovations fear and hate the logical and scriptural pen of Brother David Lipscomb. From what I can find out he has held the churches in Tennessee, and other places as well, nearer the apostolic simplicity, than can be found almost anywhere. While it might be impossible to find, not inspired, who would not get upon the wrong side of some of the many questions now agitating the religious (?) world, yet in Brother David Lipscomb is found a man, to say the least, who is nearly always right when viewed from, and in the light of the New Testament. . .[11]

NASHVILLE CHURCHES

On the whole there was perhaps no city in the nation where the plea for the ancient order of things had been more successfully advocated than Nashville. In 1891 Lipscomb boasted that Tennessee had fifty thousand disciples, four hundred and fifty congregations and three hundred and fifty preachers, the bulk of which was located in middle Tennessee, in the environs of Nashville.[12] Seven years later the *Christian Guide* asserted there were five hundred and thirty congregations in Tennessee. When the editor of the *Christian Standard* visited Nashville in the spring of 1901, he reported there were eighteen congregations of New Testament Christians in the city—sixteen white and two colored. The whole population of Nashville was then a hundred thousand, and there were four thousand, five hundred members of the church.

[10]J. A. Harding, "The Nashville Bible School," *Gospel Advocate,* Vol. XLVIII, No. 24 (June 14, 1906), p. 369.

[11]J. T. Showalter, "Jottings from Virginia," *Octographic Review,* Vol. XXXV, No. 12 (March 22, 1892), p. 5.

[12]David Lipscomb, "The Convention," *Gospel Advocate,* Vol. XXXIII, No. 43 (October 29, 1891), p. 677.

The first congregation to plead for original Christianity in the city had its origin in 1820. The account of that earlier history has already been given. That year—1820—Nathan Ewing donated a lot on Spring Street (now Church) between Sixth (High) and Seventh (Vine). This was the lot where Loew's theatre now stands. Here, a six thousand dollar building was erected. On January 1, 1826 P. S. Fall moved from Kentucky to Nashville to preach for the church there.

The congregation very early belonged to the Baptist denomination, but the restoration principles, as advocated by Alexander Campbell, became thoroughly implanted in the church. In the summer of 1827 the congregation withdrew from the Concord Baptist Association. A year later the church voted to reorganize in full sympathy with the restoration plea. Out of one hundred and fifty members only six dissented.

In 1831 P. S. Fall returned to Kentucky. The church now had over three hundred members. Tolbert Fanning and A. Adams now preached here. After 1841 W. H. Wharton, a physician, preached for the congregation, but in 1847, after the church had succumbed to the eloquent charms of Jesse B. Ferguson, there was a change of preachers and Ferguson located here. The next decade was one of "advance through storm." In 1849 the congregation decided to erect a new building on Cherry Street (Fourth Avenue) below Spring (Church Street). The new building, completed by 1852, was the most pretentious thing in the city. At a cost of $30,000 the congregation had built a meeting house that would seat twelve hundred.

Then came the Ferguson fiasco. The congregation divided and a new congregation was established near the present site of the Sam Davis Hotel. Meanwhile, it filed suit to get possession of the new building on Cherry Street. A year later, Campbell came to Nashville to try to save the church. It was December, 1856 before the group finally got possession of the new building. Early the next spring, a remnant of fifty-seven members recalled P. S. Fall to come and rebuild the church. But that year, on April 8, the new thirty-thousand dollar building burned. The original building on Spring Street had been sold to the Shiloh Presbyterians, so now the congregation negotiated to purchase the old property.

The church weathered the storm of the Civil War, and gradually grew back to surpass its former numerical strength. The quiet, unassuming P. S. Fall had the respect of the towns-people as well as the congregation, and throughout the city, the congregation was spoken of as "Brother Fall's Church." The increasing infirmities brought on by age made it necessary for Fall to think of departing. In 1876 Samuel A. Kelley, one of the editors of the *Apostolic Times,* came to hold a meeting. He was urged to locate with the church, and on January 1, 1877 did so.

Kelley came with expectations of doing great things. "Consultation Meetings," as they were popularly called, had been widely accepted in Tennessee before and shortly after the war. Kelley called one to meet on November 20, 1877, and invited the brotherhood at large. Some illustrious men came. David Walk came from Memphis. Ordinarily, preachers in the church were and are plain men, dressing like common men. But, Walk had a dignity and dress that made him look more like a professional clergyman than any preacher in the church. When Joe Franklin saw him, Franklin avows that he didn't know whether to call him, "Brother Walk," or address him as an Irish Catholic would his priest.

At any rate, Kelley had not properly appraised himself of the thought among brethren in the Tennessee churches. Although "Consultation Meetings" were popular earlier, the brethren grew more and more suspicious of what they might become. William Lipscomb debated with Kelley the advisability of this meeting. The result was that its total effect was killed, and Tennessee churches henceforth allowed all "Consultation Meetings" to die.

Kelley's untimely death the next summer, paved the way for the coming of R. C. Cave to the congregation. Cave was the son-in-law of Winthrop H. Hopson. Hopson, now old and feeble, followed Cave to Nashville, where Hopson died. R. C. Cave's health was bad. He left Nashville in a year, and his brother, R. Lin Cave then settled down to preach for the church. R. Lin, like his brother, was brilliant and eloquent, and had everything to make him popular in the city. He had fought under Robert E. Lee in Virginia, and was one of those haggard, tired Confederate troops standing by at Appomatox when Lee surrendered. Consequently, at the annual Confederate reunions in Nashville, R. Lin Cave was usually the favorite speaker.

On the issues facing the church, Cave remained silent, but it was clear that his sympathies were with that larger body of northern brethren who favored innovations into the work and worship of the church. Through the years the older members of the original congregation passed. In the fall of 1876 Orville Ewing, Sr. and James Foster, Sr. died, leaving only one member of the original congregation left—Jesse March. By 1885 the congregation had eight hundred members, but the bulk of its growth was from members moving into the city from other localities. They brought their affinity to innovations with them, and the congregation became fertile soil for the use of these additions to the work of the church. Yet, the church had had great preaching. T. W. Brents had conducted a meeting here in November, 1877, which was followed by another one with Moses E. Lard, who was now sick, broken-hearted and unpopular. R. Lin Cave preached for this congregation from 1881 until 1897 when he resigned to become president of Kentucky University. His drifting with the popular current on the issues confronting the church was a pledge of things to come.

On March 27, 1887 the last service of the church was held in the old Spring Street property. P. S. Fall, now yielding rapidly to the inexorable pull of death, came back to preach the last sermon in the meetinghouse. For the next two years the church met in Watkins' Hall, awaiting the completion of its new building. In 1889 it was finished at a cost of $21,000, and henceforth became known as the Vine Street Christian Church. The introduction of the instrument came a short time later to nobody's surprise and with but little fanfare.

Brethren in Nashville who had deep convictions against the more modern additions to the church were prone to mark off the Vine Street church as no longer an effective instrument to advocate pure apostolic Christianity. They found it necessary at the same time to hold a similar view toward the Woodland Street Church in East Nashville, or Edgefield. In view of the early teaching that it had received, the reasons for Woodland Street's departure seemed less natural. E. G. Sewell moved to Nashville in January, 1870 to become co-editor of the *Gospel Advocate*. That year he baptized a number of persons as a result of some preaching done on White's Creek Pike in North Edgefield. This group moved into an Odd-Fellow's Hall on Woodland Street.

The congregation continued to meet here until July, 1878 when it completed its new building.

For twelve years E. G. Sewell preached here once a month. Except for the time he was away in meetings he was usually present to teach at a mid-week service. In 1875 the little church cooperated with the Owen's Station congregation in Williamson County to sustain an evangelist full time in the field. A good work in a small, unpretentious way was being done. But changes came in the membership. Members of the church moved in from other states. The congregations where they had formerly worshipped were in favor of Societies, and the Woodland Street church soon found itself with an element favoring these "modern fads" in the church. Sewell, by patient teaching, resisted the encroachment of the society element. An undercurrent of feeling swam through the church.

E. G. Sewell, never one to stay where he was not wanted, yielded to the desire of the church for a new preacher. The selection was a young man, W. J. Loos, son of C. L. Loos. The son was like his father. C. L. Loos had heartily sympathized with societies, and for a time was president of the General Missionary Society, and the son was strongly behind his father. Young Loos came to Nashville the first of 1883. In October, that year, he attended the national convention, and returned with the fire of Societism burning brightly in his soul. He spoke to the Woodland Street congregation in laudable terms of the work the Society was doing, and insisted that he was ashamed to admit at the Convention that he was from Tennessee. The next Wednesday night, after Loos returned, Sewell kindly upbraided the young preacher, and Loos said no more about the Society publicly as long as he was there.

The first of 1887 R. M. Giddens came to the Woodland Street Church. The Society sentiment grew. Some women organized an auxiliary society despite the fact Sewell spoke against it. Soon the Ladies' Auxiliary Society had sent letters to the churches in Tennessee, asking for money so that it—the Ladies' Society—could employ a State Evangelist. Sewell objected to the elders, but the ladies were upheld. In the summer of 1890 J. C. McQuiddy and E. G. Sewell, along with forty other members, sent a petition to the elders of the Woodland Street Church—D. C. Hall, W. A.

Corbin, and B. J. Farrar—asking them to lay aside their society for the sake of peace, but the elders refused.[13]

Yet, despite the fact that both the Vine Street Church and the Woodland Street Church adopted these innovations, other congregations planted on a more solid foundation grew up in the city. Most of these owed their origin to the sacrifices of godly men. In 1857 David Lipscomb went one bright Sunday afternoon to Fireman's Hall on Cherry Street in South Nashville. Only three women attended. Lipscomb told them that if each would come back the next Sunday afternoon and each bring one other person, he would be back to preach. From this effort the College Street congregation had its origin. The work was slow and arduous. In the spring of 1877 the church appointed a committee consisting of R. Averitt, Humphrey Hardison and Frank Anderson to receive funds to buy a lot for a building. They refused to build until they had all the funds. Later, the College Street Church began some mission work on Green Street, and the Green Street congregation resulted. In 1887 the College Street Church had a membership of one hundred thirty-six. Many of these were former members of the Church Street or Vine Street congregation who were dissatisfied with the adoption of innovations.

The church in North Nashville was started with as little pomp and show. In 1867 David Lipscomb went out to the old army barracks and started preaching. The North Spruce Street congregation resulted. Five years later Lipscomb went out to Watkins Chapel in the northwestern part of the city and preached. He conducted a protracted meeting here without a song ever being sung. [David Lipscomb could not sing.] The Line Street church grew out of this. In 1876 Lipscomb went west of the city and held a meeting in a schoolhouse. There was no town there then, but this effort resulted in the establishment of the church in West Nashville.

Meanwhile, in East Nashville, the church was likewise growing. The original members who formed the Woodland Street church were pushed out by the society element, and established the Foster Street church. Later, more people left the Woodland Street church because of its acceptance of innovations and started the church at

---

[13]David Lipscomb, "The Work of Strife," *Gospel Advocate,* Vol. XXXII, No. 36 (September 3, 1890), pp. 566, 567.

Tenth and Russell Streets. By 1895 David Lipscomb could announce that there were ten white congregations in the city. There were more members of the church in Nashville, in proportion to its size, than in any city in the world. Yet, all of this was done without the aid of a single society separate and apart from the church. This work was accomplished by the zeal of individual members, and stood as the strongest proof that the establishment of Missionary Societies is not the sign of strong missionary zeal, but rather the sign of the *lack* of it. Men never feel the need of human organizations to do the work of the church until the church loses its zeal.

Perhaps in no one year did the church in Nashville see greater success than in 1889. A large part of this was due to the preaching of James A. Harding. In the spring Harding conducted a meeting for the church in South Nashville. In May of that same year, he held a much-publicized debate with J. N. Moody, a Baptist preacher, that was well attended. Following the debate, he went to the northeast part of the city and preached for eight weeks with one hundred and fourteen additions. This was done with the Foster Street Church. Later, this congregation put up a building on Grace Avenue and became known as the Grace Avenue Church of Christ. That same spring F. B. Srygley and Granville Lipscomb, preaching under the supervision of the College Street Church, conducted a tent meeting in West Nashville. While the churches were being established, new additions were mounting, the *Gospel Advocate* announced that persons looking for money need not come to Nashville, for they were spending right in their own city, establishing churches. Whether that be a selfish attitude is open to question. Nevertheless, it is a stern fact that a part of the present-day success of the church in the city is owing to that earlier attitude.

Still the work proceeded. P. W. Harsh reported in the spring of 1895 the following:

We have arranged to have regular services at two places—one at a little house on Carroll Street, near Wharf Avenue, where services will be held as follows: Sunday School, 9:30 A.M.; preaching Sunday, 11 A.M. and 7:30 P.M.; prayer meeting Thursday, 7:30 P.M.—another in a hall, corner South Market and Molloy (two blocks from Broad), Sunday at 3 P.M. and 7:30 P.M.; prayer meeting Friday, 7:30 P.M. We have secured Jackson's hall, on South Cherry, just beyond Decatur Railroad crossing, and expect to have regular services there in a short time. . . .[14]

It was a strong point with David Lipscomb that many congregations be established in the city instead of pouring money lavishly into one large one. David Lipscomb was in Philadelphia, Warren County, Tennessee, preaching, in 1857, when word reached him that the thirty thousand dollar building that the Church Street congregation had erected burned. He arose before the church and publicly expressed his joy. Writing about it nearly forty years later, Lipscomb said: "I still think it was a blessing from God."[15] Modest houses of worship with a people strong in missionary zeal was the combination Lipscomb liked, and which the churches had in these years.

SOCIETY INVADES TENNESSEE

Late in 1889 R. M. Giddens, the preacher for the Woodland Street church, went privately to David Lipscomb informing him that the ladies in the church had raised enough money to support an evangelist in the state. He insisted that this mission work be done in Tennessee through the church, under the supervision of the elders, and he asked Lipscomb to run a notice of it in the *Advocate*. E. G. Sewell prepared an article. The *Advocate* was just ready to publish it when word came from Louisville that A. I. Myhr was on his way to Tennessee to organize a Tennessee State Missionary Society. For the next fifteen years Myhr was to be heading the conflict over the Societies in that state.

Myhr came to Tennessee from Missouri where his spiritual edification had mostly come through the liberalism of the *Christian-Evangelist*. His beliefs were very closely akin to those of R. C. Cave. He came to Tennessee advocating that the preaching had to keep abreast of the times; that the preaching of twenty years ago would no longer do any more than the preaching of John the Baptist would do after Jesus came.[16]

The first meeting of the Tennessee Christian Missionary Society was held in Chattanooga in October, 1890. Present at the meeting

---

[14]P. W. Harsh, "Nashville Notes," *Gospel Advocate*, Vol. XXXVII, No. 15 (April 11, 1895), p. 235.

[15]David Lipscomb, "Fine Houses for Worship," *Gospel Advocate*, Vol. XXIV, No. 4 (January 28, 1892), p. 52.

[16]David Lipscomb, "Further Comments on Brother Harsh's Queries," *Gospel Advocate*, Vol. XXXIII, No. 2 (January 14, 1891), p. 23.

were nine preachers from Tennessee and three from without the state. R. M. Giddens and R. Lin Cave were present from Nashville. R. P. Meeks and a student came from Henderson, Tennessee. David Lipscomb went as an observer. The convention appointed a committee of seven to contact Lipscomb and see if harmony could be reached. Lipscomb wrote out his views, presented them to the convention, but they availed nothing. Nor did Lipscomb expect they would. Later he wrote:

We went to this meeting with no anticipation of changing the current of affairs. We had seen enough of the spirit of disregard of the rights and feelings of Brother Sewell and others, and the perversion of the property in East Nashville, to know the course had been determined upon. We were satisfied they would not stop to study the will of God or consider the feelings of their brethren. But we have spent over thirty years, during which the leading purpose and end of every day's work was to build up the churches of God after the model given by him in the Scriptures. The highest and only real ambition of my life is to see the churches in good active working order in just that condition that the Holy Spirit sought to leave them. I have no confidence in human wisdom, common sense, sanctified or unsanctified, improving upon the model of organization, worship or work given by the Holy Spirit. And if we cut loose from these, there can be no restraint to the fancies and follies of humanity. The departures may not be very marked or flagrant at first, but once under headway they will grow with accelerating force. We are certain this movement will affect the churches in Tennessee. Many have come into the churches that have but little confidence in God's provisions, and are dissatisfied with the simplicity of his order. It does not afford scope for display or gratify opportunity for the ambitious. The ways that human wisdom have invented seem more effective and more attractive to many. . . .[17]

The exact cause of the establishment of the Tennessee Christian Missionary Society may never be known. Ostensibly, its devotees claimed that it was established to inaugurate, systematize and organize cooperative work in Tennessee. But Lipscomb himself could not be shaken from the conviction that the whole thing was started by the *Christian Standard* in the selfish matter of looking after its own financial interests.

This whole society movement in Tennessee has been whooped up by the *Christian Standard*. It has been well known to all

---

[17]David Lipscomb, "Convention Notes," *Gospel Advocate,* Vol. XXXII, No. 43 (October 22, 1890), p. 678.

familiar with the publishing interests that the Standard Publishing
Company has steadily sought to obtain a monopoly of the publishing business among the disciples.   It obtained its success by
being recognized as the organ of the societies, general, foreign and
state.   When it failed to control the sale of the society hymn book,
it published a rival one—Hymn and Tune book.   It now owns
the *Guide,* and it, or Russell Errett, owns a large interest in the
Courier, of Dallas, Texas, and directs its policy.   Some years ago,
through a third person, R. Errett bought the *Christian Evangelist,*
with all its publications.   The owners learned, before the delivery
of the property, that R. Errett was the purchaser, and refused to
deliver the property on the ground that they had been deceived in
the transaction.   To injure the *Evangelist* it has established an
agency for the *Standard* and its publications in Kansas City, and
encouraged other publications in Missouri calculated to injure the
Evangelist.

Russell Errett has, through several years past, made repeated
efforts to buy the *Gospel Advocate.*   When we would refuse to
sell, he would raise the price of Popular Hymns upon us.   Our
readers all used it, and we were compelled to handle it, even if we
had to do it without pay.   But this determined us to publish a
book of our own.

Five or six years ago, we made a contract to have a book prepared.   When the matter was greatly prepared, Errett learned of
it, and bought the book up; he has never brought it out.   This was
done, no doubt, to hold us at his mercy.   We then got out Christian
Hymns.   The *Standard* has never extended it the usual courtesy
of a notice, so we are told.   But it is reported that it paid it the
highest possible compliment by sending a messenger to its editor
to induce him to get out one as good for the Standard Company.

A few months ago Errett proposed to transfer the *Guide* to the
Advocate for an interest in the Advocate Publishing Company.
While we would be glad to combine the two, we did not see how
the *Guide* editors could work in harmony with the *Advocate,* nor
did we believe the present readers of the *Guide* would remain with
the *Advocate.*   So we did not see that we would get anything in
the trade.

In every proposition to purchase the *Advocate,* or an interest
in it, it was stipulated that Brother Sewell and I were to continue
to edit it, and that it should be held to its present position.   The
idea was that it was to be held to its present position as suiting the
southern brethren, and as their organ, just as the *Standard* is for
the northern brethren.   With these propositions has come to me the
assurance that R. Errett was half opposed to the societies, anyhow,
and one reason given for wishing to transfer the *Guide* to the
Advocate was his conscience hurt him because it was not being
run in harmony with the wishes and purposes of F. G. Allen, who

founded it, while the *Advocate* is being run more nearly in harmony with his wishes than any other of our papers.

I am just as sure as I could be of anything human, that if we had sold R. Errett an interest in the *Advocate,* the present effort at organizing a society in Tennessee would not have been made. Some favored it, but without the encouragement given by the *Standard,* no effort would have been made, and it would never have encouraged it, if Errett had owned an interest in the *Advocate.* These brethren are allowing themselves, consciously or unconsciously, to be used by R. Errett to break down all home enterprise among Christians in the different sections of the country, and to build up one great central monopoly in the hands of those who have no social, local or other sympathy with them, further than to use them in building up their own interests. . . .[18]

An undocumented statement has passed down from year to year for the past half century to the effect that David Lipscomb spent an entire night in prayer to God. One cannot refrain from thinking that if this event occurred, which is very likely, it must have taken place on the night of October 17, 1892. The next morning at nine o'clock the General Christian Missionary Society was to open its annual convention in the building of the Vine Street Christian Church. For several weeks the convention had been given considerable publicity. Both the *Christian Standard* and the *Christian-Evangelist* had been trying to encourage considerable enthusiasm. They pointed out that the churches of Nashville had a very great "prejudice" against the Society, and that a national convention in that city would show those people the greatness of the organization. Lipscomb was practical enough to recognize that his life's work might be undone. With the strong arm thrusts the Society was making at Tennessee, there was serious danger that the work of a life might be overthrown.

Actually, of course, it strengthened most opposers to the Society in their convictions. Society advocates had from the beginning contended their agency was but an expedient. They suggested that it made no difference to them *how* mission work was done, just so it was done. They contended that the minority who opposed the Society should submit to the majority who wanted it. Lipscomb always believed that this was so much propaganda, calculated for effect, but it was difficult to disprove it. The action of the Society in coming to Nashville was the most effective force

[18]David Lipscomb, "Convention Notes," *Gospel Advocate,* Vol. XXXII, No. 45 (November 5, 1890), p. 708.

to disprove it.   Only two congregations in the city wanted it there —Vine Street and Woodland Street—and even these were not united in that desire.   The bulk of the brethren did not want the Society, and felt that its coming might promote division.   The Society ignored the majority when that majority was against it. In their efforts to try to convert the people to the Society method of working they most effectively proved the contention that the Society was much more interested in making converts to Society-ism than it was in making converts to Christ.

But Lipscomb could not be sure of this before the Society came to his city.   Most brethren stayed away from the convention while the visitors who did attend were those from Vine Street and Wood-land Street.   C. M. Wilmeth suggested a meeting of those who opposed the Society with its advocates at the convention to see if harmony could be reached.   The advocates declined the invitation because of the lack of time.   A paper signed by David Lipscomb, E. G. Sewell, C. M. Wilmeth, M. C. Kurfees and a host of others was prepared to be read at the convention.   The following was the paper drawn up:

To the General Christian Missionary Convention, Assembled in Nashville, Tennessee.—Dear Brethren in Christ: Inasmuch as your body now in session in this city purports to represent the churches of Christ, untrammeled by creeds, and there is a conspicuous ab-sence of many myriads of brethren whose sentiments are voiced in such periodicals as the *Gospel Advocate, Christian Leader, Octo-graphic Review, Firm Foundation, Christian Messenger, Christian Preacher, Primitive Christian* and *Gospel Echo;* and, inasmuch as you have assembled in the State of Tennessee, which contains about 40,000 Christians who profess to practice the primitive order of things, and perhaps not more than 1,000 of these thoroughly sympathize with your organization; and, inasmuch as arguments and appeals have been made on the floor of your convention to win these brethren over to your ways, we respectfully submit to your august body this memorial.

1. That we, believing as we do, that all should be one in Christ, of the same mind and the same judgment, speaking the same things and endeavoring to keep the unity of the spirit in the bonds of peace, cannot countenance the corruption of the pure speech of the Bible, and do deeply deplore the grievously divided state of the church, whereby brethren are embittered against each other, congregations are torn asunder and sections are arrayed one against another.

2. That, believing as we do, that whatever is not of faith is sin,

we cannot conscientiously cooperate in the organization or workings of any missionary society, home or foreign, with officers unknown to the New Testament and terms of membership at variance with the spirit and genius of the gospel, it being our firm and abiding conviction that in building up such societies we are pulling down that which our fathers labored to build up and are sapping the strength of the church for which Christ died.

3. That, believing as we do, that the Scriptures furnish us unto all good works, and that preaching the gospel stands preeminent as a good work, we boldly affirm and earnestly contend that the Bible contains a divine system of evangelism, powerful enough to shake the Roman Empire in its day and perfect enough to carry the gospel to the ends of the earth; and we modestly submit that, putting this faith into practice, we have demonstrated that in our day this divine plan is effectual, in that without other organization the primitive gospel has been planted in this region, a mission among the Indians has been sustained for many years, a mission in Turkey has been established and the Volunteer Band in Japan supported.

4. That we, in consideration of the aforesaid truths and facts and with no desire to destroy or cripple the work of any one engaged in preaching the gospel and teaching the way of salvation in either the home or foreign field, but believing that all now engaged can be sustained and more work be done in harmony with the examples of the apostles and inspired men, come before you with brotherly love and beseech you in the name of our Lord Jesus Christ that you abandon these organizations that found no necessity or recognition in apostolic times, and that you concentrate your zeal and energies in the churches of God, under the direction of their heaven-appointed officers, which we all admit to be common and scriptural ground, thereby removing a cause of widespread division and bringing about that union and cooperation in which there is strength and which will enable us to make more rapid conquest of the earth for Christ; and to this end we present this memorial, and for this consummation devoutly to be wished for shall we ever pray.

C. M. Wilmeth,
David Lipscomb,
E. G. Sewell,
J. A. Harding,
M. C. Kurfees,
and Others.

At one point in the convention C. M. Wilmeth arose and read the paper. J. W. McGarvey was chairman that day. A few brethren smiled while the paper was being read. McGarvey suggested referring the paper to a committee made up of himself, J. H. Garrison, C. L. Loos, B. B. Tyler and F. D. Power. Garrison himself made a great joke of the whole affair.[19]

Lipscomb attended the convention to observe its proceedings. The Women's Board of Christian Missions was there and Lipscomb heard women preach. He observed that the Bible was about as popular as "last year's almanac." Not a verse of scripture was quoted. Later he wrote:

A mere girl was put up to make a rambling talk on missions to Loos, McGarvey, Tyler, Darsie, and other wise men present. It could not profit them. It injured her and lowered the standard of womanly modesty.

Candidly, if I believed the law of God iterated in precept and example all through the Bible, written from the beginning in the being and natural functions of woman, could be set aside and trampled under foot, as was done in this Convention, without sin, I would think that sprinkling could be substituted for baptism, or baptism be rejected altogether. I would think the statement that Jesus was begotten of God could be rejected with impunity, or the whole Bible set aside without harm to man in time or eternity. I cannot see, if this is allowable, why we cannot substitute a creed, a confession of faith, a discipline like the Methodists, as containing the parts of scripture we think essential or like to follow, together with such additions by human wisdom as seem to us good. Indeed, I prefer a fixed human standard to one unstable, dependent only on the passing humor of the men, women and children who come together.

If that Convention was not an open, defiant rejection of God and his holy word, I would not know how to reject God or set aside the authority of his word. I do not think delicious speeches or animal enthusiasm manifested by constant cheering and handclapping applause compensate in any way for the violated law of God. Nor do I think its being done for a worthy cause helps the cause or palliates the sin.

If the Bible is of God, let us obey it. If we are not willing to be governed by it, let us make no present; let us kick the book out of our homes and be a law unto ourselves.

Jesus Christ calls in Matt. 15:7, those who profess to honor him, yet follow the teachings of men, hypocrites. "In vain do ye worship me teaching for doctrines the commandments of men." Man's only duty is to obey God and leave results with him.[20]

---

[19] J. H. Garrison, "The Nashville Convention," *Christian-Evangelist*, Vol. XXIX, No. 43 (October 27, 1892), p. 677.

[20] David Lipscomb, "Convention Thoughts," *Gospel Advocate*, Vol. XXXIV, No. 45 (November 10, 1892), p. 709.

The meeting of the Society did very little to convert the churches of Tennessee. Most became thoroughly satisfied that they were wrong. As to the results Lipscomb wrote:

We did not see or hear of a single preacher or brother among our Tennessee preachers that was not strengthened in his conviction that these things are all wrong and lead to division and strife, and gradually school men to neglect the Bible. Quite a number even of those who had looked favorably on the societies went away disgusted. . . . I believe the effect of the convention here has been good, that the atmosphere will be purer, that the brethren and sisters who are in earnest will be more united, more content to stand upon the Bible, and be satisfied with its provisions; because they have seen in this convention to what extent good, God-fearing, strong-minded men like McGarvey, Loos and others can be carried by those organizations, unknown to the apostles, not mentioned in the New Testament.[21]

HENDERSON TROUBLES

Viewed from the standpoint of its later influence upon the cause through the next few years, the rearguard action which occurred at Henderson, Tennessee, in 1903-04 was at a particularly strategic point. Here, since 1874, had been meeting what was known as the Henderson Masonic Institute. Through the influence of J. B. Inman the school came under the influence of the brotherhood and its name was changed to West Tennessee Christian College. Inman, reared a Presbyterian, moved into McNairy County, Tennessee, in 1856. He was preparing to be a Presbyterian minister when he heard Knowles Shaw, "the singing evangelist," and was converted. Immediately afterwards he began preaching for the congregation in Henderson. Meanwhile, through his influence the Henderson Masonic Institute became West Tennessee Christian College, and Inman was accordingly its first president.

Inman died in 1889 and G. A. Lewellan became the next president of the college. Three years later the faculty of the school is found to consist of G. A. Lewellan, president; H. G. Thomas, vice-president; and R. P. Meeks, head of the Bible Department.[22] The school was rapidly attaining a high literary distinction among Tennessee schools. In the spring of 1893, Lewellan, Thomas and Meeks suddenly resigned from the faculty, and shortly afterward

[21]David Lipscomb, "Convention Items," *Gospel Advocate,* Vol. XXXIV, No. 43 (October 27, 1892), p. 676.
[22]J. C. McQuiddy, "Miscellany," *Gospel Advocate,* Vol. XXV, No. 19 (May 11, 1893), p. 396.

A. G. Freed, who had opened a school at Essary Springs, Tennessee, moved to Henderson to become president of the school. Enrollment grew and soon it was seen that a new building needed to be erected. In 1896, J. F. Robertson of Crockett Mills, Tennessee, promised to make a donation of five thousand dollars toward this end, with the understanding that the name of the college would be changed to honor his daughter, "Miss Georgia." Consequently West Tennessee Christian College became Georgia Robertson Christian College in 1897.

Freed made every attempt to improve the school. One of his methods in doing so was to build up a better faculty. N. B. Hardeman joined the faculty in 1897 as a teacher of Bible. Five years later E. C. McDougle became co-president with A. G. Freed, and about the same time L. L. Brigance became connected with the school.

It was inevitable that a struggle over innovations should occur. From the days of Inman the school as well as the church in the town had shown a decided partisan attitude favoring the more modern additions to the work and worship of the church. On his way to Chattanooga in 1890 to establish the Tennessee Christian Missionary Society A. I. Myhr had stopped at Henderson and had received assurance of the backing of the church before going on to the meeting. Henderson was undoubtedly the most influencial point from the standpoint of the plea for a return to the ancient order that could be found in West Tennessee. Developments there would doubtlessly influence the whole church in that part of the state—and as events have proved, very widely in the whole country.

By the turn of the century most Christians in Tennessee were making their viewpoint clear on these issues. Gradually, eyes turned in the direction of Henderson. R. P. Meeks, head of the Bible Department at the college, had a wide reputation for favoring the use of the instrument and the society. C. A. McDougle, co-president, had the same reputation. But A. G. Freed, N. B. Hardeman and L. L. Brigance did not have this reputation. When A. G. Freed debated J. N. Hall of Fulton, Kentucky in April, 1902, some of the brethren signed a petition that they were against the organ and "human societies." Among those to sign were J. W. Grant, G. Dallas Smith, L. L. Brigance and A. O. Colley.[23]

---

[23]John R. Williams, "Notes from West Tennessee," *Gospel Advocate*, Vol. XLIV, No. 18 (May 1, 1902), p. 283.

It was widely known what attitude the church at Henderson took. The attitude of McDougle and Meeks was also known. But, with Freed, Hardeman and Brigance on the other side of the issues, it as hard to tell about the total influence of the college at Henderson. John R. Williams, one of West Tennessee's prominent preachers, undertook to defend the school.

> . . . As to Brother Freed, one of the presidents of the college, and Brother N. B. Hardeman, one of the teachers, I am personally acquainted with both of them, have heard them express themselves publicly and privately, and know they are opposed to these things, notwithstanding the fact that they have not removed them from the congregation at Henderson nor withdrawn from it. Brother Freed had laid his plans before me and convinced me of the course he would follow; and right here I will state that in a very short time it may be seen what that course was to be. . .[24]

But questions about Freed continued to arise. The Henderson church continued its course of favoring innovations, and Freed took some criticisms. G. Dallas Smith, knowing the man, came to his defense, and wrote:

> During the past few years there has been a good deal of complaint against Brother A. G. Freed by well-meaning brethren who did not understand the man or the circumstances under which he labored. Many knew that the organ was in the church at Henderson, Tenn., and, without knowing Brother Freed's attitude toward, condemned him as being unsound in the faith. . . I have often doubted the propriety of Brother Freed's course and have so expressed myself to him and others, but I have never for a moment doubted his soundness in the faith. Brother Freed's idea was to educate them out of it, and his influence in that direction has been wonderful, as is shown in the number who have taken their stand with him recently. . . "By their fruits ye shall know them." When Brother Freed went to Henderson, if I am not mistaken, Brother N. B. Hardeman, who is now one of the very best preachers in West Tennessee, was working and worshiping in full fellowship with the progressives, for he had never known anything else. Now he is a great power in contending for the "old Book," without addition or subtraction. Why did he change? Brother Freed simply taught him out of it. Brother L. L. Brigance, another one of our splendid preachers, told me that he was not opposed to the organ in the worship when he entered the Georgia Robertson Christian College, about eighteen months ago. Now

---

[24] John R. Williams, "Notes from West Tennessee," *Gospel Advocate*, Vol. XLV, No 5 (January 29, 1903), p. 77.

he is earnestly contending for the faith unmixed with any sort of human inventions. . .[25]

The whole affair came to a head in a comparatively innocent gesture at the beginning of 1903. In November of the previous year A. M. St. John, one of the elders of the Henderson church,· wrote E. A. Elam requesting him to come and conduct a meeting for the church. Elam had, upon the death of F. D. Srygley, become front-page editor of the *Gospel Advocate* and was regarded as one of the outstanding preachers of the state. St. John in his letter pointed out that the church was using the instrument and supporting the society, and that some day these things might be discussed "dispassionately," but for the present he was to preach only on Christian living. Elam agreed to come provided St. John would get all of the elders together and they should agree upon it. If agreeable to all, he would come the second Sunday in December, 1902.

A letter came from A. G. Freed, requesting the meeting be postponed until after the Christmas holidays. The elders however had decided not to use the church house for any such meeting because they feared Elam might speak against their practices. Freed, however, assured Elam that at a meeting of many of the brethren it was urged that Elam come ahead. Moreover, the young preachers in the school wanted to hear the issues discussed. The meeting was set for the second Sunday in January, and Elam prepared to go.

Meanwhile, the brethren had made arrangements for Elam to do his preaching in the Baptist meeting house, since the building of the brethren had been refused. Elam arrived on the Saturday before the second Sunday. On the way into town he was met by a committee of five from the church led by R. P. Meeks. They asked Elam not to hold the meeting, since the roads were muddy and people could not attend. Elam knew, of course, that the real reason was they did not want their practices opposed. Meeks admitted that opposition would stir up strife and that he did not want this condition there.

The meeting was held anyway in the Baptist meetinghouse. About seventy-five people dissatisfied with the innovations that had been brought into the church in the town, decided to hold

[25]G. Dallas Smith, "A Statement Concerning Brother A. G. Freed," *Gospel Advocate*, Vol. XLV, No. 11 (March 12, 1903), p. 171.

separate services and worship according to apostolic precedent. A. G. Freed and N. B. Hardeman and "every young preacher in the school" were included in this number. The church for the present began meeting in the courthouse with Freed and Hardeman preaching.[26]

Very shortly the original congregation thought of checking this opposition. A. I. Myhr was sent for, and came to Henderson to hold a "Bible Institute" from February 23-25. W. J. Shelburne of Union City, Tennessee spoke on "Ground And Authority For The Organization of Missionary Enterprises" as the first address. R. M. Giddens also spoke in defense of these innovations. Hardeman and several of the students attended, and challenged Shelburne for a debate, but were only ridiculed.[27]

To bring things even more to a head was the debate held in Henderson between J. Carroll Stark and Joe Warlick. F. W. Smith, recently returned from a trip to Texas where he had met and learned to admire Joe Warlick, was in McMinnville preaching. Stark was also in the town, and became boastful of his opposition to those against innovations. A challenge for a debate was issued. Smith accepted, agreeing to get a suitable opponent for Stark. When Joe Warlick was contacted, he was ready to come. The debate began on November 1, 1903 and lasted for four days.

The congregation of seventy-five had now grown to one hundred and thirty and was meeting in a building of its own. Good attendance was seen at the discussion although not a single preacher, favoring innovations, came except Stark himself. R. P. Meeks was out of town. A. I. Mhyr, although in the neighborhood, refused to come. F. B. Srygley, N. B. Hardeman, L. L. Brigance, A. G. Freed, F. W. Smith, Jesse P. Sewell and John E. Dunn were among the preachers who did attend.

Debating on these issues now came prominently into vogue. The only reason they were never more popular was because advocates of innovations could not be induced to publicly discuss them. Constant sparring went on with J. B. Briney, but little success followed it. In 1903 Briney challenged the *Gospel Review*

---

[26]E. A. Elam, "A Meeting at Henderson, Tenn.," *Gospel Advocate,* Vol. XLV, No. 6 (February 5, 1903), pp. 81, 82.
[27]E. A. Elam, "no title," *Gospel Advocate,* Vol. XLV, No. 16 (April 9, 1903), p. 225.

of Dallas, Texas for a debate. Briney was editor of the *Christian Companion* at this time. Noting the challenge the *Advocate* casually announced that other papers had given Briney the same provocation the *Review* had for a discussion, and if, for any reason, the *Review* did not accept the challenge, Briney should rest assured he would not go without an opponent. Briney retaliated with a suggestion for a debate in Nashville. The *Advocate* agreed providing the debate would be repeated in Cincinnati or Louisville. Briney refused this stipulation. It was agreed to have both a written discussion and an oral one. Briney would conduct the written debate with M. C. Kurfees and the oral one with Joe Warlick. It was agreed that the written discussion should be carried in both the *Gospel Advocate* and the *Christian Companion*. Briney backed out of putting it in the *Companion* because instrumental music was no issue with his readers. Finally it was agreed to have the oral discussion in Nashville, and the discussion was to be put in tract form, but the sale of the tract, Briney's promoters insisted was not to be pushed by either the *Advocate* or the *Companion*. It was increasingly clear to the brethren that Briney would discuss the issues only before an audience where the people were against these innovations; he would never stand to see them discussed before his own people. Consequently the debate was dropped.

Before the discussions ended, Briney quibbled that he had wanted to debate with David Lipscomb, the champion of the opposition, all along. Why had he never challenged Lipscomb? Naturally, Lipscomb had to decline the challenge. He was now getting old. His sight was almost gone and his hearing extremely poor. He rarely ever was outside the house at night. Lipscomb had advised Elam and Kurfees all along that Briney was an unfair man, and had no intention of allowing those who believed like he did to hear the other side. Elam and Kurfees had tried every way to discuss issues with Briney, but as Lipscomb predicted it was of no avail. His opinion of Briney he summarized as follows:

I am told Brother Briney frequently gives me notices not very complimentary. Over twenty years ago he convinced me he was not a fair or just man. It was in a small thing, but the Master said: "He that is unjust in the least is unjust also in much." F. G. Allen about the same time published that he had never had to deal with a more unfair man than Briney, and the Old Path Guide published a cartoon of him astride a planked fence.

Knowing these things, I discouraged the brethren giving him notice and insisted all correspondence with him looking to a discussion of questions was a waste of ink and paper. I never believed he had the most remote intention of a fair discussion with any one. His reason for not publishing a discussion was, his readers did not need it; yet proposed to discuss them himself in his paper. So he proves what I say. . .[28]

By 1906 the rearguard action was nearly fought. The events preceding the break of fellowship had for the most part transpired. The overtures of the Society, the last ditch struggle of advocates of innovations had been resisted. A few congregations here and there, especially in East Tennessee, adopted these modern appendages. But the vast majority stayed with their earlier principles and were unshaken by the fiery trials. J. H. Garrison in 1890 prophesied that David Lipscomb and the *Gospel Advocate* were on their way out; that the brethren had tolerated them long enough, and was ready *en masse* to join the "progression" ranks. Garrison wrote:

. . . Let me make a little prophecy, and you can file it away for future reference. Unless there is a radical change in the policy and spirit of the *Gospel Advocate,* its subscription list five years hence will be much smaller than now. More alliance has been made for Brother Lipscomb than would have been made for any one else, but there is a considerable element and a growing one in Tennessee that is tired of just such things as D. L. is getting off weekly. Mark my words. The majority of the live members of our churches in Tennessee will in less than five years be contributing to our foreign and home missionary societies. The *Advocate* need not support these societies in order to live. It could oppose them if it were done in a fair way, and keep up for a while at least. . . Every time the *Advocate* denounces those who contribute through these societies in effect as apostates, it makes life-long enemies to the *Advocate* and life-long friends of the societies. The response to an appeal to take Tennessee for organized mission work you will find is going to be prompt and liberal, and those who are working to that end are to my knowledge counting largely on the unreasoning opposition of Brother Lipscomb to help the movement.[29]

As events proved, Garrison was a failure as a prophet.

[28]David Lipscomb, "Criticisms," *Gospel Advocate,* Vol. XLVII, No. 9 (March 2, 1905), p. 137.
[29]F. D. Srygley, "From the Papers," *Gospel Advocate,* Vol. XXXII, No. 17 (April 23, 1890), p. 257.

Chapter XVIII

THE NASHVILLE BIBLE SCHOOL

Many years before the Nashville Bible School was established, David Lipscomb had settled his mind upon the value of such schools.

We have always believed in Bible schools, Bible academies, and Bible colleges. We have believed it the duty of every Christian who teaches to teach the Bible, to teach it as thoroughly and systematically as it can be taught to the pupils.

Our objection to Bible college has been that they were especially to make preachers. The evil of the churches, the corrupting influence is found, we are sure, in the position of the preachers and the tendency to subject everything in the churches to the work of the preacher. . .

If the brethren will just teach the Bible to all who will attend whether they intend to be preachers or follow any other call ng in life, they will do a good work and none will more heartily rejoice in that labor that I will.[1]

Indeed, the real question with Lipscomb was, how a Christian could support a school where the Bible was not taught.

There has never been a question with me as to whether a Bible school is right or not. The question that has troubled me is: Can a Christian teach or support a school that is not a Bible school? "Whatsoever ye do in word or deed, do all in the name of the Lord Jesus." (Col. 3: 17) To do it in his name is to do as he would do were he in our places. Does any one believe, if Jesus were here as we are, he would teach a school in which he was not permitted to teach the Bible as the most important consideration of life? If he would not, his servants should not. Does any one believe he would send children to a school in which the Bible was not the chiefest text-book? . . .[2]

Nothing could be of more paramount interest to a Christian parent, in Lipscomb's estimation, than to see that his children were taught in a school where the Bible was studied daily.

We have long insisted that Christians ought to have Christian schools for their children, and children ought to study the New

---

[1]David Lipscomb, "Bible College," *Gospel Advocate,* Vol. XIX, No. 32 (August 16, 1877), p. 505.
[2]David Lipscomb, "Teaching the Bible," *Gospel Advocate,* Vol. XLVI, No. 32 (August 11, 1904), p. 505.

Testament, especially, daily, as they study the spelling book or the reader. The lessons of the New Testament ought to be stamped indelibly upon the impressible minds of the children, before they are filled with other things. . .

. . . If Christians were half as determined that their children should be taught the Bible at school, as the opponents of religion are that theirs should not be, there would be schools all over our land teaching the Bible. But as matters now exist in our relations with the world, the Bible will not be taught in the common schools.[3]

Shortly after the Civil War Lipscomb caught the "education fever," had the desire to establish a school, but in a few years that fever subsided. It was not that he had lost interest in schools but only that his other work overshadowed it. In the fall of 1877 he wrote:

We are glad to know of the prosperity of all our schools. We wish them much success. We wish them to stand on a solid platform of true worth, that will raise them above all jealousy and sensitiveness. We once had a very fervid educational fever. It has wholly subsided, so far as any disposition to work in that direction ourself. But we wish those who engage in it, usefulness and success. We find some who when giving our time and means to it, were lukewarm, are now quite fervid in their zeal. That is all right, we think. We find, too, that every brother who becomes identified with a location or school, thinks that the best location and school in the world. We have found they frequently change their opinions with a change of location.[4]

Members of the church around Nashville had been interested in schools since 1842 when Tolbert Fanning had organized what became Franklin College. This school flourished until the Civil War when it was forced to close. During the war, its buildings were used by the armies as barracks, but as soon as the conflict ended, plans were made to reopen it. On October 2, 1865 the school reopened. On October 28, a little boy, in the act of "burning out his chimney" accidentally caught the main building on fire. There was no insurance and the cost of the fire was estimated at forty-thousand dollars. For a short time George A. Kinnie and A. J. ("Jack") Fanning tried to continue the school but with little success.

---

[3]David Lipscomb, "Schools," *Gospel Advocate,* Vol. XXV, No. 31 (August 1, 1883), p. 482.

[4]David Lipscomb, "Schools," *Gospel Advocate,* Vol. XIX, No. 37 (September 13, 1877), p. 567.

For several years brethren were undecided as to what next to do. At a meeting of the Board of Trustees following the burning of the main building, it was decided to build a large college in Middle Tennessee. It was proposed that between two hundred and three hundred thousand dollars should be raised. There was a strong emphasis, of course, on the fact that these new buildings must be fire-proof. The school, it was hoped, would be sufficiently endowed that all worthy students could attend gratis. The people of Tennessee, however, were in hard financial circumstances. The money could not be raised, and the dream for a large school in Middle Tennessee was lost.

Tolbert Fanning's interest in educational advantages for the poor was not to be defeated so easily. He announced in June, 1867 that "Peace College" would be erected upon the ruins of Franklin College. A charter was granted and a Board of Trustees was provided. On the board were P. S. Fall, James Metcalfe, James C. Owen, O. T. Craig, David Hamilton, David Lipscomb, John W. Richardson, Tolbert Fanning and John Hill. But, one hears nothing more of "Peace College," so it likewise proved to be but a vision.

One dream, however, was realized. On December 10, 1866 the Tennessee State Legislature granted a charter for the founding of Hope Institute. On the board of trustees were E. G. Sewell, P. S. Fall, V. M. Metcalfe, W. H. Goodloe, T. W. Brents and A. J. Fanning. This school was for the education of girls. Hope Institute continued to function until 1884 when the property was given over to the establishment of Fanning Orphan School. Fanning, before his death in 1874, had expressed a special interest in educating orphan girls. His wife, Charlotte Fanning, who had constantly guided Hope Institute kept this thought in her mind. Finally in 1883 she deeded one hundred and sixty acres of land, including Hope Institute, to the new Fanning Orphan School. In 1867 Fanning had spent $17,500 for sixty acres of ground plus the buildings for Hope Institute. The buildings, however, had suffered considerable decay. A Board of Trustees consisting of John G. Houston, J. C. Wharton, C. W. McLester, John H. Ewing, J. R. Handley, Dr. E. Charleton, A. J. Fanning, S. S. Wharton, P. S. Fall, J. P. McFarland, W. H. Timmons, O. T. Craig, and David Lipscomb, was appointed. The Board spent

Christmas week of 1883 looking over the grounds and making estimates of the amount of expenditure needed to put the buildings back up in first class condition. The outlay of money needed was negligible, the work was done, and in the fall of 1884 Fanning Orphan School opened to "train white girls for virtuous Christian lives."

But such a school by its very nature obviously could not meet all the needs. Nashville, educationally, had come to be looked upon as the "Athens of the South." There was a gradual realization that so far as the plea for the ancient order was concerned it was also the "Jerusalem of the South." David Lipscomb's frequent assertion that in proportion to population the church was better established in Nashville than in any city in the world was no doubt correct. The eyes of the church in the South were turned toward the capitol of Tennessee. Mars Hill College at Florence, Alabama, which T. B. Larimore had run for seventeen years, closed its doors in 1887. Here, some of the South's influential preachers had been educated. This small school, like so many others, was constantly harassed by financial worries. When the doors closed, the youth of the South looked for other places to be educated. Bethany College, they felt, had been swallowed up by advocates of innovations which made it undesirable. The College of The Bible at Lexington had its attractions not only for its proximity to the South, but the name of scholarly J. W. McGarvey held some magic power. But one major objection attached itself to the College of The Bible: its adherence to Society plans to do the work of the Church. McGarvey, while being a strong opponent of the use of the instrument, was a devotee of Society plans. C. L. Loos, president of the College, was also president of the Foreign Christian Missionary Society, and there is ample evidence to show that he was an extremely partisan president. So, both the College of The Bible and Bethany College were strongly objectionable to many of the members in the South. It is not unlikely that many around 1890 expressed their wish to see a school established nearer home and free from these objectionable features.

However, David Lipscomb was not the type of an individual to project an institution to hurt another. No matter how correctly this might at times be said of others it cannot be correctly said of Lipscomb that he would establish a school in Nashville for the express purpose of hurting the College of The Bible. McGarvey, however, was strongly suspicious, and as soon as the Nashville Bible School was established, accused Lipscomb of jealousy toward the College of The Bible, and of having a desire to hurt it. No one knew better than McGarvey, Lipscomb's opposition to Societies and of McGarvey's inconsistent position regarding them. But still, at this time, Lipscomb would practice patience with his errors in the hope of leading him—and the school—back on more apostolic ground.

In March, 1889 James A. Harding came to Nashville to conduct a meeting. Before he left the city, he had been there seven months, and besides conducting meetings, held his great debate with J. N. Moody, the Baptist preacher. During the debate, Harding stayed in Lipscomb's home, and the two discussed the possibility of starting a Bible School in Nashville. Lipscomb asked Harding to join him in the project. Harding agreed that he would do so as soon as he had caught up on all his obligations to hold meetings, which would take him about two years. Of this talk with Lipscomb Harding later wrote,

Sixteen years ago I began a meeting in Nashville, Tenn., in March. The meetings were continued for nearly seven months. Brother David Lipscomb and I talked of the many fields that were white for the harvest for which laborers could not be found. Daily we were receiving pressing calls for evangelistic work for which we could not find workers. We did not have suitable schools in which to educate our children, and so they were being sent to sectarian or digressive institutions. The influence of these schools, so far as religion is concerned, is more or less baleful. And so we talked about starting a school in which we should teach the Bible daily to every student. I had been thinking about such a work, hoping and praying that I might have an opportunity opened to me to enter upon it, for about sixteen years. Brethren W. H. Timmons and W. H. Dodd joined us in the work. And so two years and six months after Brother Lipscomb and I began to talk about it the Nashville School was opened in a large, comfortable old brick building in Nashville, which had once been one of the fine homes in the city. Six young men were enrolled the first day. We enrolled in all thirty-two that session. Our average daily attendance, I suppose, was about twenty-five. Our students led about 250 souls to Christ during the summer vacation. During the session they had been great helpers to Brethren Allen and Mead in planting the Green Street Church, which is now one of the most earnest and faithful of the churches of the city, a congregation that has already developed from its membership several efficient preachers, including brethren Allen, Mead, McPherson, our young correspondent, James A. Allen, and others. Brother Dan Gunn at the time he began to preach, was a member of this congregation, I believe. The Bible School did a great work in that first year. . .[5]

From that first private conversation between Lipscomb and Harding the discussion of the possibility of such a school was passed around. J. C. McQuiddy gently broke the news that something was in the wind when he wrote in his column on "Miscellany" in the *Advocate:*

Nashville is justly considered the "Athens of The South." With many fine institutions of learning located here, this city certainly has a right to the title. We learn from the *Baptist Reflector* that the Baptists have completed arrangements for establishing a Female College in South Edgefield. The thought occurs to us, why have not the disciples a good institution of learning in this city? We are sure it is not because the location is not a good one, not because there is no desire for a good school here among the disciples. We have known of the subject being discussed and agitated by some and all concurred in the opinion that by all means we should have a first class school here. The Methodists are represented here by the Vanderbilt and the Nashville College for young ladies, the Catholics by St. Cecilia, and then there is the Wards Seminary, claiming to be non-sectarian, the State Norman, Woolwine's High School, Montgomery Bell Academy, The Fisk and Roger Williams Universities, colored schools. Besides these, the public schools, many small and select schools, and yet out of all these there is not one under the control of the disciples. It occurs to us that the right man could build up a first class school here among the disciples. This is only suggestive. . .[6]

Gradually, interest in establishing such a school increased, and by the following spring, McQuiddy could write,

That it is desirable to have a good Christian college in Nashville will certainly be conceded by all. Nashville deservedly has the title, the Athens of The South. While others have the finest educational facilities here, our people have not a single school in the city under their control. If we wish to educate our boys and girls we must send them away from home. Those who desire

---

[5]James A. Harding, "Bible Schools and Colleges," *Christian Leader and the Way,* Vol. XXIX, No. 15 (April 11, 1905), p. 8.

[6]J. C. McQuiddy, "Miscellaneous," *Gospel Advocate,* Vol. XXIX, No. 33 (August 14, 1889), p. 522.

to educate their sons for the ministry have usually sent them to another state. Is it possible that a great people in a great state and country cannot establish a good school for the education of their sons and daughters?

One brother is certainly in earnest about this matter. He proposes to give ten acres of beautiful ground out about three miles from the city. He says the ground is as beautiful as the Vanderbilt campus. He has thirty-five acres and, at his death will deed all the land to the trustees of the college. The street railway management now say, that the electric cars will be running there inside of twenty-four months. We would be glad to hear from all who are interested in establishing a good college here and who will work to accomplish this end.[7]

By the next January, the "rumor" that Nashville was to have a Bible School went far and wide. *The Apostolic Guide* of Louisville, Kentucky commented tersely,

It is rumored that a Bible College is to be started soon at Nashville, Tenn. in the interest of sound theology. Rumor also intimates that T. B. Larimore is to be the presiding genius.

When McQuiddy read the above in the *Guide,* he playfully rejoined,

Come now brethren, you are too old in the business to go publishing things on *rumor.* Wonder if a *woman* is editing the News Department on the *Guide.*[8]

It was not, however, until June that the public in general was allowed in on the news that the Bible School was to be a reality. David Lipscomb wrote,

It is proposed to open a school in Nashville, in September next, under safe and competent teachers, in which the Bible, excluding all human opinions and philosophy, as the only rule of faith and practice; and the appointments of God, as ordained in the Scriptures, excluding all innovations and organizations of men, as the fullness of divine wisdom, for converting sinners and perfecting saints, will be earnestly taught. The aim is to teach the Christian religion as presented in the Bible in its purity and fullness; and in teaching this to prepare Christians for usefulness, in whatever sphere they are called upon to labor. Such additional branches of learning will be taught as are needful and helpful in understanding and obeying the Bible and in teaching it to others.[9]

---

[7] J. C. McQuiddy, "Miscellaneous," *Gospel Advocate,* Vol. XXXII, No. 22 (May 28, 1890), p. 346.

[8] J. C. McQuiddy, "Miscellany," *Gospel Advocate,* Vol. XXXIII, No. 6 (February 11, 1891), p. 90.

[9] David Lipscomb, "Bible School," *Gospel Advocate,* Vol. XXXIII, No. 24 (June 17, 1891), p. 377.

As plans to establish the Bible School took on concrete form, the thought of a "superintendent" naturally arose. David Lipscomb pushed aside the thought that he might head the school. As a trustee at the Fanning Orphan School, editor of the *Gospel Advocate,* a gospel preacher and a farmer, he found his time mostly taken. He would consent to teach one Bible Class but that is all. As to a superintendent, attention turned first toward T. B. Larimore. Larimore had gained wide popularity as an eloquent preacher and a devoted Christian. Moreover, his experience at Mars Hill made it appear that he was the right man for the position. Larimore, therefore, was invited to accept the superintendency. His answer, however, was held up while he weighed the offer. By August, 1891, it was still thought Larimore would come, but no definite answer had been reached. It was planned to open the school in September, but the opening date was pushed forward to October. Early in September came Larimore's formal decline of the offer, and in his place, went William Lipscomb as a teacher. James A. Harding was made the superintendent.

What lay behind Larimore's rejection? Maybe nothing. Or again, maybe Larimore realized that his attitude toward Missionary Societies and instrumental music was not the same as David Lipscomb's and that sooner or later it may be the occasion of conflict. A few years after this, Hall L. Calhoun expressed to James A. Harding *privately* that he was against the society and the use of the instrument, but because he refused to state his position *publicly,* Harding refused to allow him on the faculty of the Nashville Bible School. When Harding spoke to Larimore about these issues, Larimore replied that he did not know what the Bible taught on them. Harding had already planned to use Larimore in a series of lectures at the Bible School, but now refused to allow Larimore to deliver them. Whether underneath, this may have had anything to do with Larimore's refusal cannot be for certain said, but it is interesting to notice the possibilities.

During the summer, Lipscomb wrote:

The responses from those desiring to attend such a Bible school as we have spoken of, has been encouraging. There are from twenty-five to fifty young men anxious to enjoy the help at once of this school. The responses from those willing to aid with their means, in such a school, have not been so encouraging. Shall we not brethren put such a school in operation and aid those who wish to devote their lives to the service of God?[10]

David Lipscomb was undoubtedly correct in asserting a few years later that the Nashville Bible School was started quietly and without much publicity in response to a widespread demand. School opened on Monday, October 5, 1891 in a dwelling house at 104 Fillmore Street. There were six students to enroll the first day. Students came from Kentucky, Tennessee, Alabama, Arkansas, California and Texas. Thirty-two regularly enrolled students entered the school that first year, twenty-four of these were preparing to be preachers. Besides these, there were twenty-one others who attended a Bible class. Nothing is said about young women being enrolled although two or three years later we are assured that from the very beginning a few girls attended "though not many." A boarding-house keeper who wanted to dispose of his belongings was bought out, and the boys moved into the house where they paid their board at the rate of two dollars a week. Tuition was three dollars a month to the boys who could pay. Those who could not, went free; no worthy young man was turned away for lack of funds. "No one," wrote Lipscomb, "is trying to make money out of the school."

Courses taught included English, Latin, Greek, Mathematics, Logic, Metaphysics, and Natural Science. In addition, the Bible was taught "above everything else." There were three daily recitations from the Bible. The first class was in a study of the Old Testament, which by the close of the first session at Christmas, was expected to complete the Pentateuch. The second class was on the New Testament, and the third studied the Bible in a topical form. Lipscomb taught the class in New Testament while the other Bible classes were taught by Harding. Every student was required to have at least one Bible class a day. He was expected to memorize the contents of each chapter of the Bible. The class in New Testament was expected to memorize all the sermons of Christ and the apostles which are recorded in the four gospels and in Acts.

The first year closed on Thursday night, May 26, 1892. Recitations, essays and addresses were made by the young men.

The school now looked forward to its second year. J. W.

---

[10]David Lipscomb, "That Bible School," *Gospel Advocate,* Vol. XXXIII, No. 28 (July 15, 1891), p. 445.

Grant, a graduate of Kentucky University, was employed to teach. Thirty-four students enrolled that fall, "all save two or three, preparing to spend their lives in teaching the lost the way of life." During the school year these young men preached constantly in the city and country around Nashville. By March, 1893 the *Advocate* reported that forty-two persons had obeyed the gospel "under their ministry."

The second year of school had closed May 31, 1893. Forty-two young men had been enrolled. J. W. Grant and James A. Harding had taught full time, and David Lipscomb, one hour a day. Expenses had been increased the second year over the first. Tuition was now five dollars a month; board, two dollars and a quarter a week, and matriculation fees were three dollars. It was estimated that total cost for the year would not run over one hundred and fifty dollars. Young men who wanted to preach, but who could not pay, were admitted free. But this worked a hardship on the school, and Harding urged others to help out.

. . . It is a fact that many young men who want to attend the school cannot pay tuition and board. In some cases congregations send and sustain them; in others, individuals have done it; some have worked their way through. In no case has a young man, properly commended to us, been turned away because he lacked means. Next sessions we will need much more help in this line. We would like to hear from individuals and churches who will take part in this good work. The man who wishes to invest means for Christ, we think, cannot find a better field for investment. Any one, male or female, wishing to study the Bible will be received in the school.[11]

Very early in 1893 plans were begun for opening the school for its third session that fall. Lipscomb was impressed with the fact the school's present buildings were very unsatisfactory. Could a new location with more suitable quarters be found he felt confident of an enrollment of one hundred students. Consequently, in the September 7, 1893 issue of the *Gospel Advocate* Lipscomb announced that a tract of land consisting of two acres or more on which was a large brick building had been purchased. This old building was made into a boarding house. Two large classrooms were erected and a home for the superintendent. W. H. Dodd and wife volunteered to manage the boarding house free of charge. In

---

[11]James A. Harding, "The Nashville Bible School," *Gospel Advocate,* Vol. XXXIV, No. 31 (August 4, 1892), p. 485.

this new location on Spruce Street the Bible School opened its third session. This term opened with Dr. J. S. Ward, a graduate of the medical school at the University of Tennessee, added to the faculty. Harding was now teaching Latin, Greek and Bible; Grant, mathematics and "the English branches"; and Dr. Ward, classes in chemistry and physiology.

Gradually the influence of the school broadened. The young preachers were encouraged to spend their summers preaching the gospel in destitute fields. Grabbing their Bibles at the close of a session, these youths would head for the country school houses and brush arbors from Mississippi to Kentucky. During the summer of 1893 all the "boys" together baptized over five hundred people and established six congregations. The next summer the number of baptisms was over one thousand, two hundred. During the summer of 1896 it was estimated that in the five years the school had been established its young preachers had led three thousand and four hundred into the church, and had established twenty-eight congregations.

The fourth session opened with the school becoming gradually a more pretentious affair. During the summer of 1894 new buildings were erected on the South Spruce Street property that added twenty-eight more rooms for the school's use. There were eighty-nine students in all during this session, eighteen of whom were girls. Forty-eight of the number were preachers. This was a great enrollment, offering bright prospects for a school with as lowly a beginning as this one. The next spring—the spring of 1895—Dr. T. W. Brents delivered a series of lectures for the Bible School. As he walked across the lawn one day, he spoke prophetically, "This is a big thing, a much bigger thing than I expected to find here; there is no telling whereunto this will grow."[12] At this time there were four buildings on the two and a quarter acres on South Spruce Street—the "Recitation Rooms," boarding department for young men, and the homes of J. W. Grant and James A. Harding.

From 1896 through the spring of 1902 the school had a yearly average enrollment of one hundred and twenty-five students. That same spring the grounds, buildings and equipment of the school were valued at twenty-five thousand dollars. In that brief span

[12]David Lipscomb, "Bible School Notes," *Gospel Advocate*, Vol. XXXVII, No. 26 (June 27, 1895), p. 407.

of time the school had grown considerably. At the turn of the century James A. Harding had resigned at the Bible School to go to Bowling Green, Kentucky to start the Potter Bible School. W. Anderson, of Maury County, Tennessee, was chosen superintendent in his place. In 1901 the first sizable bequest of money was given to the school by Fannie Pond, who stipulated in her will that twelve thousand dollars should go to it, the interest of which was to pay the way of worthy young men to get an education.

In some respects the Nashville Bible School was undergoing some changes, whether for the good or not may be a mooted question. Coming shortly after Harding left to go to Bowling Green, the Nashville Bible School was incorporated. The exact date of this was February 2, 1901. A Board of Trustees made up of seven men was appointed. So far as the records go the separation was peaceful, and was occasioned by only one factor— Harding's desire to establish a similar school in Bowling Green. However, it hardly takes more than a neophyte to know that the full truth, especially as it respects motives, is rarely put out for the public to read. It is not at all unlikely that the separation of Harding and Lipscomb at this time had occurred when Lipscomb announced his intention of incorporating the school to enable it to become a larger one.

In the attention given to degrees the Nashville Bible School also underwent some change with the turning of the century. In the summer of 1894 Harding wrote,

We confer no degrees. It is vain to use empty titles; and the degrees D.D., A.B., A.M., B.S., Ph.D., etc., in this country are just that, they are so common and so easily obtained. But when a student has finished our four-years' course, maintaining a standing of seventy and above, we present to him as a diploma book, beautifully and substantially bound, stamped as a gift from the school to him, containing a statement of the length of time he has been with us, of the branches he has studied, and giving his monthly standing in each study for the entire time. If he remains longer than four years this will be certified to in the book, and his monthly standing given. The presentation will be publicly made, and will be, we think, more valuable than any degrees we could confer.[13]

But, in the spring of 1901 Lipscomb announced,

The Nashville Bible School has been incorporated, and will

[13]J. A. Harding, "The Nashville Bible School: Extracts from Catalogue," *Gospel Advocate,* Vol. XXXVI, No. 26 (June 28, 1894), p. 405.

hereafter more rigidly encourage a regular curriculum of study, and will confer the literary and scientific degrees common in the college and higher institutions of learning.[14]

Now that the school was incorporated, and intended to give degrees and look toward more extended work, it was time to think about expansion. On Granny White Pike, two miles below the corporate city limits, David Lipscomb had his farm. He gave this to the school, which necessitated immediate preparation on the buildings. So Lipscomb wrote,

. . . To continue the school, we must have more buildings. A good tract of land outside of the city limits, near the street car line, has been secured. Stone foundations of two buildings have been built and are ready for the brickwork. One of the buildings is forty-four feet wide and seventy-five feet long. It is to be two stories high, for a chapel and eight recitation and library rooms. The other building is in the form of a T, one hundred and sixteen feet by one hundred and twenty-five feet, and is to be three stories high. This is to be for lodging rooms for the boys, and also contains a kitchen and a dining room. There is a residence on the place that, with some additions, will furnish rooms for the girls. From present prospects, we will need room for at least from one hundred to one hundred and twenty boys and at least fifty girls. These buildings will cost not less than sixteen or seventeen thousand dollars. If we could sell our present buildings for cash, we could realize twelve thousand dollars on them; but we do not think it possible to do this in time to help in the new buildings. We believe that with about five thousand dollars from friends abroad, we can place the buildings without debt. We have begun the building with the confidence that this amount would be cheerfully given for the work. We are compelled to begin now and press the work vigorously to be ready for use next September. It will not do to have the school in debt, because the income of the school will not pay debts. It really does not run the school as it should. Those conducting the school have made greater sacrifices to run it than they should be asked to do. . .[15]

And so, in the summer of 1903 the Nashville Bible School moved to its new location on Granny White Pike. When school opened that fall, classes met in two large brick buildings that had been erected during the summer. In slightly over a decade the school had made it evident that it was here to stay.

---

[14]David Lipscomb, "Nashville Bible School," *Gospel Advocate,* Vol. XLIII, No. 23 (June 6, 1901), p. 361.

[15]David Lipscomb, "The Nashville Bible School," *Gospel Advocate,* Vol. XLV, No. 9 (February 26, 1903), p. 136.

Two ideas were prominent with the founders of the school: viz. the Bible should be uppermost in the course of studies, and the school did not exist exclusively to prepare young men to preach.

The Nashville Bible School originated in the twofold desire on the part of disciples of Christ to see schools in which children, while gaining an education to prepare them for the duties of life, will be also daily taught the Bible as the most important study of life and as the only rule of faith and life, excluding all additions and devices of human wisdom from the faith, work, and worship of the Christian. This purpose was set forth in the original subscriptions to build the school, in the following clause: "The supreme purpose of the school shall be to teach the Bible as the revealed will of God to man and as the only and sufficient rule of faith and practice, and to train those who attend in a pure Bible Christianity, excluding from the faith all opinions and philosophies of men, and from the work and worship of the church of God all human inventions and devices. Such other branches of learning may be added as will aid in the understanding and teaching of the Scriptures and will promote usefulness and good citizenship among men."

It was further set forth in the deed conveying the property on Spruce Street for the use of the school in the following clauses or statements: That the property shall be used for maintaining a school in which, in addition to other branches of learning, the Bible as the recorded will of God and the only standard of faith and practice in religion, excluding all human systems and opinions and all innovations, inventions and devices of men from the service and worship of God, shall be taught as a regular daily study to all who shall attend said school, and for no other purpose inconsistent with this object. This condition being herein inserted at the request of the founders of the proposed Bible School, the same is hereby declared fundamental and shall adhere to the premises conveyed as an imperative restriction upon their use so long as the same shall be owned by said Bible School, or its trustees, and to any and all property which may be purchased with the proceeds of said premises in case of sale or reinvestment, as hereinafter provided. . . All trustees shall be members of the church of Christ, in full sympathy with the teachings set forth above, and willing to see that they are carried out. Any one failing to have these qualifications shall resign or be removed.[16]

Preachers, as a professional class of men, generally excited the contempt of many in those earlier years. Allied with the professional status of the preacher was the opinion that no man was

---

[16] J. S. Ward, "Nashville Bible School Notes," *Gospel Advocate,* Vol. XLIV, No. 32 (August 7, 1902), p. 505.

qualified to preach who did not have a college education. David
Lipscomb himself did not share this feeling. He never wanted
to view himself as a preacher. Rather he thought of himself as
doing the work which he could do. As a Christian, he must do
all the good in life that it was possible. He expounded the word
because he could not be a Christian and fail to do so, but he had
no desire to preach a day longer than he could do good. He re-
sented the popular insinuation that the study of the Bible was for
preachers to professionally qualify them, while others should remain ignorant of it. Shortly after the Civil War, a great interest
was displayed in educating preachers, and Lipscomb thought that
either consciously or unconsciously the impression was being made
that a man was not qualified to preach unless he had a college
education.

We certainly do not object to an education; but we protest
against the idea that no one but a college educated man is fitted
to preach the gospel. The great qualification of the preacher is,
to thoroughly imbue his heart with the truths and spirit of the
Gospel, and then study how to impress them upon his fellow-men.[17]

But the idea of the professional preacher was growing in the
world, and professionalized training was becoming prominent. In
view of the rising drift in thought, F. D. Srygley's lengthy comments are well worthy of consideration.

An educated preacher a hundred years ago was simply a preacher
who had a classical education. There were few, if any, schools
then especially designed and operated to educate men for the
ministry as a profession, but within the last century schools have
been established by the various denominations to give men special
education as professional preachers. An educated preacher now
means a preacher who has attended a school where men are
educated for the ministry as a profession. Graduation from such
a school is a passport to a position as a professional preacher in
any denomination; while the lack of such education and training
as these schools give puts consecrated men who know the truth
and preach it from a sense of duty in a spirit of self-denial at a
disadvantage in any denomination. The idea on which all such
schools are founded, and by which they exist, is that men who
are educated in them can preach better than men who have never
attended them. This creates a demand for preachers who have
attended such schools, and causes people in general and churches
in particular to underestimate preachers who have not taken the

---

[17]David Lipscomb, "Education of Preachers," *Gospel Advocate,* Vol. IX,
No. 8 (February 21, 1867), pp. 157, 158.

prescribed course in such institutions. Of course no man who is worthy to preach is unwilling to attempt it unless he feels that he is thoroughly furnished unto all good works and fully prepared and qualified to declare the whole counsel of God, and the people naturally prefer to hear men preach who are supposed to be best qualified and prepared for the ministry. If there is something in such schools which prepares and qualifies men to preach, and which cannot be found anywhere else, it is easy to see that such institutions have a patent on the ministry and a monopoly in the business. Moreover, a man who is specially educated as a professional preacher is poorly prepared for any other business or occupation. To try to support himself in any other way than by preaching is to forfeit all his special education and training for the ministry as a profession. It is as a doctor who gives his attention to another occupation than the practice of medicine after a special course in a medical college. This creates a class of dependent professional preachers who must have remunerative employment as preachers or come to want. When the supply of such preachers exceeds the demand, there is a glut in the ministry which cannot be relieved by opportunities for remunerative employment in other vocations, because the unemployed preachers are not qualified to engage in other occupations. Moreover, professional preachers feel that it is not in keeping with ministerial dignity to earn their bread in the sweat of their faces; and inasmuch as they have prepared themselves to preach and have made no preparation to do anything else, they consider the churches under obligation to support them in the ministry. Places must be found or created for them, and the scramble for position discredits religion in the eyes of the world. Within the last few years several secular papers and some religious papers have stated that there is now such a glut in the ministry, and have argued that schools ought not to educate so many preachers for the next few years till the situation is relieved. The burden of supporting so many professional preachers is heavy on the churches, and doubtful methods of raising money are resorted to, and inventive genius is exhausted in devising organizations and schemes to make places and create salaries for professional preachers. In this rush for places, the interest every school feels in its graduates and every man cherishes for his alma mater and fellow-students tends to clannishness in mutual efforts to promote a common interest in the distribution of patronage. Charges have been openly made on high authority in more than one denomination within the last few years that great theological schools in this way practically dominate the preachers and churches to the extent of their influence. The effect of it is to centralize in such schools what might be termed "the appointing power" over the ministry, especially in denominations which have a congregational form of church polity. Such schools, probably without intending it, gradually become a kind of ministerial "pie counter," as politicians would say, around which aspiring young men, with an eye to the main chance in a desirable profession, crowd for a chance at the crumbs which fall from the institutional table in the distribution of patronage in what Alexander Campbell aptly termed "the kingdom of the clergy." In politics all this would be called "a ring" or "a party machine," but in religion it is known by the softer name of "an educated ministry." Preachers who do not rank in this class are relegated to "our poor and country charges," if, indeed, they are not denied any recognition at all in the ministry.

The idea that men who graduate from schools designed and operated specially to educate preachers can preach better than men who have not taken the prescribed course in such schools turns the attention of the people from the Bible to the schools as the source of religious light. The philosophy of it is that something about Christianity can be learned in such schools which cannot be learned from the Bible without the help of the school. This weakens the confidence of the people in their ability to read and understand the Bible without the help of such schools. The effect of this is to discourage efforts among people who cannot attend such schools to study the Bible for themselves, form their own conclusions as to what it teaches, and preach the gospel exactly as it reads in the New Testament. Instead of robust individuality in Bible study and independent vigor in faith, people accept the doctrine promulgated from the schools, even though it is contrary to what seems to them to be the plain teaching of the Bible. They gradually come to have more confidence in the dictum of the schools than in their own understanding of the Bible. This gives the schools the power, and sometimes creates in them the disposition and desire to "lord it over God's heritage."[18]

Reaction to the establishment of the Nashville Bible School was varied. J. W. McGarvey felt "cross" at Lipscomb for starting it, thinking it might be a formidable competitor of the College of The Bible. J. M. Barnes of Alabama and M. C. Kurfees of Kentucky failed to have much enthusiasm for it, both men, as Lipscomb put it, "think they are against" such schools. *The Christian-Evangelist,* traditionally unable to see a distinction between the school and its Missionary Society, ironically reported that the Nashville Bible School had been started. Daniel Sommer coolly received the word that the School had begun, and tersely commented,

---

[18]F. D. Srygley, "no title," *Gospel Advocate,* Vol. XLI, No. 7 (February 16, 1899), p. 97.

There is a Bible School in Nashville, Tenn., which we presume is doing a good work, but if the brethren who have it in charge ever call it a college, and give the pupils a regular collegiate course, and a diploma with titles, then we predict that it will be an institution of mischief. Collegism among disciples led to preacherism, and preacherism led to organism and societyism, and these led to worldliness in the church.[19]

On the whole, the successful establishment of the Nashville Bible School ignited a flaming desire for such schools over the entire brotherhood. Colleges were springing up everywhere. At Bowling Green, Kentucky James A. Harding had established Potter Bible School at the instigation of C. C. Potter and wife. Four years later, J. N. Armstrong announced that he, A. D. Gardner, R. C. Bell, B. F. Rhodes, and R. N. Gardner would open a new school at Paragould, Arkansas to be known as the Southwestern Bible and Literary College. Six weeks after this announcement was made came another saying that the location had been changed to Odessa, Missouri forty miles east of Kansas City. About the same time Southwestern Christian College was born at Denton, Texas, and a little earlier, Gunter Bible College at Gunter, Texas. Lockney Christian College had been in Texas since 1894. A. B. Barrett received inspiration from Lipscomb and Harding to establish Childers' Classical Institute (now Abilene Christian College) in Abilene, Texas in 1906.

There were many other colleges established shortly before and after the turn of the century. The inspiration for most of this came directly or indirectly from Harding and Lipscomb, and the influence of the Nashville Bible School.

The reaction to the establishment of the Nashville Bible School was both positive and negative. The positive reaction is seen in the wave of schools and colleges later to be set up in the brotherhood. Of far greater significance is the negative reaction. Daniel Sommer, editor of the *Octographic Review,* was the epitome of this negativism.

Schools in which brethren taught the Bible were almost as old as the restoration movement itself. Alexander Campbell had taught "Buffalo Seminary" in his home and closed it only when he realized that the students were less interested in the Bible

---

[19]Daniel Sommer, "Notes and Annotations," *Octographic Review,* Vol. XXVI, No. 47 (November 21, 1893), p. 1.

than they were in getting an education in those early days. But his interest in establishing a college had never subsided, although it was delayed some by the establishment of Bacon College in Kentucky. Bethany College which he set up in 1841 was in a large measure the climax of a life-long dream, and into it he poured the best of his energies until his death.

The principle behind the Bible school was almost never discussed. It was generally assumed that the schools were acceptable, and there were almost no suggestions to the contrary. It was not until the proposal of the missionary society was before the brotherhood that people began to critically examine into basic principles involved in human institutions.

Alexander Campbell and a corps of younger preachers consisting of Isaac Errett, W. K. Pendleton, C. L. Loos, W. T. Moore, and D. S. Burnet satisfied their minds that human institutions, whatever their nature, were acceptable to the Lord. The church *universal,* not the church local, was divinely commissioned to evangelize the world, teach the Bible, and exercise benevolence in works of charity. Since God had not told the church what *methods* to use to do its work, any method the best wisdom of the church devised was permissible on the ground of expediency. And so, largely through the influence of Campbell and his younger corps of lieutenants, the missionary society was inaugurated. So also were Bible Societies, Publication Societies, Educational Societies, and Bible Colleges. The church could establish, maintain, own and operate these human institutions. In doing so it was using a method which God had left the church at liberty to use. This was one school of thought.

These, however, of this school of thought recognized prominent dangers. Chief of these was that the child of their creation might become strong enough to become their master. The human institutions must be subservient to the church, not masters over it. The church must control the institution, not the institution the church. Some, fully cognizant of this danger, launched into the promotion of these institutions with the same disquietness of an individual nursing a baby tiger. There was always the question, when the monster would grow up, would it devour the person that fed it?

In the process of time their worst fears were realized. J. H.

Garrison and the *Christian-Evangelist* cried more and more for centralization. The General Convention should become the voice of the brotherhood and the *Christian-Evangelist,* the agent of that voice. The *Christian Standard* viewed this trend with alarm, and the result was—and is—everything but an open division in these ranks.

Meanwhile others could not accept the viewpoint of Campbell and his lieutenants. They could find no scriptural warrant for the church universal acting as the church universal in an organic sense to do anything. The formation of human institutions to do the work of the church was a human addition to a divine plan, an assumption of the prerogative of God in making laws for his people, besides being a threat to the local independence and autonomy of the individual congregation. On this basis Jacob Creath, Jr. and Tolbert Fanning waged a relentless war against the Society.

For a quarter of a century it did not occur to the opponents of the Missionary Society to measure their principles against the Colleges. So thoroughly was Tolbert Fanning settled that the college belonged to a different category that he failed to notice Isaac Errett's witticism when Errett declared he could not take the opponents of the Society seriously as long as they persisted in operating colleges in which the Bible was taught.

The whole question as to the principles involved in the Bible College was opened when the trouble at Kentucky University burst before the brotherhood in the fall of 1871. John F. Rowe openly asked, "Are Colleges A Blessing Or a Curse?" and concluded with some indefiniteness that they must be a curse. Ben Franklin declared that he had always assumed colleges were permissible without examining into them, but the affair at Kentucky University had caused him to see the dangers of such schools. The brief remainder of his life was spent in opposing colleges. Jacob Creath, Jr. likewise turned against them and became an outspoken critic. David Lipscomb likewise cocked an eyebrow in the direction of Kentucky University, but his criticisms were more tempered. Kentucky University taught him two great lessons. One he was never to forget, and the other, he found easy to forget. The chief objective in the College of The Bible was to train preachers. He became convicted that this was wrong.

"We think the most fatal mistake of Alexander Campbell's life," he wrote at the time, "and one that has done much and we fear will do much more to undo his life's work, was the establishment of a school to train and educate young preachers.[20]   This lesson Lipscomb would never forget, and when he established the Nashville Bible School it must be understood that this school was not to exist "to train and educate young preachers."

Kentucky University also taught Lipscomb the lack of wisdom employed in richly endowing colleges.   McGarvey, representing a conservative element, was turned out of the school, and the "progressives," as Lipscomb called them, took over.   Thus, the endowment that had been years in being accumulated would be used to tear down the cause it was given to build up.   So Lipscomb wrote,

Endowment funds so universally are thus perverted to pull down what they are intended to build up, that we can hardly hope for a change.

Great amounts of money have been donated to build up the Christian religion.   The religion of our Saviour exists today in spite of the influences exerted through nine-tenths of the amount given to endow schools for teaching that religion.[21]

This lesson Lipscomb found it easy to forget after he had established a school of his own.

For nearly a decade during and after the troubles at Kentucky University brotherhood periodicals gave considerable attention to Colleges.   Then for a score of years almost nothing was said on the subject.   Discussion on the matter has followed pretty much of a pattern from that day to this.

David Lipscomb's views on teaching the Bible in schools followed those of Tolbert Fanning before him.   No human institution had any right, as he viewed it, to exist to do the work God gave the church.   This principle was clear in Fanning's mind.   The simple fact was that a school, as he ran it, and believed they ought to be run, did not exist to do the work God gave the church. The school to him was a "worldly" institution, not a religious. The Bible did not regulate those things on the worldly side of a

---

[20]David Lipscomb, "Schools for Preachers," *Gospel Advocate,* Vol. XVII, No. 15 (April 8, 1875), p. 345.

[21]David Lipscomb, "Kentucky University," *Gospel Advocate,* Vol. XV, No. 42 (October 23, 1873), p. 998.

man. The Bible did not tell a man what kind of a house to build, what kind of a horse to ride, how to plow his ground, how to earn his livelihood. These belonged to what Fanning would call the "worldly" side of a man. The principles of Christ may in a general way guide and control this side, but no more. The Bible does not tell a man, he reasoned, whether he ought to earn his livelihood by farming, teaching school, practicing law, build houses, or run a bank. These belong to the "worldly" side of man's life. Yet, if a man did any of these, and if that man were a Christian, he could hardly be a Christian and fail to teach the Bible in conjunction with his work. If a farmer were a Christian, he would teach the Bible to those that came under his influence; if he were a banker, a lawyer, a doctor, or a school teacher, he would do the same. He could not be a Christian and do otherwise.

Lipscomb was frequently called up to distinguish between the school, the Gospel Advocate Company, and the Missionary Society. He had condemned the Society as being a human institution doing the work of the church. Was not the school a human institution doing the work of the church? Was not the Advocate Company a human institution doing the work of the church? But to Lipscomb there was a difference. The business of sending out and overseeing missionaries was a work which God committed to a church. No human organization could do this work without usurping authority. On the other hand, the work of teaching the Bible was a work for every Christian.

The school was but a means of educating children. Lipscomb failed to see that the Bible ever committed the work of educating to anybody except parents. Yet, when children spent several hours a week learning worldly knowledge and only one hour a week learning the Bible, the result was they received the impression that Bible knowledge was a matter of indifference. So he wrote:

When we relegate the study of the Book of God to an hour in a week, and then in a loose and careless way, and study other things every day in the week, the children cannot avoid the conclusion; the one is a matter of indifference compared with the other. . .

Our effort in the Bible School is, to give Bible teaching its true importance in education; to train children to be better, truer Christians. We are doing what we believe should be done in teaching every child, whether he intends to farm or merchandise, preach the gospel or practice medicine.[22]

Early in 1891 Lipscomb found himself in a controversy with P. W. Harsh through the columns of the *Advocate.* Harsh defended the use of missionary societies. He places the societies on a par with the orphan school, the Gospel Advocate Company, and the Sunday School. But again, Lipscomb denied that the orphan school or the Advocate Company were parallel to the missionary society. He wrote:

And whenever you will convince me that the school is usurping any function of the church of God, takes out of its hands or the hands of individual Christians, what God has committed to it, I henceforth will oppose all schools. The orphan school is for the same end as Hamilton College, or any other school. Its purpose is to educate girls for usefulness that they may be able to make a living in a creditable way. While educating them, we try to make Christians out of them. Just as it is the duty of the farmer to try to make Christians of every one under his influence. . . . I have never found where the Bible committed to the church or to anybody but parents, the work of educating their children for making a living. . . I fail to see one single point of likeness in the two institutions.[23]

James A. Harding saw eye to eye with Lipscomb on the subject of a Bible School. His ideas were forthcoming in a discussion of the subject with J. M. McCaleb in 1895. McCaleb was in Japan as a missionary at this time. Aside from McCaleb, almost all the brethren in the Japanese mission at this time were behind the society. McCaleb, in an attempt to think his way through the issue carefully, wrote to Harding, asking the difference between the Bible School and the Society in principle. To this, Harding replies:

The day the Bible School becomes an organized society for preaching the gospel, teaching the scriptures, or for any other purpose, that day I leave it. The Bible School is a *school,* that is all. . .

May the richest blessings of God ever rest upon this work, and may He forbid that it should ever become a Society organized for the purpose of doing what He has committed to His church.

---

[22]David Lipscomb, "Bible Schools," *Gospel Advocate,* Vol. XXXIV, No. 26 (June 30, 1892), p. 404.

[23]David Lipscomb, "Missionary Societies," *Gospel Advocate,* Vol. XXXIII, No. 5 (February 4, 1891), p. 70.

No living man is more intensely opposed to such a thing than am I, not even Brother McCaleb himself.[24]

The relationships between the *Gospel Advocate* and the *Octographic Review* had on the whole been pleasant since Daniel Sommer took over the latter paper as editor. A few times the truculent James A. Harding thought he saw some peculiarities in Sommer, and readily pointed them out, but on the whole, while these brief skirmishes were fiery, they were good-naturedly taken by both men. In 1894 Daniel Sommer ran a series of articles in the *Review* by way of examining Lipscomb's book on "Civil Government," Sommer, of course, holding the opposite viewpoints. Lipscomb thought Sommer misrepresented him, and so, wrote out his answers to Sommer's charges, sent them to the *Review* with the request they be printed. Sommer refused and announced that the discussion was closed. Thereafter, Lipscomb wrote, "It seemed to me his misrepresentations were intentional, and his refusal arose from fear of exposure before his readers. I passed the matter over without mention, willing for him to do what good he could, satisfied we could not work together." Sommer thereafter insisted that Lipscomb's coolness toward him was occasioned because he [Sommer] had "felt called upon to expose his errors."

Lipscomb in the meantime persisted in his policy of ignoring Sommer. While other writers of the *Gospel Advocate* for the next few years felt occasionally called upon to debate with him, Lipscomb rarely did, "willing for him to do what good he could," but satisfied that he and Sommer could never work together.

In January, 1901, a Brother Young of Oklahoma Territory sent a clipping on "Marriage and Divorce" written by Daniel Sommer to the *Advocate* with the request Lipscomb examine it. Lipscomb did and wrote briefly his own comments. Sommer replied with a violent attack on the use of Sunday School citing two cases where the literature was wrong. E. A. Elam, then a young man, was writing some of the literature. He had commented that on the triumphal entry of Jesus into Jerusalem, the Lord had ridden an untrained ass, but Sommer took exception insisting Jesus had straddled two asses at once. Elam replied to this by a gentle article, intending to disarm Sommer's criticisms

---

[24]James A. Harding, "A Friendly Criticism," *Gospel Advocate,* Vol. XXXVII, No. 41 (October 10, 1895), p. 662.

by kindness, but Sommer again replied comparing Elam to an assassin that sneaked up behind his back. Elam hardly knew what to make of it, but Lipscomb was thoroughly disgusted. "Does not this," he asked, "savor more of the bravado of the slums, than of the courtesy and graces of the Christian?" And again, Lipscomb repeated his intention of ignoring Sommer,

I have no disposition to hinder Brother Sommer in doing all the good he can. But I am sure we cannot work together, with his present style; so in the future, as in the past, I shall let him do all the good he can, and I will go the way that seems best to me.[25]

Lipscomb summarized Sommer's attitude by saying that Sommer "seems to think it is discussion to dogmatically state his opinions, often crude ones, and then to abuse the person who dissents from him."

With personal feelings already at a breaking point between the *Gospel Advocate* and the *Octographic Review,* between Daniel Sommer and David Lipscomb, and with Bible schools sprouting rapidly over the brotherhood, Daniel Sommer now felt obliged to attack these schools. He began in the fall of 1901 by reprinting the old articles of B. F. Leonard (L. F. Bittle) that had appeared in the *American Christian Review* in 1873. By the next year, 1902, Sommer was ready for a full-scale war against colleges.

Daniel Sommer's opposition to Bible colleges dated back to at least twenty-five years before this. Beginning in the October 29, 1878 issue of the *American Christian Review,* he presented a series of articles on "Educating Preachers" which were intended as an attack against Bible Colleges. From 1878 to 1902 he had presented occasional articles on this subject, but it was not until 1902 that he waged a bitter war against them.

When Sommer first renewed his attacks against Bible Schools early in 1902, James A. Harding was the first to take notice and seek to reply. For a considerable time, the main force of the discussion was centered between Harding and Sommer, the *Advocate,* as a general rule, maintaining its policy of ignoring Sommer. It will be of special interest to observe what Sommer's objections were, and the answers that were commonly given to them. On the ground that the Bible Schools were unscriptural

---

[25]David Lipscomb, "Our Reason for Our Course," *Gospel Advocate,* Vol. XLIII, No. 20 (May 16, 1901), p. 312.

organizations, Sommer found many points of criticism against them. It cannot be denied, in all fairness to Sommer and to the facts involved, that on many points he was right—more correct than his enemies ever gave him credit for being. Yet, it was unfortunate that he ever went to such an extreme and became so dogmatic and unyielding on that extreme.

Sommer, in noticing the catalogue of the Potter Bible School during the summer of 1903, observed that the school was established as a "most appropriate monument" to the memory of a man, Brother Potter. Sommer then quoted scriptures such as Numbers 20: 10 and showed that it had always been a desire of man for self-glorification, but that it had never pleased God for man to do this. He leveled the charge against Bible schools that they are, essentially, institutions built up for the purpose of glorifying man.[26] A man's ego was much more highly honored if he can be recognized as the president of a college or university than if he is known simply as a preacher of the gospel. There was nothing of the pomp, the show, about the latter. Suffice it to say that there is probably more point to the objection than most men are honest enough to admit.

But in the main, Sommer leveled two charges against the schools. They were charged, first, with glorifying man and seeking the exaltation of man; and, secondly, that Bible Schools involved the mistake of the misappropriation of the Lord's money. He objected strongly to churches contributing from the treasury to this work, and he even thought that if men were giving all they could to the church to do the work of the Lord, they would not have enough left to make large gifts of money to a Bible School. If a man had five thousand dollars to give to a Bible School, it was, with Sommer, a good sign he has not been giving to the church "according to his ability," and the five thousand he gave to the Bible School was but the amount he kept back from the church.

In years to come Sommer was to accuse both Alexander Campbell and David Lipscomb of holding back from the church, of saving money that rightfully should belong to the Lord, and of using that to establish schools. But Sommer could never be made to see that this was an overstatement of the case. When,

---

[26]Daniel Sommer, "Educating Preachers," *Octographic Review,* Vol. XLVI, No. 31 (August 4, 1903), p. 1.

for example, Sommer purchased the *American Christian Review,* he promised to pay fifteen thousand dollars for it. Where was he to get this money? By his own reasoning it could be gotten only by his taking it from the Lord.

It is hard to escape the conclusion that Daniel Sommer on the one side and David Lipscomb or James A. Harding on the other were not closer together in their thinking than they admitted. In Sommer's articles of 1878 on "Educating Preachers" his major criticism is against raising up preachers as a special class and bestowing upon them special training. Ten years after this he wrote another article in which he said,

Public sentiment is generally in favor of colleges for educating preachers. As a result thereof it endangers the reputation of any one to express a sentiment in opposition thereto. Opposition to colleges in any department is supposed to result from aversion to education, and surely, it is thought, none but erratics or simpletons could be averse to educating the rising generation. But we respectfully claim that one may possess common sense in a respectable degree and yet oppose the building of colleges by the church of Christ for the purpose of educating men to proclaim the unsearchable riches of Christ. . .

Colleges for educating preachers have proved to be perverting schools among disciples of Christ. When the corner stone of Bethany College was laid, the foundation for another clergy was begun, and thus it was that a revolutionist establish the institution which tends to destroy his revolutionary work. . .[27]

Near the close of his life, Daniel Sommer wrote again,

When discussing the college question among disciples of Christ at Odessa, Mo., in 1907, I was challenged to state what kind of a school I would endorse. My prompt reply was—"An untitled school such as Buffaloe Seminary, which Alexander Campbell conducted for years before he seemed to have thought of Bethany College." Such a school did not graduate pupils, and thus did not confer on them any empty, pompous titles. To such a school pupils went to learn without any idea of degrees or titles of any kind. Any such schools could never have impoverished the brotherhood by using millions of money to pile up brick and mortar and secure furnishings.[28]

Taken at their face value, it is difficult to find any difference in

---

[27]Daniel Sommer, "Colleges Again," *Octographic Review,* Vol. XXXI, No. 47 (November 22, 1888), p. 1.

[28]Daniel Sommer, " 'Disciples of Christ' Challenged!" *Apostolic Review,* Vol. LXXXI, Nos. 9, 10 (March 2, 1937), p. 8.

these thoughts and in those of David Lipscomb or James A. Harding. Neither man believed it was right for the church to own and operate schools, or to turn its work over to a human institution like the school. They protested vigorously against schools existing to give special training to preachers to promote a class of clergymen upon the brotherhood. That it was wrong for the church to organize societies—whether missionary, Bible, Publication or Educational—these men believed. But that the individual Christian, in connection with his livelihood, could teach Bible to all who came under his influence, whether he intended to preach or not, Lipscomb or Harding both believed. From all appearances Sommer believed it too.

This made the enigma of Daniel Sommer which Harding found difficult to solve. Harding had been sparring with Sommer only about a year, when Sommer announced,

But from the first response to what I have written on subject to the last, that I recollect having seen, I have been charged with teaching that it is "wrong" to teach the Bible in connection with secular things, and that it is even "wicked" to do so. . .

In regard to the charge just quoted I state that it is utterly destitute of truth, at least so far as the *Review* is concerned. . .[29]

In the summer of 1905 Sommer proceeded to put in bold type and run in weekly issues of the paper the exact position of the *Review* on Bible Schools. He wrote:

This journal favors and advocates all schools, colleges and universities, which do not oppose the Bible, nor disregard the physical health and mental temperament of their pupils, and it contends that the Bible, or certain parts of it, should be used as a text book in every school, college and university.

Then Sommer proceeded to say:

But this journal is set in opposition to the New Testament Church establishing schools, or colleges, or universities, from either wholly or partly secular, as institutions separate from the church, and with money which should be placed in the treasury of the church. Such an institution, even if wholly religious, is as much of an innovation as a man-made missionary society. . .[30]

His announcement that he was not against the Bible being taught in secular institutions, but only against the church es-

---

[29] Daniel Sommer, "A Plain Statement and Challenge," *Octographic Review,* Vol. XLVI, No. 31 (August 4, 1903), p. 1.
[30] Daniel Sommer, "The *Review's* Position in Regard to Education and Colleges," *Octographic Review,* Vol. XLVIII, No. 30 (July 25, 1905), p. 6.

tablishing such schools with funds which belong to the Lord, immediately surprised Harding. He had not so judged Sommer's beliefs. After reading Sommer's first announcement of his position on July 25, 1905, Harding replied:

So his announcement in his issue of July 25, that he favors its use in all schools, colleges and universities, came to me "like a clap of thunder from a clear sky." I am amazed to think how successfully he kept me in the dark about his true position in all these years. While I and others were "raking him fore and aft with shot and shell," for opposing the use of the Bible in schools that teach secular learning, he was actually burning with zeal for that very thing—more in favor of it than any of us, and we did not find it out till July 25, 1905.[31]

Periodically from 1906 to the present the brotherhood has not been allowed to forget this controversy. It is difficult to escape the conclusion that if men of like thought of David Sommer understood the true nature of the colleges, they would oppose them less. But personalities, sectional pride, and prejudice have played no small part in keeping the question alive, and until time produces a more perfect work, there is little promise of a permanent cessation of hostilities.

---

[31]James A. Harding, "Another Effort to Secure a Discussion of the Bible School Question," *Octographic Review,* Vol. XLVIII, No. 34 (August 22, 1905), p. 8.

CHAPTER XIX

AUSTIN McGARY

The fictitious Praxiteles Swan of the Methodist Episcopal Church, South, Captain of the Fifth Texas Regiment, Confederate States Provisional Army is a composite character created from the yarns and legends which Lt. Col. John W. Thomason, Jr. heard from the "old timers" during his boyhood days in Huntsville, Texas. *The Lone Star Preacher,* Thomason's life of Praxiteles Swan, reads like another *Seventy Years in Dixie.* Some of the tales, woven into the fabric of Swan's life, Thomason picked up from one of the most colorful preachers the church has known in the last century—Austin McGary of Texas.

What David Lipscomb was to the church of Christ in Tennessee Austin McGary was to the church in Texas. "A. McGary," wrote J. D. Tant, "did more to stem the tide of innovations the Christian Church was making in Texas than any other man."[1] Possessing a boldness born of sagacity, the truculent Austin McGary was a match for any occasion where fearless reproof was demanded. "To be great," said Emerson, "is to be misunderstood," and McGary was often misunderstood. Some considered him too extreme, too bold to have the meekness and humility required of a Christian. Generally, a personal acquaintance with McGary convinced even his enemies that he was meek, although they were not always convinced that he was not yet too extreme. Weighed from the standpoint of the total effect of his life, Austin McGary had had few peers in the church within the last century.

Much of the colorful story of Austin McGary goes back to the days before he became a Christian, and in some cases, is intimately linked with the history of early Texas. When the army of Mexican General Cos was driven from San Antonio late in 1835, General Santa Anna, with a much larger army, determined to attack the city early the next year. The result was that on March 6th, 1836 the Alamo fell. Garrisoned by 183 men, they died to the last man. Two weeks later Texas General Fannin and his army

---

[1]J. C. Tant, "Brother Tant Answers," *Apostolic Review,* Vol. LXXX, No. 26 (June 23, 1936), p. 15.

of 371 men were captured. A week after this all were shot except the twenty who escaped. Sam Houston, a Major-General under Governor Henry Smith, in the Texas provisional government, was elevated to a full General. Gathering a small but courageous band of men, he faced General Santa Anna. It was a dark hour in Texas history. Houston's small army was poorly equipped and far outnumbered numerically. But the fate of Texas was hanging upon it. Houston skillfully retreated before Santa Anna, and received taunts and jeers from citizens of Texas as well as his own soldiers. At the San Jacinto River, however, he suddenly turned, drove against his enemy and destroyed the Mexican army. But, where was Santa Anna, the chief prize? That evening, a tired, bedraggled Mexican was brought in by Texas soldiers, who recognized him only as another Mexican prisoner. He might have remained unknown except that his own soldiers gave him away. That night, Santa Anna was placed under guard as a prisoner near the quarters of General Sam Houston. The guard who watched Santa Anna all that night, and who had fought so valiantly in the decisive battle was Isaac McGary, the father of Austin McGary.

Isaac McGary had immigrated to Texas from Ohio, had fought against superior odds to help gain Texas freedom, and afterward, entered into Texas politics. He was County Court Clerk of Walker County, and Sheriff of Montgomery County. In 1858 he ran on the Sam Houston ticket for the State Legislature, but was defeated by three votes. Since first coming to Texas, Isaac McGary had been a votary at the shrine of General Sam Houston. Houston who had been inspired to an indomitable courage by a similar devotion to his close friend, General Andrew Jackson, was thoroughly capable of similarly inspiring others. It was natural that Isaac McGary should pass his great devotion to General Houston on down to his own son, Austin McGary.

Austin McGary's childhood was spent in Huntsville, Texas which also was the home of Sam Houston. Here, as a boy before the Civil War, McGary played with Sam Houston's children. One Sunday afternoon the children were playing ball on a vacant lot. A doctor, a bitter enemy of Sam Houston, was walking down the street, and was met by Houston, coming from the other direction. Houston courteously spoke, "How are you, sir?"

To which the doctor replied, "I don't speak to a d--- rascal."

"That is the difference between you and me, sir, I do," said Houston, and walked on.

Austin McGary was born February 6, 1846 at Huntsville, in Walker County, Texas. His mother died when he was but eight or nine years of age. Educational opportunities were scant, but McGary attended McKenzie Institute, a Methodist school, in Clarksville, Texas, in Red River County. The Civil War broke out when he was sixteen. For a while Texas was uncertain on which side to plunge. The Union made pleasing overtures to her, and Governor Sam Houston pleaded with the State to remain loyal to the Union. Despite this, the Southern sympathizers were strong enough to secede. Houston himself refused to take the oath of allegiance to the new government, and accordingly, was deposed. Meanwhile, Texas regiments mustered into service over the state.

When the "Huntsville Grays" were organized in Madison County, Austin McGary, although barely sixteen, joined them. Sam Houston, Jr,. son of the veteran fighter, also joined up, although against his father's wishes. Some of the young men went off to join the Army of The Confederacy. Sam Houston, Jr was seriously wounded at the battle of Shiloh, and was officially listed as killed. But, after the battle, he was found alive by a Union army doctor, and nourished back to health. Before the "Huntsville Grays" were scattered to join Texas regiments, they marched in review before General Houston. As they marched, Houston called out,

"Eyes right!"

Then asked, "Do you see anything of the son of my friend the great anti-secessionist who has been so anxious for us to go to war to preserve the Union?"

The company answered, loudly, "No!"

Houston then called, "Eyes left!"

"Do you see anything of Sam Houston's son?"

The answer: "Aye!"

McGary was placed in the Hamilton Guards which were later connected with General J. B. Head's Brigade. McGary saw no action in the war, but was kept in coast guard service in Texas and Louisiana until the conflict ended.

Texas suffered along with other southern states at the close
of the war, but hardly as much as those on whose soil the struggle
had been waged. Coming back from the war, McGary found
that his father's horses had been commandeered for the use of
the Union Cavalry garrisoned at Navasota. About everything
on his father's homestead of any value was gone except a buckboard and a sorrel buggy horse. His father was leaving for a
trip to Tennessee, so McGary and a companion, decided to jump
in the back of the buckboard and go along. As they rode along
a narrow lane, two Union Cavalrymen came riding to meet them,
and commanded they go over, and let them pass. As the cavalrymen rode past, McGary noticed that on the horses' flank, above
the U. S. brand, was his father's own brand. McGary and his
companion grabbed rifles, commanded the soldiers to dismount,
took their horses, and rode ahead toward Tennessee.

Years later, when mounting age tried to grapple with the
more modern iron horse—the Model T Ford—McGary found
that his experiences in the Confederacy came in handy. Riding
on South Main Street in Houston, Texas, he was stopped by a
traffic policeman who severely reprimanded him for running a red
light.

"What do you mean, running a red light and giving me a ticket?"
he asked the policeman.

"You drove right through that red light," replied the officer,
"and that's a very dangerous practice. I will have to give you a
ticket for it."

"I don't know what you are talking about. What are red
lights?" queried McGary.

"Don't sit in that Model T and tell me that as long as I have
seen you driving around Houston, you don't know what red lights
are. What is your name so I can make out a ticket?"

McGary insisted that he didn't know what a red light was,
yet he had driven a Model T for several years without an accident.
He had always driven carefully, and upon coming to a corner,
if he saw the cars "bunched up," he would stop; when the way
cleared, he would drive ahead.

The policeman insisted, "I can't accept that answer. Give me
your name and address." McGary was tired arguing, and so
informed him of his name and address.

The officer was shocked. "You mean you're Aus McGary?"

he inquired. "I can't give you a ticket. My father was in the Huntsville Grays, and he would turn over in his grave if he thought I had given a ticket to Aus McGary. You are the only man in the world whose statement I will accept when you say that in all the years you have been driving that you had not known that you were to stop for a red light."

At the close of the war, when McGary was twenty years of age, he married Miss Narcissus Jenkins of Grimes County, Texas, a girl that was four years younger than he. Two children were born to them—a boy and a girl. The girl died at the age of eleven. In January, 1872 his wife died, and three years later, McGary married Miss Lucie Kitrell, who bore him nine children. Three of these died in infancy, but the others lived to adulthood. When the second wife died on June 1, 1897, her dying request was that McGary devote his entire life preaching this gospel, for by this time, McGary had become an ardent proponent of the plea for the return to the ancient order. A year later, McGary married Miss Lillian Otey of Huntsville, Texas, a young lady he had known all her life. She still lives [1950] in old age in Houston, Texas, at the old McGary home, 1709 Yale Street.

After the war, McGary entered into politics. Texas was still working at reconstruction. The country was sparsely settled, and its wide-open plains were inviting to unlawful citizens of other states. But the name of Austin McGary was soon to become legendary with Texas outlaws, and a name to be feared.

The election in Madison County, in 1872 was to be a decisive affair. Since the close of the war, the republicans or "radicals," as they were sometimes called, had politically controlled the County. McGary entered the race as candidate for sheriff on the Democratic ticket, but the election race was no tea party. The former sheriff was lax in enforcing the law. His brother-in-law was the biggest cow thief in the county; and preyed upon the herds of the ranchers in the county without fear of interruption. Ex-confederate soldiers, democrats to the last man, had become discouraged at the mishandling of justice, and were indifferent about voting. McGary saw that his only chance to win was to muster up enough interest among these ex-soldiers to get them to vote. As election time drew near, it was evident he was having surprisingly good success. But another problem now faced him.

The Republicans, sensing they were about to lose the election, felt their only chance was to get the negroes, all ex-slaves of course, to vote. However, all over the South, the negro-vote, no matter on which side it was cast, was unwelcome. McGary could not have been a Texas Confederate soldier and not resent it.

In nearby Hempstead, there was a man known widely by the distasteful sobriquet, as a "nigger voter." McGary and his supporters learned that this man was riding from Hempstead, and McGary determined to interrupt him. Saddling his horse, he rode southward out of town to meet him, and waited in a grove of trees until he saw him approach. Rider and horse galloped by. McGary pulled out of the trees, and trotted up behind the man. When the man turned, he was looking down the barrel of McGary's gun. McGary spoke emphatically,

"You're the 'nigger voter' from Hempstead, and I want to talk to you about this election. We don't want any outsiders here, and I want you to go back peacefully."

The stranger insisted that he was going to ride ahead, but McGary's gun helped persuade him to return to the grove of trees. Taking a jug from his saddle horn, he handed it to the man, and said, "Now, let's take a drink before we start talking." The man demurred, but the menacing-looking six-gun prodded him ahead. He took a swallow, vomited it out violently, and cried,

"That tastes like castor oil!"

"That's what it is," replied McGary, "and you're going to drink it all!"

The "nigger-voter" drank the jug of castor oil, and returned to Hempstead. The "niggers" did not vote, and Austin McGary won the election by only a slight majority.

During the two terms he served as sheriff, he had many hair-raising experiences against Texas outlaws. Once he disarmed and arrested John Wesley Hardin, "one of the coldest-blooded" gunmen in Texas history. Hardin had the record of killing twenty-seven men in his life-time. On another occasion McGary got the drop on a desperado, and had him standing with his hands in the air. Standing beside McGary were two of his younger deputies. The outlaw had two guns buckled on his hips. McGary told him he was coming after him, and that if he went for his guns, his deputies would shoot. As soon as McGary holstered his guns, the outlaw reached for his, and McGary's deputies shot him.

In years to come, after McGary had settled down to preach the gospel, reports circulated that he had killed a man. Actually, McGary, with all of his experiences, never killed a single person, although on this occasion, his deputies, acting upon his orders, did shoot an outlaw.

Near the close of his second term as sheriff of Madison County, McGary resigned his office to take a position as conveying agent for the state penitentiary. His job was to go all over the state and get the condemned criminals and bring them back to the state prison. This was far from a simple, monotonous job. Texas then had few railroads. The plains were infested by wild indians and desperadoes. Often McGary would start across the plains with eight prisoners, and one companion. They would ride for days at a time without passing a white settlement or seeing another man than his little party. They would sleep at night on the plains, and cook their meals over an open fire. In two years of this service, McGary did not lose a single prisoner.

It was in 1880 that Austin McGary resigned this work to return to Madison County to live. After settling down he gave himself to some serious thinking. He had thought little about religion, and had come to the conclusion that he was an infidel. He determined, however, to give the whole subject a thorough and impartial investigation, and so began by making a critical study of the Campbell-Owen debate. During the summer of 1881, an English emigrant by the name of Harry Hamilton came to Madisonville, Texas, to preach on the principles of apostolic Christianity. McGary's sister, Mrs. J. W. Gillespie, heard Hamilton, was convinced, and obeyed the gospel. She urged her brother to go hear the preacher, so McGary went. But his studies continued. It was December 24, 1881, that he was baptized into Christ.

Now McGary plunged more deeply into a search of the Bible. As he had an opportunity he preached. In 1883 he moved to Austin, Texas. For several years he made this his home, living a little west of the town.

As in politics so in preaching, McGary found his greatest felicity wherever the demand was most needed for a pugnacious style. He once received a letter from a young lady, a schoolteacher, who had recently moved to west Texas. She wrote saying that she longed to hear the gospel preached like her mother believed, and if McGary would come there and preach, she would pay his expenses. McGary wrote that other engagements prevented his going. Later, a meeting was cancelled, so he determined to go to the town. Without writing the young lady he was coming, he drove his horse and buggy the distance, arriving on a Saturday morning. Philpot, a great Methodist evangelist, he found was in town, causing considerable excitement in a large tabernacle meeting. McGary retired at a hotel that night, expecting to attend the meeting the next morning.

Sunday morning he had overslept, and when he arrived at the tabernacle, the crowd had already assembled. McGary took a seat in the rear of the building. Philpot's speech made the "Campbellites" his target, and straight toward it he drove. He announced that down in Texas was a Campbellite preacher by the name of McGary that taught people had to be baptized in running water to be saved. When Philpot finished, McGary stood up, walked casually to the front, across in front of several preachers who sat on the platform behind him, took his place and spoke.

"I am a stranger in your town. There is nobody to introduce me, so I will introduce myself. I am A. McGary from Austin, Texas. I baptized the doctor that Mr. Philpot referred to, but I did not baptize him in running water. Philpot's information is wrong, and if I can get the tabernacle this afternoon, I will be glad to tell you the facts in the case."

The owner of the tabernacle called out that he could get it. Philpot went into a rage, and announced that the meeting was closed. But McGary preached that afternoon, and on for several days. He also baptized the young lady schoolteacher who had written him, although he learned several days later that she had joined the Methodists under Philpot's preaching before McGary arrived in town.

The most prominent characteristic of McGary was his courage. Fear had absolutely no part in his make-up. At Willis, Texas, near Houston, the Ku-Klux Klan became active after the Civil War, and McGary was widely recognized as a bitter enemy. He was warned to get out of Willis, but he ignored the warning, until a stranger from another town informed him that he would be killed, and that people from another community would do it if he did not move. McGary was puzzled for a moment what to do. He conceived a plan, and sent an old Negro to every street corner in the town to shout at the top of his voice that McGary would speak on a certain Sunday afternoon at a specified locality on the subject of "Ku-Klux Klan."

The time arrived and the town was full of people. McGary laid serious charges before the Klan. The Klan was unconstitutional. He related how they had taken an old preacher out of his house at night and beaten him unmercifully. McGary's language was bitter in the extreme. He told them his door was unlocked at all times; that they could come any time they choose, but they better bring a wheelbarrow in which to haul their boys off. "I have a gun and some of you know that I am handy with it," McGary cried. The Ku-Klux Klan never bothered A. McGary.

· But perhaps the crowning work of McGary's life was the establishing of the *Firm Foundation* at Austin, Texas. The name is selected from the fact that Jesus is the Foundation upon which His church is built; hence, the church has, in Christ, a *Firm Foundation*. The paper, then a monthly, began publication the first of September, 1884. It was not intended that it should be projected for over a year, but in September, 1885, McGary announced that it would henceforth be a weekly. How long it should run in the future was indefinite.

In announcing the launching of the paper, McGary wrote in the first issue:

This pamphlet, *The Firm Foundation,* in its contemplated monthly visitations, is respectfully, fraternally, and affectionately dedicated to all that class of brethren who, believing that the New Testament Scriptures are from God, to man, through His Son Jesus the Christ, and who, regarding this book as an infallible guide through this wilderness of sin to the promised haven of safety beyond, are willing to turn their steps away from *all* human *systems, plans* and *directions* into this *one* mapped out by he apostles of our Lord.

. . . It goes forth to battle for the truth, ignoring the conventionalists of so-called "polite society" preferring to call things by their right names as did He who "spake as never man spoke."[2]

The avowed purpose of the establishment of the *Firm Founda-*

[2]A. McGary, "no title," *Firm Foundation,* Vol. I, No. 1 (September, 1884), p. 1.

tion was occasioned by McGary's growing alarm at the practice of some preachers of "shaking in the Baptists." The point, of course, was that the Baptists were baptized not "for," viz., "in order to" the remission of their sins, but because their sins had already been remitted. The question was, when a Baptist decided to abandon the Baptist Church for apostolic Christianity, should he be rebaptized? McGary discussed the issue with everybody who would discuss it, but in those days he was very much in the minority. Before long, he gained the reputation of making it a hobby; still he would not be discouraged. The "Progressives" used it to his disadvantage.

W. H. Bagby, of Bryan, Texas, was a liberal and wrote the news of Texas for the *Christian Standard.* He opens an attack on McGary:

Every phase of foolishness that ever sprang from the faithful soil of dwarfed and ignorant minds among us may be found in Texas, as I, at least, have never seen it elsewhere. From the anti-society doctrine down to the rebaptism hobby, the contemptible foolishness of which English language has no word to express, we have everything. No wonder that in many places we are regarded with contempt by intelligent and good people. . . . The whole body has to bear the reproach that belongs only to a few irresponsible hobbyists who are no more in sympathy with the feelings of God's word and the spirit of true Christianity than are the Holiness people. Their leader enjoys the liberty of a man who carries in his pocket a letter of dismissal from the church in the community where he lives. . . . [2]

Concerning McGary's idea on Baptist baptism, Bagby writes:

We know of no departure from the faith in modern times so hurtful to the cause of New Testament Christianity as this hobby which the *Firm Foundation* was established to advocate.[3]

David Lipscomb and the *Gospel Advocate* were less concerned about it as an issue. When Lipscomb was only fourteen years old, he was recovering from a spell of typhoid fever, when he sent for Tolbert Fanning to come and baptize him. He had told no one about his intention. When Fanning arrived, he asked the boy, David Lipscomb, why he wanted to be baptized, and Lipscomb's reply was, "to obey God." Forty years later Lipscomb wrote about it, still determined that he could not improve his reply. With this statement Fanning baptized Lipscomb in a box.

[3] W. H. Bagby, "Texas Tidings," *Christian Standard,* Vol. XXI, No. 8 (February 20, 1886), p. 61.

At the first gospel meeting Lipscomb ever conducted, a woman came forward to "unite with the disciples," having been a member of the Baptist Church. Lipscomb inquired of her if she had been baptized to join the Baptist Church or for another reason. This was the question he generally asked in such cases. She replied: "My friends were not Baptists, and my preference was not to join that church, but they were the only people I knew that practiced what I believed the Lord required, so I united with them."

Jesse L. Sewell happened to be passing through the community, and attended the meeting that night. Lipscomb asked Sewell his opinion of whether the woman should be rebaptized. Sewell answered, "it would be mockery for that woman to be rebaptized."[4] Lipscomb always thought so himself.

But, here was the issue: David Lipscomb believed that if an individual were baptized from the motive of wanting to obey God, that motive was acceptable whether the individual understood that baptism was in order to the remission of sins or not. Austin McGary, on the other hand, denied this, insisting that obeying God "from the heart" required an accurate understanding of the purpose of baptism. For more than fifteen years brethren discussed the issue in both the *Firm Foundation* and the *Gospel Advocate*. Many doubtlessly tired of it, and some thought the difference in viewpoint was only slight indeed. J. D. Tant, who himself sympathized with McGary on the issue, once wisely wrote:

. . . I often think of what a noted Texas preacher said to me some years ago: that the best way to bring about an understanding between Lipscomb and McGary would be to work up a big meeting somewhere, select the two to hold it, and at the close of the meeting they would find they were so near in accord on almost all things that they would be ashamed to claim a difference. . . . [5]

Nevertheless, McGary's insistence that it was wrong to "shake in the Baptists," a term he frequently used, gained for him the reputation of being an extremist. When H. F. Williams paid a visit to Texas in 1894, and met McGary, he hardly knew what to expect.

Here also I had the pleasure of meeting A. McGary, of the

---

[4]David Lipscomb, "Queries," *Gospel Advocate,* Vol. XXXIX, No. 23 (June 10, 1897), p. 355.
[5]J. D. Tant, "Our Nashville Meetings—No. 1," *Gospel Advocate,* Vol. XLI, No. 27 (June 6, 1899), p. 427.

Firm Foundation. I had heard much of him, and read from his pen. My acquaintance with him was very pleasant. He is one of the "rebaptism" folks. As I had met several of that tribe in my travels, but had never heard one of them preach, I was interested to know how they preached. I heard Brother Mc. one time. He was a plain, earnest, interesting talker; but it would surprise some people in some places to hear that he just preached like many other folks. If he has horns, I did not see them. I do not think him overly sound. He said nothing about "rebaptism," and I understand that he preaches many sermons without referring to the "baptism of Baptists." This was refreshing to me, as I had understood that many of the *Foundation* folks took their text on "baptism for the remission of sins," and seldom got further on baptism than the talking of "Baptists on Baptist baptism." It is strange how much prejudice a little fire will kindle. . . .[6]

Although McGary was a lover of music, and himself quite talented as a "fiddler" [the instrument that played his kind of music was a "fiddle," not a "violin"], he believed the use of the instrument in the worship of God to be an innovation, corrupting the simple pattern of New Testament worship. Likewise, he believed societies to do the work of the church were wrong. Consequently, Austin McGary will always be remembered "primarily for his firm and fearless stand against the wave of digression that deluged the churches of Christ in Texas during the last quarter of the nineteenth century."

In the early part of 1903 McGary moved to Los Angeles, California where he published a paper called *The Lookout*. He stayed there only a short time, and in June of that year moved to Eugene, Oregon. The next year his health failed, so he moved to Bryan, Texas. Nor did his health improve here. He thought a higher climate would help, and so moved to Springdale, Arkansas in the Ozarks. But this helped little. He decided then, to return to his native state. Houston was now to be his home.

On February 6, 1926, Austin McGary passed his eightieth birthday. The inexorable demand of nature slowly reached out for him, and, on June 15, 1928 he passed away at his home in Houston. His body was laid beside that of his mother in the cemetery at Huntsville.

---

[6]H. F. Williams, "Field Findings: In Texas," *Gospel Advocate*, Vol. XXXVI, No. 1 (January 4, 1894), p. 12.

Chapter XX

TEXAS

One of the most thrilling chapters relating to the restoration movement could be written covering the church in Texas from the close of the Civil War to the turn of the twentieth century. It would certainly include the lives of many noble preachers—Carroll Kendrick, John T. Poe, J. W. Jackson, H. D. Bantau, C. M. Wilmeth, A. J. Clark, J. D. Tant, and Joe Warlick, to mention only a few. Such a history would breathe the atmosphere of conflict, and could justly close with a crowning victory to the purity and simplicity of apostolic work and worship. It cannot be expected that one chapter could serve any more than a prelude to such a gallant and glorious history.

After the Civil War, a steady migration pushed into Texas from the east. There is an indefiniteness about the cause. Probably it was a combination of factors. The restlessness of the human soul, inherently sure that the best is beyond one's reach, probably entered. Cheap lands, with the possibility of grasping a fortune over-night, had something to do with the sky-rocketing growth in Texas population. With some, adventure and romance were attractive as there were indians and outlaws to fight. Earlier settlers had migrated to Texas, and had learned to love the state. Their letters to relatives back east urged them out to the west, to the land of golden opportunity. In the sheer desolation of wide open plains, the matchless marvels of broad, yawning valleys; in the sacred dignity of gaunt, angular peaks, bursting suddenly upward from a wind-swept mesa of sand and cactus—the westerner learned to love these scenes. Every Texan became a salesman, and with his broad arm, beckoned his friends westward.

Foremost among the immigrators to Texas were native Tennesseans. Their state, torn apart by the ravages of the Civil War, offered little inducement for them to stay. Their economic system was poor, their slaves were free, and their property gutted by the merciless sword of Mars. If start over they must, why not in a new place? So to Texas they went. David Lipscomb, in

1872, paid an extended visit to the state. Twelve years later he returned, and was impressed by the way Tennesseans had filled Texas.

Texas, within itself, is a nation in extent. A constant stream of immigration from the older states is pouring into its borders. It must soon be a nation in population and wealth. It is strange how many Tennesseans are there. For some years after the formation of its government, nine-tenths of the members of its congresses and legislatures were Tennessee born, as were several of its first Presidents, Governors and Congressmen. We have concluded that Tennessee has been the prolific spawning ground for the South and Southwest. Many shoals have gone forth to people and subdued these regions. A Tennessean may always feel at home in Texas.[1]

V. R. Stapp wrote from Coleman City, Texas to the *American Christian Review* in the summer of 1879 that the tide of immigration was astonishing. Almost half of the population in his own county, and in Runnels County, to the west, lived in camps.

It was, of course, to be expected that in the migration westward many members of the church would be found. T. W. Caskey, the Mississippi "fightin' parson," left the ruins of his home east of the River and came to Texas after the Civil War. H. D. Bantau, a native Tennessean, moved in 1870 to Waco on the advice of his physician. He had been preaching at Weatherford eleven years when he died in 1888. E. J. Lampton moved from Illinois to Denton in 1877, where he found a small congregation. P. Minor, a carriage-maker, was preaching for it. In the fall of 1871, L. C. Chisholm, a dentist by trade, took his brother with him, and left Tuscumbia, Alabama for Texas. Many congregations in southwest Texas owe their origin to Chisholm's preaching. About the same time, R. C. Horn left Hartsville, Tennessee for Texas. C. M. ("Uncle Mac") Wilmeth graduated from Kentucky University in 1871, spent the summer preaching in middle Tennessee, and then moved to Texas in the fall. Wilmeth became one of the church's most noted preachers in Texas.

The list of names of pioneer preachers pushing westward after the war could be extended endlessly. On they came, but their work in preaching the gospel was to be everything but soft. Railroad companies were only beginning to meet the challenge of the

---

[1]David Lipscomb, "A Trip to Texas," *Gospel Advocate,* Vol. XXVII, No. 4 (January 28, 1885), p. 50.

plains, and so preachers rode horseback or on stagecoachs for many miles to preach at distant appointments. They would often sleep at night on the open, rattlesnake-infested prairies, and then with the coming of daylight, push on to a school-house, or old barn, and announce a gospel meeting was about to begin. For three years, 1887-1889, J. D. Tant preached, being sent out by the brethren in Hamilton and Coryell County, Texas. He received five hundred dollars a year. His father, mother, sister and himself lived on two hundred dollars a year and spent the remainder in payments on their home. Pay amounted to very little—but so did expenses.

Typical of the experiences of these preachers were those of A. J. Bush who came to southwest Texas after the war. The church in that part of the state was very weak; here and there were a very scattered brethren. Bush got himself a "yellow-sided" Texas pony, put a saddle on him, picked up his Bible and hymn-book, and a few scattered pieces of clean linen and started out to preach. He rode twenty miles to Goliad and preached; he rode another twenty to Popolota Creek and preached. Here he learned that Lagarto in Live Oak County needed a preacher, so he started there. On the way he got lost. On Sunday morning he found himself nine miles from his appointment. He was told that he would find a Brother Stillwell, six miles on the way to Lagarto. Stillwell was supposed to be a leading member of the little congregation.

Bush spurred his pony on and finally arrived at Stillwell's home. He noted that there were several men gathered around the home, all heavily armed with knives and guns. Bush inquired for Stillwell, found him, introduced himself, and then inquired what was happening. Stillwell replied, "We are glad to see you; don't be alarmed at appearances; you go over to town, and the brethren will care for you. We have three or four Mexicans to hang, and then we will be ready for a meeting."

GROWTH IN TEXAS

One of the most intrepid preachers in east Texas after the war was John T. Poe. Through his influence many congregations were established. His naturally independent turn of mind can well be seen in his earlier religious experiences. Although reared in the Methodist Church, he was never satisfied that this was according to New Testament teaching. But he had never heard of any other kind of preaching, and so remained with the denomination. Poe was in the Confederacy during the Civil War. In 1864 he was one day sitting in camp, reading his New Testament, when he decided that he would be immersed the first time he had the opportunity. After the war, he moved back to his home in Huntsville, Texas. The next Sunday after his return, he heard J. W. D. Creath preach at the Baptist Church. He and a brother-in-law, H. C. Wright informed Creath that they objected to many teachings of the Baptist Church, but they wanted to be immersed— to obey God. An old Colonel Rogers, a Baptist deacon, discussed the unusual request, and, being thoroughly satisfied in his own mind that these men would later agree with Baptist teaching, acquiesced in the decision to baptize them.

Two years later, having learned of a people who were Christians and Christians only, who took the Bible and the Bible only, Poe "bade adieu to sectarian folly," and became a member of the church of Christ in Huntsville. He had no intention of preaching, but at the urging of some members, decided to try once. He prepared earnestly for a month, gathering scraps of quotations from Beecher and others. When he got up to deliver the sermon, he spread papers out before him, and started. He noticed women whispering to each other, and, fearing that had discovered his secret that he had borrowed his sermon from others, he sat down in confusion. He was resolved never to preach again until an old lady asked him to speak the next Sunday at her husband's sawmill, and promised to take him out there and back in her buggy. She told him not to "prepare" a sermon, but just get up and tell the people what the Lord wanted them to know about the plan of salvation. Poe obliged, and baptized two people at the sawmill meeting.

The congregtaion at Huntsville, Texas had been established in 1860. When David Lipscomb visited Texas in 1872, he found that this congregation had one hundred members, and that John T. Poe was preaching for it quite regularly. Although Poe was constantly and intrepidly fighting innovations, there were times when his life's work was lost by the congregations accepting these, and Poe had to begin again. There were strong congregations at Longview and Palestine, but both departed with innovations. In the summer of 1899 Poe sent out a call for help, got some, went back to Longview, and held a meeting. A small congregation of seven members was established. Four years later, when it had only thirty members, the Longview church sent Poe to Palestine, Texas to re-establish the cause. The old congregation now had J. C. Mason, a Texas-Arkansas preacher of definite "Progressive coloring," who was preaching for this church. Eighty-three year old, John F. Taylor, who had once been an elder in the other congregation, but was driven out when the instrument was driven in, asked for the privilege of using the old meeting house for a meeting with Poe. He was refused. An old sister, Alice Brown, borrowed a tent from a Baptist preacher, and so in this, Poe began his meeting, to plant again the cause in Palestine, Texas.

At Waco, the congregation was organized in 1870 with forty members. Three years later it had a hundred members, but no meeting house. J. H. Bantan, a district judge, from Huntsville, did frequent preaching here during the summers. At Hamilton, the congregation was established on the second Lord's Day of April, 1876. Here, J. D. Tant did considerable preaching in his earlier days. Mrs. Dillie Harris moved from Thyatira, Mississippi to Kyle, Texas around 1887. She put an item in the *Gospel Advocate,* asking someone to send a preacher there. Her home congregation saw it, contacted John T. Poe, and paid him forty dollars to establish a congregation. At Marshall, Poe went in the summer of 1888, but the meeting closed in two days with a "dyed-in-the-wool digressive" elder protesting. W. D. Ingram reported to the *Christian Leader* in the summer of 1894 that there were four hundred members of the church in Van Zandt County, although there was considerable indifference.

In Hood County, Thorp Springs became a radiating point for the churches in the early years following the war. J. A. Clark, a native Tennessean, had become a member of the church of Christ in Titus County, Texas as early as 1843. At the close of the war he had moved to Fort Worth to become the city's first postmaster. Two years later he and his sons, Addison and Randolph, opened a college. By 1873 in order to avoid the influences of an evil city, they had determined to move their college into the country. J. A. Clark purchased a two-story building at Thorp Springs, and opened school that fall, September, 1873.

The school was known as "Add-Ran Male & Female College," but more popularly, as "Add-Ran College."

There is, and has been, a wide misunderstanding as to the source of the name. The general opinion is that it was taken from "Addison" and "Randolph," the two sons of J. A. Clark. Aaron Prince Aten visited Texas in 1879, making Thorp Springs a stopping point on his itinerary. In his report on his visit, he reported that the school was named for "Addison" and "Randolph," sons of J. A. Clark, and for this mistake, the elder Clark chastised him, saying,

He says, "It is locally known as Add-Ran College, the name being formed from the first syllables of the two names just mentioned." Here, again, the writer has affirmed without being fully posted. At least, his statement is calculated to convey an idea that is not strictly true. Did the writer know this college was named for one person alone? If he did not, he knew not how it got its name, and ought not to have undertaken to tell. I can tell him, if to know will afford him any satisfaction, that the college was named for one who has for years lain buried in the graveyard at Fort Worth. . . .[2]

Clark made it clear that Add-Ran College was to have no endowment, was not to belong to the church, and yet would hold forth Christian principles. "We have never asked," he once wrote, "an endowment from the brethren; nor have we asked them to take the college under their control as church property, believing that we could do better for the brotherhood with it as individual property." James L. Thornberry expressed their point of view by writing,

A church had as well run a farm as a college. The business of the church is to "edify itself, to shine as a light in a dark place, to hold forth the word of life to a dying and lost world." When the church perceives in the body gifted men, men of faith, humility and piety, whose sole desire is to preach, men who, as the lamented R. Rice said, "can not help preaching," let the church aid such to educate themselves, send them to college and pay for it. . . . I am by no means opposed to colleges, and I am glad to see my Christian brethren conducting them; but let not the church be burdened with them, nor put in money there that ought to be used for other purposes. Nor do I like a college whose ostensible

---

[2]J. A. Clark, "Add-Ran College," *Christian Standard,* Vol. XIV, No. 33 (August 16, 1879), p. 258.

purpose is preacher-making. Let God and the church make the preacher and the colleges the scholars.[3]

Thorp Springs, then, three miles west of Granberry, county seat of Hood County, a mile west of the Brazos River, having, in 1873, a population of less than six hundred, became a strong focal point for the influence of the principles of primitive Christianity.

Churches over Texas grew up by sacrifice, slow constant toil, and for the most part amid inward turmoil. Nowhere was there more evidence of this than in the central and southern part of the state. The church at Austin had dated from 1853 when Henry Thomas had moved there from Missouri. Soon, forty members were organized, and the first meetings were held in a school house. Soon afterward, it was meeting on Congress Avenue, in an old house it had bought from the Methodists. W. H. D. Carrington was the chief spirit in building up the congregation in those earlier years. In 1879, W. E. Hall, a young man of only twenty-eight, came to Austin. He was beset by constant criticism. He, too, had a definite "progressive coloring," and the congregation was torn by dissension. John I. Poe was certain that the church was killed by the "pastor mania."

When McGary came to Austin and saw the church beset with innovations, he rolled up his sleeves and went to work. In opposing Hall's liberalism, McGary wrote articles and sent them to the *Advocate*. He succeeded in getting Hall to leave Austin and head back for headquarters at St. Louis, but that did not end the dissension. McGary then asked for a letter from the congregation, and went outside the city, at a place called Pecan Springs to worship.

Around Austin, congregations were springing up like magic. At San Marcos in 1873 there were one hundred members meeting in a new house. At Bethany, near Willis, in Montgomery County, was reported to be the strongest congregation numerically in southern Texas. This was in 1886. Small congregations were found at Goliath, Manahuella, Charco, and Harwood. In March, 1882 L. C. Chisholm came to Goliath, a village of three or four thousand people. Goliath was the site of the massacre of General Fannin and his Texans by the Mexicans in 1833. All but one of

---

[3]James L. Thornberry, "Texas Letter," *American Christian Review,* Vol. XXII, No. 22 (May 27, 1879), p. 171.

the American force had been slaughtered. This one to escape was an old brother who attended church at Goliath, and who was also a judge in the town. He escaped by playing dead, and crawling away at night. At Uvalde, 95 miles west of San Antonio, Chisholm came in January, 1882 to preach. This was a typical western town, located in a stock-raising country. It had then a population of only five hundred, and only a small congregation.

At San Antonio as late as 1883 there were only a few brethren meeting. Although the city had a population of forty-two thousand, it was difficult to plant the church here. D. Pennington came here to build up the church. He spent all of his money, got no support, and left. W. J. Barbee went in 1886 and stayed one year. When he left, he declared San Antonio to be the hardest place he ever saw to establish the truth. David Lipscomb explained that the real difficulty at San Antonio lay in the fact that the preachers who had gone there, and the few members to be found, straddled the fence on the issues before the church until few brethren were willing to support them.

The church at Houston was slow getting planted. A. E. Cloud, a businessman and member of the church, earnestly requested W. F. Barcus to conduct a meeting here. Barcus went in July, 1886, and afterward declared, correctly or incorrectly, that this was the first time the gospel had ever been preached in Houston. We are inclined to the opinion that Barcus' statement was made incorrectly for John T. Poe declared that he and D. Pennington went to Houston early in 1876 and established the church in the town. If so, it yet would seem evident that it functioned very little in the coming years. At any rate, when General R. M. Gano went here in the spring of 1888 to conduct a meeting, he found a small congregation. His meeting resulted in ten additions. By the fall of 1904 one reads of a small congregation of twenty-nine members meeting at Houston Avenue and Bingham Street.

John T. Poe was largely responsible for establishing the church at Corsicana. In September, 1888 Poe went to the city at his own expense to conduct the meeting. He rented the city hall, paying a dollar a night for it. He ate his meals in a restaurant, and again at his own expense. T. F. Driskill, a dentist and a preacher, who lived in the city, aided him. The meeting lasted ten days, and before it had ended, a congregation of sixty-two members was organized. Shortly after the congregation was organized, B. B. Sanders, state evangelist for the Texas Christian Missionary Society, came to the town, introduced the organ, and divided the church. Meanwhile, the brethren who worshipped as they had originally done before Sanders came, continued. When R. L. Whiteside left the Nashville Bible School to return to Texas, he went, in a few years, to Corsicana to live. F. W. Smith visited the city in the summer of 1903, and conducted a meeting for the church. He wrote of Whiteside, "Brother Whiteside is a strong man, and will some day take his stand among the clearest reasoners in Texas."

When "Bold and Beseeching" W. F. Black went to Fort Worth in June, 1887 to conduct a meeting, he found that the congregation had the reputation of being the largest church among the brethren in the state. The first preaching in the city was done in 1857 when B. F. Hall established a church of fifteen members. When David Lipscomb visited Fort Worth in 1872, he estimated the population of the city at less than seven hundred. This was at the time that J. A. Clark was anxious to move his school to the country to get away from the evil influences of a large city. By 1889 the congregation had grown to number four hundred members. That year it moved into a new building that cost ten thousand dollars, and was said to be the finest in the city. That year also, scholarly J. W. Lowber was called to be the preacher.

The attainments of the church became widely known, and the fact that it had the finest church building in Texas became equally as well known.

I notice an account in the Texas Department of the *Guide* of May the 24th of the grand work that our esteemed Kentucky brother, J. W. Lowber, is doing at Fort Worth. For the marvelous success of his work there, we feel truly and thankfully proud; but there are some things in the report of Brother Lowber's work to which I feel constrained to object. While Paul doubtless saw many virtues in his brethren that were praiseworthy, he saw things that he could not praise and told them so. In my judgment, if Paul were to write an epistle to the saints at Fort Worth, he would tell them that he praised their liberality, but as to the way they used it, he "praised them not." I refer to the cost of the interior finery of the house of worship. One window cost the immense sum of five hundred dollars—quite enough to have built a new little house at some destitute point. Why did they not pay about twenty five dollars for a window and send the four hundred and seventy five to some mission work? *Pride.*[4]

This original congregation by 1896 had grown to number eight hundred members, and was widely referred to as the Central Church. The brethren had two other congregations in town, although they were much smaller. Homer T. Wilson, the only located preacher in the town, was now preaching at the Central congregation. J. D. Tant came to the city in the spring of 1896 and conducted a meeting on the south side of town with a small congregation. Members of the Central Church had gone to a State Meeting in the central part of the state, and so could not support Tant's meeting. The action was a straw to tell which way the wind was blowing.

James E. Scobey came to Fort Worth in the spring of 1899. This small south side church had grown some. W. T. Kidwell now preached regularly for it. Scobey could now declare that this was the only church in the city which "maintains the apostolic work and worship." Homer T. Wilson had led the Central Church into putting in the instrument. J. E. McPherson, who succeeded Wilson, had the same policies. Wilson had taken another group and established what was called the "Second Christian Church."

In Dallas, a congregation was organized about 1855. At first its meetings were held in the Masonic Hall, then in the courthouse, then in the City Hall, and frequently afterward in other rented halls. After the Civil War, the congregation bought a lot and built a meeting house. This was the first church house of any description ever to be erected in Dallas. The congregation gradually outgrew it. About 1885 a Brother Peak gave them a lot on the corner of Pearl and Bryan Streets, and here the church continued to meet. General R. M. Gano served as an elder for this congregation for over thirty years.

After the Civil War, this congregation was known as the Commerce Street Church. Kirk Baxter, brother of William Baxter, biographer of Walter Scott, came to preach for the Commerce Street Church. At his instigation, Knowles Shaw, "the singing evangelist," came to conduct a meeting. During this meeting, Baxter and Shaw introduced the organ and divided the church. It was immediately upon the close of this meeting that Shaw took the train for McKinney, Texas at which time occurred the train wreck that took his life.

The division at Commerce Street probably resulted in strengthening the Pearl and Bryan Street church. In 1884 "Weeping Joe" Harding held a lengthy meeting here. The congregation now had four hundred members. They employed Harding the next year to work in the county, establishing congregations. W. H. Bagby reported to the *Christian Standard* in 1887 that in the county, about Dallas, there were eighteen or twenty congregations, many of which had been established by "Weeping Joe" Harding.

After the war, T. W. Caskey settled in Dallas. Here, he spent most of his last years. The truculent Caskey, like Joe S. Warlick who followed him, held many a debate that strengthened the church greatly in that general area. From April 13-14, 1874 he held a debate in Fort Worth with a Methodist preacher by the name of Price, who was widely referred to as "the Campbellite killer of Texas." Addison Clark, in describing Caskey at this time, says of him,

To those who have seen and heard him, I need not say that there is but one T. W. Caskey on this globe. A man more peculiarly *sui generis*, I never saw. I believe he told me he is 57 years old. Is 6 feet, 3½ inches high. Is dry and humorous in conversation. I don't suppose he has shed a tear since his mother whipped him, and I doubt much whether he did then.[5]

At both Denton and Sherman there were strong congregations very early. As early as 1877 Denton had a fine meeting house, but when H. F. Williams visited here in 1894 there were omens of trouble ahead. Williams observed that "they nearly all spell it with a big D, which means *one* more of the denominations that afflict professed Christendom."

For several years following the Civil War the church at Sherman, Texas had met in the court house and in the Odd-Fellow's Hall. "Uncle Charlie" Carlton and B. F. Hall did the preaching. In 1874 a new building was erected at the corner of Montgomery and Houston Streets. At this time the church had only forty or fifty members. The next year the congregation received its greatest boost. John S. Sweeney debated Jacob Ditzler, the noted Methodist. Shortly after the debate, Sweeney conducted

---

[5] A. Clark, "The Caskey and Price Debate," *Gospel Advocate*, Vol. XVI, No. 19 (May 7, 1874), p. 443.

a meeting which closed February 19, 1876 that resulted in one hundred and twenty-four additions to the congregation. In 1894 T. B. Larimore held, what was perhaps his greatest meeting, at Sherman.

At Weatherford there was a strong congregation. A lady by the name of Soward was largely instrumental in building up the church. H. D. Bantau preached here; so did John T. Poe. J. D. Tant's mother lived here for a while, so Tant was frequently "in and out." At Breckinridge, Addison Clark established a church of forty members in the summer of 1885. The city of Abilene was established about 1880. Three years later, it had a population of four thousand. That same year, 1883, T. H. Hughes came to the town and established a congregation of fifty members. There were then small churches at Anson, Buffalo Gap and Dead Man Valley, but Hughes found no preachers within a hundred miles.

Professor Bruner, a teacher at Eureka College in Illinois, made a move to El Paso for his health around 1890. Three years later a small congregation was regularly meeting with Bruner doing most of the preaching.

Texas gradually became dotted with congregations, although in many locations omens of impending strife were plainly visible. At Tioga and Collinsville were small churches. At Whitesboro Dr. H. H. Talley, formerly of Petersburg, Tennessee, had established a small church, but when H. F. Williams visited here in 1892, he found an organ and a society, "a heap of church fussing," and little interest. At Mason a church was established in 1875. At Bryan, there was a church as early as 1869. Carrol Kendrick did some of his early Texas preaching here. The church was set up in Fayette County, at the town of Liberty before the war by a Colonel I. H. Moore, "a wicked outsider," who built the meeting house because he hated to see the church suffer persecution. Afterward, Moore became a faithful Christian. In August, 1885 a congregation was set up at Benjamin, Texas. The county judge, the sheriff, the trustee, the tax collector, the county treasurer, and the justice of the peace all belonged to the church.

The struggle over the instrumental music and the missionary society was as inevitable in Texas as it had been in other places. The tide of immigration that swelled the state's population was a heterogeneous group. To no small extent this was true even within the church. From Tennessee had come a host of church members who had been taught against these innovations in the worship, and, upon their arrival in their new home, they were thoroughly determined to build up churches where these innovations would be unknown. There was one thing in their favor. Texas was a southern state, and, with the bitter prejudices that lived on for awhile throughout the nation after the war, Texas people found more affinity to Tennessee people than those migrating from the North. The fact that the *Christian Standard* was violently pro-northern made its reception somewhat slow in the state. The *Gospel Advocate* had been introduced before the war, and was widely received.

Still, as many congregations in other states back in the east had introduced the organ, more frequently than not, with division resulting, the same conflict was inevitable in Texas. As a matter of fact, definite signs had been pointing in that direction since the war.

Before the war, it was common for brethren to meet together in what was often referred to as "Cooperation Meetings," "Consultation Meetings," and sometimes, "District Meetings" or "State Meetings" depending upon their extent. These comparatively innocent meetings were nothing more than mass gatherings to discuss problems relative to the advancement of the church. Everybody was invited so there was no tendency of a segregation into "clergy" or "laity," named or unnamed. No influence toward coercion was put toward any of the churches.

Carrol Kendrick left his home of Kentucky in 1851 to move to Texas. In the west Kendrick became a most influential preacher. It was he who introduced "State Meetings" to Texas churches. These meetings were mass gatherings of brethren at specific locations to discuss the work of the church. It was not a missionary society, although in these earlier years Kendrick was not averse to societies. Before the war, Kendrick and Tolbert Fanning discussed these societies at great length through the *Gospel Advocate,* Kendrick affirming their right to exist. After the war when David Lipscomb came prominently to the front in the *Advocate,* Kendrick and Lipscomb had a great misunderstanding. When Lipscomb visited Texas in 1872, he attended the State Meeting held at Bryan, but was ignored and discourteously treated by Kendrick. Afterwards, rumors of Kendrick's disapproval of Lipscomb reached the *Advocate* editor, and Lipscomb blazed forth with a sizzling chastening for Carrol Kendrick. Although afterward, Lipscomb regretted what he had done, the harm was done, and the personal feelings between Carrol Kendrick and David Lipscomb were never the most fraternal.

Although in the last twelve to fifteen years of his life, Kendrick opposed the missionary society, for several years earlier he had spoken favorably of them. At the State Meeting held in Dallas in July, 1876 Kendrick spoke, favoring adopting a plan to do missionary work in Texas. T. W. Caskey openly objected on the ground that this "plan" was just another "Louisville Plan," "whitewashed over." So the suggestion was killed.

Nevertheless with the passing of years, and the growing influx of advocates of both the missionary society and the use of the instrument coming into Texas, the battle loomed more definitely upon the horizon. By 1885 advocates of the society hoped to get a missionary society started that year. It was thought that the State Meeting in Sherman would be the ideal time to put across the proposal. At this meeting, W. K. Homan put forth the resolution to organize a Texas State Society. Thomas Moore, W. H. Wright, R. C. Horn, J. R. Wilmeth, and C. M. Wilmeth fought the resolution down. J. A. Clark afterwards reported to the *Old Path Guide* that the opposers of the society were more interested in notoriety than in the cause of Christianity.

But the fact that the advocates of the Society had failed this once, did not mean they were through. A. J. Bush proposed in the December 3, 1885 issue of the *Texas Christian* that the Texas State Missionary Society be organized at the close of the next Bible Institute to be held at Thorp Spring. This would be in early January. At this Bible Institute there were many lively discussions on "Church Organization," "Christian Liberty," and "The Pastorate And The Work of Evangelizing," but still, the missionary society idea was not able to be put across.

Proponents of the society now looked forward to the next State Meeting to be held in July, 1886 at Austin. Early that year, W. R. McDaniel reported that the lowest estimate of the number of disciples in Texas was thirty thousand, and added, "there are more than three times seven thousand of these who will never board the progressive car." Nevertheless, Chalmers McPherson made it clear that this time there would be a society organized, so sent out word that all who were opposed, please stay away from the meeting.

According to plans, the State Meeting convened in Austin on July 7, 1886 at ten o'clock in the morning. The sessions lasted for three days. W. K. Homan, ardent proponent of the Society, was chairman. A committee on resolutions was appointed which drew up seven resolutions favorable to the establishment of the Society. A few opponents of the Society were present. These included C. M. Wilmeth of Dallas and General R. M. Gano; W. H. D. Carrington, the man who led J. D. Tant to the truth, and Carrol Kendrick who by now was violently opposed to the Society. J. D. Tant was also present, but Tant was a young preacher, and confessed later that he came, not out of interest in the meeting, but rather to get himself a wife. "He came, he saw, he conquered," and Tant went home with a wife.

When it was announced in the meeting that the resolutions had been drawn up, it was suggested that the consideration of these be put off until the next day. Opponents of the society had from some source gotten the impression that no attempt would be made to introduce the society, and so were surprised at the resolutions. The next day the resolutions were read one by one, and generally agreed upon down to number seven. When the seventh resolution was read, Society advocates knew that this was the signal for the battle to begin. Before a word could be said against the resolutions, "Uncle Charlie" Carlton, an advocate of the Society, jumped up and led in the singing of "All Hail The Power of Jesus' Name." C. M. Wilmeth later wrote in the *Christian Preacher,* "They sang as lustily as niggers at a corn-shucking, while good men and women sat and wept." General Gano stood up and begged the brethren not to introduce the society, and when they persisted, he "went to the door and wept as a child." Later, Carroll Kendrick wrote,

In July, 1886, after an absence of nine years, I attended the State Meeting at Austin, Texas, because I was urged to do so, and because I saw from the papers, that an effort would probably be made at that meeting to form a Society, or, at least, to have the work take on more of the society form. For over twenty years the meetings had done moderately well, and I was sure that such a move would cause a division and great harm. My objects were to prevent a division and encourage union and all the right ways of the Lord. I was not mistaken. The effort was made, and succeeded, after all we could do to prevent it. After the order of political management, a leading progressionist was put in the chair. He appointed his committees of his own class. The Committee on Ways and Means soon brought in their report for a Society; it was what we would, in other days, have called a *constitution*. A number of us told them plainly that we could not work on such a plan without being hypocrites, and that to urge it was to urge *division*—to *carry* it, to make a division. We implored them most earnestly to desist, and to let us work on in harmony. They persisted. The vote was a tie, and the chairman decided for the division. . . This caused us to feel that they did not desire *harmony*—that they *desired* to get rid of us, so they could add innovations without opposition! This, I think, was fully proved. Certainly they could have had harmony had they desired it. The rest of us, after they closed, called together the State Meeting, as formerly, and did what we could in the brief time we had. . .[6]

When it became evident that the Missionary Society would be launched, W. H. D. Carrington stood before the audience and asked that all who wanted to do missionary work on a scriptural basis to come to the basement. Carrington's intention, of course, was to have the work continue as it had been done. Beginning in 1867, it had been the practice of the churches to put the work each year under the elders of one Texas congregation. The work was under the Sherman church perhaps more than any other one congregation. Of this practice Kendrick wrote:

. . . The churches sent messengers, pledges, etc., and the meetings chose evangelists and a committee from among themselves to act for them from one meeting to the next. Each meeting determined the time and place for the next, and each meeting chose its own chairman, secretary, treasurer and evangelizing committee. We had very little machinery about these meetings. We had out some years from twelve to eighteen evangelists, and never any trouble with them or their salaries. . .

I think we should never have had any serious difficulty among Texas preachers or churches; but preachers came from the East, and human organizations were urged to great disadvantage. To guard against these evils, and seeing we had example for it (Acts ii. 27-30), we requested first the elders of the church at Austin to act as a receiving, managing and disbursing evangelizing committee. Afterward and for several years, the elders of the church at Sherman did all this, and the work went on increasingly

---

[6]C. Kendrick, "Our Missionary Machinery—No. III—Former and Present State Meetings," *Christian Leader,* Vol. II, No. 42 (October 16, 1888), p. 1.

well. It was hindered some, and finally, two years ago, greatly interrupted by a human organization, in opposition to all our efforts. . .[7]

W. H. D. Carrington's suggestion for a meeting in the basement met with approval, and so several retired to hold a meeting of their own. Carrington was chosen chairman and I. D. Faut, secretary. There were two brief sessions—Friday evening and Saturday morning. The elders of the Pearl and Bryan Streets church in Dallas were to oversee the work for the next year. Meanwhile, the Society upstairs announced its intention of meeting with the Commerce Street church the next year in Dallas, so the State Meeting downstairs decided to meet at Pearl and Bryan Streets.

During the 1887 meetings, held at the same time in Dallas, committees representatives of each group, met back and forth, to discuss the possibility of harmony, but to no avail. The Society took steps to appoint a State Evangelist who had about the same authority as a Methodist presiding Bishop. Churches wanting "pastors" were encouraged to contact him, so he could look after the matter. Of course, a primary qualification of the State Evangelist had to be that he was not opposed to either the Missionary Society or the use of the instrument in worship. The State Society took steps at this meeting to form a stock company with which to publish a paper, called the *Christian Courier*. W. K. Homan was made editor. The *Christian Courier* for the next several years was the *Christian Standard* of Texas.

Opposition to the State Society came from various sources. John T. Poe wrote in the *Advocate:*

Recently, certain brethren have thought we were not progressing in the work as fast as we should, and assuming that there was lack of organization, system in missionary work, they have gone to work, and sent out agents on behalf of their plan, or system of work. A large portion of the brethren in Texas protested, that this is wrong, and refuse to work in the name of the Society organized at Austin last year, contending that the church alone, is God's missionary society, and that all must be done by the church, and thus done in the name of Christ.[8]

---

[7]C. Kendrick, "Our Missionary Machinery, No. II," *Christian Leader,* Vol. II, No. 39 (September 25, 1888), p. 1.

[8]John T. Poe, "Two Sides to the Question," *Gospel Advocate,* Vol. XXIX, No. 12, (March 23, 1887), p. 179.

In the spring of 1887, J. D. Tant moved to Hamilton to work with this congregation. Tant was only twenty-six. He had been under the influence of Carrington and that probably helped settle him against the Society. Concerning the church at Hamilton and the cause in Texas in general, Tant wrote:

And permit me to say the congregation at Hamilton is under a leadership that does not know what it is to stop and discuss the insufficiency of the Bible, for they do believe the Bible will furnish them to all good works. . . They are men of too much intelligence to inquire after some organized state machinery under the name of the Society.[9]

In the same article Tant continued and wrote of the cause in general:

When I think of Dabney, Hansbrough, Durst, Burnett, Hawkins, Poe and many more of us who have left home and friends and gone through cold and rain, and have night after night slept upon the ground, whose covering was the sky, that we might preach the word, and have done more good for the cause of Christ than the little two by four society will do in a hundred years, (for when the money fails the society is going to fail also), and then when I hear those who claim to be our brethren put us down as anti-missionaries because we will not turn back from serving God that we might with them partake of the flesh pots of Egypt, it is enough to make us hang our heads in shame.[10]

The *Octographic Review* copied an article from the *Christian Messenger* from one who severely rebuked the Society in Texas.

The Society advocates and adherents have method in their madness. One might think from hearing them say that "Just so the work is done it matters not to the *how*" they care very little about the way in which it is accomplished. Really, one might suppose that they would hail him happy who preaches the primitive gospel on any plan. But the leaders of the Society men in Texas have shown a different spirit. They show very little sympathy for any preacher who does not follow after them, no matter how much he has labored or suffered for Christ.[11]

The history of the restoration movement has well shown that the Missionary Society and the instrumental music were inseparable twins. Like Mary's little lamb, wherever the one went, the

---

[9] J. D. Tant, "Notes from Hamilton, Texas," *Gospel Advocate,* Vol. XXIX, No. 20, (May 18, 1887), p. 307.

[10] J. D. Tant, "Notes from Hamilton, Texas," *Gospel Advocate,* Vol. XXIX, No. 20, (May 18, 1887), p. 307.

[11] Anonymous, "The Society Spirit," *Octographic Review,* Vol. XXI, No. 22, (May 31, 1888), p. 1.

other was sure to follow. As early as 1873 Carrol Kendrick wrote, "We have no use for organs in our churches here *yet*. We have not got that far along in our progress." L. P. Phillips moved to Johnson County in October, 1876. Two years later he remarked that he had yet to see a preacher afflicted with the "organ mania." Instruments of music in the worship of the churches in Texas were few and far between before 1890. Not until the Texas Christian Missionary Society became firmly established did the churches begin to put these in on any large scale.

At Denton the instrument was pushed into the church late in 1893. P. B. Hall who was present at the time wrote T. R. Burnett of Dallas the following:

Dear Brother Burnett: . . . I witnessed one of the saddest affairs last Lord's day that I ever witnessed in my life. The church at Denton has been in trouble for some time over the organ and other things, until a few weeks ago, when those in favor of the organ had a called meeting, with Brother W. I. Thurman for chairman, and withdrew from all the brethren who opposed them. Those who were excluded were the most faithful and devoted brethren in the church at Denton. Brother A. Alsup had been employed by the elders of the church to labor for them, but those in favor of the organ were not satisfied to let him preach in the house. So when we met last Lord's day to hear Brother Alsup, they refused to let him preach in the house. Some of those in favor of the organ went so far as to say: "That a man who would not use the organ in worship was not fit to preach in any church in Texas." Now, they may talk about the inconsistency of making rebaptism a test of fellowship, but how does it look to make the using of an organ a test of fellowship? When the brethren were refused the use of the house, they bore it patiently, and I did not hear an unkind word from any of them. They turned then and asked them if they would take the house they had built with their own hands, turn them out of doors, and for all their labors give them not a cent. They made them no reply. As the old gray-headed brethren arose and walked out of their own house, you know not how bad I felt. Now, I have tried to keep from being prejudiced towards our progressive brethren, but I just know it is wrong to take a person's property without paying him for it. . .[12]

The church at Sherman had a bitter conflict over the instrument. Before Larimore's meeting of 1894 some attempted to

---

[12] P. B. Hall, "Denton, Texas," *Gospel Advocate,* Vol. XXXVI, No. 4 (January 25, 1894), p. 61.

introduce the organ but failed. After the meeting, it was put
in, and the church divided. At Longview, the church divided
in 1895. W. H. Wright of Dallas came down and helped the
preacher, L. A. Dale put in the instrument, and about twenty-
five or thirty left to start over again. At Paris, the organ was
put in in the spring of 1891, causing fifty-three members to
separate and build again on a new platform. B. B. Sanders
came to Hamilton, Texas in December, 1893, introduced the organ,
and divided the church. The church at Commerce, Texas divided
soon after the new building was completed in 1894. R. G. Scott,
an employee of the Cotton Belt Railroad, and a member of the
church, moved to Commerce in August, 1900. He received
permission to use the building for a worship service at a time
when the others were not in it. This arrangement went well
until they invited General Gano to conduct a meeting. Gano
was refused permission to preach in the building. A turmoil
resulted when an old sister, ready to demonstrate her loyalty,
tore down the door with an axe to let the brethren in to worship.

In the summer of 1885 the church at Waxahachie put in the
instrument. Chalmer McPherson led the move, and Isaac M.
Fuston opposed it. At the sign of the first opposition, it was
temporarily dropped. But when brethren assembled on Sunday,
October 4th, they found the organ in the church. McPherson
had secretly raised the money among those who favored it, and
bought it. His wife played it at the services. The next Sunday,
October 11, when the organ was used again, Fuston stood up
and asked all who objected to it to meet him that afternoon at
the building. McPherson was present and tried to argue its
scripturalness. General confusion resulted, and the result was
another division.

Slowly those who opposed the organ were losing patience.
What could they do to stop this? It was evident that they were
losing valuable church property by these innovations. What
could be done? Some were bold enough to suggest the answer.

We want to warn the brethren everywhere against those who
divide the churches. "Mark them that cause divisions," says
the apostle, "and have no company with them." It is the work
of the Dallas committee through its agents to divide the churches
and if possible drive out all not in favor of the human plan work,
then possess themselves the church property. Let the congregations look to this. If they can succeed in driving out of the

congregations—by the introduction of the organ or other means—all those who oppose the plan and its sectarian work, the church property will be left in their hand. This is no doubt their program. They have at least worked this way to the present.[13]

Affairs then in Texas had entered this critical period. The introduction of the Society and the instrument caused several of the congregations to be lost to our brethren. There was a growing impatience. One can well see that sterner measures to counteract this influence were in the making.

---

[13]John T. Poe, "Among the Churches," *Gospel Advocate,* Vol. XXXI, No. 31 (July 24, 1889), p. 475.

Chapter XXI

THE REALITY OF DIVISION

On Sunday, August 18, 1889, six thousand members of the church gathered in Shelby County, Illinois, at the site of the old Sand Creek congregation in a great mass-meeting. Since 1873 large masses of brethren had congregated at this site to enjoy a few days of fellowship, and to have opportunities of hearing prominent preachers. With the passing of years the general condition of the church had a tendency to reflect itself upon this gathering, so they came somberly together contemplating the rising threat of division within the church. On this particular Sunday in 1889 the taciturn audience listened for an hour and forty minutes while Daniel Sommer spoke on the condition of the church. Sommer charged the "innovators" with being responsible for all the division, discord, bitterness and strife within the church. He claimed that they had constantly asked these men *not* to push their innovations, but they had been refused. The missionary society and the instrumental music were being pushed into the churches, driving a wedge between brethren. What then, was to be done?

At this point in Sommer's sermon, P. D. Warren, one of the elders in the Sand Creek congregation arose and read what later came to be called the "Sand Creek Address And Declaration." Because of its great significance the document is given in whole here:

To All Those Whom It May Concern, Greeting:
Brethren—You doubtless know that we, as disciples of Christ, with scarcely an exception, many long years ago took the position that in matters of doctrine and practice, religious, "Where the Bible speaks we speak, and where the Bible is silent we are silent." Further, we held that nothing should be taught, received or practiced, religiously, for which we could not produce a "Thus saith the Lord." And, doubtless, many of you also know that, as long as the above principles were constantly and faithfully observed, we were a prosperous and happy people. Then we were of one heart and of one soul; we lived in peace and prospered in the things pertaining to the kingdom of God and the name of our Lord Jesus Christ. Then what was written as doctrine and for practice was taught and observed by the disciples of Christ. And it may not be amiss in this connection to say that many—yes, very many—in the sectarian churches saw the beauty, consistency,

and the wonderful strength and harmony, in the plea as set forth by the disciples for the restoration of primitive or apostolic Christianity in spirit and in practice, and so came and united with us in the same great and godly work.

It is, perhaps, needless for us to add, in this connection, that we, as a people, discarded all man-made laws, rules, disciplines and confessions of faith as means of governing the church. We have always acknowledged, and do now acknowledge, the all-sufficiency of the Holy Scriptures to govern us as individuals and as congregations. As an apostle has said, "All Scripture is given us by inspiration of God, and is profitable for doctrine, for reproof, for correction, for instruction in righteousness, that the man of God may be perfect, thoroughly furnished unto all good works."

And now, please to allow us to call attention to some painful facts and considerations. There are among us those who do teach and practice things not taught or found in the New Testament, which have been received by many well-meaning disciples, but rejected by those more thoughtful, and in most instances better informed in the Scriptures, and who have repeatedly protested against this false teaching and those corrupt practices among the disciples. Some of the things of which we hereby complain, and against which we protest, are the unlawful methods resorted to in order to raise or get money for religious purposes, viz.: that of the church holding festivals of various kinds, in the house of the Lord, or elsewhere, demanding that each participant shall pay a certain sum as an admittance fee; the use of instrumental music in the worship; the select choir, to the virtual, if not the real, abandonment of congregational singing. Likewise the man-made society for missionary work and the one-man, imported preacher pastor to feed and watch over the flock. These, with many other objectionable and unauthorized things, are now taught and practiced in many of the congregations, and that to the great grief and mortification of some of the members of said congregations.

And now, brethren, you who teach such things and such like things, and those who practice the same, must certainly know that they are not only not in harmony with the gospel, but are in opposition thereto. You surely will admit that it is safe, and only safe, to teach and practice what the divine record enjoins upon the disciples. To this none can reasonably object. This is exactly what we want and for which we contend.

And now we say that we beg of you that you turn away speedily and at once from such things, and remember that though we are the Lord's freemen, yet we are bound by the authority of our Lord Jesus Christ. You know that it is by keeping his commandments, and not the commandments of men, that we have the assurance of his approval. Therefore, brethren, without addressing you further by using other arguments, and without going further in detailing those unpleasant and, as we see them, vicious things, you must allow us, in kindness and in Christian courtesy, and at the same time with firmness, to declare that we cannot tolerate the things of which we complain, for if we do we are (in a measure, at least) blamable ourselves.   And let it be distinctly understood that this address and declaration is not made in any spirit of envy or hate or malice, or any such thing.   But we are only actuated from a sense of duty to ourselves and to all concerned; for we feel that the time has fully come when something of a more definite character ought to be known and recognized between the church and the world.   Especially is this apparent when we consider the scriptural teaching on the matters to which we have herein referred.   Such, for instance, is the following:

"Be not conformed to this world, but be ye transformed by the renewing of your mind, that you may prove what is that good and acceptable and perfect will of God."

It is, therefore, with the view, if possible, of counteracting the usages and practices that have crept into the churches that this effort on the part of the congregations hereafter named is made. And now, in closing up this address and declaration, we state that we are impelled from a sense of duty to say that all such as are guilty of teaching or allowing and practicing the many innovations and corruptions to which we have referred, after having had sufficient time for meditation and reflection, if they will not turn away from such abominations, that we can not and will not regard them as brethren.

(Signed)
P. P. Warren
A. J. Nance
Daniel Baker
J. K. P. Rose
James Warren
Officers of the Sand Creek Church
Randolph Miller
Charles Erwin
W. K. Baker
Wm. Cozier
Officers of Liberty Church
Wm. R. Storm,
Ash Grove Church
J. H. Hagan,
Union Church
Isaac Walters,
Mode Church.[1]

---

[1] P. P. Warren, "Sand Creek Address and Declaration," *Christian Leader,* Vol. III, No. 37 (September 10, 1889), p. 2.

To avoid, if possible, any misunderstanding, those responsible for the "Sand Creek Address And Declaration" made it clear that this mass-meeting was not a convention to be considered a representative body of the church of Christ. It was made plain that this document was an expression only of the will of the churches that were responsible for it, and that it was presented only after it was seen that there was no other solution.[2]

The reaction for the moment was hardly dramatic. The *Christian-Evangelist* and the *Christian Standard* gave it slight notice. Samuel Magee thought it was a "foolish" move, in that it would be the means of prejudicing the popular mind. The brethren, however, were fully serious. It was plainly evident that somebody meant to do something, but what? Alfred Ellmore looked at it in this light:

I have a long and thoughtful letter from Brother Rose, of Sand Creek, Ill., in which he urges that all who are sound in the gospel come out and take a stand against this mountain of "progression" lately heaped upon the apostolic teaching. He is anxious that the *Leader* come out in clear terms, and show where it stands. Now, it seems to me that the *Leader* is pronounced against *all* this ungodliness, and has been from its birth. But we should all remember that we can't build a house in a day. This leaven of unrighteousness has been twenty-five years in gathering its mass of corruption. And like the man of sin, whom it serves, it has come in the garb of righteousness, hence the deception. As every generation must learn largely by experience, we were not prepared to meet it. Good men have wept and prayed over the matter, hoping that it might be only a transient cloud, and would soon dissipate, but in this they were disappointed. Like Catholicism and Mormonism, and every other ism, it is growing, and will continue to grow, as an eating cancer, and unless we *cut it out* the body will be ruined.

I hear that Brother Herndon is not in sympathy with the "Sand Creek" move, but he is in favor of a complete separation. But it is a great undertaking to declare a full separation in this great body. And seeing the danger to which we are exposed, and the body, as such, declining to take action, have not the Sand Creek brethren done precisely what we say the whole body should have done? And in making the advance, have they not done what many of us think is right? As I have said before, there is one of several things we can do, viz:

1. Ask the "progressive" men to return to our original plea

---

[2]Daniel Sommer, "Address and Declaration," *Octographic Review*, Vol. XXXII, No. 36 (September 5, 1889), p. 8.

in all things, viz., speak when the Bible speaks, and be silent when the Bible is silent.

2.   The brethren who are yet loyal to this plea, leave it, and go with the party who declare us only a religious "movement."

3.   Remain together as we are and go on in endless confusion and strife; or,

4.   Separate and have peace.

Now, let every thoughtful, loyal praying man decide for himself, and so act.   As to my own individual part, I have decided long ago, and intend to stand by my convictions and the word of God. . .[3]

However, if the "Sand Creek Address And Declaration" of 1889 failed to arouse the brotherhood, the one of 1892 made up for any lack.   Whereas the former declaration set forth the belief that the "innovating brethren"—those who had added instrumental music and the missionary society—had departed from the gospel, and unless they surrendered these, they could not be considered as brethren, the declaration of 1892 now went a step further, strongly recommending that every church that bought property should put a clause in the deed declaring that no instrument of music or other innovations should ever be used on the premises.

This suggestion touched off a verbal warfare that had repercussions upon all the brotherhood, and became a subject of discussion in all of the papers.   The *Christian-Evangelist* insisted that this was a new creed made binding upon the people, that Sommer was now using civil law to enforce his beliefs.   Sommer denied it.   As for the matter of using civil law in church matters, the deed itself was that.   The clause in the deed was simply a declaration that the property would not be used for other purposes than that for which it had been purchased.   Sommer observed that brethren were tired of building church houses, only to be driven from them when someone comes along to put in an organ with which they cannot conscientiously worship.

The *Christian Standard* was loud in its denunciation of the Sand Creek Declaration.   It called it a new Confession of Faith and suggested that all adherents to this must separate themselves from other brethren where the organ is used and where the society

---

[3]A. Ellmore, "Wheat and Chaff," *Christian Leader,* Vol. III, No. 51 (December 17, 1889), p. 4.

is involved. Daniel Sommer was openly accused of being a schismatic and a church divider. The *Standard* wrote:

The churches should be on their guard. They should know that Daniel Sommer has abandoned apostolic ground and is no more identified with the Disciples of Christ than Sidney Rigdon.[4]

The *Standard* of June 25, 1892, advised "without reservation" that Sommer should not be used as a preacher because of his tirades "against the progressive Christianity we teach."[5]   Probably nothing had so aroused the ire of the *Standard* in some time. The *Standard* declared it to be the duty of other papers, like the *Advocate* and the *Leader,* to say whether or not they are behind this Sand Creek Declaration.

The *Advocate* watches the proceedings with mixed feelings. Lipscomb was prone to look upon mass-meetings with disfavor. He had observed the general tendency of them to assume a legislative position over the churches and to be the voice of the congregations.   As for putting a clause in the deed, Lipscomb was not quite ready to go that far, although he saw nothing objectionable to the practice.   He merely chose to wait and hope there was a better way.   As for the *Standard's* challenge for the *Advocate* to speak out, J. C. McQuiddy wrote.

Well for our part, the *Advocate* needs no second call to express its sentiments on this momentous matter.   The Sand Creek manifesto was manifest folly, and the *Advocate* emphatically denies any sympathy with Sommerism—whatever that is—Sand Creekism, Sand Lotism, Sans-culottism, Standardism or any other partyism in religion.   The *Advocate* is for Christ and His church (chosen ones) and is in ardent sympathy with all who are drawing their life from Him who is the true vine. . .   It is not trying to build a church on the teachings of the *Standard's* Fathers, nor is it following anybody's Fathers.[6]

Lipscomb strongly defended Sommer.   He showed that Sommer, in opposing these innovations, was not going against the pioneers, but the *Standard* was.   When the *Standard* complained about di-

---

[4]Russell Errett, "A Divisive Work," *Christian Standard,* Vol. XXVIII, No. 25 (June 18, 1892), p. 521.

[5]Russell Errett, "Daniel Sommer," *Christian Standard,* Vol. XXVIII, No. 26 (June 25, 1892), p. 540.

[6]J. C. McQuiddy, "Miscellany," *Gospel Advocate,* Vol. XXXIV, No. 26 (June 30, 1892), p. 408.

vision, it should remember that the men who introduce these things are the ones causing division.[7]

The *Christian Messenger* of Dallas, Texas, after reading Errett's remarks against Sommer and division, regarded the *Standard's* remarks as altogether ridiculous, insisting it could point out churches all over the country which have been divided over the organ and the missionary society, and the *Standard* during that time had not become the least indignant. Was the *Standard* really concerned about division, or was it more concerned about protecting its innovations?

The core of Sommer's declaration was that churches should put the clause in the deed to protect the building. Brethren who had worked and put their money into a building would not be forced out when others brought in the innovations. As to the principle involved, John T. Hinds writes:

If those who desire to change the use of the house from the well-understood purpose would pay those who dissent the money they put in the building, it would not be dishonest, though it would not be commendable to thus destroy the peace and harmony of the church. But when, by majority vote, the organ is put in and the house taken without paying those who are forced to leave, it is no more honest than it would be for a majority of a business firm or corporation to take the business without paying those who must leave the firm. Many times churches would do better if all the members possessed more of the common honesty of business life.[8]

The attitude of the brethren who opposed the introduction of these innovations during these years may best be compared to the perturbation occurring at the outbreak of any holocaust. No one knew quite what to do. General bewilderment ensued. J. W. McGarvey believed that the tendency toward the use of the instrument was then a current fantasy that would soon run its course, and so wrote,

. . . the prevalent rage for instruments of music in our worship is a passion and a fashion of the hour, and that like all fashions, when it shall have endured for a time, it will pass away. As in the case of other fashions, too, its devotees are usually deaf to reason on the subject and rebellious against authority. This tide

---

[7]David Lipscomb, "Our Response," *Gospel Advocate,* Vol. XXXIV, No. 27 (July 7, 1892), p. 429.

[8]John T. Hinds, "Hearing and Doing," *Christian Leader,* Vol. IX, No. 20 (May 14, 1895), p. 6.

of feeling will not be stemmed and turned back by reason and authority of Scripture, but, like all other movements of the kind, it will go on from bad to worse until its own excesses will breed disgust for it and bring about a reaction. Such at least, is my expectation; and therefore, having little confidence in human nature but great confidence in the final triumph of the truth as it is in Christ, I shall toil on hopefully as the Master of the vineyard seems to direct.[9]

But McGarvey's prophecy itself proved to be only a vain speculation. Others lived on in hope that something providential would hinder the pushing of the instruments of music into the worship, but finally, it became evident that more stringent course of action must be devised. By 1895 T. R. Burnett of Dallas, author of "Burnett's Budget" was ready to declare:

This Budget becomes more and more convinced every day that it will become necessary to establish churches of the apostolic order in every town in the state where the so-called "Christian Church" now holds sway. The lawless determination of the society and organ people to rule or ruin every church with which they have connection, and either put in the unscriptural things, or put out the brethren who oppose them, makes this plainly evident. The loyal brethren need not waste any valuable time waiting for a reformation, for there is none in prospect. Ephraim is joined to his idols, and he would rather have his society and music idol than any kind of Christian union known to the Bible. Brethren, proceed to re-establish the ancient order of things, just as if there was never a Church of Christ in your town. Gather all the brethren together who love Bible order better than modern fads and foolishness, and start the work and worship of the church in the old apostolic way. Do not go to law over church property. It is better to suffer wrong than to do wrong. Build a cheap and comfortable chapel, and improve it when you get able. It is better to have one dozen true disciples in a cheap house than a thousand apostate pretenders in a palace who love modern innovations better than Bible truth. The battles of this reformation have yet to be fought.[10]

Since the churches were locally governed, it was impossible for them to act in any concerted action by any authorative convention. The problem of what to do about those who were adding these innovations had to narrow itself down to the action of in-

---

[9]J. W. McGarvey, "What Shall We Do About the Organ?" *Gospel Advocate,* Vol XXVIII, No. 25 (June 23, 1886), p. 386.

[10]T. R. Burnett, "Burnett's Budget," *Gospel Advocate,* Vol. XXXVII, No. 19 (May 9, 1895), p 291.

dividuals and of single congregations. That extreme measures would be taken at one time and lax measures at another seemed inevitable. There was no convention or synod to dictate measures to be taken, and so the reaction to the introduction of innovations was different in different places. Some, realizing that no representative convention of the churches ever met to declare non-fellowship with the "so-called Christian Churches," to use Burnett's phrase, have denied that there is any real division today. This thought would easily furnish occasion for an interesting little problem for those with the idle time to engage in it.

As the reality of division becomes increasingly evident, it will be of interest to trace the hopeless plight of the so-called "middle ground" that arose in Kentucky following the Civil War. J. W. McGarvey, Moses E. Lard, W. H. Hopson, L. B. Wilkes, and Robert Graham were leaders in this school of thought. Each adherent maintained and defended the right of a missionary society to do the work of the church, while at the same time, each fought the instrument of music in the worship as an innovation. In the days following the war there were no more popular preachers in the church than these men.

In 1866 the *Gospel Advocate* was revived at Nashville while the same year the *Christian Standard* was born. The *Standard* looked upon these men in Kentucky as entirely too conservative while the *Advocate* thought of them as entirely too liberal. So far as the *Advocate's* line of thought went, the missionary society was an unscriptural, unauthorized aid to the *work* of the church, and the use of the instrument was an unscriptural, unauthorized aid to the *worship* of the church. The principle in each case was the same. The *Standard* vigorously promoted the society, and undoubtedly, had it not been for the *Christian Standard* in those critical years, the Society would have died. The *Advocate* was published too far south, was too small a periodical, and the bitter feelings between North and South that prevailed, made it almost a hopeless task for the *Advocate* to exert any great influence, except in its own local sphere of influence.

Some realized this and felt that the most hopeful prospects possible before them would lie in starting the *Apostolic Times*. Over thirty years later, when Lipscomb reviewed the starting of the *Times,* and its history, he wrote of it saying,

. . . About twenty-five years ago J. W. McGarvey, Moses E. Lard, W. H. Hopson, L. B. Wilkes, and Robert Graham started the *Apostolic Times* at Lexington, Ky. It was an open secret, if secret at all, that they started it to oppose the influence of the *Standard.* Wilkes wrote he disliked to do anything that would injure the *Advocate,* but the *Advocate* was too far South to hold Northern Kentucky against the influence of the Standard; so they thought it essential to establish a paper in Lexington, in the heart of Kentucky, to check the influence of the *Standard.* They thought the *Advocate* would be smothered out (and I thought so, too) and they would get a large patronage in the South, all Kentucky, Missouri and a fair share north of the Ohio River. There was no special objection to the *Advocate* then; all of them opposed the organ, and their support of the societies was not hearty. This is proved by the fact that when they did not succeed as they had hoped, McGarvey wrote me and offered, if we would combine and come to Lexington, Brother Sewell or I, as we thought best, could be managing editor. The *Times* went into other hands. Allen had started the *Old Path Guide,* that seemed to prosper, and McGarvey went on it with him. After Allen's death McGarvey and Kurfees wrote for the *Guide.* Some of the owners sought to restrict Kurfees that he should not write on these subjects. He refused to write unless he could be free to maintain the whole truth as he saw it. McGarvey stood with him. Both left the *Guide,* and McGarvey went to the *Standard,* the influence of which he started out to oppose; but he did not go free to discuss such questions as he thought the Bible and interests of truth required. He submitted to have his hands tied; he submitted to the very restrictions on the *Standard* that he and Kurfees had refused to submit to on the *Guide.* In the *Christian Evangelist,* last year, he said: "I did my best by writing and speaking for about fifteen years to check the progress of the innovation (of instrumental music) among us; but when all the papers through whose columns I could hope to reach those who engaged in it were closed against the further discussion of the subject, and when the minds of those I could hope to convince were equally closed, I desisted, because I did not wish to whistle against the wind, especially when I had no whistle to whistle with." Which means the popular papers would not permit him to discuss questions he thought the truth of God demanded should be discussed. He sticks to them, with his hands tied, and ridicules the *Advocate* because it is not as popular as the society and organ papers. I said, "He sat on the hind step of the band wagon"; to have completed the picture, I should have said, "with his hands tied." Brother McGarvey now says he will not leave a church for perverting one part of the service. James says: "Whosoever shall keep the whole law, and yet offend in one point, he is guilty of all." Certainly it is applicable in this case, if ever.[11]

Thus, the passing of years had wrought changes. By 1890 Lard, Graham, and Hopson were dead, and Wilkes because of old age was no longer active. McGarvey remained the sole survivor of the five earlier men. The *Apostolic Times* had seen its failing days. F. G. Allen had grasped it from possible oblivion and joined it with the *Old Path Guide*. Allen's death, however, in 1886, made its future still uncertain. For awhile, McGarvey and M. C. Kurfees tried to make it steer a conservative course, but Kurfees' conservativism became unbearable to the management and he had to retire. McGarvey resigned in 1889, taking "the last of the conservative element from the *Guide.*" From here on, the *Guide* steered the same editorial course of the *Standard*.

After McGarvey ceased his editorial labors on the *Guide,* he turned his attention to writing for the *Christian Standard*. At first his articles combated the spirit of rationalism and higher criticism an interest in which was aroused in the brotherhood by the teachings of R. C. Cave. Although he still disagreed with the *Standard's* attitude toward instrumental music, McGarvey felt a closer affinity to the *Standard* than to the *Advocate*. The exact reason for this may be hard to say, but probably several entered in to it. For one thing the proximity of Lexington to Cincinnati had something to do with it. McGarvey was literally swallowed up by a people of the *Standard's* type of thinking. The *Advocate's* strict insistence that the missionary society was unscriptural aroused McGarvey's ire who always defended the society's right to exist. Then, too, Lipscomb himself had at times snubbed McGarvey's overtures of friendliness, and furthermore, had openly criticized McGarvey's course. All of these factors had a tendency to alienate McGarvey from the *Advocate,* and made him set out for himself a course which he pursued almost alone.

On March 1, 1901 McGarvey passed his seventy-second birthday. The last forty years of his life had been spent in connection with the College of The Bible and the Broadway Church at Lexington, Kentucky. In September, 1902 he passed the fiftieth anniversary of his preaching career. Thirty-two years he had

---

[11]David Lipscomb, "Brother McGarvey's Position, Again," *Gospel Advocate,* Vol. XL, No. 6 (February 10, 1898), p. 88.

spent as an elder of the Broadway Church. All of this time he had vigorously opposed the use of the instrument in the worship. In 1883 when the rumor was circulated that McGarvey had ceased his opposition to instrumental music, he wrote to Moses Porter, an elder of the church at Lovington, Illinois, the following postcard:

Dear Brother:
Yours of the 3d I answer at the earliest opportunity. I have not withdrawn my opposition to the organ. I would not hold membership with nor contract to preach for a church using one. Its introduction against the conscientious protest of a minority is high-handed wickedness, and can be prompted by no spirit but that of the world and the flesh.[12]

When it became evident that the instrument of music was to be an occasion of the disruption of fellowship in the church, many looked to McGarvey to see his attitude. The terse answer of the Lexington professor was, "I have never proposed to withdraw fellowship from brethren simply because of their use of instrumental music in the worship."

Now the enigma of J. W. McGarvey became clearly evident. On the one side McGarvey maintained his belief that the introduction of the instrument was "high handed wickedness"; on the other, he would never withdraw fellowship from those who used it. Again, McGarvey deplored the fact that Lipscomb, Sewell, and James A. Harding bitterly opposed the Society; on the other hand, McGarvey would never contract to preach at a place where the organ was used. But still, it was plain that "society churches" were the ones that planted the instrument. Srygley was certainly right when he wrote,

Brother McGarvey ought to feel very grateful to David Lipscomb, J. A. Harding, and the Gospel Advocate, if for no other reason, because they are building up and maintaining churches in which he can hold membership and for which he can contract to preach, as he cannot do in the churches he himself is helping organized effort to build up.[13]

Two months after McGarvey celebrated his fiftieth anniversary of preaching the gospel, the Broadway Church announced that

---

[12]J. W. McGarvey, "Queries," *Gospel Advocate,* Vol. XXXIX, No. 33 (August 19, 1897), p. 518.

[13]F. D. Srygley, "From the Papers," *Gospel Advocate,* Vol. XXXIX, No. 34 (August 26, 1897), p. 529.

on Sunday, November 2, 1902 a vote would be taken on the use of the instrument in that church. McGarvey, knowing that the predominence of feeling in the congregation favored the instrument, went to the preacher, Mark Collis, and asked for a letter for his wife and himself. The voting was deferred until Sunday, November 23, at which time, by a count of 361 to 202, the church voted in the organ.[14] McGarvey took his letter, and he and his wife went to the Chestnut Street Church. I. B. Grubbs, who had preceded him a few years before in going to this congregation, met McGarvey when the latter, on the third Lord's Day of September, walked down the aisle to present himself and his wife as members of this congregation. Moved with deep feeling, Grubbs remarked, "Brother McGarvey, we'd rather have you than ten thousand aids to worship."[15]

Thus McGarvey was driven from one congregation to another until his death, but it was hardly more than McGarvey himself could expect. In the words of Jesse P. Sewell,

Professor McGarvey may speak out against the use of instrumental music in the worship, as he does, and say things against it that those who refuse to use it would hardly say; but what do the people who want the instrumental music care about this thing so long as he gives his influence almost entirely (except in his home congregation) to those who use it? Brother McGarvey believes that instrumental music is wrong, and so teaches; still, he gives his name and influence to a paper that advocates its use and associates with churches that use it (except at home and possibly on a few other occasions.) So, while he believes and teaches that the thing is wrong, there is not a church in the land that uses it that will not today point to Brother McGarvey as "one of the strong men on our side." His influence goes with his fellowship, not with his faith and teaching.[16]

Thus McGarvey became the last of the vanguard of the "middle ground" whose pretentious claims were a tower of strength after the war. This distinction although of dubious value the pertinacious McGarvey will always possess.

As two groups now emerged, a prominent question became

---

[14]Daniel Sommer, "Publisher's Notes," *Octographic Review,* Vol. XLV, No. 49 (December 9, 1902), p. 1.

[15]W. C. Morro, *"Brother McGarvey,"* (St. Louis, The Bethany Press, 1940), p. 223.

[16]J. P. Sewell, "Wouldn't Stand for Organ," *Gospel Advocate,* Vol. XLIV, No. 49 (December 4, 1902), p. 771.

"What Name Shall We Wear?" Barton W. Stone, perhaps following the suggestion of Rice Haggard, had insisted that we ought to be Christians and Christians only. Alexander Campbell, on the other hand, had positively expressed his preference for the term, Disciple, because it was used in the New Testament to refer to Christ's followers before the name Christian was given, and too, because a religious group in New England, Unitarian in religious beliefs, called themselves Christians, and Campbell did not want to prejudice the restoration movement by putting this dubious title upon them. At the time Stone, John T. Johnson and many others refused to be moved by Campbell's reasoning. Stone wrote in answer to Campbell:

You well knew the great attachment thousands of us had to the name *Christian,* and many believed from your writing that you had adopted it as the most appropriate name. You also knew that many could not conscientiously be called *Disciples,* as a family name. You knew your two warmest friends, J. T. Johnson and myself, rejected the title of our Hymn Book, because it was called the Disciples' Hymn Book. Brother Campbell, ought you not to have respected the feelings of so many, who united their energies with *yours* in promoting the common cause? The reasons given by you for rejecting the name *Christian,* because you were anticipated by a people in the East and in some parts of our country, who are Unitarians, and who do not baptize for the remission of sins, nor break the loaf every first day, are the things so objectionable, and objected to by all, whom I have heard speak on the subject.[17]

Stemming from Campbell's influence came an element who strongly favored calling the church the "Disciples of Christ Church." The title "Christian Church" was perhaps most frequently used, and for many years, except on a few occasions, was very little questioned. Still the title "church of Christ" had nothing to be said against it being the most defensible title of it. The lucent pen of Ben Franklin wrote:

Those who are aiming to be simply *people of God* have nothing to do with *naming themselves,* or *choosing what name they shall wear.* They should speak of themselves in the style of scripture precisely. That is, they should speak of themselves as the Lord speaks of them. . . . The Lord did not select a name and call them by that name *exclusively.* Nor did the apostles, or

---

[17]Barton W. Stone, "Communication," *Millennial Harbinger,* New Series, Vol. IV, No. 1 (January, 1940), p. 21.

followers of Christ, select and adopt any one designation *exclu-sively.* . . . No matter whether it was intended as a reproach, by those who first applied it, or not, it is no reproach to be *called a Christian,* much less to *be a Christian.* . . . But if the whole church existed some ten years before any were *called Christians,* and the whole New Testament written, with the name but *three times in it,* it is clear that it was by no means *exclusively* used to designate the first disciples or followers of Christ.

. . . In nine cases out of ten we will be perfectly understood by saying "the church," "the body," or the "kingdom." There is no necessity for lugging in such terms as "Christian Church," "Disciples' Church" or "Disciple Church." This is as ridiculous as "Disciple Preacher." If we have simply *the mind* of the Lord, we can express ourselves *in the words* of the Lord.[18]

W. K. Pendleton disagreed with Alexander Campbell on the name. Admitting there were four terms common to the primitive church (viz., (1) disciples, (2) saints, (3) believers, and (4) brethren), Pendleton found no reason to adopt the title "Disciples of Christ," as the exclusive title. On this appellation Pendleton said: ". . . We cannot concede that it should be adopted by us as the specific name by which we would be called." The term, thought Pendleton, was "too vague and indefinite to answer the demands of a significant and definite name." However, for indi-viduals to refer to themselves as Christians, thought Pendleton, is at once "sufficiently definite and comprehensive for a significant and adequate name." As to calling the church "The Christian Church," Pendleton wrote:

Since the public name of the disciples is Christians, are we warranted in calling the church, which is composed of Christians, "the Christian Church"? We judge not. Such an expression is nowhere found in the language of the New Testament. We have "The Church of God," "The Churches of God," and "The Churches of Christ," but nowhere Christian Church or Churches.[19]

By the decade of the 1890's considerable agitation over the name was now coming up. Among the more liberal element the "Dis-ciples of Christ," as a designation, became more popular. But, was it to distinguish a new denomination? President McDiarmid of Bethany College writes in the *Christian Standard* on this usage.

---

[18]Ben Franklin, "What Name Shall We Wear?" *American Christian Review,* Vol. XIV, No. 26 (June 27, 1871), p. 204.

[19]W. K. Pendleton, "What Shall We Be Called?" *Millennial Harbinger,* Vol. XXXVIII, No. 9 (September, 1867), pp. 498-505.

F. D. Srygley copies McDiarmid's statements and adds some thoughts of his own. McDiarmid writes:

How shall one religious body distinguish itself in literature from other religious bodies *without either using an unscriptural term, or using a scriptural term unscripturally? This thing cannot be done.* And all for the reason that the divisions that make the distinguishing names necessary are themselves unscriptural. But we *have* these divisions, and while they exist we must find some terms that will distinguish them.

F. D. Srygley commented:

This is a distinct admission that the religious body which he designates Disciples of Christ is itself an unscriptural body. As long as an unscriptural body exists the world must have, and will have, some name to designate it, of course. In such a case it is courteous and proper to use such name to designate it as those who compose the body select for themselves. But what authority, according to the New Testament, has President McDiarmid or any other Christian to belong to such an unscriptural body? Does he seriously think the New Testament authorizes him to belong to a body which cannot be designated without using either an un-scriptural term, or using a scriptural term unscripturally, and all for the reason that the body itself is unscriptural?[20]

Bethany College, in those days, was publishing a student paper called the "Bethany Guardian." An item in the paper suggested that Alexander Campbell had belonged to the "Disciples of Christ Church." C. L. Loos cared very little for such designations and so replied to this statement by saying:

No, Alexander Campbell never belonged to the Disciples' Church. There was, to the best of my knowledge, no such church in his day. Yet I ought, perhaps, not to assert this too positively. There may have been in A. Campbell's time, in some remote backwoods corner of the land, where schools were poor, where the sun rises late and sets early, a Disciples' Church. If so, it must have lived in great isolation, for at Bethany, where I lived almost an entire generation, we never heard of a people or a congregation with such a name. . . . The Disciple Church is a thing of later times, born of an ignorance of the elementary New Testament teaching of our better days, of a sad lack of sound grammatical teaching in English, and, above all, of a disposition to yield to the pressure for a denominational name, so that we might be like other people.[21]

---

[20] F. D. Srygley, "From the Papers," *Gospel Advocate,* Vol. XXXVIII, No. 1 (January 2, 1896), p. 2.

[21] F. D. Srygley, "From the Papers," *Gospel Advocate,* Vol. XXXVIII, No. 16 (April 16, 1896), p. 241.

But W. K. Pendleton has shown great acumen by writing:

The *quality* of the members of a church may be Christian, and Christian Church expresses this thought; but when the purpose is to state the possessor and head of the church—that is, the relation of founder and proprietor—we say "church of Christ." It is very plain to me, therefore, why the Holy Spirit never used the phrase "Christian Church." The grand idea is not in it. Brethren, is not this another striking example of how dangerous it is to depart from the rule of calling Bible things by Bible names? There is a mighty difference between the "church of Christ" and the "Christian Church." Let us be careful to mark it.[22]

The prophecy of Moses E. Lard, that "expediency may well be the rock on which this reformation will go to ruin," was proving remarkably accurate. Every addition to the work and worship of the New Testament Church was excused on the ground of "expediency." How long the church might have continued without disruption had nothing but the missionary society been involved is difficult to say. It is certain that the Missionary Society did not present the impetus to division that the instrument did. Individuals could have attended worship services, and otherwise worshiped acceptably, even though there were differences of whether the church should support the society. Those who conscientiously believed the instrument a sinful addition to the worship could not have gone to the service where it was used, and worshiped with it, without directly violating their own consciences. Therefore, once the instrument was introduced, they, believing as they did that its use was sinful, had little other choice than to leave, and band together and worship without it.

This problem being settled in the individuals' minds, there came now other problems. Could this band of people who came together determined to worship without the instrument and the former group that worshiped with it continue in fellowship? Considered from a practical standpoint, this was impossible. That body of people who refused the worship with the instrument soon found that if they allowed preachers who favored the instrument to come in, that in time it was a reoccurrence of the old trouble, a division within the congregation. To prevent this constantly recurring division they were forced to use those public teachers who did not believe in the use of the instrument, and, also, teach

---

[22]W. K. Pendleton, "Christian Church or Church of Christ," *Christian Standard,* Vol. XI, No. 18 (April 29, 1876), p. 140.

the flock against it. Thus, from the practical standpoint there was no other step to take.

In taking this drastic step, which was clearly unavoidable, they must now meet the accusations of proponents of the instrument, viz., that they were making the instrument a test of fellowship, and were, therefore, causing division. Actually, of course, these lines of fellowship were definitely drawn by both sides. Advocates of the instrument were as consistent in their refusal to use preachers who would preach *against* the instrument as those opposed to the instrument were in their refusal to use preachers who would preach *for* it.

Basically, the action is to be understood only in the light of the real issue involved. On the one side, the following statement from W. K. Homan in the *Christian Courier* expresses the viewpoint of advocates of the instrument:

One who admits that the New Testament is silent as to the use of an organ as an aid to the worship of God in song, and yet refuses Christian recognition and fellowship to Christians who exercise the liberty that God has left them to use such aid, is guilty of flagrant sectarianism in attempting to make a law for God's people where God has made none, and is a divider of the Body of Christ. . . .

This sentiment was expressed hundreds of times in different words by the numerous advocates of the instrument. It was precisely the argument of J. Carroll Stark to Joe S. Warlick. God had not said, "Thou shalt not use instrumental music in the worship." Since God had made no law against it, the use of it is a violation of no law of God, and is, therefore, not sinful. But opponents of the instrument regarded this as a dodge of the basic issue. God had not said, "Thou shalt not count beads as an act of worship." If someone introduced the counting of beads, as Catholics practice it, as an act of worship, would any person objecting be the cause of division? The principle could be applied in a thousand such cases. To adopt that as a principle of restoring the New Testament church is suicidal, for it would, as McGarvey pointed out, open the floodgates to an endless number of unscriptural practices.

The basic issue lay, not merely in an innocent-looking thing like an instrument, but in a principle beneath it. Moses E. Lard forceably put it:

The question of instrumental music in churches of Christ involves a great and sacred principle. But for this, the subject is not worthy of one thought at the hands of the child of God. That principle is the right of man to introduce innovations into the prescribed worship of God. This right we utterly deny. The advocates of instrumental music affirm it. This makes the issue. As sure as the Bible is a divine book, we are right and they are wrong. Time and facts will prove the truth of this. The churches of Christ will be wrecked the day the adverse side triumphs, and I live in fear that it will do it. Our brethren are now freely introducing melodeons in their Sunday schools. This is the first step to the act, I fear. As soon as the children of these schools go into the church, in goes the instrument with them. Mark this.

And so, by 1906, the work of division had taken its full course. The "Christian Churches" or "Disciples of Christ," as they preferred to be called, took their instruments and their missionary society and walked a new course. The battles had been long, treacherous, costly and bitter. Many brethren, still licking their wounds, looked to the future to start all over again.

Chapter XXII
HORIZONS OF DESTINY

Nearly half a century has passed since J. W. Shepherd compiled and submitted the first religious census on the numerical strength of the churches. With the year 1906, the date of that census, the scope of these volumes closes. But, before drawing the curtain across this study a final word should be said about the various congregations of the church of Christ—their problems, past and present, and the destiny awaiting them.

When the innovations began to be introduced into the work and worship of the church a century ago, strong opposition resulted. With the passing of a few years some, even of the more intrepid opposers, sensing that these were going to be popular despite their opposition, relaxed and joined the popular movement. Others, however, with more trenchant consciences found it impossible to yield. Driven from their former places of worship, they were forced to start all over. Since they were in the minority, the majority forged ahead. The churches of Christ at the present time are realizing an astonishing growth, but this has not always been true. It would be vain—not to mention untruthful—to deny that there have not been problems internally that have delayed this growth. It is toward some of these problems that we now turn our attention.

EXTREMES

Certainly one of the major concerns of the church has been presented by the extremists who have frequently arisen. The sincerity of this class is hardly open to question, but that the total effect of their influence has been a retarding influence is equally undeniable. These extremes owe their origin to a jealous concern over the full import of Thomas Campbell's famous motto, "Where the Bible speaks, we speak; where the Bible is silent, we are silent." Since the Bible is silent, they reasoned, about the Sunday School, the use of literature, etc., these cannot be allowed. Thus, the extremes were created.

The Sunday School. The prime objection to the Sunday School

449

was expressed in the words of Lydia L. Bowman in the *Christian Leader* in 1890 when she wrote:

There are many advocates of the Sunday School, but surely these have not seen the evils of this institution as they now exist. In the first place, there is no authority for it in the word of God, and those who plead that it is essential to the growth of the church must admit that God overlooked a very important item in the plan of salvation, and man, being wiser than God, has supplied the deficiency with a Sunday School. . . .[1]

Thus, the very existence of the Sunday School has far-reaching implications, according to one extreme view. But it is obvious that the very ambiguity of the term, Sunday School, is one cause of the discussion that has centered around it. David Lipscomb wrote: ". . . A Sunday School as a distinct organization or under the direction of or composing a part of any organization except the simple churches of Christ, is open to all the objections laid against the missionary society." If the Sunday School be organized as a separate organization from the church to do the work of the church, it differs, according to Lipscomb, in no major principle from the missionary society. But, if the term, "Sunday School," connotes this, it need not necessarily be so. Lipscomb wrote:

To have clear conceptions, let us go back a little. The only manifestation or development of the church on earth is the local congregation. The church cannot be approached save in and through the local congregation. It cannot act save in and through the local congregation. The local congregation can act as a whole or through its individual members. Just as the human body to which the spirit likens it, can act as a whole or through the individual members. The idea of a church on earth, save as it manifests itself in the individual congregations and through its members as parts of this body, is contrary to every presentation of the church in the Bible.

Now any Sunday School other than the local church through its members, or individual Christians, directed by its elders, teaching the word of God to those who assemble to be taught, is wrong. It is the duty of the elders to direct in this teaching and to control and guide the Sunday School as much as it is their duty to direct the Lord's day worship. It is simply the church doing the work committed to it. No officer, no organization outside of the regular

---

[1] Lydia L. Bowman, "The Sunday-school," *Christian Leader,* Vol. IV, No. 24 (June 17, 1890), p. 1.

organization and officers of the church is needed or is allowable. Any association with any society outside of the church is sinful. I do not mean the elders are to do all the teaching in the Sunday School, any more than they ought to do all the reading, exhortation, thanksgiving at the worship. But they should direct it all and see it is properly done. The only allowable Sunday school is the teaching of the word of God in classes under the direction of the elders of the church, or by individual Christians. A separation of the Sunday School into an organization distinct from the church and the teaching done in it, without the superintendence of the elders, is the source through which many of the corruptions work into the church of God.

With this understanding of a Sunday School there is no principle in common between it and the missionary society. The one is the church in a perfectly scriptural manner doing the work God has laid upon it, without any organism outside of or separate from the church and without any unscriptural organisms in the church. The society is a distinct organism from the church doing the work God committed to the church. It takes the work from the officers of the church, and gives it to officers of its own body and all the evil before mentioned, necessarily grows out of this perversion of the order of God. . . .[2]

And so, with David Lipscomb the principle to be followed was, ". . . whatever can be used to enable a man to do more of the service of God or to do it better without entering into or modifying that service or without adding to or taking from the appointments or institutions of God, is an allowable expedient. Whatever modifies or changes, adds to or takes from the services and appointments of God is sinful."[3]

It is right for the church to study the Bible when it comes together to worship; it is wrong for it not to. The segregation into classes according to age or knowledge attained is but a convenient arrangement to do the thing God requires—study the Bible. So, E. G. Sewell wrote:

. . . But while God has thus required his people to know and to do his will, he has not fixed the time and place where the reading and studying shall be done; whether alone, in the family when all are together, at prayer meeting in the week, or in the meeting on the first day of the week. This part of it is left to our wisdom. The Lord requires that we shall study, shall know his will, but

---

[2]David Lipscomb, "Is It An Unauthorized Practice?" *Gospel Advocate,* Vol. XXXI, No. 5 (January 30, 1889), p. 70.

[3]David Lipscomb, "Is It An Unauthorized Practice," *Gospel Advocate,* Vol. XXXI, No. 5 (January 30, 1889), p. 70.

the precise time, place and circumstances under which the reading shall be done are not given. It is certainly right for a man to sit down alone every day at some hour that may suit his other engagements, and read the word of God. It is unquestionably right for a husband and father to read the word of God to his family, and thus teach them the will of the Lord while he himself is studying, for he is required to bring up his children in the nurture and admonition of the Lord. It would certainly be right for a man to sit down in the morning when he first rises from sleep, and read a few chapters of the word of God, and thus begin the duties of the day with a lesson in God's word. And yet there is just as much authority for several members to sit together when assembled on the first day of the week and read and study a chapter of the Lord's word as for one to sit alone and do it on that day or any other. That we must study and learn the Lord's will is positively required. But as to when and where we shall do the studying is not fixed. This is left to our discretion. . . . Some of the strongest churches, and most thoroughly enlightened members we know, are those that have Bible classes on Lord's day, and read, investigate, and talk over a chapter or more each Lord's day, and that do not allow anything they control to keep them from it. Yes, there is just as much authority for the Bible class on Lord's day as there is to sit down and read a chapter alone at home. No one needs be afraid of starting an innovation in the church by having a Bible class in it. Nay, verily, have more of them, and study the lessons more at home.

The Bible class is simply a help in doing a thing which the Lord has commanded to be done, but has not prescribed the precise manner in which it shall be done. God has required Christians to meet together on the first day of the week to break bread, but does not tell how they shall travel to get together. This is left to them. They walk, ride on a wagon, horseback, in a buggy, or on a train. But come together they must, or they will not obey the Lord. But that one that walks to the place can worship God just as well when he gets there as the one who came horseback or on a train. The whole manner of getting there is left to man's choice. But he that willingly fails to go sets at naught the authority of God and endangers his soul's salvation. . . .[4]

Literature. Closely allied to the extreme of the Sunday School was the contention that the use of the literature in the Sunday School was a sinful practice. It is difficult for one to escape the conclusion that the origin of this extreme lay in jealousy over commercial interests between publishing concerns. The *American*

---

[4]E. G. Sewell, "Shall We Have Bible Classes?" *Gospel Advocate,* Vol. XXVIII, No. 32 (August 11, 1886), p. 497.

Christian Review, while under the editorship of John F. Rowe, complained of the *Christian Standard* that one of the departures it fostered was the use of lesson leaves. The *Standard* was shrewd enough to single out this extreme and make capital of it.

Actually, of course, the use of literature was a very innocent practice. Extremists showed the utmost folly in comparing it to the creeds of denominationalism. Lesson leaves represented no more than a *written* method of teaching, whereas public preaching was *oral.* No more authority was attached to it than was attached to oral declamation.

The Preacher. Extremists have generally made a field day of the preacher—his work, his pay, and in fact with nearly every phase of his life.

The problem of "located preachers" came in for the usual critical examination. One extreme begets another, and so it is here. D. S. Burnet fathered the idea of making the preacher the "pastor" of a congregation. In Bible times it is generally understood that the term bishop and the term pastor referred to the same func tion—that of overseeing the flock. This function belonged to the elders of the New Testament church. By the time of the Civil War, it was becoming an increased practice in the church of placing a preacher in "charge" of a congregation, and giving to him the title "pastor." Usually the responsibility of overseeing the flock belonged almost exclusively to him.

This tendency very correctly came under the critical eye of many brethren. But in their application of a remedy, many concluded that a "located preacher" was to be tabooed. The idea was slow taking hold that a preacher might possibly establish himself in a certain geographical area for a lengthy period of time and preach the gospel under the oversight of a scriptural set of elders without assuming the function of those elders. The failure to sense this possibility greatly deterred the forward progress of the churches for many years.

Still connected with the preacher was the problem of his pay. In the earlier days Alexander Campbell preached without receiving financial remuneration for it. There were two reasons for this. The first reason was that Campbell did not have to be paid. From the farm which he received from his father-in-law Campbell managed to make considerable money, so that when he died he was a relatively wealthy man. The second reason for taking no money

showed the sagacity of the Bethany sage. Leaders in any movement are subjects of considerable criticism, and by his refusal to
take money for his religious work, Alexander Campbell was never
criticized for leading a religious reformation as a means of making
money. Likewise, David Lipscomb seldom accepted pay for his
preaching. It was not because he believed this wrong, but only
that he made a sufficient living from secular work that he did not
need it.

The economic condition of the country, particularly in the
South, reflected itself upon this whole problem. After the war,
people had no money, and nearly everyone was in exactly the same
condition. If preachers had refused to preach because there was
no money in it, few communities would have had any preaching.
Consequently, that preacher was looked down upon who would
refuse to take the gospel to the poor. The poor were far more
prevalent than usual. A cardinal virtue of the preacher was his
willingness to preach where he would receive little or no pay.
Most preachers, then, were farmers, doctors, teachers, or merchants. They made their living in this way that they might preach
the gospel free of charge.

In the course of time churches began to expect to receive all
preaching without paying the preacher. If, in a few cases, they
could get Alexander Campbell to preach for nothing, they could
hardly see why they should pay another preacher with less ability
than Campbell. As economic conditions bettered themselves in
the country, church members had more money, but they still
wanted their preaching for nothing. No one can read the files of
the *Gospel Advocate* from the close of the Civil War until after
the turn of the century without noting the swinging of the pendulum on this subject. At first, every encouragement was given
for preachers to earn their living at a secular work and preach the
gospel free of charge. It was a case of necessity. By 1901 and
after, E. A. Elam felt frequently called upon to censure the selfishness of churches who refused to pay their preachers anything adequate for their labors. When John Augustus Williams, biographer
for "Racoon" John Smith, wrote his reminiscenses of the restoration, he could not fail to notice this attitude. He wrote:

As for the churches, though they were zealous enough for the
ancient faith, they had not yet been fully trained in the ancient
work. They had been quick to learn from Mr. Campbell the evils

of a hireling spirit in the ministry; and they curiously reasoned among themselves that if it is wrong to work for hire in the Lord's vineyard, it is equally wrong to pay hire to those who labor. The gospel, many thought, should be freely dispensed, and as freely enjoyed. Hence it was, in those early days, that so many earnest preachers were doctors, or farmers, or schoolteachers, or merchants, or dentists, or even phrenologists, or, in fact, anything by which they might, like Paul, earn an honest support while preaching the Word. . . .[5]

But the pendulum was slow in swinging. Any preacher who undertook to teach the congregation out of its selfishness, and to stress their duty to support their laborers, immediately ran the risk of severe criticism for preaching for money. Many were silent, preferring insufficient support to the criticism that they were preaching for money.

Acts 2: 42. Another problem closely allied with those of the preacher was the "order of worship." The originator of this extreme was Alfred Ellmore. Ellmore, born near Elnora, Indiana (then called "Owl Prairie," after an Indian chief by the name of Owl), was reared south of Frankfort, Indiana. About 1886 he moved to Covington, Indiana, from whence radiated his ideas. Ellmore, despite the fact that he promoted an extreme position on the "order of worship," was one of the most tireless gospel preachers in the church of his day, and one of the most devoted to Christ. It is one of the tragedies of promoting extreme positions that in future years one's good points are forgotten in the objections raised against his extremes.

The point in his position was that Acts 2: 42 furnished a divine pattern of worship. This affirmation arose chiefly as an answer to those promoting "innovations." As the use of the instrument came to be more widely advocated, objectors raised the point that it was a human addition to a divine pattern. This was in turn met by a fervent denial that there was no divine pattern laid down for us in the New Testament. And to meet this, Alfred Ellmore conceived of the idea that Acts 2: 42 was the divine pattern of worship. He said:

Within the last seventy-five years, Acts 2: 42 has been quoted perhaps ten thousand times as describing the order of the worship of the first church, and yet, in about nine thousand nine hundred

---

[5]John Aug. Williams, "Reminiscences—VII," *Christian Leader,* Vol. XII, No. 9 (March 1, 1898), p. 2.

and ninety and nine and a half times, the advocates have failed to adopt this order. I have often heard of men carrying dark lanterns, but I am inclined to think that nothing is so dark as the man who is religiously blind. Fifty years hence, children in the gospel will wonder at our stupidity in not being able to see the harmony of the order of the worship in the Jewish temple and that of the Church of Christ.

And upon this divine order I comment again. Let the bishops go up into the stand: one read and another offer the opening prayer. (1) Then, under the supervision of the bishops, let a half-dozen occupy five minutes each in the lesson, which was announced the Lord's Day before teaching. (2) Take up the fellowship. And I would be understood here as teaching that they should *take up the fellowship,* and not do something else in the place of it. (3) Break the loaf. (4) The prayers. Let from two to five offer prayers of two to three minutes each time. Now, if Acts 2: 42 is the divine model, then nothing else is. And I insist that we wheel into line at once. Professing to be apostolic, let us be apostolic. . . .[6]

Ellmore was vociferous in insisting that all the churches adopt this "divine model." "Why continue in that hireling-pastor-every-Sunday system?" he once asked. If it be inquired, if Acts 2: 42 is intended to be the "divine model," why does it exclude singing, Ellmore's reply was that it was implied in the "teaching."

Ellmore's known love for the truth and knowledge of the Scriptures gave a ready impetus to the spreading of these ideas. Churches grew up, particularly around Ellmore's home in Indiana, thoroughly imbibed with this point of view, and have in some cases remained so unto this day. This extreme very early became planted in Indianapolis. The ancient order was first preached in the city in 1833. After the Civil War, the original congregation, called the Central Church, put in the instrument of music. It was about 1878. A group refused to worship with the instrument and left. Leader in the group was Dr. Joshua Webb, the man who converted S. K. Hoshour from the Lutherans. The little church met on Mulberry Street in a house built on the property of Dr. Webb. No preacher was allowed to preach at the morning worship. Each man read a scripture and "exhorted" as far as time permitted. The evening service, if any, was given to evangelistic type of worship with the preacher, if any, preaching.

---

[6]A. Ellmore, "Wheat and Chaff," *Christian Leader,* Vol. II, No. 9 (February 28, 1888), p. 5.

It can be safely said of all of these extremes that they represent only a small minority in the churches of Christ today. Here and there are geographical areas where pockets of extremist-colored congregations are found, but this is not generally characteristic of the church. Consequently, members of the church seldom fail to feel some chagrin when one of these extremes is held up as being representative of the church when this is far from the case. The extremes actually owe their origin to a reaction against the introduction of "innovations," and to genuine desire to be wholly acceptable to God.

MISSIONS

Because many brethren objected to the missionary society, they were accused of not believing in cooperation, having no love for lost souls, and generally, of having no interest in mission work. While this may have been true in some instances, it was far from being predominantly the case. Most of those who objected to the society were busily engaged in establishing churches throughout the nation. Their work was less glamorous, received less publicity, and the preachers themselves received far less money. But they did considerable mission work.

While Tolbert Fanning was objecting to the Society, the church established at Franklin College was sending J. J. Trott to the Cherokee Indians in Arkansas. Later, when the Cherokees were pushed further west into Oklahoma Territory, the churches were not lax in preaching the gospel to them. R. W. Officer, supported by the Gainesville, Texas, congregation, began work among these Indians about 1880. Two years later, the church at Paris, Texas, undertook this mission work, sending Officer among the Indians. In 1888 there were over fifty-six thousand Indians in "Indian Territory" divided among the Choctaws, Cherokees, Creeks, Chickasaws, and Seminoles. That year there were about nine hundred members of the church of Christ among the number, mostly the converts of R. W. Officer. Among the converts was H. C. Collier, a full-blooded Cherokee, who was instrumental in establishing a church at Muskegee, a town one hundred miles north of Atoka, Officer's headquarters.

Foreign missionary work received little concern from the churches of Christ until after 1880. That year, Jules DeLaunay went to Paris, France, to establish a congregation. At his death about fifteen years later, he had a congregation of four hundred people worshiping after the pattern of New Testament teaching. DeLaunay, reared a Roman Catholic, was educated in Rome. After becoming a Jesuit priest, the Roman Catholic Board of Foreign Missions was preparing to send him to China. Once, while walking in the catacombs of Rome with two friends, De-Launay was struck with the idea that the religion of the early martyrs was that of the New Testament, not of the papacy. His friends told him not to say that publicly or he would disappear. Soon after he came to America, he heard for the first time the preaching of the apostolic gospel, and espoused the cause of New Testament Christianity.

During the summer of 1889, three congregations in Nashville undertook to send Azariah Paul to Armenia. Paul, born near Harpoot in eastern Asia Minor in the ancient province of Cappodicia, came to the College of the Bible in 1884. During the summers he was in school, he preached for a colony of Armenians at Worcester, Massachusetts. The Nashville churches banded together to send him to Turkey. The Turkey mission, however, closed in only a few years with the untimely death of Paul.

Perhaps the most publicized foreign mission work the church undertook was in Japan in 1892. Early the year before, W. K. Azbill of Indianapolis proposed a Japanese mission and asked for several volunteers. Major repercussions were started in the Society. The General Society, fearing it would lose some of its support by the congregations giving to the Azbill mission, notified Azbill that he could expect no help from them, and asked him to raise his money from churches other than "society churches." Young J. M. McCaleb, reared in Hickman County, Tennessee, and educated at the College of the Bible at Lexington, counseled with David Lipscomb about going. Lipscomb encouraged him and was a great help in raising his support from Tennessee churches. The first of March, 1892, Azbill and McCaleb, with five others in their party, started for Japan.

Mission work among the churches of Christ, and especially foreign mission work, has subjected itself to considerable criticism. Foreign missionaries, so to speak, live in glass bowls, and are, therefore, open to the scrutiny of all. The Japanese mission, at first, was subjected to servere criticism. It was complained that Azbill was a "Society Man." Actually, while Azbill was hardly as opposed to the Society as some brethren, yet he did not solicit funds from it. When The Society offered him money, he was inclined to take it, which was the occasion for a difference between McCaleb and Azbill. Others complained of the Azbill mission that it was getting too much money, forcing the preachers at home to have less.

Foreign mission work has been received by churches of Christ with varying degrees of enthusiasm. Criticism of this type of work has generally followed a set pattern.

1. It is suggested that there is so much mission work to do at home that this ought to be done first.

2. The foreign missionaries themselves are criticized for desiring too much the glamor and publicity of the thing. If five people are baptized in Russia, news is spread all over the religious periodicals, but five baptisms in Kentucky may hardly find space in a news report.

3. Foreign missionaries are criticized for taking "sight-seeing trips" at the expense of the church. They must ride airplanes, go first-class on ships, or ride pullman on the train whereas the preachers who stay at home cannot afford such "luxuries."

4. The results achieved in the foreign field on a per dollar basis hardly measure up to that received at home. Hence, it is argued that foreign mission work is too expensive for what it costs.

Other criticisms, growing out of particular circumstances, generally follow this set pattern. Suffice it to say, those aspiring to foreign mission work have become more cognizant of these criticisms and have been wise enough to try to avoid them.

PRESENT-DAY PROBLEMS

Suggestions have been made as to some of the problems that faced the church in the past. We turn our attention now to some of the more modern problems facing the church.

The problem of fellowship. The matter of drawing lines of fellowship against individuals in the New Testament Church was an act of the most serious import. It was done generally as a last resort after all other efforts to correct the incorrigible had failed. Still, when being exercised it was done reluctantly and regretfully and with the hope that it would correct the error of the individual.

The problem of who to fellowship remains acute in the churches of Christ today. The action of brethren has had a tendency toward two extremes. On the one side, there is a laxity of drawing lines of fellowship against the disorderly, while on the other, the practice of disfellowshipping individuals is promiscuously used by a clique in power, generally spearheaded by the preacher, as a whip to keep the flock in line. Both extremes are revolting to individuals having a desire to pattern after the New Testament order.

How much error must one imbibe before the church disfellowships him? This problem was faced by David Lipscomb many years ago. Lipscomb believed that it was sinful for a Christian to participate in warfare, and to participate in civil government. The next question was, Would he disfellowship those who did? Consequently, when R. C. Horn asked Lipscomb how far a man may go in sin without being withdrawn from, Lipscomb replied:

We are not much of a believer in capital punishment either in church or state. We are never willing to give a man up finally, until we believe he has committed the sin unto death. So long as a man really desires to do right, to serve the Lord, to obey His commands, we cannot withdraw from him. We are willing to accept him as a brother, no matter how ignorant he may be, or how far short the perfect standard his life may fall from this ignorance. We do not mean either to intimate that we are willing to compromise or to hold in abeyance one single truth of God's holy writ, from any motive of policy or expediency. We will maintain the truth, press the truth upon him, compromise not one word or iota of that truth, yet forbear with the ignorance, the weakness of our brother who is anxious but not yet able to see the truth. I feel sure, if I am faithful, and he willing to learn the truth, he will come to the full measure of my knowledge. Why should I not, when I fall so far short of the perfect knowledge myself? How do I know that the line beyond which ignorance damns, is behind me, not before me? If I have no forbearance with his ignorance, how can I expect God to forbear with mine?

What is needed is patient instruction and discipline in the church, instead of withdrawal from the weak. Final withdrawal is the end of discipline. I have no doubt it is much too often hastily resorted to, without previous instruction and discipline. . . To withdraw from and turn over to Satan, is just the opposite of discipline. It should be resorted to only when all discipline has wholly failed. So long then as a man exhibits a teachable disposition, is willing to hear, to learn and obey the truth of God, I care not how far he may be, how ignorant he is, I am willing to recognize him as a brother. No matter how wise or how near the truth or how moral a man may be, if he sets up a standard of his own or another and is not willing to learn of God, take his law and obey him, then I can withdraw from him. Not until he is beyond the reach of all instruction, expostulation or exhortation would I then surrender him.[7]

Colleges. There is so much pride in the human heart that it is very often difficult to learn from one's enemies. The question of the Bible College has already been discussed, and will not be repeated here. The oft-repeated statement of Sommer's that the colleges were the beginning points of all digression probably would not bear up under more thorough investigation. As L. F. Bittle pointed out as early as 1873 in his letters to Jacob Creath, it had rather been the tendency of colleges to fall in line behind the popular sides of issues in the brotherhood. Colleges, as a general rule, will as a matter of policy pursue for a time a midway "safe" course until it is known which side will be the most popular, and then will jump with full force on that side. Colleges, as a general rule, have not fostered the thinking of brethren on certain issues, but rather have reflected the opinion of the majority after the issues have arisen. Consciously or unconsciously, this has been the tendency. The reason is clear: colleges must have money to operate and if they get too unpopular, they will not have enough funds to run.

The charge, therefore, that the Bible schools have been the cause of digression is a generalization of very little historical accuracy. Rather, just the opposite is true. The chief forces of opinion and policy in the brotherhood have always been the brotherhood publications. Here the issues are discussed. Here the merits of any issue are weighed. Here the opinions are finally fixed. Churches all over the nation reflect the attitudes and opinions of the papers that are most read. The churches in the North where the *Octographic Review* was read came to be modeled after the policies and views of that paper, just as churches in the South came to be modeled after the views expressed in the *Advocate*. Digression began in the restoration movement not with colleges but with papers, which is to say with influential editors and writers. It was not until after they had swung the opinions of the brotherhood into one line or another that the

---

[7]David Lipscomb, "Queries on Civil Government," *Gospel Advocate,* Vol. XVII, No. 17 (April 22, 1875), pp. 399, 400.

colleges began to take up the issues and become champions of them. The popular side in the restoration was swung after the *Standard* and the *Evangelist*. After they set the pattern of thought, the colleges, one by one, fell in line behind them.

The outlook for the future of the church is far from being dark and the subject-matter is not all distasteful. There is little question that the church is now enjoying one of its greatest surges of growth. New congregations, though in some cases yet small, are springing up in cities and towns like magic. Churches more and more are arising from the decadence of indifference to be filled with strong missionary zeal. Individual congregations are awakening to their possibilities and are putting forth strenuous efforts to convert the lost in their own community.

The coming generation of gospel preachers is in some respects one of the most optimistic signs in the church. They are, on the whole, young men of talent and sincere love for the truth. Many have gone to higher universities and are proving themselves capable of understanding and meeting the mightiest thrusts of liberalism and modernism. Grounded in the truth that they love so well, they are extending whole-heartedly the warm hand of sincere love to each other, so that the absence of jealousy and suspicion is noticeable.

So also is the interest in Christian education an encouraging sign. With the passing of each year one finds additional plans being made to establish a school in which the Bible may be taught as well as other subjects. It is to be hoped that in a few more years there will be hundreds of schools dotting the nation—schools in every city and town where boys and girls can be taught to love God from the moment they enter school until they graduate from college. While, as has been noted, there are always problems, God-fearing men will find the solution.

The wide interest in foreign mission work it is hoped will not prove to be only a current fad. Despite its culpable points, it is good to see the gospel preached successfully and correctly in foreign lands.

Likewise is it encouraging to witness the extreme positions that formerly faced the church gradually fading away, and a vigorous program of launching the truth daily planned.

But there has never been a time when the church did not have problems. After the present generation is dead, there will still be others. But, whatever their nature, there are principles that will guide the church on safe ground if the church but remembers them. In the light of this we can think of no words to serve as a more fitting close for this volume than those spoken by F. G. Allen a few years before his death.

While we remain true to the principles on which we started out, there is no earthly power that can impede our progress. But the day we leave these walls and go out to take counsel with the world, will mark the day of our decline. We have nothing to fear from without. Our only danger lies in the direction of indifference and compromise. While we are true to God in the maintainence of these principles, the divine blessing will be upon our work. But should they ever be surrendered, ruin will as certainly follow as that the Bible is true.[8]

---

[8]F. G. Allen, "It Came to Pass," *Gospel Advocate,* Vol. XXXVIII, No. 4 (January 23, 1896). p. 54.

INDEX